TALES FROM THE TIBETAN OPERAS

The Library of Tibetan Classics is a special series developed by the Institute of Tibetan Classics aimed at making key classical Tibetan texts part of the global literary and intellectual heritage. Eventually comprising thirty-two large volumes, the collection will contain over two hundred distinct texts by more than a hundred of the best-known authors. These texts have been selected in consultation with the preeminent lineage holders of all the schools and other senior Tibetan scholars to represent the Tibetan literary tradition as a whole. The works included in the series span more than a millennium and cover the vast expanse of classical Tibetan knowledge—from the core teachings of the specific schools to such diverse fields as ethics, philosophy, linguistics, medicine, astronomy and astrology, folklore, and historiography.

Tales from the Tibetan Operas
This anthology contains most of the *lhamo* stories that are portrayed in Tibetan opera, many of which are written by anonymous authors, and it includes more than fifty gorgeous photos of the operas performed on location in Tibet and India. In a uniquely Tibetan literary style, the dialogue in these Tibetan "plays" is in verse meant for singing. Included are *Drimé Künden*, a story modeled on the Buddhist Jātaka tale of a prince who pushed the practice of generosity to its limits, causing complications of all kinds; *King Norsang*, a love story between a human king and a celestial princess who is caught in a web of intrigue fueled by the jealousy of court members; *The Story of the Chinese and Nepalese Princesses*, in which a minister skillfully manipulates to bring the emperor's two brides from China and Nepal back to Tibet; *Nangsa Öbum*, a Dharma teaching of a noble ḍākinī who took birth as a woman, and her quest for enlightenment; *Drowa Sangmo*, a story of dissension sown among a king, a queen, and their two children by an evil concubine who is envious of the queen's good fortune; *The Brothers Dönyö and Döndrup*, a tale of how the love between two brothers helped them overcome their diverse trials, such as banishment from home; *Sukyi Nyima*, a story of a hermit's daughter becoming a queen; and *Pema Öbar*, in which a young prince quests to find a wish-granting jewel.

Like India's *Pañcatantra*, the Middle East's *Arabian Nights*, and well-known works from ancient Greece and medieval Europe, the narration and performance of these stories have served a vital role in teaching moral sensibilities and civic responsibilities in their land of origin.

THE LIBRARY OF TIBETAN CLASSICS • VOLUME 31
Thupten Jinpa, General Editor

TALES FROM THE
TIBETAN OPERAS

Translated by Gavin Kilty

in association with the Institute of Tibetan Classics

Wisdom Publications
199 Elm Street
Somerville, MA 02144 USA
wisdompubs.org

© 2019 Institute of Tibetan Classics
All rights reserved.

No part of this book may be reproduced in any form or by any means, electronic or
mechanical, including photography, recording, or by any information storage and
retrieval system or technologies now known or later developed, without permission in
writing from the publisher.

Library of Congress Cataloging-in-Publication Data
Names: Kilty, Gavin, translator.
Title: Tales from the Tibetan operas / translated by Gavin Kilty.
Description: Somerville, MA: Wisdom Publications, [2019] | Series: Library of
    Tibetan classics; volume 31 | Includes bibliographical references and index. |
Identifiers: LCCN 2018038910 (print) | LCCN 2018047111 (ebook) |
    ISBN 9781614295822 (ebook) | ISBN 9780861714704 (hardcover: alk. paper)
Subjects: LCSH: Tibetan drama—Translations into English. | Folk drama, Tibetan.
Classification: LCC PL3771.E5 (ebook) | LCC PL3771.E5 T35 2019 (print) |
    DDC 895/.42—dc23
LC record available at https://lccn.loc.gov/2018038910

ISBN 978-0-86171-470-4   ebook ISBN 978-1-61429-582-2

23 22 21 20 19   5 4 3 2 1

Cover and interior design by Gopa&Ted2. Typeset by James D. Skatges. Set in DGP
10.5/13.5.

Wisdom Publications' books are printed on acid-free paper and meet the guidelines
for permanence and durability of the Production Guidelines for Book Longevity of the
Council on Library Resources.

♻ This book was produced with environmental mindfulness. For more information,
please visit wisdompubs.org/wisdom-environment.

Printed in Canada.

Message from the Dalai Lama

THE LAST TWO MILLENNIA witnessed a tremendous proliferation of cultural and literary development in Tibet, the Land of Snows. Moreover, owing to the inestimable contributions made by Tibet's early spiritual kings, numerous Tibetan translators, and many great Indian *paṇḍitas* over a period of so many centuries, the teachings of the Buddha and the scholastic tradition of ancient India's Nālandā monastic university became firmly rooted in Tibet. As evidenced from the historical writings, this flowering of Buddhist tradition in the country brought about the fulfillment of the deep spiritual aspirations of countless sentient beings. In particular, it contributed to the inner peace and tranquility of the peoples of Tibet, Outer Mongolia—a country historically suffused with Tibetan Buddhism and its culture—the Tuva and Kalmuk regions in present-day Russia, the outer regions of mainland China, and the entire trans-Himalayan areas on the southern side, including Bhutan, Sikkim, Ladakh, Kinnaur, and Spiti. Today this tradition of Buddhism has the potential to make significant contributions to the welfare of the entire human family. I have no doubt that, when combined with the methods and insights of modern science, the Tibetan Buddhist cultural heritage and knowledge will help foster a more enlightened and compassionate human society, a humanity that is at peace with itself, with fellow sentient beings, and with the natural world at large.

It is for this reason I am delighted that the Institute of Tibetan Classics in Montreal, Canada, is compiling a thirty-two-volume series containing the works of many great Tibetan teachers, philosophers, scholars, and practitioners representing all major Tibetan schools and traditions. These important writings will be critically edited and annotated and will then be published in modern book format in a reference collection called *The Library of Tibetan Classics*, the translations into other major languages to follow later. While expressing my heartfelt commendation for this noble project, I pray and hope that *The Library of Tibetan Classics* will not only make these important Tibetan treatises accessible to scholars of Tibetan studies but will also create a new opportunity for younger Tibetans to study and take interest in their own rich and profound culture. It is my sincere hope that through the series' translations into other languages, millions of fellow citizens of the wider human family will also be able to share in the joy of engaging with Tibet's classical literary heritage, textual riches that have been such a great source of joy and inspiration to me personally for so long.

The Dalai Lama
The Buddhist monk Tenzin Gyatso

Special Acknowledgments

THE INSTITUTE OF TIBETAN CLASSICS expresses its deep gratitude to the Ing Foundation for its generous support of the entire cost of translating this important volume. The Ing Foundation's long-standing patronage of the Institute of Tibetan Classics has enabled the institute to support the translation of multiple volumes from *The Library of Tibetan Classics*. We are deeply grateful to the foundation for offering us the opportunity to share many of the important texts of the Tibetan tradition with wider international readership, making these works truly part of the global literary, knowledge, and spiritual heritage. We also thank the Scully Peretsman Foundation for its generous support of the work of the institute's chief editor, Dr. Thupten Jinpa.

Publisher's Acknowledgments

THE PUBLISHER WISHES TO extend a heartfelt thanks to the following people who have contributed substantially to the publication of *The Library of Tibetan Classics*:

> Pat Gruber and the Patricia and Peter Gruber Foundation
> The Hershey Family Foundation
> The Ing Foundation

We also extend deep appreciation to our other subscribing benefactors:

Anonymous, dedicated to Buddhas within
Anonymous, in honor of Dzongsar Khyentse Rinpoche
Anonymous, in honor of Geshe Tenzin Dorje
Anonymous, in memory of K. J. Manel De Silva—may she realize the truth
Dr. Patrick Bangert
Nilda Venegas Bernal
Serje Samlo Khentul Lhundub Choden and his Dharma friends
Kushok Lobsang Dhamchöe
Tenzin Dorjee
Richard Farris
Gaden Samten Ling, Canada
Evgeniy Gavrilov & Tatiana Fotina
Ginger Gregory
Rick Meeker Hayman
Steven D. Hearst
Heidi Kaiter
Paul, Trisha, Rachel, and Daniel Kane
Land of Medicine Buddha
Diane & Joseph Lucas
Elizabeth Mettling

Russ Miyashiro
the Nalanda Institute, Olympia, WA
Craig T. Neyman
Kristin A. Ohlson
Arnold Possick
Quek Heng Bee, Ong Siok Ngow, and family
Randall-Gonzales Family Foundation
Andrew Rittenour
Jonathan and Diana Rose
the Sharchitsang family
Nirbhay N. Singh
Kestrel Slocombe
Tibetisches Zentrum e.V. Hamburg
Richard Toft
Timothy Trompeter
Tsadra Foundation
the Vahagn Setian Charitable Foundation
Ellyse Adele Vitiello
Nicholas C. Weeks II
Claudia Wellnitz
Bob White
Kevin Michael White, MD
Eve and Jeff Wild

and the other donors who wish to remain anonymous.

Contents

A sixteenth-century statue of the fourteenth-century Tibetan yogi Thangtong Gyalpo, reputed founder of the Aché Lhamo tradition.

General Editor's Preface

THIS VOLUME CONTAINS the so-called eight great operas of the Tibetan-speaking world. In these operas, some aspects of the portrayal of the characters, such as names and places, do display classical Indian Buddhist influence. However, the narrative style of the stories themselves reflects unmistakably Tibetan aesthetic and cultural sensibilities. In addition, the third opera, "The Story of the Chinese and Nepalese Princesses"—which tells the story of the sixth-century Tibetan emperor Songtsen Gampo's marriage to princesses of Tibet's two neighboring kingdoms—and the fourth, "The Story of Noble Ḍākinī Nangsa Öbum"—which is based on the life of a woman in eleventh-century Tibet—are entirely Tibetan in character. For many Tibetans, the most loved are the second, fourth, and seventh, not least because the main story in each opera presents an innocent woman's struggles against, and ultimate transcendence of, great adversities. Most Tibetans of my generation would have seen these three operas performed many times over and would know portions of the libretti by heart.

The texts of these operas are used also by bards, known as *manipas*, who sing the stories aloud during live storytelling performances. Typically, the bard sets up an altar by hanging a thangka, or painted scroll, depicting the specific opera on a wall or a pillar and creates a mandala offering in front of the thangka atop a piece of cloth. Then, sitting on the floor aside the thangka, he or she blows on a conch shell to call the townsfolk together. During the performance, the bard indicates specific parts of the thangka with a metal pointer to signal which part of the story he or she is now narrating. In Tibet this kind of storytelling, done mostly by a wandering bard, is an important medium of dissemination of basic Buddhist values and teachings. So to see these operas now made accessible to an international audience through this volume is a source of profound personal satisfaction.

Two primary objectives have driven the creation and development of *The Library of Tibetan Classics*. The first aim is to help revitalize the appreciation and the study of the Tibetan classical heritage within Tibetan-speaking communities worldwide. The younger generation in particular struggles with the tension between traditional Tibetan culture and the realities of modern consumerism. To this end, efforts have been made to develop a comprehensive yet manageable body of texts, one that features the works of Tibet's best-known authors and covers the gamut of classical Tibetan knowledge. The second objective of *The Library of Tibetan Classics* is to help make these texts part of a global literary and intellectual heritage. In this regard, we have tried to make the English translation reader-friendly and, as much as possible, keep the body of the text free of unnecessary scholarly apparatus, which can intimidate general readers. For specialists who wish to compare the translation with the Tibetan original, page references of the critical edition of the Tibetan text are provided in brackets.

The texts in this thirty-two-volume series span more than a millennium—from the development of the Tibetan script in the seventh century to the first part of the twentieth century, when Tibetan society and culture first encountered industrial modernity. The volumes are thematically organized and cover many of the categories of classical Tibetan knowledge—from the teachings specific to each Tibetan school to the classical works on philosophy, psychology, and phenomenology. The first category includes teachings of the Kadam, Nyingma, Sakya, Kagyü, Geluk, and Jonang schools, of miscellaneous Buddhist lineages, and of the Bön school. Texts in these volumes have been largely selected by senior lineage holders of the individual schools. Texts in the other categories have been selected primarily in recognition of the historical reality of the individual disciplines. For example, in the field of epistemology, works from the Sakya and Geluk schools have been selected, while the volume on buddha-nature features the writings of Butön Rinchen Drup and various Kagyü masters. Where fields are of more common interest, such as the three codes or the bodhisattva ideal, efforts have been made to represent the perspectives of all four major Tibetan Buddhist schools. *The Library of Tibetan Classics* can function as a comprehensive library of the Tibetan literary heritage for libraries, educational and cultural institutions, and interested individuals.

It has been a real joy to be part of this important translation project. I had the pleasure of editing the original Tibetan of these texts, offering me a chance not only to closely read the texts themselves but also to reflect on the possible sources of their inspirations. To those who have the facility to read Tibetan, I draw your attention to my introduction to the Tibetan volume, which brings together my explorations on the historical, cultural, and literary context of these Tibetan operas.

I wish first of all to express my deep personal gratitude to H. H. the Dalai Lama for always being such a profound source of inspiration. I thank Gavin Kilty for producing a masterful translation of these much-loved Tibetan operas in a language and style that speak to English readers, and for his important introduction on the history of the *lhamo* operatic tradition. Thanks also to our long-time editor at Wisdom, David Kittelstrom, and to his colleague Mary Petrusewicz; and to my wife, Sophie Boyer-Langri, for taking on the numerous administrative chores that are part of a collaborative project such as this.

Finally, I would like to express my heartfelt thanks to Nita Ing and the Ing Foundation, whose long-standing patronage of the Institute of Tibetan Classics made it possible to fund the entire cost of this translation project. I would also like to acknowledge the Scully Peretsman Foundation for its generous support of my work for the institute. It is my sincere hope that the translations offered in this volume will be a source of joy and benefit to many.

Thupten Jinpa
Montreal, 2018

Translator's Introduction

ONE OF THE DELIGHTS of living in Dharamsala throughout the 1970s and '80s was spending an entire day at an outdoor performance of a folk opera put on by the local Tibetan Institute of Performing Arts. The atmosphere was one of a great picnic attended by the entire refugee community of Dharamsala. Food was packed in baskets, large thermoses were filled with Tibetan tea, maybe a bottle or two of beer was brought, and the whole family, children in tow and babies on backs, made their way up the half-mile dirt road to the performance.

The weather was guaranteed to be good because the local yogi, or *ngakpa*, had been hired to keep away the rain clouds with a ritual aided by his thigh-bone trumpet. Many a time I sat with him on the hill above the performance as he kept a lookout for any threatening cloud coming our way. If one was spotted, he would repel it with short blasts from his trumpet. I do not remember a single performance being rained off.

The audience sat cross-legged on the ground, the food and drink spread out around them. They would chat with one another, eat and drink, applaud the performances, join in the songs, laugh at the jokes, and spend the entire day in merriment. They all knew the operas, and the stories within, because there are only eight main operas and they had enjoyed them all many a time.

In the center, sometimes on a stage, sometimes on the ground, the performers enacted the opera. In beautiful, colorful costumes they sang, danced, and chanted the storyline while musicians crashed cymbals and banged drums in accompaniment.

But also on show was evidence that a race of people whose country had only recently been savagely invaded by an alien force, their whole way of life turned upside down and either forced to flee into exile in India or remain in Tibet to suffer the heavy yoke of oppression, had nevertheless retained their fortitude and cheerful disposition in the face of such adversity. That struck me then and still does today.

The Chinese and Nepalese Princesses, staged by the Tibetan Institute of
Performing Arts (TIPA), Dharamsala, 1963. The cloth backdrop
depicts the Potala Palace in Lhasa.

Lhamo

The tradition of performing arts is known as Dögar (*zlos gar*) in Tibetan,
which is described as a visual display of the human and nonhuman char-
acters of history and folklore, together with the performance of songs and
expressions of inner emotion through dance and movement.

In seventh-century Tibet, the emperor Songtsen Gampo instructed his
minister Thönmi Saṃbhota to devise a Tibetan script as a means of trans-
lating sacred Buddhist texts written in Sanskrit that were being brought into
Tibet from India. As a result, early Tibetan translators, meditator-scholars
who had studied the true meaning of the teachings with Indian masters,
were able to render Indic works into Tibetan, and it was then that the term
dögar was created.

The Tibetan word *lhamo*, in a performing arts sense, refers to the folk
operas of this tradition and is the term used to describe the eight works in
this volume. Lhamo literally means "goddess," and its application to the per-
formance of a folk opera is said to have originated in the fourteenth cen-
tury to describe the seven beautiful maidens who first performed songs and

dances at Chusur in Central Tibet under the instructions of the yogi Thang-tong Gyalpo, the reputed founder of this tradition. Lhamo is also known as Aché (*a che*) Lhamo, *aché* meaning "sister," although in the dialect of Tsang in western Tibet it just means "woman." According to Tashi Tsering, the first literary use of this term was in 1691 when it was employed to describe performances given at Tibetan government ceremonies in Lhasa.

In Tibet, and in now in exile, folk opera is the dominant performing art of the tradition. Folk opera also encompasses the individual artistic disciplines of singing, dance, mastery of musical instruments, and storytelling. Therefore the two terms *dögar* and *lhamo* are often interchangeable.

COMPONENTS

Alongside the main actors, a folk opera should possess five types of supporting participants: a director, musicians, costumed performers, comic performers, and a supporting cast. The director is the organizer, arranger, and overseer of the performance. He or she is likened to the main or head bead on a Tibetan rosary, in dependence on which the other beads have their required order.

Aché Lhamo supporting cast. The male actor, right, depicts a female goddess. The character on the left represents a Tibetan government official.

Musicians playing the traditional double-skin drum and cymbals
during a revival of the Shotön Festival in India.

The musicians augment the physical expressions, dramatized movements,
and storyline being acted out by the performers. Musical instruments are of
three main types: wind, percussion, and string. Wind instruments include
the transverse flute, the recorder, the *gyalin*—which is a long clarinet or
oboe-like instrument—the trumpet, the whistle, the conch-shell, and so on.
Percussion is divided into idiophones, or shaken and vibrated instruments—
such as small and large cymbals, bells, double-headed hand drums, and so
on—and membranophone drums, such as the kettle drum and the deco-
rated and colorfully painted double-skinned frame drum. This last instru-
ment together with the large cymbals are the two main musical instruments
used to accompany an opera performance. String instruments include the
Tibetan lute, the hammer dulcimer—which according to Samuel (1986)
probably came from China, and before that from Europe—the two-string
fiddle, the tambura, and so on.

The costumed performers occupy the stage and, through their dance and
movement, provide support to the various vocal and physical expressions of

Aché Lhamo at Chitishö, Central Tibet, 1938–39. Juniper is burned,
center stage, as an offering.

the main actors. They are divided according to which side of the story they
support and are graded as main, ordinary, and supporting performers. Their
contribution helps build the appropriate atmosphere of the performance
for the audience. Generally the costumes are colorful, stylized, and usually
include masks.

The comic performers are participants who intervene in a long perfor-
mance and provide light relief by way of jokes, topical asides, and interac-
tion with the audience. Satire as a way of gently ridiculing and criticizing
authority was commonly used by the ordinary people of Tibet, whose cul-
ture frowned on direct confrontation and outright rudeness. Therefore,
under the protection of tradition, a comic interlude within a performance
was a perfect front for expressing mild criticism of secular and religious
authority. Hugh Richardson (1986, 10) describes "the clever miming of
an oracle priest with rolling head and wild gestures" and "a remote dig at
the British when two girls in a little dance shook hands and sang 'Good
morning.'"

Nevertheless, the biting humor was not visited everywhere. Tradition
and respect dictated that some figures and topics were left untouched. Even

comic attacks that were within bounds sometimes invited the rebuke of the authorities if it was felt that the comic performers had gone too far.

The supporting cast—the singers, storytellers, helpers with costumes and scenery, and so on—conclude the five supporting elements of a folk opera performance that enhance the portrayal and telling of the story by the main performers, and the entire cast contributes to the daylong colorful spectacle enjoyed by the eagerly awaiting crowd.

The Performance

A performance should be able to convey through movement and song nine essential expressions: (1) beauty and poise, (2) splendor and radiance, (3) aversion and repulsion, (4) wonder and delight, (5) power and wrath, (6) sudden fear and fright, (7) wretchedness and pity, (8) desire and attachment, and (9) peacefulness and gentleness. The first three are expressed solely by movement, the remaining six by movement and song.

A performance consists of three main sections: the preliminary performance of the hunters, the opera, and the concluding ceremonies.

The performance of the hunters can last for an hour and is a preparatory act for the actual opera. It utilizes three kinds of performers: hunters, headmen or princes, and goddesses. The hunters' task is to purify and tame the performance space. After that the headmen bring down showers of blessings to consecrate the stage. This is followed by the songs and dances of the goddesses.

Before the hunters walk on stage two drummers beat out a signal informing the audience that the performance is about to begin. A second signal from the drummers alerts the performers to get ready. At a third signal the hunters emerge onto the stage.

They perform prostrations, offerings, and rituals, accompanied by songs, dance, and conversation, with the headmen and goddesses occasionally joining in. Since 1981 the first ceremony is a prayer to the yogi and reputed founder of the Lhamo tradition, Thangtong Gyalpo. The hunters are dressed more like fishermen than hunters and are said to represent the fisherman who appears in the opera Norsang, the second opera in this volume. They wear full face masks bordered by white hair that has the topknot of a yogi. General instructions for their performance say they should be "dignified, elegant, and imposing" and their movements should resemble "a vulture spreading out its wings." The leader of the hunters is also the teacher of the troupe and has the responsibility of reciting the opera narrative.

Hunter dancers, holding decorated arrows, prepare an auspicious
beginning for an opera performed in Tibet.

A headman, played by a senior
troupe member in Darjeeling,
West Bengal, India, 1964.
Wearing a conical felt hat
and carrying a long staff,
he performs special songs
accompanied by hand gestures
to "let fall the rain of blessings."

Young Tibetan women play the part of goddesses for a performance in India.

The two headmen (*gyalu*) are portrayed as pious and dignified, and are usually played by older members of the troupe. Their task is to perform a dance ritual to consecrate the performing area. The goddesses are played by younger members and portrayed as charming and gracious. They perform songs and dances in the third part of this preliminary section, and also as an accompaniment to the hunters and headmen.

As an ending to the hunters' performance, the goddesses line up in a semi-circle around the stage, the play is announced, the narration begins, and the main actors emerge onto the stage. The performance proceeds in a way that has much in common with folk operas around the world. The narrator, who is usually the leader of the hunters, maintains the continuation of the story and announces the characters as they appear. This he does from memory for the whole of the performance, mostly in prose, and in a drone-like parlando or declamatory style. Traditional instructions say that the narrative should maintain a rhythm like that of "threading pearls on a string" but with a clarity resembling "flowing water." Sometimes the actors themselves will recite the narration.

A character also announces his or her entrance on stage with a dance particular to the role. Dances can be performed by the actors individually or in groups, and by goddesses in unison. The goddesses will dance in between scenes.

The actors play out the story in verse, song, and prose. A lot of the dialogue between them is sung in verse "songs" known as *namthar*. In classical religious literature, *namthar* refers to the biography of a lama, but here the term encompasses the unfolding narrative. The songs are initially delivered solo and a cappella. The *namthar* style of singing is of a high register, without going into falsetto, and makes frequent use of a glottal vibrato and inflection. It is a skill that demands much training. The songs can be "long tune" or "short tune." Those of long tune often begin with a long, drawn-out sound without meaning and rising in pitch. They may also contain extra syllables that add no meaning to the message but serve to lengthen the tune. Long-tune singing is the most distinctive voice heard in Tibetan opera and is a skill difficult to master. Of the types of voices, the male and female voice are the most prevalent. The male voice is low in pitch, loud, and open-throated. The female voice is pitched high and is constricted. After a few lines the solo singer is supported by a chorus intervention sung by the goddesses, who have remained on stage since the preliminaries. Finally, the whole troupe joins in. Thupten Jinpa tells an amusing anecdote from a performance given in India, soon after exile, where a member of the Indian audience was overheard attempting to explain the performance to others: "First one cries, then another cries, and finally they all start crying!"

The *namthar* style of singing is unique to Tibetan opera. It is combined with swirling dances, fast narration delivery, the accompaniment of drums and cymbals, the occasional folk song, and comic interludes, all performed in striking costumes. The result is a daylong treat for the audience, a rich and colorful presentation of a well-known myth or story, to be enjoyed by young and old, rich and poor alike.

Traditionally, the cymbal and the large double-sided drum were the only two instruments used in a Lhamo performance, but trumpets and other instruments can make an appearance. Skillful playing of these two main instruments can illustrate for the audience the personality of the character they are accompanying or the atmosphere of the scene.

The libretto of an opera used by the performers bears little resemblance to the literary texts of the operas presented in this volume. In these literary works, most text is in conversational dialogue, but there is none of the stage direction, repetitions in *namthar* singing by the chorus, and so on. Performers in a troupe were illiterate and learned their lines orally from the teacher or director. However, there is anecdotal evidence that even some of

Actors are presented with white offering scarves, at the
conclusion of a Lhamo performance, Chitishö, Tibet, 1938.

the greatest Lhamo teachers were also illiterate and had learned the librettos
by heart from someone else orally.

The conclusion or epilogue of an opera consists of statements about the
play, salutations to the Dalai Lama, and prayers and wishes of auspicious-
ness for the future. It will also include the well-known barley-flour-throwing
ritual ending with the cry, "May the gods be victorious!"

The Eight Operas

Tibetan Lhamo brings to the people the fundamental ethical laws of
behavior and teachings of natural justice based on Buddhist doctrine, with-
out the need for literacy or scholarly pursuit. The operas show that good is
the right way and will ultimately prevail, and that the bad, no matter how
successful they are in the beginning, are doomed to fail and to suffer for
their actions.

The operas revolve around the fundamental impulses and urges of the
human condition: the desire for power, the seduction of attraction, thoughts
of revenge, the fear of pain, the longing that comes from separation, the wish
to be free from oppression, the attachments of family, and so on. They are

set in India or Tibet, in places often mythologized by the telling of the story. The characters are often kings, queens, and ministers; ordinary folk such as children, young men and women, and elderly mothers and fathers; and yogis, monks, and various beings from other realms, such as gods and nāgas. The action involves plotting, kidnapping, exile, fighting and death, journeys to faraway lands, separation, reconciliation, and often a quest to attain some seemingly impossible treasure.

The stories are long and involve many plot twists. Sometimes their storylines span many years. But they all end in happiness, where the good achieve their goals and the bad receive their just deserts.

Some operas in this volume tell of events, real or mythologized, that occurred in old Tibet, some can be traced to Indic Buddhist works, such as those that tell of the previous lives of the Buddha, and some are myths centered on the past lives of a great lama or teacher. They all seek to teach, entertain, and enthrall their audiences.

The eight operas in this volume form the mainstay of Tibetan performance troupes in the past in Tibet and these days in exile. Each takes many hours to perform.

1. Drimé Kunden

This is a story declaiming the virtues of selfless giving, which refers to a willingness to give to others without the slightest attachment to wealth or possession. The eponymous hero is driven by a longing to give away everything he owns to those who merely ask. This desire lands him in trouble with his father, the king, because ultimately he gives away a precious wish-granting jewel that kept the kingdom safe from enemies. As a punishment he is banished into exile with his wife and children. Even in exile he continues his giving and parts with his children, his wife, and his eyes. Finally, however, the beggars who requested such impossible gifts reveal themselves as gods and announce that they were only testing the prince. His family and eyesight are restored and they return to their repentant father.

This story has its origin in a well-known Jataka, or past-life story, of the Buddha when he was born as Prince Viśvantara. This particular Jataka is the ninth in the *Garland of Past Lives* by the Indian master Aśvaghoṣa.[1]

2. Norsang

In this long and winding tale a malicious king of a southern Indian kingdom eyes enviously his more prosperous northern neighbor and attempts to lure the nāgas of the northern lakes, who are the source of its prosperity, to the southern kingdom. He employs an immoral yogi to do this, but he is thwarted by a valiant hunter who lives by the side of the lake. The nāga queen in gratitude invites the hunter to the nāga realm deep in the lake, and there she gives him a special wish-granting jewel. The hunter takes the jewel and approaches a well-intended yogi, who explains its powers. The hunter learns of a nearby celestial bathing pool visited by goddesses, and he persuades the yogi to take him there.

The hunter becomes smitten by Manoharā, the most beautiful of the goddesses, and returns to the nāga queen to obtain from her a jewel with lasso-like powers capable of ensnaring anyone. He persuades her to part with it, and returning to the celestial bathing pools with the yogi, he seizes Manoharā. The goddess is saddened by the prospect of having to spend her life with a low-class hunter and would rather die. Concerned, the yogi persuades the hunter to offer Manoharā to the noble king of the northern kingdom, Norsang, in return for a position of power.

Norsang takes Manoharā for his wife and rewards the hunter. His other queens begin to resent Manoharā, calling her a wanderer who was brought into the kingdom by a hunter. They approach a yogi called Hari and deceitfully persuade him to separate the couple. Hari causes the king's father to have troubling dreams, as a consequence of which he approaches Hari and asks for a divination. Hari tells him there are wicked wild men of the north plotting to overthrow the kingdom, and only Norsang can defeat them.

After a great ceremony, Norsang is sent away to do battle in the north. Meanwhile the queens plot to kill Manoharā. Hari persuades Norsang's father that Manoharā is in fact a demon, and that her heart should be torn out and its fat used in a bathing ritual as a way to appease the troubles that were befalling the kingdom. The father is persuaded and provides weapons for the queens to attack Manoharā's palace. However, she is able to escape by flying into the skies using a special necklace given to her by the yogi who helped set her free from the hunter.

Manoharā disappears and sets off to her celestial realm, but before she reaches it she visits her yogi friend and tells him how Norsang should navigate his way to her home, if he decides to come and bring her back.

After a long journey and a battle, Norsang defeats the enemies of the north and returns home. There he finds his beautiful wife has disappeared. He realizes what has happened and sets out to search for her. Receiving directions from the yogi, he eventually travels to the celestial realm that was her home. Skillfully negotiating the traps laid for him, he meets up with Manoharā again. However, her father, the celestial king, is unwilling to let her go back to the human realm and has other suitors in mind. An archery contest is arranged, with the winner to take Manoharā as his queen. Norsang wins and leads her back to his kingdom. They are welcomed back, Hari and the queens are punished, and all is restored.

This complex story is said to be based on a Jataka tale of the same name retold in *Wish-Fulfilling Tree of the Bodhisattva's Lives*, a collection of stories told in a rich poetic form by the thirteenth-century Kashmiri author Kṣemendra, and which was translated into Tibetan alongside the Sanskrit original and placed in the Tengyur.[2] Later, in the seventeenth century, the Fifth Dalai Lama oversaw its publication, thereby ensuring its popularity. Also, Thupten Jinpa points out that in the thirteenth century the Tibetan master Karma Rangjung Dorjé compiled a collection of Jataka tales from the Sutra and Vinaya collection of the Kangyur, known as *The Hundred Jataka Tales*, and the Norsang Jataka is the eighty-eighth of that collection. The folk opera of Norsang reproduced in this volume and other versions found these days in the Tibet canon differ considerably from their Jataka origins, although the characters and basic exploits run through all versions. The version in this volume was compiled by Dingchen Tsering Wangdü, an eighteenth-century official at Shelkar Dzong Monastery in southern Tibet.

Norsang is considered to be the oldest written opera in Tibet, and melodies from other operas have been copied from those performed in it. Moreover, the hunter and the prince who appear in the prologue of all Tibetan operas are based on the hunter and the prince Norsang of this opera.

3. The Chinese and Nepalese Princesses

This opera recounts how the Tibetan emperor Songtsen Gampo brought his two brides from China and Nepal in the seventh century. However, much of the story is taken up with the skillful manipulations performed by the minister Gar Tongtsen, who was charged with bringing the princesses back to Tibet. He managed first to persuade the Nepalese king to part with his beloved daughter, who was considered to be an incarnation of Tārā, by matching his demands. As part of her dowry the princess brought four statues to Tibet, two of which reside in Lhasa's main temple, while another was brought to India and resides now in the temple at Dharamsala.

The main characters of *The Chinese and Nepalese Princesses* opera,
staged at Conium House, Dharamsala, 1966.

Gar Tongtsen's exploits in China are even more elaborate, and mostly
involve tricking the Chinese emperor into parting with Princess Kongjo.
However, he is also portrayed as self-sacrificing and willingly remains in
China, where he marries a Chinese woman to ensure that the princess is
delivered safely to Songtsen Gampo. Eventually, through more trickery, he
escapes and returns to Tibet. The ability of this Tibetan minister to fool and
make mockery of a Chinese emperor is not lost on the Tibetan people and
is played up as much as possible. In recent times the Chinese have reinstated
productions of this opera in Tibet, mainly in order to instill in the recalci-
trant Tibetans a sense of patriotism for the motherland. However, it is dif-
ficult to imagine that the clever exploits of Gar will take much of a place in
their production! The Chinese princess brought with her the famous Jowo
statue of the Buddha that now graces the main temple in Lhasa.

The opera text is based heavily on two Tibetan works: *Maṇikabüm*[3] and
Mirror Illuminating the Royal Genealogies.[4] The first of these is a renowned
work said to be mainly composed by Songtsen Gampo and revealed as a
treasure text by three later masters. It focuses on meditative practices around
the deity of compassion, Avalokiteśvara. As Songtsen Gampo is considered
to be an incarnation of this deity, his life is recounted in the fourth section

of the work. The second text is a fourteenth-century Tibetan chronicle attributed to Lama Dampa Sönam Gyaltsen.

4. NANGSA ÖBUM

This is an indigenous Tibetan story based on events that occurred around the eleventh century near the town of Gyangtsé, west of Lhasa. Nangsa was a beautiful young woman who wanted to devote herself to the Dharma, but her beauty attracted the attention of the local governor who was seeking a bride for his son. Her parents were in no position to resist the authority of the governor and Nangsa was taken away to become a bride.

After seven years she gave birth to a son. One day while she was working with others in the fields two cotton-clad yogis appeared asking for alms. Filled with devotion, Nangsa gave some of the harvest to them. Her husband's sister, who witnessed this, flew into a rage and beat Nangsa, but then ran to her brother saying that Nangsa had beat her. Nangsa's husband believed his sister and he too beat his wife.

Later a lama, who had manifested as a beggar and his dancing monkey, arrived at the house. Nangsa wanted to give them something and brought them secretly into the house. This was discovered by her husband, who beat her again and took away her little son. The pain and grief was too much for Nangsa and that night she died. Filled with remorse, her husband placed her body on the mountain top. There her consciousness wandered off into the intermediate state, where she came into the presence of the Lord of Death. He saw that Nangsa was no ordinary woman and told her that she should return to her life and do good in the world.

Nangsa returns to life and, entreated by her repentant family and her son, takes up her place again in the family. She teaches the Dharma and involves herself in worldly life. Yet she becomes discouraged by the lack of response to her teachings and by having no time to devote herself to the Dharma. Seeing her sadness, her husband sends her to her parents, hoping to wean her away from the religious life.

Back with her parents, she still yearns for the religious life, much to their annoyance. After one particular incident when Nangsa starts weaving in the courtyard and singing beautiful allegorical songs using the parts of the loom as metaphors for the Dharma, her mother becomes enraged and throws her out of the house. That evening she leaves the house and finally arrives at the monastery of the lama who had previously manifested as the beggar and the monkey. After a series of tests, she is taken in by the lama to become his disciple, and after a few months of meditation she gains many realizations.

Sometime later her husband and his army arrive at the monastery to take her back. They attack and scatter the monks. Fearful that her lama would be killed, Nangsa rises into the air and shows her powerful supernatural feats. Her husband and his army are cowed. They repent their ways, her son takes over the kingdom, and Nangsa is free to continue her spiritual journey.

This story is considered to be based on actual events, and the text of this volume mentions that while Nangsa was at the monastery she meditated in a cave and that imprints of her cloak can still be seen on its walls "like impressions made in butter."

Nangsa is often cited as an example of the phenomenon of a death-returner (*'das log*), one who returns to life after death. Many accounts of death-returners are to be found in Tibetan literature, but Nangsa is the only one to have been made into an opera.

5. DROWA SANGMO

Drowa Sangmo was the beautiful manifestation of a celestial ḍākinī, born to poor and aged parents in India. Upon her birth, the ḍākinīs made predictions, including that her life would be obstructed by a demon and so at that time she would fly off to the celestial realms. One day a king who had lost his hunting dog came to their little hut in search of the dog. Seeing Drowa Sangmo, he was smitten and took her against her wishes to be his wife. Eventually she gave birth to a son and daughter. The king's other queen was the manifestation of a demon and developed great hatred for Drowa. Recalling the prophecy, Drowa Sangmo sent her children to the king and flew away to the ḍākinī realms.

Meanwhile the demoness fed poison to the king to drive him insane and hatched a plot to kill the children. Feigning illness, she told her minister that only the warm hearts of the two children would cure her. The children were given to two butchers to be killed, but they were unable to carry out the task. They sent back the hearts of two dogs instead, but the demoness queen discovered the deceit and gave the children to two fishermen to carry out the deed. They too could not kill the children and set them free in the forest.

In the forest the children suffered much. The boy is killed by a snake, but their mother manifests as a medicinal snake and he is brought back to life. Finally, they are recaptured by the demoness queen and given to two outcaste men to be killed. Out of pity one of the outcastes releases the girl, but the other throws the boy off a cliff. Their mother manifests as a hawk and catches him. He lands in the sea and his mother, now a fish, carries him to the water's edge. Eventually, with help from more manifestations of his mother, the little prince is taken to the land of Padminī, where he is crowned king. Finally, his sister makes her way to Padminī, and brother and sister are reunited.

Meanwhile, the demoness queen hears that the young son has become king of Padminī and at once assembles a large army to attack it. However, the young son defeats her in battle and she is killed. Their father is cured of his madness, released from prison, and is reunited with his children.

This story appears to have a connection with the tribal peoples of Mön, a region of Tibet that spills over into the far northeastern part of Arunachal Pradesh in India. The region is mentioned in the text, and according to Snyder the people of Mön can identify the ruins of Mandal Gang Palace, where the king lived.

6. THE BROTHERS DÖNYÖ AND DÖNDRUP

This story is set in India, where a pious king and queen long for a son. After performing many rituals, a very special son was born to them. The royal couple were overjoyed, but soon after the queen died. Not long after that, the king became attracted to an ordinary woman he had seen in the crowd. He took her for his queen and she too gave birth to a son. These are the two brothers of the title, and they became inseparable.

Soon the queen began to resent the older brother because he was destined to inherit the throne over her own son. She feigned an illness, saying that the only cure was the heart of the older son, who was a demon who had killed his own mother and now was hurting her. The king was persuaded but could not bring himself to kill his own son. Upon hearing all this, the older son was determined to flee the palace. His brother begged to go with him. So one night they stole off into the forests. They suffered much on their journey across desolate plains, and one day the younger brother died of his deprivations. His surviving brother carried him on his back until he found a suitable place to inter him. In grief, he went on his way.

The gods Śakra and Brahma manifested as humans and with medicine brought the younger brother back to life, who immediately went off in search of his brother.

Meanwhile the older brother had found a teacher living the life of a solitary hermit in the forests. He remained with his guru, serving him devotedly.

One day he was seized from the guru by a nearby king who was searching for a youth to offer as sacrifice to a lakĕ, which in the past had attracted a dragon whose arrival was responsible for bringing good harvests and prosperity to the kingdom. The dragon had not been seen for some time and the land was in famine. The king, in keeping with the words of a soothsayer, planned to offer the older brother as sacrifice. The king's daughter, meanwhile, had fallen in love with the handsome prince and was unable to bear his sacrifice. Seeing this, the compassionate prince arranged for the sacrifice to take place secretly while she was asleep.

In the lake the prince did not die but gave teachings to the nāgas there. Later he returned to his guru in his forest abode. The prosperity of the land increased and the king invited the guru in order to thank him for providing his disciple as sacrifice to the dragon. The prince accompanied his guru, his face hidden by a cloth. While in the palace the cloth slipped from his face and the king and his daughter were overjoyed to see that the prince had not perished. The prince married the daughter and was installed as king.

One day on a picnic, the older brother, now a king, wandered off in the forests. There he met a bedraggled youth calling out his name and declaring that he had his brother's share of food. The two brothers were reunited and returned joyfully to the palace.

Later the two brothers returned to their father's palace. The king, happily reunited with his sons, forgave the queen her misdeeds, and the two kingdoms were shared between the two brothers.

This story explicitly expresses Buddhist concepts throughout and even ends with the guru making predictions concerning the future rebirths of the main protagonists in Tibet. According to tradition, this story was written by the Fifth Panchen Lama, Losang Yeshé (1663–1737), and Thupten Jinpa has seen a woodblock print of this story in which the colophon reads: "The secret life of Panchen Losang Yeshé." Also, there is a widespread view that the two brothers and the relationship between them represent the Dalai Lamas and the Panchen Lamas, and the bond that exists between them. However, the twenty-first story in the ancient *Vetala Stories*[5] tells a tale of two brothers whose names match those of this opera.

7. SUKYI NYIMA

In this story a non-Buddhist king in India is on his way to make blood sacrifices to his god when he sees a beautiful low-caste maiden collecting water.

He becomes infatuated with her and takes her for his queen, despite the dire warnings of his clairvoyant talking parrot.

As the story goes, a hunter in pursuit of a pig comes across an extraordinarily beautiful maiden coming to fetch water. The hunter thinks to tell the king of her, hoping for a reward if the king takes her for his bride. Although the maiden, who was Sukyi Nyima, refuses to answer any of his questions, the hunter reports her presence to the king. The king, accompanied by the hunter, sets off to see for himself. Agreeing that she was the most beautiful woman he had ever seen, the king makes repeated attempts day after day to engage her in conversation, but to no avail. Finally, they follow her and see that she is living a religious and ascetic life with her yogi guru. After much persuasion, the yogi agrees to let Sukyi Nyima be taken by the king for his bride, although it is against her will. The yogi secretly gives her a special rosary for her protection, and she leaves for the palace to be married to the king.

The king adopts the Buddhist path, and when he no longer pays the first queen any attention, she becomes resentful of Sukyi Nyima. A woman in the queen's retinue then offers to help her get her own way. The woman, skillful in dance and singing, uses her charms to inveigle herself into the king's inner circle. There she wins the trust of Sukyi Nyima and cleverly manages to exchange the protection rosary for a lookalike fake. With the protection removed, she drugs the king and his entourage. While they are unconscious she kills his extraordinary elephant and makes it so that the blame falls on Sukyi Nyima. When this and other ruses do not convince the king, she kills the king's own son and smears Sukyi Nyima with his blood.

The king is angry but is unable to kill his beautiful queen. Instead she is given to three butchers to be dragged off to a cemetery and cut to pieces. However, they too are unable to kill her and cut her free from the cemetery slab.

Sukyi Nyima wanders abroad and makes her way to her guru's hut, which she finds in ruins. The guru had died and only his relics remained, worshipped by the animals. She stays there for many years engaged in meditation.

Finally, she receives a vision of her guru, who tells her to go among the people and teach the Dharma. Disguising herself as a low beggar woman, she teaches the Dharma in the towns and cities until finally the first queen, in a state of regret for her deeds, confesses, though unaware that she is confessing to Sukyi Nyima. However, a wise minister recognizes her and informs the king that Sukyi Nyima is still alive. The king is overjoyed. Sukyi Nyima becomes queen again, and after a while a son is born. When he grows up, the king is persuaded to become a monk. The son becomes king and Sukyi Nyima and the former king go off to a remote monastery and spend their lives in meditation.

Some say this play is based on the Indian play *Śakuntalā*, which was adapted from the Mahabharata by Kālidāsa, but there seems little resemblance. However, the prologue states: "The story of brahman Sukyi Nyima, whose message is to urge those of great desire to renounce samsara, was translated into Tibetan long ago by Lotsāwa Vairocana and She'u Lotsāwa. This version follows the translation of She'u Lotsāwa." Moreover, there are Sanskrit references in the story and one or two Sanskrit names. Others say it was composed by a lama from southern Tibet who, of course, may have been familiar with Sanskrit.

8. PEMA ÖBAR

In India a non-Buddhist king is fearful that Sudhana, a wealthy merchant, will eclipse him in wealth. Therefore the king sends him, on pain of death, on an impossible mission to find a wish-fulfilling jewel far away in the ocean. On the journey Sudhana's boat is capsized by nāgas and the whole crew is captured by a race of female cannibals who take them as husbands. Deciding to escape, they ply the cannibals with beer and then flee to a desert to meet with a flying horse who will carry them all to safety. However, the crew, with the exception of Sudhana, make the fatal mistake of looking back as they fly through the skies on the horse. This causes them to fall, and they are devoured by the cannibals. Sudhana is taken to Tushita heaven.

Meanwhile, Sudhana's wife miraculously gives birth to a son, who is an incarnation of the great Indian yogi Padmasambhava. As the child grows up he becomes curious about his father, but his mother does not tell him the truth. One day as he engages in the business of selling yarn with an old woman in a market, she lets slip some information about his father. Pressed to reveal more, she tells him the whole story of Sudhana and his journey.

Meanwhile, the king in his palace sees from afar the yarn in the market and is attracted by its glow. Sending his minister to make inquiries, he learns about the existence of Sudhana's son. Fearful of him, he sends the boy on a difficult mission to find a special jewel in the ocean. Before Pema Öbar leaves, a ḍākinī gives him a powerful mantra to say in times of danger.

Pema sets out with his crew, and thanks to the mantra he is able to subdue the nāgas who caused his father so much trouble. The same mantra helps to gain the jewel from the nāgas, and he returns home to his mother.

A *Pema Öbar* performance at the Norbulingka palace, Lhasa.

The king is even more worried and sends him out again, this time to fetch a golden pan from the land of the cannibals. On each of the four stages of the journey he meets a fierce cannibal woman but is able to escape her clutches and even win her friendship and trust with help from the mantra. Finally, he arrives in the land of the queen of the cannibals with her sixty sons. He wins her over with his courage and his mantra and manages to evade the hungry sons. She gives him the golden pan, and through the mantra she is transformed into a beautiful ḍākinī. Together they fly off to Tibet. On the way they pick up the other four cannibals, and they too are transformed into ḍākinīs. Pema also picks up an item from each cannibal land.

Upon Pema Öbar's arrival back home, the king is even more fearful of him and orders that he be burned in sacrifice on a high mountain. This is done and his ashes scattered to the winds. The ḍākinīs go to the place of sacrifice and restore Pema back to life. They invite the king and his wicked ministers to fly with them in the golden pan. Taking them over the cannibal lands, they tip the pan and the king and his ministers fall out to become food for the cannibals below. Pema comes down from the mountain and is crowned king.

It is widely accepted that the story of Pema Öbar is an account of a past incarnation of Padmasambhava, as the text itself makes clear.

LING GESAR

Worthy of inclusion in a volume on Tibetan performing arts would have been the epic of the legendary Tibetan hero Ling Gesar. However, it is a vast story divided into six main episodes and spanning over a hundred volumes.[6] Gesar is the archetypal warrior king, lord of the land of Ling, whose conquering exploits have been told in song, poetry, and prose throughout Tibet, Mongolia, and Central Asia for centuries. It is one of the few oral epic traditions to survive as a performing art. Whether Gesar was an actual person is still a matter of debate. Li Lianrong (2001, 317) states: "After nearly a half-century of research, scholars have reached basic agreement that either the epic's protagonist Ling Gesar was a real person or he is a synthetic character created by the combination of historical figures."

There is a general consensus that the epic began around the twelfth century. The core story has been summed up by Samuel:

> King Gesar has a miraculous birth, a despised and neglected childhood, and then becomes ruler and wins his (first) wife Drükmo through a series of marvelous feats. In subsequent episodes he defends his people against various external aggressors, human and superhuman. Instead of dying a normal death he departs into a hidden realm from which he may return at some time in the future to save his people from their enemies. (2005, chap. 8)

The Origins and Development of the Lhamo Tradition

The tradition of singing and dancing in a community must be as old as humanity itself. Songs and dances are a natural expression of the inner feelings that are an innate part of the human condition. Jikmé Wangyal (2009, 51) says that the inner pain and joy of Tibetan people spill into physical and outer expression "like Tibetan tea and soup bubbling up in the pot and causing the lid to rattle," and that such singing and dancing were the beginnings of the performing arts tradition in Tibet. These songs and dances were later codified and organized into performances for the entertainment of local communities.

Jikmé Wangyal also describes the mythical origins of performance art in ancient India. Long ago in antiquity, singing and dancing was widespread in the celestial realms of the gods. However, the gods pointed out to Brahma, the celestial ruler, that the age of plenty had come to an end and that now living beings were plagued by all kinds of suffering, and they pleaded with him to find a way to end their miseries. Therefore Brahma created the four Vedas, in which can be found storytelling, melodic intonation, movement and dance, and expression.

In Tibet, texts of the Bön tradition, which was the dominant religious tradition before Buddhism found its way into Tibet in the seventh century, describe types of ritual dances that were in existence during the time of the tradition's founder, who some say predates the Buddha. Other indigenous works on Tibetan history describe the existence of a tradition of singing and dancing during the time of the first Tibetan emperor, said to have ruled in the first century BCE.

In the seventh century, the Tibetan king Songtsen Gampo brought his two brides from China and Nepal, an event depicted in the opera *The Chinese and Nepalese Princesses.* There are mural depictions on the walls of the Potala and the Jokhang Temples in Lhasa portraying the festive singing and dancing that welcomed the brides as they arrived in Tibet. When the eighth-century emperor Trisong Detsen built the great temple of Samyé, southwest of Lhasa, the local people put on a great festival of song and dance for the consecration celebrations that went on for days. This too is recorded on portico murals around Samyé. It is also said that the emperor asked the children of the Kongpo region to perform a dance in order to distract the spirits while the temple was being built.

The Tibetan literary tradition of performing arts seems to have begun in the thirteenth century with the composition of works by Sakya Pandit (Sakya Paṇḍita Kunga Gyaltsen, 1182–1251). He translated many ornaments of poetics found in the *Mirror of Poetics,*[7] composed by the seventh-century Indian grammarian Daṇḍin, and wrote his own works on the performing arts, such as *Treatise on Music.*[8] Jikmé Wangyal thinks that this period also marked the time when performances were first written down.

Nevertheless, Thupten Jinpa remarks that although it might have been deemed necessary to incorporate the various phonic rules taught in these analytical works into the Lhamo tradition, it seems that they have remained the preserve of the scholars while Aché Lhamo was valued and sustained by the common folk.

Mahāsiddha Thangtong Gyalpo

According to oral tradition, the founder of the Aché Lhamo performing arts tradition was the fourteenth-century Tibetan yogi Thangtong Gyalpo. He was born in Tö Yeru in Tsang, in western Tibet, and died in Riwoché in Tsang. His dates are either 1361–1485 or 1385–1464. If the first dates are accepted, he lived to be over one hundred twenty years.

As a child he was intelligent and caring. His parents placed him in Jangding Monastery. Eventually he took the vows of a monk and was given the name Tsöndrü Sangpo. He studied the major texts and at the age of eighteen visited Nepal and India, where he studied with tantric masters.

One day on his travels in Tibet, he was unable to pay a ferryman the cost of the journey across the river. The ferryman hit him over the head with his paddle and threw him in the river. At first humiliated by this experience, he became determined to relieve the hardships of travelers who had to cross large rivers and steep valleys and set about becoming a bridge builder. He began digging for and smelting iron ore and built his first bridge in Kongpo district, in southwest Tibet. Soon he spread his bridge-building expertise to other parts of Tibet and he became known as Chaktsampa (iron-bridge builder).

His work involved seeking out large quantities of iron, and for this he needed funds. Among his workers were seven sisters from Lhokha in southern Tibet who had beautiful singing voices. Thangtong Gyalpo taught them songs and dances. Some sources say two maidens played the hunters, four played the goddesses, one was the musician, and Thangtong himself played the drums. They performed for local communities in order to raise money to buy the iron. This was the first Lhamo troupe. The sisters were so beautiful and such perfect singers that audiences soon referred to their performances as those of "goddesses" (*lhamo*). Thus the tradition was born and Thangtong Gyalpo, the yogi and bridge builder, is said to be its founder. In the end he was able to raise enough money to construct fifty-eight bridges.

However, in the written biographies of Thangtong Gyalpo there is no mention of his Lhamo fundraising activities or that he was the founder of the Lhamo tradition.[9] It is only in the oral tradition that he is credited as such. As to why his Lhamo activities are not found in his older biographies, Tashi Tsering thinks that it could be because his Lhamo activities rank below that of his other deeds, which, apart from bridge building, include constructing temples, publishing scriptures, creating shrines, and so on. Alternatively, his name as the founder of Aché Lhamo could have been added posthumously, or it might be because singers and performers were not afforded that much respect in Tibetan culture and performance art was not deemed an appropriate deed to be included in a written biography. However, Tashi Tsering cites incidental references from other texts that point to Thangtong Gyalpo being the founder of at least a tradition of Lhamo.

Whatever the case, paintings and drawings of Thangtong Gyalpo are always there in any present-day Lhamo environment, and since the 1980s a prayer to him is always recited at the beginning of a performance. He is indelibly linked to the performing arts tradition of Tibet and has become its patron saint.

Development of Lhamo and Other Troupes

Outside the Lhamo tradition, other song and dance traditions flourished in Tibet. Some were performed by troupes of minstrels and dancers who entertained the Lhasa aristocracy. Their two main types of performance were Nangma songs and Western songs. Nangma were elegant renditions, whereas Western songs from Tsang were more from the folk-dance traditions and often quick-stepping in tempo. The term *nangma* means "inner" and is said to have originated in the seventeenth century from Lhasa, where Desi Sangyé Gyatso, the prime minister of the Fifth Dalai Lama, and other officials would watch musical performances in the rooms of the Potala inner circle. The Fifth Dalai himself contributed to the development of the performing arts tradition by designing masks and costumes for hunters in the introductory section of a Lhamo.

Another tradition was that of the Gar dances. On these, Jamyang Norbu writes:

> Gar was an ancient musical and dance tradition maintained in the court of the Dalai Lamas and certain monasteries of Tibet. It was of an entirely secular character and had no relationship to the Tantric dances, although it bore the same name.[10] The maintenance of a Gar troupe and its accompanying orchestra was considered the prerogative of a king, and its performance the symbol of royalty. The dances were, for the most part, performed by a troupe of thirteen small boys, each carrying a small battle-axe,

and accompanied by an orchestra of paired kettle drums and double-reed oboes. (1986, 132)

According to one source, Gar was introduced to Central Tibet at the beginning of the seventeenth century, during the time of the Fifth Dalai Lama, by the ruler of Tsang in western Tibet. He in turn had brought it from Ngari in the far west, which was ruled by descendants of the emperors of old Tibet, such as Songtsen Gampo. Other sources say it came from the former Buddhist kingdom of Ladakh, which region historically included the Baltistan Valleys, the entire upper Indus Valley, and much of Ngari.

Outside of Lhasa, circle dancing and royal songs were popular in western Tibet. In eastern Tibet troupes performed Ling dances in honor of the legendary hero Ling Gesar. Also in eastern Tibet roving troupes called "the cotton-clad ones" performed songs and dances handed down from Rechungpa, the disciple of the eleventh-century yogi Jetsun Milarepa. In southern Tibet, villages performed the famous drum dance.

By the eighteenth century many Lhamo troupes were in existence, especially in Lhasa. According to Snyder, there were ten established troupes that performed at events such as the Shotön Festival. Of these, the Kyormolung, Gyalkhar, Chung, and Shang troupes were the best known.[11]

The Kyormolung was the largest and most popular troupe, originally hailing from the town of Kyormolung, twelve miles west of Lhasa, and founded by a woman called Dangsang Lhamo. It was the only "professional" troupe in the sense that its members, about forty in all, had no land and were not tax-paying farmers, but were obliged, nevertheless, to perform at certain events, which was considered as a tax in kind. Their upkeep was assigned to Kundeling Monastery by the Thirteenth Dalai Lama. Their standard Lhamo repertoire was *Pema Öbar*, *Sukyi Nyima*, and *Drowa Sangmo*.

The Gyalkhar troupe originally came from Rinpung in Tsang and belonged to the Kagyü Buddhist tradition. They were a semimonastic troupe insofar as they dressed as monks and often performed in monasteries, but they were laymen and allowed to marry. They had about twenty members and membership was handed down to sons. This troupe excelled in their performance of *Norsang*, and its standard Lhamo repertoire also included *Nangsa Öbum* and *The Chinese and Nepalese Princesses*.

The Chung troupe was affiliated with Chung Riwoché Monastery, near Ngamring, southwest of Lhasa. This monastery belonged to the Nyingma

The wandering Kyormolung troupe, Chitishö, Tibet, 1938–39.

school of Tibetan Buddhism and was closely connected with Thangtong Gyalpo. It numbered about fifteen members taken from the sixty or so families that lived in the Chung Valley. This troupe did not perform regularly at the Shotön Festival in Lhasa because of its remote location, but it became a yearly performer when it became a favorite troupe of the Thirteenth Dalai Lama. Its repertoire included *Norsang, Nangsa Öbum*, and *The Brothers Dönyö and Döndrup.*

The Shang troupe was from Namling district in Tsang. Numbering around fifteen players, it was the lesser known of the four troupes. For a while it replaced the Chung troupe at the Shotön Festival. Its repertoire included *Drimé Kunden, The Chinese and Nepalese Princesses*, and *Nangsa Öbum.*

There were six lesser groups that did not perform full plays at the Shotön Festival. The Tashi Shöl troupe was from Yarlung, southeast of Lhasa in Lhokha district. They numbered about ten players and counted *Norsang* and *Nangsa* in their repertoire. Other sources speak of three Tashi Shöl troupes from Yarlung. It seems that this name refers to the type of performance given rather than the name of one particular troupe. The Shedra Nyemo and

The Tashi Shöl troupe from Lhoka province, performing the
preliminary songs of *The Chinese and Nepalese Princesses*
at the Norbulingka, Lhasa, August 1921.

Thönpa Nyemo troupes came from Nyemo between Lhasa and Tsang, and
were named after the aristocratic families they were bound to. The Pundun
Drok Kharpa troupe came from Chongyé in Lhokha, and were farmers
bound to the Phalha family. "Pundun" means seven siblings and is said to
refer to the seven maidens employed by Thangtong Gyalpo, as described
above. The Nangtsé and Tshomé troupes, numbering about eight members
in each troupe, were from a place west of Lhasa.

Except for the Kyormolung, the Lhamo troupes consisted of farming
families who worked the lands owned by their aristocratic or monastic land-
lords. They were also taxpayers, and their performances during the Shotön
Festival served as partial exemptions to their tax-paying liabilities. As men-
tioned, the Kyormolung troupe had no land and were a wandering group of
performers. Their income from their performances was often in the form
of goods, such as butter, flour, tea, and so on, and they also received money
from the government and sponsors. All troupes received gifts on the day of
the performances, often from members of the audience. Outside of Lhasa,
the troupes were often required to perform at certain monasteries as they
made their way back home after the festivities in Lhasa. These too provided
income.

Aché Lhamo performed in a paved courtyard
of Drepung Monastery, Lhasa, late 1930s.

All troupes, especially the Kyormolung, were ultimately answerable to the government, or specifically the Potala Treasury Office. No member of the Kyormolung could leave the troupe without its permission. The Treasury Office kept a list of the actors and maintained control over their movements. For some of the other troupes, such as the Chung, the families of the area in which the troupe was based were obliged to provide new members to ensure that the troupe could continue to perform at the annual Shotön Festival in Lhasa. Moreover, if the wandering Kyormolung saw a promising recruit in a family somewhere on their travels, they could apply to Treasury Office to have him press-ganged into their troupe.

Socially, members of the landless, wandering Kyormolung troupe were not highly regarded. One informant interviewed by Schuh said that their status was little more than that of wandering beggars singing for their supper. Consequently, social mobility and marriage outside the troupe was rare. An actor in the troupe primarily knew how to act and was without any other formal education.

Lama Manipa

No discussion about the performing arts in Tibet would be complete without mention of the colorful Lama Manipa. These were itinerant storytellers who traveled from town to town. They would set up a large scroll painting as a backdrop and often have a mandala in front of them. They attracted a crowd by blowing a conch shell and intoning the mantra *O ma o ma ma ṇi pemé hūṃ*, a chant often taken up by the onlookers. They would then sing songs and tell stories from the Lhamo operas. Thupten Jinpa says he clearly remembers seeing them even in South India in the Tibetan communities when he was young.

Shotön Festival

The Shotön or Yoghurt Festival began on the twenty-ninth or thirtieth of the sixth Tibetan month. Officially it lasted until the fifth of the seventh month, but unofficially it could continue for about seven weeks. It contributed greatly to the development and consolidation of the performing arts tradition in Tibet, even though it appears that the festival in its origins had little to do with the performing arts but lay with the annual summer retreat followed by the monasteries in Tibet that had been laid down in the Buddhist monastic code since the time of the Buddha. This retreat was held over three summer months and required the monks and nuns to not wander from the monasteries during that time. In the large Sera and Drepung Monasteries in Lhasa, officials from the lay community would serve yoghurt to the monks during the retreat. This follows the tradition of the Buddhist monasteries of ancient India, where the lay community would put on a "feast of milk and yoghurt" for the monks during the summer-season retreat.

The offering of yoghurt to the monks in the Sera and Drepung Monasteries took place on the last day of the sixth Tibetan month, and thus was the start of the Shotön Festival (lit. "Yoghurt Festival"). On the following day, which was the first day of the seventh month, up to the fifteenth of that

Senior monk officials watching a dramatization below the
Dalai Lama's personal viewing tent. The Dalai Lama's chief
secretary sits on the left. August 1921.

month, these monastic communities would engage in debates on the major
treatises of their curriculum.

The Fifth Dalai Lama, Ngawang Gyatso (1617–82), began the tradition
of song and dance troupes performing in front of the Ganden Phodrang
government building in Drepung Monastery on the first day of the Shotön
Festival.[12] This was also the start of the practice of draping the great embroi-
dered portrait of the Buddha on the face on the cliff at Drepung, a practice
still seen today during the Festival. Therefore it seems that the use of the
term *shotön* to refer to a performing arts festival dates from this time.

However, there are other explanations of the term. Some people these
days say that the word *shotön* (*zho ston*) is a corruption of *shöltön* (*zhol ston*),
with *shöl* being the administrative area below the Potala Palace, and that
therefore the festival has nothing to do with yoghurt. Whether this expla-
nation means that the festival was organized by the Shöl offices or that the
first performance of the festival was outside the Potala Palace by the Shöl
buildings is difficult to say. However, the fact that there is a written record in
1635 referring to the festival as "Shotön" long before the practice of holding
the performances outside the Potala would suggest that *shotön* is the correct
spelling and that the festival originated in monastic communities during the
summer retreat.

During the time of the Eleventh Dalai Lama, Khedrup Gyatso (1838–56), the Shotön Festival was extended to performances by renowned troupes outside the Kalsang Palace in the Norbulinga estate, the Dalai Lama's summer residence. This extension contributed greatly to the growth and establishment of Lhamo troupes in Tibet. In particular, Dedruk Rinpoché (d. 1872), regent of Tibet and teacher to the Twelfth Dalai Lama, took a great interest in the performing arts. Also at that time the Lhasa monastery of Meru Gönsar specialized in Lhamo performances, including a three-day staging of *The Brothers Dönyö and Döndrup*. During the breaks in performance locals from Lhasa would take to the stage and perform. As late as 1940 Meru Gönsar staged a Lhamo performance at the enthronement of the Fourteenth Dalai Lama.

The Thirteenth Dalai Lama, Thupten Gyatso (1873–1933), instructed renowned theater groups and singers from Central Tibet and Lhokha to give annual performances at the Shotön Festival specifically to strengthen the performing arts tradition. He said that during the performances they should retain and develop the individual characteristics and features of their troupes. He made every attempt to watch the performances.

From that time on, the Shotön Festival became an important event in the Tibetan calendar. Beginning on the twenty-ninth, or penultimate day, of the sixth Tibetan month, the above-mentioned Lhamo troupes would congregate one after another outside the main gates of the Potala Palace and in the large courtyard called Deyang Shar to perform the inaugural offering songs and dances. Each group took about thirty minutes. The same procedure was repeated at the Norbulinga, where the Dalai Lama was often present, and then again in the evening at Drepung in front of the Ganden Phodrang government building. On the following morning they performed an offering ceremony and inaugural songs and dances in front of the giant embroidered depiction of the Buddha that was draped across a rock face at Drepung. This was also the occasion for the ceremony of installing the new proctors of the monastery. After the ceremonies each troupe went to an allocated monastic house within the monastery, where they would perform and stay the night. This whole event was called the Drepung Shotön. On that day it was said that a hundred thousand ḍākinīs made offerings to Drepung Monastery.

Laypeople could attend these performances in the monastery, but monks were not allowed to attend performances at the Norbulinga estate and elsewhere, as they were still under the vows of the summer retreat.

The hunters' purification dance performed prior to a Lhamo performance
at the Shotön Festival, the Norbulingka, Lhasa, 1940–41.

On the first or second day of the seventh month, the Lhamo perfor-
mances began at the Norbulinga. This was the Norling Shotön. Richardson
describes visiting these with great delight and adorns his firsthand account
with amusing anecdotes. He remembers the time when the band struck up
a version of the British national anthem, "God Save the King," which had
been purloined by the Tibetans and dedicated to the Dalai Lama. On hear-
ing the first notes, the British dignitaries present stood to attention abruptly,
much to the amusement of the Tibetan audience.

The official performances at Norbulinga would last until the fifth day,
after which the various troupes wandered throughout Lhasa giving private
and public performances in return for donations. From the fifteenth day, for
four days, four troupes would perform historical plays at Norbulinga.

Present-Day Status of Tibetan Performing Arts

On the status of the performing arts tradition in Tibet these days, Jamyang
Norbu, writing in the 1980s, says:

> It would not be an exaggeration to say that, for all practical pur-
> poses, the old performing traditions are dead in Tibet. While
> the religious dances have been absolutely proscribed, and its

musical instruments, masks and costumes destroyed, there has,
on the other hand, been a systematic and wholesale perversion
of Tibetan folk songs, dances and operas to serve as vehicles for
Communist propaganda and a buttress for racist and pseudo-
historical claims. (1986, 5)

Certainly from 1959 when China invaded and occupied Central Tibet,
and during the disastrous Cultural Revolution of the 1960s, all opera was
banned. Mao Zedong's wife, Jiang Qing, oversaw the reconstruction of
opera in China and therefore only those approved by her were allowed to
be performed.

During the 1980s Tibetan opera began to reemerge. However, as Jamyang
Norbu points out, the storylines were often changed to suit the communist
ideology that the Chinese occupiers wanted to impose on the Tibetan peo-
ple. For example, the Nepalese princess was conveniently omitted from *The
Chinese and Nepalese Princesses*, and in *Nangsa Öbum*, the eponymous her-
oine is turned into a firebrand revolutionary cadre wreaking revenge on her
imperialist masters.

As for the music and performance itself, most reports are of a rigid display
with singers performing to prerecorded instrumental music. Indeed, when
I was in Lhasa recently I attended a performance in which the singers were
clearly miming, while the whole effect was high-pitched and very shrill.

Tibetan Performing Arts in Exile

In 1959 the Tibetans fled in their thousands across the border to India. The
Fourteenth Dalai Lama was given residence in Mussoorie, in Northern
India, where an administration in exile was formed. His Holiness was of the
opinion that the creation of a performing arts society would serve to counter
the destruction of Tibetan culture by the Chinese Communists and help to
publicize the Tibetan cause. He conveyed these thoughts to his ministers.
They in turn gathered five former government officials and instructed them
to travel to Kalimpong in West Bengal, close to Sikkim and Bhutan, and
there to covertly set up a performing arts troupe.

Kalimpong was chosen because of the connections it had with Tibet. It
had been frequented for a long time by traders from Tibet who exchanged
goods. Jamyang Norbu describes it as "home to a flourishing community of
Tibetan traders, craftsmen, and a few émigré aristocrats and lamas" (2001,

142). Moreover, the itinerant Kyormolung troupe would perform there from time to time.

As a result of the efforts of these five men, a troupe of twenty-six members was assembled, and on August 11, 1959, the first Tibetan performing arts society in exile was founded. In celebration, a public performance in Kalimpong Town Hall was held over three nights, boasting a repertoire of twenty-two songs.

The fledgling troupe continued to hone their skills, and consequently a second major performance was given in the presence of the Dalai Lama in Mussoorie. The repertoire consisted of two historical plays, intertwined with folk songs and dances.

From April 9 to 11, 1960, the troupe participated in the cultural events put on for a conference of Afro-Asian countries in New Delhi, India. The performance was enjoyed by senior Indian officials, representatives of nineteen countries, as well as Tibetan dignitaries and officials. The songs included the elegant Nangma songs described previously, as well as those from Central Tibet, Tsang, Kham, and Amdo, while the dances portrayed aspects of Tibetan life—such as the stages of cloth making, from sheep shearing up to the finished article, or the work of the farmer, from tilling the ground up to the alcohol-fueled celebrations of a good harvest, or the life of nomadic herders, from milking a cow to making butter. The performances ended with a joyful song and dance, after which the Tibetan flag was held aloft during the singing of the Tibetan national anthem.

On April 15 the troupe traveled to Mussoorie, where they performed for the Dalai Lama. Later that month His Holiness and the Tibetan government in exile relocated to the Himalayan hill station town of Dharamsala in the state of Himachal Pradesh. There on July 6 the Kalimpong troupe put on a performance in celebration of the Dalai Lama's twenty-sixth birthday.

In 1961 the troupe performed at Calcutta and at Buxa Fort in Bengal, where a temporary monastic residence had been set up for refugee monks, and also at Darjeeling and at Dalhousie in the Chamba district of Himachal Pradesh. In April the troupe was officially affiliated with the Department of Education of the Central Tibetan Administration, and eventually was relocated to Dharamsala. Until then, the troupe had no official name, and after a list of suggested names was put to the Dalai Lama, he chose a name that translates as Cultural Performing Arts Society of the Exiled Tibetan Community. They were moved to an estate called Conium House, built during

An early Tibetan Institute of Performing Arts (TIPA)
performance in Dharamsala.

the time of the British Raj, located above the village of MacLeod Ganj,
where they reside to this day.

Jamyang Norbu (2001, 143) quotes Tashi Tsering as saying that there were
at least two other performing arts troupes among the exiled community in
India: a troupe formed from the Tibetan Handicraft Centre in Dalhousie,
and another formed from the road workers of the Chamba Road Camp in
Himachal Pradesh.

Once established in their own residence, under the aegis of the govern-
ment in exile, the Cultural Performing Arts Society regularly performed at
official functions, anniversaries, and celebrations. They not only entertained
the community but also kept the Tibetan cause fresh in people's minds, and
new dramas were written to highlight the political situation of the Tibetan
people and the repression in Tibet. By performing outside of Dharamsala,
they brought Tibetan culture to Indian audiences.

In 1965 Phuntsok Namgyal Dumkhang, a talented performer, was
appointed director of the Society. During his tenure operas were once again
performed for the Tibetan people; the first two being *Drowa Sangmo* and
Sukyi Nyima. In 1967 he persuaded the great Kyormolung opera performer
Norbu Tsering to come from Kalimpong and join the Society as an opera
teacher. Norbu Tsering had escaped from a Chinese labor camp near Lhasa
and had set up a small opera company in Kalimpong.

Phuntsok Namgyal Dumkhang, director of the Music, Dance, and Drama Society, with the troupe that performed *Drowa Sangmo* on July 6, 1967, in Dharamsala, in honor of the Fourteenth Dalai Lama's birthday.

Norbu Tsering, 1964. A former Kyormolung actor, he became the director and teacher at a newly formed Lhamo troupe in exile in Kalimpong, India.

Also in 1965 it was decided after consultation between the Department of Education and the Society to appoint music and dance teachers to schools run by the Tibetan administration in exile. This was done to bring the Tibetan performing arts traditions to children in exile. As a result, more Tibetans learned their culture's folk songs and dances and were able to present them to other cultures without the Society's oversight.

In 1967 a craft center was established in order to meet the growing need for costumes, wigs, boots, and props. In 1969 the Society was named the Tibetan Performing Arts Society, or just Dögar, as the locals called it, and in 1971 a new auditorium and hostel was built at Conium House.

The Society's first international tour was in 1975, from June to December. It began with a performance of *Pema Öbar* at the Volkhaus in Vienna, an event covered by the press in interviews and photos. This was followed by performances in Amsterdam, Basel, and Zurich. In September the Society gave performances in twenty-eight US states and in six cities in Canada. The performances were well covered by the media, which afforded the opportunity to present the case for Tibet and counter the propaganda put out by the Chinese regime. In February 1976 the Society toured Australia, where members performed at the Festival of Perth, as well as in venues in Sydney, Canberra, and Adelaide. After their return to India, they gave performances in Singapore.

Gradually the great operas described above were reintroduced into the repertoire. A re-creation of the Shotön Festival was begun in 1981, although it was not until 1993 that it became an annual event that included Lhamo troupes from the various settlements. Performances took on a more modern look with the introduction of Western instruments and new songs influenced by modern culture. Nevertheless, the Society still struggled in terms of finance and resources. Tuberculosis was rife among the Tibetan community in exile, and those at the Tibetan Institute of Performing Arts (TIPA), as the Society was renamed in the 1980s, were not exempt from this ravaging disease. Another setback was the huge fire that destroyed the auditorium in May 1984. I well remember seeing the billowing smoke as I walked down the hill that morning. The auditorium, six houses, workshops with equipment, including all broadcasting and recording equipment and half of all costumes and props, were destroyed. Fortunately, the generosity of institutions and the community, the refusal to be discouraged, and the volunteer labor offered saw to it that eventually all these were replaced.

Up until 1990 TIPA was under the jurisdiction of the Department of Education, and by then had conducted six teacher training courses, which resulted in the creation of about a hundred qualified artistes and musical instructors, many of whom are teaching performing arts in Tibetan-run

Director Jamyang Norbu with trainees of the first music curriculum,
TIPA, 1982.

schools. After 1990, TIPA was placed into the Department of Religion and
Cultural Affairs.

Over the following years TIPA continued to tour in India and abroad. As
of 2010 it had been on ninety-two tours covering thirty-two countries, all
of which helped to spread the message of the Tibetan cause and showcase
Tibetan culture all over the world. The music and performance have been
recorded on CDs and DVDs. In addition, many books on various aspects of
Tibetan music and dance have been published.

Other song, dance, and theater groups can be found in Tibetan settle-
ments in India and Nepal. The Tibetan community in Switzerland set up a
troupe, and in San Francisco two former members of TIPA formed Chak-
sampa, a theater company that has toured all over the United States for the
benefit of Tibetan communities and to sow the seeds of this rich tradition
in their children.

Since its inception on August 11, 1959, TIPA, under its various names, has
ensured the preservation and development of the performing arts traditions
of Tibet in an admirable manner worthy of recognition. I leave the last word
with Jamyang Norbu:

> If some Spring evening you were to take a walk up the mountain
> road from McLeod Ganj to the Tibetan Institute of Performing

Arts, you might come across cheerful groups of men and women proceeding rather unsteadily downhill. They will probably be clinging to each other in boozy camaraderie, helping to prop each other up. They will all be singing, at the top of their voices, a peculiar yodel-like air. These people are returning from a daylong performance of the Tibetan folk opera, or Lhamo. (2001, 153)

Acknowledgments

These operas are written in the vernacular of a particular region of Tibet, and the verse is often charged with emotion. Consequently, the full meaning expressed can be difficult to grasp. There are also a few somewhat enigmatic sayings and proverbs. Therefore I have sought out the help of others. I particularly want to thank Geshé Thupten Jinpa, president of the Institute of Tibetan Classics, for giving his time to answer specific queries, which he did enthusiastically. I would also like to thank him for entrusting this translation to me. It has been a pleasure to work with such beautiful poetic expressions of the range of human emotions.

I would also like to express my gratitude to Gen Losang Samten, artistic director at Tibetan Institute of Performing Arts, Dharamsala, India, for his valuable insights into these time-honored stories. He also gave freely of his time in the midst of a busy schedule.

Thanks too must go to my old classmate and longtime friend, Geshé Kalsang Damdul, director of the Institute of Buddhist Dialectics. Geshé-la was never less than enthusiastic to help me resolve queries whenever I walked into his office.

Nevertheless, there will be misunderstandings and errors that I have made within the text of the operas, for which I ask the reader to make allowance.

No author is complete without an editor, and no text shines as much as it does without the thorough and insightful hand of an editor. Therefore I must give ample thanks to Mary Petrusewicz, editor at Wisdom Publications, for her thoughtful suggestions and corrections to the text.

The photos in the book are the result of painstaking work by the photo researcher Jane Moore. Jane has included many historical photos of operas in Tibet, which she has identified and provided captions for. The more recent color photos bring out the full glamour of the Tibetan performing arts tradition and are an essential visual addition to the book.

Finally, I would like to thank my wife. Though it has become almost cliché for writers to thank their spouses, I am truly indebted to Jacquie for her support and patience in my pursuit of the often solitary and insular undertaking that is a career in written translation.

Technical Note

THE TIBETAN TITLE of the work translated here is *Bod kyi lha mo'i 'khrab gzhung che khag gces btus*, which translates as *Selected Great Folk Operas of Tibet*. The Tibetan text was prepared specifically for *The Library of Tibetan Classics* and its Tibetan equivalent, the *Bod kyi gtsug lag gces btus* series, where it also appears as volume 31 (New Delhi: Institute of Tibetan Classics, 2012. ISBN 978-81-89165-31-3).

The operas presented here are Tibetan operas and are commonly known by their Tibetan names, such as Sukyi Nyima, Pema Öbar, Norsang, and so on. However, all but two of the eight are set in India. Moreover, some have Indic sources, as described above. Therefore names and places in the operas are mostly Indian. Nevertheless, the operas have taken on a Tibetan coating, and references to Tibet and its culture, such as yaks, tsampa (roasted barley flour), indigenous Tibetan deities and rituals, and even a few people and place names are found throughout the stories. This presents the problem of whether to back-translate into Sanskrit. I have decided where possible to use Sanskrit names for the eponymous protagonists and all other proper names within the body of the text, but to keep in Tibetan all references to the operas outside of the text. Many Westerners will know the Tibetan names, and in the introduction, the table of contents, and story titles, the Tibetan names of the operas are used.

Moreover, there is the issue of aesthetics. These are operas that rest a great deal on flowing song and verse, and quite honestly, Sanskrit trips off the tongue more fluidly than Tibetan. "Manoharā," the name of the beautiful goddess in Norsang, looks and sounds more appealing than "Yitrokma." "Amogha and Siddhārtha" are easier to the eye than "Dönyö and Döndrup."

"Nangsa Öbum" and all other proper names in that story are left in Tibetan because it is an indigenous Tibetan story based on actual events. "Drowa Sangmo" has also been left as it is because the story seems to have its roots in the Tibetan region of Mön on the Tibet-India border, although many of the names have been back-translated when they are clearly of Indic origin.

The conventions for phonetic transcription of Tibetan words are those developed by the Institute of Tibetan Classics and Wisdom Publications. Transliterations of the phoneticized Tibetan terms and names used in the text can be found in the table in the appendix. Sanskrit diacritics are used throughout except for Sanskrit terms that have been naturalized into English, such as *samsara*, *nirvana*, *sutra*, *stupa*, *Mahayana*, and *mandala*.

Finally, there are some names clearly of Tibetan origin. These have been left in Tibetan.

PRONUNCIATION OF TIBETAN PHONETICS

ph and *th* are aspirated *p* and *t*, as in *pet* and *tip*.
ö is similar to the *eu* in the French *seul*.
ü is similar to the *ü* in the German *füllen*.
ai is similar to the *e* in *bet*.
é is similar to the *e* in *prey*.

PRONUNCIATION OF SANSKRIT

Palatal *ś* and retroflex *ṣ* are similar to the English unvoiced *sh*.
c is an unaspirated *ch* similar to the *ch* in *chill*.
The vowel *ṛ* is similar to the American *r* in *pretty*.
ñ is somewhat similar to the nasalized *ny* in *canyon*.
ṅ is similar to the *ng* in *sing* or *anger*.

1. A Pearl Garland: The Life and Deeds of Dharma King Viśvantara (Drimé Kunden)

Oṃ maṇi padme hūṃ hrīḥ

Homage to the noble Avalokiteśvara!

COUNTLESS EONS AGO in the great Indian city of Vidarbha lived the lord and king Bhūpāla Yaśas Śrī. With three thousand ministers he ruled over sixty vassal kingdoms and possessed an inconceivable wealth of riches and jewels, such as the wish-granting jewel. Moreover, he owned the fabulous and greatest of all jewels, known as the all-fulfilling and all-conquering jewel, which would instantly grant his every wish.

This mighty king had five hundred queens of noble birth, five hundred queens of great wealth, and five hundred queens of great beauty, and yet he did not have a single son. This made him very sad. Therefore he performed divinations and made astrological calculations. These foretold that if he made offerings to the gods, presented ritually consecrated food to the eight classes of spirit beings, and gave alms to the poor, he would be rewarded with the birth of a son who would be the incarnation of a bodhisattva. This made the king very happy, and accordingly, he made offerings to the gods, presented ritually consecrated food to the eight classes of spirit beings, and gave alms to the poor. Not long after, a queen named Kuśalāvatī Bhadrā, who was agreeable to all, who lacked the eight faults of women, and who possessed excellent qualities, came to know that she was bearing a son. She had many good dreams and went before the king:

> Great and mighty king, please hear my words.
> There have been excellent signs during the day,
> and I have passed the nights with excellent dreams.

Within the three hundred and sixty channels of my body,
at the cakra of bliss within the crown of my head,
I dreamt of a blazing golden vajra,
whose tip reached to the skies.

I dreamt of light rays filling the ten directions,
of palaces made of rainbows and light,
and of white conches being blown throughout the universe.
Such auspicious dreams have I had.

In the celestial mansion of my body,
a great and noble son has arrived.
On an auspicious date and time,
a boy of great joy will be born.
Perform the rituals throughout the land!

The king was overjoyed and replied:

Kuśalāvatī, who is in harmony with my mind,
and from whom I will not be parted for an instant,
in the sacred celestial mandala of your body,
at the cakra of bliss within the crown of your head,
the blazing and golden vajra portends
that the lord of all guides and protectors will appear.

The palaces of rainbows and light
portend that an emanation of the Buddha will appear.
White conches being blown throughout the universe
are a sign that the banner of his great renown
will fly throughout the ten directions.

By the blessings of making offerings to the gods,
by the fruits of the practice of giving to the poor,
and by the grace of the infallible objects of refuge,
this sonless king has received the signs of a son.
By these signs you have fulfilled my wishes.
As you suggest, I will perform the rituals as best I can.

Drimé Kunden, performed at a harvest festival in Batang,
eastern Tibet, in the 1920s.

Recital of *Drimé Künden* in
Yatung, Chumbi Valley, Tibet,
May 1948.

The wise, ethical, and compassionate gurus,
with great pandits numbering five hundred,
will recite the scriptures and mantras.

All space and every direction will be sealed by mudra.
Five hundred *phurpa*-wielding tantric yogis
with their constant cries of *hūṃ* and *phaṭ*,
will hurl the wrathful mantra tormas at the enemies.

Those who have degenerated their pledges,
the hostile and the hinderers, will all be ground to dust.
Summon here all that is auspicious and wholesome,
and cast the thread-crosses and the tormas.

The rituals and ceremonies were performed accordingly.

After nine months and ten days the royal prince was born. As soon as
the boy emerged from the womb, the only sound he would make was "*oṃ
maṇi padme hūṃ hrīḥ*,"[13] and tears would come to his eyes. He had a mind
of love like that of a mother for her only child. The king and his ministers
were overjoyed and he was named Prince Viśvantara.[14] He was presented
with immeasurable offerings and given a jewel-like palace called Place
of Joy.

By the time he was five he had mastered reading and arithmetic. He
became learned in the five sciences and understood all the scriptures. The
prince declared that all living beings were his parents and proclaimed:

Alas! When I think that we have been sunk for so long
in the fierce sufferings of the great ocean of samsara,
with this beguiling mind attached to illusory wealth,
living beings, how sad, how sad.

Alas! Within the sufferings of the three realms,
Woe, oh woe! What can be done!

In the city of the great conflagration of desires,
no parting from the mind that clings to self, how sad!

In the great fire-pit of endless samsara,
wherever one looks, no freedom.
Sentient beings of the three realms, how sad!

Undertaken but not completed,
the deeds of the world will never end.
What suffering! How sad!

Married couples, in their deluded minds,
hoping they will be together forever, how sad!

One's country is like a nomad's encampment.
Clinging and attachment to it, how sad!

Beings of the six realms are equal in being our parents,
yet we divide up into self and others, how sad!

This honey-like wealth gathered with greed
will be used by others, how sad!

Carrying the great load of evil deeds,
we fall into the chasm of suffering realms, how sad!

Although the truth is taught, it is not believed.
Living beings deceived by ignorance, how sad!

I, Viśvantara Arthasiddhi Śrī,
in the midst of confused beings, how sad!

Father, the wealth you have so carefully amassed,
is without essence, is without meaning.
Should I not give it away?

His father replied:

My Viśvantara Arthasiddhi Śrī,
until you were born, I suffered greatly.

Now this wealth I have accumulated,
is yours to do as you will. Give it away!

The prince proceeded to make countless acts of giving, and the people were liberated from the suffering of poverty.

There was an evil minister called Taradzé who came before the king and said:

Great lord of men, please hear me.
All the wealth you have gathered
has been reduced to nothing by Viśvantara.
A king without wealth will become the servant of others.
Therefore it would be good to find a bride for the prince,
and to hold onto your wealth.

The ministers convened to discuss the matter. In the country of Padmā-vati lived King Sucandra with a daughter called Mandé Bhadrā. She was beautiful and alluring, possessed of a fair complexion and a beautiful aroma. She was a young woman of great faith and had a love for the Dharma. She was blessed with a broad mind and was generous. She was like a goddess and loved by everyone. Adorned with precious jewels, she was taken as a bride by Prince Viśvantara.

She regarded the prince with great esteem and took him to the crown of her head like a guru. With joy she spoke these words of praise to the prince:

Unstained by fault you are like the buddhas,
possessed of all qualities stretching beyond imagination,
a wealth of glory and endowments that surpasses all thinking,
able to accomplish all, you are a wish-granting jewel.
Great universal monarch, looking upon you,
Bhadrā is happy and her mind fills with joy.

The prince looked at Bhadrā and replied:

Such uncontrived and timeless beauty, a goddess-like form
that becomes a dance of bliss with the sweetest voice.
Bhadrā, beautiful goddess, looking upon you,
I too am happy and filled with joy.

We have come together through the power of prayer.
Let us live in the glory of joy and be happy!

The prince and princess lived in the palace in great joy within the Dharma. Gradually, three children were born. The eldest boy was called Sādhuvadin, the middle son was Sādhuvardhati, and the youngest was a daughter called Sundarī. Great festivities were held at their births.

One day the prince, together with his ministers, went to look at the flowers in the palace gardens. People gathered at all the gates of the palace. Like sheep in a slaughter house they stared wildly at the prince. The prince exclaimed, "Father deity, Avalokiteśvara,[15] look on this!" Tears came to his eyes. Sobbing, he returned to the palace overwhelmed by great pain. He recited *oṃ maṇi padme hūṃ hrīḥ*, refused to eat, and took to his bed. His father came to him and said:

Viśvantara, in this palace called Place of Joy,
all pleasures are to be found, all desires will be met.
Instead of enjoying them, why do you grieve?
Tell me in all honesty why this should be.

The son replied to his father:

Mighty godlike father, please hear me.
Alas! When I look upon and think about
the sufferings of this samsaric existence,
it becomes a cause for grief and sadness.
The blind persecuted by their karma and the six
    types of beings,
in danger of falling to the chasm of birth, sickness,
    old age, and death.
If I could prevent that and free them,
I would be cured of my grief.

His father spoke:

Viśvantara, my son, listen to me.
The sufferings of living beings are caused by their karma.
Grieving for them does not good at all.

Viśvantara, enjoy the glories of pleasure.
To disobey my word is a great fault.

Again his son replied:

Mighty godlike father, please hear me.
Outside the palace gates I have seen the six kinds of sufferings.
If you, my father, would give the wealth you have gathered
to the poor and needy who have nothing,
I would be free from my grief.

The king replied:

My Viśvantara, I think of nothing but you.
My son, do as you please, and give up your grief.

The king gave over his treasury to the prince and instructed him to do with it as he wished. The prince gathered the riches into one place. There he called together the people of the world and showered upon them the rains of generosity. The people were encouraged to recite *oṃ maṇi padme hūṃ hrīḥ* and were freed from the suffering of poverty.

* * *

At that time, King Shing Tritsen of the uncivilized land of Jema Shingdrung entertained unvirtuous thoughts. He called his retinue before him:

My retinue, listen to my words.
I have heard that in the great city of Vidarbha,
Prince Viśvantara has vowed to give away his wealth
to all who ask, without prejudice or favor.
In his possession lies the all-fulfilling and all-conquering jewel.
Who will go to him to ask for it?
Speak now and I will give him half my kingdom.

Those in the retinue thought that not only would they not be given the jewel but would also be in danger of losing their lives. Therefore no one accepted the task. Then an old brahman with not a single tooth in his mouth stood up and said: "Great king, I will go. Give me clothes, shoes, and provisions."

The king gave him all he needed and the brahman set out on his journey. After crossing many a hill and valley he arrived at Vidarbha. Outside the palace he stood with his head in his hands and sobbed. A minister came to him: "Old man, where are you from? What is it you want?"

"I am from Jema Drung," the brahman replied. "I have come to beg food and provisions from Prince Viśvantara." The minister reported this to the prince, who was overjoyed and came to the palace gates to meet the brahman:

> Alas! My friend, you have come a long way.
> You have hastened over hills and valleys.
> Are you not tired and worn out?
> What it is you want? Tell me quickly.
> I will fulfill your wishes.

The brahman placed his hands together and sobbed:

> You who are the eyes of limitless sentient beings,
> my country is called Jema Shingdrung.
> Our ruler was King Shing Tritsen.
> Three years ago he died of a stomach complaint,
> leaving his country and people in ruin.
>
> I am named brahman Mati, the father of a hungry family,
> surrounded by children who are like hungry ghosts.
> Not finding food we go hungry in the day.
> Not being covered by clothes we go naked at night.
>
> You have love for all, whether close or distant.
> You give to all, without prejudice or favor.
> To this poor and destitute brahman family,
> Viśvantara, king of Vidarbha,
> I ask you to give me what I ask for.
> I give you my word that till the end of my days
> I will recite the six-syllable mantra.

The prince led the brahman to his treasury and gave him the wish-granting jewel and many other fantastic jewels. The brahman said:

> Great king, please listen to me.
> I did not come for these jewels.
> I came for the all-fulfilling and all-conquering jewel.
> Dharma King Viśvantara, I ask that you give me
> the all-fulfilling and all-conquering jewel.

The prince replied to the brahman:

> Brahman Mati, hear my words.
> This precious all-fulfilling and all-conquering jewel
> my father has not given to me, nor will he give it to me.
> To give away the people's wealth would be a cause of much
>   dispute.
> Therefore take the jewels that I have the power to give.
> Do not think about the all-fulfilling and all-conquering jewel.

The brahman spoke:

> Prince, listen to me.
> Having heard much about your renowned acts of giving,
> I have come from afar, enduring great hardship.
> If my hopes are to be answered this way, then I have lost
>   my faith.
> If you will not let go of the all-fulfilling and all-conquering
>   jewel,
> your pledge to give to others whatever they desire is a lie.
> Alas! You have reneged on your vow.
> I will return to my country.
> I do not want these jewels. You keep them!

With these words the brahman angrily left. The prince ran after him and pleaded:

> Friend, do not turn against me like this.
> Think on me with affection.

The story of this jewel is as follows.
The white nāgas from the depths of the ocean
offered it to the Buddha Amitābha,
and Amitābha presented it to my father.
The king has not given it to me.

The stability and greatness of the kingdom
comes from the all-fulfilling and all-conquering jewel.
The three thousand ministers, such as Sucandra,
come from the all-fulfilling and all-conquering jewel.
The happiness and wealth of the country
come from the all-fulfilling and all-conquering jewel.
The wealth of the king comes from this jewel.
It is a precious vase from which all desires are fulfilled.
The armies of enemies are destroyed by this jewel.
It is a jewel rare in the three realms.

Now, even though it may cost me my life,
but because the act of giving is the path of Dharma,
this jewel, superior in the universe,
I give to you brahman Mati.

With these words the prince put the jewel into a quartz casket and presented it to the brahman. He also gave him the gift of an elephant and said:

Good and great brahman, stand up.
Quickly, place this great jewel treasure
on this young and powerful elephant.
If my father hears of this he will pursue you
and take back the jewel and the elephant.
It will not do to be caught, for you will lose your life.
Do not be slack, and with urgency be on your way.
Accomplish great things for yourself and others!

The brahman replied:

This is well decided, son of a king!
Sole refuge for the beings of the three realms,

manifestation of the buddhas of the three times,
supreme guide and path to freedom for the beings of the
    three worlds,
great illuminator of the teachings of the Buddha,
ferry that rescues those from the great river of samsara,
with an army to defeat the samsara of the six realms of beings,
great king, brave and skillful, I honor and prostrate to you.

Placing the jewel on the elephant, the brahman set out. The prince prayed:

Buddhas and bodhisattvas of the ten directions,
I beg you, please hear my words.
So that I may fulfill all wishes of living beings,
and complete the Great Vehicle deed of giving,
I pray that the jewel is not stolen by others,
and that he arrives safely in far-off Jema.

The brahman arrived in Jema Shingdrung. He presented the jewel to the king, who was very pleased. He gave the brahman a reward and venerated the jewel.

A month or so passed. When it became known that the jewel had been given away, the ministers and the people were in distress. Having discussed the matter, the evil minister Taradzé went before the king:

Lord and king, please hear my words.
Your all-fulfilling and all-conquering jewel
has been given away thoughtlessly to our enemy by the prince.
If you think this is untrue, please look in your treasury.
What is to be done with this son who gives away such a jewel?
Should he not be brought before the law?

The king replied:

How can this be true!
Taradzé, rumor is half true, half false.
There is time to question, investigate,
and come to the right judgment.

Minister, do not spread these malicious lies!
He could not have given the jewel to an enemy.

The minister said:

With my own eyes I saw him give away
the all-fulfilling and all-conquering jewel to an enemy.
He gave it to a brahman from a far-off land.
If you hold my words to be untrue,
I will not prevent your son from giving.
I don't mind. Do as you please!

With these words he stormed out. The king became very sad. Like one
who had drunk strong poison, his body became numb and was in shock.
His face darkened. The next day before the sun had risen he went to his son's
palace. The prince sat with his face to the ground. His father addressed him:

My Viśvantara, speak to me truly.
That precious treasure that will fulfill the wishes
of those descendants born from a mighty lord
whose light has shone in countless beautiful towns and cities,
have you given it to an enemy?
Viśvantara, tell me the truth.

His son bowed before him, placed his hands together, but could not reply.
Again his father spoke:

I have ninety-two thousand cities,
sixty vassal kingdoms, thirty thousand ministers,
five hundred precious wish-granting jewels,
many treasuries filled with silver and gold,
quantities of jewels and special gems,
but I have no jewel like the all-fulfilling and all-conquering.
Is it true or not that you have given it to an enemy?

The son thought to himself: "I cannot show the jewel. It is impossible to
keep this secret. Now I must be honest." He addressed the king:

Great lord and king, please hear my words.
A man arrived who had traveled from afar with great
    hardship,
a man bereft of wealth, deprived of food,
from a land stricken with hunger and thirst,
to this brahman from a far-off land, I gave the jewel.
Father and master, do not reprimand me.

On hearing this news, the king fainted. The queens too were overcome with grief. After a while the king recovered and said:

In the northern land of Svara, of the five *bhīma* trees,
the ruler and king Dundubhisvara has great power,
but he does not possess such a jewel.
In the south, in Jambudvipa, land of jewels,
the King Ananta Yaśas has great power,
but he does not possess such a jewel.
In the middle kingdom of Jeru Indra,
King Indrabodhi has great power,
but he does not possess such a jewel.

With this precious and excellent wish-granting vessel,
outwardly, enemies are destroyed,
internally, powers are granted.
You wicked person, you have cast away
this precious and priceless treasure!
My kingdom has been cast to the winds!

The son addressed his father:

Lord of men, my father, please listen to me.
I have such great love for the practice of giving.
I have promised to give whatever anyone asks.
If someone asked, I would give away my sons and daughter.
I would even give my life.
Therefore, father, lessen your attachment to this jewel.

His father replied:

> When I had this precious jewel
> the kingdom was safe and happy.
> Now that I no longer have this all-conquering jewel,
> my kingdom has been lost to a rival.
> Enemy from a past life, what have you done!
> Without asking your father, without speaking to your mother,
> why did you give this special jewel to an enemy?

The prince replied:

> Lord of the gods, my father, please hear my words.
> Previously, you and I made a pledge;
> I would happily give to all those tormented by poverty,
> even the sons and daughters of my own blood,
> even my life, and even the all-fulfilling and all-conquering jewel.
> Father, did I not say this to you?

His father replied:

> Jewels such as the wish-granting jewel,
> gold, silver, copper, iron, and stores of grain,
> horses, elephants, and buffaloes—
> these I agreed that you could give.
> I did not agree that you could give your life,
> and the all-fulfilling and all-conquering jewel.

The son replied:

> Father and king, please hear my words.
> Bees work hard to accumulate honey,
> but their efforts are ultimately fruitless.
> Father, you have great attachment to wealth,
> but the wealth held tightly by your miserliness has no essence.
>
> Even the king who rules over the wealth of the entire universe,
> when he leaves this world must travel on empty-handed.

Therefore why are you deceived by wealth and material
     possession?
Father, lessen your attachment to wealth.
Though your niggardly mind is reluctant to see it go,
the all-conquering jewel has gone and will not return.

His father replied:

Enemy from a past life posing as a son!
The all-conquering jewel has gone!
The risen sun has set in the evening sky.
My kingdom has been cast to the winds.
Alas! Alas! Look at what has been done.

The prince again addressed his father:

Do not cling to a self, show love to all.
If you abandon the jewel of miserliness and clinging to self,
the sun of the joy of fulfilling the needs of self and others
     will rise.
Put all your efforts into the Dharma.

His father replied:

You pretense of a son! Even though you were raised with love,
with perverted aspiration, you have emptied the kingdom.
An enemy who has lost the all-conquering jewel,
I have no need of one such as you. Let the law take its course!

Prince Viśvantara was handed over to the jailers. They seized him,
stripped him naked, and bound his hands behind his back. A rope was tied
around his neck and he was paraded around the palace walls. Bhadrā, the
prince's queen, took her three children and followed the prince. Pulling her
hair out, her eyes filled with tears, and in great despair, she cried out:

Alas! Alas! Such suffering, such pain!
My Viśvantara Arthasiddhi Śrī,

today without dying I have seen hell.
Will the armies of the gods not come here!
Will the buddhas not be witnesses!

Look with compassion upon this innocent prince.
My Viśvantara has so much love for the righteous path,
and the king and his ministers with no understanding
have carried out this uncompassionate act!

Between your son and a jewel, you have chosen the jewel.
How is such impossible punishment made possible?
Please think of him. Won't you show compassion?
He may be your enemy, but how could you do such a thing!

Gods and yakṣa spirits, great lords of men,
Powerful earth lords, the half-human kiṃnaras,
and all those with power and ability that exist in the world,
can you shelter this mother and her children from such pain?

If so, please protect us! I will quickly repay the kindness.
Alas! Alas! My heart cannot bear such pain!
How can my mind take any more!
Why didn't I die before seeing this?

With these words she continued to follow Viśvantara. The jailers carried weapons such as cane arrows, bows of bone, swords, and spears. They rode on elephants, blew conch shells, and so on. All were dressed in a frightening array of costumes. Some pushed the prince from behind, while others pulled him from the front. In order to show him to others, he was paraded through the town in the daytime. At night he was kept in a dark pit.

All the people of the town gathered. Bhadrā and her children were overwhelmed by grief, and tears filled their eyes. Beating her breast, Bhadrā wailed:

Viśvantara shows the good path.
He is a father with great love and compassion
to those without wealth, stricken by poverty,

a courageous man satisfying others by giving whatever
    they want.
Today, without the fruit of giving maturing,
he is subject to such dreadful deeds.
It is as if all good fortune of mother and children is at an end.

Then the king called about him those ministers skilled in discussion
and said:

Ministers, hear my words.
This unworthy son has given the jewel to an enemy.
Look at such an unspeakable act.
Now what kind of punishment is to be inflicted upon him?
Think on this, my ministers.

One minister replied: "He is the son of a king, but he is not above the law.
Therefore his skin should be ripped from him." Another said: "He should
be impaled on a stake." "His limbs should be cut off," said another. Another
suggested ripping out his heart and lungs. "Put him on the torture rack!"
said one. "He should be killed by drawing blood from all parts of his body,"
said another. "Beat him to death," said another. "He should be beheaded and
his head stuck above the palace gate," said one. "The prince with his wife and
children should be cast into a filthy, stinking pit," said another. Everyone had
their own suggestions, but they all agreed that the prince should die.

The king was affected by these comments and said to the ministers:

My son has great love for the good path.
He is of the lineage of the bodhisattvas.
Who would dare kill him?
Think again on this matter, ministers.

One minister, Sucandra, a man of deep faith and of great liking for the
Dharma, said:

Listen, assembly of ministers!
What kinds of things are you saying?
The king has only this one son.
If there is no king, what will the people do?

Thinking about this, I have become sad and troubled,
and am thinking of leaving for a far-off land.
Father and king, do not be of a petty mind.
Do not listen to the talk of these evil ministers.

Oh my! This Viśvantara, a wonder in this world,
an extraordinary and wonderful manifestation of the
    Buddha!
A crown jewel of qualities beyond description, beyond
    imagination;
while he was being paraded around the palace,
Bhadrā and her children followed him.
Looking at his face, they wept.

The townsfolk, old and young, men and women,
looked on the prince and were stricken with grief.
There were many there who would have gone in his stead.
"To see the prince like this is unbearable," they cried.
"Release the prince and kill us instead," they begged.

Think again, king and ministers.
There are Mongolian and Tibetan systems of justice.
Is it right to put two saddles on one horse?
Let what has already happened to the prince
be punishment enough for giving away the jewel.
I ask that you release him.

"Bring the prince here," said the king. Minister Sucandra quickly went to the palace gates, where he untied the prince, offering him soft clothes and beautiful adornments. "Precious prince, come into the palace," he said. As the prince was leaving, Bhadrā and the children thought that the prince was being led away to be killed. With their eyes filled with tears, they clung to him and would not let go. At this, Sucandra became very sad. Tears welled up in him and he could not speak. He returned to the palace and said to the king: "I untied the prince and invited him in the castle. Bhadrā and the children think he is being led to his death and they refuse to let go of him. I became very sad. What can be done, precious king?"

"Bring them all here," said the king. Sucandra went and brought the prince, his queen, and his children to the king. They all prostrated to the king and sat before him. The king said:

Enemy from a past life posing as a son,
you gave my precious jewel to a rival,
and you have emptied my treasuries.
My enemies are delighted and I am ruined.
This is the consequence of your many deeds.
This is the consequence of your many plans.
Flee to the great demon mountain
known as the "Kem-kem" Hashang Mountain.
Stay there for twelve years.
Go now. Do not remain in this land.

His son replied:

Celestial lord, my father, please hear me.
A kingdom not ruled according to Dharma is the fault
    of the king.
My father, showing me little compassion,
put me into the hands of low-caste jailers.

They beat the bones of my four limbs,
hit my body with a whip of thorns,
tied and dragged me everywhere like a wild horse.
I was encircled by jailers like an enemy,
paraded through the town like a hero's sword,
divested of clothes, naked like a corpse.
In the daytime I was circumambulated like the faithful,
and at night hidden in a pit like a robber's loot.

Like a criminal, weapons rained down on me.
May the sufferings visited upon me
never be experienced by other living beings.

I have no need of illusory wealth.
I will do as my father commands.

May my mother and father be well,
and their entourage be content.

The prince, his queen, and the children returned to their own palace. The prince gave the remainder of his wealth away and prepared to leave for Hashang Demon Mountain. Everybody came and presented him with parting gifts. Each of the sixty vassal kings presented him with a gold coin. The three thousand ministers gave him a silver coin each. The ninety thousand subjects presented him with many horses, elephants, and so on.

However, the prince even gave these away, and without a possession to his name, he turned to Bhadrā and said:

Bhadrā, listen to me.
As my father commands, I leave for Hashang Mountain.
Lotus Palace is the palace of my father.
Return there with the three children.

Live happily, my dearest of friends.
I pray you keep well for twelve years,
and that again I will meet you, the children, and your retinue.
Live in peace and happiness!

Bhadrā bowed before the prince and said:

How could I possibly return to Lotus Palace
and be separated from you, noble prince?
How could I and our children live there,
while you must travel to Hashang Mountain?

How can I go from the happy times of being with you
to the sad times of being without you?
How can I bear it, how can I face it?
Take me with you to where you are going!

The prince replied:

Bhadrā, do not say such things.
In your own happy country

in a beautiful part of this land,
you have your parents when you need advice.

You will have your children, the love of your life.
You have male and female servants to do your worldly tasks.
You will be with those who are of like mind.

When you are hungry, sitting on lotus and pañcāli[16] seats,
you can eat of food endowed with the eight great tastes.
When thirsty you can drink from a stream of nectar.
When sad, you can listen to music or watch dance.

In Kem-kem Hashang Demon Mountain,
when hungry there is only fruit, when thirsty only water,
only leaves to wear and only grass to sit on.

Your friends when sad would be the birds and animals.
In the daytime there are no people,
at night many ghosts roam abroad.
It is a place of great fear.
Day and night rain and snow fall constantly.
There is no place for you there.
Stay here. I will soon return.

Bhadrā took the prince by the hand and said:

Prince, if you do not take me with you,
then today Bhadrā will end her life.
Without you, who can I give my life to?
Don't do this. Take me with you as your companion.

The prince replied:

Bhadrā, listen to me.
I have a great liking for giving.
If asked, I would give my wife and children.
If someone wanted it, I would even give my life.

At such a time you would hinder my giving.
Therefore you and the children should stay here.

Again Bhadrā pleaded:

Great prince, please hear me.
Take me as your helper in giving.
Even if you give me and the children away,
to fulfill your wish, I will do as you say.
Therefore take us with you.

Hearing this, the prince promised to take Bhadrā and the children with him. Then Viśvantara went to his mother and bowed before her:

Great mother who gave birth to the buddhas of the three times,
endowed with the four immeasurable attitudes and the ten
    perfections,
mother who fulfills all hopes, wishes, and needs, bringing all
    to fruition,
mother, great mother, please hear my words.

I gave the all-conquering jewel to an enemy,
and have been reprimanded many times by father.
I have been expelled for twelve years
to Kem-kem Hashang Demon Mountain.

For such time I pray that there be no hindrance to your life,
that you will not suddenly be stricken with illness,
and if I do not lose my life, that we quickly meet again.

At these words, the queen fell into a faint. After she had recovered she took her son by the hand and with tears in her eyes said:

Viśvantara Arthasiddhi Śrī,
I am the mother that gave birth to you.
How could you leave me, you who are my heart,
and go away to this frightening mountain!
If you go for twelve years to Hashang Mountain,

as an old woman I could not survive for so long.
Without you, who do I devote myself to?
Alas! To be on the brink of old age without a son!

What was the great king thinking?
First he had the great suffering of having no son.
Then by the blessings of making offerings to the gods,
by the fruit of giving alms to the poor,
and by the blessings of the infallible objects of refuge,
a rare son was born to me.

With the hopes and devotion of the world on you,
what is the point of sending you to a far-off place?
Before you were born he was in despair.
Now you are with us and he does something like this.
Is the great king not possessed by a spirit?

Her son replied:

My great mother, wipe away your tears.
All living beings in this three-realm samsara
that come together will have to part.
This is the nature of all things.

Mother, I am your own flesh and blood.
This great longing you have for me is natural.
One day I will arise as exonerated.
Mother and son will meet again in this life.
But if we cannot, I pray that in future lives
we will meet again in a pure realm.

His mother took her son's hand and cried. Then she thought: "My son
has to set off on a long journey. It is inauspicious to cry." She dried her eyes,
bowed to the deities of the ten directions, and prayed:

Great host of powerful buddhas abiding in the ten directions,
sons of the buddhas, arhats, and bodhisattvas,
powerful protectors, the four great direction guardians,

treasure protectors, wealth deities, formless ḍākinīs,
earth lords, local deities, nāgas, and demons,
hear me, give me your attention!

When my son sets out on the road,
keep him to the right path, don't let him be lost.
When he travels swiftly over high passes and through valleys,
see that he does not become exhausted or suffer in any way.

When he arrives at Hashang Demon Mountain,
may he see it as the beautiful palace of Indra.
When he eats the cold fruit there,
may it become nectar endowed with the eight supreme tastes.

When he drinks water to ease his thirst,
may it become an unending stream of milk.
When he wears clothes of leaves and sits on seats of cotton,
may they become pañcāli and seats of lotus.

When the wild and fearful animals roar,
may they become the sounds of the Great Vehicle.
When the rushing rivers roar,
may he hear them as the six-syllable mantra.

When he is tormented by the heat
of being in the deep valleys and gorges,
may the goddesses give him shade and shelter.

When he dwells on that fearful mountain where no humans live,
may he be comforted by the buddhas,
and when illness strikes, may medicine and doctors effortlessly
    appear.
In short, wherever he roams, may he experience no suffering
and may he dwell in happiness.

Having conquered all opposing forces
and gathered all favorable circumstance,

may the wish-fulfilling tree that is the mind of prince Viśvantara
break out in full leaf and blossom.

By these words of truth issuing from my heart,
I pray that mother and son are quickly reunited.

When the time came for the prince and his family to leave for Hashang
Demon Mountain, they set out on the road, with the prince in one char-
iot pulled by two horses, his queen and three children in another two-horse
chariot, and provisions for the journey loaded on three elephants. They were
accompanied for a considerable distance by the fifteen hundred queens led
by his mother Kuśalāvatī Bhadrā; the sixty vassal kings, such as King Bhadra;
the three thousand ministers, such as Sucandra; and the citizens, entourage,
and servants, such as the layman Śrīmān, all in a state of great mourning.
After they had passed through many valleys, the prince turned to them
and said:

> Great mother and all other assembled queens,
> King Bhadra, minister Sucandra, and all other ministers,
> Śrīmān and other citizens, retinue and servants,
> with great kindness you have accompanied me for a long way.

> The dispersal now of this harmonious gathering
> reflects the transitory nature of all composite phenomena,
> and so my mind too is resigned to it.

> Now return to your lands.
> Live there in harmony with the Dharma.
> Death will come, so give away your bodies.
> Trust in the Three Jewels in this and future lives.
> For blessings, imagine your guru on the crown of your head.
> To remove obstacles, make offerings to the ḍākinīs and
>   protectors.

> As for me, I pray that I remain healthy, and after twelve years
> I will return and we will meet again.
> If we do not meet again in this life,
> I pray we meet again in some pure realm.

With sighs and cries of great sadness, the entourage prostrated to the prince and left for home. His mother, Kuśalāvatī Bhadrā, took hold of her son's hand and said:

> My Viśvantara Arthasiddhi Śrī,
> you are the very heart inside of me,
> a karmic debt from a previous life.
> Now my heart has gone and been expelled to a fearful
>   mountain.
> Today your mother has been left without a heart.
>
> The sun that shines in this life has set.
> Who can I turn to in this life?
> Your father has been guided by an evil minister,
> who encouraged him to carry out this unworthy punishment.
>
> My loving son, you are about to leave.
> Each time I think of you and bring you to my mind,
> three times I will call out, "Viśvantara!"
> without ever getting weary of it.
> During the three summer months the blue dragon
>   thunder roars,
> and at that time, my son, I will clearly remember you.
> Three times I, your mother, will call out, "My son!"
> Three times I will call out, "Viśvantara!"
> You, my son, call out three times, "Mother!"
> Three times call out, "Kuśalāvatī Bhadrā!"
>
> During the three winter months the cold winds blow,
> and at that time, my son, I will clearly remember you.
> Three times I, your mother, will call out, "My son!"
> Three times I will call out, "Viśvantara!"
> You, my son, call out three times, "Mother!"
> Three times call out, "Kuśalāvatī Bhadrā!"
>
> During the three spring months, the blue cuckoo sings,
> and at that time, my son, I will clearly remember you.
> Three times I, your mother, will call out, "My son!"

Three times I will call out, "Viśvantara!"
You, my son, call out three times, "Mother!"
Three times call out, "Kuśalāvatī Bhadrā!"

I will always hold you with the greatest of love.
I pray that we meet again in this life.
If not, I pray that in future lives,
we meet on the path to enlightenment.

With these words, and her eyes brimming with tears, she returned home.

When the prince, his queen, and the children came to a stop on the road, they looked back and saw their escort party far in the distance. At the next stop on their journey, three beggars appeared and asked for alms. The prince was delighted:

These precious elephants, excellent for traveling,
possessions of inestimable value, the wealth of the Jewel
    Continent,
though I surely need them for the journey,
in order to fulfill your wishes, dear brahmans,
I give them now to you.

With these words he gave the elephants to the beggars. One league further on they arrived at Kalinga Happy Valley. There they met five beggars who asked the prince for his horses. "Excellent!" the prince replied, and then said:

These precious horses, as fast as the wind,
these beautiful chariots, adorned by garlands of flowers,
by giving them to you with the purest of minds,
may they be endowed with miraculous power.

With these words he gave the horses and chariots to the beggars.

The family continued their journey, with the prince at the front, the children in the middle, and Bhadrā at the back carrying a bundle of provisions. After a while they arrived at a place called Place of Glories. There, one path led to a clean and pleasant grassy plain covered with flowers and surrounded by hills. The water there was pure, and deer and birds played all around.

Under the cool shade of a *tāla* tree the family rested for a while. Bhadrā went to drink some water. She took a mouthful of water and looked back and forth and all around. All she saw were the deer playing and no sign of human life. This made her sad, and she remarked:

> Alas! In whatever direction I look,
> there are no like-minded people to see.
> Coming to quench my thirst at a time like this,
> I see the pointlessness of gathering wealth.
> How it came to this, I do not know.
> It must be something bad from a past life.

The prince thought to himself: "Bhadrā is unhappy in this empty land without people. The road ahead is difficult and there is the danger of wild animals. She should return home." He spoke:

> Bhadrā, listen to me.
> We still have far to travel.
> There will be countless hardships in the valleys and passes,
> and much fear of wild animals.
> This is no place for you.
> Would it not be better to return home?

Bhadrā bowed to the prince and replied:

> Great prince, please hear my words.
> Just now I was thoughtlessly talking aloud.
> Without you who would I turn to?
> How could I possibly be without you?
> There is no question. Wherever you go,
> take me as your companion.

With these words they journeyed on. After a while they rested on a grassy meadow. Again Bhadrā became very sad. Out of the hearing of the prince, she said:

> This place with its shiny colored clothes of green,
> a place without people, but where bees play in song and dance,

where birds call in their different voices;
wherever I look, it just makes me sad.
When mother, father, and children are expelled to a far-off land,
I wonder if in Vidarbha the kingdom is safe.

Again they journeyed on. After a while they came to high hill, where deer played, and which was clean, pleasant, and bountiful with fruit trees. Bhadrā said:

Great prince, please hear these words.
This place is beautiful, adorned with flowers of all kinds,
clean running water, the sweet sound of the cuckoo,
fruit trees, and the musical sounds of deer playing.
Why not consider staying here?

The prince replied:

It would be wrong to disregard my father's command.
We will not stay here but journey on to Hashang Mountain.

Thus they journeyed on.
The three children began to suffer from swollen feet and were lagging behind. The prince prayed:

Gurus, meditation deities, ḍākinīs, possessed of great
    compassion,
earth lords, local deities, possessed of great power,
help me fulfill my prayer.
We two have the strength to carry on walking,
and by moving swiftly, to arrive at our destination soon,
but our young children do not have such ability.
May the Demon Mountain be nearer!

With these words the mountain moved five leagues nearer.
The family journeyed on and arrived at a place called Valley of Fluttering Banners. There they rested at Lotus Grove with Joyful Smile. Bhadrā gazed at a lotus and said:

Water-born lotus, free from water,
of joyful smile, adorned with stamens;
those stamen hands, their palms together,
raised in devotion at your crown,
they flutter and dance.

They traveled on and arrived at a place called Copper Land of Glorious Light. There they met three brahman beggars who prostrated before the prince and asked for alms. "Where are you three from?" asked the prince. "Aren't you tired and weary?"

"We are from the Land of Golden Sands," said one. "I am eighty-one years old," he continued. "I had a young brahman wife, but she did not like me because I was old and would often disparage me. So I gave her to the other two brahmans. She told us, 'Go and ask Prince Viśvantara to give me his three children for my servants.' I replied that it was not possible that he would give away his own children, but she said that the prince had pledged to give whatever was asked of him, and as he possessed them, he would give them away. So this is why we are here."

"The three children are so young. They are not ready to be servants," replied the prince. "And what a pity to take them from their mother!"

"We are not here to destroy your pity," the brahman replied. "We are here to search for servants."

The prince thought to himself: "I have vowed to give whatever is asked of me. Therefore I will give them." Thinking that Bhadrā would be unwilling to let her children go, the prince said to her: "Bhadrā, go and find some fruit and bring it for our three guests."

Bhadrā went off in search of fruit. To ensure that there would be no hindrance to the act of giving, a virtuous deity made sure that no fruit was to be found nearby, thereby ensuring that Bhadrā had to travel far to find some. Meanwhile, the prince took the three children by the hand and said to them:

Sādhuvadin, Sādhuvardhati, Sundarī, my three children,
our long association today comes to an end.
This parting of harmonious ways comes about
because all composite phenomena are transitory.

> I am not someone with little love for you,
> because all living beings of the six realms
> having come together will one day part.
>
> My children, do not be attached to your father,
> do not think of your mother,
> but to fulfill the wishes of the brahmans, go now.

With these words he gave the children to the brahmans. The children being young, and particularly because they feared they would not meet their mother again, refused to go and resisted the brahmans for a while, all the time hoping they could just see their mother again. The brahmans tied the children to a tree, pulled their clothes over their heads, and beat them with a branch from a thorn bush. The prince wept. He could not watch and buried his face in his clothes. The children cried and called out, "Mother! Mother!"

The brahmans took the children by the hand and started to leave. Sādhu-vadin asked them to be allowed to say goodbye to their father. Crying, he said to his father:

> Great father, my king, in order to accomplish your great
>   purpose,
> you made a pledge to give away even us three children.
> In keeping with your pledge, I will go.
> Not to meet my mother, who nourished us with kindness,
> and gave us love from heart, makes me sad.
> But sadness is of no use. Keep well, my parents.

Then Sādhuvardhati, who was also crying, said:

> Father, you made the promise to give whatever was asked of you.
> Not to leave would be to go against my father's vow.
> To fulfill your wish, I too will go.
> Not to meet my mother at this point leaves me sad.
> I wonder if we will meet again in this life.
> If not, I pray we meet on the path to enlightenment.

Sundarī, also in tears, said to her father:

> This little peacock known as Sundarī
> must step out of the great trees of my parents
> and become the servant of this wicked brahman.
> I too will do as my father says and go.
> It makes me sad not to meet my mother,
> who cared for me with love and gave of her milk.
> If we do not meet in this life, I pray we meet in the next.

Their father, his eyes filled with tears, said to his children:

> My three children, you are my heart,
> and I have the suffering of my heart being torn out.
> But now I am on the Dharma path of giving.
> Be brave. Do not shed tears.

> Compassionate divine guru, Three Supreme Jewels,
> as soon as these children set out on the road,
> may they be beset by no sudden illness,
> and by the words of truth that come from my heart,
> may mother, father, and children soon be together again.

The brahmans led the children away. Far along the road, the children were split up and taken to individual homes.

Meanwhile Bhadrā had picked some fruit and now returned to the prince. She saw that the brahmans and her children were no longer there. Realizing that they had been given away to the brahmans, she threw herself to the ground and in great grief and sorrow exclaimed:

> My three beautiful, sun-like children
> have been overcast by the clouds of the brahmans,
> and my bountiful harvest has been destroyed by a hailstorm
>   of grief.

> Powerful gurus, meditation deities, ḍākinīs,
> mighty earth lords and local deities,

in one moment, this act of impermanence has occurred.
Why such a thunderbolt?

The loss of my children, who are my very heart,
has now brought me death without dying.
This suffering of mother and children,
is it not all the work of these evil brahmans?

With these words she fainted from great sorrow. "Ah, poor Bhadrā," said the prince to himself, and sprinkled water over her. When she recovered, he said:

Bhadrā, listen to me.
Do you not remember what we talked about?
When we set out from Vidarbha to Demon Mountain,
didn't I explain to you that I had great love for giving,
and that if someone asked, I would give away
my children, my wife, even my life?

You said you would not obstruct my giving,
and you came with me having promised to help me
fulfill the two accumulations of merit
necessary for the attainment of enlightenment.
But now you grieve like this.

Having crossed over many a valley and mountain,
I have only you for my companion in times of sorrow,
and your grieving disturbs my mind.

With these words the prince burst into tears. Bhadrā wiped away the tears and said:

Great king, please hear what I have to say.
I was not able to see the children before they left,
and so I cried many tears of love and compassion.
I did not cry to disturb the mind of the prince.

My three beautiful children, who are my very heart,
have now been separated and each led away.
My three beautiful children, who are my very heart,
their eyes now are bulging out of their head.

To imagine and to think of it makes me sad.
I have not gone against the words of the prince.
I will do whatever you say to fulfill your desire.
Now let us journey on. I will be your helper.

With this, the couple journeyed on. After some time they arrived at a thick forest whose trees were laden with fruit. Bhadrā picked a fruit and brought it to the prince. He took a bite from it and discovered that it was delicious. Taking it in his hands, he said:

This mango fruit with eight supreme tastes,
delicious and sweet, the best of all foods,
if I were to see my children I would give it to them.
Without my children I am so sad.

At this, Bhadrā again began to cry. The prince said:

Ah, anything can slip from an unguarded tongue.
Anything will arise to a thoughtless mind.
Thinking about this, maybe I was wrong.
Bhadrā, please eat this delicious mango.

They traveled on. After a while they came to a river. Being very wide and deep, it was difficult to cross. The prince made a prayer:

Gurus, meditation deities, ḍākinīs, possessed of great
    compassion,
earth lords, local deities, possessed of great power,
you who dwell as witnesses to the truth,
show us a path across this river.

If we do not cross the river and are left here,
we would be contravening my father's commands,
and how in the future would we attain enlightenment?
Please show us a way across the river.

As a result of this prayer, the river swirled, the flow was stopped, leaving a path in between on which they crossed. The prince realized that the drying up of the river would adversely affect many creatures, and so prayed: "May the river be as it was." In response, the river flowed normally as before.

After some time they arrived at a place called Windswept Path. There, Indra, king of the gods, and Brahma both manifested as brahmans. They wanted to see if Viśvantara's acts of giving were merely conventional acts or ultimate acts. In front of the prince they asked for alms. The prince thought to himself: "Nobody comes to this place. I wonder if these are non-human manifestations." He asked: "Where are you two from? I have nothing to give."

"We are from the land of Phava," replied the brahmans. "We are miserable because we have no friends or helpers, and so we are asking you to give your queen to us."

The prince thought to himself: "If I refuse to give Bhadrā to these brahmans, my previous acts of giving will amount to nothing. In this faraway place she is very attached to me, and if I do give her away, then she will have to bear the pain of being separated from me. Poor thing! But I have no choice." He turned to Bhadra and said:

My beautiful Bhadrā,
by the accumulation of merit from previous lives
you have attained a human form.
For the Dharma we have to give up our bodies and lives.
Giving away what we have is the essence of Dharma.

For long you have been with me,
but, although I cannot bear to do it,
if I do not give you to the brahmans,
I cannot perfect my practice of giving.
You too will not find happiness in the future.

Therefore go now and fulfill the wishes of the brahmans.
I am one with the minds of these brahmans.
Keep these things in your mind, my beautiful lady.

With these words he gave Bhadrā to the brahmans. Bhadrā said: "If you give me to the brahmans, you will have no one to serve and wait upon you. Please don't give me away." The prince replied:

Bhadrā, don't say this. Listen to me.
I have made the pledge to give of whatever is asked.
Be an aid in my accumulation of merit
for the attainment of enlightenment.
Don't think of me. Be the servant of the brahmans.
That is how you can be of service to me.

Bhadrā, with tears in her eyes, agreed to go with the brahmans. The prince said to the brahmans:

You two brahmans, listen to me.
This Bhadrā, a true companion in all lives,
is of royal caste and lineage,
skilled in making nourishing and delicious food.
This beautiful Bhadrā, I no longer need.
Brahmans, make her your own.

The brahmans led Bhadrā away. But after a hundred steps or so, they turned back and offered her back to the king, saying:

Great lord of men, we have been pretending.
How wonderful it is that you have meaningfully used
this human life of opportunity and endowment
with acts of ultimate giving, great lord of men.

We pay homage to the prince,
possessed of the courage of giving,
who would give even his own life away.

After this praise, the prince said: "Once I have given something I cannot take it back. Please carry on with your journey."

The two brahmans revealed their celestial form and said: "Great king, we were testing you to see if you had attachment or not. We do not need your queen." With these words Indra cast his eyes around the sky. Immediately he brought all the gods under his control, and they transformed into a large camp of nomads who began to serve the prince and his queen. Indra, king of the gods, bowed to the prince and said:

> Mighty one of the gods, venerable and supreme being,
> you have given up this life to attain great things in the future.
> You are a peerless buddha who has perfected working for others,
> a being of extraordinary deeds, a beacon in this world.
> Great being, we prostrate to you, and may we please you
> in a way that is without parallel in the world.

The prince and his queen traveled on. Looking back, they saw the group of nomads disappear like a rainbow.

After a while they came across a white child holding a white crystal rosary in his hand. "Great prince," said the child, "About one league ahead you will come across an offering made to you by the god Brahma." With that, the child disappeared.

Further on, by the side of a river, Brahma manifested a large town. There for seven days Brahma made offerings to the couple. As they were about to leave, Brahma in his form as the white child said:

> Great prince, stay in this place.
> A home and all the possessions you need, I will offer.
> A world of servants and helpers, I will offer.
> The punishment of your father ends here.
>
> In the dreadful Demon Hashang Mountain,
> the demons, vicious cannibals, and wild animals
> are hard to endure, and you will return in fear.
> It is a harsh place, a black mountain, and of great fear.
> Prince, it is not a place for you.

The prince replied:

Through the power of merit gathered in previous lives,
unending wealth and possession have appeared.
With faith in deeds of virtue, I make offerings.

If I were to develop attachment and desire
for this wealth of all that one could desire,
my virtuous deeds would not increase
but diminish from the distraction.

Especially if I were to ignore my father's commands,
I would be breaking my pledge.
Therefore now I will leave.

With this, the couple journeyed on, and the city vanished like breath on a mirror. The prince said: "The fruit of my prayers to the Three Jewels has been realized in this life."

After a while they came to a very gloomy place in the midst of a thick forest that blotted out the sun. Looking here and there, they did not know which way to go. Soon they came across a yogi with his hair tied up on his crown, a yellow beard and eyebrows, holding a *ḍāmaru* drum and a thighbone horn. He addressed the prince: "You are very bold. Where have you come from? Where do you intend to go? What is your name? About five hundred leagues from here is Black Demon Mountain of Hashang. It is a wild place with harsh valleys, where rocks of salt cast black shadows like lances, where the flowers of poisonous trees abound, where poisonous lakes boil and bubble, where the breath of venomous snakes fill the air like clouds, where malicious demons gather day and night and indulge in killing. Vicious animals such as lions, tigers, and bears give terrifying chase as soon as they scent a human, and devour their victim. Merely the sight of this place brings great fear. Moreover, on the road to this place terrifying sufferings beyond the imagination will be encountered."

To this the prince replied: "I am Prince Viśvantara. I have traveled from Vidarbha. I am going to Hashang Demon Mountain."

The yogi spoke: "I have heard that this Prince Viśvantara gave away his wealth and a kingdom. To see him now brings me much merit too. About one league from here is the river Nagara. Keep to the right of it and you will see a narrow track used by animals. Take this path. I pray that we meet in future lives." With these words he vanished.

After a while they came to a dark forest that obscured the sun. All kinds of demons and cannibals were seen, even in the daytime. Wild animals ran toward them roaring, and boiling poisonous pools bubbled loudly. Bhadrā in terror exclaimed:

> Alas! What kind of place is this!
> Cannibals, demons, and spirits roam, even in the daytime.
> These apparitions, these ghostly displays,
> are reminiscent of the demon city of the Lord of Death.

> I see tigers, lions, bears, and other wild animals,
> all with their vicious fangs bared.
> I see boiling poisonous pools.
> My mind is defeated.
> Never will we be free from this place!
> It is as if my life were spent.

> Gurus, and the precious Three Jewels,
> lead us out of this place!

Seeing that Bhadrā was frightened, the prince proclaimed:

> Demons, spirits, gods, nāgas, yakṣas,
> kiṃnaras, and powerful earth lords,
> tigers, lions, packs of jackals and wolves,
> bears, and all other wild animals who roam here,
> listen to me for a while.

> As I have a mind that is completely empty,
> I possess no cherishing of body and life.
> But for the well-being of Mandé Bhadrā,
> I ask that you relinquish your harmful and malicious minds,
> generate the mind of enlightenment, do no harm,
> and rest in a state of peacefulness.

With these words all the malicious demons and cannibals stopped causing harm and remained in a peaceful state. The wild animals also ceased their attacks and like pet dogs wagged their tails and came up to greet the couple. Even the birds sang beautiful songs and welcomed the prince and Bhadrā.

Finally, they arrived at Demon Mountain. Its peak was a white snow mountain. Its base was rock, and in between small streams flowed down. Merely by the prince's arrival, the dry trees burst into life and arid springs burst forth with water. All the gods, nāgas, yakṣa demons, smell-eating gandharvas, rakṣa cannibals, flesh-eating piśācas, kumbhāṇḍa demons, elemental spirits, walking corpses, garuḍa birds, half-human kiṃnaras, and all the other creatures that lived there—many wild carnivorous animals, such as tigers, leopards, bears, wolves, hyenas, and so on, and grazing animals such as elephants, buffaloes, and bulls, and all types of birds, such as cranes, ducks geese, and peacocks, as well as every other kind of animal that lived on that mountain—all came together to welcome the prince and his wife.

The couple looked at Demon Mountain. They saw that in its southern part, the sun rose early and set late. There were no distracting sounds. The water there was clean. Birds chattered back and forth. There were mango trees, and the ground was clean and adorned with flowers. In this place that clarified and brightened the mind, they built huts made of leaves. The prince lived in one hut contemplating the perfection of his mind of enlightenment. Bhadrā lived a little further away. From time to time she would gather fruit and offer them to the prince.

After a long time living this way, one day Bhadrā went before the prince and said:

> You whose mind is pure and who refrains from speaking,
> youthful Viśvantara, please hear these words.
> Twelve years have passed in this sacred place.
> The journey here was six months, the journey back six months.
> I think it is time we were back in our country.
> Shouldn't we start our journey home?

The prince replied:

> Bhadrā, listen to me carefully.
> In this sacred forest, prophesized by the Buddha,
> all distracting and nonconducive chatter has been left behind.

In this joyous and happy place of meditative concentration,
virtuous activity will increase.
I am not going. Here I will stay.

With these words he returned to his meditation. Bhadrā went to the far
edge of the forest in search of fruit. There she saw a finely plumed parrot that
spoke. Bhadrā said to the bird:

Beautiful bird, endowed with the power to speak,
you are a handsome creature, and very attractive,
with the fine color of your throat and your red beak.

Since arriving in this uninhabited Demon Mountain,
I have found no fine food fit for humans,
and so I come to the forest in search of fruit.

You in the form of a bird, who knows how to talk,
I ask you great bird to show me
where I can find the fruit I seek.

The parrot hopped back and forth three times on the tree and said:

Bhadrā, in the prime of your youth,
of complexion beautiful and smooth, of an aroma supreme,
of the kind who fulfills all alluring desires,
your face is like the full moon.

My mind has fallen for you like falling into an ocean.
With your bright smile, to see you, goddess, brings joy.
What fruits you desire, I will show you.

With these words the parrot led Bhadrā to a place where fruit was to be
found. The bird flew to the top of a mango tree and caused the fruit to fall.
Bhadrā was overjoyed, and having feasted on the mangoes, she said:

Possessed of the winged power to fly through the skies,
virtuous bird, you have satisfied me with fruit.

May you play in joy with those of your own kind.
I pray that I too am soon reunited with those of my own kind.

The bird flew down from the tree, escorted Bhadrā for eighty steps, and said:

You are virtuous, beautiful, of good lineage,
of ethical mind and beautiful conduct,
in the form of an alluring goddess, with a lotus smile.
Go now in peace.
If we do not meet again in this life,
I pray that we do in the future.

With these words the parrot flew away. On the way back Bhadrā came across a powerful gushing river. She thought to herself: "This river probably flows all the way to Vidarbha. Maybe it passes my children on it way." She exclaimed:

Great river, water dressed in white silk,
waters of ambrosia quenching the desires of thirst,
water clear and clean, forever flowing,
your pleasing sounds delighting my mind.

On your long journey to places far from here,
I hope you will meet my three children.
If you do, give them this message.

"Mother and father are well and happy.
We hope the life of our three beautiful children
has also not been blighted by illness.
It has been a long time since we were parted,
and so for a long time our hearts have been heavy.
Not for a moment have we not borne
the pain of having our hearts taken from us.
Twelve years will soon have passed,
and parents and children will soon be together again."

With these words she left. Sometime later, far away, the three children were sent to the river's edge to collect wood, and the river delivered the message to them. The children thought of their mother, called out her name, and wept. The daughter, Sundarī, went to the top of a high hill. There she saw a kalaviṅga bird that possessed the mastery of beautiful speech, coming out of the sky. Sundarī was upset and, on seeing the bird, she hoped it would be flying to Demon Mountain and that it would meet her mother and father. She said:

> Kalaviṅga bird, you delight in flying over the snowy peaks
> with your beautiful "kyu-ru-ru" song,
> but to hear your song leaves me sad.
>
> Great bird, do not be nervous,
> but listen to my sadness.
> Are you flying over Demon Mountain?
> Our mother and father are there.

Say this to them:

> "Mother and father, are you well and happy?
> Here, we three have not had the misfortune of being ill.
> The suffering of being separated from our parents
> torments our minds day and night without end.
> And so look upon us with pity.
>
> Your message has reached us.
> And if it is within your power to meet us soon,
> think of your children and come to us quickly."

The bird took the message and flew off to Demon Mountain. There he delivered it to their mother and father. On hearing the message, they were plunged into sadness and wept. Their tears formed a lake from which grew a lotus plant bearing a thousand flowers. Each flower gave birth to a buddha and from the essence of these thousand buddhas Avalokiteśvara was born. The couple offered their devotion and praise to him by way of prostrations, circumambulation, and so on.

Then Bhadrā thought of the children. Bowing to the prince, she said:

> Wise prince, please listen to me.
> Twelve years in this sacred place has passed.
> It took six months to get here, six more to return.
> Thirteen years is more than the king's command.
>
> Now I ask that we return to our land.
> I think of my children, who are my heart,
> my mother, my father, my country, and so on.
> Think on me with love, and let us leave.

The prince felt great compassion at the sight of Bhadrā's sadness and said to her: "Bhadrā, do not cry. We will leave right now." He rose from his seat and made preparations to leave. Immediately, the gods, nāgas, yakṣa demons, animals, birds, and other creatures that lived on the mountain all gathered in front of the prince. In their own languages, and with tears rolling down their faces, they implored the prince and his princess to stay. The prince looked with compassion on the demons, cannibals, and other creatures, and with his right hand in the gesture of giving refuge, he said:

> Demons, spirits, yakṣas, smell-eating gandharvas,
> and all you other creatures that dwell here,
> for long you have viewed us as your parents,
> and as friends have acted lovingly toward us.
>
> But today our long acquaintance comes to an end.
> This is composite phenomena being impermanent,
> a truth for all living beings in the three realms.
>
> Place your faith in the Dharma, do no harm to others,
> live in peace, my like-minded friends.
> If we should not meet in this life,
> I pray that we will in the next.

With this, the prince and his queen left. The creatures of the mountain were very sad and escorted the couple for a long time before returning.

After a while the couple came to a place called Light-Gathering Wind. There they met a blind brahman, who held out his hand and asked for alms. The prince said: "I am happy you are here, but I have nothing to offer. What can I give you?"

The beggar replied: "Give me your two eyes."

The prince was overjoyed and immediately sat down cross-legged on the ground. "Now I can complete my practice of giving," he thought. "Bhadrā," he said, "do not have attachment and desires for me now. Since the beginning of samsara, no matter how many bodies I have taken, they have all been wasted. Now, I will make this one meaningful." With his right hand he took a sharp knife, and with his left he pulled back the eyelid to expose the eyeball. He plunged the knife into his eyes, and blood spurted forth. Bhadrā screamed in grief and, unable to bear it, seized hold of his hand.

"Bhadrā, don't do this," said the prince. "If you do this, you are no longer close to me but far away, and we will not meet again for a very long time. Therefore sit down and do not obstruct my giving." He took the knife again, put it into his eye-sockets, and took out his eyes. Bhadrā could not bear to look and buried her face in the ground and lost consciousness.

The prince took his eyes in his hands, placed them into the eye-sockets of the brahman, and said:

> Listen well, my good brahman.
> I have given you my eyes, which are difficult to part with.
> Having fulfilled your wish, may you gaze upon the three realms!
> And may I, endowed with the faultless eyes of the Dharma,
> be a beacon of freedom, dispelling the darkness of ignorance.
> May I complete the practice of giving!

So saying, he stood there in splendor. The brahman discovered that he could see. He prostrated to the prince and exclaimed:

> Kind one! Noble son of a king!
> Compassionate one who satisfies by giving whatever is asked for,
> great beacon dispelling the darkness of the three worlds,
> a prince unrivaled in the three-thousandfold universe.

> Generally you are kind to all living beings,
> but specifically you have shed the suffering

brought on by the bad karma of this brahman.
I pay homage and praise you, most kind prince.

With these words the brahman left for Vidarbha. On his arrival, the townsfolk gathered around him and asked him where he had obtained his new eyes. "These eyes are those of Prince Viśvantara," he replied. The king and all his subjects were amazed. The king sent the minister Sucandra and his retinue to invite the prince home.

Meanwhile, Bhadrā had recovered her senses. She turned and looked at the prince sitting upright with blood over his face and body. She burst into tears and exclaimed:

Alas! Twelve years we spent on that terrifying mountain.
Now we are on our way home,
and I was thinking of meeting again with our beloved friends.
But now all our efforts have come to nothing. Oh no, no!
Alas, alas! What kind of karma is this!

The prince said:

Bhadrā, do not grieve, place yourself in the Dharma.
In all lives, in this beginningless and endless samsara,
up to the present life with this human body,
all my deeds have meant nothing.

Now I have extracted the essence of this life.
So Bhadrā, do not grieve, let us go now.
Lead the way.

They left for home, with Bhadrā leading the prince. After some time, they arrived at Hari Meeting Place. There they were welcomed by the minister Sucandra and his retinue, who bowed to and circumambulated the couple. The minister said:

Great being of great mind!
Such hardships you have undertaken!
Truly wondrous! You are a glorious ocean of great qualities.

So that we all may be held in your great mind,
we request that you accompany us to Vidarbha.

The minister shed many tears. The prince placed his hand upon the head of minister Sucandra and said:

Sucandra and your retinue, are you here?
I too have not died and am just about alive.
But I joke. Sucandra, listen.
Is the kingdom of Vidarbha sound?
Are my mother and father, and their subjects all well?

Minister Sucandra and Bhadrā supported the prince on his left and right and they proceeded toward Vidarbha. After a while the prince took a rest and said:

Sugatas and bodhisattvas of the ten directions, please hear
    my plea.
To dispel the sorrow of Bhadrā, and to fulfill the wishes of
    Sucandra,
may my eyes be restored to have sight even clearer than before.

Instantly his eyes were restored with a sight keener than before.

After a while they came to Place of Glories. There, King Shing Tritsen of the uncivilized land of Jema Shingdrung welcomed Prince Viśvantara, his queen, and entourage. He served them and made offerings. He offered the prince priceless and unimaginable jewels, including the all-fulfilling and all-conquering jewel he had taken previously. Addressing the prince, he said: "Holy prince, I take the blame for the hardships that you have endured for such a long time. Therefore, in order to earn your forgiveness and to right my wrong, I offer you my kingdom and my subjects. And I ask that you lead me from samsara." With this he made many prostrations and circumambulations. The prince accepted his offers and requests. In this way a rival to his father the king was brought under control.

The party proceeded. After a while they met the three brahmans who had taken their children. The brahmans made many prostrations to and circumambulations of the prince, and said:

Can it be that the wonderful and extraordinary parents are here!
Your three wonderful children have been most useful to us.
Now, so that we may repay the kindness of the prince,
we offer them back to you.

The brahmans made to offer the children to the parents, but Prince Viśvantara said: "Once I have given something, I cannot take it back. Give them some work that they can do."
Bhadrā said:

Great prince, listen to me.
These three children born of my body,
for twelve long years have served as servants to the
    brahmans.
You do not find an udumbara flower[17] on the road,
and these three children, even rarer than that flower,
are of the lineage of a noble king,
but as servants of these ignoble brahmans
have endured countless hardships.

"In that case, we will take them," said the prince. He addressed the brahmans:

Brahmans, come to my country.
You will be compensated for the children

They continued on their way. For twelve leagues on the road to Vidarbha the vassal kings of his mother, their ministers, and their subjects all welcomed the prince with offerings. Even his father, King Bhūpāla Yaśas, welcomed his son by offering incense for seven leagues outside Vidarbha. From the Lotus Palace in Vidarbha to the city of Radiant Light the streets of every town were filled with parasols, victory ensigns, banners, cooling fans, tail fans, pavilions, music, offerings, singing, tambourines, cymbals, bells, horns, and so on, all to welcome the prince.

The prince, his queen, their children, and the brahmans reached the city of Radiant Light. There in the city, the prince's own vassal king, Samanta Darśin, prostrated to and circumambulated the prince and his entourage. Having made many offerings to the prince, he said:

Like the sun that has set in the west,
only to rise again in the east,
great prince, mother and father of all living beings,
went to Demon Mountain and has now returned.
So very kind to all living beings,
you have removed all our sorrows.

Here we have heard that Viśvantara Arthasiddhi
gave to others his own children and his eyes.
If that be so, why should the king, your father,
care about you giving a jewel to a rival king.

Great and powerful being, lord of men,
a victory banner on top of Mount Meru;
sacred being, with the name that radiates purity,
in the great palace known as Place of Joy,
may you nourish your kingdom in the ways of the Dharma.

May I too, when I depart from this life,
be reborn again and again in your company.
I make this auspicious prayer with single-pointed mind.

Then the prince was greeted by the people, the ministers, and the vassal kings, who prostrated to and circumambulated him. King Kāñcanavati and the other vassal kings each presented him with one gold coin. Subhadra, Arthavat, and the other ministers each presented him with a silver coin. The townsfolk, and the people from the neighboring areas, presented him with silver, beryl, coral, grains of precious metals, and many other jewels.

Then in the town called Heaped Flowers he met with his father. The prince, his queen, and the three children prostrated to the king. They took the king's hand and wept. The king said: "Today is the auspicious occasion of father and son meeting. There is no reason for tears." The prince and Bhadrā dried their eyes. "Come and sit on my lap," said the king to the children. However, the children were unwilling. "Why is this so?" asked the king. Sādhuvadin replied:

The fruit falls from the wish-granting tree,
into the ocean where it is eaten by nāgas.

Though we are children of a renowned lineage,
through punishment we were sent to a far-off land.

After many miles, in an isolated valley,
our faultless father gave us to three brahmans.
I along with Sādhuvardhati and Sundarī,
sons and daughter of his own flesh and blood,
were given away as a practice of giving.

We each worked as servants for the brahmans,
ate impure food and wore unclean clothes.
Contaminated and unclean, we have become dirty.
Great father, we may bring contamination to you.
And so we will not sit on your lap.

    The three children were bathed in jeweled baths with scented water and dressed in new clothes. The brahmans were given five hundred gold coins as compensation for Sādhuvadin, five hundred silver coins for Sādhuvardhati, and three hundred elephants for Sundarī. Then, with provisions for the journey, they returned to their own country.

    Then prince Viśvantara addressed the king:

Lord of men, sole father and king, please hear me.
I have carried the burden of punishment
as decreed by King Bhūpāla Yaśas Śrī.
On the long road I was tormented by troubles and weariness.
On that fearful mountain were vicious animals,
malicious spirits, yakṣa demons, and the like.

There in their midst we lived a terrifying life.
We wore leaves for clothes, used grass as beds,
ate fruit for food, drank cold water to quench our thirst,
and turned to birds for companions in our sadness.

May such suffering as I have experienced
for a virtuous act concerning worldly wealth
never befall on any living being.

By the act of giving away my father's all-conquering jewel,
up to the act of giving away my own eyes,
may I fulfill the practice of giving.

By the sum of these virtuous deeds,
may all beings without exception be happy.
In particular, for my father and lord, great protector and king,
down to his retinue, entourage, and subjects,
may all karma, obscuration, and imprints be removed.

I pray that in all future lives we meet again,
and that in future, by the power of this giving,
I gain the fruit of complete enlightenment.
Thus I dedicate my virtue.

The king replied:

It is true, exactly as you say.
Through the fault of not understanding,
you were subjected to punishment and expelled,
and made to experience many trials and troubles.
I and the ministers were poor in our discussions.

I heard that when my son had traveled far,
he gave away his children and his eyes,
as well as his horses, chariots, wealth, and grain.

That being so, I no longer had any remorse
about you giving the jewel to my rival.
Now I have heard of all you have done,
and I feel profound joy and faith in you.

For all the wrong that has been done to you,
I ask you please for your forgiveness.
Hereafter, in order to right the wrong I have done,
I give my vast treasury to you,
to give away as you please.

With these words the father took his son and Bhadrā by the hand. The children were put into a chariot, and together they proceeded to the palace. At the gates of the palace they were welcomed by the queens, led by the prince's mother, Queen Kuśalāvatī. All were holding incense. Gods led by Indra showered down flowers and played cymbals. The prince, his queen, and the children prostrated to the queen and wept. The prince's mother said to her son:

> Viśvantara, my son, listen to me.
> Alas, the violent winds of karma
> has visited much suffering upon
> Viśvantara and his wife.

> But now it is over, and we can be happy.
> The sorrow of a mother has today come to an end.
> Grieving over my son for twelve years,
> I have pulled out my hair,
> and a river of tears has fallen onto my breast.

> I have been tormented by the fires of grief.
> But the waters of your enlightenment
> have today put out that fire.
> My grief has been dispelled, my son, Viśvantara.

At the gates of the palace they gathered and the king spoke:

> Youth Viśvantara, you who possesses the courage to give,
> I ask that you accept the jewel of my crown.
> This supreme all-conquering jewel
> was given to a rival but was returned due to our merit.

> Now, please accept the fine words, the royal documents,
> the crown jewels, as exemplified by the all-conquering jewel,
> the treasuries of gold, silver, pearls, and silk,
> the horses, elephants, and buffaloes,
> the kingdom, the vassal kings and ministers,

the subjects, the armies, all of these,
my compassionate son, please accept.

With these words the prince was garlanded with jewels and the ministers and the vassal kings prostrated before him. He was led to the sandalwood throne, where he was handed the emblems of a king, beginning with the great wheel. The king spoke again:

My Viśvantara, so dear to my heart,
Take my wealth and offer it as you please,
look after the vassal kings and their subjects,
maintain the law in the manner of the golden yoke,[18]
and for the Dharma law, plant the victory banners of liberation.

Turn your back on the powerful who are of wicked ways,
revere the monastic community and those worthy of offerings.
For the sacred Dharma, build precious temples
and other centers of virtue for worship and offering.

See that the faithful are held up as examples to others.
Conquer your outer enemies with love and peaceful means,
and with a broad mind and a smile, nourish your friends.

This garland of light created by your father
is composed for you, my Viśvantara,
you who are like Indra, lord of the gods, incarnated as a man.
This well-constructed garland of advice,
hold it in your heart, my dear young son.

With these words the king presented the prince with the great sapphire seal marked with a foot, the great endless-knot crystal seal, and the white coral seal, thereby crowning prince Viśvantara as his successor. In celebration, festivities were organized over a distance of forty-five leagues.

Prince Viśvantara reigned over the kingdom. By the power of his merit, the rule of the kingdom was more established and more extensive than before.

One day the prince invited Indra, the king of the gods, and made this prayer in his presence:

This vast and busy kingdom
is nothing but a large prison of samsara.
But now to go against my father's will
would to be to haul something up on high.[19]
Without asking, this kingdom has come to me.
My father's commands are said once only.

Having taken up these reins,
I have found happiness in this life,
but it will not help in future lives.
So through this prayer, bless me that I
will gain what I strive to accomplish.

In the future, in a pure realm,
may my mother-and-father living beings
attain complete enlightenment
and wash away the stains of the impure realm.

Especially, may the great protector and king
be reborn as a meritorious preserver of the doctrine,
and may we as his entourage and retinue
worship and please him at his lotus feet.

May my mother, Kuśalāvatī Bhadrā, also
live her life in the Great Vehicle Dharma,
and having eradicated all faults in the three worlds,
may she become the lady who cares for all living beings.[20]

By the power of my merits
may the queens, the vassal kings,
Sucandra and the other ministers,
the people, the workers, and the entourage
walk the path to enlightenment and omniscience
and reach the stage of happiness.

At that stage, may they eradicate all faults
and liberate samsara completely.

Having freed all beings from samsara,
may they live totally in the Dharma.

Indra, king of the gods, said to the prince:

With the many excellent qualities of your wisdom,
you are a radiant wish-fulfilling tree.
The banners of your fame flutter in the ten directions,
and you have flown the great flag of stainless purity.
Great king, may your power spread everywhere.

From the time you were born until now,
the great ocean of your deeds
has been as one with the Dharma.
Recalling just a fraction of them,
I offer up this praise to you.

At the age of five you had completely mastered
the sciences, calculation, and grammar.
When you were ten you gave away
the jewels of your father's treasuries,
and dedicated the virtue of such an act.[21]

Without constraint, your father banished you to Demon
    Mountain.
You bore the burden of much suffering,
and for the sake of all living beings,
you gave away your sons and daughter.

At the age of twenty-two you gave away your eyes,
and then gained the supreme sight clearer than before.
You returned home and took the reins of the kingdom.

Thinking that this vast, busy kingdom is essentially without
    meaning,
you again gave it away to sentient beings,
and made a prayer to gain complete enlightenment.

Finally, you have become a mighty being of unexcelled fame,
a sole beacon ablaze on this earth.
A universal ruler greater than you is hard to find.

Viśvantara, on passing from this life,
on Potala Mountain in the east,
you will be born as Bhadravyāsa, a son of the Buddha.
You will become the guide of mother sentient beings,
turn the wheel of Dharma, and become a complete buddha.

Moreover, your father and lord, Bhūpāla Yaśas,
during the eon known as the Luminous,
millions of eons from now, will be born as the Buddha Himal,
to nourish and extend the great kingdom of Dharma.

The queen, Kuśalāvatī Bhadrā, after this life will be born
as Prajāpati in the great realm known as Leaves of Turquoise.
The queen, Mandé Bhadrā, having left this life,
will be born as King Śaṅkara in the great land of Siṅgala.

Your two noble sons, in the life after this,
will take birth in the south of India:
the eldest as the great King Arthavat,
the youngest as Megaśrī Dhara.

Your daughter, Sundarī, after this life,
will take birth in Oḍḍiyāna as the son of King Sukhā,
and will come to wield the reins of power
over the kingdoms of Sata and Mahāsata.

The great minister Sucandra
will be born as the son of King Ānandabhadra
in the land known as Nené.[22]

By the fruit of the wonderful tradition of virtue
initiated by Viśvantara, who has completed his
    meritorious deeds,

may mother, father, ministers, subjects, sons, and daughter
be brought to happiness.

Buddha born in a human realm, of a royal dynasty.
Prince, endowed with that extraordinary lineage,
may you always grow and flourish along this path.

You are a wonderful lotus garden, in whose skilful mind
endowed with method and wisdom
are shoots that are the fruits of virtue.
May they blossom with beautiful flowers of many wonderful
    qualities,
whose pure stamens would adorn Mount Meru.

May you have happiness in your future lives,
and in this life, may the renown of the one whose name
    means purity
resound with a dragon-like roar that covers the entire earth.

May I too, when my days as a god are over,
take your precious feet to the crown of my head,
and I pray that I will never be separate from you,
as the body is never separate from its shadow.

With these words Indra disappeared.

Then Bhadrā said to the prince: "That beautiful celestial form just disap-
peared. Why is that?"

The prince replied:

Bhadrā, listen to me carefully for a while.
The hollyhock flower will fade and disappear
when the song of the lark comes around.

The dew on the grass in autumn
dries as soon as the golden sun appears.
The beautiful colors of the rainbow
remain but for a short time and then are gone.

We too, mothers, fathers, and children,
come together in joy and happiness for a while,
and then like the flowers of the fig tree are gone.

The things of this world do not last for long.
This being together now will not last for long,
and it makes me sad.

I have been in this world for one hundred thirty years
and prayed to be of benefit to others.

My two sons, take this jewel of my reign,
accept it willingly, and work for the welfare of others.

With these words he handed the kingdom over to his two sons, who took five hundred wives for their queens, led by the ḍākiṇī daughter of King Śrīharṣa—an emanation of Yeshé Tsogyal. The coronation and the festivities were celebrated over a distance of twelve leagues. The daughter Sundarī was betrothed to the son of brahman Śaṅkara.

Prince Viśvantara, his queen Bhadrā, the minister Sucandra, the son of minister Kīrtikara, and the minister Jinadhara set out for Sinhala Mountain, where they meditated. The two sons maintained the kingdom as before.

After five years had passed the prince and his queen transformed into a pair of vermillion lotuses. They were carried away by the wind in South India and were gone. The ministers returned home and announced that the prince and his queen had attained nirvana. The two sons were overjoyed and commissioned the printing of a thousand copies of the hundred-thousand-line *Perfection of Wisdom Sutra* in gold ink in honor of their parents.

May all be auspicious!

2. The Story of Dharma King Sudhana (Norsang)

Oṃ svasti

The magician who in all directions, and in all times,
turned the thousand-spoke golden wheel of the sacred Dharma,
the eighty-four thousand Dharma gateways, and the Three
    Jewels,
I venerate with the crown of my head.

Sun-like friend, born of the ikṣvāku lineage,[23]
son of Śuddhodana, supreme of all princes,
who took on the burden of guiding living beings
in these times of the five degenerations,
I bow to the Śākya king and protector.

With limitless emanations born from great compassion,
you said, "I will reveal narratives in all languages—
in those of the gods, of nāgas, yakṣa spirits,
of kumbhāṇḍa water demons, and the languages of humans."

THEREFORE, WITH GREAT COMPASSION and skillful means, the perfect
and complete Buddha took births that exhibited pure and impure forms.
Of these births, the story of the wonderful deeds of the noble Dharma King
Sudhana, as found in the precious Kangyur, have been clearly presented as
the *Life of Sudhana* in more than one version by the great masters. These
narratives are not just beautifully sounding stories but possess great purpose,
such as planting the seeds of liberation. However, the meaning is couched
in terminology, poetic devices, and idiomatic expressions so that to the ears
of those of little learning, such as myself, it would be like the Amdo dia-
lect to a Tibetan ear, and we would not understand a word. Those of little

learning, such as myself, require something that is more appropriate, just as, for example, a craftsman requires his tools. Therefore crazy Tsering Wangdü from Dingchen,[24] while working in Shelkar Monastery, compiled this *Life of Dharma King Sudhana.*

Part 1. The Southern King, Shakpa the Young, Develops the Deluded Intention to Summon the Lake and Nāgas of the North.

In the past, countless eons ago, in a land of eastern India, there were two kingdoms. In the north was Vaśin and in the south Kulika.

> In their history and founding they were alike,
> in the dynasty of hereditary princes they were alike,
> in their power, caste, and size of kingdom, there were
>   no differences,
> and in the size of their palaces, they were similar.
> All in all, the two kingdoms were alike.
>
> However, in the fruits of the practice of giving sown in the past,
> in more immediate activities, in success, good fortune, and
>   so on,
> and particularly in the capabilities of succeeding generations,
> there were ups and downs, as is the way of things.

The king of the southern land of Kulika was Shakpa the Young. He was an arrogant and fierce man, who was also very selfish and miserly. As someone who had no understanding of the workings of karma and its effects, he took over the kingdom and cast aside the good and decent ways of the past and turned his back on the great gurus of old that the people had turned to for refuge. He refused to recognize and respect the wise deities but placed his trust in spirits and ghosts. He took refuge in charlatans and perpetual liars. He sought to know what was right and wrong by relying on deceptive fortune tellers. Elders who gave wise council were relegated to the ranks of the common people, while dissemblers and those with biased views he regarded as trustworthy and reliable.

As all his unworthy acts accumulated, meritorious activities such as making offerings to the Three Jewels, honoring the monastic community with donations and service, making regular torma offerings to the deities,

Norsang performed at the Tibetan Music, Dance, and Drama Society, India, 1971. The opera master Norbu Tsering, originally from the Kyormolung troupe, plays Sudhana.

The hermit from *Norsang*. Khorchag Monastery, Tibet, 2010.

giving to beggars, and so on, had consequently decreased. As a result, the rains did not arrive on time, the waters for irrigation were not good, and disease among humans and cattle was unending. Internal strife and famine plagued the land, leaving poverty and destitution in their wake. Finally the king could stand it no more and addressed his ministers:

> Assembled council of ministers, hear my words.
> Pay attention and listen to what I say.
> Here in eastern India are two kingdoms, north and south,
> whose power and prosperity were once the same.
>
> But these days the northern kingdom Vaśin is happy and
>   prosperous,
> while we in Kulika in the south are destitute and poor.
> My subjects and the people are fleeing to the north.
> What causes and conditions have brought this about?
>
> How can we bring the kingdom to prosperity?
> Should we not make preparations and go to war?
>
> Assembled council of ministers, hold discussions.
> Come up with a plan of how best to proceed,
> and bring it to me quickly!

The ministers were speechless and stared at each other in amazement. After a while they discussed how best to prepare for war, because for fear of the king's wrath they did not dare come up with an alternative plan. Among them was one elderly minister who had some understanding of right and wrong. He placed his hands together and addressed the king:

> Lord of men, and son of a king, please listen.
> Pay no heed to other reports, but hear my words.
> Several years have passed since we arrived at this wretched state.
> It would not be good to make an enemy of the northern state
>   of Vaśin,
> or to hold wrong views of the Dharma King Sudhana and his
>   father.

It is reported that the number of men in an army consisting
  of all our subjects
could be found in any town close to the Vaśin Palace.
Isn't it deluded for the ministers to discuss fighting them?

If we were to look at how our kingdom has deteriorated,
I have heard that the people have been secretly lamenting to
  the ministers.
So as to what is to be done about this, ask your people, great
  king.
But I don't know who among the ordinary people will know
  the answer.

Do you hear what I say, lord of men?
Do you hear and consider my words, great lord?

The king scowled and said:

Listen again, council of ministers! Pay attention and listen!
Assemble now all our subjects, high and low, in Iron Hill Palace.
Send out the summons to all regions at once.
As the minister says, I will ask the people.

The ministers rushed to the very top of the palace. They beat the great
drums that had never before been beaten, blew great horns that had never
before been blown, and flew great flags that had never before been flown. All
the people of the southern county, high and low, young and old, wondered
if the king would give them something they wanted, and immediately gath-
ered inside Iron Hill Palace. The king stood in full view at one side of the
palace, greeted his subjects, and addressed them as follows:

Listen to me, people assembled here.
Pay attention. Listen to what I have to say.

Here in the eastern part of India
there are two kingdoms, north and south.
In their history and founding they are alike,
in the dynasty of hereditary princes they are alike,

in their power, caste, and size of kingdom, there are no
    differences,
and in the size of our palaces, they are similar.
All in all, the two kingdoms are alike.

But these days the northern kingdom Vaśin is happy and
    prosperous,
while we in Kulika in the south are destitute and poor.
Many towns and regions are abandoned, and houses are in ruins.
What causes and conditions have brought this about?
How can we make this country prosperous again?
Speak now! Do not be secretive, don't be timid.

The townspeople took off their hats, put their hands together, and were
unable to speak. After a long time, an old man, aged around a hundred and
eighty, whose white hair stood up like that on a goat, who could barely see,
and who did not have a single tooth in his mouth, stood up, offered three
stumbling prostrations, and said:

Please listen, lord of men, and son of the gods.
My name is Ānanda Utkarṣa.
I am close to a hundred and eighty years old.
I was an attendant to your father and his father before that.

From the age of twenty until I was ninety,
I served your father, grandfather, and their sons.
When I reached ninety, my faculties declined.
No longer being able to serve, I returned home.

Soon after, the fortunes of the southern kingdom declined,
and my fellow countrymen went elsewhere.
I could not follow and was left alone in my house.
Unable to make a living, I wandered as a beggar.

In my mind I want to speak kind and pleasing words,
but I am in the presence of the king for today only,
so in answer to your question I offer you
good words, given in honesty, without equivocation.

With these words he sat on the ground and began his speech:

> Hear what I have to say, great king, ministers and people.
> The northern kingdom of Vaśin is happy and prosperous
> because life and the deeds of the king are in keeping with
>   the Dharma.
> The ways of decency and goodness have not declined there.
>
> In particular, Prince Sudhana has since birth
> made offerings to the Three Jewels, given alms to the poor,
> offered to the gods and nāgas, shown respect and veneration
>   to his parents,
> and cared for and benefitted his people and retinue according
>   to their needs.
>
> His virtuous Dharma life has pleased the celestial nāgas,
> especially in the great Lotus Life-Force Lake,[25]
> where lives the nāga queen Janmacitrā, the eight great nāgas,
> many lesser nāga kings, and many great nāgas of the lotus and
>   jewel caste.
>
> Making offerings to these nāgas, his kingdom has prospered.
> The people bask in the fortune of bountiful harvests and
>   good health,
> and enjoy the glories of possessing all that they could wish for.
>
> The old kings of our southern kingdom
> up to your father and lord, Tridhātu Balavat,
> made offerings to the Three Jewels, gave alms to the poor,
> restored shrines and temples to their former glory,
> and cared for and benefitted the people appropriately.
>
> Moreover, in this land in the east, on the high ground
> are the abodes of local gods, life-force trees, and life-force lakes.
> On auspicious days during the waxing moon,
> regular offerings were made to the gods
> and mountain tops were covered with prayer flags and incense
>   smoke.

Cairns were built for those gods who valued the way of virtue,
and tormas and purification incense ceremonies were held
for the nāgas during the times they appear on land.

The harvests were good, and such words as "illness" were
    not known.
The streets were filled with the songs of the people,
and even the northern land of Vaśin envied us.
The old kings fostered such a glorious time!

Then your father, Tridhātu Balavat, passed away.
Whether it was the fault of the prince's young age,
or whether it was the low merit of the people,
the behavior of the king is clear to see.

The king is angry and his behavior unpredictable,
he has no faith in the good and decent ways.
He relies upon many new gurus and deities,
while disparaging and belittling the refuges of old.

He has expelled venerable ministers and subjects, punishing
    them by law,
while promoting novices and slanderers to positions of
    authority.
He does not foster the kingdom according to the Dharma,
but does whatever comes to his ears.

He has stopped all offerings being made to the Three Jewels
and halted veneration and support of the monastic community.
he has taken offerings intended for gods and nāgas and given
    them to demons.
The king has become deluded by charlatan fortune tellers.

Twenty years have passed since the kingdom slid into decline.
In the highlands the abodes of the gods have fallen to devils,
    they say.
The life-force lake has dried up, the life-force trees have
    fallen down.

Even the nāgas, it is said, have moved to the northern kingdom,
and live by the side of the lotus lake there.

The richness of the soil has gone and the rains are not on time.
The harvests are bad, the land dry, disease and troubles are
    widespread.
Please find a way to reverse all of this.
Please find a way to bring back the celestial nāgas.
Bring back the essence and richness to the soil.

Do you hear me, great king, ministers, and people?
If you think I am wrong, then put this old man in prison,
and I pray that in my next life I be born in the northern
    kingdom.

With these words the old man gave a heavy sigh and fell back in his seat.
The ministers and the people assembled there all thought that the old man
spoke the truth. The king replied:

Listen, all you learned people gathered here.
What the old man says seems to be the truth.
I had not heard that on the uplands the life-force trees
    had fallen down.
I was not aware that in the valleys the life-force lake
    had dried up.
Nor did I know that the nāgas had moved north,
or that the abodes of the gods had fallen to devils.
Tomorrow I will go to the east and look myself.

The next day, the king with about thirty ministers traveled to the east of
the country. He saw clearly, just as the old man had said, that of the seven
life-force trees, five had fallen down, and the life-force lake had almost dried
up and was reduced to a small pool in its center. The king was very unhappy
and returned to the palace, where he addressed the ministers:

Listen, my assembled ministers.
What the old man said yesterday was true.
I saw the dried-up life-force lake and the fallen life-force trees.

If it is true that the nāgas have moved to the lotus lake,
we must work to retrieve our lake and bring back the nāga queen.

Send out word and quickly assemble the tantric practitioners
    of the south.
If they announce that they possess the power of summoning,
they will be rewarded and venerated by all.
If they lack these powers, then what are they doing as tantrikas?
Tell them these things and I will discuss with them.

As the king had commanded, the ministers sent out the message to the tantric practitioners. The following day the tantric practitioners assembled early and came before the king, who, smiling from his throne, addressed the tantrikas:

Listen and consider this, assembled tantrikas.
Pay attention and listen to your king.

In this country all around the uplands,
I, the king, possess life-force trees and a life-force lake,
but the life-force trees have fallen down
and the life-force lake has all but dried up.

The celestial nāgas who live there have moved to the north
and play by the side of the lotus lake, it is said.
Is this not the sorcery of the venerable Hari of the north?

You gathered here are of an authentic tantric lineage.
The bond that brings the protectors to your minds remains
    strong,
you know without question practices supplemented by mantras,
you have without doubt completed the required sets of mantras,
and the necessary repetition rituals in retreats.

You certainly have confidence in the practice
of your mind arising as the form of a deity,
and you show signs of having the powers
to bring under your control the eight classes of deities.

Now you must perform a tantric ritual for me.
You must move to the south the lotus life-force lake.
You must summon to the south the nāga queen who lives there.
You must summon to the south the minor nāga kings and
    their retinue,
and you must summon to the south the happiness of the north.

The king performed the rituals of service for the tantrikas. At that time
a young man from the company of tantrikas, of strong build and dark com-
plexion, with a flat nose and an ugly face, stood up and said:

King of the south, please hear and consider my words.
Please listen carefully, king and lord of men.
For those of us gathered here, your command is weighty indeed.
Summon the northern lake and nāga queen, you say.
Summon the happiness of the north to the south, you say.

Generally in tantric practice the bonds are most important.
If you maintain the mantra repetitions, the bond of speech does
    not weaken.
If you maintain the bodily mudrā, the physical bond does not
    weaken.
If you maintain the mind as deity form, the mental bond does
    not weaken.

To find someone here with all three bonds intact will be difficult.
To be able to bring the lotus lake and the nāga queen here
would require the presence of someone like Guru
    Padmasambhava.

Moreover, the completion of such actions depends on the
    motivation
of achieving victory for oneself and inflicting defeat upon
    others.
To bring happiness and well-being, the purpose of the teachings,
one must be without doubt well protected by Guru
    Padmasambhava.

The activity of achieving victory for oneself and defeat for others
is not something I have seen expressed in the tantras.
If such activities exist in the core instruction compendiums,
I ask my friends assembled here to look for them.

Then another tantric practitioner, with a high-bridged nose and dark-blue hair, addressed the king:

Hear my words, assembled nobles and subjects.
Pay attention. Listen to this tantric practitioner.
I will tell you what this old yogi thinks.

Among this assembled company of tantra practitioners,
there are none who can fulfill the desire of the king.
However, I have heard a certain story,
one passed down from father and mother.

It is not something I have seen with my own eyes,
yet I offer what I have heard to the king.
Please listen, assembled nobles and subjects.

With these words he began his story:

In a place very far from here,
three hundred and forty leagues to the south,
in a land whose mountains and valleys are covered with forest,
there lives, it is said, a yogi rare in this world.

It is said that his family lineage is the Holders of the Black Shawl,
and that his name is Kṛṣṇasarpa Kokila.
Above him the skies are thick with ḍākinīs and protectors,
below he uses the eight classes of deities as servants.
He enjoys the offerings of uncontaminated nectar with the
    ḍākinīs.

If the king were to send a messenger to his dwelling,
this holder of tantric practices would fulfill the king's wishes.
Other than that, there is no hope anywhere else.

Do you hear my words, great king and lord of men?
Do you hear me, my tantric friends and brothers?

The king was delighted and made the following announcement:

Listen, you assembled holders of tantric practice.
Listen well, you venerable tantric yogi.
The story you have told delights me much.
Merely hearing it fills me with joy.

This place where this king of tantrikas lives,
three hundred and forty leagues from here, is not so far.
You from the company of tantric practitioners, go there.
Go quickly to where this king of tantrikas lives.
Ten of you go now, headed by this elderly yogi.

Take with you whatever you need to make offerings to him.
Whatever money and food you want, I will provide.
Whatever type of transport you need, such as mules and horses,
    I will give.
Whatever beasts of burden you need, such as yaks, I will send.

Deliver this message to the king of tantrikas:
"In the capital of the northern kingdom of Vaśin
lives the venerable Hari, a sorcerer by trade.
Through his practices born of malicious thought and deed,
he has planted a curse on our southern country.
It has disturbed the mind of the king and weakened the
    kingdom.
The people are in poverty and have gone elsewhere.
The life-force lake has dried up, and many life-force trees have
    fallen down.
Most of the nāgas and local deities have moved to the north,
where they live besides the lotus lake, it is said.

The earth has lost its goodness, so fruit cannot grow.
People and cattle are falling sick and dying in numbers.

People indulge in meaningless arguments, disturbing each
    other's minds.
So many bad omens are appearing in our southern land.

The rituals performed by the southern tantric practitioners
have not put a stop to this, and the kingdom continues its
    decline.
Our southern kingdom lies in poverty and destitution,
while the northern kingdom basks in bountiful happiness.

Therefore with much bravado venerable Hari boasts:
"Among those who hold the practices of the tantrikas,
who, apart from me, has actually beheld the face of the deity?
Who, apart from me, can lead the nāgas and deities around
    like dogs?
Who, apart from me, can conjure up anything he desires?"
This he boastfully proclaims like thunder in the summer.

Not being able to bear this, we of the south,
the king, ministers, and people, come before you, master.
In the great Lotus Life-Force Lake of the north,
lives the lord of that lake, the nāga queen Janmacitrā,
as well as the eight great nāgas and many minor nāga kings.
Many nāgas from the south also dwell there.

We want to summon to the south the nāgas and the lake.
We believe that you, powerful one, can help us.
If you accomplish what I, the king, desires,
I will give you a third of all my estates,
    a third of all my servants and serfs,
and gifts of every kind of temple.

In Search of the King of Tantrikas

Ten capable tantrikas equipped with provisions were sent to the abode of
the yogi, carrying a letter setting out the above. They explored the land and
eventually came to an area covered by forest where no man had been before.
They wondered where the dwelling of this king of yogis could be, and set
out in pairs to search for it, but after a few days none had found it. Even-

tually, having followed a long path into the forest, they came across a place bordered on three sides by water. In its south was a large rock, very tall and steep, the mere sight of which was frightening. At its base the birds and animals did not dare utter their loud cries or chatter. A river rushed through a narrow valley, filling it with the clamoring and crashing sounds of water.

The rock was so large that they could not find the yogi's cave. However, one evening they saw in the distance the light of a fire and headed toward it. In a crevice in the rock where the sun never reached, they saw a black door, above which a poison horn was hanging, from which a blue flame blazed like an eternal fire. The tantrikas did not dare go up to the door, and so from a safe distance they chanted in unison:

> We go for refuge.
> To the guru, meditation deity, and ḍākinīs we go for refuge.
> To the local deities, earth lords, region protectors, we go
>   for refuge.
> Grant us quickly our wish that all anger and malice will
>   be pacified.
> We go for refuge.
> Especially to this great tantric master who lives in this
>   solitary place,
> we go for refuge.
> We make this prayer so that we may soon see your face
>   and hear your words.

Three times with long, drawn-out chanting they called out. Finally from within the meditation hut came the "Aang! Aang!" sound of a human thighbone trumpet. All around the ground shook, and then the door opened and the yogi emerged.

His body was large and coarse. His dark, yellowish hair came down to the folds of his clothes at his waist. His eyes were red and he glowered at his audience with a ferocious scowl. He wore a black flowing cloak and a black hat that had the appearance of a wrathful skull, tied up with a strap made of a recently killed snake. In his right hand he brandished to the skies a ritual dagger tied with black ribbon. In his left hand he held a skull cup filled with poisonous blood used as a liquid ritual substance. The dry ritual substances[26] were strung on his shoulder. He was uttering cries of *hūṃ* and *phaṭ*, and with a ritual dancing movement he moved closer and said:

Hūṃ, hrī la!
For many years have I lived in this solitary place.
For many years have I bound myself in wrathful retreat.
For many years have I gazed on the faces of the deities.
For many years have I used the eight classes as servants.
For many years have I been trained by the ḍākinīs in sustaining
    myself.
For many years have I had no need of sustaining myself with
    human food.

Whatever this calling with loud voices may be,
whoever these tantrikas here today may be,
be they gods with or without form, be they humans, whoever
    they be,
do not stay in the presence of a yogi who is out of retreat.
Do not stay in the face of a brandished ritual dagger,
do not stay in a place where the poison horn is uncapped.
If you stay, untimely conditions may change your path.

If you understand my words, keep them in your mind.
What is the meaning of this calling?
Speak now, speak quickly, and speak the truth.

With these words he stood there staring up at the sky. At the mere sight
of him the tantrika messengers were terrified and merely prostrated, unable
to approach. Instead they became intoxicated by the smell of the poisonous
blood carried on the wind and they were all reduced to a state of trembling.
After a while the old tantrika gathered his courage and confidence and spoke:

King of tantrikas, great sphere of meditative concentration,
please listen. I offer these words to you.
We are ten men who have come here
from our country, the southern land of Kulika.

The name of the king is Shakpa the Young.
There is no one there who can fulfill the desires of the king,
and so we have been sent to you, king of tantrikas.
The reason for our loud calling I will tell you.

Once more I ask, please listen, king of tantrikas.
Consider this well, powerful and mighty one.
The words of our king are as follows.
I offer them to the ears of the great tantrika.

"In the capital of the northern kingdom of Vaśin,
lives the venerable Hari, a sorcerer by trade.
Through his wicked mantras born of malicious thought
    and deed,
he has planted a curse on our southern country."

This has disturbed the mind of the king and weakened
    the kingdom.
The people are in poverty and have gone elsewhere.
The life-force lake has dried up and many life-force trees
    have fallen down.
Most of the nāgas and local deities have moved to the north,
where they live besides the lotus lake, it is said.

The earth has lost its goodness, so fruit cannot grow.
People and cattle are constantly falling sick and dying in
    numbers.
People indulge in meaningless fights and disturb each
    other's minds.
So many bad omens are appearing in our southern land.

The rituals performed by the southern tantric practitioners
have not put a stop to this, and the kingdom continues
    its decline.
Our southern kingdom lies in poverty and destitution,
while the northern kingdom basks in bountiful happiness.

Therefore, with much bravado, venerable Hari boasts:
"Among those who hold the practices of the tantrikas,
who, apart from me, has actually beheld the face of the deity?
Who, apart from me, can lead the nāgas and deities around
    like dogs?"
This he boastfully proclaims like thunder in the summer.

Not being able to bear this, we of the south,
the king, ministers, and people, come before you, master.
In the great Lotus Life-Force Lake of the north
lives the lord of that lake, the nāga queen Janmacitrā,
as well as the eight great nāgas and many minor nāga kings.
Many nāgas from the south also dwell there.

We want to summon to the south the nāgas and the lake.
We believe that you, powerful one, can help us.
If you accomplish what the king desires,
he will give you a third of all his estates,
 a third of all his servants and serfs,
and gifts of every kind of temple.

We ten tantrikas who have arrived here
are messengers come to invite to you to our land.
If you come, you will fulfill the wishes of our king.
You not coming would mean losing our lives
and our families imprisoned.

We beg that you come to fulfill the king's wishes.
We beg that you come so that our lives will be saved.

The great tantrika looked hard at the ten men headed by the old tantrika, but said nothing and returned to his cave. After some time he sent out a monkey to give to the men syllables, mantras, substances, skulls, and all-purpose protection, together with instructions, which read: "By attaching these protective substances to your body, may you be free from the taint of doubt when you enter the cave."

Following the instructions, they entered the cave. In its center they saw a mandala of the wrathful deities of the eight classes of the great and glorious Heruka, which was inseparable from the wisdom beings and glowed like a fire. In one corner of the cave the king of tantrikas was sitting on his tiger-skin seat. In front of him were the implements of the four types of tantric activities, each of which was giving off a radiant glow. Having requested blessings from the implements, they sat in front of the yogi, who gave some food to the monkey and began questioning them about the king's request.

Finally the yogi agreed to come to the southern kingdom and dictated his response to the king:

> Listen, messengers of the king of the southern kingdom.
> Pay attention, you ten holders of the tantric tradition.
> I have listened to what the southern king has had to say.
> Not only have I listened but I have considered it as well.
> I will restore the ruined kingdom of the king.
> I will restore peace to the troubled mind of the king.

> The king's offer of houses does not please me.
> The offer of servants and serfs does not please me.
> The offer of deity temples does not please me.
> If I wanted to fulfill the desires of this life,
> gaining control over the world would be easy.
> A yogi divorced from such entanglements
> has no thoughts that cling to a self.

> With a good motivation, I will challenge the power of Hari.
> If he has a way of using the eight classes of deities as servants,
> what kind of way is that? I will see.
> If he has a method to lead the deities and nāgas around
>   like dogs,
> what kind of method is that? I will see.
> Does he have a way to summon the lake and the nāgas?
>   I will see.

> King, ministers, and people of the southern kingdom,
> prepare these various substances.
> I need eight or so ritual daggers, each the size of a man,
> made from the various metals used to kill humans, dogs, and
>   horses.

> I need about one elephant-load of silken pennants.
> I need the skull of a leper man as the receptacle for the dry ritual
>   substances.
> I need the skull of a leper woman as the receptacle for the wet
>   ritual substances.

I need poison and blood of many different types, as much as
   possible.
I need as many medicinal substances as possible, such as the
   five precious gems.

I need you to build a lake the shape of the lotus lake.
I need you to gather various birds around its perimeter.
I need trees and streams at its edges, as many as possible.

Make these preparations completely and without question.
In two months evidence of their power will emerge.
Take this message to the king of the southern kingdom.
Five of you go ahead. I will come after a week.

With these words five young tantrikas were quickly sent ahead. When
they arrived at the southern kingdom they reported to the king in great
detail the accounts of their meeting with the great yogi. The king was aston-
ished. He gave gifts to the messengers and appointed people to fetch the
substances, and whatever was needed from his treasury was taken. Any sub-
stances that were not there he ordered to be prepared elsewhere.

The king of tantrikas emerged from his retreat and made the "golden
drink" offering to satisfy the local deities, nāgas, and earth lords. On that
day he sent the five messengers away. As the evening arrived, he made the
threatening gesture with the fingers of his right hand and everywhere was
filled with light. If you looked closely, you would see that his beard, poison
horn, and ritual dagger were ablaze.

On his arrival in the southern kingdom he was greeted and led into the
city with a welcoming procession, songs, and so on. In the palace a throne the
same height as that of the king was arranged, and he was presented with offer-
ing scarves and treated to a lavish banquet, where much discussion was had.

The next day the great yogi went into retreat for three weeks. He saw that
the fifteenth day of the following month was the right time for going to the
lotus life-force lake in the northern kingdom of Vaśin.

THE NĀGA QUEEN SEEKS THE PROTECTION OF THE HUNTER
At the same time, the nāga queen who lived in the northern lake saw with
her uninterrupted and uncontaminated clairvoyance that this yogi of the
south was coming to cause harm at the lake. She transformed herself into an

eight-year-old boy with long hair hanging down his back, emerged from the lake and walked along its shore. In the southeastern corner of the lake there was a hunter in a little hide coracle casting his net over the fish. In order to find out about the fisherman, the nāga queen said:

> Listen to me, man in a boat.
> Why are you putting a boat on the lake?
> What is the name of this lake?
> What is the name of this place?
> Man in a boat, what is your name?
> Tell me these things. Don't keep them secret.

The fisherman replied:

> Listen to me, eight-year-old boy on the bank.
> Pay attention. Listen to this hunter.
> Child, when you came here today, where did you come from?
> Child, when you leave this evening, where will you go?
> Child, what kind of place, what direction, are you from?
> Child, why have you come here?
> If you answer truthfully and not keep it secret,
> I will answer your questions honestly.

The nāga, disguised as a boy, said:

> Listen, and think about this, man in a boat.
> The land of this child is in the south,
> under the rule of the king of Kulika.
> Resources were scarce and my old father went begging.
> I followed him, and so now I am here.
> Now answer the questions I have asked you.

The hunter replied:

> Listen, child on the bank.
> Pay attention and hear these words.
> The name of this country is the northern kingdom of Vaśin.

The name of this lake is Lotus Life-Force Lake.
The name of this man is Phalaka.

My father's name was Rāhula.
He has long since passed away.
For work I patrol around the lake,
and for food I catch fish.

Again the child asked:

Listen again hunter Phalaka.
Pay attention to this child.
What is the name of the palace in Vaśin?
What is the name of its king?
What kind of celestial nāgas live in this lake?
What are their names?
How are they venerated?

The hunter replied:

Listen again, my articulate child.
Why do you ask such meaningless questions?
You should be asking if I have seen your father.
Why ask the name of the palace, the name of the king?
Why ask about the lake, the celestial nāgas?
Why ask about the offerings made to the celestial nāgas?

However, the child was very appealing, and the fisherman thought that he should maybe answer the questions fully:

My sweet child, listen to me.
I will tell you everything you want to know.
I am a subject of the king of this northern kingdom,
but I have not seen the king or his palace with my own eyes.

Yet I have heard their names.
The king is called Dharma King Sudhana.
His palace is named Land of Joy.

This lake is called Lotus Life-Force Lake.
Its master is the nāga queen Janmacitrā,
who has many minor nāga kings in her retinue.

The name of this lake is Lotus Lake
because its shape is that of a hundred-petal lotus,
and at each lotus-petal valley a river flows,
and at each riverhead is a nāga dwelling.
There, each month tormas and purification incense
    are offered.
Each year a treasure pot is hidden and lake substances
    are planted.

The happiness of the king and his people in the north
depends on this lake and its nāga queen.
In particular, my well-being, food, and clothing
depends on this lake and its nāga queen.

The nāga queen, in the form of a child, said:

I have heard you well, fisherman.
Because I too am the son of a nāga,
tomorrow I will tell you something important.

With that he disappeared into the lake. The fisherman was astonished.
The next day he was by the lake, where he fell asleep. The nāga queen again
took the form of the boy and in a long, drawn-out voice said:

Fisherman, do not sleep now! Fisherman, wake up!
A sleeping fisherman is of no use.
I the nāga have something important to say to you.

He tugged at the fisherman's hand. "What is it!" said the fisherman with a
start, and stood at up. The nāga continued:

Listen to me, powerful son of a hunter.
Pay attention. Listen to the king of the nāgas.
The reason I came to you is as follows.

On the evening of the fifteenth of the fourth month,
an evil-minded person from the south
is coming to do harm to this lake.
He is an enemy that frightens me.

Will the queen of nāgas be protected by this hunter?
Hunter, if you can do it, please promise to help.
If you cannot, this nāga will go elsewhere.

For all the creatures that live in the lake,
there will no recourse but to die untimely deaths.
This is the sad state of mind of this nāga.
Can you bear it, Phalaka?

The hunter, with his hair clinging to his head, sang out:

Oṃ mo maṇi padme hūṃ! [27]
I pray to the Three Jewels!
Listen to me, wealthy nāga queen.
Hear me without mistake.
Keep your mind attentive.

My father also used to patrol this lake.
In his time no harm ever came to the lake.
I have been patrolling this lake for many years,
and in that time no one has ever brought harm to it.

So do not think that harm is coming to the lake.
Do not be mistaken. Return to the land of the nāga queen.
This is meaningless talk. Return to the lake.

So saying, he went back to sleep. The nāga again pleaded:

Listen well, powerful son of a hunter.
Pay attention. Listen to this wealthy nāga.
This nāga is not mistaken. This is a time of truth.
These things have been seen by the nāga queen with her
    clairvoyance.

Hunter, do not be deceived. This will bring about my downfall.
If I am harmed, the northern king and his subjects will also
    be harmed.
If I am harmed, you too will be harmed.
Hunter, do not say these things.
Won't you accept what I say?
Could you bear to send the nāga queen to another
    human land?
Think on this, powerful son of a hunter.

The hunter could not tolerate this and replied:

Listen to me, wealthy nāga queen.
Pay attention and listen to this fisherman.
It is not true that harm is coming to the lake and the nāgas.
It is not true that someone from the south is coming
    to cause harm.

However, if some fearful enemy were to come to the lake,
as the wealthy nāga queen has said,
then because this is the life-force lake of the great king,
and all happiness and prosperity of the north comes from it,
and specifically because it is the source of wealth for this hunter,
and my food, clothing, and good name all come from it,
if anyone should come here intending to cause harm,
I will confront him and kill him, without thought to my life.
Do not be afraid, nāga, return to your home.

The nāga queen was pleased and said:

Listen, powerful son of a hunter.
The enemy from the south is very powerful,
but by past prayer and karma you have the merit to overcome
    him.
Any blade sharpened with this sharpening stone made from
    nāga gems
cannot be stopped by anything,
and will not be hindered by any tantric substance or protection.

Sharpen your knife with this stone, hunter,
and strike at the enemy, powerful son of a hunter.

With these words she gave the hunter the precious gem-sharpening stone, whose hue shone green and blue, and returned to his nāga home. The hunter sharpened his knife accordingly and rested.

THE TANTRIKA TRAVELS TO THE NORTHERN LAKE

On the twenty-ninth of the third month, the tantrika emerged from his retreat in the king's palace in the south. He addressed the king:

> *Hūṃ hri.*
> Listen to me, lord of men and great king.
> Pay attention and listen to this yogi.
> I have been in meditation in the palace of the king.
> For twenty-one days the investigation was good,
> but for a short while I experienced some disturbance.
> Was this a sudden hindrance to the retreat?
> Or was it a hindrance from allowing this tantric
>   retreat to be known?
>
> Great king, requisition twenty young tantrikas,
> and send the substances and elephants immediately.
> If I do not leave right away, hindrances will come.

With this, the yogi left with twenty young tantrikas. The journey was seven hundred leagues. For five hundred leagues he was accompanied by his companions. Then the yogi feared that if he took the tantrikas with him to the lake, they would learn his practices and more beings could be harmed, so he sent them home. For the next two hundred leagues the yogi loaded food on the elephants by himself and journeyed on.

On the fifteenth of the fourth month, just as the moon was rising, he arrived at the northern lake and set down at the northwestern corner. There he set up the offering torma and made the golden-drink offering and the propitiation:

> *Hūṃ.*
> To Samantabhadra down to my root gurus,

I present this offering torma and golden drink.
Accept it and grant powerful blessing to us yogis.

To the deities of the eight classes of great and glorious Heruka,
from the palace of the realm of exalted wisdom,
I present this offering torma and golden drink.
Accept it and grant all powerful attainments.

To all guardians and Dharma protectors who have gained
the power of direct wrathful action,
I present this offering torma and golden drink.
Accept it and be my powerful support today.

To those guardians of the community of tantrikas,
oath-bound land protectors, and celestial envoys,
I present this offering torma and golden drink.
Accept it and fulfill my wishes.

In particular, to the exalted-wisdom garuḍa[28] deities,
powerful beings who kill ferocious nāgas,
I present this offering torma and golden drink.
Accept it and accomplish this task I am undertaking.

Furthermore, celestial nāgas, and gandharvas,
and noncorporeal ones who moved from the south,
be sated with this food and drink.
Each of you return to your abodes.

He entered into generation-stage meditation, and after a while the
celestial nāgas who had moved from the south were dispersed like a flock of
birds pelted by stones. The yogi imbued the area with the smoke of burning
nutmeg and sal-tree resin to pacify the nāga queen, and began the summon-
ing invocation:

Wealthy nāga, master of the lake, who lives in its depths,
do not stay under the water, come to the surface now.
Come and meet this man on the surface. Come and talk.
I have three things to say to you that you will like.

The nāga thought: "He is trying to beguile me with sweet words. The hunter must be asleep." She wrapped a snake around her head, surfaced in the middle of the lake up to his waist, and waking the fisherman, addressed the yogi:

> Listen to me, man at the lake.
> What kind of place have you come from?
> Why have you come to this lake?
> Why are you calling the nāga?
> What is it you have to say?

Meanwhile the hunter had fallen asleep again in a hollow by the lake. The yogi piled the five precious jewels, fine silks, medicines, grain, and so forth by the side of the lake, and filled the area with the smoke of burning nutmeg and sal-tree resin. Holding an arrow decorated with silk pennants, he spoke reverentially to the nāga queen.

> Listen to me, wealthy queen of the nāgas.
> Pay attention. Listen to this yogi by the lake.
> I have come from the happy land of the south.

> The reason for me coming I will offer to the queen of nāgas.
> Listen well, wealthy nāga of the north.
> I wish to worship and serve you, great nāga.
> For a long time this has been in the mind of the yogi,
> but you live so far away, I was not able to carry it out.

> Nāga, do not stay here. Come to the south.
> The south is a happier place than here.
> There is abundant white and red sandalwood,
> fruit trees of apricots, walnuts, and so on,
> all that you could wish for.

> The varieties of grain are more abundant in the south.
> Even if you wanted birds large and small, they are in the south.
> If you want peacocks and parrots, they are in the south.
> If you want apes and monkeys, they are in the south.

If you want frogs, snakes, and insects, they are in the south.
If you want gold, silver, copper, and iron, they are in the south.
The water is more abundant in the south.
All the young men and women you could wish for are in
   the south.

All the jewel garlands are in the south.
Nāga, do not stay here. Come to the south.
All the things that delight you, I, the yogi, will provide.

With these words he beckoned the nāga with the arrow. The nāga replied:

Dear oh dear. This is strange. This is very strange.
Veneration from a yogi of the south, how strange.
Coming to fulfill the wishes of a nāga, how strange.

"Leave my own happy country
and go to another unknown human land," he says.
This veneration by the king of tantrikas is well received,
but you should return to your happy land of Kulika.

It may be happier than this land, but this nāga is not going
   south.
It may be purer than this lake, but this nāga is not going south.
Its lake may have a more wonderful shape than this lotus lake,
but this nāga is not going south.

Trees may be more abundant there, but this nāga is not
   going south.
It may have fruit trees of apricots, walnuts, and many more,
but this nāga is not going south.
Grain may be abundant there, but this nāga is not going south.
There may be large and small birds, but this nāga is not going
   south.

Yogi, you prattle a lot. Go back to the south.
If the king hears you, you will lose your life.

Go back to your beloved Kulika in the south.
This nāga may be miserable but will stay in the northern lake.

The nāga disappeared back into the lake. On hearing these words the yogi became angry. He broke open the bundle containing the substances, smeared the eight daggers with poisonous blood, and said:

Wealthy nāga queen living in this lake,
you do not respond to summoning by peaceful means.
Let us see now if your boastful words come true!
All you have accomplished in your life,
look now and see if it is worth anything!
This blazing poisonous blood,
look now and see if it is worth anything!

With these words he planted the eight ritual daggers at the eight compass points of the lake and spoke:

Corporeal and noncorporeal beings living around this lake,
do not remain where this yogi has placed the daggers.
If you stay in places where the daggers have been planted,
I think you will experience something very unpleasant.

He planted the eight daggers around the lake and adorned them with interlinking garlands of pennants to make a network with eight points. He placed the wet and dry ritual substances and other substances on the lake, and blew a fanfare from his thigh-bone trumpet from the four corners of the lake. Staring at the sky, he said: "Homage to the truth of the guru, the buddhas, and the monastic community! Homage to the truth of the deities of the eight classes of great and glorious Heruka! Homage to the truth of the essence mantras, the mudras, and the tantric substances! Through the power and abilities of these great truths let the nāga queen and her entourage who dwell in this lake be taken from their home, from their wealth, and from any form of refuge! Summon them! Kill them! Let this lake boil as if it had been placed upon burning coals! *Vajra aṃ kuśaya jaḥ!*"

Turning his back on the lake, he cast an effigy of the nāga into the triangular iron ritual pit, stood on it, and entered the generation-stage meditation on the black garuḍa. After an hour or so the lake started to boil like tea. The nāga queen rose in agony to the surface, and all the minor nāga kings and other creatures in the lake lost consciousness. The nāga cried out:

> Alas! Such sadness in my mind!
> What wicked deeds did this nāga do in a past life
> now visited upon me by the evil deeds of one from the south?
>
> He has planted iron daggers at the eight corners of the lake,
> and woven upon them a network of pennants.
> Poisonous blood in the skull of a leper,
> and other substances, he has cast into the lake.
> The lake boils uncontrollably like Indian tea.[29]
> The minor nāga kings and the other creatures are suffering
> dreadfully.
>
> Listen to the distress of this sad nāga.
> Nothing like this has happened before in other worlds.
> Hey! Mighty hunter! Can you tolerate this!
> How could you send this nāga to another land?
> Today is the day of your promise.
> Do not go back on your word, son of a hunter.

With this, the nāga called to where the hunter was sleeping. The hunter woke up with a start. "What was that?" he wondered, and looked to see the nāga standing beside him. He quickly got up and looked around. Everywhere from the lake came gurgling and hissing noises. The nāga stood there writhing in pain. At the sight of this, the hunter tied his hair up on his head, tucked his clothes inside his belt, picked up his fish knife, and strode off. Seeing a ferocious-looking yogi standing by the lake, he plucked up his courage and said:

> *Oṃ mu oṃ mu maṇi padme hūṃ!*
> Hey! You beside the lake, listen to me!
> Why have you come here?
> Have you come to harm my lake?
> You have placed ritual daggers at the corners of the lake,
> and created on them a network of five colored pennants.
> The lake is boiling and the nāga queen has come to the surface.

Why are you bringing harm to this lake?
Explain this now to me!

Without hesitation, he thrust his knife at the yogi, knocking off and ripping his black hat and causing a small wound on his head. The yogi was afraid and said:

Hear my words, brave son of a hunter.
Pay attention. Listen to this yogi of the south.
Hunter, do not be so agitated. Listen to me.

This is not the greed of the yogi but the insistence of a king.
You must do as the northern king commands.
Likewise, I had to come here on the orders of the southern king.
Hunter, what you suspect is true, but listen to the words of this yogi.

Send the lake and the nāga queen to the south.
You too, hunter, come to Kulika in the south.
You will be honored by the king.
Whatever he has pledged, I the yogi can give to you.

If you want houses, I the yogi can give them to you.
If you want gold, silver, copper, or iron, I the yogi can give them
    to you.
If you want the finest silks, I the yogi can give them to you.
If you want cattle, horses, or sheep, I the yogi can give them to you.
If you want a constant, trustworthy companion, I the yogi can
    give them to you.
If you want fame and reputation, I the yogi can give them
    to you.
All the above, with the unchanging deities as my witnesses,
I the yogi can give to you.
Nāga and hunter, come to the south.

The hunter replied:

Listen to me, southern yogi at the end of his life.
Pay attention. Listen to this powerful hunter.

Carry out the commands of the king in your own country.
If you carry out the affairs of the southern king in the north,
won't the life force of the yogi be wandering aimlessly on
    the plains?[30]

There is no need for the hunter to go to the south.
There is no need to send the nāga to the southern land.
I do not want to be honored by the king. Make the lake as it was.
I do not want houses and land. Make the lake as it was.
I do not want gold, silver, copper, and iron. Make the lake as it was.
I do not want to wear fine silk. Make the lake as it was.
I do not want a constant, trustworthy companion. Make the
    lake as it was.
I do not want cattle, horses, or sheep. Make the lake as it was.
Rather than send the nāga to another country,
this hunter would be happy to lose his life.

With these words he again brandished his knife. The yogi replied:

What you say is true, very true, brave hunter.
Hunter, pay attention. Please listen!
Don't kill me. Set me free.
By killing me, the Dharma protectors will not die.
By killing me, the lake and the nāgas will not be restored.
With such a sinful act, you harm the yogi and the nāgas.
Hunter, please consider this, and I will do as you ask.

The hunter said:

If you are to do as I ask, then the lake must be left as before.
Remove the power of the substances and the mantras.
Revive the minor nāga kings and all the other creatures.
Do that and the yogi will not be parted from his life force.
If you value your life, do these things now!

The yogi gathered the daggers and the pennants from around the lake. He
removed the substances and the skull he had placed in the lake, and uttered
the reversal mantra. In their place he put medicines, the five precious jewels,

and other nāga substances. The lake was restored to its former condition. The minor nāgas and all other creatures were revived. The nāga queen too returned to the lake. The yogi said:

> Brave hunter, please listen to me.
> The tantrika has done what you ask.
> The daggers around the lake, the pennants and substances,
> have all been collected. Mantras and medicines have replaced
>   them.
> The lake has been restored to its pristine state, the nāgas are
>   revived.
> If all that you wished for has been accomplished,
> I ask that you send me back to my country.

The hunter replied:

> Listen to me, evils deeds in the form of a yogi,
> you create enemies of the teachings of the Buddha,
> you disturb the minds of the southern and northern kings.
> Enemies of the teachings are to be killed,
> they are not objects of compassion.

With these words he plunged his knife into the legs of the yogi, who collapsed and was unable to get up. He raised his head and said:

> Forgive me, forgive me, son of a hunter.
> I see this as the hindrance come to the yogi who has weakened
>   his pledges.
> I see this as the ripening for the attitude of victory to self, defeat
>   for others.
> I see this as the hindrance I saw suddenly arising in my retreat.
> I see this as me being the servant of self-grasping and
>   self-concern.
> I have the great remorse of dispatching my life while doing the
>   work of others.
> With the eight worldly attitudes as the practice of the yogi,
> I have applied myself to harming myself and others.

The view of the profound completion stage I have not
assimilated into my mind.
With the imprints of a malicious mind I will wander the
intermediate state.
Not existing in this or the next life, this yogi is filled
with regret.

The hunter stabbed the yogi and killed him.

Powerful actions in the past cannot be changed, so let us consider the killing of such a yogi by the hunter. Most yogis these days practice just by looking at the texts without taking any initiations or tantric teachings at all. They do whatever practices they have made up themselves. They act as if they had mastered the profound thinking of the generation and completion stages of tantras, and while holding their own interests at heart, think that it is not necessary to keep the pledges or do retreats. These people who have mastered the act of sorcery, curses, and repression, and who constantly tie ritual daggers, poison horns, and skulls to their bodies, are taking a dangerous gamble in this and future lives. This promiscuous Tsering Wangdü may risk catching syphilis and other sexually transmitted diseases, but he does not have this fear!

* * *

Thus ends part 1, on how the southern king, Shakpa the Young, developed the deluded intention to summon the lake and nāgas of the north.

Part 2. An Insignificant and Low-Caste Hunter Accomplishes Great Things for the King and Subjects of the Northern Kingdom.

THE NĀGA QUEEN SHOWS GRATITUDE TO THE HUNTER

The hunter used the corpse of the yogi as a pillow, half of his hair as a mattress, the other half as a blanket, and went to sleep. The next day the nāga transformed into a young woman and appeared before the hunter. She said:

> Listen to me, brave son of a hunter.
> You who have shown great kindness to the northern
>   kingdom,
> and, specifically, constant kindness to me, the nāga queen,
> do not sleep here, kind one. Come to the nāga world.
>
> Hunter, I will repay well your kindness there.
> Whatever delights you, hunter, I the nāga will give you.
> Hunter, do not sleep here. Come to the nāga world.

Lying on his side, the hunter sang:

> Listen to me, nāga queen, jewel in the crown.
> Pay attention, nāga queen. Listen to this hunter.
> For many years I have lived by the side of this lake.
> I have never seen what the nāga kingdom looks like.
>
> To go into the lake without good purpose
> would cost this hunter his life.
> Nāga, if you have something to repay my kindness,
> bring it to the surface of the lake.

The nāga insisted:

> Kind hunter, listen to this nāga.
> Why this meaningless and harmful doubt?
> The nāga palace is extraordinary.
> Its roof is made from precious gold,
> its middle is made from precious silver,
> and its base from precious agate.

For your mouth, food and drink of supreme taste,
for your body, soft, silken clothes,
for your ears, the sweet music of song and dance,
for your nostrils, the beautiful aroma of medicinal incense,
for your eyes, the beautiful bodies of the singing girls;
the nāgas possess a treasury of jewels and gems.
Do not stay here. Hunter, come quickly.

The hunter replied:

Wealthy nāga queen, listen to me.
Your offer of service and gratitude is well received,
but I cannot go into the depths of the lake.

If I were a golden goose, I could go into the lake's depths,
but how will this hunter, an unformed deity, be rescued?
If I were a little black-hide coracle, I could go on the surface,
but how will this hunter, more splendid than a god, be rescued?

If you have any sugar, bring it to the side of the lake.
If you have any beautiful women, bring them here.
For the survival of the nāgas, this hunter is definitely needed.

The nāga replied:

Hunter, do not say these things. Come to the nāga world.
Hunter, this wealthy nāga will carry you on her back.
Now, come quickly, my brave hunter.

The nāga seized the hunter by the hand and placed him on her back. As soon as they touched the surface of the lake, they arrived at the nāga palace. Just as the nāga had described it, the palace was extraordinary, irresistibly splendid—a tall and vast building made entirely of precious gems, the roof adorned with parasols and tasseled victory standards. The countryside around was green and lush with vegetation, and carpeted with grassy meadows, through which clean streams and rivers flowed gently. A variety of birds sang sweet songs. There was an abundance of horses, goats, and sheep, and cattle too, all with fine hair and hides.

In one jeweled house with a crystal door, the hunter was seated on a beautiful throne. He was treated to a feast of the best-tasting food and drink, while beautiful nāga sons and daughters played sweet music and sang songs. The environment of the hunter had completely changed, and of course his perception did too. "This is really a perfect place on earth," he thought. Without noticing the passing of the days, he spent a month there.

Finally the hunter said to the nāga queen:

Listen to me, wealthy nāga queen.
Listen to this hunter.
The gratitude of the nāga has been much appreciated.
It has been a wonderful and extraordinary experience.
I have had the best food and drink, and all that I could desire.
This hunter has spent many happy days here.

But now I will return to my own land.
This precious sharpening stone I do not need,
and I offer it back to the nāga.
Help this hunter to return to his country.
Help him return to the shore of the lake.

With these words he returned the jewel to the nāga. The nāga said:

Listen, hunter. Pay attention. Listen to this nāga.
You have been kind, and I must show gratitude.
Returning to the surface, your work will be nothing but
    evil deeds.
Leave behind the evil mind. Stay here in the nāga world.
Whatever the hunter commands, I will happily comply.

The hunter responded:

Listen again. Think again, wealthy nāga queen.
Pay close attention. Listen to this hunter.
Even though someone may be kind,
    those who repay kindness are truly rare.

I have great respect and faith in this nāga,
as one who remembers the kindness of others.

Again, if this is worth asking, please consider it.
Today I will not stay here. Take me to my world on the shore.
I miss my little red dog. Take me to the shore.
I miss my little black boat. Take me to the shore.

The nāga said:

Listen to me, brave son of a hunter.
There may be many men of great kindness,
but the brave and kind hunter who brought happiness
	to the north
is one of a much greater and very special kindness.

Kind Phalaka, savior of the lake and the nāgas,
if you will not stay here but return to the surface,
I will offer you a jewel of your choice.

The nāga queen ordered Śaṅkhapāla, Upananda, and the other great nāgas to open the treasury and place every type of jewel before the hunter. The nāga said:

Listen to me, hunter of immense kindness.
I have described in detail to the other minor kings
the wicked deeds of the tantrika from the south,
and how the brave hunter saved the lake and the nāgas.

Having heard of your kindness, they happily promise
to relinquish all attachment to any of our jewels.
I offer you a choice from these jewels
I offer you a choice from a hundred jewels, from a thousand
	jewels.
I offer you a choice from twelve thousand jewels.
Examine well, brave son of a hunter.
Take a jewel that pleases you, kind hunter.

The hunter replied:

> Nāga queen of most kind thoughts,
> Śaṇkhapāla, Upananda, and the other great nāgas,
> lend your ears to me, the hunter.
> For work this hunter patrols the lake.
> For food he eats the flesh of fish.
> For drink he takes the water of the lake.
>
> The glories of the lake and the great nāgas,
> I have seen this only once.
> How will this hunter know the qualities of these jewels?
> Nāga queen and all you other nāgas,
> give me a jewel that will grant my wishes.

The nāga queen replied:

> Listen well, brave son of hunter.
> Whatever you ask for I will give.
> Here we have jewels with qualities beyond imagination.
> Some fulfill the wishes of gods and nāgas.
> Some fulfill the wishes of gurus and ministers.
> Some bring the rains, some make the trees grow.
>
> Some increase the wealth of humans.
> Some give protection from demons above.
> Some give protection from demon below.
> Some bring victory in battle.
> The qualities of the jewels are beyond imagination.
> Now in gratitude I give you this jewel.

With these words the nāga queen took out of an agate jewel box the precious gem known as the granter of all wishes and needs, wrapped in silk of five colors, and said:

> Listen well, brave son of a hunter.
> The crown garland jewel is the jewel of the gods.
> It is a jewel indispensable to the gods.

The amoghapāśa[31] jewel is a jewel of the nāgas.
It is a jewel indispensable to the nāgas.

The granter of all wishes and needs is the jewel of men.
You are a jewel among men, and with this excellent jewel
I, the nāga queen, repay your kindness.
Hunter, whatever you wish for, it will quickly accomplish.

Enjoy as you will the glory of fulfilling all your desires,
good harvests, spreading the rule of the king, and all good
    fortune,
where even the name of disease, war, and famine is not heard.

The nāga queen gave the jewel to the hunter by placing it on his head. The
hunter said:

Ah! Such joy in my mind!
Happiness such as this in the mind of the hunter!
In this life I am born of a poor caste,
and yet through merit gathered in past lives
not only have I been to an extraordinary nāga palace
but I have also been given such a precious jewel
by the nāga queen and her retinue in gratitude for kindness.

May the nāga kingdom prosper!
May the nāga queen live in peace!
Now the hunter will return to his own land.

With the jewel the nāga sent the hunter back to the shores of the lake.

THE HUNTER TRAVELS TO VISIT THE SAGE
The hunter spent five days by the lake. In that time, thanks to the blessing of
the jewel, he became more radiant than before. His senses were sharper. His
body was lighter but stronger. His voice became beautiful and his mind was
happy. So much so, he remarked to an old couple who lived there:

Listen to me neighbors. Hear what I say.
Listen carefully to this hunter.

Something wonderful has happened to me.
Something I could never have dreamed about, I actually possess.
Dear neighbors, have you ever seen anything like this?

He took the jewel out of its box and showed it to the couple. The old
brahmans were amazed and said:

Ah! Listen, brave son of a hunter.
Of course, we have never seen anything like this.
We have never even heard of it.
How did it come into your hands?
Is this something gained through wicked ways?
Tell the truth to this old couple.

The hunter replied:

Listen to me, my two old neighbors.
I will tell you truthfully what happened.
On the evening of the fifteenth of the fourth month,
a tantrika from the south called Kṛṣṇasarpa Kokila, with an
    evil mind
came and brought harm to our Lotus Life-Force Lake.
The lake boiled, the minor nāgas almost died,
and the nāga queen cried out in agony.
The lake was being harmed and I could not bear it.

"What is this," I wondered, and saw that the lake had been
    circled by a yogi.
Ritual daggers festooned with pennants had been planted
    around the lake,
substances had been put into the water until it began to boil.
At the side of the lake I saw this fearsome tantrika from the south,
uttering mantras and performing mudras.

Immediately I said to him: "Evil one, what are you doing to
    this lake?
The lake is boiling, the nāgas are in agony. What is the meaning
    of this?"

I struck at him with my knife and wounded his head.
This made him agitated and he swore to restore the lake.

He became subdued and said he would do as I asked.
He pulled out the daggers and gathered the pennants.
He removed the substances from the lake,
replacing them with medicinal substances.
The lake was restored and the nāgas were revived.
Again I stabbed the yogi and killed him.

This was a great kindness, said the nāga queen,
and I was given this jewel.
Apart from that, what wicked deeds have I done?

Brahman couple, you are not of unintelligent minds.
Examine this jewel and declare its qualities.
Do not judge it without examining it.

The old brahman husband and wife said in reply:

Listen to us, brave son of a hunter.
Pay attention to this old couple.
Our wondering if this amazing jewel
came to you through improper ways
was an honest question asked with affection.
We did not mean to accuse you.

The shape and color of this jewel is in keeping with
the type of jewel that came to you as you described.
Therefore it is something rare on land.
This jewel brings happiness to all beings, not just to you.

We do not know the details of its name, its type, and so on.
However, near here, about seven leagues to the south,
are background mountains shaped like a giant helmet,
in front of which is a mountain shaped like two hands
    in prayer,
behind which is a region abundant with grain and flowers,

in which is a very special place known as Ke'u cave,
in which lives a sage known as Prakāśamati.

He is one who has gained the power over life and death,
who with a mind of great nonapprehending compassion,
has perfected a life and practice dedicated to the welfare
of others,
who for food lives on meditative concentration,
who for clothes wears robes of pañcāli cloth
who for friendship puts his faith in the Three Jewels,
who for enemies holds with suspicion the poisonous mental
afflictions,
who for a weapon constantly wields the sword of wisdom,
who for a shield is never parted from the forbearance
of no-self.

Go to the cave where he lives, hunter.
Ask him about the qualities of the jewel.
This is the declaration of the brahman couple.
Since we brahmans were little children,
No aging or deterioration has visited this sage.
Ask him about the jewel, you will receive a clear reply.
Go quickly, brave son of a hunter.

Just by hearing the name of the sage, the hunter was filled with joy and wanted to meet him straightaway. At the same time, the great sage with his clear light mind knew that the hunter was coming with the jewel. The hunter set out to find where he lived in accordance with the brahman couple's instructions.

After traveling for three days in the uplands, he came upon a delightful and extraordinary area entirely covered with trees and flowers. Streams flowed and various sweet-smelling medicinal plants grew. Various breeds of deer, antelopes, and so on played and amused themselves. Peacocks, kalaviṅga birds, soaring birds, hoopoes, parrots, and many other varieties of birds produced a chorus of song. The trees there were tall and straight.

He wondered where the sage lived, but searched without success. He placed the jewel on his head and prayed to meet with the sage. From the trees a flock of kalaviṅga birds sang out in unison and flew off in a northeasterly direction. The hunter took this as a sign showing him the path to take. He followed the birds as best he could and came to a part of the forest where he clearly heard the birds singing. Heading in that direction, he came to a large area with grassy south-facing hills, in the middle of which was a white rock shaped like a stack of scriptures, at the base of which were fruit trees radiant with blossom. The hunter went there and by a spring saw signs of human activity. A little further on, kuśa grass was stacked like a retreat boundary marker. Beyond that was a stone wall with a stone gong and striker. Thinking that this was the residence of the great sage, he sang out:

> *Oṃ mo ma ṇi padmé hūṃ.*
> Again I prostrate to the Three Jewels.
> Earth lord of the gods and nāgas who live in this lonely place,
> today give protection to this son of a hunter.
> Alone I have come from afar to visit Ke'u cave.
> Here, it is said, lives a great sage venerated by gods and men.
> If this is the dwelling, I will beat the stone gong.

> Great sage, I beat the stone gong!
> Dweller in excellent meditative concentration, I beat the
>   stone gong!
> Dweller in exalted wisdom, I beat the stone gong!

Three times he beat the gong. After a short time, under the tree blossoms the great sage emerged. He was radiant and glowing, and had white hair tied up on his head, white eyebrows and beard, and wore cotton robes. Looking around, he said:

> You who stand in front of the retreat stone, pay attention.
> What is the purpose of you coming here?
> Why do you beat the gong and call the sage?
> Tell me everything. Tell me truthfully.

> This morning in my dawn postmeditation session,
> while mixing the state of sleep with clear light,
> there appeared to me a vision in which trees
> that for many years had withered and dried
> came back into bloom and again produced fruit.

Examining this sight increased this old man's practice,
for it was a sign of fruit coming to maturation,
and brought joy in my mind and ease throughout my body.

The sound of you beating the stone gong
brought me to a similar state of joy.
Because of past prayers and karma you came here.
Otherwise, it would not be possible to come to such a special
    place.
Speak! Talk to me now.

   The hunter recounted in detail how he was a fisherman living by the side
of the life-force lake in the north, how a yogi from the south came to cause
harm to the lake, how he, the hunter, had killed the yogi for the sake of the
nāgas and the lake, and how in gratitude he been taken to the nāga world
and been given the jewel. Then he prostrated to the sage, and with the jewel
in his hands, said:

Listen to me, great sage,
I will tell you all. I will speak the truth.
I am here to ask for evaluation and advice on this jewel.
After the nāga had given me the jewel I spent five days on
    the shore,
after which I visited a brahman couple who lived nearby.
I showed them the jewel and explained how I came by it.
They were unable to pass judgment on it,
and said that for evaluation I should come see you, great sage.

They told me how to find you and sent me here.
Hearing your name filled my mind with joy,
and I set out with eagerness to find you where you lived.
But in the middle of the forest I became confused.
I prayed to the jewel, and a flock of kalaviṅga birds
has led me to this very special place.

Please evaluate this precious jewel for me.
Give it a name. Give it a description.
Is it a dream or is it for real?

I am of little fortune, born into a hunter family.
For work I do wicked deeds. For food I eat fish.
I wear ragged clothes and suffer from the cold.
I have no friends, no wife, and live alone.
I am an outcast from society, and low caste by name
    and family.

Such a person, by great fortune, went to the land of the nāgas,
and such a jewel came into my hands.
Great sage, I have actually met you!
Such good fortune is greater than I could have dreamed of.

The great sage replied:

Listen well, son of a hunter.
Your act of saving the northern nāga lake was excellent,
and was of great importance for living beings and the doctrine.
This jewel is an extraordinary and astonishing jewel.

When Buddha Krakucchanda generated the mind of
    enlightenment,
he saw that for the sake of others a relic jewel
that would grant anything and make anything possible
would be of great benefit for beings in the future,
and gave it the name of granter of all wishes and needs.

Through karma of the past it came to the land of the nāgas,
and through karma it fell into your hands.
This sage has been alive for close to five hundred years,
and has not seen such a wonderful jewel until now.

Hunter, this is not a dream, it is for real.
You are one who can do great things for living beings.
Hunter, it is a jewel that will give you whatever you want.

The sage took the jewel on the crown of his head and went with the hunter
into Ke'u cave. The great sage satisfied the hunter with tasty and nutritious
food and drink, with fruit and juice, and so on. That evening the hunter lay

in the presence of the sage. During a break in the sage's recitation session, the hunter asked:

> Hear me, great sage.
> Lend your ears to hunter Phalaka.
> This hunter has seen all kinds of people,
> but apart from my neighbors, the brahman couple,
> I have not seen anyone of an advanced age.
>
> They told me that since they were children,
> that had not seen any aging in you, great sage.
> What is the cause and reason for this?
> I ask you to please tell me this.

The sage replied:

> Listen to me, brave son of a hunter.
> The reason why no aging occurs in this sage
> is not something I explain to ordinary people.
> However, just this once, a hunter of good fortune
> has brought a supreme jewel to this place.
> So now I will explain all to this hunter.
>
> Hunter, pay attention. Listen well.
> In a place a few leagues from here,
> about three leagues to the east,
> reached by a difficult and very narrow path,
> are the Brahma court[32] bathing pools.
> Upon their beautiful groves and gardens,
> enclosed in structures of crystal and aquamarine,
> with turquoise-studded golden roofs,
> spacious and tall—one gazes insatiably.
>
> Inside, the ground is strewn with various flowers,
> and adorned with groups of bathing pools.
> Guardhouses of ruby are in the four directions.
> Outside grow many varieties of trees,
> and the songs of peacocks and kalaviṅga birds are heard.

In this special place on auspicious days during the waxing moon,
first the daughters of the gods come to bathe,
followed by the daughters of the spirit gods,
and then the daughters of the gandharvas,
especially the princess of the king of the gandharvas,
the beautiful Manoharā Devī with her hundred thousand
    servants.

They come with parasols, victory standards, banners,
perfumed silk streamers, and military banners.
They come to the gods' ambrosia bathing pools.
The air is filled with song, dance, beautiful sounds,
the flutes of the gandharvas, and other sweet music.

Seeing this and drinking the ambrosia of the gods,
and bathing each month in this special place,
this sage became long-lived and free from disease.
This is the cause of my freedom from aging.

When the hunter heard the story of the Brahma court bathing pools, he was unable to sleep that night. The next morning as soon as he got up, he said to the sage:

Listen to me, great sage!
Consider my request, master of meditative concentration.
Having heard the story of the Brahma court bathing pools,
I was unable to sleep last night.
I wish to see such a wonderful sight,
and to drink the ambrosia of the gods from the bathing rituals.
Take me to the bathing pools.

The sage replied:

Hunter, pay attention. Listen to this sage.
I am venerated by both gods and men.
Except for me, no other beings could possibly go
to the Brahma court bathing pools.
If it were possible, I would like to take you there,

but it is strictly for gods, spirits, and gandharvas.
Forget about going there, brave son of a hunter.

The hunter insisted:

Listen to me, great sage.
You are venerated by both gods and men.
You are a being of immense power and magical ability.
In particular, we have a jewel that accomplishes all wishes.
With the combined power of the sage and the jewel,
could I not go to this special place?

This is a request made with complete sincerity.
Do not cut me off from your great compassion.
Take me to the Brahma court bathing pool.
Even if the punishment of the gods means my death,
the mind of this hunter is made up to see such a sight.

The sage replied:

Listen to what I say, brave son of a hunter.
You refuse to listen and are determined to go.
But your body is tainted by your being of low caste,
your mind is tainted by the wicked deeds of being a hunter.

If, in order to purify these, you perform body purification
    rituals,
develop remorse, make prostrations, circumambulations,
    and so on
for about a month, then on the eighth of the following month,
when the beautiful maidens of the gods, spirits, and gandharvas
come to bathe and sing at the Brahma court bathing pools,
the hunter and the sage will go to that sacred place
to listen to the songs of these beautiful women.

The hunter was overjoyed. Therefore each day the sage instructed the hunter on bathing and purification bathing rituals. He gave the hunter teachings on a correct mental attitude, developing remorse, taking pledges and so forth in order to purify his mind, and encouraged him to make circumambulations and so on.

THE HUNTER AND THE SAGE JOURNEY TO THE BATHING POOLS

They arrived on the appointed day at the bathing pools. The great sage held up to the sky fumigating incense with his right hand and a mirror with his left, and intoned:

> *Oṃ mo ma ṇi padmé hūṃ*
> Again I supplicate the buddhas of the ten directions.
> Ḍākinīs of Buddha Vajrasattva in the east,
> as today is an auspicious day, come to the bathing pools.
> Ḍākinīs of Buddha Ratnasambhava in the south,
> as today is an auspicious day, come to the bathing pools.
> Come to bathe at this happy and special place.
> Ḍākinīs of Buddha Amitābha in the west,
> as today is an auspicious day, come to the bathing pools.
> Come to bathe at this happy and special place.
> Ḍākinīs of Buddha Amoghasiddhi in the north,
> as today is an auspicious day, come to the bathing pools.
> Come to bathe at this happy and special place.
> Ḍākinīs of Buddha Vairocana in the center,
> as today is an auspicious day, come to the bathing pools.
> Come to bathe at this happy and special place.

With these words the ḍākinīs and the gods associated with them descended like falling snow, and as the air became filled with music they performed the bathing rituals. They performed their songs and dispersed. Again the sage intoned:

> Daughters of the formless spirit gods,
> wherever you may dwell in the ten directions,
> as today is an auspicious day, come to the bathing pools,
> come to bathe at this happy and special place.

All the different types of spirits came from the sky like hail and performed their bathing rituals. Having sang their songs, they left. The sage addressed the goddesses of the celestial realm of the Thirty-Three:

Daughters of Indra, dwelling in the realm of the Thirty-Three,
beautiful maidens of the Thirty-Three, captivating ḍākinīs,
as today is an auspicious day, come to the bathing pools.
Come to bathe at this happy and special place.

The deities of the realm of Thirty-Three descended like a swirling snow-storm. They performed their bathing rituals, sang their songs, and left.

Then the sage addressed the gandharva daughters that lived on the middle ranges of Mount Meru:

Gandharva maidens living on the four levels of Meru,
Manoharā, daughter of the king of Vṛkṣaḥ gandharva realm,
and your entourage of hundreds of thousands,
raise your banners and come to the bathing pools.
Today is an auspicious day. Come to bathe.

The gandharva daughters, headed by Manoharā with her entourage num-bering in the hundreds of thousands, came to the bathing pools like pearls threaded on silk, bringing with them various offering substances. By the side of the pool Manoharā was enclosed by a jeweled silken curtain. Five circles of her entourage stood outside the curtain holding banners and musical instruments. Inside, many attendant goddesses stood in their posi-tions. Some held vases of gold, silver, crystal, sapphire, and so on, of various shapes and colors. Some held up mirrors of silver, crystal, bronze, and so on. Prompted by Manoharā chanting the bathing ritual, the goddesses inside sang in unison and the entourage outside played their musical instruments in accompaniment:

Hosts of tathāgatas, headed by the victorious Vajradhara
in the Ghanavyūha celestial palace at the top of the realms
    of form,
    I offer this bathing ritual to you.

Hosts of tathāgatas, headed by the venerable guide Maitreya
in the celestial palace of Uccadhvaja
in Tuṣita, a pure place of the desire realm,
I offer this bathing ritual to you.

Hosts of tathāgatas, headed by victorious Akṣobhya,
in the eastern celestial realm of Abhirati,
I offer this bathing ritual to you.

Hosts of tathāgatas, headed by noble and venerable Tārā
in the southern celestial realm of Leaves of Turquoise,
I offer this bathing ritual to you.

Hosts of tathāgatas, headed by the guide Amitāyus
in the western celestial realm of Sukhāvatī,
I offer this bathing ritual to you.

Hosts of tathāgatas, headed by Bhagavan Vajrapāṇi
in the northern celestial realm of Jaṭila,
I offer this bathing ritual to you.

All buddhas of the ten directions,
today the goddess Manoharā, in particular,
offers this bathing ritual to you.
By the power of this deed,
may living beings equal to space
be purified of evil acts, mental afflictions, and obstacles.

Gods, nāgas, gandharvas, spirits,
today the goddess Manoharā
offers this bathing ritual to you.
In particular, great father Turaṃvadana,
in the celestial palace of Vṛkṣaḥ,
today the goddess Manoharā
offers this bathing ritual to you.
Great mother Ḍākinī, I offer this bathing ritual to you.

In this sacred place I offer this bathing ritual to myself.
I offer this bathing ritual to purify the outer body.
I offer this ritual to purify the inner channels and chakras.
I offer this bathing ritual to the host of upper gods.
I offer this ritual to purify Manoharā's obstructions.

> By bathing from the top of this maiden's head to her feet,
> the obscurations of the body are washed away.
> Those who hold the mirrors, Darśanamukti and entourage,
> bring them here, I need to look upon my body.

The air was filled with the delightful melodies of song and sweet music. The birds, deer, and wild animals listened to the song of this beautiful maiden. The hunter and the sage too were entranced by this astonishing spectacle, so much so that they were unaware of the day passing by. Finally Manoharā and her entourage left.

The sage and the hunter also bathed at the pool used by Manoharā for her bathing ritual. The mind of the hunter had been turned, and he said to the sage:

> Ah, listen, great sage. Pay attention to me.
> Today has been an astonishing spectacle.
> If only this hunter could gain just one of these
>   beautiful women.
> Would that be possible? If you say that it is,
> I will give the precious jewel to you.
> Help me with this. Give me instructions.

With these words the hunter made many prostrations to the sage, who replied:

> Hear my words, brave son of a hunter.
> Do not entertain these mistaken notions.
> Be at ease in body and mind.
>
> Those gods and spirits that came to bathe here today
> are mostly without physical form and are beyond capture.
> Even to catch those you could catch
> would be like catching sunlight with your hands.
> They are not real, brave son of a hunter.
> Let us not stay here, let us return.
> Let us return to Ke'u cave.

With that they left. Back in the cave, again the hunter pleaded with the sage:

Please listen to me, great sage.
Consider this, great being of exalted wisdom.
The confidence in thinking that I must capture one
   of these maidens
comes mainly from the compassion of the great sage,
but particularly from the power of the precious jewel.
I have no desire other than the thought
to capture one of these beautiful women.

Today I have no hope,
but if a beautiful maiden were mine,
the wishes of the hunter would be fulfilled.
If she does not materialize, what is the point
of this jewel renowned as granter of all wishes and needs?

Moreover, the great sage himself said
this was a jewel granting the hunter all he wished.
Well, I have no other wish whatsoever
than to have just one maiden from this group.
Great sage, please do this. I do not need the jewel.

The sage replied:

Listen to me, brave son of a hunter.
Do not think these wrong and deluded thoughts.
Previously when I was evaluating the jewel,
I said that Buddha Krakucchanda generated the mind
   of enlightenment
and spoke of the jewel as "for the sake of living beings."
I did not say that it was for satisfying your desires
with gods, nāgas, gandharvas, and other noncorporeal beings.

We humans do not possess a way of capturing these beings.
The nāgas have the amoghapāśa jewel.
It is the life force and the prosperity of the nāgas.
If you had possession of this jewel,
maybe you could capture yakṣa spirits and gandharvas.
There is no other method.

The hunter said in response:

> Listen, great sage.
> If the nāgas have such a jewel,
> it is possible they will give it to me,
> because no one kinder than me has been to the nāgas.
> I will go at once to seek the amoghapāśa jewel
> and return the granter of all wishes and needs.
> Once I have the jewel, I will return to the guru.

The sage said:

> As the nāgas owe you a great debt of gratitude,
> they will give you the amoghapāśa jewel,
> and when they do you will take a pledge for the nāga world.
> For the other god realms you must take a pledge.
> But do not take the pledge for the land of Vṛkṣaḥ.
> If you gain the amoghapāśa jewel,
> you will definitely fulfill your wishes, brave son of a hunter.

The hunter replied:

> Hear my words, great sage.
> You explained the qualities and functions of the jewel.
> Now again I will act according to your word.
> I will go quickly to the lake, and when I have the amoghapāśa
>   jewel,
> I will return to the presence of the guru.
> May I never be separated from the great refuge,
> a great realm of meditative concentration,
> who grants help in fulfilling the wishes of the hunter.

The Hunter Seeks the Amoghapāśa Jewel

He made farewell prostrations to the guru, placed the jewel on his head, and left. He traveled continuously day and night with great effort and arrived at the lake after three days. At the western shore he called out to the nāgas in song:

Wealthy nāga, mistress of the lake, who dwells in its depths,
listen to me, hear these words of the hunter.
I have come here for a purpose and have a few words to say.

He waited for a while but no response was forthcoming. So he went to
the northern shore and called out:

Listen to me, take notice, wealthy nāga queen.
Pay attention, listen to this hunter.
I am the very hunter who killed the yogi.
Please listen to a few words from this hunter.

There was no response. He went to the eastern shore and said:

Again I say, listen to me, nāga queen Janmacitrā.
Do not be distracted. Listen to this kind hunter.
Remember my kindness and come to the surface.
There is something important that I need.

Still there was no response. The hunter became irritated:

Listen I say, shameless nāga queen.
When I came to your nāga world,
what was it that was decided between us?
You promised to do whatever I wanted.

Today, not even bothering to reply to my call,
shows that you are as shameless as an animal.
I regret that I ever showed you kindness.
I will not stay here but go to the south,
where there are seven yogis
more frightening than the previous one,
and he was the weakest of them all.

Also, in the hunter's hide tent right now
are the dagger and poison horn of the yogi I killed.
Best comply, my shameless nāga queen.

He fetched the dagger and the poison horn of the yogi and prepared to cast them into the lake. The nāga queen thought to herself: "I know that in the south there are no yogis greater than the previous one, but if the poison horn of the old yogi is placed into the lake it could bring much disease to the nāgas. Moreover, the hunter has been very kind to us, and it would not be right to disappoint him."

She rose to the surface and spoke to the hunter:

> Listen to me, brave son of a hunter.
> Pay attention. Listen to the nāga queen.
> What is the reason you call the nāga?
> Do not be so agitated. Be peaceful.
> Nāgas are not to be threatened.

The hunter replied:

> Listen to me, wealthy nāga queen.
> Pay attention and listen to this hunter.
> Do you recognize this hunter today?
> Have you forgotten the yogi from the south?
> Do you remember how the nāga called the hunter
>   at that time?
> Why did you not reply to my call today?
> Have you forgotten the kindness of the hunter?
>
> If you have not forgotten,
> I have something to ask of you.
> This jewel that the nāga gave the hunter before
> gives me many things, whether they are my wish or not.
> But I do not want it. I return it to the nāga.
> This jewel has no fault. Take it back.
> I ask instead for the amoghapāśa jewel.
> Pray give it to the hunter.

The nāga replied:

> Pay attention hunter. Turn your ears this way.
> The granter of all wishes and needs is a jewel for men.

The amoghapāśa is a jewel of the nāgas.
It will grant no powers to anyone except nāgas.
Hunter, why do you want the amoghapāśa?

If your need is genuine, I will offer it to you,
as you have been so kind to us,
even though it may harm the nāgas.
Return the granter of all wishes and needs,
and I will fetch the amoghapāśa
and offer it to you now.

The nāga went below the surface and quickly returned with the amoghapāśa jewel. Addressing the hunter, the nāga said:

Listen well, brave son of a hunter.
This amoghapāśa nāga jewel is the source
of the happiness of the nāga kingdom,
and, in particular, is the life-force residence of every nāga.

If anyone but me has anything like this jewel,
hunter, you would find it difficult even to see it.
Because you have been kind, I offer it to you now.
But in the future, return it to the nāga queen.

With these words she presented the jewel to the hunter. It was jewel that no one could have ever created. It shone with five colors, possessed a noose-like shape, was made of an unknown material, and emitted a light of long and fine beams. Holding the jewel by its noose-like tip, the nāga spoke the oaths that the hunter had to swear:

Hunter, listen to me. Pay attention.
Having taken the jewel, you must take the pledges.
Take the pledge of the upper realms of the gods.
Pledge not to capture the daughters of the gods.
Take the pledge of the realm of Thirty-Three.
Pledge not to capture the goddesses of the Thirty-Three.
Take the pledge of the four levels of Meru.
Pledge not to capture the yakṣa spirits and gandharvas.

Take the pledge of the noncorporeal spirit world.
Pledge not to capture the spirit daughters.
Take the pledge of the lower world of the nāgas.
Pledge not to capture the nāga daughters.
If you take these pledges, you may take the jewel.
Otherwise, to take the jewel becomes a cause for wickedness.

The hunter replied:

Hear me. Take notice, wealthy nāga queen.
Pay close attention. Listen to this hunter.
Remembering my kindness, the nāga has wisely given me
    the jewel.
The hunter can take the pledge of the upper realms of the gods,
and pledge not to capture the daughters of the gods.
He can take the pledge of the realm of Thirty-Three,
and pledge not to capture the goddesses of the Thirty-Three.
He can take the pledge of the noncorporeal spirit world,
and pledge not to capture the spirit daughters.
He can take the pledge of the lower world of the nāgas,
and pledge not to capture the nāga daughters.
He has no need to take the pledge of the four levels of Meru,
and has no need to pledge not to capture the gandharva maidens.
Therefore it makes no difference if he takes the amoghapāśa
    jewel or not.

With these words he took the jewel, and traveling nonstop day and night,
he reached Ke'u cave in two days. Prostrating to the guru sage, he said:

Hear me, guru and great sage.
I have acted according to your instructions.
Three times I called the nāga, but received no reply.
So the hunter took the poison horn of the dead yogi,
told the nāga that she was a shameless creature,
and prepared to throw it into the lake.

The nāga immediately appeared on the surface,
and I told her how I wanted the amoghapāśa.

Her face showed some expression of not wanting to give it,
but I addressed her with a few strong words,
and, cowed by that, she gave me the jewel.

She told me that the hunter had to take pledges
not to cause harm to the gods, spirits, nāgas, and so on.
Except for the gandharva realm, I took the pledges.

Guru, please look to see if this is the amoghapāśa.
Risking my life, I accomplished a great deed.
From now on nothing will be out of my reach.
Summon the beautiful and captivating celestial maiden.

With these words the hunter wiped his face with his sleeve. The sage replied:

Listen to me, brave son of a hunter.
You went quickly to the northern life-force lake,
and you brought back the amoghapāśa jewel.
No one possesses another jewel like this.
For the nāgas there is no jewel more precious.

With this jewel I will perform a bathing ritual.
On the auspicious fifteenth day of this month,
at the Brahma court bathing pools,
the gods, spirits, and gandharvas will gather.
On that day we will go to the bathing pools.
Hunter, take food and drink as you wish.

The sage gave the hunter fruit and juice. The sage thought to himself: "If the hunter gets what he wants, at that time it will be a wrong thing to do. However, in the long term, it seems as if it could be of great benefit for the doctrine and living beings. Therefore I too must make a well-intended prayer." With this thought he placed the Amoghapāśa on his head and prayed:

Homage to the ḍākinīs, the guru buddhas of the ten directions,
to the sacred community, Dharma protectors and guardians.

If the action of this hunter is of benefit to doctrine and living
    beings,
let him quickly accomplish what he desires.

You powerful gods and nāgas who watch over virtuous deeds,
help this hunter achieve what he desires.
Summon all good fortune and auspiciousness necessary
for this skillful and brave hunter to fulfill his wishes.

The Hunter Captures Manoharā

At dawn on the fifteenth day of the month the hunter, with the jewel carried
on his head, arrived with the sage at the Brahma Court bathing pools. The
hunter, as he did previously, hid among the flowers. The great sage chanted
the tunes of invitation to the gods, and one after another the groups of god-
desses, spirits, and gandharvas from the form, formless, and desire realms
came to the pools. In particular, Manoharā, the gandharva princess, and
her entourage, adorned with an even greater number of precious gems than
before, arrived and bathed. Manoharā said to her entourage:

Listen to me, daughters of my entourage.
For time without beginning in this samsara,
countless times we have taken bodies,
and now we have come together in the kingdom of Vṛkṣaḥ.
"King" and "subjects" are determined by the turning wheel
    of karma.

Our mother-and-father sentient beings are equal to space,
and through the ignorant self-clinging to "self" and "others,"
we have accumulated the stains of desires and anger.
So with the purification of remorse I myself now bathe
    my mind.

This bathed body, this beautiful body, is the body of a goddess,
but will not remain here forever.
Daughters, look in your mirrors of exalted wisdom,
I fear we may be snared by the magic noose of bad karma.
Do not stay here daughters. Flee to the land of Vṛkṣaḥ!
Right now there is danger. An obstacle is arising!

As they were about to leave, the sage made a sign to the hunter. Immediately, the hunter threw the noose jewel at Manoharā, who flew up into the air, but the noose caught her and she dropped to the ground like a bird hit with a stone. The celestial entourage flew off like a flock of birds. The hunter was overjoyed, and quickly and roughly pulled in the noose. He exclaimed:

> *Oṃ mo oṃ mo ma ṇi padmé hūṃ.*
> I pray to the Three Jewels.
> Listen to me, captivating goddess.
> Do not resist, captivating goddess.
> Do not resist, do not struggle, beautiful goddess.

> The aromatic thousand-petal lotuses in the lotus garden,
> the various gentian flowers that grow abundantly in meadows,
> by the force of karma they come together
> as offerings to the Three Jewels.

> A captivating goddess, a daughter born of a god,
> and a hunter, a brave man born of a human,
> by the force of karma have come together in this special place.
> That karma today has come to fruition.
> Today my wishes have been fulfilled.

As the hunter pulled in the noose, Manoharā cried out:

> Guru, meditation deities, ḍākinīs, protectors,
> powerful gods, and nāgas who watch over virtuous activity,
> and especially my objects of refuge in the land of Vṛkṣaḥ,
> come today to give help to the goddess Manoharā!

> Whether by the ripening of bad karma
> I have gathered in past lives,
> or by the bad circumstance of an obstacle in this life,
> this maiden has been captured by a low-class hunter.

> I am powerful and can perform miraculous feats,
> but he is difficult to beat.
> Peaceful and wrathful gods, produce your powerful armies.

The great sage is an object of veneration by the gods.
Won't you look at this daughter whose life is at risk!

Manoharā turned her back on the hunter and wept. The sage realized that if the hunter were to touch the goddess, she would run the risk of being tainted, so he stepped in between her and the hunter. Taking the amoghapāśa in his hand, he said:

Hear me, brave son of a hunter.
She is of celestial breed, and very pure.
You are of hunter breed, and very tainted.
For a tainted human to touch a goddess is harmful.
It would be best if I deal with this.

The hunter replied:

Listen to me, great sage.
I have undertaken a task at great risk to my life,
and today the fruit of that task has come to my hands.
This expression of distaste for me on the face of the goddess
is very hard for this hunter to bear.

The hunter walked around the sage and stared closely, again and again, at the goddess's face. The goddess exclaimed:

Alas! Alas! Such distress in my mind.
Such despair as this in this daughter's mind.
Such sad karma for one who has taken the body of a goddess.
This daughter with her bad karma has fallen into the hunter's
    noose.

Hunter, do not come near. Go away!
If the breath of the hunter should land on me,
it will be like autumn flowers being destroyed by frost.
If the body of the hunter should touch me,
it will be like summer flowers being destroyed by hail.

The blue mane of the white lion from the high snows
should not adorn the shoulders of a street dog.
How can I, Manoharā Devī, a princess of the gandharvas,
be the companion of a low-caste hunter?
Hunter, do not do this. Let me go.

The hunter replied:

Listen to me. Take notice of what I say, beautiful goddess.
The high upper plains are the abode of the deer,
but the wild hunting dogs will bring the brown antlered stags
of the upland plains down to the lowlands.
Likewise, in the upper god realms
the goddess may possess magical powers,
but I have captured her to be the hunter's companion.

On the high cliff the hunter set a trap,
and the white eagle was caught at the bathing pool.
The hunter cast the noose and caught the princess Manoharā.
How could the hunter release Manoharā Devī?
The constant companion I have had in my mind has appeared,
but how long we are together is determined by our past karma.

Far from letting her go, the hunter moved to seize her. Manoharā addressed
the sage:

Hear me, great sage!
Pay me heed, great one of exalted wisdom!
I have not been aware of any humans coming to these pools.
So now what is this hunter doing here?
Sage, you are an object of veneration by the gods.
I have not caused disturbance in your mind.
Help to set me free!

Manoharā took a ring off her finger and placed it in the sage's hand, and
again pleaded with him:

Alas! Listen to me, great sage.
Deliver this to the ears of this powerful hunter.
Among the gods, Manoharā is a princess.
She is chaste and a celestial lay practitioner.
Among humans, the hunter is of the fisherman caste.
He does evil deeds and is without shame.
Rather than spend a single day in his company,
this maiden would happily die right here.

All the jewels of the world piled together cannot compare
with just one of the gemstones set in this maiden's ring.
Take the ring and help set this daughter free.
Great guru, deliver these words of this daughter.
Great sage, loosen this knot tied by a snake.

The sage replied:

Hear me, princess Manoharā Devī.
I will tell the hunter exactly what you said.
He may be of a lower caste,
but he is strong and clever in magic.

Do not be upset, Manoharā Devī.
I will explain to the hunter as best I can.
Do not doubt that he will listen to me.

The sage gave the ring to the hunter and told him what she had said. The
hunter replied:

Listen to what I have to say, great sage.
Pay great attention, one of exalted wisdom.
Manoharā says that she would rather die
than spend just one day as my companion.

As an answer to that, deliver this message from the hunter.
Having caught a wolf, you may want it to be a house dog,
but if the wolf dies, then all you can do is take its hide.
Having caught Manoharā, I want her as my companion,

but if she dies, then I can only take her jewels and robes.
If the goddess dies, she will die in sight of the hunter,
and I will have lost all hope today.
All will be decided today.

The sage said:

Hunter, don't say this. Listen to me.
You have captured the beautiful and celestial Manoharā princess,
but this will be of no benefit to you.
This ring of the goddess is rare in the world.
Take it and let this maiden go free.

The hunter replied:

Listen to what I say, great sage.
I did not capture her because I wanted her ornaments.
I captured her because I wanted Manoharā as my companion.

If I capture the brown stag on the uplands,
then its beautiful antlers belong to me.
If I capture the white lion from the high snows,
then its blue mane belongs to me.
If I capture princess Manoharā Devī,
then her crown jewels belong to me.

Great sage, take these words from the hunter
and tell them clearly to the beautiful princess.

The sage delivered these two messages to Manoharā, who reacted angrily
and glared at the hunter, saying:

Evil hunter, pay careful attention.
Never will you and this daughter be companions.
I ask you peacefully to let me go,
and I offer this ring as ransom.
Having humbled myself, this wretched situation
is more than this daughter can bear! Be sure of that!

When called peacefully, I am Manoharā Devī,
When called wrathfully, I am the flesh-eating yakṣa.
If you would lose your life, hunter, then come here!

Manoharā raised her hand in the air, and as she was about to slip from his grasp, the hunter became a little frightened. He picked up the noose and backed off somewhat. Regaining his courage, he said:

Listen to me, you young gandharva.
If you have no hesitation to commit wicked acts,
then I have no fear to kill all that I see,
my young gandharva Manoharā.

The hunter went to seize her hand, but the sage came between them. He addressed the hunter:

Listen, brave son of a hunter.
Listen well to this sage.
Do not be so proud. Listen to me.
Everything you have accomplished in your life,
would you lose it all in just one meaningless hour?
If you commit the act that finally leads
to the death of this beautiful maiden,
it will be hard to find any happiness in this world.

The hunter held back for a while. Manoharā put her face to the ground and cried. A few goddesses, headed by her sister Darśanamukti, appeared in the skies above, the distance of a bowshot away, circling like garuḍas. They cried out in grief:

Alas! Alas! Our sister!
The good fortune of the goddesses is at an end.
Our mother and father of the Vṛkṣaḥ kingdom
have many princesses, but one such as Manoharā is rare.

She is an incarnation of the Buddha in goddess form,
possessing devotion to her parents, great affection
    for her siblings,

and a mind of love and compassion to her entire entourage.
The sun of happiness of the Vṛkṣaḥ kingdom has set.

Manoharā looked up at the entourage in the skies and said:

Sister Darśanamukti and entourage who rest safely in the skies,
of good and bad karma is this sister Manoharā Devi.
With good karma I was born in the Vṛkṣaḥ kingdom,
born as the adornment of the family of Vṛkṣaḥ princesses,
regarded as the jewel among the gandharva royalty and subjects.

With bad karma this sister had been captured by a hunter.
Not only made captive, but look at this torment and suffering!
Take this message to this daughter's mother and father.
Tell them that Manoharā, born with bad karma,
has been taken today by a hunter.

Today their daughter is close to an untimely death.
Tell my kind parents to come to ransom their daughter.
Tell them to come, bringing many jewels
as ransom for their daughter.
Tell them to bring gold, silver, and silk
as ransom for their daughter.
Bring elephants adorned with jewels
as ransom for their daughter.
Bring the best horses with beautiful saddles and bridles.
Bring ordinary Vṛkṣaḥ girls as replacement for this daughter.

The hunter too looked up in the skies and said:

Entourage of the beautiful maiden,
dwelling high in the pure skies,
listen to what I have to say.

Take this hunter's message to the kingdom of Vṛkṣaḥ.
Say this to the king and people of Vṛkṣaḥ.
Tell them I have captured my desired Manoharā.

Tell them that Darśanamukti and her entourage have returned.
The hunter does not want them.

They may have many jewels there,
but the hunter does not want them.
They may have gold, silver, and silk,
but the hunter does not want them.
They may have elephants adorned with jewels,
but the hunter does not want them.
They may have the best horses clothed with beautiful saddles
    and bridles,
but the hunter has no desire for any of them.

If there are common Vṛkṣaḥ girls as servants, then bring them.
Even at the cost of my life, I will not release Manoharā.
If there is a dowry, you can give it in good time.
Give my answer and this message
clearly and without error.

With these words he sat right in front of Manoharā. The maiden's celestial body pained by the bonds of the noose and her mind deeply saddened, beads of sweat glistened on her face and her breath shook like a little bird being pursued by a hawk. The sage addressed her:

Hear what I say, beautiful princess.
The hunter does not hold back from committing evil deeds,
so no matter what you do, you sit there pained by this noose.
The crown jewel necklace that you wear,
this evening you should give it to the hunter.
It will be good, I think, if you are released from the noose.
Do not be upset, daughter Manoharā.

Manoharā said:

Listen to me, great sage.
I do not have a choice between happiness and suffering,
but you are the messenger between men and gods.
Great sage, please consider me.

This pain and suffering is difficult for this maiden to bear.
Can you bear to see it, great sage?

May the suffering experienced by this daughter
never be experienced by other beings.
Take the crown ornament and give it to the hunter.
Set me free soon from this noose.
Release me from the danger to my life.

The sage took the crown jewel necklace from Manoharā and addressed
the hunter:

Listen to me, brave son of a hunter.
This crown jewel necklace of Manoharā
is the pair of wings with which she flies into the sky.
It is like the earth on which she sits.
Without this ornament Manoharā cannot fly.
Take the ornament and free her from the noose.
The maiden is not far from death.

The hunter took the ornament and released Manoharā from the
amoghapāśa noose. Manoharā, with long, drawn-out sighs, went to the
bathing pools, where she bathed herself with her hands, sipped the water,
and dressed. That evening the sage, hunter, and Manoharā went to Ke'u cave.

Darśanamukti and the entourage returned to Vṛkṣaḥ. She related to
her parents, the king and queen, and their subjects, how the hunter seized
Manoharā from the bathing pools. Her mother, Ḍākinī, fell into a faint and
had to be revived by a sprinkling of sandalwood water. The king and his sub-
jects talked about how to get Manoharā back by peaceful or wrathful means.
That evening the king, Turaṃvadana, saw with his worldly clairvoyance that
there was no immediate danger to Manoharā's life, and that in the long term
all would turn out for the good. He told this to his people, and for the next
seven days gave advice and reassurance to his people.

The same evening in Ke'u cave, Manoharā lay down. The hunter lay close
to the cave door and the sage slept in between. Manoharā thought to herself:
"If the hunter touches me tonight, I will die," and so she lay there without
sleeping.

The sage thought to himself: "My whole life, I have practiced the Dharma, but tonight if the hunter touches the girl and she dies, my prestige will suffer." He too did not sleep.

The hunter thought to himself: "I have gone through all this trouble, but I have not joined with Manoharā even once. Maybe I will lose her." He also did not sleep.

In his clear light mind between his meditation sessions, the sage had a vision in which the gods Brahma and Indra appeared in the skies around the Palace of the Land of Joy in the northern kingdom, holding flowers in their hands and standing in a pose of veneration. That evening Dharma King Sudhana had a dream full of auspicious signs, in which the sun rose over the Palace of the Land of Joy, many flags and banners flew from its roof, and trumpets and conches and many other instruments sounded, while the king himself held a radiant *utpala* lotus in his hands.

As soon as he got up in the morning the sage said to the son of the hunter:

Listen to me, brave son of a hunter.
Pay attention. Listen to the sage.
I have received some excellent signs.
If you agree with what I have in mind,
you will fulfill the wishes of yourself and all others.
Does that not appeal to you?

The hunter replied:

Hear me, great sage.
Take notice, Prakāśamati.
In the past I have asked you for advice on what to do.
Again I ask you to teach this hunter.

The sage said:

Listen, brave son of a hunter.
I will tell you truthfully what is on my mind.
You are a low-breed hunter of wicked ways.
Manoharā is a celestial princess, chaste and pure.
There is no way that you two could be companions.

However, in a place some leagues from here,
three hundred and sixty leagues to be exact,
lies a great palace known as the Palace of the Land of Joy
in the capital city of the happy northern kingdom of Vaśin.

There lives Dharma King Sudhana.
This Dharma king has many queens,
but none like the princess Manoharā.
If you were to offer her to the king,
she would become supreme queen to that king,
you would have all you desire,
and Manoharā would be freed from the risk to her life.
Consider this, son of a hunter.

The hunter replied:

Listen once more, great sage.
The hunter will express his thoughts in detail.
The northern king is this hunter's lord and master.
Up to now I have not seen him,
but I have heard of his renown.

This Dharma king known as Prince Sudhana
is a king of good deeds and magical power.
It is said that he is rare in this world.
If I give Manoharā away,
who would I give her to except him?

When I think of the hardship I have undergone to capture her,
and when I gaze at the face of beautiful Manoharā,
I find it very difficult to do as you ask.
Especially not spending even one night with her,
I find it difficult to let her go, great sage.

However, if a powerful master takes her from me,
then even if I get nothing in way of recompense,
there is nothing I can do about it.

With all these thoughts in my mind,
it is difficult for the hunter to make a decision.

He gazed at the face of Manoharā and sat close to her. The sage addressed
him:

Listen to me, brave son of a hunter.
Think about this very carefully.
Your thinking is profound and your thoughts are many,
but as you have just said, hunter,
if the king takes her away, who can prevent that?
Moreover, you would also lose your life.

You have much on your mind, but listen to me.
Go quickly to the northern kingdom,
offer Manoharā and the crown ornament to the king.
Take the rewards that satisfy you.
Tell the king the story of how all this came about.

The hunter replied:

I risked my life to capture Manoharā,
and what I need I have not enjoyed even once.
If I am able to offer her to the gracious Sudhana,
it will be a loss, but there is no one else I would offer
    her to.

In the past you have given me advice, great guru,
and again the hunter will follow the words of the sage.
I will leave to offer the goddess to the great king.
Do not fret, beautiful goddess Manoharā.
We will leave at once for the northern kingdom.

On my right I will lead the goddess with the amoghapāśa
    noose,
on my left I will carry the crown ornament.
Guru, give me assistance as you have done in the past.

THE HUNTER OFFERS MANOHARĀ TO KING SUDHANA

The hunter tied a scarf around his head and prepared to set off to the northern kingdom to offer Manoharā to Dharma King Sudhana. Manoharā addressed the sage:

> Listen to me, great sage.
> Even if the hunter offers this daughter
> to the Dharma king, as the great sage has advised,
> if the king, out of compassion,
> pays a ransom for the life of this daughter,
> can I still be sure that my life is safe?
>
> If the king does not ransom me, my life will surely be in danger.
> In whatever way I think, my mind is disturbed.
> Great sage, I plead that you ask the hunter to pledge
> that he will protect the life of this daughter.
>
> By the power of the buddhas of the ten directions,
> may this daughter be quickly freed from this distress,
> and may she again see her country of Vṛkṣaḥ
> and be reunited with her mother and father.

With these words she prostrated in all eight directions and made prayers with tears in her eyes. The sage spoke to her:

> Listen, Princess Manoharā.
> Do not worry. Listen to me.
> The northern Dharma king and Manoharā
> are united by prayer and karma. Have no fear.
> Go quickly with the hunter to the northern kingdom.
>
> Brave hunter, do not break your promise,
> offer the daughter to the hand of the northern king.
> I will pray that the wishes of the hunter and Manoharā
> are fulfilled exactly as you wish.

The hunter and Manoharā made farewell prostrations to the sage and left.

After three days they arrived at the iron walls of the Palace of the Land of Joy. Many people stopped and stared in wonder at Manoharā. Soon a crowd had gathered around her. The gatekeeper wondered what was going on and came to see. The hunter addressed him:

> Hear me. Take notice, head gatekeeper.
> Keeper of the gate, listen to this hunter.
> This hunter has come from Ke'u cave.
> He has come from the residence of a great sage.
>
> I have come here to be at the Land of Joy.
> I have come to be in the presence of King Sudhana.
> Take this request to the ears of the great king.
> Tell him a pleasant-voiced hunter has arrived,
> and tell him that on his right
> he brings a beautiful young maiden.
>
> Tell him I need an audience as soon as possible.
> Head gatekeeper, do this quickly.

The gatekeeper looked at the beautiful form of Manoharā, and quickly returned into the palace. He reported to palace attendants what the hunter had said. They in turn reported this to the king, who was delighted and said:

> Attendants, pay attention. Hear what I say.
> The auspicious dreams I have had recently
> come together well with these words you bring me.
> Bring the hunter and the young maiden to me.
> Arrange seats and cushions in my central chambers,
> and prepare tea, ale, and other necessary food and drink.

Attendants made the preparations the king had ordered. The king welcomed the hunter and Manoharā at the entrance to his private chambers. As he brought them over the threshold, peals of thunder rang out. The hunter prostrated, and holding the jewel ornament in his hands, said:

> Hear me, lord of men, son of the gods.
> Take notice, great Dharma king.

This goddess Manoharā that I bring here today,
is the daughter of Turaṃvadana, king of Vṛkṣaḥ.

At the Brahma court bathing pools,
many goddesses, such as Manoharā, would come to bathe.
Among them, this hunter captured this princess with
   a noose.
However, the great sage Prakāśamati of Ke'u cave
said these words to me, the hunter:

"The celestial princess Manoharā is chaste and pure.
You are the son of a hunter, of low breeding.
She cannot be of any benefit to you.
If you offer her instead to Dharma King Sudhana,
she will become his supreme queen.
The king in return will give you all you desire."

Together with the goddess, I come to offer this crown
   ornament.
I come to ask for food, clothing, and prestige.
Accept this extraordinary jewel necklace.
Accept this beautiful celestial princess, Manoharā.
Later I will tell the circumstances of how all this came to be.

The hunter laid the crown ornament in the hands of the king. The king
was delighted. A turquoise throne was erected in front of the king's golden
throne and Manoharā was sat upon it. The hunter was placed on three lay-
ers of soft tiger skins. The ministers were astonished. The king said to the
hunter:

Listen to me, skillful son of a hunter.
What is your country? Who is your lord?
Tell us in detail how you and the sage of Ke'u cave
came to capture your companion.
Your gift of the ornament and the maiden is extraordinary.
Hunter, whatever you wish for, I will give.
Now tell us of these matters.

The hunter replied:

Hear my words, lord of men and son of the gods.
Take notice. I will speak fully and truthfully.
In a place several leagues from here,
over three hundred leagues to the southeast,
is the life-force lake for the king and his subjects of the north.
Its name is the Lotus Life-Force Lake.

The patroller of the lake is this hunter before you.
My father's name was Rāhula, mine is Phalaka.
For food, I eat fish. For drink, I take the water of the lake.
I am a subject under the rule of the northern king.
I have no fixed home, I am not taxed or yoked under
    any serfdom.
This is the first time I have seen the king and his palace.
For a little man, I have notions greater than others.

The king of the southern kingdom filled his mouth with desires,
and wanted to summon to his own country in the south
the nāga and entourage who lived in the northern life-force lake.

To this end, on the evening of the fifteenth of the fourth month,
a very powerful tantrika came to the shores of the northern lake.
Around the lake he planted ritual daggers
and interwove them with banners.
In the lake he planted ritual substances
and a skull cup of poison blood.

The lake began to boil and the minor nāgas almost died.
The nāga queen was in great pain and called out to the hunter,
saying that such and such dreadful events had occurred.
"What is this?" I thought, and walked around the lake.

There was the frightening yogi from the south,
uttering mantras and performing mudras to enhance his deeds.
As soon as I saw him, I said to him: "You wandering, evil-
    hearted man,

why have you come here to harm the lake!"
I went to kill him with my knife,
and struck him in the head.

With a fearless roar, I gave him this final demand:
"Return the lake and the nāgas to their former state!"
The yogi was chastened and promised to do what I commanded.
He gathered the iron daggers and banners from around the lake,
removed the substances from the water,
and replaced them with medicines.
The lake became as before, and the nāgas were revived.
There and then the hunter killed the yogi.

The next day the nāga queen came to me and said:
"The hunter has been so kind to us.
Below the water lies the nāga palace. Come there now."
So I went. It was happy place with wonderful sights to see.

I spent a delightful time there,
and then, as I was about to leave,
they gave me a jewel as a gift,
and I returned to the shore of the lake.
Not being able to evaluate the jewel,
I went to ask the great sage in Ke'u cave.
This guru gave me much excellent explanation.

This sage, it is said, was almost five hundred years old.
I asked what was the cause of such a long life.
He said that a few leagues away from the cave
were the Brahma court bathing pools, and that many goddesses,
spirits, and gandharvas came there to bathe.
Seeing them and drinking the ambrosia water of the baths
was the cause of his longevity, he explained.

I said that I wanted to go, and so I did.
Many beautiful goddesses, spirits, and gandharva maidens
I saw coming to that place to bathe.
They captivated my mind, and as a way to capture them

I procured the amoghapāśa nāga jewel and seized Manoharā.
In keeping with the sage's word,
I offer her as queen to the king.
Such an amazing and extraordinary story,
will the king and his subjects believe it, I wonder?

The king and his ministers were astonished at this story. However, some workers whose work it was to go to the lake to look after the special substances placed at the lake recognized the hunter, and so the story was believed.

That day the king and the goddess met. The gods sent down a rain of flowers as a joyous sign of Manoharā's enthronement. From the skies came the sound of music, and many wonderful and astonishing signs were witnessed. The king and subjects of Vṛkṣaḥ were also lifted from their grief.

The king addressed the hunter:

Mighty hunter, listen to me.
It is wonderful indeed that through your great kindness,
more than once the northern kingdom been protected.
In particular, such a goddess as Manoharā,
no king on earth has ever had before.
Hunter, in recognition, you are worthy of reward.
Whatever your wish, I will fulfill.

Beginning tomorrow, for several days
we will have celebrations with great festive gatherings,
the entire kingdom will enjoy this joyous enthronement.
Hunter, we will talk about your reward tomorrow.
Today as an auspicious token, please accept this.

The hunter was presented with a complete set of the best silk clothes, a ceremonial scarf in honor of his bravery, and the finest food and drink. He was lodged in a house and given four servants.

The mother and father of Sudhana heard of these events and were overjoyed. They came to the Land of Joy and were lodged in private chambers. The father, Mahādhana, took charge of organizing the people. He had discussions on the great events and ceremonies to be held throughout the kingdom, beginning on the following day with the singing and dancing, and the horse races, archery contests, and so on that would make up the festivities, and decisions were made about such things as the order of the participants and so on. At the same time, because the sun of a happy day had risen for the people of the northern kingdom, he ordered that drums be beaten and great flags flown throughout the land as encouragement to the people to participate. He offered to Manoharā jeweled ornaments and silken clothing, beautiful beyond imagination, and gave her Ānandaśrī and Sukhasamājā and eight other ladies-in-waiting.

On the day of Jupiter, the twentieth day of the eighth month of the earth dragon year, an auspicious day when the moon occupied the lunar constellation Puṣya,[33] in the Land of Joy Palace reception hall known as The Coming Together of All That Could Be Desired, the prince and his father were seated on a golden throne, and Manoharā and the great mother on a turquoise throne. The five hundred queens were seated on wooden thrones. At the head of the front row the hunter sat on three layers of soft tiger skins. Officials and other people were seated all around according to rank. An unprecedented and lavish banquet was served. From the top of the palace, offerings were made to the gods, drums were beaten, and flags were flown.

Within the walls of the palace there was singing and dancing. Outside there were horse races and archery contests, with everyone, high and low, attired in their best clothes. Within and outside the great palace walls there was no room to walk, no place to sit, and it was not possible to take in all the shows. When everybody had gathered to watch the shows, to which the gods had come in admiration of the people of the north, the hunter was presented with his rewards in recognition of his actions. The official proclamation read:

> Possessed of unshakable faith in the Three Jewels, beloved by the heroes, ḍākinīs, and Dharma protectors, possessed of armies of gods and nāgas protecting the good, the guide and guardian of sentient beings whose numbers equal limitless space, constant companion of all beautiful celestial and human maidens, destroyer of the malicious enemies of the doctrine and living beings, Sudhana, holder of the northern royal lineage, declares:
>
> This is for the consideration and understanding of all those, who by the causal factors of fixed channels, moving winds, and placed bodhicitta, possess various languages, livelihoods, and

forms, and in particular, for those beings of the north and south kingdoms of India, monastic and lay, high and low, however near or far away they may live.

The hunter Phalaka lives by the Lotus Life-Force Lake, and at the time of the wicked actions of a person from the south, he protected the nāgas there for the sake of the northern king and his subjects, and killed the yogi. In particular, at the Brahma court bathing pools he captured a celestial princess from the kingdom of Vṛkṣaḥ and offered her to me. He also recounted the extraordinary account of how these events unfolded. In all ways he is a worthy recipient of an unparalleled reward. He shall be rewarded by being presented with the title Vajrapāti Ghihana. He shall be given a vast estate of Phuntsok Tongmon in Bird Country. His list of possessions will include external wealth and household goods. He will have five hundred Sehruk servants, and fifteen nomadic homesteads, the profit from which shall remain with him. These servants are guaranteed not to diminish. No one will resent his right to land and water. Vajrapāti Ghihana together with his succession shall live happily hereafter.

This proclamation has been written in the earth dragon year on an auspicious date, in the great Palace of Land of Joy Victorious in All Directions.

The hunter was presented with a set of clothes, horses and mules, gold and silver, coral and amber, and given the choice of a queen from the five hundred, and on that day was relieved forever from the suffering of poverty.

* * *

Thus ends part 2, on how an insignificant and low-caste hunter accomplished great things for the king and subjects of the northern kingdom.

Part 3. Hari Agrees to Carry Out the Wishes of the Demon-Possessed Five Hundred Queens, and They Experience the Subsequent Shame of Their Wicked Deeds Not Coming to Fruition.

THE FIVE HUNDRED QUEENS PLOT TO KILL MANOHARĀ
The festivities of the earth dragon year went on for over a month. During that time the hunter stayed in the palace. After the celebrations ended, he traveled to the lands he had been presented with, together with a witness authorized to oversee the transference of the estate.

Everybody who gathered at the palace at that time was talking about the incredible beauty of Manoharā. They spoke about her noble deeds and said that her qualities were those of a wise woman. Having seen Manoharā, secretly they gossiped that the five hundred queens looked like monkeys!

As for the king, after Manoharā arrived he almost forgot about the five hundred queens. Manoharā thought to herself that in the god realms there was never a more handsome and radiant man than the king. With a broad smile of joy, she said to the king:

> Listen to me, supreme lord of men.
> Listen well to this maiden.
> Great king, your radiance and splendor
> steals the glory of the sun and moon.

> If we look at your great deeds of bravery and heroism,
> then even the gods Brahma and Indra would feel inadequate.
> That one such as you, unrivaled in the three realms,
> should become the companion of this maiden
> is fortune gained by the compassion of the Three Jewels.

> Merely by seeing you, all sufferings caused by the three poisons
> are relieved, all darkness vanishes, all happiness is gained.
> Profound thoughts arise in my mind, my faculties are sharp.
> Food has the best taste, and all suffering is forgotten.

> I have found this long-lived but quickly passing joy.
> It is a happiness rare even in the god realms.

Therefore, you who kindly ransomed the life of this daughter,
I ask that you never abandon me.

The king took the hand of Manoharā and said:

Beautiful, captivating young maiden,
Listen well, celestial princess Manoharā.
You are an ornament of beauty for every god realm,
the main ḍākinī in the realm of Cakrasaṃvara,
who has come to be my consort for the sake of living beings,
to produce the union of clarity and emptiness,
found in the bliss of the mudrā embrace.

You are like a lamp that dispels the darkness
when traveling on the paths and levels,
illuminating all phenomena and showing
what to avoid and what to embrace.
Who else apart from you could reveal these to my mind?
Be happy, joy of my heart.

They could not bear to be apart for even one moment of all the joyous moments they spent with each other. Seeing this, the people also became free from suffering and their hearts were full of happiness. In the land the Dharma flourished, and the harvests were good and the crops bountiful. All famine, war, and sickness disappeared, and here began the enjoyment of the glories of a golden time.

However, it is said:

Wherever one works for the welfare of others,
there the hinderers reside.

Accordingly, the minds of the five hundred queens became influenced by demons and they began to resent Manoharā. Also, during the festivities her seating position, and the ceremonial offerings made to her, such as the silk scarves, and so on, had been superior to those of the other queens. The general talk, moreover, was universally of her beauty and noble ways. The king too had obvious affection for Manoharā, and he had given the hunter the choice of a queen from among the five hundred. All this had disheartened the queens. The people did not hold them in high regard, regarding them as inferior even to Manoharā's attendants. For the queens this was unthinkable. This led to talk of Manoharā, of her not being wanted in their company, and there were discussions about how to get rid of her, peacefully or violently. However, fearing the effect this would have on the king, nothing was done and time passed. Finally Arthasiddhi Lakṣmī, one of the more senior queens, practiced in the art of deception, spoke up:

> Listen to me, community of five hundred.
> Through that ill-omened and low-caste hunter,
> and that destructive mountain-dweller Prakāśamati,
> this wandering woman, the so-called Manoharā Devī,
>   came here.

> Some trouble-making ministers and citizens
> informed the king about this new and exciting prospect,
> and as soon as she arrived, he greeted her and gave her gifts.

> The lords and people were all assembled and a celebration
>   was laid on.
> Ornaments, clothes, servants, whatever she wished for,
>   she was given.
> Even when presenting gifts, the people showed us little respect,
> as when an official meets his servant.

> If the king is to have such high regard for a maiden
> merely escorted here by some homeless fisherman,
> we think it is shameful for a king to show so little respect
> to we five hundred queens, who by our fathers' names alone
> were met and royally escorted when taken as brides.

> In the past, we five hundred would catch the king's eye,
> and he would hold us in great esteem.
> Since this wandering, so-called Manoharā has arrived,
> it is not possible for us to be in the king's presence.
> If we do not devise a way to be rid of Manoharā,
> in the future it will become difficult
> even to have the esteem of servants.

The yogi Hari, the object of veneration for the king's father,
possesses many methods, oral traditions, and great magical
    ability.
Some of us should go to him
and seek a way to be rid of Manoharā.

Everyone agreed with what the senior queen had said. The following day
four suitable candidates for the journey prepared to leave the palace secretly.
Some of the other queens told them that if it meant finding a way to destroy
Manoharā, even if they had to offer their own clothes to the yogi, they
should have no regrets.

The four queens left the palace secretly and traveled to the place where
Venerable Hari lived. With their hands held high they presented him with
jewel offerings and requested:

Hear us, great object of veneration.
Take notice, most powerful of beings.
Turn your attention to us queens.
Events have occurred in the northern kingdom.

A wandering woman who goes by the name of Manoharā,
brought to the palace by a low-caste hunter,
has now been taken by the king to be a queen.
Unprecedented and lavish festivities were held and gifts
    were given,
and she was presented with many ornaments, clothing, and
    servants.

Now the king no longer pays his five hundred queens any
    attention.
As a result, the servants and entourage despise us.
Many months have passed since even one of the five hundred
    queens
has been in the presence of the king.

Consequently, Manoharā is by his side day and night
lavishing her with gifts and praise.

We five hundred are disheartened and find it hard to bear,
but for fear of disturbing the king's mind we have been tolerant.

Accordingly, with her officials and attendants,
Manoharā has become bold.
Thinking that there is no one on earth like her,
her self-regard grows stronger by the day.
She speaks with bravado, posing and strutting.

For we five hundred, there is now nothing we can do.
Therefore we four have come before you, great guru,
to ask, whether by curse, burning, power, or torma,
for a way to destroy Manoharā.

Whatever, great guru, you ask for we will offer.
If you are able to fulfill the wishes of the queens,
as a reward, we will fulfill any wish
the great object of veneration may have.
With your great compassion, look quickly upon this request.

Hari replied:

Listen to me, you four queens who come here.
Pay close attention to this ritual yogi.
Everybody says that the qualities of a wise and noble woman
are complete within Manoharā, and I have heard this too.

That the king had lost affection
for his five hundred queens, and so on,
had not reached my ears until this moment.
However, if what you say here is true,
then the king's actions can be seen to be at fault.

Especially if Manoharā and entourage have become bold,
their behavior arrogant, then the queens are correct.
The ears grow first, the sharp horns grow later,
and this situation bothers me greatly.

I will do what I can to fulfill the queens' wishes.
If I am able to do that, then for my reward,
I ask only the same as was given to the hunter.
How could Hari possibly be greedy?

The four queens fervently requested that the promise Hari made would not be undone. They returned home and reported back to the other queens, who were all very happy.

Meanwhile, Hari turned the prince's father's head and caused him to have a succession of bad dreams. In particular, one night the father dreamt that a flock of sheep, which were the life-savers[34] of the father, mother, and son, were attacked by a greater number of wolves and were all killed. Some of the sheep's heads were carried far away by the wolves. King Mahādhana wondered about the meaning of these dreams and together with several official and attendants went before Hari, his great object of veneration, and asked:

Hear me, great object of veneration.
Take notice, lord of the wise.
For many days now my mind is disturbed
with a succession of bad dreams.

In particular, last night there was a terrible storm.
I come before you to ask for a divination.
Please speak clearly, great object of veneration.

Hari replied:

Hear me, great father and king.
Pay attention, and listen to this ritual yogi.
You have had bad and troubling dreams,
and last night we saw a forceful storm.

Wondering what they meant, you decided to ask,
and today you came here. That is excellent.
Bring here the materials for divination.

A white, unwoven woolen cloth was laid out in front of him. On it were placed flour mixed with butter, an ale offering, meat from the right leg of

an animal, and ceremonial arrows. The divination charts were opened, and
Hari began:

> I invoke the gods! I invoke the gods!
> From the peak of great Mount Meru,
> I invoke Indra, lord of the gods,
> and the other gods from the Thirty-Three.

> From the levels of great Mount Meru,
> I invoke the four great kings and retinue.
> From the regions of this earth
> I invoke the twelve local goddesses.

> Invoking and making offerings to you today,
> I ask for an explanation of these events.
> I do not know the answer and so I ask the gods,
> who possess the eye of transcendent wisdom.
> If the answer is favorable, reveal a favorable sign.
> Be clear and distinguish between the good and the bad.

> For the first divination,
> concerning the throne of the king and father:
> The flag hoisted upon the high mountain
> is moved by the wind, and all is good.
> However, when moved by the violent winds
> that blow in all directions, it is otherwise.

> For the second divination, concerning the well-being of
>   Sudhana:
> On the banks of the river that runs through the narrow gorge,
> the flowers of the rhododendron tree are radiant in bloom,
> but when the thunder roars as the winter clouds gather,
> the flowers are quickly destroyed by hail.

This was the divination. Hari addressed the king:

> Listen to me, great father and king.
> In the charts spread out before me

a more troublesome divination this ritual yogi has not seen.
There is a great storm coming for the kingdom of father and son.
Specifically, a great enemy to the northern kingdom has arisen.

King Mahādhana said:

The explanations of both divinations do not bode well.
Their significance is that an enemy has arisen, you say.
From which direction will this enemy come?
Is he near, far away, or in between?
I ask that you perform divination again.

The ritual yogi declared: "I invoke the retribution gods and nāgas in the northern kingdom. Speak clearly on the divination for the fortune of the northern kingdom."

Hari explained the third divination concerning the forthcoming enemy:

A former enemy of the northern king
has become a tribe of many wild and unruly men
living far away in the north.
If an army does not set out this year to conquer them,
next year they will come to conquer you,
and the king's rule will be lost.

The king asked: "Is there a ritual to repel this enemy without sending an army there?"

Hari replied: "According to your request I will perform a fourth divination to see if there is a ritual that will stop them."

He performed the divination and said:

Even if you are to defeat this unruly tribe with an army,
you should apply yourself to the victorious army ritual,
the Mahākāla battle thread-cross, the torma of Yama,
the wrathful female divinities thread-cross, and suppressing
    rituals
such as the fixed-stare concentration of the wrathful deities.
Also, you should send Sudhana there with an army.

This is revealed as the best way to defeat these foes.
It is best to send him as soon as possible.

The father, Mahādhana, replied: "The divination indicates that rituals
and an army should be employed, but I dare not send the youth Sudhana so
far away. If someone has to go, it should be me that goes."
Hari replied:

Generally, bad omens have appeared for the northern kingdom.
Specifically, the great king and father is thinking wrong.
You asked me for divination, and if you do not listen to the
     clear results,
and say you will not send Sudhana to conquer this enemy,
there will be no outcome other than the enemy seizing the
     kingdom.

With these words Hari gathered up the divination materials. The king
pleaded:

Alas! Listen to me, great object of veneration.
Pay attention. Listen to this father.
I am only saying this because of my love for Sudhana.
I cannot bear to send him and would go myself.
I am not saying that your divinations are not correct.

If Sudhana does not go and the enemy is not defeated,
the consequence will be on our kingdom.
I have no choice but to send him,
though I will be sending away what I cherish most.
Whether that is sooner or later will be my son's wish.

Hari did not reply but only showed an angry face. Sadly, the king returned
to the palace and sent a minister to request that Sudhana come to his rooms.
The young Sudhana came at once, and his father said to him:

Alas! Listen to me, my son close to my heart.
You with the name of Sudhana, hear these words.

Previously, for several days I had inauspicious dreams,
and one night there was a terrible ill-omened storm.

With a troubled mind I went to see Venerable Hari for
    divination.
The divination indicated great disturbance and enemies, he said.
A former enemy of ours has arisen again
to become an unruly tribe in the north.

If they are not defeated this year with an army,
the following year they will come and defeat us, he said.
The responsibility for defeating this enemy was not given to me,
but my young son Sudhana was given this task.

This is the divination of our ritual yogi.
Therefore, my dear son, it is right that you go.

Sudhana replied:

Kind father, listen to me.
An enemy of the northern kingdom has arisen,
and if there is danger that these tribal men
will come here to conquer us, I will go there.

How could I refuse my father's command?
I have never gone against my father's words.
Now, on such an important matter, why would I refuse?
It is right that I go, as my father wishes.

However, mother is very loving and Manoharā adores me.
The worry that comes from their attachment
could turn into destructive consequences, I fear.
When I think about this, it makes me sad too.

There is no way I can go against my father,
but if mother, father, and Manoharā were of one mind,
this young son would be happy.

With a grim face Sudhana returned to his rooms. Manoharā saw that his face had changed. She took him by the hand and said:

> Ah! Supreme lord of men, of unparalleled kindness,
> lend your ears well to this maiden.
> Usually your young face is as bright and clear as the full moon.
> Now your complexion has changed and my mind is sad.
> In my heart I find this difficult to bear.
>
> Have your mother and father scolded you?
> Are you troubled because the five hundred queens resent me?
> Are your mother and father not well?
> Maybe you wish to cast me out of your thoughts.
> Has some wicked servant put doubts in your mind?
> Why do you wear such a grim expression?
> Tell me true, my most kind prince.

The prince put his tea to one side, looked lovingly at Manoharā, and with a deep sigh said:

> Beautiful princess, who I love from my heart, listen to me.
> Mother and father are well. They have not scolded me.
> Neither the queens nor the servants have disturbed my mind.
> Manoharā, the love in my heart for you has not changed.
>
> Today my father has spoken to me.
> He had disturbing dreams and approached Hari for divination.
> The results were bad. An enemy has arisen in the north.
> The instructions came that it was I that should go
> far in the north to tame these wild men.
>
> No way can I go against my father's words.
> Because I love my mother and you, Manoharā,
> I cannot bear it, and I wear this black face.

Manoharā took his hand and laid her head upon his shoulder. With tears in her eyes, and in great grief, she told Sudhana why he should not agree to go north:

Compassionate lord of men, of unparalleled kindness,
lend your ears to this maiden.
The command your father has given to you,
is the divination of Hari, his object of veneration,
saying that in the north a wild tribe has arisen
and it is you have that must go to subdue them.

Mahādhana is sending you to a land he knows nothing about.
There is no other prince in this northern kingdom aside
    from you.
That your father should dare send you is shameful.

An enemy has arisen when before there was none,
and dearest Sudhana is ordered to go to conquer them.
I do not know if this enemy is without or within.
I will go at once to see the great mother.
Would she dare send Sudhana, I wonder?

Sudhana replied:

Listen to me, celestial princess Manoharā.
I have no choice but to go to the enemy far in the north.
If Manoharā and my mother were to ask father
for me to be excused, I doubt he would agree.

The following day, as soon as she rose, Manoharā went to the great mother
and said:

Hear me, great and kind mother.
I have heard news that brings pain to my heart.
Not being able to bear it, I come before you.

To Sudhana, who is my very heart,
his father has spoken these words.
A wild tribe has arisen in the north, it is said,
and to subdue them Sudhana must go there.

This is the divination pronounced by Hari,
and if this enemy is not destroyed by an army this year,
the following year they will come and quickly destroy us.
It is the nature of Sudhana never to disobey father's command,
and so he will not go against his father and has decided to go.

I come to you, great mother, to offer you these thoughts.
Has there ever been a tradition of enemies in the north?
Why now do these wild men suddenly arise?
Has the great father not been tricked by others?

Is it not right, great mother, to approach the king
and ask that Sudhana might be relieved?

With these words she started to cry. The mother too was disturbed by this news. She said:

Listen to me, celestial princess Manoharā.
My young son is not to be sent so far away.
I could not possibly do this. We will go to father.
Who could possibly rely on this divination from Hari?

If this son, so close to my heart, were no longer here,
who would maintain the kingdom?
Today I have heard unpleasant news,
such news to make a mother sad.
We will go now to the king.

The mother held Manoharā and cried. Then together they went to the king. The mother said:

Hear me, lord father and king.
The king has said that tribal enemies have arisen in the north,
and that our young son should go to subdue them.

It makes no sense that enemies should arise in the north.
How can we be sure? Even if there were such enemies,
here our kingdom is powerful and prosperous,

and we can send an army, with as much support as necessary.
Who could possibly send the young Sudhana?

What suffering we two experienced
in the past when we had no son.
We made offerings to the Three Jewels,
gave alms to the poor,
cast tormas, erected thread-crosses,
invoked divination deities,
and I wore protection wheels on my body
and performed ritual bathing.
In response, our son Sudhana appeared.
To a mother her only son is like her heart.

If you send Sudhana to another land,
who will take care of the kingdom?
Without Sudhana there will be no need for subjects.
I come to ask you to excuse Sudhana of this duty.
Great father, you of great pity, you must relieve him.

The mother and Manoharā, with tears in their eyes, made many prostrations to the king. He replied:

Lady mother and Manoharā, so much talk.
Take these words of mine to heart.
Recently I had bad dreams that troubled me,
and I went before the master to seek divination.

It is not possible for his divination to be faulty.
He said that many wild men had arisen in the north,
and if they were not conquered by an army this year,
the following year they would come and conquer us.

In particular, the task of conquering them falls on Sudhana.
For that reason I am sending Sudhana to the north.
In an important matter, it is the destiny of a king to fight,
so do not come here with the foolish hope of excusing him.

Mother and Manoharā, with respect for what you asked,
I will delay his leaving by some days.
Do not cry for no good reason. Do not assault my ears
with your gloomy thoughts. Return to your rooms.

The father was angry, and in a state of despair the mother and Manoharā
went to Sudhana's rooms. His mother said:

Listen to me my son, who is my heart.
Hearing the news that you will have to go
to subdue this enemy makes your mother sad.

Manoharā and I went to your father,
where we pleaded for you not to be sent to the north.
The answer came that the divination of Hari could not
    be mistaken,
and that in important affairs the king's merit is to fight.

Therefore you are not to be relieved, but must go to the north.
He scolded us, and now if there is nothing we can do,
I, a mother of an only son, am distraught.

Sudhana replied:

Mother is advancing in age, and I am concerned about this,
but I cannot go against my father's command.
Listen to me, my mother.
Hear me and do not be distracted.
Mother and Manoharā, do not be troubled.

Manoharā said:

Listen to me, compassionate mother and son.
Lend your ears to this maiden.
The lord father has been listening to evil people,
and without pity is sending Sudhana to the north.
Though we begged him to excuse you, he was minded
    to scold us.

If the king is to go to the north for no good reason,
I ask that you take me with you.
Otherwise I will return to my country of Vṛkṣaḥ.

King Sudhana replied:

Manoharā, dear to my heart, listen to me.
There is no way for me to contravene my father's words.
My princess, do not say these things, Manoharā.
After I go to this northern land,
who will take care of mother and father?

My mother is old and she loves me dearly.
Manoharā, you must be her companion and comfort her.
There is the risk that what I am doing may kill her.
Do not speak this way, celestial princess Manoharā.

Father is about to send me to the north,
and this anxiety from mother and Manoharā,
will it ease my inner mind or help conquer my outer enemy?

Mother and Manoharā, if you were not to worry,
this young son would have no fear
about vanquishing the enemy in the north.

The lady mother said to Manoharā:

Celestial princess Manoharā, dear to my heart,
it is not possible to go against the lord father's word.
Let us perform rituals to ease Sudhana's mind.
We will hoist prayer flags and make firm prayers.
My young son will accomplish his task of crushing the enemy.
Come and let us do whatever is auspicious to help.

In keeping with the lady mother's suggestion, Manoharā and many male
and female helpers carried ritual substances for supplicating the gods to the
peak of the central mountain. At the king's fort on the central mountain,
Manoharā hung flags, made purification incense offerings, and then per-

formed the golden drink offering to the gods. Manoharā held in her hands a golden vessel complete with the five butter markers. Her attendant Ānandaśrī held a silver bowl filled with various grains and powdered gold. The attendant Sukhasamājā held a tea urn filled with ambrosia. Manoharā intoned:

> Gurus and buddhas of the ten directions,
> deities of the four classes of Tantra,
> I offer this precious golden drink offering.
> Grant me the power to accomplish my wishes.

> Blood-drinking Heruka with consort and retinue,
> direction protectors, and oath-bound ḍākinīs
> in the celestial mansion of Cakrasaṃvara
> on the vajra seat in the north,
> known as the white mountain of Kailash,
> I offer this precious golden drink offering.
> Destroy all hindering enemies and perverse guides.

> Dharmarājā and consort from the city of Yama in the south,
> and all your entourage of retribution deities,
> I offer this precious golden drink offering.
> Generate the mighty force to kill enemies of the doctrine.

> In the great lake of the northeast,
> mistress of the desire realm, Rematī,
> Queen Palden Lhamo, and your retinue,
> I offer this precious golden drink offering.
> Lead the divisions of Sudhana's army.

> Personal deity of the king of the northern land,
> Gertso Nyenpo,[35] together with your retinue,
> I offer this precious golden drink.
> Be a companion to king Sudhana.

> Five long-life sisters, the twelve local goddesses,
> and the powerful gods who live in the north,
> I offer this precious golden drink offering.
> Be a friend to king Sudhana.

Also, those deities, wherever they may abide on this earth,
who guard and maintain the ways of virtue,
and those fierce deities and their servant retinue,
who maintain the ways of worldly cause and effect,
I offer this precious golden drink offering.
Fulfill the wishes of this daughter.

Having completed the golden drink offerings successfully, Manoharā went to the top of a mountain to plant the fortune flag of the king and made many prayers. Then looking northward, she saw far off in the distance a similar snow-covered mountain peak, where snow was falling constantly. Thinking sadly how the king would have to travel far beyond that place, she became anxious and began to cry. Looking at her attendants, she said:

Listen to me, maidens who have gathered here.
Generally, nothing is forever with the phenomena of samsara.
Specifically, when I think of my own fortunes in life,
I fell into the hands of a low-caste hunter
from among a multitude of other celestial maidens,
and experienced the fear of almost losing my life.

Then, through the words of an unparalleled sage,
I was ransomed by the kind King Sudhana.
He loved me and became my affectionate companion.

Now by unwanted circumstance, suddenly we must part.
When did this maiden collect such bad karma!
I cannot bear that this young man travels alone
to those hostile lands in the far-off north.
Even though it may cost me my life,
I will not stay here but will go along with the king.

With these words she lost consciousness. Nothing that any of the attendants tried was of any help, and so a message was sent to the king in the palace. When he heard the news, Sudhana was beside himself with grief. Saddling the finest horse, which could travel like the wind, he immediately rode out and was soon with the princess. When he saw Manoharā unconscious with her beautiful dewdrop-like shining face nestled in the lap of an attendant, his heart almost broke. Taking water in his own mouth, he was able to give water to his beautiful maiden. After a short time, she regained consciousness. For a while they sat and held each other. Observing this, the attendants became worried. Then the king spoke:

> Truly beautiful and dearest Manoharā,
> do not be troubled. Listen to me, beautiful girl.
> When I heard that you had lost your life
> on top of this high mountain,
> I was distraught and came at once.

> I gave you water, and by the grace of the Three Jewels,
> you were among us again. This is truly a wonder.
> I am reminded of the compassion of the Three Jewels.
> Let us not stay here but return home.
> Let us return to the Land of Joy Palace.

Once they were safely in the palace, Manoharā said to Sudhana:

> Kind prince and leader of men,
> just by seeing you, the pain of this maiden disappears.
> Just by hearing your name, my body and mind trembles.
> Young Sudhana, listen to this maiden.

> On the high mountain I looked in all four directions,
> and when I looked to that place far off in the north,
> just by seeing it, I felt sad and troubled.

> I cannot allow the great king to go there alone.
> Even though it might cost me my life,
> I ask that you take me along as your attendant.

> Could you bear it if you left me behind?
> Please consider this, kind prince.

With these words she began to cry.

Around the time that Manoharā arrived back with the king, Hari again brought about false omens in the sleep of the father. He dreamt that father and son were naked and surrounded by many men. Everywhere, inside and outside the palace, was filled with people dressed in strange costumes. As soon as he awoke he went to the great reception rooms of the palace and gave the order to summon Sudhana, the lady mother, Manoharā, and all ministers and officials of the palace. When they had assembled, he spoke:

> Listen to me, Sudhana, son of your father.
> Recently, mother and Manoharā came to me
> and spoke of the outcome of my previous bad dreams,
> which was the existence of this enemy
> and that Sudhana had to go and defeat it.

> They asked me to postpone this venture,
> and I agreed to delay it for a few days.
> However, again I have had troubling dreams.
> Therefore, Sudhana, you should leave quickly.

> Tomorrow the necessities for the military camps will be
>   arranged.
> Make an inventory on the open ground by the southern gate.
> As for officials and aides, their weapons can be found in
>   tiger-skin chests
> marked alphabetically up to the letter *pa*[36]
> in the sealed great hall situated on top of the armory.

> They are the abode of our tutelary war god, and are usually
>   unopened.
> Our weapons are complete and in plentiful supply.
> However, Sudhana has not been to battle before,
> and I will provide you with special weapons.

> Those officials traveling with Sudhana and his retinue,
> announce your departure simultaneously to the people.
> Those officials and people who are staying behind,
> such as lady mother and Manoharā, do the following.

> Tomorrow morning, on the roof of the palace,
> hoist many standards, parasols, and banners.

On the plain at the southern gate, erect thrones.
In the center prepare butter flour, beer offerings,
  various grains,
food and drink, and so on, for a large military festivity.
Dress in auspicious clothing appropriate for the event.
Tomorrow is the presentation of the weapons,
and on the following day the army will set out.

Mother and Manoharā, the young prince has to go.
Do not conduct yourself with inauspicious behavior,
such as meaningless talk, shedding tears, and so on.

Thus the king gave orders to the officials and the people, and all carried out their duties accordingly. On the next day, all military officials and attendants who were leaving and all those who were staying behind assembled in their best clothes on the ground by the southern gate. The keys to unlock the weapon chests from the great hall above the armory were given by the king to lady mother, Manoharā, and the ministers. The king said:

Hear me, lady mother and Manoharā.
In the sealed great hall above the armory,
are kept the weapons of our forefathers of this northern
  kingdom.
The weapons are many and complete.
Sudhana has not been into battle before.
These special weapons I give to my dear son.

With these words the chests numbered from *ka* to *nga*[37] were opened and the weapons taken out. The king spoke:

All assembled here, especially Sudhana, listen to me.
This great helmet is known as the Sun Shining on Snow.
This armor is known as The Radiant Army.
This arrow quiver is known as The Thunderbolt Palace.
This arrow is known as The Thunderbolt Striker.
This leopard-skin sheath is known as Light in the Darkness.
This shield is known as the Intertwined Rainbow.

The weapons were placed before the king and an auspicious offering of food was made. Manoharā gathered her courage. Presenting the weapons one by one to Sudhana, she said:

> The king placing this great helmet on his head
> raises the glory of the Buddha's teachings higher than the
>   heavens.
> The king placing this armor on his body
> is like the turning of the wheel of the Buddha's teachings.

> The king placing this arrow quiver on his body
> is like the pleasant sun shining in the heavens.
> The king placing this bow sheath on his body
> is like clearing the darkness of ignorance in living beings.

> The king holding this sword in his hand
> is like firmly establishing the iron mountain of the teachings.
> The king strapping this great shield to his body
> is like entering a vajra pavilion.

> From the bows of the thick rain clouds of past imprints
> that float in the unbounded skies of the great aspiration,
> may the arrows of the hail of wrathful ritual activity
> destroy every sprouting shoot of the enemies of the teachings.

After the weapon presentation was concluded, the palace officials were given a list of weapons taken and a general inventory was conducted. As a token of auspiciousness, the king, the lady mother, Manoharā, and others presented Sudhana and his attendants with silk scarves of honor.

On the open ground at the southern gate, flags hung like falling snow, and after the festivities were complete everyone returned home. Sudhana, the lord father, the lady mother, and Manoharā assembled in one room. Sudhana spoke to his mother and Manoharā on the subject of Manoharā wanting to travel with him to the north:

> My most kind mother and my dearest celestial princess,
> pay attention and listen to me.

Manoharā has told me again and again
that she wants to travel with me,
and it makes me sad.

Mother and Manoharā, this young man
in all sincerity asks this of you.
Until I have returned from my journey to the north,
mother and Manoharā, please stay together in one house.
Maiden, willingly do everything my mother asks of you.
Mother, just as you love and cherish me,
similarly, take loving care of Manoharā.

The king placed the crown jewel of Manoharā in the hands of his mother
and said:

Manoharā and this crown jewel I entrust to you, mother.
Manoharā and I have no other refuge than you.
Unless there is a danger of her losing her life,
keep a close watch on this crown jewel, great mother.

Maiden, do not cry. I also am sad.
It is not possible for us to plead to my father for me
    not to leave.
The only outcome of coming together is parting.
This is what I say to you. Keep it in mind.

His mother replied:

Hear me. Listen to me, my son, Sudhana.
To die and to be separated is the way of the world.
Not to die and yet to be separated from one's life
is what has happened to this mother and son.
It would have been better had you not been born.

Yet my only-born son is being sent to an enemy country.
It could take many years for him to defeat this foe.

His mother's life cannot be sustained until
her young son finally returns from the north.

If I live a long life I will, of course, do as my son asks.
If I should die, I pray that mother and son
will meet again in a pure land.

Manoharā said:

Listen to me. Take notice, great king, you who are my heart.
The golden goose entrusts itself to the great lake,
but if the lake freezes and closes up,
the goose returns to the borders.

Goddess Manoharā entrusts herself to you, Sudhana,
but if the king goes north, this maiden returns to her country.
It is not that this maiden does not wish to serve your mother,
but wicked people will plot evil things against me.

Greatest of great kings, take this maiden with you.
Otherwise, send her back to the country of Vṛkṣaḥ.

The king replied:

Maiden, do not say this. Listen to me.
How could Manoharā possibly go to this enemy country?
This is no journey for this maiden to make.
In the daytime no human life is to be seen.
At night every type of demon emerges.

Moreover, we will both fall into the hands of the enemy.
They will be victorious and I will be defeated.
Do not say these things. Princess, stay here with mother.

Finally, Manoharā agreed to remain with the lady mother, who promised,
in keeping with the king's request, to give the crown jewel back to Manoharā
if the princess's life was ever in danger. That evening the mother took the
crown jewel and everyone went back to their chambers.

SUDHANA LEAVES FOR THE NORTH

Early the following day, the father summoned Sudhana and the other nobles in the great reception room. After presenting them with farewell presents, he addressed them:

> Listen to me, all nobles and attendants gathered here.
> For the farewell escort for my son who leaves today,
> I, his father, will bid farewell from the courtyard.
> The five hundred queens will say their farewells by
>   the southern gate.
> His mother will escort him as far as the first
>   mountain cairn.
> Manoharā will escort him to the second cairn.
>
> For the initial ceremonies of my son leaving,
> make the necessary arrangements as best you can,
> as I have described previously.
> Take note of all this, nobles and attendants.

The father gave orders to his own attendants and proceeded to the courtyard, where he gave Sudhana a farewell cup of ale and a ceremonial scarf, and addressed him thus:

> Listen to me, Sudhana, son of my heart.
> Going away today to conquer an enemy
> is for the sake and glory of our kingdom.
> And in this matter I am sending Sudhana
> because of his glorious abilities,
> and not because my heart is distant from him.
>
> Have no fear about conquering these savage foes of
>   the doctrine.
> Merely seeing you wearing this special armor and these
>   weapons
> will cause the enemy to weaken and fold.
> There is no need for anxiety. And when you have routed
>   the enemy,
> I pray that we are quickly reunited.

Sudhana prostrated to his father, and said:

Hear me, take notice, my great father.
You are kind with your words and the farewell ale.
For conquering this enemy, I will do as you have said.

I ask that father take these words to heart.
Defeating this enemy could take many years.
Father, you must lovingly take care of mother and Manoharā.
If by the designs of others you hear of enemies arising,
I ask that you do not let down mother and Manoharā.

Please father, keep this in your mind.
I hope that this son, by leaving will be worthy of leaving.
Kind father, do not disappoint mother and Manoharā.

With these words and the farewell prostration, Sudhana left. On the open ground by the southern gate the five hundred queens saw off the king with these words:

Hear us, Prince Sudhana.
Lend your ears to these five hundred queens.
Accept this auspicious farewell food.
We pray that when you have crushed this enemy,
we soon meet you here again.

Sudhana replied:

Hear me, my constant companions, my five hundred queens.
Pay close attention. Listen to Sudhana.
In obeisance to my father's words, I am going to subdue
    an enemy.
Stay well and healthy, my five hundred queens.
If I do not die, then by and by we will meet again.
I thank you for your kindness with this farewell ceremony.

With these words he cast a portion of the food as an offering and left.

When he arrived at the first mountain cairn his mother and her retinue offered him a cup of farewell ale. She addressed her son:

My son, you who are my very heart, listen to your mother.
For twelve long years this mother and son will not meet.
For twelve long years this mother's life cannot be sustained.
I am a mother, you my only son. You are like my heart,
but the end of all companionship is none other than separation,
and today that separation has come about.

You have to go away in order to vanquish an enemy.
It seems that it is by karma of the past that you must do this.
And so, without concern for me, develop courage,
and subdue this enemy, as your father wishes.
I will not again hold his words to be wrong.

The protection of the all the gods and men of the north
will travel with you as your army.
I, your mother, also send with you my heartfelt prayers.

With these words she offered a silver bowl filled with ambrosia to her son. Sudhana took his mother's hands and said:

Loving and most kind mother, listen to me.
There is no need to be anxious about your son going north.
The command to defeat this enemy has come down to me,
    your son.
Mother, you are advanced in age, and I am concerned.
The kindness of a mother is not something to be taken away.

Thinking how she lovingly placed me on her lap, I remember her.
Thinking how she gently covered my body, I remember her.
Thinking how I drank from her breast, I remember her.
Thinking how she looked at me with loving eyes, I remember her.

When I return from the north, and if you are still with us,
the wishes of mother and son will have been fulfilled.

If that is not for certain, and we do not meet,
I pray we meet in the next life.

Sudhana made his farewell prostrations and left. He traveled to the second stone cairn, where Manoharā and her retinue were to offer him farewell ale. Manoharā stood with a silver bowl filled with the best food offering and said:

Kind and loving prince, supreme lord of men,
listen to this Manoharā of little merit.
Soon you will leave from this place,
and until you return and we meet again,
I pray that no illness strikes you down,
and that having conquered all enemies of the teachings,
I pray that your hopes for bringing to happiness
all living beings who are limitless as space
are fulfilled exactly as you have wished.
I ask that you do not cast Manoharā from your mind.

With these words she placed the silver bowl in the king's hands and wept. With his right hand the king held the bowl and with his left he held Manoharā, saying:

Listen to me, my dearest Manoharā. Do not be troubled.
As we spoke of before, do as my mother says.
Do not listen to the prattle of evil people.
For yourself and others, strive to make offerings to
    the Three Jewels.
As soon as I have vanquished this enemy,
I will quickly return to this land.
Manoharā, love of my heart, this farewell ale
is elixir for my body and mind.
I cannot stay. Now I must go north.

As he made to mount his horse, Manoharā said:

Oh, no, no. I am so sad!
However I try, I cannot bear to be parted!

Seizing hold of the king's arrow quiver, she started to cry. The king said:

Oh, the mind of this young man is so sad!
I am about to go subdue an enemy at my father's behest,
and princess Manoharā on my right holds on to my arrow
    quiver.
Yet if I were to side with this maiden's mind,
I would be going against my father's command.
Whatever I do is difficult. My mind is so sad.
Maiden, do not do this. Think carefully about this.

Manoharā replied:

Hear me. Listen to me, my prince who is my heart.
Many days I have spent thinking about this.
However I try, I cannot bear to be parted from you.
A mare and its foal may be parted, but they are still within
    the stables.
When they think of each other, they call to each other.
The king and I will be separated by many passes and valleys.
Looking out, there is no way to see each other.
Calling out, there is no way to hear each other.

The mother yak and its calf may be parted,
but they are tied to adjoining stakes.
With calls of affection they can talk to each other.
Sudhana and I are to be separated by many passes
    and valleys.
Looking at the acts of affection that exist
between a mother and its offspring even in the animal
    world,
how can Prince Sudhana and I possibly be parted?

Prince, do not say these things. Take me to the north.
Even if it costs me my life, I will not remain here.
Down on the lake the pairs of golden geese congregate.
There are no single golden geese on the lake.
Up on the high cliffs the pairs of eagles congregate.

There are no single birds on the high cliffs.
In the four-cornered willow groves the nightingale[38] pairs
   congregate.
There are no single nightingales in the willow gardens.

Having been born, it is a certainty that all beings are parted
   by death,
but to be parted without dying is something that happens
   only to me.
Infallible Three Jewels dwelling in the unseen realm,
look on this maiden with her destructive bad karma
from within your realm of exalted wisdom.

As she spoke these words, she wept. The king replied:

Maiden, do not say this. Manoharā, you who are my heart,
I have no wish to be apart from you.
We are being separated by my father, a powerful lord of men.
My father's command came upon me like a thunderbolt.

Manoharā, do not cry. It oppresses our lives.
When a great horse is sold to another, one retains its bridle rope.
This is a custom of the past done for auspiciousness,
and as I am going to the north, I offer you these remembrances.

This helmet I will need to conquer the enemy,
but this headscarf I give to this beautiful woman
as a token of remembrance.
This long-sword I will need to conquer the enemy,
but take this Chinese knife, beautiful woman,
as a token of remembrance.
This horn thumb-ring I need to gauge the arrow notch,
but accept this finger ring, beautiful woman,
as a token of remembrance.
This quiver I need to conquer the enemy,
but take this heirloom, beautiful woman,
as a token of remembrance.

Do you hear me, celestial princess Manoharā?
Now help this young man on his way to the north.

The king wiped away the tears from Manoharā's face. She said:

Listen to me again, prince, who is my very heart.
Your tokens of remembrance are most kind.
Thinking of you, days and nights will have no end.
You are going into battle. Keep the Chinese knife.
Leave your vest behind for this maiden.
In that, she will place her hopes.

The king took back the knife and gave Manoharā his vest. She buried her face in it, wept, and sat down. In a moment the king and his entourage were gone. For a while Manoharā sat there surrounded by her attendants. Finally, she stood up and gazed far off in the direction the king had taken.

In the palace that evening she went to see the lady mother. Manoharā held her and wept. The lady mother said:

Listen to me, celestial princess Manoharā,
the sole child that was born to me
today has had to go to a far-off land.
In his place is a daughter who was not born to me.
Mother and son are of one mind in caring for you.
Do not be troubled, my Manoharā.

Manoharā replied:

Listen to me, great lady mother.
The mother who gave birth to me remains in Vṛkṣaḥ.
My companion husband has gone far away.
Apart from you, my mother from whom I was not born,
no one else close by is to be seen or heard.

They delighted in each other's company and loved each other more than mother and son.

After traveling for many days, King Sudhana came to a high and cold place known as Tiger Pass. In front of the stone cairn on the pass, he performed purification and offering rituals:

Ki ki so so![39] Glory to the gods!
I invoke the infallible Three Jewels.
Be my refuge now and in future lives.
I invoke the peaceful and wrathful meditation deities.
Grant me fulfillment of all my wishes.
I invoke the ḍākas, ḍākinīs, and Dharma protectors.
Watch over the teachings of the Buddha.

I make offerings to the twelve local goddesses.
I make offerings to the worldly gods, wherever they dwell.
I make offerings to those who guard the ways of virtue.
I make offerings to the gods of this northern land.
I make offerings to my personal protector.
I make offerings to the war-gods of men.
I invoke all the gods and deities who dwell on this
    mountain pass.

Be my refuge on my journey to the north.
Aid my army in destroying the enemy of the north.
Relieve the minds of my mother and Manoharā from
    their sadness.
Moreover, may all my wishes be fulfilled.
Ki ki so so! Glory to the gods!

They traveled on for ten days and came upon a place where water and vegetation were scarce and there was not even a bird or animal to be seen, let alone any semblance of human life. The king felt sad and said:

Hear me, my guru! Most kind root guru.
Sudhana goes to defeat an enemy, in accord with his father's
    command.
I do not know where to find the land of these wild men, enemy
    of the teaching.

After much traveling, coming across this desolate uninhabited
   northern plain,
where there is no vegetation, water, or trees, makes this young
   man sad.

Great refuge god, show me the path that leads to the land
of this enemy of the teachings, this breaker of the bond.
Gertso Nyenpo, personal protector of the northern land,
come as my refuge to deliver me from this evil place.

Having made this request to his personal protector, in the northeast a
white cloud suddenly appeared in the cloudless sky. Sudhana understood
this to be a sign and set off in that direction. After a long journey they came
across a spring with grass growing around. Here they made camp. For the
most part, the men and horses were close to exhaustion. Stopping at this
place was the rest they needed. The following day most of the men stayed
at the camp while Sudhana set off in the northeast with a few nobles and
servants to search for the path and for more grass and water. After a while
they came across a herd of wild asses. Sudhana gazed on these animals with
delight and affection, and said:

Having crossed many a pass and valley,
this son has arrived in this unknown land,
an evil place with no grass, no water,
and from which we must escape.
Today we have come across this herd of white wild asses,
and I see that compassion depends upon
the love between mother and child.

The male asses that are fathers go in front.
The female asses that are mothers stay behind.
The fortunate children run under the bodies of their parents.
They drink their mother's milk,
and the love of the mother is great indeed.

Seeing this, this young son thinks of his mother and Manoharā.
Just thinking about the love of these animals on this northern plain,

I see that mother and Manoharā are not separate from my mind.
Before my eyes my mother roams.
Before me as I walk, Manoharā fleetingly appears.

Although I am made sad remembering mother and Manoharā,
the infallible Three Jewels lift up my mind.
Being sad is of no use.
Now I must go to conquer this evil enemy.
I must follow my father's command and set off to conquer.
I will not stay here. We will set off.
Gods, show Sudhana the road to victory over the enemy!

Sudhana and the nobles left, and after a while they came across a place abundant with grass and water. Sudhana stayed there while one attendant was sent back to the military camp with the order to proceed to this place. Two days later the army arrived. There they made camp and the men and horses rested.

Four attendants took four good horses and were went ahead as scouts to search for enemy territory. Everybody else stayed in the camp. After traveling for three days, the scouts saw many cattle herders of the same race as the tribe they were seeking. They asked where the tribe was. They were told it was five days hence, and so they set off in that direction.

Arriving at the enemy territory, they saw that there were no buildings of stone and earth but only tents made of leather. For food, they ate and drank flesh and blood, and for clothing dressed in animal hide. For weapons, they had only knives. The four scouts returned to the king and gave their report. The king was delighted and said:

According to your report on your arrival,
the land of the enemy of the teachings is not far.
Now our army will prepare to head straight there.

Sudhana and the entire company decamped. When they reached the outskirts of the enemy territory, the wild men were terrified at the sight of Sudhana's army and in a state of anxiety they ran to the head of the clan. They told him of an army whose number was too large to count, and in their midst was a man the mere sight of whom rendered any enemy impotent. The head of the tribe spoke:

Listen to me, my clan. It has been reported
that an army has arrived in this northern land.
Are they here to attack us or seek refuge?
There can be no reasons other than these two.

The father and son tribe will go to meet them.
Bring all my weapons.
Sons, make ready the provisions.
Let us go together to meet this army.
Śuklā, don't sleep. Śuklā, get up.
Get up Śuklā. Prepare an incense purification offering.
There is no one to rival me. Come and see.

The tribe father together with his sons went to meet Sudhana. He said:

Having left your country behind, where are
    you headed?
Why do you come to the land of my tribe?
Are you seeking provisions—food or clothing?
Are you seeking a place of safety?
Why are you here? Explain in detail.

Sudhana replied:

Listen to me, father and son tribe.
I have come from the northern kingdom.
Where I will stay is not certain.
I go by the name of Sudhana.

My purpose is to keep watch over the Buddha's teachings.
I am the guide and protector of all living beings.
I am the butcher who kills all common enemies.
Apart from that I have no other purpose in coming here.
If you understand me, hold that in your mind.

Most of the tribe became afraid at the mere sight of Sudhana. The tribal
father was also afraid but pretended not to be. He replied to Sudhana:

You are a very boastful young man.
What enemy are you going to fight against?
Do you regard me as a friend or enemy?
You will be short-lived, coming and going on our land.

If you are willing to listen to me,
and do not stubbornly follow your own desires,
but show us some courtesy and respect,
then you can stay here as if it were your own land.
Whatever food we have, we can share.

If you stubbornly follow your own way, all pleasantries
    will be over.
For refuge here in this tribal land we have four kinds:
those of the hinderers, spirits, demons, and nāgas.
If you understand me, keep that in your mind.

Sudhana replied:

Pay attention, you corrupt doer of evil deeds.
Let alone coming to just your land,
I am master of the entire world.
Your refuge of hinderers, spirits, demons, and nāgas,
we regard as belonging to the realms of ghosts and animals.

Listen to me, you violator of oaths,
you enemy with your perverse objects of refuge.
If you do not know who I am, let me tell you.
I am the Dharma King Sudhana.

For my refuge, I am cared for by the Three Jewels.
I am aided by the meditational deities.
I have the support of the armies of the Dharma protectors.
I use spirits, demons, and nāgas as servants.

I have vajra armor to protect my body.
I have a horse that will go wherever I wish.

I have the trust of this long white spear,
I have the messengers of arrows.

I have the diamond, blood-drinking sword
of the murderous piśāca flesh-eating demons.
In you the ten qualities of an enemy of the teachings
are complete, and you deserve to die.
Surrender quickly, father and sons.

Hearing these words, the tribe immediately retreated and for a while occupied an area close to their town. There, weapons were handed out to the tribe. The father said:

Listen to me, my tribe.
The message of that man at the head of his army,
delivered beautifully in all his fine clothes,
is that he demands our surrender.

He portrays the posture of wishing to attack.
Now, think about how we are going to fight.
This old man thinks it would not be wise to fight them close,
so let loose your arrows and stones from a distance.

The tribe let fly a shower of arrows and stones upon sight of Sudhana and his army. Sudhana approached them and said:

Listen to me, tribal army.
Before I came here, you asked me to show myself.
Now I am here, you do not know how to fight.
As a practice for your entire army,
Sudhana will send a messenger of just one arrow.
If you can withstand this arrow, there will be battle with me.
If you cannot withstand it, you are all mistaken to fight me.

Sudhana shot a single arrow. In its wake many died, and the wind created by the arrow caused several men to lose consciousness. All realized that it was hopeless to fight Sudhana, and they began to prostrate to him. Sudhana said:

Listen to me, barbarian army.
I am not partisan toward any living being.
Alas! What a pity that you beings of evil deeds
do not hold the Three Jewels as your refuge.

Following my father's command, I am here to conquer.
If the father and his two sons were to flee,
out of necessity I could not let them go free.
For the rest, to kill them would be a sin.

If I am not to transgress my father's words,
convert to the Dharma and stay here.
If you understand me, hold that in your mind.

The tribe bowed their heads to Sudhana and happily promised to do what he demanded. The father and two sons came forward and said:

Listen to us, Sudhana and your army.
The reason for you coming here
is to kill us, father and sons, you have said.
In order to keep the lands held by us,
I launched an attack on you, Sudhana,
but I have not committed any wrong act.
Do not kill us. Let us go free.

We will share with you our entire land.
We will share all our servants with you.
We will share all our wealth and possessions
    with you.
We will share with you all our delicious food.
We will exchange our companion dancing girls.
Do not kill us. Set us free.

Sudhana said:

Pay attention, father and sons. Listen to me.
You are holders of a perverted refuge who deserve to die,

but you are not an enemy that has done harm to me.
Yet I cannot go against the command of my father.

Father and sons, the time has come for you to die.
It is a great pity, but you must die. It is my father's command.
Though it be cruel, you must die. It is my father's command.

Sudhana drew his sword and said:

Enemies, who in past lives made perverted prayers,
conquering you for the sake of self and others
is designed by karma.
You are not objects of my anger or hatred,
but I kill you in obedience to my father's command.

Over the crown of your heads is placed a weapon.
Meditate on consciousness transference
as learned from a qualified guru.
On your bodies of one fathom square is placed a weapon.
Meditate on giving your bodies to meat-eating birds and dogs.

Thus he killed the father and his two sons. By caring for them he had
blocked the door to the three lower realms. The tribe converted to the teach-
ings of the Buddha, and with great delight Sudhana said:

Ah! Such joy in my mind, such happiness as this.
Carrying out my father's command, such joy naturally arises.
Accomplishing for the Buddha's teachings, such joy naturally
arises.
Achieving all I set out to do, such joy naturally arises.
This without doubt is the compassion of the infallible
Three Jewels.

On the high snow mountain a marker will be placed.
Until the snow melts, no enemy of the teachings will arise.
In the depths of the lake a marker will be placed.
Until the lake dries up, no enemy of the teaching will arise.

Until the eon is over, no enemy of the teaching will arise.
Until the era of the teachings is ended, no enemy of the teaching
   will arise.
Having achieved all I set out to do, this all will naturally arise.

Having made this rallying victory speech, he continued:

We will stay no longer, but return home.
I think of my father. Let us return home.
I think of my mother. Let us return home.
I think of dearest Manoharā. Let us return home.
I think of the Land of Joy Palace. Let us return home.

THE QUEENS PLOT TO KILL MANOHARĀ

At around the same time, back in the northern land of Vaśin, the five hundred queens earnestly entreated Hari for a way to kill Manoharā, now that Sudhana was gone. Again the ritual yogi conjured up false omens in the dreams of the father. He dreamed that the saddled horses of Sudhana were fleeing back to the northern kingdom, and after them came an army and surrounded the palace. The flags were torn down and the father was expelled from the palace. The king was disturbed by these dreams and sent a messenger to Hari, telling him to come to the king with his divination implements. Hari arrived and made homage. The king said:

Hear me, great ritual yogi.
These days I have very bad omens in my dreams.
I ask that you perform divination to learn
if the purposes of sending Sudhana to the north
have been accomplished as the previous divination predicted,
and to learn about the fate of our throne.

Hari replied:

Listen to me, great father and king.
I, your object of veneration, could give you a divination,
but previously, on the matter of sending Sudhana to the north,
I presented you with you an honest divination.
If you have doubt and have lost confidence,

and think my divination instructions are not effective,
even if you receive divination, it will just be a cause of
  superstition.

Previously, if you had sent Sudhana off immediately,
his purpose would have been accomplished.
However, you delayed his leaving by a month.
The present bad signs are a result of this.

These things I tell you, great king and father,
but although you hear them, you won't like them, I fear.

Mahādhana replied:

Ritual yogi, pay attention. Please listen.
When Sudhana was being sent to the north,
Manoharā and his mother came to me asking for postponement.
Therefore I put off his leaving for a while.
I did not think to change the yogi's instructions.

Now I am asking for a divination about these disturbing omens,
and I will perform any ritual that is indicated by it.
Please give me a clear divination, mighty adept.

Hari replied:

I cannot go against the words of the great father,
and I will give you a clear and unmistaken divination.
Carefully lay out the butter dough, the ale mixture, various
  grains,
the red decoration, the purification incense, the decorated
  arrow, and so on.

The offering materials were laid out in front of him. Hari chanted:

I invoke the gods! I invoke the gods!
I invoke the gods of this world!
I invoke Pehar, Thanglha, Dorjé Lekpa.

I invoke the local gods, the earth lords,
and all-powerful gods, nāgas, and spirits,
wherever they dwell, I invoke you!

Today I ask you the question put by the king of the north.
Hari does not know the answer, and so I ask the gods.
Gods, clearly reveal the good and the bad.
Do not confuse right with wrong.

The words of the first divination concerned the future of the throne:

The light of the glorious sun in the high heavens
shines equally over all four continents,
but over your land the sun and moon are eclipsed
and the northern country is plunged into darkness.

In the valley waters of Swirling Turquoise Lake
the white-bellied fish swim in their shoals.
Though they are skilled in their dancing quick movements,
the waters will soon dry up and the fish will be cast on the land.

This is a bad sign that a kiṃnara spirit, never before seen,
is being sent as a ransom for all the gods.
Your prosperity has moved into an inferior divination house.
Now all manner of bad circumstance will arise without end.

Hari explained the divination:

Hear me, great father and king.
This divination is more disturbing than the previous.
The sun and moon in your land being eclipsed
and the northern kingdom plunged into darkness
is a sign indicating harm to Sudhana at the head of his army.
It signifies decline, and rituals to avert it are necessary.

The fish being left on dry land after the lake quickly dries
indicates bad fortune for the kingdom of Mahādhana.
It is a sign that the kingdom will be lost.

Rituals to reverse the signs of this bad divination
include those of the retribution deities,
the cross-thread ceremony, and the casting of tormas.
Father Mahādhana, perform the extensive bathing ritual.
If these are done as best as you are able,
all those bad events portended will be avoided
and the kingdom of the northern king will flourish.

Mahādhana replied:

Listen, great object of veneration.
The divination is disturbing, but there are remedies.
I will at once arrange all rituals the divination suggests.
Tell me what is needed. I am an old man.
I ask that you please perform the rituals.

Hari replied:

Great king and father, if, as you say, you will listen to me,
then prepare ingredients for the wrathful repelling torma.
One hundred twenty loads of *tsampa* for the resident and
    casting tormas,
and thirty loads of barley as grains for offering are needed.

For the meat torma, ten pieces of meat and one whole carcass.
For the butter torma, ten loads of butter
as well as purple dye are needed.

For the torma parasol and the dagger, five-colored silk strips,
for the ritual seat, four yak hides with heads still attached,
one hundred silk-decorated enemy-arrows, together with
    thread-crosses,
four sets of iron cooking pans, together with tripods—
these are the necessities for the torma casting ritual.

As a list of necessities for the extensive bathing ritual,
there is a bathing pool in front of the palace
with a three-cubit-square rock at the mountain base.

On that rock will be needed ten kinds of fat for anointing—
three kinds of animal fat, such as that of tiger, bear, and leopard,
three kinds of water-creature fat, such as fish, otter, and frog,
and especially the heart fat of a kiṃnara spirit.[40]

As well as the ten types of fat, the feathers of a crow and owl,
the flesh of a golden goose, the five-colored thread,
a knife that has killed a human, a horse and a dog,
firewood from the barberry tree, and a triangular cooking pan—
all will be needed for the bathing ritual.
If you say that you can perform a well-arranged bathing ritual,
your wishes, great king, will be quickly fulfilled.

The provisions for the torma ritual were prepared exactly as ordered. The
materials for the bathing ritual were mostly prepared, but the king did not
fully understand what the flesh of a kiṃnara spirit was, and asked Hari for
clarification. Hari said: "You will not have to search outside to find a kiṃnara
spirit. As this is a matter concerning the throne of the king, the kiṃnara is
none other than Manoharā. You should bring the fat from her heart."
The king's face darkened. He said:

Listen to me, great ritual yogi.
Listen well, powerful Hari.
This Manoharā is the beating young heart
of my young and dearest son, Sudhana.

How can it be right that we should kill her?
It would bring lifelong hostility between Sudhana and me.
And you, venerable one, would lose your life.
If there is any other way, please tell me.

Hari replied:

Listen to me, great king and father.
I performed divination and told you what would occur.
If you choose not to follow the divination instructions,
It will just be a cause for superstition.
This I told you previously but you did not listen.

If you choose to cherish something insignificant
over your son's life and your kingdom,
it makes no difference to me. Do as you wish.

For a while the king said nothing. He thought to himself: "Since Manoharā came here these troubles have all begun. Maybe what the venerable yogi has said is correct." He said to Hari:

Listen to me, great and venerable yogi.
Even though my son has great love for Manoharā,
it is our kingdom that is the issue here.
It is right to take her fat, as the venerable yogi has instructed.
Instruct us on the best way to kill her.

Hari replied:

Great father, Mahādhana, hear me.
It would not be good if Manoharā was killed by another.
If she was killed by the five hundred queens out of envy,
it would look better to the people.
Therefore you should give the instruction to the queens.

Immediately, Mahādhana sent a messenger ordering the five hundred queens to come before him. They arrived at once. The father addressed them:

Listen to me, five hundred queens.
Turn your ears to this old father.
Previously, I had troubling dreams,
and I asked our ritual yogi for a divination.

From the vast north a corrupt enemy had arisen,
and to conquer him, Sudhana had to be sent.
This was the divination given by our venerable yogi.
Because this was a matter involving our very kingdom,
I sent my young Sudhana to the north.

After that, I have had even more disturbing dreams,
and again I approached our yogi for divination.

He indicated that to avoid any oncoming trouble,
I must perform torma and thread-cross rituals
as well as an extensive bathing ceremony.

In the list of materials needed for the bathing ritual
was the fat of a kiṃnara spirit.
This will not be found by seeking elsewhere,
because the divination indicated that Manoharā
was the kiṃnara spirit sent as ransom for the gods.

Wherever she remains, trouble will follow.
The fat of her heart must be taken.
Therefore go you five hundred queens and kill her.
And quickly bring me the fat of her heart.

The queens were delighted. They replied:

Hear us, great king and father.
the king has given us his instructions.
They are given only once. Who could disobey them?
We ask, supreme king and father,
that you grant us a weapons requisition.

The father provided the five hundred queens with a requisition for all
the weapons they would need. A few days later the queens' military division
led by Hari surrounded the Land of Joy Palace with great noise and clamor.
Manoharā and her attendants heard the noise and wondered what it might be.
Looking outside, they saw Hari and the army of the queens. Immediately she
signaled to the gatekeepers to close the doors. All outer and inner gatekeepers
shut their doors. Manoharā ran to the lady mother, where she exclaimed:

Listen to me, great and kind lady mother.
I beg you, lend your ear to this daughter.
This morning a great commotion surrounded the iron-walled
    palace.
Hearing it, I wondered what it could be.
When I looked, I saw Hari and the five hundred queens
brandishing weapons, clamoring and baying.

This army of the five hundred queens surrounding
   the palace,
who are they after if not me?
When Sudhana was first instructed to travel north,
it was said that he in particular had to go,
and had to go at just that time.
At once this maiden expressed to mother and Sudhana
her thoughts that she did not know if this enemy
that Sudhana had been sent to conquer was within
   or without.

Those doubts have today come to pass.
I will not stay here but will return to Vṛkṣaḥ.
I pray, give me back my crown jewel necklace.

The mother became worried and agitated. She said:

Alas! Listen, celestial goddess Manoharā.
Until my son has returned to this land,
Manoharā and her necklace have been entrusted to me.
When it was entrusted to me I had to look after it.
When it is time to return it, I must give it.
Do not say these things, Manoharā.

The mother went to the turret of the gate of the outer iron wall with a few
officials and attendants. There she addressed the crowd:

Listen to me, you five hundred queens.
Pay attention, you black yogi, Hari.
Have you heard that Sudhana has been lost to the enemy
   in the north?
Have you heard there is to be a change in the reign of the king
   and father?
Other than these, you have no reasons for this wicked act.
If you know how to control yourselves, it would be best
   to do so.

A senior queen, well versed in the ways of deceit, stepped forward and spoke:

> Listen to us, great and precious mother of Sudhana.
> We have not heard that Sudhana was lost to the enemy
>   in the north,
> nor have we heard that the reign of the king will change.
> We have come here to carry out the instructions of the
>   lord father.

> These high cliffs are surrounded by traps and snares.
> Does the white eagle have anywhere to go? Look and see!
> These high plains are surrounded by wild hunting dogs.
> Does the brown stag have anywhere to run to? We will see.
> The willow groves are surrounded by birds of prey.
> Does the nightingale have anywhere to go? Let us see.

> This palace is surrounded by the five hundred queens.
> Does Manoharā have any place to flee to? Let us see.
> In obedience to the command of the great father,
> we have come to take fat from the heart of the goddess.
> Great and precious mother, come to watch the spectacle.

As the hearts of the five hundred queens had clearly been taken over by a demon, the mother paid no heed. Moreover, they stood in front of her in various provocative poses. She raced to Manoharā, told her what the queens had said, and began to cry. Manoharā said:

> Listen to me, kind lady mother.
> If it is true that compassionate Sudhana has not been lost
>   to the enemy,
> then Manoharā has no fear of the queens' army.
> Having given the crown jewel necklace to the lady mother,
> King Sudhana said that it be returned if this maiden's life
>   was in danger.
> Therefore, kind lady mother, you must return it to me.

The lady mother took the necklace from the higher-offering temple. She gave half of the necklace to Manoharā and kept half for herself. She said:

> Listen to me, celestial goddess Manoharā Devī.
> In the north the wicked deeds of an oath-violator have
>   come about.
> Although now you have to return to the land of Vṛkṣaḥ,
> when my son returns from the north, come back, Manoharā.
> Sudhana, my son born to me, has been sent to northern regions,
> and Manoharā, my daughter not born to me, must return to
>   her land.
> This I feel to be a bad omen for a life of suffering.

Manoharā replied:

> Kind lady mother, listen to me.
> Do not trouble yourself on my behalf.
> Perform long-life rituals for Sudhana,
> make offerings to the Three Jewels,
> look after your health, do not be anxious over me.
> My attendants will protect me with their lives.
> Today for the five hundred queens,
> Manoharā will put on an extraordinary show.

With these words Manoharā placed the necklace around her neck and went to the roof of the palace. In response to the queens' demands, she said:

> Listen to me, queens and Hari.
> These high cliffs are surrounded by traps and snares.
> The white eagle does not stay but flies to the pure skies.
> He shows off his wings and soars through the heavens.
>
> These lakes are encircled by fishermen's hooks and nets.
> The fish does not stay but travels down the stream of
>   the Ganges.
> She shows off her golden eyes and swims down the
>   best currents.

These high plains are surrounded by wild hunting dogs.
The stag does not stay but moves to the higher hills.
He shows off his ten-branch antlers and goes
to where the grass and water is best.

The willow groves are surrounded by birds of prey.
The nightingale does not stay but goes to the deep tamarisk
    forests.
She gives forth with beautiful voice and flies to the trees.

This palace is surrounded by the five hundred queens.
Manoharā does not stay but flies to the celestial realms on high.
She shows off her necklace and travels to the Vṛkṣaḥ palace.

Having given her message clearly to the ears of the five hundred queens,
she acceded to their demands and ordered the gates to be opened. Hari led
the army and, accompanied by the clamor of the five hundred queens, they
stormed into the palace. As soon as the queens reached the roof of the pal-
ace, Manoharā flew into the air like a bird and posed before them in the
skies, saying:

Listen to me, you wise queens.
Listen well, black and powerful Hari.
If you have a good arrow, then fire it at this maiden.
If you have a long spear, then throw it at this maiden.
If you want to challenge this maiden, fly to the open arena
    of the sky.
If you want the fat of this maiden's heart, come here to
    the high skies.

Is this a good show for you, you five hundred queens?
Are your wishes fulfilled, black Hari?
Eventually, I will put on an even greater spectacle than this.

One queen, who was clever with words, pointed at Manoharā and gloated:
"So-called goddess Manoharā, you wanderer of no abode, what good is it
now you no longer live in the Vaśin palace of the northern kingdom?"
Manoharā flew away like an eagle soaring through the sky. The queens

felt foolish and started blaming one another. The air became filled with the noise of infighting. Hari intervened and said:

> Listen! Listen, you five hundred queens!
> Stop all this shouting and listen to Hari.
> In the beginning you had all kinds of wild thoughts.
> The task of bringing about those thoughts fell to me.
> The banner of disgrace has been raised high today.
>
> Now what will we say before the lord father and king?
> When Sudhana returns from the north, what will we say?
> Stop all your shouting. It is making me depressed.

The queens looked at one another and were almost in tears. Hari went to the lord father and said:

> Listen to me, great king and father.
> Manoharā, the destructive force who has brought
> all these bad omens to the northern land, has today left.
> The obstacles to the lord father and king are almost dispelled.
>
> The materials for the bathing rituals are not complete,
> but it will be sufficient, I think, to perform with what you have.
> The obstacles to the lord father and king are almost dispelled.

Various substances were put in the newly fashioned bathing pool and the king took part in a so-called bathing ritual. He had been deceived by the lie that future obstacles would be averted this way.

Up in the skies Manoharā thought: "Gracious Sudhana is a man of great love, and when he returns from the north he will miss me greatly. It is possible that he will come after me. I must send a message back to him warning him of enemies and bad spirits on the road to Vṛkṣah. That message I must entrust to the great sage from Ke'u cave." Manoharā went to the stone retreat marker of Ke'u cave in the midst of the hills and cried out:

> Great one who lives in this cave,
> possessing the excellence of meditative concentration,

pay attention. Listen to this maiden.
I have something heartfelt to ask of you.

Inside, the sage thought: "Today someone whose voice sounds like that of Manoharā is calling." Seeing that it was indeed her, he invited her into the cave and said:

Hear me, celestial princess, Manoharā.
Pay attention. Listen to this sage.
When the hunter captured you and you came here,
by my words you were sent to Sudhana in the north.

Even this sage was made aware of the renown
of this perfect union entrusted with karma and prayer.
Why have you suddenly appeared here today?
Tell me, without fabrication, of this heartfelt request.

Manoharā responded:

In the presence of the one who possesses
the nonapprehending ārya mind of enlightenment
with compassion for all living beings, infinite as space,
great treasure skilled in sending down rains of Dharma,
a second venerable and wise Avalokiteśvara,
lend your ears and listen to Manoharā.

This maiden was captured by the hunter
and was in a state of great torment.
Then the hunter, in accord with the words of the great sage,
offered this maiden to Sudhana in the northern kingdom.
I was freed from the danger that may have cost me my life.
The hunter received wealth and recognition in this very life,
and I met my companion who loved and cared for me.
The kindness of the great sage is hard to measure.

However, misfortune has fallen upon this maiden.
The lord father has been deceived by a wicked person.

For no good reason Sudhana was to be sent to a far-off
    enemy land.
As he was about to leave, the lady mother and I
presented a fervent petition to the lord father,
pleading that Sudhana not be sent away.
He did not agree, but postponed the leaving for a while.

On the day of his leaving, when his father offered him
    farewell ale,
Sudhana made an affectionate plea to his father,
that until he returned from his travels in the north,
father and Hari should meet and agree to care for me
    with great love.

However, not long after Sudhana left for the north,
father and Hari met and armed the five hundred queens.
The palace was quickly surrounded by an army
and the queens were shouting for the fat of my heart.
I immediately escaped. I had to return to my land.

Sudhana has great love for me and he may try to follow me.
Great sage, please get this maiden's message to him.
Tell young Sudhana that at best, he should follow the holy
    Dharma.
Next best is that he rules the kingdom according to his
    mother's wishes.
At least, if there is a possibility that he may try to follow me,
please place this ring in the hands of Sudhana.
Guru, please give the following message to him.

Manoharā took the ring from her finger and gave it to the sage. She
continued:

A few leagues further on from this place
are the Brahma court bathing pools.
If the Dharma king bathes in these pools,
he will be freed from dangerous paths.

A few leagues further on from that place
the air is filled with flesh-eating insects.
Waving this maiden's ring at them, he should move on.

A few leagues further on from that place
is a white shrine endowed with blessings
created by the consecration of a former buddha.
There the Dharma king should prostrate and
    circumambulate,
and all that he wishes for will come true.

A few leagues further on from that place
is a square, flat crystal rock, the size of a tiger-skin seat.
Underneath it is a piece of fine white Varanasi silk.
Carrying it on his right shoulder as he would a bow,
will ensure that the Dharma king be free of the dangers
    of the path.

A few leagues further on from that place
is a self-arisen rock in the shape of a sleeping elephant.
Next to it is a hammer made of iron.
With it he must pierce the back of the neck of this
    stone elephant.
Inside is a pot of immortality-granting nectar.
If it passes the lips of the Dharma king,
he will not be cursed by unwanted illness.

A few leagues further on from that place
there is a thick forest with many wild animals.
Waving this maiden's ring at them, he should move on.

A few leagues further on from that place,
in the midst of flowers, are a number of small paths.
Which to take and where they lead is hard to know.
Waving this maiden's ring at them, he should move on.
The honey-like, soft drizzle will lead him on.

A few leagues further on from that place,
below a particularly high and steep pass,
are venomous snakes and pools of boiling poisonous water.
Waving this maiden's ring at them, he should move on.
The brown stag will show him the right path.

A few leagues further on from that place
he will arrive at a high mountain pass.
From there you can see the realm of Vṛkṣaḥ.

A little further on from that mountain pass
is a spring known as Resembling a Heap of Jewels.
From it you can drink the water of Vṛkṣaḥ.
If the Dharma king arrives at this spring,
he will be freed of all obstacles on the path.
Please tell of these things, great sage.

The sage promised to relate to Sudhana exactly what the maiden had said.
In an instant Manoharā arrived in Vṛkṣaḥ.

SUDHANA RETURNS HOME
At around this time Sudhana had successfully left the wicked lands of the
north and was approaching the outskirts of his own country. With joy he
remarked:

Ah! Such joy in the mind of this young man!
Ah! Sudhana is experiencing such happiness as this.
According to my father's command, I have conquered
    all enemies.
For the Buddha's teachings, I have accomplished great things.
Having traveled to the evil enemy land, I am approaching home.

My mother, who created this body and mind, I long to meet.
Manoharā, who is like my own heart, I long to meet.
In my mind I recall the compassion of the buddhas.

Leaving the army encamped, Sudhana and a few nobles and attendants went
ahead to Tiger Pass. There he performed thanksgiving and praise to the gods:

Nondeceiving Three Jewels and meditation deities,
great compassionate ones who work for others,
granting the power of accomplishing whatever is wished for,
Sudhana offers his prayers to all refuges and guides.

Ḍākas and ḍākinīs, Dharma protectors,
all guardians of the teachings of the Buddha,
the young Sudhana today offers his prayers.
Also, to all powerful gods and nāgas who delight in me,
today I offer my prayers.

The blue smoke of the purification-offering ritual swirled up from the pass. From the east two crows appeared. The king thought to himself: "Since I left for the north until I arrived here today I have not seen any crows. These two birds might well be manifestations of the local deities of the northern kingdom." He called to these two birds:

Birds, whose color is that of dark sapphire,
flying through the skies at a moment's thought,
you are manifestations of the protectors of the northern
    kingdoms.
Listen today to the words of this young man.
Is all well with my lord father?
If it is, fly clockwise and come to eat of this butter dough.
If all is not well, then fly counterclockwise.

The two birds flew in a clockwise circle, came to land near Sudhana, and ate the butter dough. Sudhana was delighted and said:

The actions of these birds are signs that my father is well.
Is all well with my lady mother?
If so, fly in a clockwise circle and eat of this butter dough.
If all is not well, then fly counterclockwise.

The birds flew as before, and Sudhana was very happy. He said:

Ah! The mind of this young son is so happy!
The mother who created this body and mind is well.

When leaving for the north, I prayed that we would meet
    in the next life,
but by the compassion of the Three Jewels, it seems we
    will meet in this one.
Thinking this, such happiness naturally rises in my mind.
Birds, I have one further question to ask of you.

The maiden, Manoharā, so close to my heart,
if all is well with her, fly in a clockwise circle,
eat butter dough and utter three friendly cries.
If things are not well, fly counterclockwise,
scratch the ground with beak and claws and beat
    your wings.

The bird flew far off for a while. Returning, they flew counterclockwise and landed on a rock, where they scratched with their beaks and claws and beat their wings. Sudhana's face turned black and he kicked at the materials for the god-offering ritual, saying:

Infallible Three Jewels who dwell in the unseen realm,
the law of cause and effect, whether gross and subtle,
will produce its individual results.
Accordingly, to the gods and people of this northern kingdom,
as exemplified by the lord father, I made heartfelt pleas
for the protection of my mother and Manoharā.

However, on returning home it seems that Manoharā
    is no more.
The men and gods of the north have no love, compassion,
    or care.
These birds are not celestial birds but demon birds.
My life has been taken away by these two birds.
Demon birds, you will not escape my arrows.

He prepared to shoot the birds. The birds were unable to fly away and just bowed their necks toward Sudhana. The bodhisattva mind took hold of Sudhana. He felt remorse, and said:

Alas! By the fruit of evil deeds gathered long ago,
much unwanted suffering is brought to this life.
If now I do not subdue my own mind,
even though I subdue outer enemies the whole of my life,
it would be like the unceasing ripples on the water.
Sudhana, do not be proud. Subdue your self-clinging.

Having conquered his pride, he sat on the pass lost in thought. After a while he turned to the birds and said:

Listen to me, you pair of mating birds.
Today, by examining the behavior of birds,
I learn that my Manoharā is no more.
If that is so, and I were to return home,
it would only be a cause for sorrow.
However, to meet my mother, I will return once.
Birds, carry this message for me.

Sudhana wrote these words on the arrow message:

This letter is offered to my mother and father, who are the refuge and the guide for all beings in the northern kingdom, and to all subjects and citizens, exemplified by the celestial princess, Manoharā. The good health of my mother and father, the happiness of the maiden Manoharā, and the safety and well-being of the entire kingdom are fundamental. I, Sudhana, and my army traveled successfully to the north and destroyed without trace all the enemies of the north. Those who could be tamed by whatever means, and were worthy of entering the Dharma of the Buddha, I placed into refuge and established religious and secular rule. Through this twin system of government, I developed the land as a soft piece of silk.[41] I, Sudhana, and my army are now on our way home at Tiger Pass, where I have performed a thanksgiving offering and ceremony for various refuges. Soon I will be at the Land of Joy Palace. The sequence of welcoming parties is to be determined by the lord father, and the welcoming parties, as exemplified by Manoharā, must come to the meeting places along the route. In this way I will learn the details of my mother and father's health.

This letter is sent by Sudhana on an auspicious day on Tiger Pass
by way of these two birds.

The two birds took the arrow letter, flew to the north, and landed in front
of the king as he was walking on the palace roof. The crows called out loudly
and the king took the arrow letter. Seeing that it was from Sudhana, he was
delighted. He sent out a summons calling before him the lady mother, the
five hundred queens, attendants, and prominent citizens. They came at once,
and the king declared:

> All you gathered here, exemplified by the five hundred queens,
> pay attention and listen well to what I have to say.
> This morning on the roof of the palace,
> I was doing my morning circumambulations
> and two crows brought me this letter.
> It is a letter from Sudhana.
> It says the following. Listen well.

He read aloud the letter for all to hear. The five hundred queens and Hari
stared at one another and said nothing. After a while the lady mother stood
up, bowed to the lord father, and said:

> Listen to me. Pay attention, lord father and king.
> In this arrow letter from our son returning from the north
> is the good news that he has conquered the enemy and will
>   soon be with us.
> But Manoharā is not here and I, the mother, am very sad.
> How does this sit in your mind, lord father and king?
> How does it sit in your mind, five hundred queens?

> In my simple mind I know not what to think.
> Do I think about the joy of seeing my son return from
>   the north?
> Do I think of the pain of there being no Manoharā here
>   for him?
> This mother is pulled between pain and joy.
> Lord father and king, give your orders.
> Quickly arrange the order of the welcoming parties.

The lord father said:

Listen to me, people of the northern kingdom gathered here.
Pay attention. Listen to this old man.
Lady mother, do not be sad that Manoharā is not here.

The welcoming parties can be arranged as follows.
Prepare for the lady mother's welcome at the second
    mountain cairn.
When you meet him, he will ask the following:
"Why is the welcome of Manoharā not first?
Why does the welcoming ale of the mother come first?
Please explain this to me, lady mother."

Then you should answer him, lady mother, by saying:
"Manoharā has gone to Vṛkṣaḥ to see her family.
But once Sudhana has returned, she will soon return."
Do not talk too much, lady mother. Keep this in your mind
and perform the welcoming ceremony in this way.

Arrange for the queens' welcoming to be at the first cairn.
Present him with fine clothes and offer to clean his face.
Show him smiles and joyful expressions as best you can.
Arrange for my welcoming to be at the southern gate.
I will see that father and son meet under auspicious
    circumstances.

Everything was arranged as the king ordered. A few days later the lady mother and her entourage traveled to the second mountain cairn, where preparations were made for welcoming Sudhana with food and drink.

A horseman was sent to see where Sudhana was. He returned and reported his sighting of Sudhana to this mother. Soon Sudhana appeared over the mountain and could see the preparations made in his honor by the second cairn. He thought that although Manoharā was not at the preparations, his mother probably was, and so he headed toward it. At the site he saw his mother, and from about a bow shot's distance he dismounted and walked toward her carrying a ceremonial scarf in his outstretched hands.

The lady mother also walked forward. They met and exchanged ceremonial scarves and greetings. Sudhana prostrated to his mother and said:

Hear me, most kind lady mother.
I have served well the duty of one who left his land.
Has the kingdom performed its duty as those who stayed
    behind?
Lady mother, are you in good health?
Why does the welcoming ale of lady mother come first?
Why is the welcome of Manoharā not first?
Most kind mother, please tell me honestly.

His mother replied:

Welcome, my young Sudhana!
It is excellent that my son has been a worthy traveler.
We residents have served our duties remarkably.
Apart from her body and mind being wracked with worry,
your mother has not been afflicted with any troublesome illness.
Sit down my son, and slowly I will tell you all.

Sudhana looked grim. He sat down and said:

Listen to me, my lady mother.
What the birds said on Tiger Pass is true.
Is my celestial princess Manoharā no more?
Mother, tell me, how did this maiden die?
If by illness, it is regrettable, but nothing can be done.
Did this maiden die by evil thoughts and doubt?
Was she killed by a wicked adversary?
Tell me of the circumstances under which she died.

The lady mother replied:

Listen to me. Pay attention, my dear son.
Do not be distracted. Listen to your mother.
It is simply that Manoharā is not in the palace.

There have been no such acts that have deprived her of her life.
My son, do not worry. Take some of this welcoming ale.
I still have more to tell you of in detail.

Sudhana accepted the drink from his mother and said:

Listen to me. Take notice, my lady mother.
If what you say is true, it appears that Manoharā did not die.
If this maiden is alive, then the mind of this young son is happy.
Is my mother turning my mind with her words, I wonder.
Previously, on Tiger Pass, when I heard the message of the birds,
I had no desire to come to this northern kingdom.
I came here just this once to meet my kind mother.
It is so wonderful to meet the mother who gave birth to me.
But I am so sad that my celestial princess Manoharā is not here.

His mother replied by way of acrostic verse:[42]

ka) Sudhana, young son of a mother endowed with the
primordial activity,
kha) obedient son who has successfully returned from the
north,
ga) victorious in where he was sent, subduing my enemies,
protecting my friends.
nga) Son and mother have met. Accept this delicious
welcoming ale.
ca) Complete with the five butter markers in the yellow Dakpo
wooden cup,
cha) and in keeping with all good customs, accept this ale from
your mother.
ja) This tasty ambrosia spirit has been poured into this tea pot.
nya) Do not be reluctant, my son. Drink up!
ta) On this second pass, your mother holds up the welcoming ale.
tha) The vile and wicked Hari has not polluted this ale.
da) Stay seated where you are and I will slowly reveal all.
na) Young Sudhana has successfully returned from the north.
pa) The lord father and king has been deceived by a wicked
person.

pha) Powerless, the lord father let loose the army of the queens.

ba) This beautiful goddess, more precious than a hundred other maidens,

ma) I had no choice but to send her to the celestial realms.

tsa) The situation was critical, and the useful jewel garland

tsha) I placed in the hand of the maiden.

dza) Without hesitation she went to the land of Vṛkṣaḥ.

wa) The army of twenty-five hundred clamored like yapping foxes.

zha) They did not descend on this crippled old mother.

za) This confused army filled my body with unease.

a') Mother and son have met. Drink this welcoming ale.

ya) My remarkable son has happily returned to his homeland.

ra) These answers in the conversation between mother and son

la) I have given on this mountain pass without addition or omission.

sha) It has been a speech of affection. Take it to your heart, my son.

sa) Do not remain here but go inside the palace.

ha) Have you mostly understood, my son Sudhana?

a) Alas! Before I die, return to the kingdom, Sudhana.

Once back on his horse, Sudhana rode to the first cairn, where the five hundred queens offered him welcoming ale, washed his face, and presented him with fine clothes. Standing in front of mounted Sudhana, they said in unison:

Hear us, great king, possessed of the name of Sudhana.
Turn your ears toward your five hundred queens.
Having destroyed without trace the far-off enemy,
you return in glory and splendor to your country.
The sun of happiness of the northern kingdom has risen.

At the queens' welcoming ceremony, Sudhana did not dismount. Sitting on the horse with his feet in the stirrups and his horsewhip on his knees, he said:

Listen to me, my five hundred constant companions.
I have lived up to my duties away from home.

Have you lived up to your duties at home?
You are well and we have met face to face.

I, Sudhana, have destroyed completely the tribal enemies.
I still have many enemies, but now is not the time to
    conquer them.
It has been most kind of you to offer me this welcoming ale,
but if Sudhana had a craving for ale, he would inflict harm
    upon himself.

With these words he left. The queens stood there crestfallen and worried.
Sudhana arrived at the southern gate for the welcoming ale to be given by his
father. He dismounted and offered a ceremonial scarf and prostrations to his
father. His father said:

Welcome! Sudhana, my son.
Have you conquered all those enemies of the teachings?
Your body was not afflicted by the torment of illness?
Did you think of your mother and father after so
    long apart?
Sudhana, tell me of your travels.
Today father and son are reunited.
Accept this welcoming ale from your old father.

Sudhana did not sit down but leaned on his bow like a walking stick
and said:

Listen to me. Take note, lord father and king.
As was my father's wish, I have conquered all enemies.
This son has lived up to his duties away from home.
Has father lived up to his all-encompassing duties at home?

As I was leaving for the north, you agreed to do what I asked
    of you.
Did that promise remain with you?
I do not see my beloved Manoharā where she should be.
Most kind lord father, show me Manoharā.

His father replied:

Sudhana, do not be foolish. Listen to your father.
The words that passed between father and son
remain as before. Of that there is no doubt.
The celestial princess Manoharā has left for Vṛkṣaḥ.
She has gone to meet her mother and father.

Sudhana, there is no reason to grieve for Manoharā not
    being here.
You have the five hundred queens you took previously.
As many queens as you desire I can get for you.
Although the goddesses herself is not here,
we can search for a maiden resembling a goddess.
You can give her the name "beautiful goddess."
You can tie a precious necklace to her body.
Sudhana, do not be sad. Sit here a while.

Sudhana replied:

Listen to me one time, lord father.
As I was leaving for the north,
I spoke these heartfelt words.
If this son was to remain many years away,
that you would not cast mother and Manoharā from
    your mind.

Although the entire northern kingdom had to keep this
    in their minds,
the result is that Manoharā and I cannot see each other.
Lord father, how could you dare do this?
The people of the northern kingdom have no love or compassion.

Of what benefit is it for me and Manoharā to be apart?
A lookalike goddess I have no need of.
A kingdom without Manoharā I have no need of.
I will go in search of Manoharā until I find her.

Until I find Manoharā there is nothing to do but to be
elsewhere.

You did not listen to what I asked you to do, father.
If you are prepared to take the words of another as true,
this son now asks his father to be excused.

Sudhana made no attempt to enter the palace but instead prepared to set
off in search of Manoharā, as he had announced. His father was ill-tempered
and became very angry. He said:

Wicked Sudhana, you degenerate son. Listen to me.
If you are going to leave because of cherishing
one young woman over your parents and kingdom,
you damage your reputation in the eyes of all
and are a disgrace to this royal family of the north.
If you say you are leaving for another land,
take off my treasured weaponry and armor.
You drifter, wherever you want to go, go now!

His father was close to beating his son. Sudhana was crestfallen, and said:

Lord father, do not be so agitated. Hear me.
Although they had no intention to attack us,
following my father's wish, I conquered blameless people,
which has become a cause for pity and regret.

From now on I have no external enemies to conquer.
Following the wishes of my parents, I offer this armor completely.
With the bad motivation of protecting self and killing others,
I wore this armor and weaponry and conquered.
Now I have no need of weaponry and armor.
Please accept them undamaged, my father.

Sudhana placed all his belongings before his father and said:

Infallible Three Jewels who dwell in the unseen realm,
what evil karma have I collected in lives gone by?

First, I was sent to an unknown land for an unknown
   number of years.
Second, a wicked act was hatched to get rid of Manoharā.
Third, the lord father has stripped me of my possessions.

Even if I were such an enemy, how could he do this?
If I, Sudhana, who has acted honorably, am the enemy,
then the actions of my father,
who has been deceived by another,
have defeated me.

He looked at his mother, who began to cry. She said:

Listen to me, father and son.
Now that Sudhana returned from the north,
it is true that his father has punished him,
but to leave here without entering the palace once,
how can that be right?
My son, do not say these things. Listen to your
   mother.
I will tell you all in great detail.
Do not do this, Sudhana. Be brave.
Come into the palace.

His mother took Sudhana by the hand and led him into the palace. There
Sudhana said:

Listen to me, my kind mother.
An evil person has disturbed my father's mind.
Without fault, I traveled to the enemy land in the north.
While there, the deed of destroying Manoharā was started.

As soon as I returned, I was punished and my possessions
   taken.
Even if I were such an enemy, how could this happen?
Mother, please tell me of the wicked deeds
inflicted on my dear, celestial Manoharā.

In tears his mother related to her son the actions carried out by Hari and the five hundred queens against Manoharā. Sudhana became troubled and refused to eat. After three days, he said to his mother:

> Mother, whose kindness is unceasing,
> even if I were to stay in this palace,
> I would know no end to the pain of missing Manoharā.
> My father's punishment brings satisfaction to the queens.
> Even if I stayed, this mountain of suffering would torment me,
> and without doubt I would die before my time.
> I will go in search of Manoharā.
> Do not let this trouble you, my dear mother.

As the full moon rose on the fifteenth day of the fourth month, Sudhana left the palace alone. Sudhana now gone, his mother and father, the attendants, and the people were all distraught, and the five hundred queens and Hari were deeply embarrassed.

* * *

Thus ends part 3, on how Hari agreed to carry out the wishes of the demon-possessed five hundred queens and the subsequent shame of their wicked deeds not coming to fruition.

Part 4. In Search of Manoharā

Sudhana left the palace just as the full moon was rising. It was not possible to find any trace of his beloved Manoharā flying into space, and so he wandered along a ridge of the central mountain. He reached the king's fort just as dawn broke. Reaching the summit of the mountain just as the sun rose, he looked in vain in all directions. In great sorrow and distress, he called out:

> Three Jewels, I call on the compassion you have for me.
> In this world a rare and beautiful maiden has arisen,
> and here on this mountain top that I have reached,
> where she has gone and where she stays, I do not know.
>
> From here I will call out her name in the four directions.
> Manoharā, wherever you are, come to this mountain top.
> As you are so close to my heart, how could I not do this?
>
> Three times I will call out in each of the four directions.
> Beautiful maiden, if you have magical powers, respond to
>   my call.
> Manoharā, would you leave this young son alone?

With long, drawn-out cries he called out in the four directions, but no answer came. Sudhana became troubled. He spoke:

> Buddhas of the ten directions, their spiritual sons and disciples,
> look with your compassion upon this faultless Sudhana.
> I cry out in despair for my long-lost Manoharā.
> In four directions I have clearly called,
> but no answer was heard.
>
> If I do not meet Manoharā in this life,
> then on this mountain top I shall quickly die,
> and I pray that I meet her in the next life,
> and that we will recognize each other.

Without thought or care for his body, he threw himself, like a collapsing wall, in prostration on the ground in each of the four directions. Suddenly a rainbow pierced the earth far off in the direction of Ke'u. Sudhana wondered what it might mean and realized that when Manoharā first came to him, she had come from Ke'u, and that now this rainbow was a sign pointing the way that he had to go. With gladdened heart Sudhana made his way to Ke'u cave. In front of the stone boundary marker he called out:

> Master of excellent meditative concentration dwelling in this
>   isolated place,
> I ask that you show your face to this traveler from far away,
> and that you give him an answer to his question.
> Object of refuge, I beseech you.
> From my heart I beseech you.
> Look upon me quickly with your eyes of compassion.

Merely hearing the king's voice, the sage was overjoyed and came out at once to meet him. Just by seeing the man in front of him, who was a pleasure to behold, the sage was uplifted and said:

> Listen to me carefully, you who stand by the boundary marker.
> What faraway place have you come from?
> What is your purpose in coming to this isolated place?
> Why do you call on this meditator in retreat?

The king prostrated and said:

> Dance-like manifestation enacted in order to care for others,
> by your wonderful deeds in the form of a man
> you are a second Mañjuśrī, a mighty sun that dispels
> the darkness of confused sentient beings.
> Please hear what I have to say.
>
> My country is the northern land of Vṛkṣaḥ.
> My family is of the royal caste,
> but by poor fortune I am destined to wander alone.
> I will tell you of these bad events in great detail.
> You who dwell in the great realm of meditative concentration,
> please consider what I have to say.

Sudhana went down on one knee and said:

My country is known as the northern land of Vṛkṣaḥ.
The name of my father is Mahādhana.
My mother's name is Bharat Devī.
I am called Sudhana.
I am the sole heir to the northern kingdom's throne.
Previously I had taken five hundred queens.
No other powerful king could rival me.

On an auspicious day in the earth dragon year
the great sage with his peerless compassion
said that the goddess Manoharā, held by the hunter,
was connected to me by karma and prayer,
and thus she became my companion.

This goddess, complete with all the qualities of
    a learned woman,
never before seen in this land of humans,
loved me, respected my parents,
and showed affection for the people.
Her deeds and qualities were beyond compare,
and consequently, she was cherished by us all.

By the black-magic powers of a host of demons,
the five hundred queens rose up in envy of Manoharā.
They turned the head of venerable Hari with the promise
    of wealth,
who with wicked intent created an illusory effect
in order to trouble my father's mind.
I was sent to a far-off land for no good reason,
and while I was away the innocent Manoharā
was surrounded by Hari and the army of the queens.
They bayed and shouted continually for her death,
but Manoharā has powers and escaped by flying
    into the skies.
Hari and the queens could do nothing.

When I returned home, Manoharā was not there.
I asked my father, my mother, and the people what had
    happened.
When I heard the events of which I have just told you,
I was unable to bear it and went in search of Manoharā.

Previously you showed us great compassion, great sage.
Now again I ask you to tell me, for good or bad,
have you seen my goddess Manoharā?
Are there no words of hope about seeing or hearing of her?

The sage led the king into his cave and treated him with all hospitality.
He addressed the king:

Listen to me, Sudhana, son of a king.
Your excellent deeds in learning
for the benefit of all have been made known to me.

In the capture of Manoharā, the goddess from Vṛkṣaḥ,
the hunter's actions were guided by me.
After she had been taken and then offered to the king
    as a queen,
those unwanted and dreadful events occurred,
created by demons who produce obstacles.
But this is the nature of the phenomena of samsara.

Prince, do not trouble yourself. Listen to me.
No other king in this world has a kingdom such as yours.
How can it be right to abandon such a kingdom?
How can it be right to abandon your parents and the queens?
How can it be right to abandon your possessions and entourage?

Return to your country today, great king.
If in the future I see or hear news of Manoharā
worthy of passing on, I will at once tell you.
Up to now I have not seen nor heard of her.
Great king, please take this to your mind.

The king looked grim. He said:

> Incomparable great sage, please hear these words.
> It was with a mind of self-interest, thinking about my kingdom,
> that I killed many tribal fathers and sons in the north.
> In the kingdom it is Manoharā to whom
> I have entrusted my heart.
> She not being there, I became troubled
> with remorse and so have left alone.
>
> Should I find Manoharā, I will again rule the kingdom.
> If I do not, I will wander elsewhere.
> This is my only intent.
> For this I came here seeking answers.
> Great sage, if you have nothing else to say,
> I will not stay but continue my search for Manoharā.

With these words he strode out and left. When he was almost out of sight, the sage called him back by waving his robe. The king returned to the sage, who said:

> Great king, do not be sad.
> Listen to what I have to say.
> If you will not take my advice but insist on continuing
>   your quest,
> I must tell you I have a message and instructions from
>   the goddess.
> Do not be troubled, great king. Listen to what I say.
>
> The message from the goddess is as follows:
> "At best, the king should follow the holy Dharma.
> Next best is to rule the kingdom according to his
>   mother's wishes.
> If not these, then he should go after Manoharā."
> These are her words.
> The maiden then gave me this ring and told me of
> the obstacles and assistance you will meet on the road to Vṛkṣaḥ.

The sage presented the ring to Sudhana and told him in detail of the hindrances on the road ahead. Sudhana clasped the ring and immediately fell unconscious for a while. The sage revived him by dabbing his face with water. Sudhana said:

> Ah! With Manoharā in my thoughts,
> I called for her in the four directions.
> But no answer at all came to me.
> I thought that my beloved Manoharā had cast me aside.
> But this maiden, with great love, left me a message.
> I see now I was wrong in thinking she had left no trace.

He clutched the ring to his heart and wept. The sage gave him some assistance on how to avoid the dangers on the road ahead and accompanied him as far as the Brahma court bathing pools.

Following the maiden's instructions, Sudhana successfully overcome the obstacles on the road and finally arrived at the Spring Resembling a Heap of Jewels. There in the distance he saw a large, tall, and joyful-to-behold palace whose roof resembled a flower. Merely looking at this beautiful sight filled him with happiness and joy, and he stopped there by the spring. Nearby was a resting place, and on the ground was the imprint of a pot. Sudhana waited there for some time. After a while three goddesses lead by Darśanamukti came to fetch water. Seeing the king, they looked at him with many expressions of delight. Being coy, the three goddesses would not come close to the spring, and from a distance they sang in unison:

> Handsome youth by the Spring Resembling a Heap of Jewels,
> hear the words of these three beautiful maidens.
> Why have you come to this place?
> What is your name? What is your caste?
> What is the name of your country?
> This is the drinking water for the gandharva king.
> It is not good that you stay here.

Sudhana replied:

> Listen to me, you three young maidens.
> Why do you ask about my country?

Why do you stand there for no reason?
If you are coming to the spring, then come!

The king moved away from the spring a little, and the three maidens approached. They put down their pots and began to fill them with water. The king said to the three maidens:

Listen to me, you three maidens collecting water.
What is the name of this place?
What is the name of your mistress?
What will you do with the water from here?
Answer truthfully these questions.
If not, I will not give back your pot.

Sudhana snatched the silver jewel-encrusted pot from the goddesses. Darśanamukti responded:

Listen to me, you abrasive young man.
There is no reason to snatch that pot.
As you clearly do not know this land,
that palace is the palace of the gandharva king.

There the father's name is Turaṃvadana.
The mother is the beautiful Ḍākinī.
Our mistress and sister is the goddess Manoharā.
My name is Darśanamukti Devī.
These two maidens are my helpers.

This water is for our mistress, the beautiful Manoharā.
She was captured by a hunter at the Brahma court pools.
She is weakened and tainted by a long stay in the
    human realm.
This water is water to bathe her body.

I have answered your questions clearly.
Give back my pot at once.

Sudhana said:

> Listen to me, maiden Darśanamukti.
> Today I have come here from far away.
> By prayer and karma I have ties to this sacred place.
> Darśanamukti, tell your mistress the following:
> that she should bathe as long as there is water in the pot,
> and when the water is gone, to shake the pot.
> Be sure to say this, you three maidens.

In his hand Sudhana held the precious ring belonging to Manoharā. He put it in his mouth, held up the pot, and dropped the ring into the pot without the goddesses noticing. The goddesses returned to Manoharā, where Darśanamukti said:

> Listen to me, mistress Manoharā.
> Today at the Spring Resembling a Heap of Jewels,
> was an extraordinary man we had never seen before.
> On first sight, he was frightening and terrifying,
> but on closer inspection he was someone who gladdened
>   the heart.
> He said that mistress should wash with this water until
>   it is gone,
> and when finished, you should shake the pot.

Manoharā thought that the three maidens were just teasing her and began to bathe. When the water had been used up, she shook the pot and the ring that she had left at Ke'u fell into her hand. She realized that the maidens' story had been true, and on examining the ring she knew that the stranger was Sudhana. Manoharā fell into a faint. Darśanamukti became afraid and ran to Manoharā's mother. She told the mother about the stranger at the spring, the message he had sent to Manoharā, and of her fainting. The mother and father at once sent a message to the people that no one should talk to the stranger.

When Manoharā had revived, she said:

> Listen to me, Darśanamukti.
> When I had been taken from the Brahma court pools

by a low-caste hunter and was placed in fear of my life,
kind Sudhana of the northern kingdom
paid in wealth the ransom for my life.
He has come now to this land, I think.
I will not stay but go at once to the spring.

She prepared to leave. However, her parents had forbidden anyone to approach this man, and the gatekeepers reminded her of this order. She went at once to her parents and said:

My kind parents, please listen to me.
When I had been seized from the Brahma court pools
by a low-caste hunter and was in danger of losing my life,
Darśanamukti and my retinue returned here to our land,
and gave a message from this maiden to her parents.

It said that Manoharā of poor merit had been captured
by a hunter,
and asked that mother and father provide a ransom.
I asked that jewels, gold, silver, silk, horses, and elephants
be quickly brought to that place in exchange for this maiden.

In this land of Vṛkṣaḥ there was no one at that time
among the people who gave my capture a second thought.
But now the prince who saved the life of this maiden
has come to this land. In such circumstances
how could it not be possible to meet him?
I ask that I be allowed to go to the spring.

Her father replied:

If the man who is waiting at the spring
is the kind being who provided ransom for your life,
then in gratitude we will give him food and possessions as
he desires.

For fear of human contamination upon us celestials,
it would not be right to admit him to the palace.

Therefore meeting him face to face would bring the scorn
   of others.
If you wish to meet him, then at a place within speaking
   distance only,
and hidden behind drapes, you may talk with him.

Her father's permission granted, officials set up drapes at the eastern gate
of the palace and Sudhana and Manoharā were brought together to talk.
Sudhana sang:

Ah! Of all the sunny days, today is the warmest.
Of all the special places, this is the happiest.
It has been worth Sudhana coming to this place.
This must be the residence of Manoharā.

Hearing the melodious words of Sudhana, Manoharā replied:

One voice I hear, and the day becomes sweeter.
Great king who has waited long, you have come to this
   special place.
Your clear, melodious voice this maiden has heard.
Remove this white silk veil that hides me.

Sudhana immediately replied:

To hear the melody of Manoharā's voice brings me joy.
The swaying movements of your body are veiled by this
   white silk.
I am not a tainted person to be cut off by this curtain.
Sudhana will wrap this veil around his right hand.

With a flourish of his right hand he whipped the veil away, and the Vṛkṣaḥ
officials who were holding it were thrown to the ground. The golden faces of
Sudhana and Manoharā met. Manoharā took Sudhana's hand and tears fell
from her eyes. She gazed lovingly at his face. Falling to one knee, she took
hold of a corner of his robes and said:

Dharma King Sudhana, lord of men,
with a mind that works for others, greatly compassionate,
performing wonderful deeds for the benefit of living beings
who are equal in number to the vast reaches of space,
incomparable youth, Sudhana, please hear me.

Great king, you have traveled far from the northern kingdom.
Did you meet any adverse conditions on the way?
As the lord father instructed, has the enemy been defeated?
Returning from the north, did you meet your mother
    and father?
Coming here shows you love me, gracious Sudhana.

Holding his hand, she sat there weeping. Sudhana said:

My beautiful and beloved Manoharā,
do not be distressed. Today our prayers are answered.
As my father ordered, I traveled to the north.
There all enemies of the kingdom were destroyed.
All those who asked for refuge I placed on the path of happiness.

I did not meet any adverse conditions or hindrances,
but I thought of my mother and Manoharā, so I hurried back.
At the top of Tiger Pass, Vaśin gods in the form of crows
indicated that all was not well with Manoharā.

In great anxiety I hurried on and at the second cairn
my mother was waiting to offer me welcoming ale.
I asked her if Manoharā had met with misfortune.
She replied that Manoharā was not in the palace,
but that no harm had come to her life.

At the southern gate my father awaited with welcoming ale.
I asked my father where Manoharā had gone.
He replied that she had left for the land of Vṛkṣaḥ,
and had gone in order to meet with her mother and father.
Although his answer had not been clear and detailed,
because Manoharā was so dear to me, I said to him:

"As I was preparing to leave for the north,
with firm intent I asked father to protect
with great affection mother and Manoharā.
Did you cast aside that promise?

The gods and people of the northern kingdom
have thoughtlessly cast aside my heartfelt request.
I will not stay here but go in search of Manoharā.
If I find her, I will return to reign over the kingdom.
If not I will wander elsewhere."

These words I spoke to my father.
He is of an ill temper, and replied:

"You have the five hundred queens you took previously.
If you desire more, I can get them for you.
Although the goddess is not here,
we can search for a maiden resembling a goddess.
You can give her the name 'beautiful goddess.'
You can tie a precious necklace to her body."

This he said and showed signs of anger.
However, I said to my one and only father:

"I have no need of a lookalike goddess.
I have no need of a kingdom without Manoharā.
Sudhana will leave and go in search of her.
I have no plans other than that."

With that my father became angry and said:

"You wicked person, you disgrace to the family,
if you leave because you cherish something of little value
more than your parents and your kingdom,
you damage your reputation in the eyes of all.
If you say you are leaving for another land,
take off my treasured weaponry and armor,
and wherever you want to go, go now!"

He was about to strike me, and I was crestfallen,
but there is no way to resist my father's commands.
I took off the apparel and prepared to set off
from the southern gate in search of Manohāra.

But I could not resist the fervent pleas of my mother,
and so for three days I stayed in the palace.
She told me in detail how the queens and Hari with their
    wicked deeds
rose up against you, and how you escaped with your powers.

Because of your great love for me you left a message,
which the great sage delivered to me.
I cleared the obstacles on the road
as you described and have come here.
Our hopes and wishes have today come true.

With these words they held each other for a while. The Vṛkṣaḥ officials
who held the drapes were surprised at the strength of Sudhana. Manohāra
took hold of Sudhana's hand, and with her eyes full of tears she said:

Incomparable great king that I can never tire of looking at,
having tamed the wild tribes of the north for the sake of
    the teachings,
out of love for me, you came to this land.
When I think of the hardships you endured for my sake,
even though I tried until the end of the eon,
your kindness would be hard to repay.
Come now into the palace.

Manohāra led Sudhana into her turquoise temple rooms and pleased him
with perfect hospitality. The Vṛkṣaḥ officials went before the mother and
father and told them of Sudhana's radiating presence, his fame and glory, and
so on. The gandharva rulers and the people were amazed and apprehensive.
Meanwhile, Sudhana said to Manohāra:

Listen to me, celestial princess Manohāra.
From the time we became companions to this day,

we have always seen the good in each other,
and our love and trust has never waned.

Father's mind disturbed by the tricks of black-hearted demons
and the subsequent unwanted troubles of the past have all gone.
Now in order to heal the mind of the lord father,
and to comfort the mind of my unceasingly kind mother,
we should live again in the Land of Joy Palace,
and return quickly to the northern kingdom.

We will seek an audience with your Vṛkṣaḥ mother and father,
where you can request permission to leave.
It is right that I meet with your mother and father.
Ask your parents, maiden, for an audience.

Manoharā replied:

Lord of men, of unceasing kindness,
caring for others, guide of living beings—
to see, hear, or remember you brings joy to the heart.
Youth, listen to this young maiden.

It is not possible for this maiden to go against the word
of a prince ordained by karmic deeds that have no beginning,
but the destructive acts of Hari and the queens are many,
and the deeds of your father were those of a mind deceived
    by demons.
For Manoharā to go there would be a mistake.

Whether or not the prince stays here in this kingdom,
as is Manoharā's wish, depends upon your compassion.
As you request, I will seek a meeting with my Vṛkṣaḥ parents.

Sudhana replied:

Maiden, do not say these things, my princess.
I think of the troubles my kind mother has experienced
    on my behalf.

Especially when I was about to leave in search of Manoharā,
I went secretly to my mother one evening.
The suffering she endures for me threatens her life.

Maiden, my princess, do not say these things.
If we return to the northern kingdom together,
my wishes would all be complete.
If I am parted from either mother or Manoharā,
I would have no happiness in my mind.

Manoharā, the love you have for me, you have said,
rests upon having faith and confidence in me.
If these words of yours still hold true,
do not distract Sudhana, who is skilled in settling these
  matters,
from seeking permission from your parents.
Go to your parents and request an audience for me.

Manoharā replied:

Listen to me, compassionate prince.
The love you have for me is unrivaled in the world.
In particular, the lady mother of the great prince
has greater love for me than the mother who bore me.

Thinking of the troubles the kind mother and the prince
  have endured
for the sake of this maiden, I cannot refuse the prince.
The Vṛkṣaḥ mother and father cherish Manoharā greatly,
and it will be difficult to gain permission to leave.
Great king, you may be skillful in gaining the permission
  you seek,
but I will make efforts to take the egg from the bird
who has no wish to fly from the nest.

Manoharā hurried to the rooms of her father Turaṃvadana and her
mother Ḍākiṇī, where she prostrated and said:

You who dispel the darkness of the torment
of the living beings of the gandharva desire realm,
and who are the illuminating answer to the prayers of the world,
my kind mother and father, please listen to me.

The torment of being captured by the hindering hunter
at the Brahma court pools almost cost me my life.
The kind Dharma king called Sudhana who at that time
provided the ransom in exchange for my life,
by the power of his great love for me,
has come to this great land of Vṛkṣaḥ.
Now he stays with me in my rooms,
and asks me to request an audience.

Therefore, incomparable mother and father of the
      gandharva realm,
I ask that you quickly grant,
as an ornament for this young maiden's head,
an agreeable reply to this request
from Prince Sudhana, a guide of living beings.

The father, Turaṃvadana, said to Manoharā:

Daughter, Manoharā, listen to me.
You suffered the karmic circumstance at the bathing pools
of being taken by the low-caste hunter,
and your life was exchanged for wealth by the man
who recently arrived at the Spring Resembling a Heap of Jewels.

At that time, daughter, you told us of his kindness,
and I replied that as repayment for saving your life,
he should be given in gratitude gifts of food and clothing.

However, by your own volition, Manoharā,
you have taken him to your rooms.
There is the risk of human contamination to the gods.
Now you want us to meet him face to face?
Manoharā, is not your brazen wish very selfish?

Manoharā replied:

> Please hear what I say, most kind king.
> Sudhana is an incomparable human being.
> He is the guide of all beings in this world.
> If his qualities could be described,
> they would be unimaginable.
>
> How could he possibly be compared to ordinary humans?
> He has come as a bodhisattva in human form.
> Through his supernatural powers he has traveled here.
> He is here because of his love for me.
> How could it be because of being bereft of food and clothing?
>
> He has not come as one tainted by human contamination,
> of an impure lineage or possessed of an evil nature.
> Mother and father, discuss this and quickly grant him
>   an audience.
> Please hear these words.

Ḍākinī, the mother, supported Manoharā's request, and made a fervent plea to the king:

> Incomparable great leader of the gandharvas,
> listen for a while to my thoughts expressed in words.
> Of all our princesses, she is the most important.
> This maiden Manoharā, by the power of previous karma,
> was seized and taken by a hunter of low caste,
> and became the companion of this great king in the
>   human world.
>
> In the face of the queens' wicked deeds brought on by envy,
> Hari conjured up an illusion to trouble the mind of the father.
> What happiness have Sudhana and Manoharā had?
> In his love for this maiden,
> Sudhana's mind has not wavered for an instant.

This is extraordinary, and now he has come to this special place.
When I think about this, I believe he has special powers.
The prince requests an audience out of devotion,
not for us to listen to him, and it would be right
to meet him face to face.

The father replied:

With respect to Manoharā's request,
mother has made a heartfelt plea for us to agree.
Sudhana is here in pursuit of our daughter,
he is not seeking an audience out of devotion.

However, mother has made this fervent request.
Therefore, in a day or two, so that we may meet,
prepare a throne in the Spontaneous Creation Palace,
and send Sudhana to us.

Manoharā was delighted at her father's response. She hurried back to her rooms, where she told Sudhana that he would meet with her mother and father in two days. On the day, in the great reception hall, three thrones were arranged: a golden throne for the king, Turaṃvadana; a silver throne for mother and daughter; and a slightly lower silver throne for Sudhana. Around the thrones were seated the nobles and the people of Vṛkṣaḥ. The scene resembled the bright reflected rays of the sun, master of the seven horses, shining upon the gold of the river Jambu.[43] Into the midst of this glittering assembly Sudhana was led from Manoharā's rooms by Manoharā herself and her entourage. Lutes, flutes, and other musical instruments led the way as he came into the Spontaneous Creation reception hall to be in the presence of the mother and father.

Sudhana offered a white silk scarf to the leader of the gandharvas. The mere presence of Sudhana terrified Turaṃvadana and he almost fell off his throne. The prince and the nobles had to hold him before he fell. Sudhana spoke:

Alas! Lord of the gandharvas, listen.
I come here to this audience in peace.
I have no malicious intent for any wicked deed.

Great king, do not do this. Sit on your throne.
Accept the offering of this scarf made of celestial silk.
Grant me your informality. Grant me freely your words.

The gods of Vṛkṣaḥ gathered there felt ashamed and adjusted the height of Sudhana's throne to be the same as that of the gandharva king. Sudhana sat on the throne. After a short while, and in a trembling voice, the gandharva king spoke:

Youth, who goes by the name of Sudhana,
you who have come from the human world of Jambudvipa,
Was your journey pleasant? Are you not tired?
What is the purpose of you coming here to meet us?
Tell us in detail, Sudhana, lord of men.

Sudhana smiled and said:

Leader of the herd, horse-headed[44] lord of the gods,
sun that brings happiness to the gandharva gods,
friend of Brahma, dancer that dispels the gloom of ignorance,
listen to me, the youth known as Sudhana.

The circumstances, driven by the strong winds of beginningless
    karma,
by which your daughter, the celestial Manoharā, and I,
united by past prayer and karma, came together in this
    human life
are that at the Brahma court bathing pools
Manoharā was captured by a powerful hunter,
and by the words of the Ke'u sage, Prakāśamati,
she was sent to me as my queen.

By the power of past karma, we loved each other.
The people of the northern kingdom for over a month
celebrated with gratitude this auspicious enthronement.

Her reputation of being without fault
and endowed with excellent qualities,

attested to by whoever saw this celestial goddess,
was talked about in all corners of the world.
Because of this my mother and father were also pleased.

After Manoharā arrived, in northern India the harvests were
    on time,
disease vanished, and the age of warfare disappeared.
Because of this, the northern kingdom was happy,
but by the destructive force of the five hundred queens and Hari
brought on by the black powers of the hosts of hindering forces,
my father's mind was disturbed, and by his subsequent actions
many undesired events occurred, because of which
Manoharā returned here to the kingdom of Vṛkṣaḥ.

However, this I could not bear and I have come here.
Gandharva mother and father, the reason I seek this audience
is to take this celestial princess, Manoharā, to be my royal queen
once again in the human realm of northern India.
I ask mother and father to grant the leaving
of this goddess Manoharā, so dear to my heart.

The gandharva king responded:

Listen to me, you who have come from afar.
My daughter, this young Manoharā,
has a little connection with you by way of prayer and karma.
When this maiden was in torment, having been taken by
    the hunter,
the king was kind in providing ransom by way of wealth,
and in generous repayment I will fulfill your hopes
with material wealth such as various jewels, gold, and silver,
but I cannot let Manoharā go elsewhere.

There are many suitors from other celestial realms
who seek and would wish for the hand of this maiden.
Therefore if I were to offer Manoharā to you, great prince,
the angry resentment generated in other celestial realms

would bring to this land the torment of nonvirtuous deeds.
Please consider this, lord of men.

Sudhana replied:

Great king, do not say this. Listen to me.
I love this celestial Manoharā anointed by karma,
and because of that I have come to this special place.
I did not come because I am in need of wealth.

If there is power and ability in all those celestial realms,
where exists this longing for Manoharā,
then when she was taken by the low-caste hunter,
were these other celestial worlds not aware of it?

If mother and father were to give permission to this maiden,
Sudhana is not a man to shrink from these other realms,
be they with or without form.
If the gandharva king and inhabitants are fond of wealth,
I will satisfy you with whatever wealth you desire.
Please quickly grant Manoharā permission to leave.

Ḍākinī, the mother, spoke:

Young prince of the northern kingdom, listen to me.
It is true you have great love for Manoharā,
but the king and the inhabitants of Vṛkṣaḥ will convene
and the results of our discussion will be presented to you.
Sudhana, you have come far. You are weary.
It would be best if you rested in this gandharva land awhile.
I ask that you please take this for consideration.
Today we will delight you with our offerings.

Sudhana was treated to the best food and drink of all kinds, and to such an extraordinary and delightful spectacle of gandharva singing accompanied by many kinds of musical instruments that the day passed without him noticing. After the festivities had ended, Sudhana was escorted to his rooms by Manoharā and her entourage. Over the next few days Sudhana was taken to the groves and parks of Vṛkṣaḥ, where he was encouraged to rest and enjoy himself by way of songs, dance, and amusement provided by Manoharā and many other young gods and goddesses.

Meanwhile, the father and mother and other gandharva dignitaries convened and discussed their unwillingness to allow Manoharā to go to the land of humans. Some said it would not be proper to allow her to go. Others said that they could not dare let her go. Some said that Manoharā would never give up Sudhana and the king and queen ought to let her go. Others said the matter should be settled by fighting. Some suggested recruiting an army from the yakṣa spirits. There was no agreement, and so King Turaṃvadana announced:

> Listen to me, people of gandharva.
> He is a lord of men from the human world.
> He has all the signs of possessing magic powers,
> and is clearly unlike other men.

> He came here by way of magical powers.
> When he appeared at the eastern gate
> all those holding the curtain were cast to the ground.
> Just seeing him struck fear into my heart.
> It seems there is no one who can match him.

> However, we will hold various contests over the course
>   of a few days.
> To the winner, I will give the maiden.
> In this way we shall see if he is capable or not.

Everyone agreed with the gandharva leader. Consequently, nobles and common folk of special prowess were gathered and the four best were chosen. They were assigned to other vassal kings.

One day Sudhana was invited before the king in the reception room. Additional thrones for the four men were also arranged. After treating them to a great feast followed by singing and dancing, the gandharva king spoke:

> Listen to me, prince of the human realm.
> There are so many suitors who desire my daughter,

it is difficult to know what to do.
Here are gathered four representatives from the yakṣa
    spirit world.
Together with Sudhana, five kingdoms are gathered here.
I will give my daughter to one of them. Four will be
    disappointed.

We will not descend into unwanted fighting,
but over the next few days you five will compete,
and to the one who shows the greatest skill I will give Manoharā.
Take this to your mind, representatives of the five kingdoms.

Sudhana spoke:

Hear me, lord of the gandharva.
I have risked my life for the sake of Manoharā,
and having been her companion for so long, I have come here.
It makes no sense to fight for the one you are a companion of,
but in order to comply with the king's wishes,
I will happily meet with any competitor.

On the first day, the archery contest was held in a park. The four competi-
tors from the four kingdoms fired their arrows at the target trees and they let
off a great roar of victory as they each pierced three trees. Sudhana hung an
iron pan on each tree and split each pan with each shot. In doing so he split
nine trees and their pans. All were amazed and despaired of beating him.
Sudhana said: "May each tree pierced by the arrows be removed undamaged
from root to tip and be transported before the king."
The nine trees were split by Sudhana's arrows as easy as opening a curtain
and were carried before the king at the eastern gate. The other competitors
could not even shake the trees. All the spectators were amazed at Sudhana's
strength. In front of the king Sudhana said:

Listen to me, gandharva king and people.
The great king declared that skilled contestants
from five kingdoms should take part in a contest of prowess,
and to the one who emerges as winner he would present
    his daughter.

In no other way would it be right to hand over the maiden,
   he declared.
Once spoken, the word of a king cannot be changed.
People of this land, do you not know today
who has emerged superior in this contest?

Manoharā now belongs to me.
Put your fingers in your mouth and go home.
To Manoharā who has been ordained by karma,
mother and father, now give your instructions for her farewell
here at this place where we are gathered.

The gandharva king was embarrassed and could say nothing. A gandharva senior minister called Śrīmati spoke:

Listen to me, king and subjects of this gandharva land.
This celestial goddess, Manoharā, is to be offered
to the winner of various sporting contests.
This has been the command of our great king and father.

However, nothing is decided by the one contest of today.
There are still other contests to be held.
Should Sudhana win them all, he will be presented with her.
Tonight, return to your homes.

Sudhana showed some anger in his response:

Listen well, king and subjects of this gandharva land.
In a northern kingdom of India, Jambudvipa,
I have left behind my kind and dear mother.
This I cannot bear, and I must return there.
Manoharā, young men, gandharva lord,
if I wish to do so, that I can do.
But if this senseless fighting has any purpose,
then let us continue the contest!

Manoharā and her entourage immediately took Sudhana back to his rooms. That evening the gandharva nobles and citizens convened and discussed what was best to do. Some said that this man had the power of Brahma and Indra, and that no one could overcome him. Others said that for the sake of Manoharā even the king had come close to defeat. The room was filled with talk on what was best to do. Suddenly the mother spoke:

> Listen to me gandharva king and subjects.
> You competitors have been mistaken to think
> that Sudhana, a manifested lord of men, cannot be beaten.

> Tomorrow by the eastern gate we will gather many maidens
> of the kiṃnara spirit realm, from high and low families,
> and in their midst we will place the maiden Manoharā.
> The five kingdoms will shoot decorated arrows into the air.
> The maiden on which the arrow lands will be given to
>   that archer.
> If no arrow falls on Manoharā, she will not be given away.
> If by past karma an arrow falls upon Manoharā,
> she will be given. About that there is nothing we can do.
> These are my thoughts. Consider them, gandharva people.

Everyone liked the mother's suggestion. They all agreed that by firing arrows into the skies above a crowd of goddesses, the arrows could fall on any of them. They would not fall on Manoharā alone. The next day Sudhana and the others gathered before the gandharva king as they had done previously. Turaṃvadana addressed them:

> Sudhana and others gathered here, listen to me.
> In the archery contest yesterday, Sudhana emerged triumphant.
> There are still other tests of prowess that could be held.
> However, each contest would require a winner,
> and that would be difficult to do.

> So now, with the Three Jewels as witnesses,
> many gandharva maidens will be gathered at the eastern gate,
> and Manoharā will be placed among them.
> The contestants from the five kingdoms
> will take their arrows and adorn them with silk ribbons.

They will send their arrows into the skies.
Wherever each arrow lands, that maiden will be theirs.
If an arrow lands on Manoharā,
then I, without attachment, will give her away.
There is no other way. Adorn your arrows,
and tomorrow bring them to the eastern gate.

Sudhana said:

Hear me one time, gandharva lord.
It is possible that you may send to another land
my long-time companion Manoharā,
but if you wish to hold on to your gandharva land,
do not tell senseless, sweet-talking lies.

If there exists among you anyone
worthy of taking part in a contest,
who has the confidence to say
they will compete in any test of prowess,
then say so now!

Manoharā spoke:

Listen to me, lords and subjects, both gods and human.
I have none other than the body of a woman.
In particular, Manoharā holds her body as an enemy.
It has brought strife between two great leaders of gods and men.

Being captured by the noose of a low-caste hunter,
this maiden troubled the mind of her mother and father.
Where these deeds done for my sake will lead I do not know.

Now the lord father's present edict
calls for the Three Jewels to be witnesses,
and where the arrow lands, that maiden will be given.
There is no turning back from this command.
Incomparable youth, Sudhana, you too,
take what has been said to mind.

Thus it was decided that the king's words could not be undone. Sudhana was escorted back to his rooms by Manoharā and her entourage. The gandharva king gave the command that the beautiful maidens of the kingdom should gather in two days' time at the ground by the eastern gate. In his rooms, Sudhana chose an arrow whose feathers, arrowhead, and notch were completely unworn, and adorned it with ribbons of five colors. It was placed in a container of grains in front of an altar on which were arranged various offerings. Manoharā and Sudhana, as a single virtuous vessel of pure resolve, made prayers to all objects of refuge in general, as exemplified by the buddhas and bodhisattvas of the ten directions.

On the day, headed by the gandharva king, everyone gathered on the open ground by the eastern gate. Every maiden of the gandharva kingdom, numbering almost fifteen hundred, was assembled in one spot. In their midst was placed Manoharā. The purpose of the gathering was announced. In unison the maidens wondered hopefully if Sudhana's arrow would fall on them. Some spoke their thoughts and said: "Even if I do not become the companion of Prince Sudhana, if I could only spend just one day with him in his home!" Others said: "If I could only just touch a part of his body." All looked upon him in delight.

The five human and celestial contestants took their arrows simultaneously from the gandharva king. Sudhana prayed and cast grains to the four directions:

> Buddhas, bodhisattvas, and their disciples of the ten directions,
> bless this arrow today.
> Gurus, meditation deities, ḍākinīs, and protectors,
> bless this arrow today.
> Great sage, Prakāśamati, bless this arrow today.
> Deities of Vajrasattva in the east, bless this arrow today.
> Deities of Ratnasambhava in the south, bless this arrow today.
> Deities of Amitābha in the west, bless this arrow today.
> Deities of Amoghasiddhi in the north, bless this arrow today.
> Deities of Vairocana in the center, bless this arrow today.
> Earth lords of the world, twelve local goddesses, bless this
> arrow today.
>
> Personal protector of my family, and in particular,
> Gertso Nyenpo and his entourage,

accomplish the work of this arrow today.
Through this arrow, fulfill today the hopes contained within
this single virtuous vessel of pure resolve,
the celestial princess Manoharā and I.

Turaṃvadana made a prayer and the five arrows were fired into the sky.
The arrows of the four other contestants traveled for about a spear distance
and then fell to earth. The arrow fired by Sudhana traveled far into the sky
and fell to earth upon Manoharā and her entourage. The ribbons fell about
the neck of Manoharā like the kind of ceremonial scarf presented to a war-
rior. Everyone there was amazed and full of faith. Sudhana said:

Hear me, king and subjects of this gandharva realm.
With perverse minds you long to have Manoharā,
who has been ordained by beginningless karma,
but the Three Jewels have today given her to me.

Those who believe, do you see? Do you hear?
Grant your farewells to your daughter, mother and father.
Sudhana will not stay here,
but will return to the northern kingdom.

The gandharva king replied:

Hear me, Sudhana, you of great prowess and magical powers.
It seems there exists a powerful karmic connection
between you and my daughter, the celestial Manoharā.
The object of desire that would fulfill your hopes
is clear today for everyone to see.

This matter has been decided on.
All you others, return now to your homes.
In accord with Sudhana's wish
I will send my daughter with him.
This I promise I will do soon.

That evening everyone departed. The next day Manoharā was called to
her father and mother. Her father said:

Alas! My daughter, Manoharā, listen to me.
This manifested Dharma king from the human world
is your companion. It has been decided.
When I think of his prowess and his qualities,
I am sure there is no one in the three realms who can
    match him.

Manoharā, you are supreme among the daughters of gods
    and men,
and dear to my heart, but I have no choice than to let you go.
Manoharā, whatever dowry a fortunate one such as you desires,
your mother and father will provide for you.

Go with Sudhana to the human realm of Jambudvipa.
Whatever objects of desire you wish for, tell us now.

Manoharā answered:

Mother and father of unending kindness,
please listen to this young Manoharā.
By powerful and virtuous karma I have amassed
    in the past,
I have been born as the daughter of a god,
but I must travel to the land of humans.
This is karma of the past that cannot be reversed.
I make this plea to my kind parents.

For the dowry of this daughter as my support,
I ask only that you please give to me
a representation of the enlightened body, speech, and mind.

Sudhana and Manoharā made their own preparations for leaving. On the
day of leaving, a large feast was set out in the reception hall, attended by all
the gandharva inhabitants and headed by the mother and father, along with
Manoharā and Sudhana. As farewell gifts the couple were presented with
family heirlooms, ceremonial scarves, gold, silver, and many other types of
precious gems, silks, the best horses, chariots, and many other unimaginable
gifts. After the speeches the father addressed the couple:

Hear me, son of a king from the human realm.
By the infallible process of karma and prayer
that exists within you and my daughter, the young Manoharā,
this celestial princess has become a queen to a lord of men.
When I think of the circumstances that have led to this,
the signs are all there that this is for the sake of living beings.

In particular, Manoharā, keep this in your mind.
Manoharā, your mother and father are attached to you,
but no one can turn back the strong winds of karma,
and to fulfill the hopes of Sudhana,
with compassion I send my daughter away.

With you two as a single virtuous vessel of pure resolve,
may you always dispel all doubt and be without taint
in your pledge to be free of fault and to gain all excellent
    qualities,
and furthermore may you fulfill your destined great purpose.

Black and white karmic actions are the root of samsara
    and nirvana.
Have the greatest respect for the law of cause and effect,
    Manoharā.
From the very depths of your mind, Manoharā,
entrust yourself constantly to the infallible Three Jewels.

To your mother-and-father living beings as extensive
    as space,
develop the nonpartisan compassion, Manoharā.
Miserliness-creating wealth and goods are the burdens
    of hell.
Whatever you have, Manoharā, give away as acts
    of generosity.

External enemies are endless like ripples on water.
There is no time when they are all defeated, Manoharā.
The internal enemies of the three poison mental afflictions
are defeated by relinquishing them through no-self.

The activities of this life are like illusory dreams.
give up attachment and bias, Manoharā.

As a scriptural heirloom the father placed upon Manoharā's head a copy of the *Ratnākara Sūtra*,[45] transcribed by the king himself. Manoharā placed her hands together and said:

In your methods and excellent knowledge of phenomena,
your mind possesses the compassion of impartiality.
Supreme of all the leaders of the yakṣa spirits,
most kind dear father, please hear me.

The compassion of mother and father toward me
has lent itself to a kindness of love and caring,
because of which I have enjoyed a perfect happiness
that all gandharvas, both high and low, can clearly see.

Nevertheless, by the force of previous karma
I was captured by a low-caste hunter,
and yet by the counsel of a great sage
I became the companion of a king of Jambudvipa.

Through the interfering power of black-hearted demons,
many bad events took place, as well you know.
Joy and sorrow have followed this maiden a few times.

Meeting with this youth Sudhana
was not even in this young maiden's mind,
and in keeping with my father's words,
I will hold him closely in my mind.

May the lotus feet of my father stand firm for a hundred eons.
May his activities increase, and for we sentient beings,
may he cause the rains of happiness to constantly fall
from the expanse of the dense clouds of his great compassion.

With these words she prostrated. Her mother, Ḍākinī, presented to Manoharā an heirloom turquoise statue of Tārā, which was known to speak. She said:

My daughter and my beloved Manoharā,
This is the first time you have left us by consent.
You are respectful to your mother and father.
You show affection for the nobles, compassion for the people.

When I think of your beautiful face and beautiful qualities,
sending you off to another place becomes hard to bear.
However, leaving behind your parents and your country,
and turning your mind to another land is the lot of all
      our daughters.

Do not be lax, my daughter. Listen to these words of your
      mother.
This Sudhana is a manifested Dharma king,
with whom you share a connection by way of prayer and karma.
These are circumstances difficult to overcome,
and we have no choice but to give you away.
Take these sincere words of your mother to heart.

To the one ordained by karma to be your husband in this life,
always express your intentions with a beautiful smile.
Follow the ways of your mother and father.
Look after your entourage and servants according to their status.

Do not listen to the slanderous gossip of others.
Be wary of the tasty food of those skilled in ways of envy.
Do not defeat others with harsh or arrogant words.

Rebuke others gently and with a smile,
but praise with high-sounding words,
thereby maintaining the regal ways.
Be happy with ordinary food, and be content.
Whether at home or abroad, shun alcohol and bad friends.

This extraordinary speaking Tārā made of turquoise,
was relied upon by my father and his relatives.
You are one of compassion, and I give it to you, my daughter.
Keep it always on your person, Manoharā.

The mother placed the statue on Manoharā's head and started to cry. Manoharā said:

> Incomparable, most kind mother, whom I gaze at insatiably,
> Ḍākiṇī, queen of indestructible exalted wisdom,
> I ask you please to listen to this young Manoharā.

> By the power of virtuous prayer and karma gathered in
>   the past,
> I have been born as the daughter of this Vṛkṣaḥ mother
>   and father.
> The entire kingdom has treated me with care and love,
> but the body of this maiden became her enemy,
> and she was captured by the noose of a hunter at the
>   Brahma bathing pools.

> When she was at the point of losing her life,
> a king from Jambudvipa provided the ransom for her life.
> Although the kindness of his love is impossible to measure,
> hindrances arose, as I have explained to you previously.

> However, Sudhana, because he loves me, came to this place
> and performed peaceful and wrathful magical feats for my sake.
> The entire kingdom developed great faith in him.
> As he was worthy to be my companion, I was given to him,
> and in keeping with my parents' wishes, I happily accept.

> Great mother, may your lotus feet be planted firmly,
> and may your wonderful deeds flourish.
> From within the vast space-like expanse of your enlightened
>   deeds
> may the light of the sun of happiness bring forth joy,
> and merely by thinking of it,
> may it pervade the four continents completely.

> Now I am leaving and it will be difficult to meet again,
> but I ask that you dwell in the great expanse of exalted wisdom
> that never casts me from your love and your mind.

288 Tales from the Tibetan Operas

Thus with great emotion she made this plea to her mother. Sudhana spoke:

This great realm, this special land of Vṛkṣaḥ
is difficult to travel to but Sudhana arrived here.
He met the difficult-to-meet gandharva leader,
reached the difficult-to-reach queen, Manoharā,
and received the difficult-to-receive spiritual and secular advice.

This world of gods and men, united in friendship,
if not for the great purpose of helping living beings, then what
    is it for?
May all gathered here live long lives.
I pray that all their deeds are done in accord with the Dharma.
May Sudhana and Manoharā also quickly reach
without hindrance the northern kingdom in Jambudvipa.

The couple made farewell prostrations to the mother and left. Headed
by the three princes and princesses, a large force of gandharvas carrying
various standards made their way to the Brahma court bathing pools. Song
and music resounded through the land and the skies, and gods from other
realms gathered to watch this extraordinary event at the pools. As soon as
they arrived at the bathing pools the two sisters, Darśanamukti and Puṣpa
Mayūrañgī, and the brother, Yauvana, sang in unison:

Alas! Listen to us, sister Manoharā.
By the long-time powerful winds of karma,
our sister must leave irreversibly for the human realm.
Although it is for the sake of the teachings and for living beings,
for we three it marks the end of our fortunate karma.
When the parent birds spend a long time elsewhere,
aren't the baby birds left to wander on the plains?

We think of when you went to the human realm previously, sister,
and others with wicked minds of envy did many bad things.
Who knows what will happen again?

Going to that place, great king Sudhana,
our sister will have no place of hope other than you.

Youth, do not disappoint our sister.
Sister, revere this king, and to your servants
   and entourage
have impartial love and compassion.

Sudhana and Manoharā, may you have long lives,
and may the enlightened activities that come from
your single virtuous vessel of pure resolve
increase and flourish like the waxing moon,
and bring perfect happiness to Jambudvipa!

The three took Manoharā's hand and wept. Manoharā said:

My beloved brother and sisters, listen well to Manoharā.
our incomparable mother and father in Vṛkṣaḥ
have we princesses and prince as offspring.
But I alone of little merit will now go elsewhere.

Do not entertain thoughts of sadness,
but pay homage to the infallible Three Jewels.
Willingly do what our mother and father ask.
Care for your celestial retinue with love and compassion.

Take to heart the irreversible karmic situation of this sister,
and have great consideration for the law of cause and effect.
Today is the end of our companionship in this life.
I pray that we meet in a pure realm in the next.

Thus Manoharā returned the silk ceremonial offering scarves. Puṣpa Mayūrañgī took hold of Manoharā's hand and cried loudly. All who were gathered there did not know what to do and stood there in silence. Finally, the host of gandharva gods and goddesses, headed by the three siblings, flew off like a flock of birds.

THE RETURN TO THE NORTHERN KINGDOM
The couple made their way to Ke'u. When they arrived they stood at the retreat-boundary marker and beat the stone gong. The sage at once came out. The couple prostrated to him and Sudhana said:

Compassionate guide for the teachings and living beings
    in the world
whose knowledge illuminates[46] the vast space-like range
    of phenomena
like a great beacon appearing in samsara,
incomparable great sage, please hear these words.

The message left for me by this goddess,
and given to me by the sage, I followed exactly,
and gradually negotiated the perilous way to Vṛkṣaḥ,
arriving without harm in the land of the gandharvas.

There I met face to face with the goddess Manoharā.
I asked for an audience with the Vṛkṣaḥ mother and father,
and asked that they grant Manoharā permission to leave.
In reply they said in many ways that they were unwilling.

They set me various tests, both fierce and gentle,
and by the power and blessing of all objects of refuge,
and particularly by the compassion of the great sage,
Sudhana was successful in all he attempted.

The other side gave up the competition and said
that they would happily do whatever I asked.
Not only was I given Manoharā, but a farewell party
of many gandharvas was sent as far as the Brahma
    bathing pools.

That I have accomplished all I had wished for
is due to the compassion of the incomparable great sage.
From now until I attain the very essence of enlightenment,
may I always be cared for by you
within the refuge of your meditative concentration.

As a representation of this prayer, Sudhana presented the sage with the precious royal jewel and other unimaginable emblems. The sage invited the couple into his cave. After affording them every hospitality, he said:

Listen to me, fortunate son of a noble family.
By the excellent deeds born from your excellent resolve,
you destroyed the wild northern tribe for the sake of beings
    and the teachings,
and brought all those of wrong views to the Dharma.

You traveled to the celestial realm of Vṛkṣaḥ
and outshone the gandharvas and the yakṣa spirits.
Furthermore, with Manoharā you came to this place.
How excellent that you have accomplished all your intentions.

From now on, Sudhana and Manoharā,
you will face no more unwanted and hostile situations.
Go quickly to your great palace.
Repair the bond between father and son.

Toward those violators who acted with wicked intent,
apart from one or two out of necessity,
show them the kindness of gratitude.

Make offerings to the Three Jewels and give alms to the poor.
Accomplish great things for all living beings.
I will pray that we meet again soon.

Manoharā spoke:

Compassionate guide of living beings, including the gods,
who performs excellent deeds for the sake of others,
a master of the speedy path to freedom,
to hear, think of, or remember you closes the gates to the
    lower realms.
You who possesses a knowledge that illuminates phenomena,
please listen to these words.

This maiden Manoharā, born from gods, by the power of karma
was sent to be the companion of a lord of men.
Previously, by the tricks of violators from the north,
many unwanted evil acts were carried out.

However, by the peerless compassion of the great sage,
the obstacles of these hindering violators had not power,
and once again I met with this loving youth.

May we be cared for always within the fenced protection wheel
of your meditative concentration that ensures that from now on
no hindrance or obstacle will ever arise again.

The couple made farewell prostrations and left. The horses, chariots, and oxen that had been presented to Manoharā as farewell gifts from Vṛkṣaḥ traveled with the force of magic powers and soon the couple arrived at a place called Land of Fulfillment of Wishes, which was in the domain of the northern kingdom. The regional governor, the estate supervisor, the military commander, the committee of ten elders, and so on, all knew that the couple was Sudhana and Manoharā and were overjoyed to see them. They waited on the couple and made available to them all they had. The local householders beat drums, hung flags, sang, and danced. The couple too was delighted with the reception. Sudhana addressed them:

Hear me, estate governor, officials, and committee of elders!
As was my father's command, I traveled to the north.
There I defeated completely the wild tribe of the north,
but thinking of my parents and Manoharā, I hurried back.
When I arrived home, Manoharā was not there.
Asking my parents, attendants, and servant where she was,
I was told she had returned to her country of Vṛkṣaḥ.

Being unhappy, I asked my mother for more details,
and in her reply she described how the army of the queens
    and Hari
arrived at the Land of Joy Palace, and that Manoharā had to flee.
She said that they had carried out these wicked acts
by saying with bravado that they were ordained by the words
    of my father.

My mother talked to them and tried to turn them away,
but they made it clear that there was no going back.
Their minds had been turned by a demon from the north.

She was not able to tell me everything in detail,
but because of these events, Manoharā returned to her country.

This I could not bear. I went away and called out her name.
and by the compassion of the Three Jewels I fulfilled my aim,
and now Sudhana returns to his country.

To mark this remarkable and trouble-free arrival
faithful people, prepare an auspicious celebration!

It was with a smile of joy that Sudhana gave this frank address. Tashi Wangpo,[47] the estate governor, prostrated with great happiness to Sudhana and said:

Lord of men, guardian of this world, listen to me.
What I have heard, I will pass on to you.
After you, great king, had left for the north,
Hari, in his list of substances needed for his so-called ritual,
called for the fat from the heart of a kiṃnara spirit.

This would be achieved by killing Manoharā,
and to this end he pleaded with the king, your father.
The king discussed this with the five hundred queens and Hari,
and their army surrounded the palace, I heard.

What you, great king, have just described
and what I have heard are similar.
But with great kindness you and Manoharā
have by magical powers come to this place.

Two days after they arrived, Sudhana called the estate governor before him and said:

Tashi Wangpo, governor of Land of Fulfillment
    of Wishes estate,
listen to my words with great attention.
Go to the great palace of the northern continent,
and take this message to my mother and father.

Tell them that Sudhana returns from the Vṛkṣaḥ land,
and brings with him a well and healthy Manoharā.
Now I am staying at the Fulfillment of Wishes estate,
and soon I will be arriving at the great palace.

They should tell my servants, my household attendants,
    my officials,
and the ten young female attendants to the goddess
to come to the place of the welcoming party,
and to please make whatever other preparations are necessary.

In particular, say to my lady mother
that Sudhana traveled to the gandharva land,
and the journey there and back was without hardship.
Tell her that he is overjoyed to have found Manoharā,
and especially it makes him happy in both body and mind
to think that he will soon meet again with his mother.

Sudhana presented him with a large offering scarf as a greeting for his
parents. The estate governor carried out the wishes of Sudhana. He set off
with about ten servants, traveling day and night. As soon as he arrived at the
Land of Joy Palace, he informed the palace officials of the importance of his
visit and that he needed an audience with the mother and father. He was
immediately ushered into their presence, where he related Sudhana's mes-
sage. Sudhana's parents were overjoyed. In particular, his mother took the
ceremonial greeting scarf offered by Manoharā and Sudhana in her hands
and said:

Governor of the Fulfillment of Wishes estate,
is the news you bring today true?
If so, my dreams have come true.
I have only one child, and in my later life, he had to go away,
and his presence at home was like a star in the daytime.

Especially when Manoharā left for her country,
my son disappeared one night and could not be found.
How could he possibly go to the land of Vṛkṣaḥ?

From then on I thought I would not see my son again,
and in my mind I did not have a single day of happiness.
Is the news you bring today really true? Tell me more!

Tashi Wangpo spoke:

Listen to me, lady mother.
The words I have just delivered to you,
are the unmistaken instructions of king Sudhana himself.

In particular, in his closing remarks to his mother
he says that in his journey to the land of the gandharvas
he was well and the journey back was without problem.

More than this, he was overjoyed to have found Manoharā,
and especially the thought of meeting with his mother again
brought him joy in both body and mind.
He delivered these pleasing words with a ceremonial scarf.

Moreover, on the day he arrived at the Land of Fulfillment
    of Wishes,
he was accompanied by all his previous wealth,
such as horses, elephants, chariots, and so on.
Issue the command for an unmistaken welcoming ceremony.

Mother and father were overjoyed. Tashi Wangpo was treated with lavish
gifts. The father ordered the nobles and all prominent people before him. As
soon as they had arrived, he announced:

Hear me, assembled nobles and people.
Tashi Wangpo from the Land of Fulfillment of Wishes
was recently here and brought us this news and tidings.

My incomparable son, Sudhana, in search of Manoharā,
had traveled far to the land of gandharvas.
In that land he found her and is now on his way back,
and has reached the Land of Fulfillment of Wishes.

He possesses all his previous power and glory.
He had particular words and a ceremonial scarf for his mother.
He has definitely arrived. There is no mistake, the governor
  has said.

Sudhana asks that his servants, household attendants, and
  officials,
and the ten young female attendants to the goddess,
come to meet him at the place of the welcoming party.
You should all leave early tomorrow.

When I think of the supernormal endeavors of Sudhana
I am filled with regret and feel ashamed.

As Sudhana will soon arrive, make the following preparations.
The day after tomorrow set up a throne in the reception hall.
Put on the best of feasts and prepare a list of foods to be offered.
On the palace roof, beat the drums and hoist flags and banners.

Dignitaries, form the best welcoming procession.
Householders, put on shows of singing and dancing.
Those, such as his mother, traveling by horse to welcome him,
should leave for a place about a day's ride from here.
The relevant departments should take note of all this.

For those, such as the queens and Hari,
not joining the welcoming party,
there will be no need to make any arrangements.
You can do as you wish.

An investigation, which all of you will be able to trust,
into the matter of the broken bond
between father and son
will soon be undertaken by this old man.

  With these words he stared at Hari and the queens. Everybody just stood
there gasping. Most were delighted to hear the news of Sudhana's impending
arrival. They covered Tashi Wangpo with hero-ceremonial scarves in grati-

tude for bringing good news, and rushed away to hand to the all people of the kingdom notices telling them to beat drums and fly flags on the day of Sudhana's arrival.

On the next day household attendants, officials, and female attendants belonging to Sudhana and Manoharā left the palace dressed in their best clothes. Two days later they reached the encampment at a place called Tashi Palsang. Immediately they went before the couple, offering ceremonial scarves and making prostrations. As soon as they had sat down, Sudhana addressed them:

My servants, household attendants, and officials,
and the ten young female attendants to the goddess,
it is wonderful that today we have met again.
Tell me, in the northern kingdom Palace of the
    Land of Joy,
are my mother and father in good health?
Are the harvests good? Is the kingdom happy and well?
In particular, has my mother not suffered excessively
    on my behalf?

An official called Devendra placed his palms together at his heart and said:

Celestial prince, most kind Dharma king,
sole refuge and hope for living beings, lord of men,
great king of extraordinary supernatural powers,
turn your ear to me for a while.

In our northern kingdom in the land of India,
your mother and father are well, the harvests are good.
But because of the obstructions brought on by hindering
    violators,
we were tormented by the prince leaving for we know
    not where,
and so remained troubled with no merit accumulated.

Since you have been gone, have you been free of illness?
Have you not cast the people of the northern kingdom
    from your mind?

This joy of seeing your face today,
it cannot be real. This must be a dream?

Sudhana replied:

Devendra, and all of you gathered here, listen to me.
My father, the ruler of the land, was deceived by wicked people.
For no good reason I was sent far away to the north.
At home they plotted the death of innocent Manoharā.

This maiden was forced to flee to the land of Vṛkṣaḥ,
which I could not bear, and I went in search of her,
but in doing so I had to keep it secret from all of you.
It is true that you were tormented by not knowing where
    I had gone.

However, today the dawn of reconciliation has finally risen.
I did indeed turn my mind against my father for his deeds,
but thinking about it thoroughly, I see it was the work of others.
My father bears no blame, and I regret my thoughts.
More on this I will speak later.

Thus with a smile Sudhana addressed them. They were all delighted, and
tears of joy mingled with those of sadness fell from their eyes. Manoharā said:

My attendants, Ānandī and the others,
you ten young maidens, listen to me.
After I left the Land of Joy Palace,
were all of you untroubled by illness?
Your hearts did not become diseased by wicked thoughts?
Has your dwelling place been in the palace?

The attendant Ānandī replied:

Beautiful princess, in the glory of youth, endowed with love,
possessed of the magical power to travel through the skies in
    an instant,

a ḍākiṇī who captures the mind[48] of gods and men alike,
please listen to this maiden of little mind.

Since you flew off into the skies,
we have not been tormented by illness,
but without our refuge, we have despaired,
and this has been very hard to bear.

However, apart from words from elsewhere
that have torn away at our hearts,
by the compassion of the most kind mother,
we have not wanted for food and clothing.

The lady mother has been troubled with worry for you,
and because of that we too have been without joy.
But today we have been delivered from that pit of dark despair.
The sun of happiness, the goddess Manoharā,
shines on all from the peak of the eastern mountain.
The demon-like birds of Hari and the five hundred queens,
have they not once again been cast into the darkness?

The sweet chirpings of the ten baby cuckoos
are bothersome to the owl but have to be expressed.
From now until we attain enlightenment,
may we be cared for by the exalted-wisdom ḍākiṇī.

With these words, all who were assembled there broke out in smiles.
The party proceeded and eventually arrived at a place called Tiger Peak
Plain, where they made camp. All officials and householders living in the
surrounding area came for audience and offered their service and hospitality.
Moving on, they came to a place called Stream of the Ganges. There too the
local population came to render their services and hospitality.

Two representatives of the lady mother arrived to greet the prince. They
explained that on the following day the lady mother would arrive at a place
called Land of Spontaneous Creation. The couple was overjoyed.

Early the next day the lady mother with about one hundred nobles and
servants and a welcoming party of officials and ordinary people, making a
total of almost five hundred horse riders, arrived at Land of Spontaneous

Creation. Just after midday Sudhana, with an escort consisting of a large number of bodyguards, arrived at the welcoming camp set up by his mother. His mother said:

> Sudhana and Manoharā, both so dear to my heart,
> how wonderful that we actually meet without hindrance.
> Again and again I have thought of you, and with tormented
>   mind
> again and again with a clear voice I have called out to you
>   in prayer.
> Again and again the prayers I have made have today come true,
> and the sun and moon of happiness have clearly risen.
> If this old woman were to die tomorrow, she would have
>   no regrets.

She took Sudhana and Manoharā by the hand and shed tears of joy. Sudhana placed his mother's hand on his head and said:

> Mother ordained by karma without beginning,
> who could have been mother to all living beings,
> but became my mother who nursed me with great kindness.
> When I think on the love and compassion you gave to me,
> I see it as being impossible to repay, even over an eon.
> Until you are placed upon the path to enlightenment,
> I vow to be the one to fulfill your every wish.

Mother, son, and Manoharā were seated on thrones. Manoharā said:

> By the excellent deeds within the realm
> of phenomena vast and profound,
> has your body stayed well?
> Have your meditations bloomed?
> Did the wickedness from elsewhere not disturb your mind?
>
> One by one I have met with mother and with father,
> with the great sage, Sudhana, and others,
> and every bad circumstance has arisen as a friend.

Especially meeting with you, great lady mother,
is as if this maiden has been brought back from the dead.

The lady mother replied:

Manoharā, my daughter not born of me,
my physical virtuous practices have flourished,
but when you left for the land of Vṛkṣaḥ,
the mental pain of thinking I would not see you at
   the end of my life
meant that I had not a moment of joy in my mind.

However, by the compassion of the infallible Three Jewels,
all my pain and torment has today come to an end.

Mother, son, and Manoharā spent that evening in a tent and discussed the good and bad that had happened at home and abroad.

The next day, the welcoming procession of dignitaries and the shows of singing and dancing stretched from the palace for about half a day's journey along the road. Everybody—officials and ordinary householders—beat drums and waved flags. King Mahādhana and his entourage had arranged a welcoming party on the open ground by the southern gate. The five hundred queens were not allowed to welcome the couple and stood glumly hidden among the crowd of townsfolk to watch the event. As for Hari, it was being said that he was no longer fit to receive food and provisions from the community, and as a result he pretended to be mad.

Sudhana and Manoharā arrived at the open ground by the southern gate at the head of an army complete with all four divisions,[49] looking even more glorious and radiant than before. Celestial offerings and many wonderful standards and banners lined the road as the sound of music filled the air. Sudhana and Manoharā offered ceremonial scarves and prostrated to the lord father. When they were seated on thrones, the father spoke:

My young Sudhana, listen to me.
One night you left the palace in secret,
and thinking about that, I your father had regrets.
Now it is wonderful that father and son have met again.

You traveled to the land of the gandharvas,
and by your extraordinary powers you have returned.
As you have done so before your old father died,
there will be the appropriate celebrations,
and during a break in the festivities
father and son, with mutual trust,
will separate out the good from the bad.

Sudhana replied:

Great father, please hear my words.
When I returned home from the north,
Manoharā was not here, and I asked father where she had gone.

She had left for the land of Vṛkṣaḥ,
and when I set out in search of her,
I did so in secret,
and did not offer a farewell to my father.

However, if I had not kept secret my wandering off alone,
I feared that some harm would come to your reputation,
even though I have no choice over my circumstances.
Therefore, I left without meeting anyone,
and held our refuge, the Three Jewels, constantly on my head.

Without problem I arrived at the gandharva land.
Today I have returned and met again with my father.
Put on a wonderful and glorious celebration!

Great father, you did initiate some activities,
but I do not hold them as wrong, my compassionate father.

With these words he prostrated to his father, who was overcome with
repentance. Manoharā addressed the father:

Alas! Listen to me, great king and great father.
Hari, the incomparable, mighty practitioner,

the sole refuge for father in this and future lives, is he here?
Was the powerful long-life ritual successful?

The father replied:

Celestial goddess, Manoharā, listen carefully to me.
The thoughts behind the maiden's words are true indeed,
but if the name "hell" is not well known,
the wish for the freedom "buddha" will not truly arise.

It was by the evil deeds carried out by Hari
that I came to see the qualities of Sudhana and Manoharā,
and with everyone proclaiming them with great faith,
are they not known throughout the worlds of gods and men?

Having been tricked like this, the remorseful mind
of this old father will begin its investigation very shortly.

They then proceeded to the great reception hall, where a great and unprecedented celebration was held. Sudhana addressed the nobles and the people gathered there, and told them in great detail of Manoharā's message left with the sage when he had set out for Vṛkṣaḥ, how he successfully negotiated the hindrances on the way to the gandharva land, how he met with the rulers and people of that land, how he performed various feats, wrathful and gentle, in order to win Manoharā, and so on. Everybody, from the nobles to the ordinary people, was astonished and amazed.

After the feast had ended, the main guests went to their rooms and the father issued orders concerning the staging of the following celebrations.

Tsering Wangmo and Samdrup Drölma, who were two queens from the five hundred that Sudhana previously had affection for, were told to come before him. They arrived crying and in a state of terror. Immediately, they offered ceremonial scarves and prostrated to Sudhana and Manoharā. Sudhana addressed them:

Tsering and Samdrup, listen to me.
After I was sent away to the north,
you five hundred queens, together with Hari,
surrounded the palace with an army and declared

that this was the order of the king, my father,
and that Manoharā was to be killed
and the fat of her heart was to be taken.

Although all five hundred queens were present then,
you two and I share a bond of friendship.
Why did you do these wicked things?
Tell me in detail everything that happened.

If you tell me everything, honestly and without deceit,
I promise I will not have you killed.
If you do not speak the truth,
you will know no mercy.

The two queens in a state of great fear spoke in unison:

Loving and compassionate lord of men,
listen to we two maidens of inferior merit.
Of the wicked deeds carried out by the five hundred queens,
we will tell what we know, with all sincerity.
Please do not let it cost our lives.

They went down on one knee and began:

The wicked deeds of the demon-possessed queens,
we will now relate in detail. Please hear our words.
During the festivities when Queen Manoharā first arrived
    at the palace,
she was placed at the head of the row upon a turquoise throne,
while the five hundred queens were in lesser rows on wooden
    thrones.
The offerings from those attending the outer and inner
    celebrations
showed a lack of respect for the five hundred queens.

Because of this, the queens slandered Manoharā to the people.
The people all responded by talking of her beauty and noble ways.

When such praise reached the ears of the queens,
they were tormented as if bad food had stuck in their stomachs.

For over a month they were not to be in the presence
    of the king.
Some of the elder queens began meeting and discussing at night.
Most of us were unaware of what they were doing.
One day they called us all to a meadow outside the palace.
Even our servants were to be left far behind.

We engaged in all kind of arrogant and wasteful talk
about how we did not want the celestial princess to be here.
In our midst, a senior queen, Arthasiddhi Lakṣmī, spoke:

"Through that ill-omened and low-caste hunter,
and that destructive mountain-dweller Prakāśamati,
this wandering woman, the so-called Manoharā Devī,
    came here.

Some trouble-making ministers and citizens
informed the king about this new and exciting prospect,
and as soon as she arrived, he greeted her and gave her gifts.

The lords and people were all assembled and a celebration
    was laid on.
Ornaments, clothes, servants, whatever she wished for,
    she was given.
Even the gifts presented by the people showed us little respect,
and were like an official meeting his servant.

If the king is to have such high regard for a maiden
merely escorted here by some homeless fisherman,
we think it is shameful for a king to show so little respect
to we five hundred queens, who by our fathers' names alone
were met and royally escorted when taken as brides.

In the past we five hundred would catch the king's eye,
and he would hold us in great esteem.

Since this wandering, so-called Manoharā has arrived,
it is not possible for we five hundred to be in the king's presence.
If we do not devise a way to be rid of Manoharā,
in the future it will become difficult to be regarded even
    as servants.

The yogi Hari, object of veneration for the king's father,
possesses many methods, oral traditions, and great magical
    ability.
Some of us should go to him and seek a way to be rid of
    Manoharā."

All listened to her words and all were agreed.
We formed a pact that this decision would not be changed.
Arthasiddhi Lakṣmī along with three of the other queens
one night left to seek an audience with Hari.
On returning we were overjoyed to hear from them
that Hari had agreed to our request.

After the king had left for the north,
the senior queens went often to Hari.
One day the lord father called us all before him.
This he told us:

"This Manoharā has been sent as ransom for all the gods.
Wherever she stays trouble will follow.
Queens, take weapons and go and kill Manoharā.
The fat of her heart is needed for a bathing ritual."

With these words he gave us a weapons requisition
for much armor, as well as many arrows and swords.
The senior queens were delighted and said:
"Today our hopes and wishes have all come true.
All of you queens, young and old, let us go."

For the other younger queens, such as we two here,
we had no power to do anything, good or bad.

If you ask the older queens as well as Hari,
it will be clear in your mind, great king.
Please, do not let this cost us our lives.

Sudhana felt compassion in his mind but maintained an outward wrathful expression. Manoharā spoke to the two queens:

Listen to me, you two young queens.
What you have said, I hear as honest words.
This inner enemy of the three poisons, this angry self-grasping,
is a cause for the destruction of oneself and others.
The power of the elder queen, Arthasiddhi Lakṣmī,
meant that you had no power to do anything.
Do not trouble yourselves. Have some food and drink.
I will ensure that your lives are not at risk.

With this, Manoharā took from the food and drink provided for the couple and gave some to the two young queens. The two queens prostrated many times to Manoharā and said:

Mistress of compassion, bodhisattva ḍākinī,
embodiment of the forbearance of no-self,
untainted by the stains of pride and anger,
please hear these words.

We have been ruined by the low-merit, wicked deeds of others.
Do not cast us from the place of refuge that exists for the sake
    of others,
lying within the great Dharma realm of your wonderful
    compassion.

Again they wept and made prostrations. Sudhana wrote down what the two young queens had told him and went to his father. He said:

Most kind father, please hear what I have to say.
I called before me two young queens from the five hundred,
and asked them to tell all that had occurred.

All that they said I have written down in detail,
and I come before you to present it for your perusal,
and to make the events clear in your mind.
The good and the bad, in every detail, is all within this
    document.

Sudhana presented the document to his father. He studied it carefully
and the expression on his face changed. Slapping his hand against his knee,
he said:

My beloved son, listen to me.
I had my suspicions that this homeless fraud Hari
was plotting trouble by using ritual substances with wicked
    intention
to accomplish the wishes of the destructive queens.
I will without delay carry out a thorough investigation.

Sudhana returned to his rooms. The lord father called before him the
two young queens who had given the account of the events to Sudhana. The
father questioned the two queens by going through the contents of the doc-
ument. They replied:

Listen to us, great father and king.
That report of the questions posed to us
on past events by the prince Sudhana
is a sincere and honest report of what we know.
There is nothing to be changed to that document.
For more detail, if you were to ask Hari and the elder queens,
it would become clearer for father and son.

Having verified the document, the two queens left. The lord father called
his inner and outer attendants and told them to seize Hari and the five
hundred queens. They were all taken at the same time and put separately
into dark rooms.

One day after the celebrations had finished, the lord father went to a park,
taking with him an effective number of attendants. "First, bring me Hari!"
he ordered.

Hari, his hands bound by rope, was brought before the lord father, who addressed him:

> Evil and deluded, ignorant of deeds and their effects,
> black-hearted Hari, listen to me!
> This is an account compiled from the questions
> Sudhana asked of two young queens.
> Listen to it and tell me the truth.

The document was read aloud. Hari replied:

> Lord father and king, listen to me.
> The divinations that I made concerning the fortunes of
>   the north
> came to pass in accord with their wording.
> As for the circumstances of the army surrounding of the palace,
> that occurred in keeping with the lord father's instructions.
>
> I was also instructed to arrange the killing of the goddess,
> and suggested to you that as it was not proper for others to
>   kill her,
> it would look better if the five hundred queens carried it out.
>
> The lord father himself instructed the queens,
> and provided the weapons to them and to me.
> Although we surrounded the palace,
> Manoharā flew off into the skies and escaped being killed.
>
> All of this the lord father probably remembers.
> I know nothing about the events in this document.
> You should ask the queens.

The lord father became angry. Hari was rebound and taken away. "Bring Arthasiddhi Lakṣmī to me," he demanded. When she was brought before him, the lord father said:

> Pernicious Arthasiddhi Lakṣmī, listen well!
> This is an account of your evil and wrong deeds.

Tell me if this account by two young queens
is actually what happened or not.

The document was read out, and Arthasiddhi Lakṣmī replied:

Great king, do not say these things. Listen to me.
The lord father called the five hundred queens before him,
and these are the words you spoke to us:

"Hari has performed a divination for some disturbing dreams.
He said we must perform rituals to thwart any trouble,
and the list of materials needed for an extensive bathing ritual
includes the fat taken from a kiṃnara spirit.
This kiṃnara spirit sent as a ransom for all the gods,
is none other than the maiden known as Manoharā.
Therefore, kill her and take her fat."

We accepted this task and asked for a weapons requisition.
The queens, together with Hari, surrounded the palace,
but Manoharā flew off into the skies.
We did not get the fat, and there was nothing we could do.
Hari came to the lord father, and at the bathing pool
performed the bathing ritual for the lord father.

All of this can be remembered by everybody.
I do not recognize the contents of this document.
Confirm it with those who provided it.

Neither Hari nor Arthasiddhi Lakṣmī had accepted the account. The lord father became very angry and subjected Hari to forceful questioning. Hari cried out helplessly and said:

Hear me! I know these things. Lord father,
this is what the five hundred queens did.
One night while I was sitting in my hut,
four of the queens came to see me.
This is what they told me.

"Events occurring in the northern kingdom are as follows.
A woman who goes by the name of Manoharā,
brought to the palace by a wandering fisherman,
has now been taken by the king to be a queen.
Now the king no longer pays his five hundred queens
    any attention.
It is not possible for us queens to be in his presence.
Manoharā is by his side day and night,
and, moreover, the king lavishes her with gifts and praise.

Previously, for fear of disturbing the king's mind,
we five hundred have been very tolerant,
but her self-regard grows stronger by the day.

Now we five hundred queens cannot put up with this anymore.
Therefore we four have come before you, great guru.
Whether by curse, burning, power, or torma,
we must find a way to destroy Manoharā."

Again and again they pressed me, and I could not say no.
I agreed to fulfill the demands of the queens.
I perverted the dream omens of the lord father.
When you requested divination, I gave false readings.
Once Sudhana had left for the north, I deceived the father
by suggesting that Manoharā should be killed.

My wicked deeds did not bear fruit and now I am ruined.
Please do not deprive me of my life.

With these words he had confirmed the account given by the two queens.
Then the three queens who had accompanied Arthasiddhi Lakṣmī to Hari's
dwelling that night, and who had been identified by her, were summoned.
They were presented with the account in the document as well as Hari's con-
fession, and asked to explain. They replied:

Lord of men, great father, please hear our words.
The demon-possessed deeds of the five hundred queens,

as have been recounted by the two young queens,
and then accepted by Hari in his confession,
we accept as true without question.

Although Manoharā was not liked by any of us,
and there were some younger queens implicated
alongside the senior queen, Arthasiddhi Lakṣmī,
who had initiated the discussion on the wicked deed,
most of us had no say in what was to be done, good or bad.
Hari promised to carry out what could not be done.

Such wicked deeds have ruined self and others.
Great king, apart from your mercy,
we have no place of hope.

That evening Hari and the queens were returned to their places. The lord
father returned to the palace, where he called the lady mother, Sudhana, and
Manoharā before him. He said:

Lady mother, Manoharā, Sudhana,
and others gathered here, listen to me.
This father is old, his faculties have become weak.
I relied upon this trouble-making fraud, Hari, for a guru,
and with wicked intent he performed some trickery
and placed perverted omens in my dreams.
I could not rely on my own mind. It had been manipulated.
Whatever he did, I believed to be true and put into practice.

For no good reason I sent Sudhana into enemy territory
    in the north.
After that, Hari said we needed to perform rituals,
and so senselessly I did them. Whatever he said, I did.
I organized a plot to be rid of Manoharā.
After Sudhana returned from the north, we fought.
Through the trickery of Hari this old father was like
    a madman.
What I have done, I regret and confess.
At the end of my life I will turn to the Dharma.

The accounts of the two queens have been confirmed,
and accepted as true by Hari and the five hundred queens.
From tomorrow Hari and the five hundred queens
will feel the wrath of the law and all be sentenced to death.
Their servants and dependents will all be evicted.

I am a disgraced descendant of the royal northern lineage,
and when I think about it all, I have no joy in my heart.

The lord father was close to despair. Sudhana spoke:

Alas! Most kind father, please listen to me.
Do not trouble your mind so. Do not be so sad.
By removing the stains of suspicion that hung over
the broken bond between father and son, and Manoharā,
we have examined in detail all the trouble that occurred,
and our minds have become clearer and trust is restored.

I ask that I be allowed to request in a while
that the forceful punishment of death not be carried out.
In particular, I ask that with your great compassion
you release at once the two queens
Tsering Wangmo and Samdrup Drölma.

The lord father pardoned the two queens. Later when the king was appointing the executioner to carry out the killing of the remaining queens and Hari, Manoharā addressed the king:

Listen to me, lord father and king.
Hari and the queens, who troubled and disturbed your mind,
are to be forcefully destroyed, you have decided.
This would be a victory for self and a defeat
over these ordinary beings, Hari and the queens,
but great father, as the lord of religious and secular rule,
you are the great protector for all beings and the teachings.

When you examine all that has occurred,
looking in the detail at the good and the bad,

the purposes of living beings and the teachings have been served.
Disregarding whatever you hear,
and just holding to whatever comes to mind
is a very rushed way of doing things.

You held as a guru a fraud unworthy to be held as a guru.
Whatever he said you held as true and followed it through.
You cannot bear to hear talk of it.
Your upper body is squeezed by tension.
Lord father, do not be in such a frenzy.

For Hari, enemy of the teachings who has truly caused harm,
whatever is appropriate according to the law,
great father you know best what to do.
But of what benefit is it to kill the young queens?
Please give an order about what is best to do.

The lord father replied:

Manoharā, do not say this. Listen to me.
The five hundred queens, exemplified by Arthasiddhi Lakṣmī,
seduced Hari with wealth and then deceived me.
These were pointless, wicked deeds, unheard of in the kingdom,
deeds where word and fact were not in agreement.
It looks as if these serious acts were carried out by me,
and everywhere the blame falls on me.
There is no way to set them free.
Who knows what would happen again in the future?
Do not be foolish, Manoharā.

The lady mother then spoke:

Lord father and Manoharā, listen to me.
If we look at the deeds of Hari and the queens,
they are difficult to tolerate and beyond the bounds
    of compassion.
However, lord father, please consider that which
    Manoharā asks.

It is the mere sparing of their lives that she asks,
not a way of allowing them do as they please.

This evening we should return to our rooms.
Tomorrow I will assemble four government officials,
and we will discuss what is best to do.

Everybody returned to their rooms. The next day the four government officials and all distinguished members of the palace entourage assembled in the lord father's rooms. As the lord father was arranging the execution he had decided on, Manoharā again spoke up:

I, Manoharā, am a maiden of little merit.
For my sake many innocent tribal men were killed.
I have given Sudhana and the lady mother much trouble.

If my fervent request for the lord father to refrain from
the wrong deed of depriving Hari and queens of their lives
is not listened to, I will not stay here but return to my own land.

As she said these words, she began to weep. Sudhana addressed his father:

My lord father and all assembled here,
please listen well to what Sudhana says.
If we look at the deeds of Hari and the queens,
they are indeed as the lord father has described.

However, in consideration primarily of the advice of the sage,
and of the request made now by the goddess Manoharā,
I, Sudhana, offer this suggestion to the lord father.

Hari is an enemy of the teachings and should be killed.
Arthasiddhi Lakṣmī initiated the discussion of being rid
   of Manoharā—
her eyes should be plucked out and she sent to some
   loathsome land.
As for those senior queens involved with Arthasiddhi Lakṣmī,

cut their ears off and cast them into a beggar colony.
Some of the other senior queens below them
should be given as wives to low-caste blacksmiths.
The rest should be given to poor serf families.
Please consider these suggestions, lord father.

The lady mother, Sudhana, and Manoharā made a fervent prostration request to the lord father, who replied angrily:

Looking at the deeds of Hari and the queens,
nothing has changed from my previous assessment,
but in the face of requests from the lady mother, my son, and
    Manoharā,
it is acceptable to do as Sudhana has suggested.

On the following day, the townsfolk gathered on the open ground by the southern gate. Hari and the queens were brought out. The judgment was read out, which described how black-hearted Hari, with wicked thought and deed toward all people of the northern kingdom, and for the sake of fame and fortune, had issued his instructions and so forth.

Then at sunrise on the fifteenth day of the first month of the earth tiger year, a day when constellations and planet were all in harmonious positions, in the reception hall called Coming Together of All That Could Be Desired, in the Land of Joy Palace, upon a high throne supported by stone lions, the Dharma king Sudhana was enthroned. By way of an auspicious and lavish celebration, the father made offerings to Sudhana, including a ceremonial scarf, the eight auspicious substances, and the seven royal emblems. The presentation of the emblem known as the Meditation Vajra Amassing All and the enthronement gifts were magnificent beyond imagination. All officials and householders continually made so many offerings that the men stacking the offerings could not complete their task. Music as rare and renowned as the sun and moon occurring together in the sky filled the regions far and wide, so much so that from far off, thick clouds of visitors from minor kingdoms such as the Dzungar and the Alchi arrived constantly from places months and years away in order to offer celebratory gifts.

By the great kindness of Dharma King Sudhana, in the northern regions of India and throughout the entire world, the rains of happiness fell when needed, cattle and crops were abundant and healthy, and famine, war, and disease were unheard of. His first task as ruler was to initiate prayers for the teachings. He invited the monastic heads to the palace and for over a month honored them, served them, and gave them generous donations. He restored to the people what had been gathered in tax penalties, and with acts of giving alleviated poverty.

The lord father, now of Tashi Chödé Monastery, said: "Previously, I treated Hari with great kindness, but he ignored the law of cause and effect and repaid my kindness perversely with many deeds. In particular, when I think of the demon-possessed actions of the five hundred queens, they were actions of malevolent thoughts and deeds. Using the trickery of black mantra, he organized the sending of Sudhana to the north and the fleeing of Manoharā to her own land, wicked actions where word and fact were in contradiction. Having examined these actions, by his own confession they were wicked acts based on lies. Therefore, to set a good example for all hereafter, he will be subjected to the harshest of punishments. Look now at the one who is to be killed!"

With these words Hari was impaled on a stake. Then the five hundred queens were led out. Arthasiddhi Lakṣmī had her eyes plucked out. Those senior queens who were involved with her had their ears cut off. One group lower than them were married off to low-caste blacksmiths. Their younger companions were given as wives to poor serfs.

Although the queens had to be sentenced to die, they were saved by the late intervention of Manoharā, and after much thought it was decided that they would remain in their residences to reflect wisely and cautiously upon what they had done.

The stains of suspicion that hung over the broken bond between father and son and Manoharā had been removed. The father organized celebrations for handing over the throne to Sudhana that lasted for over a month. For his own people from the districts and estates far and near who had come to the enthronement to offer gifts, he provided sweet food for the grand displays, singing and dancing, horse races, archery contests, and so on. He visited his own officials and servants, wherever they lived, engaged in pleasant conversation with them, and then left to live in solitude. The two young queens were enrolled as nuns in Samten Monastery. Everywhere and at all times, the great blessings of excellent deeds done for the sake of living beings and the doctrine were sown.

* * *

Thus ends part 4, describing how Sudhana's wish to become a great guide for the glory of the teachings and living beings, and so on, was fulfilled, and how by merely seeing, hearing, remembering, and touching him, people developed devotion toward him.

Inspired by *The Life of Dharma King Sudhana*, written in forty-six chapters, and in order to fulfill the wishes of the monastic administrators and other dignitaries, and for patrons in the land who put on this opera in regions big and small, what I have to say as expressions of dance movements, by way of addition and omission, is for the time being complete.

3. The Story of the Chinese and Nepalese Princesses

THE EMANATED KING Songtsen Gampo was born in the female fire-ox year[50] in the Jampa Migyur Ling Palace at Maldro Gyama, in the Tibetan central region of Lön. His father was Namri Songtsen and his mother was Driza Tökar. At his birth the self-arisen face of Buddha Amitābha was visible on his head. His father used a piece of red silk as a headscarf for his son's head. As it is said:

> In order to hide the face of Amitābha,
> the father used a red silk cloth as a headscarf.
> Those of the inner circle with fewer obscurations
> saw it as the crown ornaments of the five buddhas.

> The two young boys Gar and Tönmi[51]
> followed the devoted offerings made by the ministers,
> saw the face of Amitābha, and spoke of it.
> The child, therefore, was the "prince with two heads."

> Countless celebrations were held for days and months,
> and the child was given the name Trisong Tsen.
> However, endowed with every excellent quality,
> and of a profound (gam po) mind, he became known as
>   Songtsen Gampo.

When he reached the age of thirteen Songtsen Gampo ascended to the throne of the kingdom, and this mighty universal lord took on the role of a Tibetan emperor. Then this great emanated king moved to Lhasa and lived in a fortress on Red Hill, which resembled a tiger entering a mouse hole.[52] There he thought to himself: "To the people of this snow-capped land I have brought the happiness of gods and men and the happiness of the Śrāvaka and Pratyeka Buddhists, but this is of no great significance. Therefore I must propagate the peerless path to enlightenment."

He prayed and made offerings to the snake-heart sandalwood[53] statue of Avalokiteśvara. Immediately the statue responded: "You must create a statue of me."

The king gathered the material needed for creating the statue. These included cow-headed sandalwood,[54] sand from the Nairañjanā River,[55] and special grass and clay from the island of the Southern Ocean. As soon as the desire to create a statue in the likeness of his personal deity, Avalokiteśvara, had arisen, the next day a statue of Avalokiteśvara miraculously arose exactly as the king had wished. The king thought how wonderful it would be if this new statue would dwell inside the snake-heart sandalwood statue in the form of a wisdom-being. Immediately the clay statue dissolved into light from the soles of its feet upward and disappeared into the heart of the sandalwood statue.

When the king reached the age of sixteen, he decided to abide with the worldly convention of taking a bride. To this end he made prayers to the self-arisen statue of Avalokiteśvara. From the heart of the statue came two rays of light. One radiated out to Nepal and the other to China. The king looked at these places on which the light had shone. He saw that in Nepal, King Aṃśuvarman had a daughter known as the princess who was sixteen years old and endowed with every sign of beauty. She was an emanation of the goddess Bhṛkutī,[56] was accomplished in all the arts and sciences, and was rich in possessions and wealth. Looking toward China, he saw that King Tang Taizong had a daughter called Princess Wencheng, who was sixteen and endowed with every sign of beauty. She was an emanation of goddess Tārā, was accomplished in the arts and sciences, and owned a treasury filled with precious gems. These and other visions he was shown by the clear light deities in dreams.

The next day the Dharma king Songtsen Gampo put on his great brocade cloak. He covered the image of Amitābha on his head with a red silk headscarf. In his right hand he held a precious wheel amulet studded with jewels and emblazoned with the six-syllable mantra that is the very essence of Ārya Avalokiteśvara. In his left hand he held a milk-crystal rosary of one hundred and eight beads. With the six-syllable mantra on his lips, he called his inner ministers to him, such as Gar and Tönmi Kuntu Sangpo, and sang to them of the visions he had received in dreams:

Characters from *The Chinese and Nepalese Princesses* opera,
performed in India, 1962–63.

An itinerant storyteller of the *Buchen* Lhamo tradition of Spiti,
northern India, recounting the tale of *The Chinese and
Nepalese Princesses* in Langsa, 2007.

Listen to me, my ministers and subjects.
Do not be distracted. Hear what I say.
I have been granted revelations in dreams.

There are two emanations of Tārā,
one in China, and one in Nepal.
If I bring them to Tibet as my brides,
long-lasting happiness will come to this kingdom.

The inner ministers headed by seven high ministers, such as Gar and Tönmi Kuntu Sangpo, gathered under a shady tree by the side of Otang Lake to talk.[57] They had each brought to the meeting place a choice piece of leftover meat. When they placed their respective pieces of meat together, a complete carcass was formed. This was an auspicious sign for the discussions. Minister Gar spoke with great joy:

Assembly of ministers gathered here,
turn your ears to Gar Tongtsen.
The goddess revelations in the dreams of the king
speak of two noble emanations of white and green Tārā
appearing as daughters of kings in China and Nepal.
We must discuss if they are suitable to be queens to the king.

The assembled ministers all agreed that these two special princesses should be taken by the king for brides.

Seeking the Nepalese Princess

The king gave the ministers instructions. "At dawn on the eighth day of the first of the three autumn months when the moon is in the Puṣya lunar mansion, one hundred horsemen headed by minister Gar are to take one hundred golden coins and a suit of golden armor inlaid with precious stones, together with these scrolls containing my words. Pray to Tārā by the name of Bhṛkutī, then go west to Nepal and you will achieve your objective. The Nepalese king will not wish to give his daughter and will question you three times. At each question present the king with one of my scrolls in the correct order." With these instructions, together with the three scrolls, they left for the western land of Nepal.

The messenger ministers soon arrived in Nepal. They went before the Nepalese king, Aṃśuvarman, and presented him with an auspicious offering scarf. This was followed by the gifts of the golden, jewel-studded armor, and so on. Minister Gar addressed the Nepalese king:

> King of southern Nepal in the west,
> listen to this minister from Tibet.
> Headed by the auspicious offering scarf,
> we have presented you with the golden armor and so on.
> We ask that you give as queen for our king
> your daughter the princess Bhṛkutī.

The Nepalese king gave a scornful laugh. He said nothing but closed his eyes for a long time in thought. Finally he said:

> Listen to me, ministers from Tibet.
> The remote land of Tibet lacks the law of the ten virtues.
> It is not a fit land to have my daughter taken in marriage.
> If it were to abide by the law of the ten virtues,
> I would give my daughter to Tibet.

It would not be possible to establish in Tibet the law of the ten virtues. However, the first question had been asked and the Tibetan king's answer was required. Minister Gar brought to mind the emanated king's instructions. "I have a letter written by our ruler," he said to the Nepalese king. He presented to the king the scroll holder containing the letter written with gold ink in the Nepalese language.

The king looked at the letter. It read: "In one day I will manifest five thousand bodies and establish in the snow-capped land of Tibet the law of the ten virtues. Is that not amazing?" The king wondered if this was true or not. "If true," he thought, "it will be difficult to match him."

Finally the king replied:

> The Tibetan ruler's promise is impressive,
> but the remote land of Tibet has no temples or images.
> If he builds temples and the three representations,
> I will give the princess to be his queen.

Tibet had no representations of the Buddha's body, speech, and mind, but this was the second question and required an answer. The minister presented the second scroll written in silver ink to the Nepalese king. It read: "Having manifested five thousand bodies in one day, I will build one hundred and eight temples in Tibet, and the main door of each will face west toward Nepal. Is this not amazing?"

The Nepalese king thought to himself: "It will be difficult to match this. If I do not give him my daughter, that number of manifestations will lead an army here. I will be killed, my city destroyed, and the princess taken away. Therefore I will have to give her away."

However, he did not make a promise to give her away, but instead asked the ministers a third question to see if they were serious in their quest:

> Here I am wealthy in the pleasures of the five senses.
> The far-off country of Tibet is poor and has few resources.
> If your resources can match mine,
> I will give my princess as queen for your king.

Minister Gar presented the third scroll to the Nepalese king. It read: "If you grant me the princess, I will manifest the pleasures of the five senses and other attractive enjoyments until finally all the wealth and resources of other kingdoms will come to depend on my kingdom. Is that not amazing?"

The Nepalese king became very afraid. He pondered: "There is no end to these scrolls from this far-off king. Also, this Tibetan king has the power to create countless emanations. It would be best to give him my daughter." He called the princess before him and said:

> My beloved princess, listen carefully to your father.
> It is proper that you go to fulfill the desire
> of the Tibetan ruler, the emanated king Songtsen Gampo.

The princess fell to her knees and prostrated to the king, saying:

> Compassionate father, listen to this maiden.
> That snowy land has no Dharma. It is very cold there.
> There are no relatives of mother and father.
> I am distraught. Do not let me go there.

The king again said to the princess:

> Daughter, the Tibetan king is an emanation of a god.
> If you do not go to that snowy land,
> he will raise an army, kill me, and destroy the country.
> You too will be captured and taken away.

Although she had no desire to go, the princess again prostrated and skillfully said to her father:

> Alas! Listen to me, father and king.
> Tibet is a low-caste country. It has no shrines and so forth.
> Please give me the Śākyamuni statue, the object of your
>   devotions,
> and your treasury of precious jewels.

The king replied: "The patron of this statue of Śākyamuni,[58] my object of devotion, was Indra, the lord of the gods. It is made of precious stones and was crafted by the celestial artisan Viśvakarman. It was consecrated and blessed by the Buddha himself. The Buddha said that making offerings to this statue is no different from making offerings to the actual Buddha. It is a meditation deity that has these and limitless other qualities. This statue and the Noble Wati Sangpo,[59] the Maitreya Dharmacakra,[60] and the sandalwood statue of Ārya Tara[61] are the objects of devotion closest to my heart. I cherish them dearly but I give them to you, my beloved daughter, as your dowry. Moreover, from my seven treasuries I will send the best jewels as your inheritance."

The king continued: "Daughter, when you go to Tibet, see that your thoughts and behavior remain as follows." The king spoke these words:

> Daughter, having arrived in the snow-capped land,
> keep your views pure and have faith in the Dharma.
> Have respect for your companions and affection for your
>   subjects.
> Look after your body and know your possessions.

The king ordered the preparation of the dowry and gifts, seven elephant-loads of jewels taken from his seven treasuries, skilled craftsmen, many attendants, a white mule for the princess, an escort of ministers to see her off, and a bodyguard of Nepalese warriors.

The princess had been unable to dissuade her father and so agreed to go to Tibet. The Śākyamuni statue was placed on an elephant. The princess was seated on a white mule and held the sandalwood Tārā statue, and together with the other three statues[62] they set out accompanied by many elephant loads of jewels and the escort of Nepalese ministers and warriors. They headed for the eastern forest of Bheta, where they were met by a Tibetan escort. The path from Gyekhuk at the Nepal Tibet border up to Kyirong was difficult and narrow. Therefore the Nepalese soldiers and the elephants turned back. The jewels were carried on the backs of the ministers and attendants, and it is said that the statues actually walked the journey. At Kyirong in Tibet, the princess was escorted by five hundred horsemen carrying the jewels, while she rode ahead on her white mule. The Noble Wati Sangpo statue of Avalokiteśvara was left behind at Kyirong.

Finally the princess and the deity statues arrived at the center of Lhasa. The Tibetan king, Songtsen Gampo, welcomed the princess at the site of the festivities. When they met, wonderful visions appeared all over Tibet. From three jeweled containers the princess took Nepalese sugarcane juice, grape juice, and rice wine, and offered these and many other delicious foods and drinks to the king. She then presented the king with a jeweled mandala as a gift.

At that time this event was perceived by ordinary beings, bodhisattvas, and the tathāgatas in three different ways.[63]

The king would spend all his time in the presence of the deity statues. The princess wondered: "This king's features are insatiable to look upon, but why does he never venture outside the palace? I would ask him, but he does not speak Nepalese and I do not know Tibetan. It must be that he is apprehensive of an attack by some foreign army. I must remedy that."

Therefore in the female wood sheep year, using the fortress on Red Hill as a foundation, the princess built a walled palace covering an area of one *yojana*. Its four walls rose to a height of thirty-six rows of stone bricks. Tall and vast, each side covered a distance of one *krośa*.[64] Each of the four main doors had a portal with a room above the porch. The ramparts contained windows, lodges, parapets, and guttering, all surrounded by jewel-inlaid terraces, and were adorned with pearl garlands, tinkling bells, fans, and banners.

These mighty ramparts resembled those of the cities of Sudarśana or Gandavatī. Inside there were nine hundred and ninety-nine small strongholds, and in the middle of Red Hill, with a tall tower, was the thousandth. Red banners with multicolored middles flew from the roofs, each of which was built with ten red beams. The strongholds bristled with various weapons and were decorated with garlands of banners.

On the southern side of the rampart a nine-story stronghold was built, modeled on the style of a Mongolian fortress and called Draklha Auspicious Mansion.[65] The king's stronghold and the princess's palace were linked by a silver walkway with beautifully decorated windows, along which the king and queen could walk back and forth.

Even if an army a hundred million strong attacked, the whole fortress could be defended by five guards. It was an extraordinary accomplishment and as insatiable to gaze upon as the Vijayanta Palace.[66] However, it shone like the sun and was difficult to look at. At the same time, it was as menacing and terrifying as the city of Laṅkapurī.[67]

Outside the eastern gate was the king's racetrack, nine hundred arm spans long, eighteen arm spans wide, and two arm spans deep. It was built of wood and bricks and covered with copper. The sides were decorated with garlands, drawings, and embossed murals of auspicious symbols, adorned with colored paints. Small bells made various musical sounds. Inside and outside were like gold. Inside this racetrack, the sound of the hooves of just one of the king's racing horses was like the sound of a hundred thousand horsemen.

It is said that the designs for such red palaces and large towns were drawn up by the Nepalese princess.

SEEKING THE CHINESE PRINCESS

One day minister Gar went before the king and asked for permission to bring the Chinese princess to be his bride. The king said: "Take one hundred gold coins as an offering. Take a suit of armor studded with rubies as a gift in exchange for the princess. The Chinese king will say three different things to you, one after the other. At those times present these three." The king gave the minister three written scrolls.

Provisions for the journey, clothes, ornaments, and so on were loaded onto mules and the minister and his party set off. The king told them to pray to venerable Tārā day and night, regardless of the conditions on the road.

Minister Gar, carrying all the items the king had sent, set out for China with the pack animals accompanied by a hundred horsemen on the eighth day of the fourth month, when the moon occupied the constellation of Puṣya, in the male fire monkey year.[68] They passed through the Chinese cities of Zinshing[69] and Drangyan, until they finally arrived at Tashi Trigo,[70] and then at the gate to the city palace of Emperor Tang Taizong. Within the palace's four walls were a hundred thousand households. Each wall took a day to traverse and contained one large gate. The compund was at once extraordinary and terrifying to behold.

At the same time four other ministers arrived at the city to seek the hand of the Princess Kongjo[71] for their kings. The minister of the Dharma king of India arrived with a hundred horsemen. The minister of the war king Gesar arrived with a hundred horsemen. The minister of the wealth king of Tasik[72] arrived with a hundred horsemen, and the minister of the Bhata Mongolian king arrived with a hundred horsemen. Five hundred horsemen of five different races arrived before the emperor at the same time. The Indians stayed at the eastern gate. The Gesar horsemen stayed at the southern gate. The Tasik stayed at the western gate. The Bhata Mongolians stayed at the northern gate. The Tibetans stayed between the northern and the eastern gate.

The son of the Chinese emperor remarked: "The war king Gesar is heroic and skillful. The princess should be given to him." He sent a messenger accordingly.

The mother of the princess said: "My wealth is vast. The wealth of the Tibetan king cannot compare with ours. A king without wealth is like a beggar. The Tasik king has great wealth, and when times are bad, food and wealth are needed. The princess should be given to the Tasik wealth king." She sent a messenger accordingly.

Princess Kongjo said: "We would have to spend our whole life together. It is the man himself that is important. The Bhata Mongolian king is handsome. Therefore I will go to Mongolia."

The Chinese emperor said: "The sacred Dharma spread from India. This king has been very kind. Therefore the princess should be given to the Dharma king from India."

All the other ministers sent their offerings and were granted an audience immediately. The Tibetan ministers requested an audience but were told to wait. Seven days passed, until one day the Chinese emperor ventured outside the city with his retinue. Minister Gar presented him with the offering of seven gold coins.[73] He placed before the emperor the armor studded with rubies and addressed him: "Great king, the qualities of this armor are many. When disease strikes the people and the cattle, if you wear this armor and circumambulate the city, all disease will vanish. When hail and frost strike, wear this armor and circumambulate the fields, and the frost and hail will be repelled. When war breaks out, wear this armor and you will be victorious in battle. In this world there is no one who could put a price on this armor. It is being offered in exchange for the princess. I ask that you please grant this wise princess to be the bride for the Tibetan king."

The emperor stared at minister Gar with bulging eyes, and with his retinue burst into contemptuous laughter. He said: "This fantastical talk is extraordinary. I am an emperor in an unbroken line from the emperor of all China. Your Tibetan king cannot match my power and might. However, you have come a long way. So when you return, ask your king if he is able to establish a royal-decree law based on the ten virtues. If he can, I give him my daughter. If not, I will not give her."

Minister Gar replied: "It would be a long journey if I were to travel between China and Tibet with this message and its answer. This would mean it would not be possible to bring the princess to Tibet. As a reply to your question, my king gave me this to present to you."

He gave the first scroll to the emperor. He opened it and looked at it. Written in the Chinese language in gold ink on blue paper, it said: "You, emperor of China, possess the law. I, king of Tibet, have no such law. You take great joy in possessing the law of the ten virtues. Therefore if you give me your daughter, I will manifest five thousand bodies and will establish the law of the ten virtues in one day. Is that not amazing?"

The emperor replied: "This Tibetan king is very boastful. Do you have the power to construct temples in Tibet? If you do, I will give my daughter. Otherwise, I will not. Now return and ask him."

Gar replied: "Great king, I have brought the reply to your question. Please look at it." He presented the second scroll to the emperor.

The king opened the scroll. It read: "The Dharma has spread in your country, and you have the ability to construct temples. I, king of Tibet, do not have the ability to build temples. Great king, as you delight in the building of temples, if you grant me your daughter, I will emanate five thousand bodies and construct one hundred and eight temples, with the gates of each facing in your direction. Is that not amazing?"

"Your king is truly boastful," replied the emperor. "In your country do you have resources for the delights of the five senses? If you do, I will give my daughter. If not, I will not. Now go and ask him!"

Again, minister Gar presented the emperor with the third scroll, saying: "The answer to your question is here. Please look at it."

The king opened the scroll. It read: "Great king, you possess great wealth and resources. I, the king of Tibet, do not possess such wealth. Great king, as you delight in the possession of wealth and resources, if you give me your daughter, I will emanate five thousand bodies and produce gold and silver, grains, silks, ornaments, food, and clothing that even the wealth of the gods cannot rival. Furthermore, I will start up commerce in all four quarters of the country. All your far-off wealth will inevitably end up at my door, and I will possess every resource and wealth. Is that not amazing?"

The emperor thought to himself: "There are many who want my daughter, but eventually it seems I will have to give her to the Tibetan king." In an unhappy state he returned to the palace.

Inside the palace the princess's father and emperor, her mother and queen, their son, and the princess herself assembled for discussions. The emperor said: "The Dharma has spread here from India. The Indian Dharma king therefore has been very kind, and the princess should be given to him."

The queen, who had a great fondness for wealth, suggested that she should be given to the wealth king from Tasik. Their son loved skill and bravery and said that she should be given to the Gesar, the war king. The princess herself was fond of handsome men and was attracted to the Bhata Mongolian king. She remarked that a life-long companion was the important thing.

The following day the suitor ministers assembled before the king. The Tibetan ministers said that, as they had requested first, the princess should be given to them. The Mongolian ministers said that if the princess was not given to them, they would fill the country with their warriors. The Tasik ministers said that they would ravage the entire country with fire. The Gesar ministers said that they would flood the whole country if the princess was not given to them.

THE CONTESTS TO WIN THE PRINCESS

The emperor replied: "Ministers, I have no favoritism toward any of you. I will give my daughter to the one who has the sharpest mind. We will have a contest of wits."

The king possessed a life-source turquoise, circular in shape and about the size of a small bowl. It glowed and was penetrated by a hole beginning at its middle, which wound its way round and round inside and emerging at its edge. The hole wound its way inside like the terrace-like markings on a shield. The emperor gave the turquoise and a thread to the ministers, saying: "I will give my daughter to the one who can thread this turquoise."

Minister Gar said: "Four sets of ministers, the emperor likes you. Moreover, you are more powerful. So see if you can thread the turquoise first."

The ministers gathered together awls, bristle brushes, and various threads. Each tried unsuccessfully before handing the stone to another. Finally they handed it to minister Gar, saying: "We cannot do it, no matter how we try. See if you can thread it."

The clever Gar had previously fed an ant with food and milk till it grew to the width of a thick needle. He then tied a silk thread to its waist. He folded up the thread, put the ant into one of the holes in the turquoise, took the loose end of the thread in his hand and blew into the hole. The force of the air blew the ant and the thread out of the other hole. He untied the thread from the ant's waist, and little by little pulled the silk thread through the turquoise.

"I have done what was required. Now please give me your daughter," said Gar.

The king refused, saying: "We must have further contests."

The following day the king gave each of the five ministers a hundred sheep and said: "The man who by tomorrow can kill these sheep, eat the flesh, and tan the hide will be given my daughter."

Each of the Tibetans killed one sheep and placed its carcass and skin in separate piles. Small strips of the flesh were rubbed in salt and the Tibetans were told to eat them. Forming a row, each skin was rubbed and passed down the line. At the end of the row each skin was ready to be greased. Working backward, the skins were greased, rubbed again, and in this way each skin was tanned.

The other ministers had not finished. Gar said: "I have done as you required. The others have not. I ask that you give me the princess."

The emperor said that there were still more contests to be had and refused to give him the princess.

The following day, the emperor gave a hundred containers of beer to each of the ministers, saying: "Whoever can finish this beer by tomorrow without spilling any or getting drunk will be given the princess."

Gar gave small amounts of beer in small bowls to his ministers, saying: "Drink a little at a time." Doing so, they were able to finish the beer without spilling any and without getting drunk. The other ministers, for fear of not finishing in time, filled large bowls with beer and gulped it down. They became drunk, sick, and spilled their beer.

"I have done as you required," said Gar. "The others have not. I ask that you give me the princess." But the emperor said that there were still more contests to be held.

The ministers were each given a hundred mares and their hundred foals, and the emperor said: "To the one who is able to identify each mother and child, I will give my daughter."

The other ministers did know how to accomplish this. Minister Gar put the mares and the foals in separate enclosures. For a day he denied the foals grass and water. Then he released the foals among the mares.[74] Each foal sought out its mother and drank her milk. In this way he had identified each mother and child, and said: "I have identified them. The others have not. I ask that you give me the princess." But the emperor refused, saying that there were still more contests to be held.

On the following day the ministers were each presented with one hundred mother hens and their brood of a hundred chickens. The king said that he would give his daughter to the minister who could identify the mothers from the offspring. The other ministers did not know how to do this. Gar scattered mash on the ground and led the chickens there. The chickens immediately paired off and began eating. Those who ate from below the neck and whose behavior was unruly, he identified as the offspring. The others were the mothers. "I have identified them," Gar said. "The others have not. Please give the princess to me."

But the emperor refused, saying that there were still more contests to be held.

For the next contest the ministers were given a hundred sticks of pine wood each. "I will give my daughter to the one who can identify the top from the bottom," said the emperor.

Again the other ministers had no idea how to do this. Minister Gar took the sticks to water's edge and threw them in. The root end of each stick was heavier and therefore sank down in the water. The upper end pointed upward in the water.

"I have identified which is which," said Gar. "The others have not been able to do so. Please now give the princess to me."

But the emperor refused and said that there were still more contests to be held.

One day the large bell inside the palace was sounded. The other ministers at once proceeded into the palace. The hostess in charge of the Tibetan ministers said: "The other ministers have gone into the palace. Are you not going? You should go."

"We have not been asked," replied Gar. "I do not know what that bell means."

The hostess said: "The other ministers have gone. Even though you have not been invited, it is right to go."

Gar suddenly realized the sounding of the bell was a ruse. He took his ministers to their guest house and marked the door in red ink. On the upper threshold he drew a vajra, and on the lower a swastika. He counted the doors on the way to the palace and marked each with paint. Then he entered the palace. The other ministers were already there.

That evening the emperor laid on a great feast for the ministers. After darkness had set in the emperor said: "Now all you ministers should return. Go and find your guest houses. I will give my daughter to the one who can find it."

Gar borrowed a lamp from the palace. He went through each door following the paint marks he had made earlier and arrived at his guest house. The next day they got up and went to look for the other ministers. Some had entered the wrong houses, while others had been unable to find the right door and had slept on the streets.

"I found my guest house," said Gar. "The others did not. Now please give me the princess."

The emperor replied: "In three days, three hundred beautiful women adorned with jewelry and ornaments will be lined up outside the eastern gate. The princess will be among them. I will give her to him who can identify her."

Gar went back to the guest house and initiated an intimate relationship with the hostess. With great charm and gentle disposition, he said to her: "One year has passed since we Tibetans arrived in China. I have won every contest of wits. We have won the princess, but out of contempt the emperor does not give her to me. This magical Princess Kongjo's fame and renown reverberates like thunder. However, I have never seen her. You and the princess are very close. What does she look like? Describe her to me. This is very important. In three days the princess will be placed in a line of three hundred maidens and paraded outside the eastern gate. The emperor has stated that whoever recognizes her will be given her. The other ministers are powerful and will choose first. If any of them recognizes her, she will probably be given to them. It will be difficult for me to win. Even if they do not recognize her, and I do, because of his contempt for us, the emperor will probably not give her to me. Even if by the power of karma I had the opportunity and did meet her, I don't know what she looks like. Please describe her to me. I will give you anything you want." With this he gave her a small bag of powdered gold as a gift.

The hostess replied: "You Tibetan ministers are right. The emperor is very biased. He is hoping that one of the other ministers wins his daughter. If any of them are smarter just once, they will be given the princess. The magical Princess Kongjo is my niece and I know her very well. She is well-versed in Chinese elemental divination.[75] If she uses it to identify this plot I will be killed. I cannot talk to you."

Gar replied: "I have a way to ensure she does not detect it with her divination." He locked the door and set out three large hearth stones. On top he placed a large copper pot filled with water. On the water he scattered feathers from various birds and covered the pot with a red shield. He sat the hostess on the shield and covered her head with a clay pot. He covered the pot with mesh. In the side of the pot he made a hole and inserted a copper pipe through the mesh and the pipe. If she spoke through the pipe, even if it were picked by the divination, it would not be believed. "Now, speak," said Gar.

The hostess replied: "Great minister, keep this in your mind. This magical Princess Kongjo in size is no bigger than the other maidens. In beauty she is no more extraordinary than the others. In dress and adornments she is no more elegant. Her special qualities are as follows. She has a bluish complexion with a reddish hue. From her mouth comes the sweet aroma of the blue lotus. Around her delightful bodily aroma, a turquoise-colored bee hovers. On her right cheek is a small mole. On her left is the figure of a lotus. Between her eyebrows on her *sindhūra* mark[76] is the figure of Ārya Tārā, the size of a barley grain. Her white, conch-like teeth are set firm.

"Princess Kongjo will not be at the end of the line of three hundred, nor will she be in the middle. She will be after the sixth maiden counting from the left. Her body and her clothes have protection on them and are not to be touched. Therefore you must carry an unused arrow wrapped in square red cloth. When you come to where the princess is standing, she will be wearing a five-pleated silk garment, over which is a cape. Hook the collar of the cape with the notch of the arrow and pull."

Gar took this in carefully. His body and mind were filled with joy. He addressed the other Tibetan ministers: "Previously we Tibetans have prevailed, and now we have to prevail once more. We did not come to China to engage in trade or to nurture friends. If we can gain the princess, we will have prevailed. Therefore we must think very carefully and not make any mistake."

Three days later, three hundred maidens adorned with jewelry and ornaments were assembled on the grounds outside the eastern gate. The Chinese people, young and old, men and women, came to watch the spectacle. The emperor announced: "Ministers, in the order followed previously, make your choice."

The ministers of the Dharma king of India came forward. They picked out two beautiful, well-dressed maidens from the middle of the line and led them away, saying: "If it isn't one, it's the other." They went off whistling and chattering among themselves. After them the ministers of the Tasik king came forward. They also chose two beautiful maidens, repeating the words and actions of the previous ministers. Then the Gesar ministers made their choice. They followed the example of the previous ministers by choosing two beautiful maidens and leaving in the same manner. The Bhata ministers did exactly the same.

Gar watched all this and saw that none of the choices had been the princess. He was delighted, and a smile came over his face. He took the arrow and, leading the Tibetan ministers, went to the left end of the line. Beginning with the maiden at the end of the line he said:

This one seems to be the daughter of a butcher.
It is usual, I think, for their hands to be red.

This next maiden seems to be a potter's daughter.
It is usual, I think, for their hands to be cracked.

This maiden seems to be a wood-cutter's daughter.
It is usual, I think, for their clothes to be grayish.

The next maiden seems to be the daughter of a dancer.
It is usual, I think, for their upper garments to be bright.

The next appears to be the daughter of a cleaner.
It is usual, I think, for them to have many straps.

This maiden is a blacksmith's daughter, it seems.
It is usual, I think, for their pockets to be black.

This next maiden is a silk weaver's daughter, it seems.
It is usual, I think, for them to wear fine silk.[77]

This next maiden appears to be Princess Kongjo.
Her complexion is bluish with a reddish tinge.

The sweetness of the blue lotus comes from her mouth,
around whose aroma a turquoise-colored bee hovers.

Her cheeks display a mole and a lotus,
her forehead is marked with noble Tārā.

Her teeth are close together and set firm.
This magical maiden is more beautiful than the rest.

Having spoken of her qualities, he hooked the collar of the princess's garment with the notch of the arrow and pulled her toward him. The princess followed the minister and began to cry. Seeing her tears, minister Gar, aided by the ministers Tönmi Kuntu Sangpo and Driseru Gongtön, sang a song to lift her spirits:

Ah, it is all so wondrous.
Princess Kongjo, hear these words.
Be of a happy and cheerful disposition.

In the sovereign land of Tibet,
within the palace of the king,
made from the five precious gems,
rules the celestial lord of men.
Songtsen Gampo is of noble race and handsome in form.

Beholding him, your mind will be captivated.
He is Avalokiteśvara, ruling his kingdom in keeping with
    the Dharma.
His subjects heed his word.

Ministers, retinue and people sing songs of joy.
They have gained a happy life.
They have hoisted the beacon of glory.

On the mountains are to be found various trees,
while on the wide plains fields of the five grains
grow side by side, with no space between.
Gold, silver, copper iron, and many other precious
metals abound.
There are yaks, horses, and sheep in great numbers.

Such delights are to be found.
Ah, it is all so wondrous.
Princess Kongjo, hear these words.

The princess thought to herself: "If all that is true, Tibet must be like my own country." She dried her eyes and followed the minister.

Minister Gar mounted a horse and rode around town, saying: "Now Tibet is greater than Mongolia and China. I have won the princess. All of you, put your fingers in your mouths and be quiet."[78]

The people were in despair, saying: "Our wise and beautiful princess is being taken away by the Tibetan ministers!"

The emperor said: "You other ministers, you are China's kinsmen. Take the maidens you have chosen and return to your countries."

Gar sent the princess away, saying: "Get ready to leave for Tibet."

The princess returned to the palace, where her father said: "You must go to become the queen of the Tibetan king."

She replied: "I cannot go if I have to leave my father and mother behind."

"Do not say this," said her father. "You must go. The Tibetan king possesses clairvoyance and has magical powers. Also, he is very intelligent. He rules his kingdom skillfully with courage and wisdom. His subjects obey and venerate him. It is a magnificent country, a happy country. Therefore it is good if you go."

The princess prostrated to her father and said:

Are these the instructions of my father and emperor?
Were they spoken by my mother?

Did they fall from the lips of my brother?
Life is very strange indeed!

I am to be sent to Tibet,
but there in that snow-capped land
the climate is very cold, the land is high.

There are malicious spirits, nāgas, cannibals, and demons,
and many wild animals amid the snowy mountains.
The mountain crags are like wild yak horns.
No grain grows there. It is a place of famine.

They are low-caste people, of a cannibal race,
of coarse behavior, deserving of the name "barbarian."
It is an uncivilized place where the Buddha has never trod.

Her father spoke to her lovingly:

My daughter, more precious than my own eyes.
This snow-capped land known as Tibet
is a country more special than others.
Its snow mountains form natural shrines.
Its four great lakes are arranged like a turquoise
    mandala.

It is a place abundant with amazing golden flowers.
Cool but beautiful, it is a mansion of the gods.
The land is beautiful with forests of green trees.
Four great rivers flow and the five types of grains grow.
It is a resource for a variety of precious stones.
Animals roam everywhere and butter is enjoyed.

In that extraordinary and supreme place,
inside a palace adorned with precious ornaments,
dwells a ruler of men, a wise and celestial king,
in reality the noble Avalokiteśvara,
a king who is both skillful and compassionate.

He has abandoned the ten nonvirtuous acts,
and abides in the law of the ten that are virtuous.
He has power, wealth, and all that he desires.
He is a king with limitless qualities, a son of the gods.
His entourage, epitomes of courage and wisdom, are
  bodhisattvas.
To such a place, my daughter, you must go.

This statue of the Buddha, object of my veneration,
and the basis, my beautiful daughter, for your gathering
  of merit,
was patronized by Indra, the lord of the gods.
It was built from the ten precious stones,
crafted by the celestial artist, Viśvakarman,
and was consecrated by the Buddha himself.

If you see, hear of, bring to mind, touch, or pray to
such an incomparable statue of the Buddha,
the Buddha has said you will quickly gain enlightenment.
This I send with you, my beautiful daughter.

Whole libraries written in gold and turquoise,
three hundred and sixty classical works,
many ornaments made of gold and turquoise,
all these I send with you, my beautiful daughter.

Many varieties of food and ingredients,
many recipes to make drinks,
and golden saddles, studded with turquoise,
all these I send with you, my beautiful daughter.

Soft brocade cushions adorned with eight lions and birds,
trees whose leaves are adorned with the drawings of jewels,
these I will send to amaze the king.

The three hundred and sixty Chinese divination charts,
mirrors of karma that foretell what is good and bad,
these too I will send with you, my beautiful daughter.

Texts on the science of design and construction,
made special with beautifying ornaments,
texts on the sixty sciences of arts and crafts,
these I send with my beautiful daughter.

Medicine to destroy the four hundred and four diseases,
the hundred means of diagnosis, the five therapies,
the six purification techniques, the four types of medicinal
    preparation,
these too I will send.

Silks and brocades that will keep you warm your whole life,
twenty thousand ornamented garments of many a color,
these too I send with you, my daughter.

As your retinue I will send twenty-five maidens
of agreeable minds, as companions to comfort you,
beautiful to look at and of noble lineage.

In order to tame the people of Tibet,
maintain your behavior as follows.
Have a broad mind, examine your conduct.
Be gentle of voice, wise in your speech.
Be skillful in all your deeds, outer and inner.

Be respectful toward your lord, affectionate to your retinue.
Be modest, considerate, and conscientious.

Alas! I cannot bear to be separate from you, my daughter.
These have been loving words of advice from my heart.
Keep them in your mind.

Thus the emperor gave this and much other advice on necessary codes of
conduct in the world.

The princess held on to her father's hand, not wanting to leave. But realizing she had to go to Tibet, she finally parted from him and left the palace. With her attendants she went to Gar. There she said: "Great minister, I have the statue of Jowo Śākyamuni to bring to your country, and I am bringing a limitless amount of wealth and other things. In your country do you have porcelain clay? Multicolored stone? Rose bushes? Tough *drema* grass? Turnips?"

"We have them all, except for turnips," replied Gar. "However, we could sow them in Tibet," he said. She took some turnip seeds, wrapped them in a red cloth, and put them in her hair.

The statue of Jowo Śākyamuni was placed on a carriage and pulled by Lhaga and Luga, two strong Chinese men. The statue was followed by the princess, accompanied by four attendants in a carriage pulled by two white mules. After them came the twenty-five companions adorned with beautiful ornaments and each riding their own horse. The emperor had laid on a lavish feast for the Tibetan ministers and furnished them with gifts. Various jewels, ornamented clothes, and immediate provisions were loaded on horses, mules, and camels. Her mother and father gave the princess much advice on proper worldly conduct. They and their ministers accompanied the princess for a short distance as they set off for Tibet.

MINISTER GAR REMAINS IN CHINA

A Tibetan minister, Driseru Gongtön, had grown jealous of Gar. He said to the emperor: "If one intelligent minister were to remain in China in the place of princess Kongjo, it would ensure that relations between Tibet and China would remain very cordial."

The emperor said: "You Tibetans have won my wise and beautiful daughter. Now in order to keep good relations between Tibet and China, Gar must stay here."

Minister Gar was aware that Driseru Gongtön had acted out of jealousy, but said: "I will see to it that good relations are maintained between our two countries." And he promised to remain. However, he took Tönmi and Nyang aside and said: "I will not stay in China for more than five months. At that point send someone to me disguised as a beggar."[79] The ministers and retinue circumambulated the Jowo statue and the princess, and they set off for Tibet.

At the end of the first day's travel they set up camp. The Jowo Śākyamuni was draped in a white silk curtain. A bowl of rice soup was made and given to the princess. That day the ministers and attendants relaxed and enjoyed themselves. They partook in horseracing, athletic competitions, archery

contests, and other tests of skill. Princess Kongjo set up an altar of the five
types of offering, took up a silver three-string tambura, and to its accompa-
niment sang this praise to Śākyamuni:

> When you, lord of men, were born,
> you took seven steps upon this earth,
> declaring, "I am supreme in the world."
> At that time the wise bowed to you.

> Of five pure bodies, of supreme and excellent form,
> an ocean of wisdom, renowned like a mountain
>   of gold,
> splendid and bright within the three worlds,
> guide supreme, I go to you for refuge.

The next morning, before the day was drowned out by the cries of the
crows, they set off on the road with the statue in front and the princess fol-
lowing behind.

Gar was left on his own in China. The emperor, knowing that Gar was
an intelligent man, and hoping to increase his family stock, presented Gar
with a niece of the princess as a wife, as well as a fine estate. But Gar was very
unhappy. He thought to himself: "If I am not sent to Tibet, those four sets
of ministers who came to win the princess will seize her on the road." He
demanded that a hundred brave and skillful young men, aged twenty and
from good families, should be sent to accompany her. This was done.

Minister Gar, from fear of increasing his family line, refused to go to his
wife and stayed alone in his little room. He refused all food given to him and
spent the whole day on his bed. He became very thin and his face took on a
dark complexion. Inside his right cheek he smeared indigo and inside his left
cheek lac. His saliva now had the dark-red color of pus. Under his mattress
he had placed a freshly killed animal hide. His Chinese wife became aware of
the smell and exclaimed:

> Alas! Great minister, please get up.
> Listen to the words of your wife.
> Your sick-looking face and the bad smell—
> tell me truthfully, what is the cause of this?

Gar replied: "Can't you see that I have a fever?"

One day the emperor, his ministers, and his entourage visited Gar. "I have much to discuss with you," said the emperor.

"Great emperor, I am tormented by fever," replied Gar. "I might die."

The emperor looked and saw that Gar was indeed sick. He was trembling, had become thin, and was coughing up dark-colored phlegm. He saw dried spittle everywhere around the room. He became concerned that Gar would die, and thought: "He is a wise minister of the far-off king Songtsen Gampo. If he dies, that king will manifest five thousand bodies and wage war against me. That will not be good for me." The emperor became frightened. He summoned a skillful doctor and told him to cure the minister.

Minister Gar stayed in the house and said: "I have a bad smell. It might harm others." And he locked the door. He dipped one end of a piece of rope into water and hung the other end out of the window for the doctor to examine.[80]

After he had looked at it the doctor said: "His illness has the nature of the water element. There is nothing else wrong with him. He should be treated for a cold disorder."

The next day the doctor came again. This time Gar held the rope over fire and hung the other end out the window for the doctor to examine. "What is this?" exclaimed the doctor. "The minister's illness has changed. Now it has the nature of the fire element. He should be treated for a heat disorder."

The following day the doctor again visited. This time Gar tied the rope to a revolving millstone and passed the other end through the window. The doctor, upon examining it, remarked, "What is this? The minister's illness has changed. Now he is as cold as a stone. His pulse circulates and is disturbed."

The next time the doctor came, Gar suspended a cat upside down. He tied the rope to its leg and fed the other end to the doctor through the window. "What is this?" He exclaimed. "The blood from the lower part of his body has traveled to the top, and all the upper blood has gathered in the lower part of his body. His pulse is none other than that of a low animal. I do not know how to treat him." With this he left.

The emperor became very afraid. He summoned another wise doctor. Meanwhile, minister Gar said to his wife: "Tonight, sleep outside the room. You are a woman and are defiled. Tomorrow the doctor will not be able to read my pulse. If that were to happen, I would die and you would become a widow." He sent his wife outside. He then lifted the bottom of his bed up high and lay with his head facing downward. This had the effect of disturbing all the pulses.

The doctor examined him and said to the emperor: "Great emperor, this illness of the minister does not arise from the winds and it does not arise from the bile humor. Similarly, it does not arise from the phlegm humor or from the eighty thousand types of demonic forces, and so on. It is a serious illness other than these. I do not know how to treat it."

Then the emperor said to Gar: "You are a wise man. What is the best way to produce a good harvest? What is the best way to ensure that the seeds will grow to maturity?"[81]

Gar replied: "If the seeds are parched and then planted, they will grow very strong, and in three months they will be ready for harvest."

Chinese farmers followed Gar's advice, and after three months there were sprouts but no further growth.

"Now I am going to be punished," thought Gar. "I must have a plan." He said to the emperor: "Now after seven days I will die. I have been left behind by my ministers who accompanied me to this faraway land. My body is tormented with illness. I think longingly of my king and loved ones, but it is in vain. No matter what I do, death awaits me." He covered his head and lay down.

The emperor was disturbed. "Great minister, you are a wise man. There must be something that can be done. I will do whatever I can to help."

Gar thought to himself: "Now I have an opportunity." He said to the emperor: "I have a better way to cure my illness than you do. A Tibetan protector has become unhappy. If I could go to the summit of a tall mountain from where I could see the mountains of Tibet and make offerings to this protector, it would help. For this I would need the following substances: One sack of ash produced from burning the best silk; a stomach sack filled with blood from the spleen of a slaughtered gray sheep; a charcoal lance, one arm span in length, with no cracks; and a brown horse with a reddish head. However, these things are difficult to find, difficult to bring together. Emperor, you too will find it hard. Therefore I will die. There is no alternative. After I die eighteen bad omens will appear, and much disaster will befall Tibet and China."

The emperor replied: "I will do whatever I can to help you. Lay down and rest." With that he left.

Even though the emperor burnt every forest, no charcoal lance could be made. Every gray sheep was killed but not even half a cup of spleen blood was gathered. However, he did find a brown horse with a reddish head. He said to the minister: "I could not find all the substances. I did find a brown horse with a reddish head."

Gar replied: "Without the other substances the method is useless. This brown horse with a reddish head will be my corpse horse. Put me on it. On another fine Chinese horse load the corpse food[82] and the corpse garments, and let me go to a high place from where I can see the mountains of Tibet."

Preparations were made for the minister to leave. He was seated on the brown horse with a reddish head. The corpse food and clothing were loaded onto the other horse. Fearing that the minister might flee, the emperor sent four strong men along. Finally they set out to a place where the mountains of Tibet could be seen, in order to make offerings to the protector.

Then the emperor said to his seers: "Make divinations to see if anyone showed my princess to the Tibetan ministers."

After they had made the divination, the seers came back to the emperor and said:

> Upon three mountains, there was a swirling ocean,
> upon which various bird feathers floated.
> A woman, whose head and body were of equal size,
> who was covered with eyes, and who had lips of copper,
> was seated there and was talking.[83]

"This is impossible!" exclaimed the emperor. He lost all faith in the divination works and threw them all on a fire. The eighty works on Portang divination[84] had already been taken to Tibet, thereby leaving China bereft of divination techniques.

Minister Gar led his four escorts to the road that led to Tibet. Via Gyalmo Tsawa Rong[85] they reached a place from where the mountains of Tibet could be seen. Up to this point the escorts had not been given any food. As soon as they arrived at this place they were given dry meat laced with salt. Gar prayed to the protector:

> I plead, I plead. To the gods I plead.
> To the gods, nāgas, and protectors of Tibet, I plead.
> To the nine deities at the time of creation,[86] I plead.
> To the thirteen gods of the masters' songs, I plead.

> To the twelve local protectors of Tibet, I plead.
> Fulfill the wishes of this minister.

Gar added wild honey to good beer and offered it to the protectors. Then he gave it to his escorts. Having drunk this and a lot of ale besides, his four escorts became drunk and fell asleep. Gar broke their weapons, put nails in the hooves of their horses, got on his own horse, and fled to Tibet.

GAR ESCAPES

When the four men awoke, Gar was gone. Their weapons were broken and their horses were lame. They said: "If we return, the emperor will punish us. We should go after the Tibetan minister." With this they set off in pursuit of Gar.

At a safe distance the minister began placing pieces of bread at distances within human sight. Then he arrived at an inlet of the River Gyachu,[87] where he set about filling the area with horse dung and hoof-prints. The horns of antelopes were reshaped in fire to make bows. Many arrows were fashioned and placed in the ground up to their feathers.

After a while his pursuers arrived. Looking around, they said: "He has been met by many powerful horsemen. We could never match them. It would be better to return." And so from Gyachu River they left for home.

Meanwhile, Princess Kongjo, her retinue, and the Tibetan ministers arrived at a place called Denma Rock.[88] There by the rock the princess constructed a seven-cubit statue of Maitreya and inscribed the *Prayer of Excellent Conduct* on the side of the rock. They waited there for one month, but Gar did not arrive.

They traveled on to Phungpo Hill. There the princess initiated the construction of a path to the summit. It became known as Chinese Princess Path. They also captured animals and milked them. Still the minister did not arrive.

They traveled on to Pema Thang in Kham. There the princess initiated farming methods and introduced water wheels for grinding grain. They stayed there for two months, but Gar still did not arrive.

They moved on to Godong Gomo.[89] Because of China's sudden loss of fortune and prosperity,[90] the Chinese protector deities had blocked the way out of Gomo and the princess was forced to stay there for two months. Finally Gar arrived. He realized that Gomo being cut off was retaliation from the angry protectors. Therefore he performed an incense purification ceremony producing vast clouds of smoke, and chanted:

> I plead, I plead. To the gods I plead.
> I plead to the gods of China.
> I plead to gods of Tashi Trigo.[91]
> I ask that you raise up the fallen trees.
> I plead to the gods of Tibet.
> Welcome and escort Princess Kongjo.

They prayed and made offerings constantly, and that evening the trees returned to a standing position. The next day they were able to continue their journey.

Gar sent messengers ahead with a message that read: "Prepare to welcome Princess Kongjo and the meditation statue of Śākyamuni from the four directions of central Tibet. People of Tibet, welcome them with a great celebration. Beat the drums, fly the flags, and fill the land with horsemen."

The message reached the ears of the Tibetan king, who immediately sent out instructions to his ministers and people:

> I have received a message that the Chinese princess
> and the meditation deity will soon safely arrive.
> Ministers and horsemen in your hundreds, households,
> men and horses beautifully adorned and clothed,
> make preparation for a great welcome,
> on a happy day three days from now.

The king also ordered: "The princess is an extraordinary emanation of goddess Tārā, and we cannot be sure from which direction she will arrive. Therefore repair all defects in the mountain roads leading into Lhasa from the four directions and prepare lavish welcomes." Accordingly, ministers and hundreds of horsemen set off to form welcoming parties, and the people repaired the roads in the four parts of the town and waited.

THE CHINESE PRINCESS ARRIVES IN LHASA

The princess Wencheng Kongjo, an emanation of venerable Tārā, adorned with all the marks and features of an enlightened being, mistress of all scripture and insight, together with the meditational deity, Śākyamuni, arrived in Lhasa from the northern gate. The sky was blotted out by the number of flags flying. The land was filled with people. Horns and trumpets were blown, drums and musical instruments were played. On the right beautiful maidens performed folk operas. On the left singers sang and dancers danced. The sounds emanating from the music, dance, and song were beyond anything imaginable.

The people, old and young, men and women, aristocratic and ordinary folk, rushed forward with ceremonial offering scarves to present to the princess and Jowo Śākyamuni.

It is said that the people living in each of the four directions of Lhasa welcomed the princess arriving from their part of town. And reasons are given for that.[92]

Princess Kongjo, adorned in beautiful silk, wearing ornaments of gold, turquoise, and other precious gems, arrived at the festivities on the plain of Draklha accompanied by the music of silver tamburas and lutes. There, together with the ministers and her retinue, she watched the extraordinary display of music, song, and dance.

King Songtsen Gampo arrived at the festivities and met with the Chinese princess. As soon she met with the king, the princess placed a long, fine silken ceremonial scarf in her hands and said:

> This pure white auspicious ceremonial scarf,
> I offer to the king as a token of our meeting.
> This Chinese princess has come from China,
> a journey three years in the taking,
> and today she has laid eyes upon the face of the king.

King Songtsen Gampo was overjoyed and asked about her journey:

> Ah! Hear my words, Princess Kongjo.
> Are you not tired after your long journey?
> How did the princess, the Jowo, and your retinue
> negotiate the rivers, gorges, and difficult paths?
> That you have arrived in Tibet without hindrance
> displays the glory of you two.

In reply, Princess Kongjo said:

The great Jowo was placed upon a carriage,
and pulled by Lhaga and Luga, two strong men.
We crossed the Gyachu River by boat.
The trees fell to the left and we could pass.[93]
In the darkness we held aloft lamps to show the way.
Although the way was long, by various methods we managed it.
May happiness and prosperity reign in Tibet!

There were three different perceptions of this event. To the buddhas of the ten directions, the king and his queen were working for living beings by way of the twelve deeds. To the perception of the bodhisattvas of the ten levels, noble Avalokiteśvara had emanated as King Songtsen Gampo, venerable Tārā had emanated as Princess Kongjo, and both were working for living beings. To the minds of ordinary beings, the king and queen were establishing a loving relationship by exchanging drinks, enjoying pleasant conversation, and so on.

The Chinese princess summoned many fine Chinese craftsmen and constructed on top of a nāga palace the Gyatak Ramoché Temple in the style of temples in China. In the temple the joined and separated arrangement of Chinese lettering on the frame of the Jowo statue was written in Chinese by the princess herself. With these and other deeds, the Chinese princess completed countless tasks in Tibet.

Thus ends the story of the two princesses.

4. The Story of Noble Ḍākinī Nangsa Öbum

Namo guru deva ḍākinī
To him born into the Śākya clan,
endowed with skillful means and great compassion,
not overcome by others, conqueror of all hindrances,
of radiant form like a great golden mountain,
to the king of the Śākyas I prostrate.

Born from the green syllable *tāṃ*,
within the supreme place, Potāla,[94]
the light from your *tāṃ* liberates living beings.
I bow before the great mother Tārā.

I will teach the Dharma in all languages—
in those of the gods, in those of the nāgas, yakṣa spirits,
and gandharvas, and in the languages of humans.

OUR TEACHER OF SKILLFUL means, possessed of great compassion, partial to no one and loving to all, taught the eighty-four thousand volumes of Dharma to disciples in accordance with their dispositions. These teachings can be condensed into the three turnings of the wheel of Dharma. For me, and those like me, who cannot understand the meanings of these celestial teachings, he told stories, such as *Parable of the Birds, Tales of the Corpse, The Story of Hanuman, The Exploits of King Gesar*, and so on, and taught legends such as those of Prince Rama, Goddess Manoharā, Dharma King Viśvantara, and others that were drawn from the Vinaya teachings.

From among these narratives our performance today, offered for the eyes of our chief guests, the assembled nobles, as well as for the ordinary folk gathered here, has been taken from the story of Nangsa Öbum and is presented as a teaching to cause the desirous to renounce samsara and turn their minds toward the Dharma.

There are different versions of the story of Nangsa, such as Nangsa Lha Yulma and Nangsa Shalü, but here we are concerned with the true story presented as a Dharma teaching of the beautiful and noble ḍākinī Nangsa Öbum who took birth as a human. All of you gathered here, listen carefully and without distraction.

* * *

Our Tibet is divided into the upper area consisting of the three regions of Ngari, the lower area consisting of the six mountainous areas of Dokham, and the four districts of the central area of Ütsang. In Yeru of Tsang from the central area, in the district of Nyangtö Gyangtsé, in an ordinary homestead called Jang Phekhu Nangpa, there lived a husband called Kunsang Dechen and his wife Nyangtsa Saldrön. They recited every day without fail the praise to Khadiravaṇī Tārā. One night, after they had completed one hundred thousand recitations of the prayer, the wife had several astonishing dreams. She told them to her husband:

With devotion and veneration I bow to Khadiravaṇī Tārā,
the activities of all the buddhas revealed as a goddess.
You who are destined by karma to be my companion for life,
my husband, Kunsang Dechen, listen to what I have to say.

Last night as I lay sleeping, I had dreams
in which wonderful events occurred.
In the sacred realm of Turquoise Leaves,
upon a jeweled and blazing conch-leaf throne,
sat Tārā, the female buddha of the past, present, and future.

From the letter *tāṃ* in the heart of this mother of the conquerors
emerged a light that entered my crown through the Brahma
     aperture,
traveling through my central pathway and coming to rest
     in my heart.
My body became a lotus flower, and ḍākinīs worshipped
     at its stem.
Swarms of bees came to it from all directions,

and sated themselves with the essence at the center
    of its petals.
Such a dream must surely be auspicious.
Tell me, husband, the meaning of this dream.

Her husband was overjoyed and said in reply:

My companion for all lives, my beautiful lady,
Nyangtsa Saldrön, my wife, listen to me.
It is true that dreams are not real and are deceptive,
but this dream is an omen of future events.

The light emitting from the *tāṃ* at the heart of venerable Tārā,
entering and dissolving into the center of your heart,
is a sign that the blessings of venerable Tārā,
personification of the activities of the buddhas of the three
    times,
have entered your heart.

Your body becoming a lotus flower
is a sign of the child being the supreme of all ḍākinīs.
Swarms of bees gathering from all directions
to partake of the essence at the center of its petals
is a sign that she will work with body, speech, and mind
for the swarms of pure and impure disciples.

When young and white of teeth we had no son,
and now when old and white of hair we have a daughter,
and she will surely be greater than any son.
Perform devotions in all directions!
This is an auspicious dream, Nyangtsa Saldrön.
Kunsang Dechen is a happy man!

The couple performed the higher devotion of making offerings to the
Three Jewels, the lower devotion of giving alms to beggars, and the inter-
mediate devotion of making donations to the monastic community. Conse-
quently, in the male earth horse year, in the waxing fortnight of the monkey
month, on the tenth day when the ḍākinīs hold their celebrations, when the

weekday of the planet Jupiter and the constellation Puṣya were in conjunction, the child was born.

As soon as she was born, she took the first portion of her mother's milk, cast it into the air, and with her palms folded said these words:

> Great mother of the buddhas of the three times,
> I offer and prostrate to the venerable Tārā.
> I **appear** here for the sake of working for all beings.
> May there be happiness and prosperity on this **earth**,
> By the **light** of enlightened activity permeating in all directions,
> may I lead **hundreds of thousands** of living beings to the
>   Dharma.

Her name, Nangsa Öbum, was taken from this verse,[95] and was the name given to her unanimously by all the people of the area. What other children developed in a year, she developed more in a month. What other children developed in a month, she developed more in a day. In her beauty and calm personality she was unlike a human child and more like a child of the gods. Her parents were overjoyed and praised the body, speech, and mind of their daughter:

> Daughter of an excellent father, you are of an excellent family.
> Daughter of a beautiful mother, you are of beautiful features.
> Sole ornament amid any gathering of gods and humans,
> Daughter, Nangsa Öbum, hear what we have to say.

> If all the beautiful things in the world were made into one,
> it would be given to you as an adornment.
> Just to see you brings joy to the eyes.
> We praise your beautiful goddess form.

> The combined songs of the kalaviṅga bird, the nightingale,
>   the cuckoo,
> and all other birds could not compete with your melodious
>   voice.
> Just to hear it brings joy to the ears.
> We praise your sweet voice, daughter Nangsa.

You have devotion to those objects of refuge,
the guru and the Three Jewels,
and toward all living beings you show great love.
Just to think of you brings joy to the mind.
We praise your mind, daughter Nangsa Öbum.

Like a brown mule born from donkey stock,
like a white yak born from the stock of the black bull,
for you, a goddess, to be born from these two old parents,
is something truly remarkable.

Nangsa replied:

Personification of enlightened activity,
mother of every buddha within the three times,
I prostrate to the noble and blessed Tārā.
Listen to me, mother and father of this daughter.
Hear what I have to say.

Certainly this daughter has her parents,
but they alone are not sufficient,
for she has outer, inner, and secret parents.

Her outer father is Kunsang Dechen,
her outer mother is the kind Nyangtsa Saldrön.
Her inner father is Avalokiteśvara,
her inner mother is venerable white and green Tārā.
Her secret father is the bliss of the great vehicle,
her secret mother is wisdom, clear and empty.
To my outer, inner, and secret mothers and fathers
I prostrate from the complete union of bliss and emptiness.

Thus she offered praise and prostrations to her parents. Also, every day
without fail she would recite the six-syllable mantra of Avalokiteśvara and
the praises of white and green Tārā. Her compassion, wisdom, and enthu-
siasm were highly developed, while ignorance, pride, and misconception
remained weak. Consequently, Nangsa comprehended perfectly the mean-
ings of the sutras and tantras of the Dharma.

In worldly affairs too she excelled. She would be the first to get up in the morning and the last to go bed. She worked hard and became skilled in cooking, weaving, farm work, and so on. As a result, the Jang Phekhu household became very prosperous.

By age fifteen her renown had spread throughout the Ütsang, Dakpo, and Kongpo regions. Many suitors came in search of her hand. However, Nangsa thought only of practicing the sacred Dharma and had no desire to follow the worldly life. Moreover, her parents had no other children and Nangsa was worth more than a hundred sons. She was wise in the Dharma and skilled in worldly affairs, and consequently was not given to any of the men who sought her but remained as a helper to her elderly parents.

In Gyangtsé Rinang Tsochen there lived a governor called Drachen. He was of a temper hotter than fire, more turbulent than the waves on the ocean, as intolerant as a thin horse tail, with a tongue hotter than Indian pepper, as stubborn as a well-rounded bean, and in pettiness as fine as well-ground flour. He had married a woman called Sönam Gyalmo, who had given birth to a son called Drakpa Samdrup and a daughter called Nyimo Netso. However, his wife had died, leaving him and his son without wives. He thought to himself: "I must find a beautiful woman from a good family to be a wife for my son."

Around this time, Nenying Monastery held its annual consecration ceremonies,[96] and it was customary for everyone, male and female, monastic and lay, the old with their white hair and the young with their white teeth, to watch the spectacle and to receive the audience blessings. So Drachen and many attendants, all dressed in the best finery, went to view the Nenying consecration ceremonies and to receive the general audience blessing.

The maiden Nangsa had never witnessed the Nenying consecration spectacle or received the blessings, and wished to go to the ceremony. Moreover, her mother and father wanted to see her stand out in the crowd with her fine clothes and jewelry offsetting her radiant beauty. So they helped her to wash her beautiful full-moon face and her silky rice-shoot hair, and she adorned herself with the best clothes and adornments. Offerings and ceremonial scarves to be presented to the physical, mental, and verbal representations of the buddhas at Nenying Monastery, initiation offerings for the lamas, and provisions for the journey were given to her attendant Dzomkyi, and they set off to the consecration and the blessing ceremony at Nenying.

Nangsa presented the offerings to the lamas and received the blessings. She made prostrations to and circumambulations of the sacred objects and presented them with offerings. After these events she went to watch the festivity dances and sat with the other maidens from the locality. The Rinang governor Drachen also attended the dances and sat in the Labrang Rapsal quarters of the monastery. Drachen did not pay any attention to the dances and other events, because he could not take his eyes off Nangsa, watching her wherever she went. His mind was completely taken by her. He gave instructions to his official Sönam Palkyé, who went among the crowd and led Nangsa to governor Drachen like a bird snared in a trap or a rabbit carried by an eagle. With his left hand governor Drachen took hold of the flaps of Nangsa's dress, and with his right hand he handed her his cup of unfinished ale, saying:

> Beautiful body, pleasant voice, delightful aroma,
> the sweetest of tastes, and so soft to touch,
> you possess the five sensory delights.
> Tell me honestly, whose daughter are you?
> That of a god, a nāga, a gandharva, a human?

> What is the name of your father?
> What is the name of your mother?
> Maiden, what is your own name?
> What is the name of your district?
> What is the name of your household?

> I am the master of Nyangtö Rinang,
> I am governor Drachen, whose renown resounds like thunder.
> My offspring is Drakpa Samdrup.
> He is my outer fortress and my inner jewel.
> He is now eighteen years of age.
> Will you not be his bride?

Nangsa thought to herself: "My face and my body have become my enemy. My desire is one that longs for the celestial Dharma, but my fate, it seems, is to enter the householder life. What can I do!" With these thoughts, she sang:

> Venerable Tārā, great mother of the buddhas,
> look with compassion upon this girl without Dharma.

Listen to me, governor Drachen.
Turn your ears to the maiden Nangsa.

My district is Nyangtö Gyangtsé.
Where I live is Jang Phekhu.
The name of my father is Kunsang Dechen.
The name of my mother is Nyangtsa Saldrön.
My own name is Nangsa Öbum.
I am the daughter of an ordinary household.

The poisonous rhododendron tree is very colorful,
but who would use it to adorn the vase on the beautiful altar?
The *dolo*[97] stone is of a beautiful blue color,
but how could it compare with the reddish luster
     of the turquoise?
The little lark is very skilled in flying,
but when it comes to soaring high in sky,
how could it ever compare with the great eagle?

The maiden Nangsa may have an attractive form,
but how could she be a bride to a high official?
Please, I ask you to let this maiden go.
She will not stay here but will go to the Dharma.

Governor Drachen's official, Sönam Palkyé, handed the governor the master's life-force turquoise with its dark-blue glow and threaded with a red silk ribbon, together with an arrow decorated with five different-colored ribbons, and said:

As the saying goes, "Pretending to like something
     that is unpleasant
are the words of a young man going to war.
Pretending to dislike something that is pleasant
are the words of a young woman becoming a bride."

"Will this girl enter the householder life?" asked the governor.
The official replied: "In her mind she wants to, but because she is in the midst of a crowd she makes out that she does not want to. If you adorn her

with the turquoise and place the arrow upon her, she will make up her mind immediately. Is this not the way to proceed?"

The governor agreed with this, and again he spoke to Nangsa:

> Beautiful Nangsa Öbum, like a daughter of a god,
> insatiable to gaze upon. Listen to me.

> The renown of governor Drachen resounds like thunder.
> In this world I am a powerful lord.
> You may be a maiden endowed with intelligence,
> but not to obey the word of a powerful lord is foolish.

> This maiden who desires the Dharma,
> will not be sent to the Dharma.
> This maiden living at home
> will not remain at home.

> The sun on his path high in the sky
> and the lotus dwelling on this lowly earth
> may have differences in being high and low,
> but by the power of karma they are in harmony,
> and they become each other's friend.

> The long arrow with its vermillion notch and eagle feathers
> and the short bow covered with wild goat hide
> may have differences in being short and long,
> but by the power of karma they are in harmony,
> and they become each other's friend.

> The great and mighty outer ocean
> and the little golden-eyed, white bellied fish
> may have differences in being small and large,
> but by the power of karma they are in harmony,
> and they become each other's friend.

> The powerful official Drakpa Samdrup
> and the ordinary maiden Nangsa Öbum
> may have differences with an inequality of power,

but by the power of karma they are in harmony,
so why would you not become his bride?

This five-colored decorative arrow in my hand
and this life-force turquoise with its deep blue glow
I place upon the crown of the head of Nangsa Öbum
and take her as the bride for my Nyangtö Rinang son.

All you people gathered here, listen to me.
Drakpa Samdrup of Nyangtö Rinang
has been given this maiden Nangsa as his bride.
From now on, she is not to be seized by the powerful,
she is not to be kidnapped by the poor,
she is not to be courted by the middling ranks of society.
Do not say that she has flown high to the skies.
Do not say that she has sunk into the earth.

The maiden Nangsa is now owned by the Rinang governor.
All of you, understand this.

He adorned the head of Nangsa with the crown turquoise and the arrow. Nangsa and her attendant, Dzomkyi, hid the arrow and the turquoise and returned home. There Nangsa continued to serve and wait upon her parents with perfect devotion. Governor Drachen and his attendants returned to Nyangtö Rinang.

Sometime later, governor Drachen and his official arrived unannounced at the Jang Phekhu household, bringing marriage ale, ornaments, and suckling money.[98] Sönam Palkyé knocked at the door. The mother, Nyangtsa Saldrön, looked out of the window and recognized the callers as governor Drachen and his attendant. Immediately she turned to her husband, Kunsang Dechen, and said:

Listen to me, Kunsang Dechen.
Turn your ears to Nyangtsa Saldrön.
Governor Drachen and his attendant are at our door.
Should we not take their horses, invite them in,
and offer them our hospitality?

Her husband replied:

> Listen to me, Nyangtsa Saldrön.
> Turn your ears to Kunsang Dechen.
> Whether governor Drachen has arrived
>   at our door
> or an owl has landed on our roof,
> makes no difference to me.
>
> Greeting and welcoming is not known to me.
> Tell them I am not here, and to go away.
> If they are insistent and do not leave,
> you should ask them what they want.

Nyangtsa Saldrön fetched a jar of ale and a ceremonial scarf and went to the door. The governor and his attendant told her in detail of the events at the monastery. The mother was delighted and ran to tell her husband, who was also very pleased. He said: "If you have no business here except to seek the hand of my daughter Nangsa, I am happy to give her. In this land there is no one greater than the Nyangtö Rinang master. By all means, I accept your request. I am happy to invite the governor and his attendant into my home."

The two men were invited in and afforded all hospitality. The governor in return gave Nangsa's parents the marriage ale and the suckling money. To Nangsa they gave the most beautiful ornaments. The governor declared:

> Maiden Nangsa Öbum and her parents, listen to me.
> The girl Nangsa, daughter of this mother and father,
> from this day forward is the bride of Drakpa Samdrup,
> son of the Rinang governor Drachen.
>
> Do not say that she has flown to the skies.
> Do not say that she has sunk into the earth.
> The powerful cannot snatch her away.
> Wandering vagabonds cannot kidnap her.
> Her mother and father cannot refuse to give her away.
> Nangsa herself cannot refuse to go.
> Now she is a queen of the Rinang lord.

Not tomorrow, or the day after, but the day after that,
five hundred horsemen will come to escort her away.
Prepare her inheritance and her parting gifts.

Hear me one more time, maiden Nangsa.
When you came to the show at Nenying Monastery,
the moon shone among the stars
and I saw your beauty among the crowd.
Do you not remember the crown turquoise and the arrow?
Where are they? Bring them to me now.

Nangsa replied: "I thought my parents would think I was flirting, and not that you and your attendant had used your authority over me. I thought they would scold me, so I hid them."

"Get them now," said the governor.

Nangsa fetched the crown turquoise and the arrow and handed them to the governor, who immediately placed them again on her head. The governor and his attendant then left the house.

Nangsa had no wish to enter the worldly ways of married life and longed to devote herself to the Dharma. She pleaded with her parents:

My kind parents who gave birth to this body, listen to Nangsa.
Seeing companions whose coming together must end in
    separation,
I have no wish to be the life-long companion of Samdrup
    Drakpa.
For her companions this maiden will put her trust
in the never-ending companions of the Three Jewels,
and she will practice the divine Dharma.

Seeing wealth whose accumulation must end in dispersal,
I have no wish for the Rinang wealth-lord.
For her wealth-lord this maiden will put her trust
in the never-declining seven jewels of the ārya beings,
and she will practice the divine Dharma.

Seeing buildings whose construction will end in destruction,
I have no wish to be the mistress of the Rinang governor's estate.

For her home this maiden will have the never-deteriorating
    remote cave,
and she will practice the divine Dharma.

My kind parents who gave birth to this body,
by whatever means, send this maiden to the Dharma.

Her parents replied:

Daughter of human parents, but with the body of a goddess,
beautiful Nangsa, please listen to us.
The Rinang lord, Drakpa Samdrup,
has a temper hotter than fire,
more turbulent than the waves on the ocean.
He is a powerful man of renown throughout the land.
Do not say that you will not be his bride.

If you insist on following the path of Dharma,
The Rinang lord will kill your parents.
If that should happen, you may practice the Dharma,
but how will you walk on the path to liberation?
Do not say you will follow the Dharma,
but go and be the mistress of the Rinang lord.

MARRIAGE

Her parents were very insistent and, not wanting to go against their wishes,
she agreed to become the Nyangtö Rinang mistress. The escort from the
Rinang estate arrived to take the bride. Her mother and father gave Nangsa
her inheritance and parting gifts, and these words of advice:

Nangsa, more valuable than a hundred sons,
listen to these words of your parents.
You are leaving here as the Nyangtö Rinang bride,
and we give you your inheritance and parting gifts.

There are representations of the enlightened body, speech, and
    mind,
exemplified by a turquoise Tārā statue, which is known to speak.

There are gifts of gold, silver, turquoise, coral, pearls, and so on,
gems and jewels, all of a value beyond estimation;
clothing of silk, brocade, wool, and so on,
as well as wheat, barley, beans, and other grains.
Dzomkyi and these other maidens
are your attendants in your new home.

Take this cockerel tied to its peg as your example,
and be the first to get up in the morning.
Take this watchdog as your example,
and be the last to go to bed at night.

Serve the father and son with great consideration.
Make few friends and be of a modest disposition.
Toward your life-long companion as ordained by karma,
show devotion, respect, and serve him well.

Toward the servants and attendants in your retinue,
develop affection that shows no favoritism.
We pray that Nangsa and her old parents meet again
    and again.

Her parents presented Nangsa with the inheritance and parting gifts.
Nangsa and her attendants set out for Nyangtö Rinang, accompanied by
the escort. Upon arriving, she was welcomed with joyous songs, music, and
dance, and an extensive bridal celebration was held.

About seven years after mistress Nangsa arrived at the Nyangtö Rinang
estate, she gave birth to a son who was unlike a human child and more like
a son of the gods. He was given the name Buchung Lhau Darpo, and great
birth celebrations were held.

Mistress Nangsa had cast off the five faults of womanhood and was pos-
sessed of the eight qualities of a wise woman. Consequently, she worked hard
in serving the Nyangtö Rinang father and son. She showed great devotion
and was very virtuous. Toward all the household servants and attendants,
and the ordinary subjects, she skillfully developed an impartial affection.
Her work on the land, her preparations of food and drink, her weaving skills,
and so on, all produced excellent results and were hugely beneficial. All of
this meant that she was cherished by the Rinang masters and attendants.

Moreover, not only was mistress Nangsa a mother of a son but she was also attractive in all she did, and very beautiful. This meant that governor Drachen and his son had so much love for her that they could not bear to be separated from her even for an hour.

They had planned to entrust her with all the keys to the storerooms. However, Nyimo Netso, her husband's sister, was in charge of the keys, which meant that she controlled how much was to be distributed to everyone. Therefore she feared she would lose her power to Nangsa. Moreover, although Nangsa showed the same respect for Nyimo as she did for the master and his son, Nyimo was not very good at anything she did and everybody ridiculed her behind her back. They all, however, spoke fondly of Nangsa. As the saying goes, "Women make desire and anger as one." Consequently, Nyimo made life unbearable for Nangsa with many vindictive acts, such as spreading false reports about her in order to cause trouble and create a rift between the two masters and mistress Nangsa, and wrongly accusing Nangsa of various things in front of the servants and attendants.

Nyimo did not give the storehouse keys to Nangsa but kept them for herself. She took the most delicious food and the warmest clothes for herself and gave the poorest food and clothing to Nangsa. As a result, Nangsa lost enthusiasm for her daily tasks. Although she still held the sacred Dharma in her heart, she could not wait upon the governor and his son but stayed in her room with her son Lhau Darpo on her lap. Kissing him and with tears falling down her cheeks, she gave him her milk and sang this sad song:

> I go to you for refuge, Three Jewels.
> Bless me, deities and ḍākinīs.
> Remove all obstacles, Dharma protectors and guardians.
> Fulfill the desires of this maiden.
>
> Son, you are a rope that pulls me into samsara.
> If you had not been born,
> Nangsa could have practiced the Dharma.
> But I cannot bear to leave you here,
> and taking you with me
> would be an obstacle to Dharma practice.
>
> To stop me doing my Dharma practice,
> my master has crowned me with turquoise.

To stop me doing my worldly practice,
Nyimo has shown nothing but envy.
I have no freedom to go and be with my parents.
Alas, alas! This maiden is so sad!

This beautiful body, this lovely son,
and my dear relatives are all enemies of the Dharma.
It is Nyimo Netso alone who is the lama
that urges Nangsa toward the Dharma.

Lhau Darpo, when you are able to look after yourself,
and if death does not visit itself upon Nangsa,
this maiden will not stay here but go to the Dharma.
Nangsa will not stay but will go to the mountains.

Putting Lhau Darpo on her back, Nangsa went into the flower garden to refresh herself. Drakpa Samdrup also came into the garden. There he washed his hair and placed his head upon Nangsa's lap so that she could pick out the lice and their eggs. It was the beginning of autumn and the fading flowers were being attacked by frost. Golden bees and turquoise bees were buzzing around one or two fresh flowers. This scene caused Nangsa to reminisce. "My two parents, who are the necessities of this life, are as good as dead to me. The sacred Dharma, which is the necessity of the next life, is denied to me. Moreover, Nyimo with her hostility has made my married life impossible." Her sadness became overwhelming and she started to cry. Her tears fell into the ears of her husband, causing him to wake up. He looked at Nangsa and saw her tears:

Captivating maiden, irresistible to gaze upon,
mistress Nangsa, hear me this one time.
Your face and body are adorned with silks and turquoise.
You are wise in all Dharma and worldly acts.

In your lap you have the beautiful turquoise jewel of a son.
You are the wife of the lord of Rinang.
Nangsa, you have no reason to be sad.
Why are you shedding these tears?
Tell me honestly. I will grant whatever you wish.

Up to now, Nangsa had not been able to tell her husband of Nyimo's wicked ways for fear that it would cause trouble between brother and sister. However, she thought to herself: "Now that I have been asked, if I could reveal a little of my trouble, at best he might give me permission to follow the Dharma. Even if that did not happen, since they are close as brother and sister, he might tell Nyimo to mend her ways. She would stop her hostility and I could bear to live here again." With this in mind, Nangsa sang this response:

> To my father lamas I prostrate.
> To the hosts of my mother ḍākinīs I pray.
> You who are ordained by karma to be my companion
>   for life,
> lord Drakpa Samdrup, please listen to me.
>
> When this maiden lived with her parents,
> when she was dwelling in her own country,
> her face and body became her enemy,
> and without Dharma she had to leave for the home
>   of another.
>
> When I arrived at the home of the Rinang lord,
> I lovingly served him and devoted myself to him.
> In particular, though there is no harmony between Nyimo
>   and me,
> I had no regrets that I had done any wrong.
>
> However, like returning ale with water,
> the good that I have done has been returned with hostility.
> If I keep quiet, they say this maiden is stupid.
> If I answer back, they say she is arrogant.
> If I go outside, they say I am of loose morals.
> If I stay inside, they say I am a temple mural.
>
> When I think of the kindness of governor Drachen,
> I am minded to serve and to be an attendant.
> When I look at the face of Drakpa Samdrup,
> I am minded to be his constant companion for life.

When I look at the face of little Lhau Darpo,
I am minded to devote myself to worldly tasks.
When I look at the attendants and servants,
I am minded to be the Rinang mistress.

When I look at the face of Nyimo,
I am minded to argue with her.
When I think of the transience of all of this,
I am minded to turn to the sacred Dharma alone.

The Dharma that I need for the next life I do not have.
The parents that I need for this life I do not have.
How happy I would be if my mother and father
could hear this sad song of a daughter thinking
    of her parents.

Drakpa Samdrup replied: "Nangsa, it is only right that you miss your parents. A long time has passed since you last met them. You must go and see them as soon as you can. Do not be unhappy. I do not know if Nyimo Netso has been so spiteful. If she has, I will talk to her. Now it is time to gather the harvest from our fields. Therefore, not tomorrow but the day after that, we must go with the farm workers to harvest the crops. Go and get the provisions from Nyimo."

Nyimo gave ale and food to Nangsa and the workers and came along as supervisor of the work.

Nyimo Turns the Master against Nangsa

During the gathering of the harvest a cotton-clad yogi and his disciple arrived from Latö Dingri. They looked at Nangsa and sang this religious song:

I prostrate to the father lamas.
I beseech that you lead mother sentient beings
of the six realms onto the path of freedom.
I come here to ask for alms and in return
I give teachings on the sacred Dharma.

Nangsa, your human life of leisure and opportunity
is like the rainbow over the eastern hills.

Its colors are beautiful, but it has no essence.
Now is the time to practice the essence that is the Dharma.

Nangsa, your human life of leisure and opportunity
is like the cuckoo of the southern forest.
Its beautiful song has every expression, but it has no essence.
Now is the time to practice the essence that is the Dharma.

Nangsa, your human life of leisure and opportunity
is like the nāga in the western ocean.
She may possess all possible wealth, but it has no essence.
Now is the time to practice the essence that is the Dharma.

Nangsa, your human life of leisure and opportunity
is like the roar of the blue dragon thunder in the north.
It is of great renown, but has no essence.
Now is the time to practice the essence that is the Dharma.

Nangsa, your human life of leisure and opportunity
is like the murals on the temple walls in central Tibet.
They are astonishing and beautiful paintings, but have
    no essence.
Now is the time to practice the essence that is the Dharma.

When that enemy, the transience of death, arrives,
the might of the warrior can do nothing.
the meek, they may run but can do nothing.
No beautiful seductress can beguile it.
The wealth of the rich cannot tempt it.

The authority of the noble minister can do nothing.
The petitioning of the ordinary people can do nothing.
The swift can run but they cannot escape it.
Only this once do you have this opportunity and leisure.
Do not leave empty-handed. Practice the Dharma.

Mistress Nangsa thought to herself: "These verses were sung with me in mind and are very true." She felt great faith and wanted to give alms to the yogi. However, Nyimo Netso Lek was supervising the workers on the farm and so she was unable to make any offerings to him. She said to the yogi and his attendant: "I have no authority to give you any provisions or offerings. Over there is a woman with a shiny face and well-dressed in deep-brown clothes. You should ask her." Nangsa pointed out Nyimo.

The cotton-clad yogi and his attendant approached Nyimo and begged for alms. Nyimo stopped what she was doing and said to them: "What are you beggars doing, coming to me? In the summer you beg for butter and cheese. In the winter you beg for ale. If you stay in the mountains, you can't practice the Dharma. If you stay on the plains, you can't work. If have something, it is because you are bandits. If you don't have something, you steal it. You spend your whole lives constantly lying, cheating, and deceiving. I know of no hospitality for you cotton-clad people with your empty words. If you want alms, go to our Nyangtö Rinang mistress, Nangsa Öbum. She is more beautiful than a peacock, more sweet-voiced than a nightingale, with a mind more radiant than a rainbow, and more powerful than Mount Meru. She is over there. I am her servant. I have not power to give you anything."

Again the yogi and his attendant approached Nangsa and told her what Nyimo had said. Unable to bear it, Nangsa gave them seven bundles of grain from the harvest and said: "Where have you come from? Where will you go now? Please help this maiden Nangsa to follow the sacred Dharma for the rest of her life and make prayers for me."

In reply, the yogi again sang a song to Nangsa:

> I prostrate to the father gurus.
> I beseech that you lead mother sentient beings
> of the six realms on to the path of freedom.

> Listen once again, mistress Nangsa.
> You are very kind in giving us these alms.
> I have come from Lachi Snow Mountain in Latö.
> I am a disciple of Milarepa. My name is Rechung Dorjé Drak.
> My sole cotton-clad companion is the disciple Rinchen Drakpa.
> Now I am leaving for Central Tibet,
> specifically to the town of Yarlung Kyorpo.

> The great meditators practicing in the uplands
> and the benefactors providing in the lowlands

makes for the happy coincidence that results in
the simultaneous attainment of buddhahood.
The essence of such a happy coincidence is the
   dedication prayer.

Nangsa, who has made a connection by giving food,
and this cotton-clad one who made the connection by
   teaching the Dharma
makes for a happy coincidence of meeting the Dharma.
The essence of this happy coincidence is prayer.

Again Nangsa felt enormous faith, and once again she gave the yogi three
bundles of the harvested crop. She prostrated to him and sought his blessing.
The two cotton-clad yogis were very pleased and made pure prayers and ded-
ications before they left.

Nyimo had seen Nangsa giving alms, making prostrations, and requesting
blessings. She became very angry. She tucked up her skirts left and right, and
with a stick in her hand strode over to Nangsa. With eyes bulging, she sang
this song:

On the outside, an attractive body with a beautiful complexion,
but on the inside, a wicked mind that feeds on poison food.
You peacock-like demoness, Nangsa, listen to Nyimo.

In the monastery of Langkhor in Latö Dingri
lives the great Indian adept Dampa Sangyé,
and on Lachi Snow Mountain in Latö
lives the great Tibetan yogi Milarepa.

Because of them, here in Nyangtö Rinang,
cotton-clad yogis constantly come and go.
if you give to every beggar whatever they want,
there is little purpose in being a mother.

This long-sown field here in Nyangtö Rinang
produces the best harvest of grain and beans.
If you want to give whatever sheaves you have to a beggar,
then don't stay here, beggar. Go with them!

In reply, Nangsa sang this song:

> I prostrate to the Three Jewels, my objects of refuge.
> Please look upon this maiden who lacks the Dharma.
> Listen to me, Nyimo.
>
> I could not decide to give them alms,
> so I sent them over to you to beg.
> You told them that you were a servant,
> and could not give them alms.
> "She is the mistress," you said. "Ask her."
>
> When you sent them back to me,
> I gave them bundles of grain because
> "beggars carry talk to the lowlands
> and crows carry meat to the uplands."
> So I feared for the Nyantö master's reputation,
> had I sent them away empty-handed.
>
> Using wealth to make offerings to the Three Jewels
> and to give alms to the poor
> is what it means to be truly rich.
> Like bees that amass their honey,
> wealth amassed through miserliness is of no use.
>
> Do not call them beggars,
> those disciples of the mighty Milarepa,
> but have faith and devotion.
> Do not call her demoness,
> a maiden doing the virtuous practice of offering,
> but rejoice in her deeds.

Nyimo became even angrier than before: "You demon, you devil who is called mistress Nangsa! You gave that grain to the cotton-clad teacher and disciple because they were good-looking and spoke to you sweetly, and not from faith, devotion, or affection. Because you think you have the authority of having a child on your lap and your father's name on your back, someone says one thing to you and you come back with two things. How dare you!

You are merely married into the Nyangtö Rinang family, whereas I am a real daughter of the family. Do you still not know how to take responsibility for any work inside or outside the house? If you will not listen to words, then the time has come for you to be taught with my hands!"

With these words she threw Nangsa to the ground and beat her many times, so that she fell to the ground on her back experiencing the whiteness of dawn, and then was pushed face down on the ground to experience the darkness of night. She plucked seven strands of Nangsa's silky rice-shoot hair and put them in her pocket. She feared that if she did not immediately make up some wrong that Nangsa had done, her brother, Drakpa Samdrup, who had great affection for Nangsa, would scold her. Therefore, when she went to Drakpa Samdrup, she pretended the hair was hers. Holding it in her hand and crying, she sang:

> Brother, master Drakpa Samdrup, listen to Nyimo Netso.
> Mistress Nangsa is not doing the harvesting work required
>   of her,
> but instead indulges in various things not asked of her.
>
> Early this morning, two good-looking and sweet-sounding
> cotton-clad deceivers arrived at our long-sown field.
> Nangsa was infatuated and gave them most of her crop.
> Shamelessly, she wanted to be intimate with them.
>
> Seeing this, I could not bear it, and went to lecture her.
> But she did not listen and reveled in her shameful act.
> Then she plucked out my hair and whipped me
>   many times.
> My brother, choose carefully between your bride
> and your own flesh and blood.

Drakpa Samdrup thought to himself: "Nyimo Netso Lek would probably not make such extraordinary claims without proof. Because mistress Nangsa is a beautiful woman, as well as a mother, I and everybody here in Rinang greet her with a smile and have treated her with love and affection. Because of this she has fallen into bad habits and become spoiled. Women and children like this would not exist if they were disciplined and not allowed to fall into bad habits in the first place."

He went to find Nangsa, who was sitting in a corner of the field crying because of the beating she had received from Nyimo. Seeing her, he sang this song:

> Listen to me this one time, demoness Nangsa!
> Turn your ears to the master of Rinang.
> Turn your ears to me, Drakpa Samdrup.
> Of the work you were entrusted with, you have nothing
>   to show,
> but engaging in activities you were not entrusted with,
> you have shown hospitality to two cotton-clad charlatans.
> What do you mean by beating my young sister?
>
> The beggar's dog is tied up on the roof and now bays
>   at the stars.
> The ale jars are warmed by the sun and their bottoms are
>   above their mouths.
> The donkey has been fed with grain and now kicks the horse.
> The ferryman knows the river and now bursts the coracle.
> The beggar knows his dog and now carries his stick on his
>   shoulders.
> Look at the deeds of this immoral Nangsa!

Mistress Nangsa thought to herself: "As the saying goes, 'Not being satisfied with shooting the arrow, he shows off his bow.' It is not enough that Nyimo herself beats me, she then slanders me by telling the master that I beat her! Still, without someone getting angry, how can we practice patience? Now I should tell the master and his son truthfully, and without deception, all the terrible things she did to me, and that would abate his anger. However, that might cause a rift between brother and sister, so how can I? Even if I tell the servants, it would look like a spat between the women."

Therefore she said nothing, but just sat there. Seeing this response, Drakpa Samdrup thought to himself: "What my sister Nyimo Netso said is true. Stricken with guilt, all she can do is sit there and cry." Furiously, he grabbed her by the hair and shook her about. He kicked her and beat her many times with the back of his knife. Unable to bear the pain, she cried out. The attendant Sönam Palkyé and the maid Dzomkyi heard her cries. They rushed to her, prostrated to Drakpa Samdrup, and begged him:

Hear us, mighty master! Listen to this attendant and maid!
If the mistress has offended you,
it is right that you should scold her,
but how could you shamelessly beat the woman
who is your companion for life and the mother of your son?

Over the full-moon face of beautiful Nangsa
are gathered the clouds of blood from her wounds.
On the fresh young bamboo tree of her beautiful body
at least three branch-like ribs are broken.

Do not beat her, Nyangtö Rinang, master.
Do not shed any more tears, mistress Nangsa.

With these words they led Drakpa Samdrup and Nangsa back to their
rooms.

At that time in a monastery called Kyipo Yalung lived an excellent lama
called Śākya Gyaltsen. He was the main disciple of Lama Rongtön Lhaga,
whose coming had been predicted to venerable Milarepa by Lhodrak
Marpa Lotsāwa. He practiced the old and new tantras, but was particu-
larly skilled and accomplished in the sacred teachings of Dzokchen. He
saw with his clairvoyance that Nangsa Öbum, the mistress of Nyangtö, was
a noble ḍākinī who would return from death as a way of turning adverse
circumstance into good. Moreover, she would go on to perform unimag-
inable enlightened activities for others. In order to hurry along the circum-
stances for her to become a death-returner, and to encourage her in the
Dharma, he manifested as a young, handsome, and pleasant-voiced beggar
skilled in the art of playing with monkeys. He then appeared under Nang-
sa's window at her home. There, while encouraging his monkey to play, he
sang this song:

Lovely maiden, whose form is more beautiful than the gods,
mistress who is sitting by her window,
fix your eyes upon this monkey playing.
Turn your ear to the song of this beggar.

In the forests of Kongyul in the east,
each mother monkey has her children.

Those blessed with skills perform their dances.
Those unskilled eat their delicious fruit.

When the karma of being a child is finished,
they will fall into the hands of beggars.
When the rope is tied around their necks, they become sad.
To train them to play, they are made to perform unpleasant tasks.
This is the result of monkeys being busy creatures.

In the forests of Bheda in the south,
each mother bird has her children.
Those with powerful wings soar through the skies,
while those without sit on the tops of trees.

The talking parrot falls into the hands of the king.
When the chain is tied to its legs it becomes sad.
To train it to speak our human tongue,
it is made to perform many unpleasant tasks.
This is the result of a parrot having a clever tongue.

In the rice country of Nepal in the west,
each mother bee has her own children.
Those who are fortunate to partake of food
take from the essence of flowers.

The unfortunate hover around the smell of rice beer.
The yellow-striped bee falls into the hands of children.
When their thumbs press on their backs they become sad.
Driven from their hives they are made to perform
    unpleasant tasks.
This is the result of honey being so sweet.

In the grassy pastures of Mongolia in the north,
each mother ewe has her own lambs.
The lucky ones feed on the nutritious plains.
Those not plump with flesh are led around by faithful pilgrims.

At the end of its life the lamb falls into the hands of the butcher,
who takes it in his hands, and on the point of death it becomes sad.
For its meat it is forced to undergo various unpleasant
    experiences.
This is the result of lamb's meat being so delicious.

In Nyangtö Sershung Ringmo in the central region,
each young mother has her daughters.
Those who have good Dharma merit
leave for the solitude of the mountain hermitage.

Those who do not, stay with their mother and father.
The beautiful one becomes a bride to the lord.
In the hands of Nyimo Netso she becomes sad.
Out of envy she is forced to perform unpleasant tasks.
This is the result of this maiden being so beautiful.

If you do not hold the transience of life in your heart,
although you are beautiful, you are like the peacocks of China.
If you do not practice the sacred Dharma with this
    human body,
although your voice be sweet,
you are like the nightingale of the willow forests.
If you do not give me, this beggar, a gift,
although you may be rich in adornments,
they are like temple murals.

Listening to this song as the monkey danced and played, Nangsa was taken with the beggar's verse. Her son Lhau Darpo was absorbed by the antics of the monkey. As they watched, Nangsa thought to herself: "I must give a gift to the beggar. I cannot possibly give him tsampa, tea, butter, gold, silver, clothes, silks, and so on, without asking Nyimo. But if I did ask her, she would only beat me like before. How can I give him something? I will have to give him something suitable from the ornaments passed down to me from my father's family. In particular, beggars who wander around the country have a lot to say. I will ask him where the best monasteries are, who the good lamas are. Before I die, should I not practice the Dharma and leave behind any attachment to my little son and my parents? The words of the songs sung by the two yogis yesterday and by this beggar today were about me. I am determined that I will follow the Dharma."

Surreptitiously, she called the beggar and the monkey into her room and sang this song:

> Listen to me, wanderer throughout the land.
> Beggar who leads a monkey, listen to Nangsa.
>
> When I look at my old mother and father,
> I see that they are like the shadows in the evening.
> In old age one has no power to serve others.
> Thinking on this, this maiden becomes sad.
> Nangsa will not stay here, but will follow the Dharma
> and leave for the solitude of the mountain hermitage.
>
> When I look at my husband and companion for life,
> I see that life-long companions are like flags blowing in
>   the wind—
> they are not self-supporting but must follow the words
>   of others.
> Thinking on this, this maiden becomes sad.
> Nangsa will not stay here, but will follow the Dharma
> and leave for the solitude of the mountain hermitage.
>
> When I look at my child, my karmic repayment,
> I see that Lhau Darpo is like the rainbow over the hills—
> he is beautiful but without any essence whatsoever.
> Thinking on this, this maiden becomes sad.
> Nangsa will not stay here, but will follow the Dharma
> and leave for the solitude of the mountain hermitage.
>
> When I look toward Nyimo Netso, my husband's sister,
> I see that she is like an envious snake.
> Though I meditate on patience, she still makes me angry.
> Thinking on this, this maiden becomes sad.
> Nangsa will not stay here, but will follow the Dharma
> and leave for the solitude of the mountain hermitage.

When I look toward the servants and attendants,
I see they are like little children—
they have thoughts but cannot speak.
Thinking on this, this maiden becomes sad.
Nangsa will not stay here, but will follow the Dharma
and leave for the solitude of the mountain hermitage.

If this maiden goes to the solitude of the mountain hermitage,
which monastery is the most pleasant to live in?
If this maiden is to follow the Dharma,
which lama would bring the greatest blessing from devotions
    to him?

A beggar who wanders where he will throughout the land
certainly has something to say, something to tell.
I will give you gifts of turquoise and of coral.
Now give me an answer that is full and honest.

The beggar, in a show of respect, knelt on his right knee, placed his palms
together, and offered Nangsa this song:

Nangsa, you who have the body of a human
but the astonishing beauty of a goddess, listen to me.

There is no place that this beggar has not been.
Ü and Tsang, upper and lower Kòngpo, I have been to them all.
All that I have heard has been nothing but the truth,
and not a word of a lie have I spoken.

Here in Ü and Tsang, where the Dharma is widespread,
there are solitary hermitages that are better than others.
There are lamas whose blessing is greater than others.
There are so many. One could substitute for another.

However, these days the great yogi Milarepa,
who lives in Lachi Snow Mountain in Tò,
is the one whose activities benefit others the most.
Yet it is far and the mistress could not travel there.

North of here and not too far is Kyipo Sera Yalung Monastery.
Its background mountain resembles a lion leaping through
    the sky.
The hills in the foreground resemble a sleeping elephant.
There lives the excellent lama Śākya Gyaltsen,
a lama wise and adept in the Dzokchen practice.
Mistress, if you are to follow the Dharma, go there.
Nangsa, if you are to meet a lama, meet him.

As soon as Nangsa heard the name of Śākya Gyaltsen, she felt a great faith that brought tears to her eyes and a devotion that made the hairs on her body tingle. With great affection for the beggar she chose five large coral stones and three good-quality turquoise stones as gifts for him. At the same time, governor Drachen thought that he should see how hard the harvest threshers were working. As he reached the bottom of the stairs he heard the sweet and melodic voice of a young man as well as an exchange of songs coming from Nangsa's room. He thought to himself: "The female voice is that of Nangsa, but that young man's voice is much sweeter than that of my son, Drakpa Samdrup. What is going on?"

He peered through a crack in the door. Inside he saw Lhau Darpo completely absorbed playing with the monkey, while Nangsa was with the beggar, taking turquoise and coral ornaments from her body and giving them as presents to him. He thought to himself: "Yesterday while working in the fields Nangsa gave many bundles of our harvest to a cotton-clad wanderer and his attendant and intended to flirt with them. My daughter, Nyimo, told her she should not do that, but Nangsa did not listen and beat Nyimo in return. Nyimo told all this to Drakpa Samdrup. As a result, he gave her a little whipping. Yet now she invites a beggar into her room and happily gives him her turquoise and coral ornaments. When I look at these shameless acts, I wonder how this immoral woman of such base behavior came to be the mistress of my Nyangtö Rinang estate. Moreover, if she remains on this path, the child, Lhau Darpo, will also be ruined."

He decided to confront Nangsa, and as soon as he opened the door, the beggar and the monkey jumped out of the window and were gone. He seized Nangsa by the hair and said to her:

Listen to me one time, immoral Nangsa Öbum.
Turn your ears to the master of Rinang Nyangtö.

As if it were not enough that yesterday
you gave bundles of grain to two cotton-clad wanderers,
why are you today giving ornaments to this beggar?

What do you mean by inviting beggars into my home?
What Nyimo said is true. What Drakpa thought is true.
This mistress Nangsa is a prostitute, a woman of low morals.
She is a devil of base habits, a doer of immoderate deeds.

Without giving her time to reply, governor Drachen beat her with his hands many times, even though the wounds on her arms and legs from the beating that Nyimo and Drakpa Samdrup had given her had not healed and the pain from her three broken ribs had not subsided. Moreover, he seized the child, Lhau Darpo, like a bird being snatched by a hawk, and gave it to the daughter of a tenant on the estate to suckle and to be its foster mother.

NANGSA DIES
Separated from her child, Nangsa sank into immeasurable suffering. That evening the vital winds around her heart moved upward and she died.

Her child, Lhau Darpo, separated from his mother, cried from evening until morning and did not sleep at all. It was as if he knew she had died. Consequently, the daughter of the tenant who was looking after the boy decided the next morning to take the child to Nangsa without the governor, his son, or Nyimo knowing. Upon arriving at Nangsa's room, she wondered why she heard no sound. Opening the door, she went to Nangsa's bedside and saw her lying there with her black hair hanging loose. "She must be asleep," she thought. "Mistress Nangsa, do not sleep. Get up," she said.

There was no reply. She put her hand inside the bedding and felt the cold of Nangsa's body. Not wanting to believe it, she checked more thoroughly and came to realize that Nangsa had died. She ran to governor Drachen and his son and told them that Nangsa had died. They went at once to see for themselves. Seeing her lying on the bed as the girl had described, they decided that this was an expression of her unhappiness with the beating she had received at their hands for giving bundles of grain to the cotton-clad visitors, and for giving turquoise and coral to the beggar with his monkey, and that now she was pretending to be sick or ill. Not wanting to believe that she was dead, Drachen took her by the right hand and Drakpa Samdrup by the left, and together they pulled her up while singing in unison to her, as if she were alive:

> Hear us, our beautiful companion.
> Mistress Nangsa, listen to this father and son.
>
> Up above in the realm of the deep blue sky,
> it is as if the clear bright moon is eclipsed.
> It is true that the moon is veiled by clouds,
> but without being full, how could it be eclipsed?
> Maiden do not lie there. Get up now.
> Do not sleep, Nangsa. By all means, wake up now.
>
> Down here in the pleasant gardens of the king,
> it is as if the lotus has been taken by the frost.
> It is true that the lotus has been attacked by the hail,
> but before autumn how could it be withered by the frost?
> Maiden, do not lie there. Get up now.
> Do not sleep, Nangsa. By all means, wake up now.
>
> In the soft and warm bed in this pleasant room,
> it is as if mistress Nangsa has passed away.
> It is true that her body has been struck by sickness,
> but it makes no sense for this maiden to have died.
> Maiden, do not lie there. Get up now.
> Do not sleep, Nangsa. By all means, wake up now.

The father and his son had taken Nangsa by the hands and pulled her up from the bed, but she did not reply and her body was cold to the touch. There was no sign of life, her breathing had stopped, and they realized that she was dead. Father and son were overcome with remorse, but there was nothing that could be done. Therefore, in order to fulfill her final intentions, they immediately arranged for the higher devotion of making offerings to the Three Jewels, the lower devotion of giving alms to beggars, and the intermediate devotions of making donations to the monastic community.

They called in an astrologer. His corpse and funeral divinations indicated that she had not lived out her lifespan, her karma was not finished, and her share of food and clothes had not yet been used up. Therefore he said:

"Her body should be placed on the top of the eastern mountain, and for seven days it should not be disturbed or touched. After seven days you can burn the corpse, cast it into the river, or feed it to the dogs, as circumstance dictates."

Accordingly, the body of Nangsa was placed upon a wooden platform, bound well in a white cotton cloth, and tied down with white woolen cloth. It was carried to the summit of a high hill to the east of the Nyangtö estate, which was shaped like the outstretched trunk of an elephant. To ensure that for seven days no harm came to it from birds, dogs, or wild animals, the men who carried her body stayed in a sheltered spot about an arrow's shot away, where they built a fire and made tea.

At that time the consciousness of Nangsa wandered about in the intermediate state like a hair that had been pulled clean from butter. Then the minions of the Lord of Death, such as Elephant-Head Awa, led her into the presence of Yama Dharmarāja, the Lord of Death. There she witnessed those who had performed good deeds walking up a path to liberation and good rebirth that resembled an outstretched white roll of cloth. Those that had performed bad deeds were being led downhill on a black path to the three lower realms and the eighteen realms of hell. Those in the hot hells were suffering greatly from being burned and boiled in vats of molten metal on the burning iron ground. Those in the cold hells were being tormented by immense and unbearable sufferings of cold, such as being encased in blocks of ice and so on. Seeing these and other sufferings, Nangsa became very afraid. She went down on her knees before Dharmarāja, placed her hands together, and said:

> Look on me! Hear me, Venerable Tārā!
> Bless me, ḍākas and ḍākinīs.
> Listen to this maiden, Yama Dharmarāja,
> you who separate black and white deeds.
>
> While this maiden was alive in the human world,
> I did not physically practice the Dharma,
> but I had a loving mind toward all living beings.
>
> Having realized that after birth comes death,
> I had no attachment to beautiful form.

Having realized that all wealth must come to an end,
I made only offerings and had no miserly mind.

Having realized that all companionship ends with separation,
I had no emotional attachment to those I loved.
Contemplating that patience is the essence of Dharma,
I had no anger toward hostile enemies.

You who separate black and white deeds,
hear this maiden, Yama, Lord of Death.

Yama Dharmarāja ordered the god and the demon who accompanied
Nangsa throughout her life to look at the black and white stones[99] and to
pile them in front of him. Only one or two black stones were produced,
whereas the pile of white stones was large. Yama looked in his mirror and
saw that Nangsa was no ordinary maiden but the incarnation of a noble
ḍākinī. He said to her:

Listen carefully to what I say, Nangsa.
Turn your ear toward Yama Dharmarāja.

The separating of good and bad deeds is performed by me.
When I lead those of good deeds on to the path of freedom,
I am known as Noble Avalokiteśvara,
the compassion of the buddhas of the three times.

When I lead those of wicked deeds to the hell realms,
I am known as Yama Dharmarāja, Lord of Death,
the wrathful warrior king who tames
those oath-breaking doers of evil deeds!

Officials do not protect the wicked.
Gurus do not save evildoers.
Once placed in the prison of Yama,
how will they escape?

Maiden, you are no evildoer but an incarnation of a ḍākinī!
By merely practicing Dharma with bodily actions,

how will you ever be able to put an end to samsara?
If you understand the Dharma with your mind,
you will without doubt reach the attainment of a buddha.

Do not stay here but return to the human realm,
and return your consciousness to your old body.
Become a Dharma-practicing death-returner,
and bring vast waves of benefit to living beings.

Nangsa was overjoyed. She prostrated to Yama and received his blessing. She climbed on to the path to liberation and higher rebirth, which resembled an outstretched roll of white cloth, and traveled along it until she arrived at her old body. There she immersed her consciousness into her body and came back to life.

BECOMING A DEATH-RETURNER

There on the peak of the eastern mountain, Nangsa covered the upper half of her body with the white funeral cloth, and the lower half with the white woolen strips used to tie her body down. In the midst of a shower of flowers, within a canopy of rainbow light, she sat in the Vairocana meditation position with its seven characteristics, such as feet in the lotus position, hands in meditative equipoise mudrā, and so on, and dwelt for a short time in the Vajrayoginī generation and completion stages. Placing her palms together at her heart she made a prayer to the five classes of ḍākinī:

I bow to the lamas, meditation deities, and ḍākinīs.
Lift this evildoer from the swamps of samsara.

Ḍākinī of the vajra family from the east,
your white body with the luster of a conch shell,
a golden ḍāmaru resounding in your right hand,
a silver bell ringing out in your left hand,
engaged in a multitude of pacifying actions,
surrounded by a hundred thousand white ḍākinīs,
pacify all hindrances and troubles.

Ḍākinī of the jewel family from the south,
your yellow body with the luster of gold,

a golden ḍāmaru resounding in your right hand,
a golden bell ringing out in your left hand,
engaged in a multitude of activities of increase,
surrounded by a hundred thousand yellow ḍākinīs,
increase all favorable and conducive circumstance.

Ḍākinī of the lotus family from the west,
your red body with the luster of coral,
a golden ḍāmaru resounding in your right hand,
a silver bell ringing out in your left hand,
engaged in a multitude of controlling actions,
surrounded by a hundred thousand red ḍākinīs,
bring the animate and inanimate of the three realms
    under control.

Ḍākinī of the action family from the north,
your green body with the luster of turquoise,
a golden ḍāmaru resounding in your right hand,
a silver bell ringing out in your left hand,
engaged in a multitude of wrathful actions,
surrounded by a hundred thousand green ḍākinīs,
destroy those enemies endowed with all ten qualifying
    conditions.[100]

Ḍākinī of the buddha family from the center,
your blue body with the luster of sapphire,
a golden ḍāmaru resounding in your right hand,
a silver bell ringing out in your left hand,
engaged in a multitude of all types of actions,
surrounded by a hundred thousand blue ḍākinīs,
grant me the ordinary and supreme siddhis.

The men who had carried the body and were keeping watch over it heard Nangsa's voice carried clearly in the air and came to investigate. When they saw Nangsa sitting upright, the top half of her body wrapped in white funeral cloth and the lower half in white woolen strips, they feared that the body had been possessed by a zombie. The more cowardly among them ran away, while those with more courage picked up rocks, intent on beating her.

Nangsa said: "Do not beat me! This is Nangsa. I am not a zombie. I have returned from the dead."

The men were amazed, and with great faith they prostrated to her. Having received a blessing, they returned to the Nyangtö Rinang governor and told him and his attendants what had happened.

Around that time, Nangsa's attendant Dzomkyi had taken the child Lhau Darpo onto the roof and was pacing back and forth with the child on her back. Since his mother's death he had not eaten in the day and not slept at night. Lhau Darpo said to Dzomkyi: "Where is the place where they laid my mother's body? Show this little child. Although mother and son cannot be together in this life, I must make a prayer that in the next life we will meet in a pure ḍākinī realm."

The attendant Dzomkyi also missed her mistress Nangsa, and feeling great pity for the little child, she wept uncontrollably. She pointed to the place on the summit of the hill where Nangsa's body lay. The little child held his right hand to his brow and peered into the distance. With a heavy heart, he sang this song:

> My loving father has killed my precious mother,
> and I am left like a baby bird wandering the plains.
> This sad song of a child missing his mother,
> if only you could hear it, my kind, kind mother.

> Look over there, my helper, Dzomkyi,
> on the hill where my mother's body lies.
> There are no wings of vultures to be seen.
> No black crows are circling the spot.

> There are rainbows and canopies of light.
> Take me to the summit of that eastern hill.
> Take me to where my mother's body lies.

At the same time, the men arrived and related to the master and everyone else how Nangsa had returned not as a zombie but as a death-returner. Governor Drachen, his son, and even Lhau Darpo, strapped to Dzomkyi's back, headed for the eastern hill to see for themselves. When they saw Nangsa sitting there, the top half of her body wrapped in white funeral cloth and the lower half in white woolen strips, bathed in a canopy of rainbow light and showers of flowers falling around, the Nyangtö Rinang governor, Drachen, and his son were full of regret for their deeds, which had disturbed the body, speech, and mind of Nangsa. They requested that from this moment on she resume her duties as mistress of the Rinang household:

> We go for refuge to the lamas, our sole fathers.
> We pray to the hosts of mother ḍākinīs.
> Hear us, Nangsa. Listen to Drachen and his son.

> Not realizing that this gently swaying young bamboo tree
> that is the beautiful body of Nangsa
> was the form of a deity, an appearance within emptiness,
> through the force of attachment we have done shameful deeds.
> All harm we have caused your body we openly confess.

> Not seeing that this music of the gods
> that is the beautiful speech of Nangsa
> was the sound of mantra, an expression within emptiness,
> through anger we have fallen into harsh words.
> All angry rebuttal of your words we openly confess.

> Not realizing that this white silver mirror
> that is the beautiful mind of Nangsa
> was the union of bliss within emptiness,
> through ignorance we have done bad deeds.
> All disturbance of your mind we openly confess.

> Whatever we have done in the darkness of our ignorance,
> disturbing the body, speech, and mind of noble ḍākinī Nangsa,
> we ask for forgiveness and to be held by your compassion.

> Although you do not think about governor Drachen,
> think about Drakpa Samdrup and return home.
> Consider that he is your life-long companion.
> Mistress Nangsa, return to your home.

> Although you do not think about Nyimo Netso,
> think about Lhau Darpo, and return to your home.

Consider that he was born from your own flesh and blood.
Mistress Nangsa, return to your home.

Although you do not think of the attendant, Sönam Palkyé,
think about the maid Dzomkyi and return home.
Consider that she has been your friend since you were young.
Mistress Nangsa, return to your home.

Although you do not think of the ordinary people and workers,
think about your mother and father and return home.
Consider how they have been your kind parents.
Mistress Nangsa, return to your home.

Nangsa, the death-returner and Dharma practitioner, replied by singing a song to father and son that explained the reasons for losing interest in worldly life and for turning her back on attachment:

I bow from my heart to the ḍākinīs of the five families
who turn the five poisons into the five wisdoms.

Listen to me, governor Drachen. Listen to me, Drakpa
    Samdrup.
Father and son, masters of Nyangtö Rinang,
pay heed to this maiden of woeful karma, bereft of Dharma.

When I, this daughter, Nangsa, was alive,
I had a fine house to call my home.
When death came to this maiden,
I came to a graveyard here on this eastern hill.
I have no interest in worldly lands and homes.
I have turned my back on the four pillars and eight beams.

When I, this daughter, Nangsa, was alive,
for traveling I would ride a stallion of fine gait.
When death came to this maiden,
I was taken without horse on the narrow path to hell.
I have no interest in riding stallions.
I have turned my back on fine horses.

When I, this daughter, Nangsa, was alive,
I was surrounded by many relatives, companions, and helpers.
When death came to this maiden,
I wandered alone without companions and helpers.
I have no interest in worldly companions.
I have turned my back on friends and relatives.

When I, this daughter, Nangsa, was alive,
I was adorned with jewels, clothed in soft silk.
When death came to this maiden,
I wandered in the bardo stripped of clothes and jewelry.
I have no interest in worldly clothes and jewels.
I have turned my back on gold, turquoise, and coral.

When I, this daughter, Nangsa, was alive,
I indulged myself in the tastiest food and drink.
When death came to this maiden,
not only my food but even my body was left behind.
I have no interest in worldly food.
I have turned my back on having the body of a beautiful woman.

When I, this daughter, Nangsa, was alive,
my guardian, the governor, listened to the words of another.
When death came to this maiden,
he confessed his faults, begged forgiveness, and feigned regret.
I have no interest in masters of great households.
I have turned my back on governor Drachen.

When I, this daughter, Nangsa, was alive,
my companion for life, my husband, beat me severely.
When death came to this maiden,
he performed good deeds, declaring,
"Nangsa's final intentions have been met."
I have no interest in worldly husbands.
I turn my back on Drakpa Samdrup.

When I, this daughter, Nangsa, was alive,
Nyimo Netso stirred up much trouble for me.

When death came to this maiden,
she put on a show and cried tears of grief.
I have no interest in worldly Nyimo.
I turn my back on Nyimo Netso.

When I, this daughter, Nangsa, was alive,
I would think of Lhau Darpo and go to work.
When death came to this maiden,
my cherished son was the rope tying me to samsara.
I have no interest in worldly sons.
I turn my back on Lhau Darpo.

This maiden will not stay here but will follow the Dharma.
She will not stay but journey instead to a mountain retreat.
Even without the presence of the maiden Nangsa,
how will the household be short of help?

Although this beautiful maiden was taken for a bride,
she waves goodbye to father and son in the prison of samsara.

It was clear to the Rinang governor Drachen and his son that Nangsa was speaking the truth, and they had nothing to say in return. They could not even return home, but with deep regret, their palms placed together and tears in their eyes, they sat there for a while in silence.

Her son, Lhau Darpo, climbed down from attendant Dzomkyi's back and sat on his mother's lap. With tears streaming down his face, he pleaded with her:

Hear me, noble ḍākinī. Mother, listen to your son.
My mother died and now has come back to life.
Is this a dream or is it for real?
If it is a dream, then this little boy is sad.
If it is for real, then without doubt he is happy.

It is astonishing that my mother comes back from the dead.
Is this a zombie or a death-returner?
If this is a zombie, then kill this child.
If she is a death-returner, then look after this child.

For a young child to be without his kind mother
is like an ordained monk without his guru.
Though he may practice, where will he find enlightenment?
Think on this and do not separate mother and child.

For a young child to be without his kind mother
is like the people and laity to be without masters.
The pay their taxes and obey the law,
but are made to do unpleasant tasks.
Think on this and do not separate mother and child.

For a young child to be without his kind mother
is like a young man without courage and skill.
He may be clever but he will never beat his enemies.
Think on this and do not separate mother and child.

For a young child to be without his kind mother
is like a young woman to be without beauty.
She may be adorned with fine clothes, turquoise and coral,
but she will never find a companion.
Think on this and do not separate mother and child.

For a young child to be without his kind mother
is like a swift horse that cannot be controlled.
It may be fast, of good gait, and strong,
but it will be of little worth.
Think on this and do not separate mother and child.

For a young child to be without his kind mother
is like a mule without a powerful back.
You can feed and nourish it with grain mash,
but it will be of little use.
Think on this and do not separate mother and child.

For a young child to be without his kind mother
is like a bankrupt trader without stock.
He may busy himself in body and mind,
but it is all to no avail.

For a young child to be without his kind mother
is like an unconsecrated roadside prayer wheel.
People pay it respect, but no one will turn it.
Think on this and do not separate mother and child.

For a young child to be without his kind mother
is like a bird that has not mastered the art of flying.
It may soar into the air but will fall to the ground.
Think on this and do not separate mother and child.

For a young child to be without his kind mother
is like the northern plains and the desolate valleys
that are deprived of water and vegetation.
Travelers may congregate there, but nobody lives there.
Think on this and do not separate mother and child.

For a young child to be without his kind mother
is like someone seriously afflicted with leprosy.
They have few friends, and those who meet them feel
    disgusted.
Think on this and do not separate mother and child.
Mother, please return home.

Nangsa felt so much love for her son, Lhau Darpo, and tears streamed down her face. However, she knew that returning to her home, as her son wished, would be a hindrance to her practicing the Dharma. Extending her arm like an outstretched roll of white silk, she caressed his head while singing this song:

I prostrate to the father lamas,
and from my heart to the mother ḍākinīs.
Listen to me, child of my heart.
Lhau Darpo, listen to your mother.

How could I, your mother, be a zombie?
I am a death-returner, come back from the dead.
How could this be a dream or an illusion?
It is for real. It is true. So be happy.

However, those that have been born have not yet died,
and all those who have died will not become death-returners.
Therefore your mother should practice the Dharma,
for there is no telling when death will come.

White snow lion with your turquoise mane,
do not be attached to me, this white snow-mountain.
The snow-mountain of Kailash is greater than me.
This snow-mountain is in danger of melting away.

Great white eagle, master of flight,
do not be attached to me, this high, rocky peak.
The mountain of Meru is greater than me.
This rocky peak might be destroyed by a thunderbolt.

Great stag with your array of eighteen antlers,
do not be attached to me, this accessible mountain meadow.
There are meadows more green and lush than me.
This meadow is in danger of being killed by frost.

Golden-eyed little darting fish,
do not be attached to me, this high mountain lake.
There are oceans greater than me.
This lake is in danger of drying up through drought.

Nightingale of perfect voice, inhabiting the willow forests,
do not be attached to me, this small, square willow garden.
The park of Luding[101] is far greater than me.
This little garden is coming to the end of her autumn.

Golden-colored bee with your silver wings,
do not be attached to me, this hollyhock flower.
There are lotus gardens greater than me.
This flower is in danger of being destroyed by hail.

Lhau Darpo, little child, son of this mother,
do not be attached to me, this death-returner, Nangsa.

The master and his son are greater than me.
There is the danger that death will come to this mother.

Do you hear what I say, my little son?
Lhau Darpo, take these things to your mind.

But again her son made this plea to Nangsa:

My loving mother who cares for me always with compassion,
listen once again to your little son.
If mother and father had not planted the seed of samsara,
how could I have become the rope that ties you to samsara?

If I, this little white snow lion from the high mountains,
were not attached to you, the white snow mountain,
then even if he survives the rain, snow, and blizzards,
there will not come a time when he sports his turquoise mane.

Until this snow lion develops his turquoise mane,
I beg you, white snow mountain, please stay.
When this young snow lion develops his turquoise mane,
snow mountain and snow lion will together follow the Dharma.
Until that time, and before the sun melts your snow,
you can invite as a guest the shades of the evening.

If I, the white eagle from the rocky cliff,
were not attached to you, the high red peaks,
even if he is not harmed by the fearless archer,
there will not come a time when his wing feathers grow.

Until this eagle develops his wing feathers,
I beg you, high rocky cliff, please stay.
When this white eagle has grown his feathers,
the rock cliff and the eagle will together follow the Dharma.
Until that time, and before this rock is destroyed by a
    thunderbolt,
you can invite a powerful tantrika as a guest.

If I, this brown stag from the high grassy meadows,
were not attached to you, an accessible green meadow,
even if I am not harmed by the hunter with his dogs,
there will not come a time when his antlers have spread.

Until the time when this young stag's antlers have grown,
I beg you, high grassy meadow, please stay.
When this young stag's antlers have grown,
meadow and stag will follow the Dharma together.
Until that time, before the meadow is killed by frost,
you can invite as guests the dark clouds from the south.

If I, this little golden fish from a high mountain lake,
were not attached to your clean blue waters,
even if he is not harmed by the ferocious hook,
there will not come a time when he knows how to dart
    here and there.

Until this little fish develops his golden eyes,
I beg you, clear blue waters, please stay.
When he has his golden eyes and his swift darting
    movements,
the lake and the fish will follow the Dharma together.
Before the lake is dried up by drought,
you can invite as guest the medicine-lake queen.

If I, this little nightingale from a square willow garden,
were not attached to you, the park of Luding,
even if I am not harmed by the hawk,
this bird would never come to know the melody of song.

Until this little nightingale knows how to sing,
I beg you, square willow garden, please stay.
When this little bird knows his song,
the garden and bird will follow the Dharma together.
Until that time and before the end of your autumn,
you can invite summer to be your guest.

If I, this little striped bee in the garden,
am not attached to you, the hollyhock flower,
even if I am not harmed by the birds,
this little golden bee will never see his silver wings.

Until this striped bee is able to collect his pollen,
I beg you, hollyhock flower, please stay.
When this bee is able to gather his pollen,
flower and bee will follow the Dharma together.
Until that time, and before you are destroyed by frost,
you can invite the rain to be your guest.

If I, this little son Lhau Darpo,
am not attached to you, my kind mother,
even if I am not harmed by the onset of death,
there will not come a time when this child becomes a man.

Until Lhau is able to look after himself,
I beg you, my mother Nangsa, please stay.
When your little son is able to fend for himself,
mother and son will follow the Dharma together.
Until that time, and before death suddenly comes,
you can request long-life initiation and do longevity practice.

Having listened to the complaints made by Nyimo,
father and grandfather beat you, it is true.
But remember that tolerance is the heart of Dharma.
Do not be angry. Please return home.
Your friends and the little son that loves you
beg you and weep their tears of grief.

If you do not look on them with compassion and listen,
how will your Dharma practice come about?
If someone has love and compassion,
even if they stay at home, that is Dharma.
Without compassion, even if they stay in solitude,
they are no different from the wild animals in the mountains.

The ordinary people of Nyangtö Rinang who were there also pleaded with Nangsa. Father and son, the attendants Sönam Palkyé and Dzomkyi, and all the servants and workers made many requests in support of Lhau Darpo. In particular, Nyimo Netso Lek came before Nangsa, confessed to her wicked deeds, and expressed sincere regret. Henceforth, she vowed that even at the cost of her life she would never do the same again.

Nangsa thought to herself: "The masters and people of Nyangtö have made these earnest requests in all sincerity. And as for little Lhau Darpo, it is truly remarkable for one so young to be able give a Dharma reply using such analogies. Moreover, Nyimo has shown remorse for what she did and promised not to do it again. This is surely the kindness of the Three Jewels. Therefore how wonderful it would be to turn their minds toward the Dharma."

Therefore, to fulfill the wishes of Lhau Darpo especially, as well as the father and son, the attendants and the people, she promised to return for a while to Nyangtö. She was presented with beautiful jewelry and fine silken clothes. The return to Nyangtö Rinang was filled with auspicious occurrences, as rains of flowers fell from the sky and three great peals of thunder rang out.

Now, with her body at one with the enlightened emanated form of appearance and emptiness, her speech at one with the enlightened enjoyment body of sound and emptiness, and her mind at one with the enlightened dharmakāya of bliss and emptiness, the death-returner Nangsa tried to turn the minds of the people, and especially the master Drachen and his son and Nyimo, toward the Dharma. She taught from the Great Vehicle on the difficulties of acquiring a precious human rebirth, the transience of life, the law of cause and effect, the faults of samsara, the benefits of nirvana, and so on, teaching each person to his or her capability. However, because of their wicked deeds, not only were father, son, and Nyimo not able to practice but they were also still tormented by the thought of Nangsa turning to Dharma. Although Nangsa waited on them and devoted herself to them perfectly, she could not turn their minds to the Dharma. Moreover, she herself could not go away to follow the Dharma, and this made her very sad. In the day she did not eat and at night she did not sleep. Father, son, and Nyimo together asked her:

Listen to us, captivating and beautiful maiden.
Mistress Nangsa, hear what we say.
Our confession of our past deeds, made with great remorse,

and our vow sincerely never to repeat them
do not go against the thinking of Nangsa,
and so there is no reason for this sadness.

Yet no food or drink passes your lips in the day
and at night you do not sleep in your bed.
There is no need for such unhappiness.
Maybe your body is wracked by illness?

Nangsa replied:

I go for refuge to the lama and the Three Jewels.
Bless me, meditation deities and ḍākinīs.
Free me from hindrances, Dharma protectors.
Fulfill the wishes of this maiden according to the Dharma.

Listen to me, master, with his son and daughter.
Listen to this death-returner, Nangsa.
I am not sad because I think the necessities of this life,
such as food, clothing, and a good name, will not be mine.
I have no illness caused by the imbalance in the four elements,
nor is there any other unwanted suffering in my mind.

You three have not embraced the Dharma,
I cannot give myself to Dharma, and so I am sad.
The temple is a place of deities, but it holds no joy for me.
Food and drink may be nectar, but it does not please me.
Those close to me may be deities, but I am not taken with them.
My son might be a son of the gods, but I have no attachment
    to him.

Master, son, and daughter, you do not practice the Dharma,
but I ask that you give Nangsa to the Dharma.
Even if there is no way you will give this maiden to the Dharma,
I miss my parents. Please send me to them.

Governor Drachen and his son considered: "Recently, when Nangsa was
innocent of any wrongdoing, we listened to Nyimo and beat her, which

resulted in the tragedy of her death and so on. That has all been forgiven. And yet these days, with not even a person as annoying as a buzzing insect around, she puts on this show of not being content. It is not right. However, if we discuss it, we will all end up having to feel remorse like we did before. If we don't talk about it, she will refuse to do any work and this continual call to follow the sacred Dharma will never end. On the other hand, since Nangsa came here as a Nyangtö Rinang bride until now, she has not been sent on a visit to her relatives even once. It has been delayed again and again. Moreover, regrettable actions have occurred, and so it is only right that she thinks of her parents.[102] Therefore, if we send her and her son to visit her parents, she will develop attachment to the child and to her parents and will not be able to pursue the Dharma. Also, her parents will teach her everything about worldly work and she will finally come to understand."

Nangsa Returns Home

Therefore it was decided that mistress Nangsa, with her son, Lhau Darpo, and fine gifts for her parents, was to be sent for a visit to her parents' home in Jang Phekhu. With Lhau Darpo strapped to Dzomkyi's back, the death-returner Nangsa, her son, and her attendant set off from Nyangtö. At that time the Nyang River was swollen and the bridges at Gyangtsé and Tsechen were impassable. They had to rely on boatmen to ferry them across in their hide boats, and so Nangsa sang this song to the boatman, asking him to send his boat:

> Ferryman on the other side of the river,
> this maiden misses her parents. Send your little black boat.
> I miss my mother, Nyangtsa Saldrön. Send your boat.
> I miss my father. Ferryman, send your horse-head boat.
> I miss Kunsang Dechen. Ferryman, send your horse-head boat.

The ferryman sang a song in reply:

> A hundred passengers cross to that side, a thousand come
>   to this.
> How can I find the time to ferry them all in my boat?
> Maiden, if you miss your parents, jump over the river and come.
> Maiden, if you miss your parents, leap over the river and come.

Nangsa sang in reply:

> Ferryman, do not speak like that. Send your boat.
> Alas! Do not say these things. Send your horse-head boat.
>
> Having fed the stallion with mash, if you then have to walk,
> it makes no difference if it is tied up in the corral or not.
> Having farmed the land, if you want to buy tsampa,
> it makes no difference if you plant grain and beans or not.
> If you follow the Dharma and the Buddha arises as an enemy,
> it makes no difference if you live as a yogi in solitude or not.
> If there is a boat in the water, and you cross the river by the ford,
> it makes no difference if you ask the boatman or not.

Again the boatman replied:

> Dry clever talk will never get wet in the water.
> In the mountain passes the bandit has the power.
> On the river the ferryman has the power.
> Maiden, if you possess magical powers, fly over here.
> Maiden, if you have the power, build a bridge over the river.
> If you are not that capable, then pay me to ferry you over.
> There is no sense in transporting a traveler without the fare.
>
> Thinking that you have to shoot arrows, you buy a bow,
> but if you do not hit the target however much you shoot,
> there is no point in having a bow.
>
> Thinking that you are going to be rich,
> you do business north and south.
> But if you had to take out a loan,
> how will you ever make money?
>
> Thinking that you are going to be beautiful,
> you cover yourself with turquoise jewelry and gold.
> But if you do not stand out in the crowd,
> what was the point of all that expense?

Thinking that a fare will be forthcoming,
the boatman makes his preparations.
But carrying someone without a fare is difficult.

"It is certainly true that the boatman on the riverside is like a bandit in the mountains," thought Nangsa. "If I do not pay him, he will not come." With these thoughts she sang this song:

Ferryman, I apologize. This maiden will pay her way.
I do not think only of my parents,
but of impermanence and death as well.
Having met my parents, I must go and practice the Dharma.
Please ferryman, quickly send your boat.

On the crown of my head I have a turquoise.
It is of reddish luster, and I must offer it to my lama.
Beneath it I have a smaller turquoise of whitish luster.
This I will offer to you, ferryman.
Having met my parents, I must go and practice the Dharma.
Please ferryman. Quickly send your boat.

I have a ring inlaid with turquoise that I must offer to my lama.
I have a clockwise white conch that I will offer to you.
Having met my parents, I must go and practice the Dharma.
Please ferryman. Quickly send your boat.

I have a turquoise and pearl headpiece that I must offer to
my lama.
I have a Kashmiri amber necklace that I will offer you, boatman.
Having met my parents, I must go and practice the Dharma.
Please ferryman. Quickly send your boat.

She took off her jewelry and offered to pay the boatman. As well as being beautiful and possessing a melodious voice, she evidently had developed bodhicitta in her mind and could easily give away her clothes and jewelry without any sense of loss. Seeing this, the ferryman felt great faith in her. "Who are you?" he asked.

"I am Nangsa, the Nyangtö Rinang mistress," she replied. Her fame was widespread and he had heard of Nangsa, who had returned from the dead and was bringing great benefit to those disciples who saw, heard, thought of, or came into contact with her. He returned the items she had offered for passage, prostrated, and requested blessing. Soon local people came to meet and hear the death-returner Nangsa. "Sing a song to benefit our minds," they asked.

Taking her clothes and ornaments as metaphors, she sang this song:

> Lama and the Three Jewels, I go to you for refuge.
> Bless me, deities and ḍākinīs.
> Remove all obstacles, Dharma protectors and guardians.
> Fulfill the desires of this maiden according to Dharma.

> Young and old, men and women, gathered here,
> listen to this death-returner, Nangsa.
> It is not because I like the sound of my voice,
> but because you have asked me to sing a song.
> With no liking for this worldly task,
> I sing this song using my clothes and jewelry as metaphors.

> The hood that covers this maiden's head,
> if it were Vajradhara, I would be joyful.
> These coral and turquoise tassels beneath it,
> if they were the lineage gurus, I would be so happy.
> This gold-encircled turquoise of reddish luster on my head,
> if it were my root guru, I would be joyful.

> This circular turquoise around my forehead,
> if it were the Buddha Jewel, I would be happy.
> These twenty-one thousand strands of hair, plaited,
> if it were the Dharma Jewel, I would be joyful.
> These red ribbons that tie my strands of hair,
> if they were the Sangha Jewel, I would be happy.

> This earring from Kongpo on my right ear,
> if it were the meditation deities and the spiritual heroes,
>   I would be joyful.

This ear ornament tied to my left ear,
if it were the ḍākinīs and the spiritual heroines, I would
   be happy.

This crown jewel decorated with a thousand pearls,
if it were the thousand buddhas, I would be joyful.
This coral and amber tied around my neck,
if it were the Dharma protectors and guardians, I would
   be happy.

This conch-shell bracelet on my right arm,
if it were the monastic conch shell, I would be joyful.
This crystal rosary I carry in my left hand,
if it were a rosary counting the six-syllable mantra, I would
   be happy.
These rings I wear on my fingers,
if they were method and wisdom united, I would be joyful.

This ornamental spoon that hangs from my right side,
if it were the bell and cymbals I would be happy.
This mirror that hangs from my left side,
if it were the world-realm mandala, I would be joyful.

This silk blouse I wear as my upper garment,
if it were monastic upper robes, I would be happy.
This blue pleated lower garment that I wear,
if it were the lower monastic robe, I would be joyful.

This woolen shawl I wear on my back,
if it were turning one's back on worldly things, I would
   be happy.
This apron I wear at my front,
if it were the taking on of Dharma practice, I would be joyful.

This death-returner Nangsa, if she were a lama
teaching the Dharma, I would be happy.
If the young and old, men and women, gathered here
were monks listening to the Dharma, I would be joyful.

I am weary of this samsara.
I will not stay but go to practice the Dharma.

All those who had gathered saw that Nangsa was skillful in singing and had a beautiful voice. Although the metaphors could be easily understood by the worldly, the meaning of the song was pure Dharma. They prostrated to her, sought her blessing, and vowed to free themselves from nonvirtuous acts and to develop virtue as best they could. Nangsa thought to herself: "This song I have just sung has been of benefit to others."

She was overjoyed, and with her son Lhau Darpo on the attendant Dzomkyi's back, they set off for her home in Jang Phekhu.

It had been a long time since her father, Kunsang Dechen, and her mother, Nyangtsa Saldrön, had met their daughter. Therefore as soon they heard that Nangsa, with her child and attendant, were coming to meet them, the father with an auspicious pure-white offering scarf, and the mother with some of the best ale, went some distance to greet them. As soon as they were reunited, the parents sang:

Nangsa Öbum, daughter of your mother,
noble ḍākinī, daughter of your mother,
Lhau Darpo, and attendant Dzomkyi,
listen well to these two old parents.

Before the white snow has been melted by the sun,
the snow lion roams the snowy mountains. What delight!
It has been long since the snow and snow lion reunited.
Is the turquoise mane of the young snow lion fully grown?

Before the high red peaks are destroyed by the lightning bolt,
the white eagle roams the cliffs. What delight!
It has been long since eagle and cliffs were reunited.
Are the feathers of the young eagle fully grown?

Before they are ruined by the frost,
the deer roams the high meadows. What delight!
It has been long since stag was reunited with its meadows.
Are the antlers of the young deer fully grown?

Before the turquoise lake is dried up by drought,
the little fish darts in its waters. What delight!
It has been long since the fish has seen its lake.
Is the golden-eyed fish skilled in darting to and fro?

Before the leaves and flowers of the willow-tree garden fall,
the nightingale roams the willow forests. What delight!
It has been long since nightingale and willow forest were
    reunited.
Little bird, is your song sweet?

Before the flowers of the garden are destroyed by hail,
the little striped bee roams among the flowers. What delight!
It has been long since bee and flower were together once more.
Golden bee, turquoise bee, are your silver wings grown?

Before these old parents meet their death,
our daughter has returned home. What delight!
It has been long since parents and daughter met.
Daughter Nangsa, is your health good?

In reply, Nangsa sang this song to her mother and father:

My kind parents, who gave birth to my body and mind,
listen to Nangsa, this death-returner.
Traveling from birth to death is common to the world.
There are not many like me who return from death.

The growth of the turquoise mane of the white snow lion
was curtailed by the rain, snow, and blizzards,
but gathering about me a host of skills,
I, the snow lion, have again come to Kailash, and in my
    mind is joy.

The growth of the feathers of the white eagle
was curtailed by the skilled archer,
but by flying into the skies,

I, the white eagle, have again come to the vajra peaks,
and now I am happy.

The growth of the antlers of the little deer
was curtailed by the hunter and his dogs,
but skilled in the game of locking horns,
I, the deer, again roam the meadows,
and I am full of joy.

The developing skills of the little golden-eyed fish
were curtailed by the sharp hook,
but skilled in darting to and fro,
I, the little fish, again swim in Manasarovar Lake,
and I am happy.

The developing song of the nightingale
was curtailed by the carnivorous hawk,
but experienced in the ways of speech,
I, the nightingale, have again seen the willow garden,
and I am very happy.

The growing silver wings on the golden bee and the
　　turquoise bee
were harmed by the harmful actions of birds,
but with the essence of honey, I, the bee,
have again found the lotus flower,
and my mind is overjoyed.

I, this mother's daughter, Nangsa Öbum,
was suddenly taken away by the transience that is death,
but as a death-returner, for this maiden to again
meet her kind parents is truly astonishing.

Nangsa proceeded to tell her parents in great detail about the birth of her son, how the master and people of Nyangtö Rinang were generally kind but that Nyimo, out of envy, had caused her all kinds of trouble, how this had caused the vital winds around her heart to move upward, bringing about her death, how her body was placed on the eastern mountain, how her consciousness came before the Lord of Death, how she received a command from him, and how she became a death-returner, and so on. Hearing this, her parents shed tears of joy and sorrow. Then with smiling faces they took her by the hand, saying: "That old saying, 'The corpse returns from the cemetery' has become a reality in our daughter Nangsa."

They led her home and lavished hospitality on her and her son and attendant. In return, Nangsa gave her parents many gifts. And so she stayed with her parents.

One day she went to the weaving room. There she saw some unfinished yarn from when she used to weave before her marriage into the Rinang household. Thinking that it would help her parents, she prepared to weave the yarn. Her mother interrupted her, saying: "We have workers who do the weaving. It would be embarrassing if the Nyangtö Rinang mistress herself began weaving."

Nangsa replied: "If that is embarrassing, then those who have gained this precious human rebirth with its leisure and opportunities and yet do not practice the Dharma, wasting their lives on meaningless pursuits, should be embarrassed. From the way you look at it, mother, now that this maiden has become the mistress of Nyangtö Rinang, she has moved up in status. The way I look at it, I have no power to serve my kind parents, who are the necessities of this life, and I have no power to practice the Dharma, which is a necessity for future lives. Whether I do worldly work or Dharma work, if the things I do are not seen through to the end, nothing is accomplished. So now I ask that I be allowed to continue this unfinished weaving without help from others." And she carried on weaving.

Many young women friends of her age in the area had heard about Nangsa returning from the dead and that she was visiting her parents. They came to see her, bringing ale and tea. They gathered in the weaving room, where they engaged in friendly chats about their clothes and jewelry, their good and bad times, and so on. Nangsa thought that she could bring the minds of her friends toward the Dharma, and so she sang this Dharma song using the parts of the weaving loom as analogies.

> I bow to the lamas, meditation deities, and ḍākinīs.
> Please look upon this maiden who lacks the Dharma.
> Listen to me, my friends of similar age.
> Listen to this death-returner Nangsa.

Using the materials of the maiden's weaving,
I sing this song to turn your minds to the Dharma.
This square hole in the ground worn down by the loom's feet,
if it were a small meditation hut just big enough for me,
   I would be happy.

This small square cushion I sit on,
if it were my meditation cushion, I would be overjoyed.
This maiden, the death-returner Nangsa,
if she were a Dharma practitioner, I would be happy.

This helper of mine, Dzomkyi,
if she were this practitioner's attendant, I would be
   overjoyed.
These wooden bobbins left and right at the head of the loom,
if it were the victory standards of the teachings, I would
   be happy.

This weaving stick that guides the weaving,
if it were instructions from the lama, I would be overjoyed.
This thick sack cast to the back of the loom,
if it were samsara cast behind me, I would be happy.

The main and secondary frame parts jointed together,
if they were bliss and emptiness joined, I would be overjoyed.
The yarn placed within that frame,
if it were the foundation-of-all, I would be happy.

These joints held firm, right and left, by the cross strings,
if they were the ethics of the ten virtuous deeds, I would
   be overjoyed.
This warping tool that guides the yarn,
if it were the life-sustaining mudrā, I would be happy.

This soft, white, and long yarn,
if it were the white path to freedom, I would be overjoyed.
This upper frame that pulls upward,
if it were the pulling up to the higher realms, I would be happy.

This lower frame that pushes downward,
if it were suppressing the lower realms, I would be overjoyed.
This separating rod that divides the yarn,
if it divided cause and effect, I would be happy.

This threading tool that threads the rows of yarn back and forth,
if it were the bodhicitta of giving and taking, I would be
    overjoyed.
This cleaning rod that cleans up the yarn,
if it were cleaning away the two obscurations, I would be happy.

This tool that packs and completes the cloth,
if it were the completion of the two accumulations, I would
    be overjoyed.
These squeezers that push the cloth inward,
if it were the eight worldly dharmas held in equanimity, I would
    be happy.

The clear clack, clack sound of the loom,
if it were the sound of the Dharma, I would be overjoyed.
This pulling to and fro of the yarn on the loom,
if it were the equalizing and exchange of self for others, I would
    be happy.

These eighty-four thousand rows of yarn,
if they were the sutras and tantras, I would be overjoyed.
This soft, white, and long yarn,
if it were the compassionate attitude of this maiden,
I would be happy.[103]

A few of the women present, whose minds were not so obscured, turned their thoughts to Dharma and made efforts to reduce wrong behavior and develop virtuous ways. However, most said: "The parts of the loom in Nangsa's song are easy to understand for ordinary people, but as they are to be applied to the Dharma, it was difficult to understand. Moreover, mistress Nangsa is young and so beautiful. She is skilled in working the land, weaving, and so on. On her lap she has a child. Behind her she has her family, and in front a good husband to be content with. She lacks neither wealth and reputation nor jewelry, clothes, turquoise, and other gems. At such a happy juncture, where does this thought of wanting to follow the Dharma come from?"

In response, Nangsa sang them a song on the transience of life in order to stimulate their minds:

> Listen again, my young childhood friends.
> This human life with its opportunities and leisure is so
>   hard to obtain.
> We have it this one time, and if we do not practice the Dharma,
> there is the danger that we will fall to the lower realms.
>
> This transient life is like lightning in the sky.
> It will flash, and in an instant it is gone.
> You, my friends, will not practice the Dharma,
> but I will not stay here
> and will leave for the mountain hermitage.
>
> This transient life is like the dew on the grass.
> It cannot withstand the slightest change and quickly dries up.
> You, my friends, will not practice the Dharma,
> but I will not stay here
> and will leave for the mountain hermitage.
>
> This transient life is like the rainbow on the side of the hill.
> Its colors are wonderful, but they are without essence.
> You, my friends, will not practice the Dharma,
> but I will not stay here
> and will leave for the mountain hermitage.
>
> This transient life is like the sheep and the goat in the
>   butcher's hands.
> They are still alive, but inevitably soon will die.
> You, my friends, will not practice the Dharma,
> but I will not stay here
> and will leave for the mountain hermitage.

This transient life is like the rays of the afternoon sun.
They are very bright but soon will set over the western
  mountain.
You, my friends, will not practice the Dharma,
but I will not stay here
and will leave for the mountain hermitage.

This transient life is like the eagle that flies through the skies.
Now it glides on high but soon disappears into the distance.
You, my friends, will not practice the Dharma,
but I will not stay here
and will leave for the mountain hermitage.

This transient life is like the mouse that burrows into
  the earth.
Now you see it but soon it is hidden in its hole.
You, my friends, will not practice the Dharma,
but I will not stay here
and will leave for the mountain hermitage.

This transient life is like the water falling on the
  mountain side.
It roars as it falls but in an instant it is finished.
You, my friends, will not practice the Dharma,
but I will not stay here
and will leave for the mountain hermitage.

This transient life is like a beggar and his food.
In the morning he is rich but by evening he is poor.
You, my friends, will not practice the Dharma,
but I will not stay here
and will leave for the mountain hermitage.

This transient life is like the crowd in the market place.
Now they are here but will soon disperse and leave.
You, my friends, will not practice the Dharma,
but I will not stay here
and will leave for the mountain hermitage.

This transient life is like the flag on the little white house.
It is moved by the slightest wind, with no power to
    remain still.
You, my friends, will not practice the Dharma,
but I will not stay here
and will leave for the mountain hermitage.

This transient life is like our beauty, maidens.
We are attractive when young but not so when old.
You, my friends, will not practice the Dharma,
but I will not stay here
and will leave for the mountain hermitage.

These wonderful teachers of the transience of phenomena
are not confined to these few examples,
but are found everywhere.
You, my friends, will not practice the Dharma,
but I will not stay here
and will leave for the mountain hermitage.

Now Nangsa's mother, Nyangtsa Saldrön, arrived. She sang a song imploring her daughter not to follow the Dharma:

You are like the heart that beats inside my body.
My daughter, Nangsa, listen to your mother.
Who would leave behind their old parents?
Daughter, how could you go to follow the Dharma?

Who would leave behind their husband, master of Rinang?
Daughter, how could you go to follow the Dharma?
Who would leave behind their little son, Lhau Darpo?
Daughter, how could you go to follow the Dharma?

Leaving behind these people, and your friends,
Daughter, how could you go to follow the Dharma?
Leaving behind your status and wealth,
Daughter, how could you go to follow the Dharma?

A pure practice of Dharma is so difficult.
How could a young maiden do such a thing?
Pretending to do something that cannot be done,
do not pretend to follow the Dharma,
but follow worldly aspirations, which can be achieved.

Nangsa replied to her mother:

My kind mother, Nyangtsa Saldrön, listen to me.
The sun, the great canopy of the skies,
circles the four continents and rises and sets.
If the sun no longer circles the four continents,
then I also will remain at home.
If the sun continues to circle the continents,
then I also will go to follow the Dharma.

The pure radiant light of the eastern moon
waxes and wanes in the two halves of the month.
If the radiant moon no longer waxes and wanes,
then I also will remain at home.
If the moon continues to wax and wane,
then I also will go to follow the Dharma.

The beautiful lotus flower in the garden
blooms in the summer and fades in the winter.
If the lotus flower no longer blooms and fades,
then I also will remain at home.
If the lotus continues to bloom and fade,
then I also will go to follow the Dharma.

The waters of the great rivers that feed the irrigation
    channels
always flow downward and never upward.
If it is said that their waters now flow upward,
then I also will remain at home.
If it is said that they continue to flow downward,
then I also will go to follow the Dharma.

The red flames of the hot and burning fire,
even if pointed downward, will still blaze upward.
If it is possible that the flames blaze downward,
then I also will remain at home.
If the flames continue to blaze upward,
then I also will go to follow the Dharma.

The flag on the peak of the mountain
is caught by the wind and flutters.
If the flag caught by the wind no longer flutters,
then I also will remain at home.
If the flag continues to flutter in the wind,
then I also will go to follow the Dharma.

For me, Nangsa, daughter of my mother,
birth is followed by death.
If, having been born, I have the power not to die,
then I also will remain at home.
If it is said that death will come to me,
then I also will go to follow the Dharma.

Mother of this daughter, Nyangtö Saldrön,
you are not young but have become an old woman.
If you are no longer old and remain forever young,
then I also will remain at home.
If, having become old, you will never become young,
then I also will go to follow the Dharma.

Her mother thought to herself: "My daughter, being the wife of a powerful lord, no longer listens to gentle pleadings. Now it is time for more forceful methods." Once more she sang to Nangsa:

Daughter, you whom I have nursed since you were
    a child,
if you no longer listen to me now you are grown up,
you are a hostile karmic debt posing as my daughter.
What is the point of giving you heartfelt advice?

You young healthy sprout from the long lowland fields,
having been given water, fertilizer, and warmth, if you do
    not grow,
and have no desire to be a friend to the gentle summer rains,
then have no regrets when you are destroyed by frost and hail.

You fully fleshed and fortunate sheep with your soft fleece,
having been saved by the faithful, if you refuse to go
    with them,
and will not remain still when being shorn in the pen,
then have no regrets when you find yourself in the hands
    of the butcher.

You sick person, in whose body the four elements
    are disturbed,
if you will not show your pulse and urine to a wise doctor,
and not take medicine and beneficial foods,
then have no regrets when you go to the next life.

You lute with your perfect and beautiful tones,
if you do not arrange your strings to their correct thickness,
and no matter what song you try to play, you fail,
then have no regrets when you are skinned and used as a ladle.

Nangsa, of beautiful form and sweet voice,
if you are not to be the wife of the Rinang lord,
and if you do not listen to kind parents,
have no regrets when you are neither one or the other.

If the daughter does not think that this is her mother,
how can the mother think that this is her daughter?
The bond between mother and child has been cut.
My daughter, Nangsa, go away and live where you please.

Nangsa's mother picked up a wooden poker with her right hand and
a handful of ash with her left. She threw the ash into Nangsa's face and
began to beat her with the poker. Nangsa's friends seized her by the hand

and begged her to stop. Consequently, her mother threw Nangsa out of the house, went inside, bolted the door, and refused to allow her back inside.

Nangsa Is Cast Out of Her Home
and Journeys to Yalung Monastery

That evening the death-returner Nangsa stayed in the house of one of her young friends and thought to herself: "To be born once and to die once is the way of the world, but I, this death-returner of poor karma, have one birth and two deaths. The first death has already occurred, and I do not know when the second will come. Therefore I must follow the Dharma. In particular, Yama, the Lord of Death, when he spoke to me gave me wise advice, which included the instruction, 'Nangsa, become a Dharma-practicing death-returner. You have the good karma to do great work for the teachings and sentient beings. So go!' Therefore, today I did not commit the wicked act of giving a disrespectful answer to my mother, the one who has been so kind to me in this life. However, as the saying goes, 'If you speak the truth, it hurts your friends.' Consequently, I have been ejected by my mother, and even my own son is not with me. These are bad circumstances arising as friends, and with such an opportunity, if I do not go to follow the Dharma, there is no knowing what kind of obstructions and delays to following the Dharma those close to me could cause. I should leave now. As for where to go, I greatly desire to go to Lachi Snow Mountain in Latö to be in the presence of the greatest of yogis, Mila Shepai Dorjé, but it is far and it is not a journey to be undertaken by a single woman. Therefore, following the advice of the beggar and his monkey, I will by all means try to meet Śākya Gyaltsen, the excellent lama of Kyipo Sera Yalung Monastery."

As soon as the other members of the household had gone to sleep, she left the house without anyone inside or outside seeing her, and by way of Tsechen Gashi came to the bridge at Tsechen. As she arrived, the white light of the full moon of the fifteenth day rose far away over the eastern mountain. Seeing this as a very auspicious sign, Nangsa was overjoyed and sang this song:

> As Nangsa arrives on the bridge at Tsechen,
> the moon of the fifteenth rises over the eastern mountain.
> This is an omen that the work done for others by this maiden,
> when held by the great compassion[104] of the lama,
> will radiate out like the light of the moon.

With this she cast into the air three handfuls of water from the Nyang River as offerings and set off.

Nangsa arrived at the foot of Kyipo Sera Yalung Monastery as the sun was rising. She came to just below the meditation hut of the lama just as the assembly conch was being blown. Nangsa took this to be an auspicious sign and was full of joy. With his clairvoyance Lama Śākya Gyaltsen knew that mistress Nangsa was a noble ḍākinī, and how she had been inspired to follow the Dharma, and so on, but he made out he knew none of this. He told his disciple, Tsultrim Rinchen, not to show this woman in directly but to go and see what she wanted. The disciple approached Nangsa and said:

> Listen here, beautiful woman.
> Listen to the disciple Tsultrim Rinchen.
> Maiden, where have just come from?
> Where will you stay this evening?
>
> Who are your parents and your family?
> Who is your husband and lord?
> What of your home, wealth, and children?
>
> Maiden, what is your name?
> What is the reason you come to this place?
> Tell me fully and honestly.

In reply, Nangsa said:

> Disciple of the lama, Tsultrim Rinchen,
> listen, I beg, to this maiden without Dharma.
> I have come from the uplands of Nyangtö.
> Where I will go this night, I cannot be sure.
>
> The estate of my birth is Jang Phekhu.
> My father's name is Kunsang Dechen.
> My mother is called Nyangtsa Saldrön.
> My name is Nangsa Öbum.
>
> I have a husband named Drakpa Samdrup.
> I have a child called Lhau Darpo.

I am not lacking in wealth and status.
Nor am I bereft of friends, clothes, and jewelry.

Having become weary of worldly life,
I have come to practice the sacred Dharma.
Disciple, do what you can to bring this maiden
to a meeting with your lama.

Again Tsultrim Rinchen addressed Nangsa:

Beautiful in form, delightful in speech,
Nangsa, listen to this disciple.

Maiden, you are like the snow lion.
With this beautiful snow lion mane,
how will you practice a pure Dharma?
Maiden, do not follow the Dharma, go back home.

Maiden, you are like the eagle from the high cliffs.
With these fully grown eagle feathers,
how will you practice a pure Dharma?
Maiden, do not follow the Dharma, go back home.

Maiden, you are like the deer from the high plains.
With these fully grown deer antlers,
how will you practice a pure Dharma?
Maiden, do not follow the Dharma, go back home.

Maiden, you are like the fish from the high lakes.
With these attractive golden eyes,
how will you practice a pure Dharma?
Maiden, do not follow the Dharma, go back home.

Maiden, you are like a peacock from Lhorong.
With these astonishing peacock feathers,
how will you practice a pure Dharma?
Maiden, do not follow the Dharma, go back home.

Maiden, you are like a nightingale from the willow
   forests.
With the beautiful song of the nightingale,
how will you practice a pure Dharma?
Maiden, do not follow the Dharma, go back home.

Maiden, you are like a flower in the garden.
With the beauty of the colors of a flower,
how will you practice a pure Dharma?
Maiden, do not follow the Dharma, go back home.

Nangsa sang this song in reply:

Tsultrim Rinchen, disciple of the lama,
I, this maiden, am like the snow lion.
This snow-lion mane formed by karma
is no obstacle to me practicing the Dharma.
Disciple, do not say these things.
Arrange for an audience.

I, this maiden, am like the eagle from the high cliffs.
These eagle feathers formed by karma
are no obstacle to me practicing the Dharma.
Disciple, do not say these things.
Arrange for an audience.

I, this maiden, am like the deer from the high plains.
These fully grown deer antlers formed by karma
are no obstacle to me practicing the Dharma.
Disciple, do not say these things.
Arrange for an audience.

I, this maiden, am like the fish from the high lakes.
These golden eyes formed by karma
are no obstacle to me practicing the Dharma.
Disciple, do not say these things.
Arrange for an audience.

I, this maiden, am like a peacock from Lhorong.
These peacock feathers formed by karma
are no obstacle to me practicing the Dharma.
Disciple, do not say these things.
Arrange for an audience.

I, this maiden, am like a nightingale from the willow
    forests.
The song of this nightingale formed by karma
is no obstacle to me practicing the Dharma.
Disciple, do not say these things.
Arrange for an audience.

I, this maiden, am like a flower in the garden.
The beauty of this flower ordained by karma
is no obstacle to me practicing the Dharma.
Disciple, do not say these things.
Arrange for an audience.

The disciple Tsultrim Rinchen was impressed with Nangsa's beauty, her command of speech, and her faith in the Dharma. He reported Nangsa's reasons for wanting an audience to Lama Śākya Gyaltsen. Nevertheless, the lama, as a teaching for Nangsa, did not grant a direct audience but closed the skylight to his upper room and sat behind it. Nangsa stood below the hatch and sang a song of her request.[105]

ka) Lama who has realized the primordial reality,
kha) I come with faith and in all sincerity for an audience.
ga) Wherever I look, I grow weary of samsara.
nga) Please grant me an audience with the lama.

ca) Other than you in this peaceful place of Sera Yalung,
cha) there is no lama in whom I place my trust.
ja) Do not cast me out like tea leaves from the pot.
nya) Hold this little fish with the hook of your
    compassion.

In reply, the lama said:

ta) Unless they are an incarnations of goddess Tārā,
tha) ordinary women cannot practice the Dharma,
da) and right now, your thoughts are not concentrated.
na) Beautiful young woman, return to your home.

pa) Even if you shave your hair and become a nun,
pha) Your mother and father and the Rinang master may
    scold you
ba) for putting a cow load of butter onto an ox.[106]
ma) Do not call out, traveler. Better if you returned home.

Nangsa replied:

tsa) Here in Sera Yalung, which resembles Tsari Mountain,
tsha) if I were unable to meditate under harsh temperature
    conditions,
dza) then coming to this hermitage out of urgency
wa) would be no better than a vixen disappearing into her hole.

zha) If even with the gait of the lame it is possible to walk the
    entire land,
za) then even without food, I can certainly practice the sacred
    Dharma.
'a) If the lama will not take care of me,
ya) then out of desperation I will stab myself.

She took out a knife from it sheath and prepared to stab herself. The disciple Tsultrim Rinchen, who was standing next to her, snatched the knife from her hand and begged her not to do it. He called out to the lama: "If you do not open the hatch and grant her an audience, she is going to stab herself!"

The lama, still from behind the shuttered window, said:

ra) For fear of a white she-goat mixing with the sheep,
la) and to separate the molasses from the wax,
sha) these forceful questions were asked, but with affection.
sa) I did not say you could not stay on this land.

ha) Such faith and devotion to the Dharma!
ha) In wonderment the lama opens his hatch!
a) Aché Nangsa, do not feel sad. The Mahayana teachings on
the two stages,
a) the meaning of the mystical syllable *a*, I will give to you.

The lama opened the hatch and brought Nangsa in for an audience. Nangsa offered what head ornaments she had to the lama, prostrated to him, and sought his blessings. The Lama knew that not only was the death-returner Nangsa a noble ḍākinī, a blessed disciple, and a worthy recipient of the tantra teachings, but that in later life her activities would bring vast benefit to living beings. Therefore he bestowed upon her a profound body, speech, and mind mandala initiation through the Sindhūra mandala of the meditational deity Vajrayoginī. He gave her explanations of the tantra, the relevant oral-tradition instructions, and encouraged her to meditate in solitude in a little hut consisting of only a meditation room.

Within three months, wonderful experiences and realizations were born in her mind. She reported these to her lama, who gave her oral-tradition instructions on enhancement practices and warding off hindrances. In this way lama and disciple lived in great delight.

THE RINANG ARMY ATTACKS THE MONASTERY

Around this time Nangsa's parents, together with her son, Lhau Darpo, went to the friend's house in search of their daughter. Nangsa was not there, and they asked the friend where their daughter had gone, but she could not say. They thought that maybe she had returned to the Nyangtö Rinang estate. Therefore Nangsa's parents and her son left Jang Phekhu and traveled to Nyangtö Rinang, only to learn that she was not there either. They told governor Drachen and his son what had happened. The masters divided their men up into search parties and sent them out to find out where Nangsa had gone.

Soon they heard that mistress Nangsa was staying at Kyipo Sera Yarlung Monastery and was practicing the Dharma under the guidance of the excellent lama Śākya Gyaltsen. They raised an army from their people, made up of men aged eighteen to sixty, and prepared to destroy Sera Yarlung Monastery, kill lama Śākya Gyaltsen, and seize Nangsa. With governor Drachen and Drakpa Samdrup as generals, the Nyangtö Rinang army rode out and arrived at the foot of the monastery. The men and women practitioners there cried out, "Because of this destructive demoness we will all be ruined!" They moved statues, books, and other sacred representations of the lama, as well as their own possessions, to a secure part of the mountain. But while they were doing so, the Nyangtö Rinang army surrounded the retreat huts. With screams, roars, and battle cries like thunder they brandished their bows, swords, lances, and other weapons. The smoke from their fire-arrows and the dust churned up by the horses' hooves blotted out the sun and was a terrifying spectacle. Some monks and nuns died in the turmoil. Some were wounded by the weapons. The rest were scattered to the four directions like a pile of beans beaten with a stick.

Tsultrim Rinchen knew he would not be able to bear it if Lama Śākya Gyaltsen died too, and so he went to him and they prepared to flee. However, the lama's body displayed signs of age and his feet could not move fast over the ground. His disciple carried the lama on his back and they made to escape, but the monastery had been surrounded on all sides and there was no escape. There was nothing they could do, and they were left behind. The lama was seized and bound by the soldiers and taken to governor Drachen and his son.

The death-returner Nangsa rose from her meditation upon space-like emptiness into the illusion-like postmeditation state. Not being able to bear what was happening, she undid her meditation belt and tied it around her shoulder. She put on her white robe and came quickly from her hut. Grasping the reins of governor Drachen's horse with her right hand, and the reins of Drakpa Samdrup's horse with her left hand, she sang this song:

> Listen to me, governor and son.
> Listen to the maiden Nangsa.
>
> Rain, snow, and blizzards, do not bring harm
> to the young snow lion traveling to the high snows.
> Skillful archer, do not bring harm
> to the white eagle that flies high in the skies.
>
> Hunter and your dogs, do not bring harm
> to the brown deer seeking the grass of the upper plains.
> Sharp hook, do not bring harm
> to the little golden-eyed fish darting in the lake.

Prey-hunting hawk, do not bring harm
to the little nightingale finding her sweet voice.
Wild planet Rāhu do not bring harm
to the sun on his journey around the four continents.

Drakpa Samdrup, do not bring harm
to the maiden Nangsa practicing the sacred Dharma.
Army gathered here, do not bring harm
to these monk and nun practitioners.

The governor and his son looked at mistress Nangsa, shorn of her worldly silk clothes and jewelry and now dressed in the garments of a yogini made of a simple cloth and meditation belt. Then they looked at Lama Śākya Gyaltsen bound and trussed and brought before them. They became very angry and did not reply to Nangsa's song but stared angrily at the lama, pointing at him in a threatening manner and singing in unison:

Listen to us, Lama Śākya Gyaltsen.
Lend your ears this way, men and women monastics.

You old bearded dog, you have exceeded all bounds
by consorting with our young snow lion. It is not right.
What do you mean by plucking the hair
from the mane of this mountain-dwelling snow lion?

You red cockerel, you have exceeded all bounds
by consorting with our celestial mountain bird. It is not right.
What do you mean by snatching away the feathers
of this high-plain celestial bird?

You Chokrong donkey, you have exceeded all bounds
by consorting with our white, wild ass filly. It is not right.
What do you mean by tearing off the mane and tail
of the wild ass filly from the northern plains?

You old black bull, you have exceeded all bounds
by consorting with our young female yak. It is not right.

What do you mean by cutting off the shaggy hair
of this rocky-mountain young female yak?

You tomcat, you have exceeded all bounds
by consorting with our tigress. It is not right.
What do you mean by snatching away the stripes
of this young forest-dwelling tigress?

You Śākya Gyaltsen, you have exceeded all bounds
by consorting with our mistress Nangsa. It is not right.
What do you mean by taking away
all the clothes and jewelry of Nangsa?

Above in the deep blue sky there are many stars,
but which of them is a match for the great light of the sun
      and moon?
When the time comes for the host of stars to disappear,
you may have regrets, but it is too late.

Down here on earth, in Ütsang, there are many lords,
but who is a match for the Nyangtö Rinang father and son?
When the monastery is destroyed and the lama is seized,
you may have regrets, but it is too late.

Governor Drachen loaded his bow, and Drakpa Samdrup raised his
sword above the lama's head and prepared to strike. At that moment the lama
revealed his magic powers. He moved the eastern mountain to the west, and
the western mountain to the east. All those practitioners who were wounded
were suddenly healed, and those who had died came back to life. The lama
rose into the sky, out of reach of the swords, arrows, and lances. Sitting in the
vajra position, he said the following:

You of human form but of animal mentality,
listen to this lama, you wicked father and son.

The sun and moon that shine in the sky above
meet their match when eclipsed by Rāhu.

The father and son masters that dwell on earth
meet their match when Nangsa is taken from them.

If you ask for the reason why she was taken,
I will explain. Listen carefully.

The lotus flower blooming in the garden,
if it is not to adorn the vase to beautify the altar,
there is no reason for it to bloom.
It will just sadly grow old in the swampy soil.

A young Gyiling stallion, skilled in galloping,
if it is not to be raced on the flat, open plains,
there is no reason to feed it grain.
I will just sadly grow old in the corral.

The straight and true arrow with its red eagle feathers,
if it is never to be used upon the set target,
there is no reason to draw it in the bow.
It will just sadly grow old in the quiver.

If Manoharā, the gandharva maiden,
were not to be the bride of Dharma King Sudhana,
there would be no reason to seize her with the amoghapāśa
    jewel.
She would have sadly grown old in the hands of the low-caste
    hunter.

If it were the case that the noble ḍākinī Nangsa
had not been encouraged to practice the Dharma,
there would have been no point in her gaining a precious
    human form.
She would have sadly grown old in the hands of her wicked
    master.

Thinking in this way, I led her into the Dharma.
Knowing the arrow, you draw the bow.

Possessing beauty, you adorn yourself with clothes and jewelry.
Being rich, you hand out loans.
Knowing the doctor, you buy the medicine pouch.
Knowing the accomplishments, you show the signs.

If you possess magical powers, it is true that you keep
    them secret,
thinking it is not right to reveal them at inappropriate times.
However, today, in order to bring to the Dharma
these enemies of the teachings, who possess all ten
    qualifying conditions,
I have revealed these miraculous powers.

Nangsa, to generate faith and belief in these evil ones,
it is only proper that you too reveal signs of your
    accomplishments.

With these words, the Dharma-practicing death-returner Nangsa spread
her white robe-like wings and flew instantly into the air, where she soared
like an eagle and swooped like a hawk, while singing this song:

Master Drakpa Samdrup, and your father,
soldiers from the people of Nyangtö Rinang,
lords and people gathered here today,
listen to this maiden, Nangsa.

You had hoped that I, a white snow lion from the high snows,
would become your house-trained dog.
You may chain up a lion, but how could it possibly stay?
Here in the high snow-mountains, I show off my
    turquoise mane.

You hoped that I, this young female yak from the rocky heights,
would become your domesticated cow.
You may thread the nose of a wild yak, but how could it
    possibly stay?
Here in the high rocky ravines, I show off my horns.

You had hoped that I, this white, wild ass filly from the
    grassy plains
would become your donkey, doomed to be a beast of burden.
You may saddle a wild ass, but how could it possibly stay?
Here in the remote northern plains, I show off my skills.

You had hoped that I, this snow partridge from the high plains,
would become a pet bird in your home.
How can a snow partridge become a crowing rooster?
Here in the mountain plains I show off my song.

You had hoped that I, a rainbow of five colors,
would become a beautiful ornament.
How can a hand grasp a rainbow?
Here I show off this illusory play
of appearance and emptiness.

You had hoped that I, a fresh young cloud in the skies,
would become a warm, soft garment.
How can anyone wear a cloud as clothing?
Here I show off my summer rain with my friends,
the thunder and lightning.

You had hoped that I, a monkey of the forests,
would become a servant and helper.
You may put a monkey to human work,
but how will it ever succeed?
Here in the tree-tops I show off my lithe skills.

You had hoped that I, the death-returner Nangsa,
would become your life-long companion.
Even though I wear the turquoise crown, how could I stay?
Here in the high skies
I show off my signs of accomplishment.

As an indication of having circumambulated Tsari Mountain,
it is customary to bring a bunch of bamboo.
After the yak has gone, it leaves behind the furrows in the fields.

If I want to soar like an eagle, I soar like this.
If I want to swoop like a hawk, I swoop like this.
Humans who are able to fly through the skies
include the venerable Milarepa in the past
and I, Nangsa, in the present.
From now on those who can fly in Tibet will be very few.

You Nyangtö governors and you soldiers,
so that you do not accumulate limitless evil karma,
have remorse and declare your wicked deeds
with faith and humility to my lama Śākya Gyaltsen.

FATHER AND HUSBAND REPENT THEIR DEEDS

The Nyangtö governor Drachen, his son, and their army, as well as all the
male and female practitioners there, were astonished and overwhelmed with
faith at the sight of the magical display of Lama Śākya Gyaltsen and the signs
of accomplishment shown by Nangsa. They offered their swords, arrows,
and lances, and all other weapons and arms as a token, and falling to the
ground in prostration, they sang this earnest song of regret and confession:

Excellent lama, Śākya Gyaltsen, and noble ḍākinī Nangsa,
listen to this prayer of regret and confession
from the wicked Rinang masters and their army.

Lama, you are in reality the meditation deity Cakrasaṃvara,
and Nangsa, you are truly the deity Vajra Varahī,
but by the mistaken perception of ignorance,
we saw you as deceiving charlatans, devoid of Dharma.

Whatever boundless bad karma we have thus accumulated
by attacking the monastery and killing monastics,
and in particular, whatever we have done that goes against
the body, speech, and mind of the lama and his consort,
we confess with great remorse, beg forgiveness,
and ask that you hold us with your compassion.

Our sins are greater than the wealth of the rich.
Our virtues are fewer than the possessions of a beggar.

We have spent our whole lives in meaningless activity.
Lama, please save us from falling to the lower realms.

Having confessed the wicked deeds we have done,
we promise on our lives never to do them again.
So we ask that you bestow upon us a sacred Dharma nectar,
beneficial to our minds and easy to practice.

The lama and Nangsa were delighted that they were able to accomplish the welfare of others by bringing the wicked masters and their people to the Dharma. They replied:

For those who were previously on the wrong path,
to make efforts to walk the path of virtue
is like the sun coming to shine on the land of darkness.
It is excellent. It is truly wonderful.

Though you may commit the five heinous sins and the ten
    nonvirtues,
if you undertake the confession and vows of the four powers,
you will definitely be purified of them all.
From now on, if you wish to pursue virtue and leave behind
    nonvirtue,
listen well to the following teaching that is easy to practice.

Like the earth is the lama, source of all qualities.
Like the rare udumbara flower is this human life of opportunity.
Like a wish-granting jewel is its value.
Like a flash of lightning is this transient life.
Like a candle in the wind is the uncertainty of when we will die.
Like stars in the night sky are the myriad causes of death.
Like stars in the daytime are the few causes of life.
Like the rising and setting of the sun and moon is the cycle
    of life and death.
Like a hair pulled from butter is the consciousness at death.
Like stones and earth is the body without a mind.
Like the honey of a bee is accumulated wealth.
Like the crowds at market are the friends we have gathered.

Like forgetting the bridge over the river are friends and
    relatives.[107]
Like your own shadow are the good and bad deeds we do.
Like the Lord of Death's prisons are the eighteen realms of hell.
Like the city of beggars is the realm of the hungry ghosts.
Like a dream of the stupid is the consciousness of an animal.
Like angry snakes are the titan antigods.
Like a borrowed ornament is the body of the long-lived god.
Like the city of the gandharvas[108] is the human form.
Like something bought for yourself are the six realms.
Like pure self-sufficiency is liberation on the path.
Like a modest young girl is the Śrāvaka and Pratyeka
    practitioner.
Like a mighty warrior is the bodhisattva.
Like a cause is the Sutra and Perfection of Wisdom Vehicle.
Like a result is the Mantra Vajra Vehicle.

If you wish to gain enlightenment in one life,
first devote yourself properly in thought and deed
to a spiritual teacher, the very root of the path.

Think how this human birth of leisure and opportunity
is very difficult it is to achieve, and now you have found it,
how great is its significance and potential.
Think how this life is transient, ending in death,
and how our time of death is uncertain, and so on,
and develop the virtuous and discard the nonvirtuous
by following the law of cause and effect.

After that, contemplate the faults of samsara,
in general terms and specifically,
and with no attachment to it whatsoever,
think on the benefits of liberation and adorn yourself
with the excellent path of the three trainings.

Leave behind the Lower Vehicle path of the śrāvaka and
    pratyeka,
and follow the activities of the great bodhisattvas

by practicing the six perfections
and the four ways of gathering disciples,
thereby shouldering the courageous responsibility
of liberating all beings.

In order to lead living beings to liberation,
you yourself must gain the state of omniscience.
If such an achievement is not reached quickly,
think about how much more sentient beings will suffer.

Therefore if you are to achieve a state of enlightenment
    quickly,
even the tantras of Action, Performance, and Yoga,
which are superior to the Sutra and Perfection of Wisdom
    paths,
will not lead to enlightenment in one short life.

Therefore enter the profound and secret Highest Yoga Tantra,
ripen your mind with the four initiations, guard the vows
    and pledges,
master the yogas of the generation and completion stages,
and achieve the unification of the four bodies.

Of those gathered there, the soldiers, whose karmic veils were greater, promised to free themselves of one or two nonvirtuous ways and to develop a few virtues as best they could. The governor and his son, whose karmic veils were lighter, actually saw Lama Śākya Gyaltsen as the deity Cakra-saṃvara Heruka and Nangsa as Vajra Varahī.

As Nangsa's son, Lhau Darpo, had reached the age of fifteen, his father's estate and possession were turned over to him, while governor Drachen, his son, and others in the presence of the lama and his consort pledged their lives to the Dharma. The lama and his consort pledged that as long as these vows were not broken, they would not die. Consequently, governor Drachen and others of an advanced age, as well as some who had been traveling far, went straight into solitary retreat to practice.

Not only did Nangsa fly into sky at that time, but the impression of her cloak and her footprints also appeared on her cave wall like impressions made in butter. These can still be seen today.

Drakpa Samdrup and others, who were younger, returned home for a while, where they oversaw the appointment of Lhau Darpo as head of the estate and region. Then Drakpa Samdrup, Nyimo, and Nangsa's parents returned to Sera Yalung hermitage, where they stayed and practiced the Dharma under the guidance of the lama and his consort.

Lhau Darpo ruled by fostering a strict code whereby all activities in the region were undertaken according to the ten virtues and the sixteen codes of decent human conduct. Accordingly, he supplied the lama and his consort, governor Drachen and his son, Nangsa's parents, and all practitioners there with the necessary provisions for their Dharma practice, and they were able to enjoy the never-ending states of temporary and ultimate happiness of the great feasts of bliss that come from possessing the wealth of Dharma.

Thus ends the story of Nangsa Öbum.

Itinerant Aché Lhamo dancer wearing a goddess headdress, Central Tibet, 1937.

Itinerant Aché Lhamo dancer in hunter mask, Central Tibet, 1937.

The Gyalkhar troupe performing *The Chinese and Nepalese Princesses* at the Tsedrung Lingka, a garden park used by monastic civil servants, Tibet, August 1921. The tent for the occasion had been lent by Sera Monastery.

A monastic setting for a recital of *Ḍākinī Drowa Sangmo* in 1930s Tibet.

Padma Prabhājvālya characters, the non-Buddhist king and a demon, during a Norbulingka Shotön Festival performance in Lhasa, 1937.

Shotön Festival at Samyé Monastery, Central Tibet, 1995.

Villagers performing "gar" dances, Namthong Festival,
Khorchak Monastery, Tibet, 2010.

Members of the Tibetan Music, Dance, and Drama Society
perform a folk opera, circa 1970.

Contemporary Aché Lhamo of the Sherdukpen people
of Arunachal Pradesh, northeast India.

An Aché Lhamo drum dance, performed on the birthday of the Fourteenth Dalai Lama, July 6, 1985, at Gangchen Kyishong, Dharamsala, India. Lobsang Samten, the present artistic director of TIPA, dances in the center.

A drummer from Gangjong Dögar, a Darjeeling-based opera troupe.

The swirling action of a dancer from Gangjong Dögar, a Darjeeling-based opera troupe.

An opera troupe from Khumbu, Nepal, performing a traditional dance at the opening ceremony of the 2015 Shotön Festival in Dharamsala.

A contemporary opera, *Life of the Lord Buddha*, written and performed by TIPA at the 2015 Shotön Festival in Dharamsala.

Goddess dancers at the Norling Shotön Festival, Lhasa, 1990s.

A dancing scene from *Ḍākinī Drowa Sangmo* featuring the yogi and the demoness, at the Norling Shotön Festival in Lhasa, 1993.

Tashi Shöl, the oldest opera troupe in Tibet, performing at a contemporary Shotön Festival in Lhasa.

A dance festival featuring the epic tale of *Ling Gesar*, Shechen Monastery, eastern Tibet, 2016. The festival is held every summer and lasts for three days.

Actors in exotic costumes at the finale of the festival.

5. The Story of Ḍākinī Drowa Sangmo

Nama Śrī Kālacakrayā

THIS IS THE STORY of the ḍākinī Drowa Sangmo. At dawn when the sun is about to rise, three pledges are to be taken: to make requests with devotion, to listen with full attention, and not to distort what you have heard.

If the Dharma is not explained, then it will not be known and other Dharmas will go to waste. Also, if the listeners listen, they too will benefit greatly. Therefore those of great merit should teach freely, like water falling from the cliffs. As this is taught in accordance with the words of the Buddha, you should listen as you have pledged to do.

> Born from the green syllable *tāṃ*,
> within the hosts of ḍākinīs and Drowa Sangmo,
> the light from your *tāṃ* liberates living beings.
> I bow before the great mother Tārā.

BIRTH AND CHILDHOOD

In this era of degeneration when lives are short, we recall a time in the past, one thousand and five hundred years after the Buddha had passed into nirvana, when the lifespan of humans was a hundred years. When the doctrines of the non-Buddhists had subsided, an exalted-wisdom ḍākinī sat within a canopy of white cloud and rainbows, gazing upon living beings. It was a wonderful time when the precious teachings of the Buddha had spread throughout the world. However, there was a land called Mandal Gang where the sounds of Dharma were not heard, where a monastic community had not been established, where meditation on the great deity Avalokiteśvara was unheard of, and where the six-syllable mantra was not recited. There, the inhabitants engaged in fights and disputes and were under the sway of anger, hatred, and pride, thereby having to suffer the unspeakable sufferings of the lower realms.

Seeing this, the ḍākinī fell into a state of great anguish. After she had regained her composure, she made a prayer, as firm as a stupa, for all living beings never to be reborn into samsara and the lower realms. By the power of this prayer a brahman woman called Sundarī had an auspicious dream one night. Upon awaking, she went to her husband, Mati, and said:

Listen to me, husband Mati.
My body feels lighter than before,
and I am of a joyous mind.

In particular, last night I had a special dream.
The sun and the moon shone from my heart,
and I saw all four continents and the minor lands.
From the peak of the great mountain in their midst
came the sound of the sacred Dharma.

Many gods and goddesses came to me
and bathed my body with water.
This auspicious dream has brought change to my mind.
A child is coming, I believe.

The husband Mati was overjoyed. He said to his wife:

Listen to me, wife Sundarī.
The wishes of this old couple will be fulfilled.
Now make your own food, wear your own clothes.
Avoid all bad food and enter into strict retreat.
In all likelihood the child to be born
will be a manifestation of a bodhisattva.

As her husband instructed, Sundarī entered into a secluded retreat. Three months into the retreat she suddenly heard a child's voice in her womb, saying: "*Oṃ maṇi padme hūṃ hrīḥ.* May all living beings be freed from the sufferings of evil rebirths and be possessed of happiness."

Ḍākinī Drowa Sangmo performed in Mussoorie, India, March 1963, to mark the anniversary of the first Central School for Tibetans in exile.

Dancers from TIPA taking part in a *Ḍākinī Drowa Sangmo* production for Tibetan children in Dharamsala.

Sundarī was very afraid and ran to her husband, saying:

> Listen to me, husband Maṭi.
> The child that dwells inside my womb,
> after three months has spoken, saying,
> "*Oṃ maṇi padme hūṃ hrīḥ.*
> May all living beings be freed from the sufferings
> of evil rebirths and be possessed of happiness."

> When we were young and our teeth were white, no child came to us.
> Now we are old and our hair is white, a child is coming.
> How can such a child be a bodhisattva incarnation?
> It could be the devilish work of the Pehar king.

> The Indian king follows the law and wields great power.
> I have been visited by a bad omen,
> and it is as if the laws of India, Tibet, and Mongolia
> are to be visited upon me.

> I feel I should jump off the peak of a high cliff,
> drown myself in the depths of a great a river,
> or die by stabbing myself with a knife!
> Tell this anguished woman what she should do.

Her husband replied:

> Listen to me, wife Sundarī.
> Concerning these syllables, *oṃ maṇi padme hūṃ hrīḥ.*
> In the northern snowy land of Tibet
> dwells the great meditation deity Avalokiteśvara.
> He is white in color and holds the hide of a deer.
> From his lips come these six Dharma syllables.

> If the child is a boy, it will be an incarnation of Avalokiteśvara.
> If a girl, a manifestation of an exalted-wisdom ḍākinī.
> Now make your own food, wear your own clothes.
> Avoid bad food and return to your strict retreat.
> Our long-cherished dream is about to be realized.

TIPA performing *Ḍākinī Drowa Sangmo* to celebrate the 83rd birthday of the Fourteenth Dalai Lama, Dharamsala, 2018.

A thangka painting illustrating the story of *Ḍākinī Drowa Sangmo,* carried by the itinerant *Buchen* traditional storytellers of Spiti, northern India.

SUNDARĪ DID AS HER HUSBAND ASKED

Nine months passed, and at the beginning of the tenth month of the male earth monkey year, on the auspicious tenth day, a daughter was born painlessly from the ribcage under her right arm. As soon as she was born, the child uttered the syllables *oṃ maṇi padme hūṃ hrīḥ*. In the skies above, a great canopy of white cloud and rainbow light appeared. The exalted-wisdom ḍākinīs of the five families assembled and in unison named the child Ḍākinī Drowa Sangmo. They made offerings and uttered this prediction: "Brahman daughter, Drowa Sangmo, for you, your life will be of the early, intermediate, and late periods. The early period will coincide with the reign of King Kālendra and his queen Hachang in the land of Mandal Gang. During the intermediate period you will bear a son and daughter. During the later period you will face many obstacles from a demoness. Therefore, without the slightest attachment to your kind parents, your husband whose face you gaze at, and your children born from your own flesh, you must fly into the skies at that time. Where should you fly? Meditate upon the exalted-wisdom ḍākinīs of the five families in their ḍākinī land in the west and fly there." With this prophecy they vanished like a rainbow.

From the outset Drowa Sangmo spoke only Dharma to her parents. To her father, she said:

Listen to me, brahman Maṭi, my father.
This life is transient, like lightning in the sky.
We do not stay here long. Death comes quickly.

Meditate on the deity Avalokiteśvara upon your head.
Recite the six syllables, the very essence of the Dharma.
Again and again examine your mind.
Never be without love and compassion.
Immerse your mind into a realm of compassion.

To her mother, she said:

Listen to me, brahman Sundarī, my mother.
This life is transient, like a flower in the garden.
We do not stay here long. We must die.
In the daytime, meditate on the nondivisibility of appearance
and emptiness.

At night, meditate on the nonapprehension of clarity
    and emptiness.
Meditate on love and compassion for all beings.

Wealth has no meaning. Practice generosity.
Meditate continually on the deity Avalokiteśvara.
Recite the six syllables, the very essence of Dharma.

Her mother and father were delighted. Her mother nourished the child with her milk. They dressed her in the finest Benares silk, and she spent her time in strict retreat in a small room.

Meeting the King

Sometime later, Kālendra, the king of Mandal Gang, hoisted great flags on high, blew great conch trumpets throughout the skies, and beat great drums from the mountain tops. All his subjects, both lords and ordinary people, gathered before him. The king addressed them, saying, "Hear me, lords and ordinary folk. When the sun rises three days from now, I will go hunting on the great mountain, at the place where the sun hits the side of the mountain. If you have guns, bows, and arrows in your homes, bring them. Otherwise, they will be provided from the royal storehouse. Lords and ordinary folk prepare to leave."

Among the people gathered there was a minister called Trinadhara. He got down on one knee, placed his hands together, and addressed the king:

Hear me, precious king.
Lend your ears to me, Kālendra.
Do not go hunting. Abandon this idea.
If you insist on going hunting,
the neighboring kings will revile you.
If the townsfolk say you are going on a hunt,
everyone will be disgusted and look down on you.
By all means, great king, abandon the hunt.

The king was very displeased with this and replied:

Listen to me, you people gathered here.
We kings say things only once.

The word of a king is like a boulder falling from a mountain.
Once fallen it is impossible for it to return.
The word of a king is like a great flowing river.
It is not possible for its waters to return and flow upward.

It is true what you have said,
but look at our neighboring kings.
They all possess substantial wealth,
whereas I have no wealth of any kind.

I have only Chaktra, my she-dog.
If I do not commit the sinful act of hunting,
there is no point in keeping this dog.
Therefore be quiet and get ready for the hunt.

The king paid no heed to the minister, and three days later, amid the gleam and flashing of bows and arrows, the king took his dog Chaktra and set off on the hunt with his ministers, servants, lords, and subjects.

They scoured the hills of India but could find no deer. On the border of Mön and India they saw many kaśa deer, and the king sent his dog after them. That day they killed thirty-seven deer. That evening in the dark the dog disappeared like a rainbow. The king was worried and said:

Ministers and subjects, hear what I say.
Today, as the sun finished his journey,
my dog Chaktra has vanished.
It is a jewel I cannot do without.
If we do not find the dog,
I will go home and die.
Tonight we will stay on the mountain.
Tomorrow, as the sun rises, we will search for the dog.

That night the king and his people put their weapons under their pillows and went to sleep. The next morning at sunrise the king addressed the minister Trinadhara:

Hear me, minister Trinadhara.
Get up, minister. Get up and go search.

Listen for any human voice or dog sounds.
Look for any dog footprints.

The minister respectfully got up. He searched everywhere but heard no sounds of humans or dogs and found no dog footprints. Therefore once more Trinadhara climbed to the peak of the mountain and looked keenly in each direction. In the east, in the midst of a forest, on a piece of level ground he saw a little well-built house with billowing smoke coming from its chimney. "That is where the dog probably is," thought the minister. He returned to the king and reported:

Hear me, precious king.
Hear me, powerful and mighty lord of men.
There were no sounds of human or dog,
and no trace of dog footprints whatsoever.

Therefore, in search of the dog I climbed the mountain,
and from its summit I looked far and wide.
In the midst of a thick forest in the east,
on a patch of level ground was a well-built home.
Blue smoke was curling into the skies.
The dog is most likely there.

The king was very pleased, and replied to Trinadhara: "Minister, you who are the very petals of my heart. You are wise in the five sciences, and so as you say, the dog could well be there."

They all looked toward this forest, known as Indian Sandalwood Heruka Forest, and set off toward it. When they arrived at the brahman's home, they saw dog prints outside the house, and Trinadhara knocked on the door. After a moment, an old brahman with hair as white as a conch shell, eyes as blue as turquoise, without a tooth in his mouth, and totally dependent on a stick to stand up, appeared through the window and said: "Who is there?"

The king produced a very special and auspicious offering scarf from the amulet around his neck and tied it to the tip of a stick, saying:

Listen to me, old brahman.
I am come from the land of Mandal Gang,
and I am called Kālendra.

Yesterday morning, for no good reason,
I set out for the low act of hunting,
and we killed thirty-seven kaśa deer.

In the evening my dog disappeared and could not
    be found.
This morning we went on a search for Chaktra.
There are clear dog prints around the brahman's house.
Please give my dog back to me at once.

The old brahman became very afraid and nervous. He had heard that the
king strictly enforced the law, was very powerful, of a temper hotter than
fire and more turbulent than the waves on the ocean, as intolerant as a
strand from the tail of a horse, as stubborn as a well-rounded mustard seed,
and as petty as finely ground flour. He had never set eyes upon him before
and now here he was at the door. Trembling, he opened the door and
went outside. Going down on his knees and putting his hands together, he
addressed the king:

Precious king! Hear me, Kālendra.
We are an old and decrepit brahman couple.
Since our youth we have never had any power,
and now we are old and close to death.

We have not seen the king's dog at all.
Even if we had, it would have been of no use to us.
If you do not believe me, great king,
please come into my home and look.

As the door was open, the king and his ministers went inside. Although
they searched for the dog everywhere in the room, they did not find it. There
were three doors in the house. In front of the middle one was the old brah-
man woman, her hair as white as a conch shell, eyes as blue as turquoise,
without a tooth in her mouth, totally dependent on a stick to stand, recit-
ing *oṃ maṇi padme hūṃ*. The king thought to himself: "The long life and
wealth of this old brahman couple is due to the blessings of the meditation
deity Avalokiteśvara." Even the king was filled with faith. However, he had
not found his dog and he was still in a state of worry. One door was shut. The

king stared at it, tapped it with his boot, and said: "Old brahman woman, open this door. My dog is inside."

The woman prostrated to the king, went down on her knees, put her hands together, and said:

> Precious king! Hear me, Kālendra.
> We are an old and decrepit brahman couple.
> Since our youth we have never had any power.
> Now we are old and close to death,
> we would not know if we had seen it or not,
> nor could we recognize the king's dog.
> Even if we had seen it, it would have been of no use to us.
>
> If you do not believe me, great king,
> and you ask me to open the door, I will do so.
> Great king, do not punish us.

The door was open and the king went inside. There on a turquoise seat was a girl unlike any human girl and more like a daughter of the gods. She was dressed in the finest Benares silk. Her complexion was fair. She exuded a beautiful aroma and her mind was pure. To look on her was to gaze upon beauty. To hear her was to hear the sweetest sounds. To smell her was to enjoy a beautiful aroma. To see her was to be captivated. She enjoyed all the signs of an exalted-wisdom ḍākinī. The king thought to himself: "My dog Chaktra disappearing and dog prints appearing outside the brahman's door are like prophecies from the five families of ḍākinīs." He took a large shiny turquoise from his amulet and tied it upon Drowa Sangmo's head. Turning to the old brahman couple, he said:

> Old brahman couple, this daughter of yours,
> I must take her as a bride for me, the king.
> From this day onward, do not say that she has flown
>   into the skies.
> Do not say that she has sunk deep into the earth.
> Do not say that she has been be seized by the powerful.
>
> Do not say that she has been seduced by the wealthy.
> Do not say that she has been stolen by the greedy.

Do not say that she has been begged for by the lowly.
Do not allow your daughter to go anywhere.

If you say that your daughter has been taken by another,
old brahman couple, you will pay with your lives.
Three days from now I will present the suckling money
    to you.
If she has no servants, I will provide whatever entourage
    she needs.
I will come to escort your daughter as my bride.
Brahman couple, make arrangements to send her off.

With these words the king and his ministers returned home.

Marriage to King Kālendra

Drowa Sangmo thought to herself: "I would rather die than be married to this wicked king." In this sad state she reflected on the blessings granted by the five families of ḍākinīs and their accompanying instruction to fly into the skies. "They told me that there would be many obstacles from a demoness. That time must be now." She hurried from her room. With her clothes she made a pair of wings, thinking that she had to fly away.

Her mother and father were aware of this. Her father, Maṭi, came to her, took hold of the right flap of her clothes, and said:

Daughter of we two old brahmans,
listen to me for a moment.
It is extraordinary for a young woman to fly.
Even if you jump far, footprints are left behind.
Even if you do leave, aged parents will be left behind.

The king of Mandal Gang abides by the law and is powerful.
Now that the king has issued his orders,
if our daughter, Drowa Sangmo, does not stay here,
these two old brahmans will surely lose their lives.

Think well, daughter Drowa Sangmo.
In order to repay the kindness of your parents,
do not, by any means, fly off into the sky.

Her father shed many tears as he beseeched her to stay. Then her mother took hold of the left flap of her clothes and said:

Daughter of your mother, listen to me.
It is unusual for a young woman to fly.
Daughter, at the moment when you were born,
the five families of ḍākinīs prophesized for you
an early, intermediate, and late period of your life.

They did not talk of flying away during the early period.
It was in the later period that you should fly away.
Now is the early period for you.
Now is not the time for flying away.
Think well, daughter Drowa Sangmo.
In order to repay the kindness of your parents,
do not leave. Stay here.

With many tears her mother beseeched her to stay.

Drowa Sangmo felt great compassion for her mother and father, and with many tears she promised to stay, as they had asked. Her parents were overjoyed.

Three days later the king and his entourage set out from Mandal Gang with horses and elephants laden with wish-granting jewels, jewel garlands, gold, silver, silks, and all manner of wealth and gems. In addition to servants and attendants, these were given to the parents as suckling money. They were overjoyed, and in return they dressed Drowa Sangmo in the finest clothes and adorned her with precious jewels. She was placed upon a black stallion with white fetlocks. The king rode a "golden" stallion and minister Trinadhara rode a "mind-captivating" stallion.

The king and his queen were met with a sumptuous welcoming party of singing and dancing that stretched for eight leagues. Having entered Mandal Gang, they went inside the palace. The king sat on a golden throne and his queen sat on a turquoise throne. The light from the golden throne fell on the turquoise throne, and the light from both thrones lit up the palace. The palace became transparent, inside and outside disappeared, and everywhere was filled with light. It became a transparent celestial mansion.

A great wedding celebration was held. The king and his queen lived in great joy and pleasure amid an abundance of everything they desired.

Sometime later Drowa Sangmo thought to herself: "As a reason for coming here, I should try to bring this bad king and his ministers to the sacred Dharma." She addressed the king:

Precious king, Kālendra, hear what I say.
Though you enjoy this world, it is just a dream.
Though you have great wealth, it is cause for wicked deeds.

All that comes together is transitory.
Now is the time to consider something meaningful for
    the future.
The time of death is uncertain. We do not stay here for long.

Meditate that the deity Avalokiteśvara is upon your head.
Recite the six-syllable mantra, the essence of the Dharma.
Give up the ten nonvirtuous acts. Take up the ten virtues.
Never be without love and compassion.
Be at ease within emptiness and compassion.

The king was delighted on hearing this advice. He said to Drowa Sangmo:

What you say is true.
I will happily follow it.

From the top of the palace, the king hoisted great flags into the blue skies, great conch trumpets sounded throughout the skies, and great drums were beaten from the palace rooftop. All the subjects of Mandal Gang gathered before their king. The king addressed them:

Listen to me, you people gathered here.
My dog Chaktra disappearing without trace,
and the dog footprints around the brahmans' house
were probably manifestations of Drowa Sangmo.

Drowa Sangpo likes the sacred Dharma.
I too like the sacred Dharma.
People, immerse yourselves in the sacred Dharma.
Give up the ten nonvirtuous deeds and follow the ten virtues.

Meditate that the deity Avalokiteśvara is upon your head.
Recite the six-syllable mantra, the very essence of the Dharma.
Never be without love and compassion,
and abide within emptiness and compassion.

If with bad minds you perform evil deeds,
I will punish you with your lives.
Understand this, people of Mandal Gang.

From then on, the king, his ministers, and his subjects all lived within the ethics of the ten virtuous deeds. The wealth and enjoyments of the land multiplied and spread as never before.

As for Drowa Sangmo, in order to protect herself from the eight fears, she lived in strict retreat in the small room known as the Tārā temple. During that time, she gave birth to a daughter. The girl was called Princess Samantabhadrā. When she was three years old, Drowa Sangmo gave birth to a son. He was called Prince Samanta Sādhu. After the birth of their son, mother and father lived in the joy of complete fulfillment of their desires. During that time, the king sang a song in acrostic verse[109] to Drowa Sangmo:

ka) My beautiful blue lotus flower,
kha) listen to this handsome king.
ga) Wherever I look, I see no essence
nga) I am enamored of the sacred Dharma.
ca) Here in this temple free from all clamor,
cha) in the garb of a great meditator, I will dwell in retreat.
ja) In your small room replete with tea, ale, and all you need,
nya) your healthy little fish of son and daughter
ta) with their mother, Drowa Sangmo, White Tārā,
tha) have come to be united.
da) Now dwell in retreat upon the sacred Dharma.
na) Take this to mind, beautiful young woman.

Drowa Sangmo replied:

pa) King, who are like a rock, listen to me.
pha) I have no power to be with my mother and father.
ba) Like a cow, I am tethered by the neck.

ma) I am like a mother ewe removed from my flock of sheep.
tsa) With its eight great fears, such as the hot and cold akin
    to Tsari Mountain,
tsha) I have arrived in this land of the dreadful demoness.
dza) If the king were to abandon his companions and follow
    the Dharma,
wa) he would be led along the path followed by the fox king.
zha) The lowly may bow to you as wise, but it is all meaningless.
za) Though I have food and drink, wealth and enjoyments,
'a) not having followed the Dharma in this busy existence
ya) has led this reckless one to the prison of Yama.
ra) The white she-goat surrounded by a flock of sheep
la) has crossed the valley and the mountain passes,
and arrived at the butcher's yard of the demoness.
sha) Though she has a loving husband,
sa) here mother and children are sad.
ha) If the demoness Hachang queen is to eat mother
    and children,
a) alas, I will not stay here but go to the ḍākinī land.

With these words mother and children retired to a strict retreat in her
Tārā Temple rooms.

DEMONESS HACHANG AND THE FLIGHT TO THE ḌĀKINĪ LANDS
Previously King Kālendra had taken a queen called Hachang. She had a ser-
vant known as Durālabhā, who one day climbed to the palace roof. From
there she spied Drowa Sangmo and her two children. She thought to herself:
"Alas, this means ruin for my Queen Hachang! The king has taken another
queen, and she has a son who will inherit the kingdom and a daughter who
will produce more kin." She hurried to the queen and said:

Great queen, hear what I have to say.
King Kālendra has taken a junior queen.
She has a son to inherit the kingdom
and a daughter to produce more kin.
Great queen, you need not have the concern
of having neither son nor daughter.

The demoness queen thought to herself:

> News from afar is half true, half untrue.
> This is news from close by,
> and these words of Durālabhā are certainly true.

She went to the palace roof and looked at the Tārā Temple rooms. There she saw Drowa Sangmo and her two children. She became angry and declared:

> What Durālabhā said was true.
> To me with the great name of Hachang,
> you, Drowa Sangmo, have become an enemy.
> If by the end of today I have not devoured mother and children,
> then may the Dharma protectors of this land take me!

She snarled three times and returned to her rooms.

In her room, Drowa Sangmo thought to herself: "When the five families of ḍākinīs told me to fly away with wings made from my clothes and gave me their blessings and their prophecies, they said obstructions from a demoness would arise. This is surely her."

She sent her beloved son to his father. Her daughter, who was like a blossoming lotus flower, she took upon her lap, and shedding many tears, said: "Daughter of your mother, listen to me. When I was born, I received a prophecy from the five families of ḍākinīs. They told me that obstructions from a demoness would arise. This woman is that demoness. If we stay here, mother, son, and daughter will be eaten by her. Daughter, take these ornaments and clothes of your mother. The fortunes of you and your brother rest now with the king. I cannot stay here but will fly to the land of the ḍākinīs."

In tears, she untied her ornaments and placed them to one side. She took off her clothes and flew off into the skies naked with her wings of cloth, until she came to the ḍākinī land in the west.

Princess Samantabhadrā decided to follow her mother and flew into the skies after her, but she was able to fly only a cubit or so. Crying, she returned to her mother's room. Like the time when the birds fly the nest, everything was empty. The clothes and ornaments were a just a pretty pile on the ground. She wept and felt as if she was going to die.

At that time Prince Samanta Sādhu arrived. Seeing that his mother was not there and that his sister was in great distress, he asked her:

> Princess Samantabhadrā, sister, listen to me.
> Where has our mother Drowa Sangmo gone?
> Sister, why do you distress yourself so?

Princess Samantabhadrā replied:

> Prince, hear what I have to say.
> While we three were enjoying a happy time
> here in the rooms of the Tārā Temple,
> Durālabhā, the servant of the queen called Hachang,
> saw we three here and reported this to her queen.
> This demoness then came to see if what her servant said
>   was true.
> When she saw we three, she became very angry and said:
> "To me with the great name of Hachang,
> you, Drowa Sangmo, have become an enemy.
> If by the end of today I have not devoured mother and
>   children,
> then may the Dharma protectors of this land take me!"

> This demoness snarled and bared her fangs three times.
> After she had shown her fearsome fangs,
> our mother was unable to bear the words of this demoness
> and gave me these instructions:
> "I have been told obstructions from a demoness would arise.
> The demoness Hachang is this very obstruction.
> Your mother cannot stay here but will fly to the land
>   of the ḍākinīs.
> Take these ornaments and clothes of your mother.
> The fortunes of you and your brother now rest with
>   the king."

> Our mother then suddenly took to the skies and was gone.
> What are we two to do?

She sat there weeping. The prince replied:

> Sister, if this is true, we cannot stay here.
> If the demoness comes, she will eat both of us.
> Let us not stay here but go to our father.

Brother and sister went to their father. Prince Samanta Sādhu prostrated to his father, went down on one knee, and with tears in his eyes said the following:

> Hear me, father. Hear me, King Kālendra.
> While we three were enjoying a happy time
> here in the rooms of the Tārā Temple,
> Durālabhā, the servant of the queen called Hachang,
> saw we three here and reported this to the queen.
> This demoness came to see if what she said was true.
> When she saw we three she became very angry and said:
>
> "To me with the great name of Hachang,
> you, Drowa Sangmo, have become an enemy.
> If by the end of today I have not devoured mother and children,
> then may the Dharma protectors of this land take me!"
>
> This demoness snarled and bared her fangs three times.
> After she had shown her fearsome fangs,
> our mother was unable to bear the words of this demoness
> and gave me these instructions:
> "When your mother was born,
> she received a prophecy from the five families of ḍākinī,
> saying that suddenly obstructions from a demoness would arise.
> The demoness Hachang is this very obstruction.
> If we stay here, no doubt she will eat us.
> Daughter, take these clothes and ornaments of mine.
> Your mother will not stay here but will fly to the land
>   of the ḍākinīs.
> The fortunes of yourself and your brother now rest with
>   the king."

Then our supreme mother, Drowa Sangmo,
took to the skies and was gone.
Father and great king, look with your great compassion
on the fortunes of this son and daughter.

The children prostrated to their father and wept. When their father and king had listened to how his wife Drowa Sangmo was no longer there, he fell into unconsciousness. His attendants brought sandalwood water and sprinkled it on his face. Recovering consciousness, and with tears streaming down his face, he said: "News from afar is half true and half untrue. This is news from close by."

He realized he had to go and see for himself. He opened the door to the Tārā Temple and went inside. Like a nest from which the eggs had been taken, it was empty. Only ornaments, clothes, and turquoise were left piled on the floor. The king almost fainted. With tears in his eyes he went to the roof of the Tārā Temple, tied a cloth around his head, and sat there in despair.

His son came to him, sat on his lap, and snuggled close to him, face to face and heart to heart. In order to soothe his father's mind, he said:

Hear me, father. Hear me, King Kālendra.
My mother disappearing into the skies
does not have to be the end of her life.
It is possible she has left for the sake of others.

There is no need to fall into despair.
Put aside your sadness, make many prayers,
and mother will probably soon return.

His father thought to himself: "This son of mine is truly a manifestation of Avalokiteśvara. He is only three years old and able to give reassurance like this."

He took the prince by his right hand and Princess Samantabhadrā by his left. From the roof of the Tārā Temple he looked to the skies and sang this prayer:

I make this request to the infallible Three Jewels.
Grant your blessings that this prayer be fulfilled.
Drowa Sangmo, hear these words.

Do not suddenly disappear into the blue skies
but return to be here in your little room.

Drowa Sangmo, who held as true
the arrogance of an angry demoness,
do not disappear into the blue skies
but return to be here in your little room.

You who dare leave behind the little prince,
you who dare abandon princess Samanta,
you who have no feelings for Kālendra,
you who have turned your back on your clothes and jewelry,
look upon all living beings with compassion,
and fulfill this request of Kālendra.

However, there was no sight of their mother and no answer was forth-
coming. Father, son, and daughter retired to a corner of the palace, tied
cloths around their heads, and sank into despair.

At that time the demoness Hachang addressed the ministers:

Listen, all you ministers assembled here.
In the past, King Kālendra made the solemn vow
to take no other queen but me.

Going back on his own words,
he secretly took Drowa Sangmo as his junior queen.
For six years he did not look upon me, his queen.
How could I bear such a thing!

Look at the kings of India. Though they all take many queens,
if they are treated equally, there will be no remorse.
When the king pursues this inequality,
how am I supposed to bear it?
Although she has flown off to the skies,
and she has leapt far, her footprints remain behind.

Give madness water to King Kālendra.
If he shows signs of having gone mad,

punish him for six years!
As a reward I will grant you all you could desire,
and you can share the rewards as you want among the people.
Ministers, understand these words I speak.

All the ministers were under the power of the demoness. They agreed
unanimously to trick the king. They brought some madness water to the
king and said:

Hear us, precious king.
Kālendra, listen to what we say.
Although Drowa Sangmo has taken to the skies,
you still have a queen that pleases you.
You have a prince to carry on your royal name
and a princess to increase your descendants.
There is no harm to your body from the four elements,
and we, your ministers, continue to prosper.

There is no reason, therefore, to feel sad.
Cast off your sadness. Take some wine.
Drink and sing songs of the Dharma!

They served the madness water to the king repeatedly. Not realizing what
it was, the king thought that the ministers had brought wine to lift his spir-
its. He was pleased and drank a large quantity. Immediately he went mad.
Sometimes he stood up, then suddenly sat down. Sometimes he would gaze
to the sky and murmur, "My Drowa Sangmo." Sometimes he burst into song,
sometimes he got up and danced. These and many other signs of madness he
showed.

The demoness said: "Ministers, throw Kālendra into a dark dungeon. For
his guard, appoint Durālabhā. For food, give him rope."

The Children Are Given to the Two Butchers

Sometime later the demoness thought to herself: "If a spark is not snuffed
out, it can become a grass fire the size of Mount Meru. If water is not stopped
early, it can flood the entire valley. If these two children are not killed while
they are young, I will not be able to defeat them when they are grown. There-

fore I need a way to kill them. If I ask the ministers to kill these two children, they will not do it. To get rid of these two I must fake an illness."

On a large bed she spread a foul-smelling hide and smeared rotten brains over her body. In her right cheek she stuffed ochre and in her left cheek indigo to produce a reddish-blue saliva, which she spat out intermittently, and lay there as if she were dying. Her ministers came and gathered around her bed. They said:

> Precious queen!
> What kind of illness affects your body?
> What kind of fever are you suffering from?
> If we made prayers to reverse it, would it help?
> If you were treated with medicine, would it help?
> What can we do to help?

The demoness replied:

> Making prayers to reverse the illness will be of no use.
> What good will medical treatment do?
> It seems there is nothing you can do to help me.

The ministers pleaded:

> Listen to us, supreme queen.
> What method is there to help you
> with the pain of this illness?
>
> The two children are still very young.
> Except for you, great queen, we ministers
> have no one to look to, no one to turn to.

Again the demoness replied:

> Assembled ministers, listen to me.
> Whatever treatment you might apply
> to this illness affecting my body, it will be of no help.
> There is a treatment, but you cannot possibly apply it.

Medicine that will cure me I will tell you.
The two children and I have opposing birth elements.
Therefore if you take out the hearts of the two children
and give them to me, this illness will be cured.

The ministers replied: "Then the prince and princess have to be killed?"
The demoness said: "As it is not right for you to kill them, there are two
butcher brothers, subjects in this land of Mandal Gang, who do not under-
stand the difference between good and evil. Call them!"
The ministers called the butcher brothers as ordered by the queen. They
went to the demoness's bedside and asked for instructions. She replied:

Younger and elder butchers, do as I say.
Go quickly now to the two children.
Elder butcher, with your butcher's knife
cut out the heart of Princess Samantabhadrā.
Younger butcher, with your butcher's knife
cut out the heart of Prince Samanta Sādhu.

It will be effective medicine for my illness,
so bring them before they lose their warmth.
As reward I will give you whatever you desire.
You can share it all among the people.
Go now and kill the two children!

As the demoness had instructed, the two butchers hurriedly left. They
burst open the door of the temple room and stared inside. Brother and sis-
ter, as is the nature of children, were sitting there playing. When he saw the
butchers, Samanta Sādhu became frightened:

Listen to us, younger and elder butcher.
In the past when you two came to our room,
we were so happy.
Now you two have come to our room,
we are so afraid.

Why have you two butchers come here?
The ministers are under the sway of the demoness.

The queen has spoken with the ministers.
Have you come to kill this brother and sister?

We two children have done nothing wrong.
Is it not heartless to deliberately kill?
Is it not a sin of great karmic consequences?
Think about this, you two butcher brothers.

The children began to cry. The younger butcher was moved. He too shed
many tears and said:

Brother, elder butcher, listen to me.
Being elder in years does not make you elder,
but being elder in wisdom you are my elder.

When the mother and father of these children were here,
we would not even dare to step on their shadows.
How can we possibly harm them now?
Spare the lives of these two children!

We could take the hearts of two puppies
from a brood under the main gate of the palace
and present them to the demoness
as the hearts of these two children.

The elder butcher was delighted, and in agreement they said to the children:

Listen well, prince and princess.
The demoness has spoken with the ministers.
We two butchers, whose ways are set in evil,
were sent here to kill the prince and princess.
When your mother, Drowa Sangmo, was living here,
we would not even dare to step upon your shadows.
Now, how can we bring ourselves to harm you children?

Beautiful children, do not play outside in the garden.
If the demoness Hachang were to see you,
there is no doubt that she will have you killed.

Even your parents could not teach you more.
Keep this in your mind, children.
We will tell the ministers in secret of this plan.

Thus they spared the children's lives. Under the main gates of the palace they killed two dogs and took their hearts to the bedside of the demoness, saying: "Supreme queen, hear us. We two butchers have without mercy killed the prince and princess. The large heart is that of Princess Samanta-bhadrā. The smaller is the heart of Prince Samanta Sādhu. These we offer to the queen to please her. We do not ask for even half the reward, but only that you regard us as before."

The demoness mixed the hearts with salt and ate them. She removed the indigo and ochre from her cheeks and put on her jewelry. She gave the butchers lavish amounts of food and money and pretended to have recovered from her faked illness.

The Children Are Given to Two Fishermen

Each day the demoness would walk on the roof of the palace. One day, the children, as is the nature of children, went out into the garden to play. At the same time the demon was on the palace roof, and she saw them. "Alas! The two butcher brothers who do not understand the difference between good and evil have not killed the children, and now they play in the garden. The ministers have great affection for the children, and so I must again feign an illness."

She lay on a large bed, placed her fine clothes and jewelry in a heap by the bed, and cried out in unbearable pain. Again the ministers came to her bedside.

Supreme queen, hear what we say.
What kind of illness affects your body?
What kind of fever are you suffering from?
What treatment would be of benefit?

The demoness angrily refused to answer and turned her head to the left and lay there. The ministers moved to the left side of the bed and pleaded:

Hear us, supreme queen!
What kind of treatment would help your illness?

The mother Drowa Sangmo flew into the skies and is gone.
The father, you have thrown into prison, and is gone.
The two children have been killed and are gone.
Except for you, great queen, we ministers
have no one to look to, no one to turn to.

Helped by Durālabhā, the queen sat up and said:

Listen to me, assembled ministers.
It seems you have no treatment that would help me.
The so-called hearts of the two children
were the hearts of two puppies from the same brood.

I am in such great pain. It is in all probability
some obstruction of impurity.
If I am to be sick, then let me be sick.
If I am to die, then let me die.

With these words she collapsed on the bed. The ministers said:

Supreme queen, please hear what we say.
A prince who will carry on the royal lineage is essential.
A princess who increases the royal descendants is essential.
However, if you say that by all means they must be killed,
then there is no other way.

The demoness said: "As it is not right for you to kill them, there are two fishermen brothers, subjects in this land of Mandal Gang, who do not understand the difference between good and evil. Call them now!"

The ministers called the fisherman brothers, as ordered by the queen. They went to the demoness's bedside and asked for instructions. She replied: "Elder fisherman, throw Princess Samantabhadrā into the ocean. Younger fisherman, throw Prince Samanta Sādhu into the ocean. I will give you whatever reward you desire. Kill them quickly!"

The two fishermen hurried to carry out the orders of the demoness. They pushed open the door of the children's room and burst in. The children were sitting there in great sadness at the loss of their mother and father. The prince said to the fishermen:

Listen to us, you two fishermen.
Before, when you came to our room, we were so happy.
Now you two have come to our room, we are so afraid.

Why have you two come here?
Speak to us honestly. Do no keep anything back.
The ministers are all under the sway of the demoness.
The queen has spoken with the ministers.
Have you come to kill this brother and sister?

How could you kill us, who have done nothing wrong?
Is it not heartless to deliberately kill?
Is it not a sin of great karmic consequences?
Think about this, you two fisherman brothers.

With these words they shed many tears. The two fishermen replied:

Listen well, prince and princess.
The demoness has spoken with the ministers.
We two fishermen, whose ways are set in evil,
were sent here to kill you children.
"Do not tarry. Throw them into the ocean," she said.

The prince said to his sister:

Listen, sister. Listen, Princess Samantabhadrā.
With the merit we have gathered,
we have gained a precious human form,
and of those precious human forms,
we have been born the children of a king.
Because of the merit we have not gathered,
we have fallen into the hands of these fishermen.

Look at that tree below. On its top sits a powerful hawk.
A helpless baby bird sits underneath it.
They are both birds, but are like master and servant.
How wonderful to be baby birds under the hawk's nest
instead of the children of the king that we are now.

All this is the result of not having our mother here.
Thinking of our mother, she is like a mother in a dream.
If she were here now, how wonderful that would be.
Supreme mother, Drowa Sangmo,
look upon your children with compassion.

They sat there crying. The two fisherman said: "You are articulate and speak well. Because of this the two butchers spared your life. You have done the same here, but we will not set you free."

They tied the children's hands tightly behind their backs. Like the capture of a deadly enemy, they were led away and dragged down the steps with the two fishermen holding both ends of the ropes. When they reached the city gates the people gathered, and in great grief they wept and wailed:

The royal children, like the sun and the moon,
are as beautiful as blossomed flowers,
but will never be taken as offerings for the temple
and will be carried away by the frost. So sad!

The people were in great distress, but because the demoness was so powerful, there nothing they could do. They just stood there, their mouths opened wide in disbelief.

The two fishermen led the children away. As they approached the sea, the prince said to his sister:

Sister and princess, listen to me.
Look over there at the great ocean.
The male duck is the father and goes in front.
The female duck is the mother and is behind.
The brood of ducklings are between mother and father.
They are all birds, but there is recognition between mother
    and child.

Instead of being the children of a king, as we are now,
how wonderful it would be to be the ducklings of those parents.
How wonderful if mother and children stayed together.
All this is the result of not having our mother.

Supreme mother, Drowa Sangmo,
look upon your children with compassion.

As they sat there in tears, the fishermen took away their beautiful jewelry and stripped them of their soft clothes. The younger fisherman picked up the prince and prepared to cast him into the sea. In response, the prince addressed the fisherman:

Younger fisherman, hear these words.
I am about to be cast into the sea.
On the point of death, allow me to make a small prayer.
If I can make a prayer, my wishes will be fulfilled.

The fisherman replied: "If it is a good prayer, you may make it. If it is a bad prayer, then no."

The prince replied: "Younger fisherman, how could I make a bad prayer? It is because I did not make prayers in my past life that I encounter these obstacles now. I will offer a song to the five families of ḍākinīs." He sang the following request:

Ḍākinīs of the vajra family in east,
send your silken rope from the east.
Ḍākinīs of the jewel family in south,
send your silken rope from the south.

Ḍākinīs of the lotus family in west,
send your silken rope from the west.
Ḍākinīs of the activity family in north,
send your silken rope from the north.

Ḍākinīs of the Vairocana family in center,
send your silken rope from the center.
Take these children to the ḍākinī lands.

This has been the result of not having our mother.
Supreme mother, Drowa Sangmo,
look upon your children with compassion.

The children wept. The younger fisherman also wept. He said to his brother:

> Brother and elder fisherman, listen to me.
> When the mother and father of these children
>   were present,
> we would not even dare to step on their shadows.
>
> Now when their mother and father are not here,
> how can we possibly harm them?
> Spare the lives of these two children!
>
> There is grain elsewhere other than here.
> We could take our wives and go to another land.
> However we look at it, we cannot kill these children.

The elder brother also started to cry. He gave back the beautiful jewelry and the soft clothes and said:

> Listen well, prince and princess.
> The demoness has spoken with the ministers.
> We two butchers, whose ways are set in evil,
> were sent here to kill the prince and princess.
>
> We two brothers cannot bring ourselves to kill you.
> Therefore, do not go now to the land of Mandal Gang.
> Else the demoness and the assembly of ministers
> will without doubt have you killed.
>
> Do not stay here. Go to the east of India.
> In eastern India, they are sympathetic to the Dharma.
> The people there are Dharma-minded and take joy
>   in giving.
> However you look at it, the east of India is best.
> There in the east, ask for food and drink.
> Even your parents could not give you better advice.

THE CHILDREN HEAD TO EASTERN INDIA

The fishermen escorted the brother and sister to a far-off place, and in sadness they returned home. They each took a bride and left for another country.

Like sheep being allowed to wander freely, the two children had no idea where they were, and for a while just stood there with their mouths hanging open. As they were the children of a king, they had not traveled anywhere. Realizing that they had no guide and no knowledge of the land, the princess said:

> Listen to me, brother and prince.
> If we stay here we will find neither food nor clothing.
> As the fishermen instructed us,
> we should leave for eastern India,
> where we should beg for our food and drink.

The prince replied: "If that is the best, then be our guide." Therefore five-year-old Princess Samantabhadrā became the guide and the three-year-old prince followed. They turned to the east and traveled on.

They came to a thick forest. The prince became tired and thirsty. He missed his mother and father. He said to the princess:

> Sister, Princess Samantabhadrā, listen to me.
> Today the road we have traveled is long.
> How long will we travel tomorrow?
> Today food and drink has been scarce.
> What will it be like tomorrow?

> Today I have been thinking of my mother.
> Will we meet her tomorrow?
> This is the result of not having our mother here.

The young boy stood there in tears. Although she had no knowledge of the land, Princess Samantabhadrā made out as if she did, and in order to soothe her brother's mind, she said:

> Listen to me, brother and prince.
> Today the journey has been long,
> but tomorrow the journey will be shorter.
> Today food and drink has been scarce,

but tomorrow food and drink will be plentiful.
There will be fruit whose taste will be delicious.

Today we have certainly missed our mother,
but tomorrow in all probability we will meet her.
We two do not possess the fortune of having
    our mother.
Supreme mother, Drowa Sangmo,
look upon your children with compassion.

With a heavy heart and many tears she took her dear brother and turned
toward the forest in the east. They entered the thick forest, which no eyes
had seen before. Inside, birds of many kinds let out their various cries. There
were many monkeys, apes, and other wild animals. Poisonous snakes roamed
the forest floor. The prince was hungry, thirsty, and tired. He wept and said
to his sister:

Listen, sister and Princess Samantabhadrā.
I have no one to turn to except you.
You cannot give me food and drink, and so all is hopeless.
Where is the place with the clear blue water?
You said you would give me water to save my life.

His sister too began to cry and said to him:

Listen to me, brother and prince.
Let us not stay here but go to that mountain.
We will look for water on the mountain.
Then we will continue on to eastern India.

Brother and sister traveled to the mountain. There was no water there,
and so the princess said: "I will and search for water. You stay here until I
return."

At that time their mother manifested as a crow and landed on the moun-
tain. The princess thought that there would be water where the crow had
landed and went to that place. There was no water except for a small muddy
pool. She began to take some, and realized she had no container. She put her
hands on her hips and saw the dyed red belt that her mother had given her.

Into its folds she put some of the watery mud and returned to the mountain slope. The summit was high and she could not travel quickly. Meanwhile, for the prince, the expected water from his sister did not arrive. But an unexpected poisonous snake did arrive. The prince was struck by its poisonous breath and, like a falling tree, he collapsed and died.

The princess arrived at the summit. Reaching for the lifeless body of her brother, she felt it to see if any warmth was present. Not feeling any, she took his body on her lap and held him close. In grief, she wailed:

> Alas! Alas! The pain of Samantabhadrā!
> Woe! Woe! What can I do!
> The pain now of this Samantabhadrā!
> When my mother, Drowa Sangmo, vanished into the skies,
> we meritless children were left behind.
>
> When my father, the king, was cast into prison,
> we children, lacking the power of adulthood, were left behind.
> Now that my traveling companion, the prince, has died,
> this grieving girl untouched by death is left behind.
>
> Alas! Alas! This suffering of mine!
> Rather than such pain and grief that I experience today,
> if only those two evil fishermen brothers
> had cast us into the sea yesterday.

She held on to the prince's body and was close to dying herself.

At that time their mother, Drowa Sangmo, was teaching ḍākinīs in the western ḍākinī land. Suddenly tears came to her eyes. The ḍākinīs asked why she was crying. Drowa Sangmo replied:

> Hear me, ḍākinīs assembled here.
> In keeping with the prophecy made by the five families
>   of ḍākinīs,
> In the remote region of Mön, against my will,
> I was made queen to a king.
>
> By the force of prayer, two children were born to me,
> and at once I was plagued by the hindrances of Mara.

Durālabhā, the servant of the demoness queen,
saw me with the two children and told the demoness.

She came herself to see if it were true.
When she saw us, she became angry and said:
"To me with the name of Hachang,
you, Drowa Sangmo, have become an enemy.
If by the end of today I have not devoured mother and children,
then may the Dharma protectors of this land take me!"

This demoness snarled and bared her fangs three times.
After she had bared her fearsome fangs,
it came to my mind that in keeping with the ḍākinī prophecy,
for the sake of living beings, I should fly off and come here.

I have left behind my two children, more precious than
    my heart,
and the demoness has brought them so much hindrance.
They were taken from the palace and wandered like dogs.

My son was struck by the breath of a poisonous snake,
and immediately fell down dead.
My daughter is stricken with grief and on the point of death.
I will leave this Dharma teaching. Today I must stop here.
Today I must reveal a special manifestation.

She transformed into a white medicinal snake and began to suck the poison from the soles of the prince's feet. The boy regained consciousness. He looked at his sister, and the two were reunited. The medicinal snake climbed to the top of a tree and flew off into the sky. The prince said to his sister:

Sister and princess, listen to me.
The water I was expecting did not arrive,
but a poisonous snake I was not expecting did.
Struck by its breath, it seems I died for a while.

A great obstruction had befallen me,
and there was nothing I could do to avoid it.

The medicinal snake that sucked the poison from my feet
flew into the skies from the top of a tree.

Did you see the snake, sister?
It was probably a manifestation of our mother.
Mother and children would have been together,
but the medicinal snake disappeared into the blue sky.

There was nothing we could do.
Nothing we do has been successful.
Give me some water, sister.

His sister replied:

Listen to me, brother and prince.
There was no water nearby,
but on the summit there was watery mud.
I had no container, so I put it in the folds of my belt.

The summit is high and I did not arrive back in time.
When I did, you had already died.
I took you on my lap and mourned.

Suddenly a medicinal snake sucked poison from
      your feet.
I was so overjoyed at the prince's recovery that
I was not able to catch the snake.
Now the water has been lost and is no more.

"Show me where you put the water," said the prince. The princess gave
him the belt. He sucked on the wet belt and was like a flower refreshed by
the rain. He said:

Listen to me, sister and princess.
If we stay here, the black poisonous snake will return.
If that happens, he will eat both of us.
Let us not stay here but set off for the east.
In the east of India we will seek food and drink.

They set off and came to a forest. Their mother manifested as a monkey and went to the forest. She looked upon the children with love and affection and spoke kind words to the children. The prince thought that the monkey must be the lord of the forest. "Tell us where we can find some fruit," he said.

"Children, sit in the cool shade of this wish-granting tree," said the monkey. She climbed to the top of a mango tree and threw down many tasty mangos. The fruit satisfied the children and they sat there eating. There were many types of fruit around, and as they sat there enjoying the delicious juices, it was a moment of happiness for them.

THE CHILDREN ARE RECAPTURED
AND GIVEN TO TWO OUTCASTE MEN

Around this time, the demoness queen was walking on the roof of the palace. From there she spied the children in a forest toward the east of India. From the top of the palace she ran up flags, sounded great conches, and beat great drums to summon the ministers. When they had assembled, the demoness spoke:

> Listen to me, assembled ministers.
> How could those two wicked fishermen brothers
> have thrown the brother and sister into the sea?
> I have seen them sitting and eating fruit
> in a thick forest toward the east of India.
> The evil fishermen have left with their families
>   for another land.

> Now, you ministers, gather weapons about you
> and bring the children back here.
> Strip them of their clothes, tie their hands,
> and lead them here holding both ends of the ropes.

As instructed, the ministers gathered weapons and set off to the ocean to search for the children's footprints. Following these, they came to the forest. Prince Samanta Sādhu spotted the ministers and said to his sister:

> Sister and princess, hear what I say.
> The ministers of the demoness are here.
> They have probably come to kill us.

Then, from afar, the ministers sang this deceiving song:

> Hear us, brother and sister.
> Your father has been released from the dark
>   dungeon.
> Drowa Sangmo has returned from the land
>   of the ḍākinīs.
> Your parents ask, "Where have our children gone?
> It seems as if this demoness has been a threat
> to the lives of our precious son and daughter.
> With fortune we will meet again in this life.
> If not, we will take our own lives."

"Your mother and father are very worried about you," continued the ministers. "Unable to bear this, we have come to fetch son and daughter."

The prince thought that this was genuine and was overjoyed. Then the ministers rushed and seized the children, stripped them of their clothes, and led them back to Mandal Gang. Their hands were tied behind their backs and the ministers held both ends of the ropes. The prince said to his sister:

> Listen to me, sister and princess.
> We are not here for long. Soon we must die.
> Visualize the Three Jewels upon your head.
> Make prayers to Avalokiteśvara.
>
> All this is the result of not having our
>   mother near.
> Supreme mother, Drowa Sangmo,
> look upon your children with compassion.

With these words they wept. Princess Samantabhadrā spoke to the ministers:

> Assembled ministers, look at me.
> When we dwelt with our mother and father
> all you ministers showed great love to us children.
> Now that we no longer have our parents,
> how can you possibly do this to us?

Ministers, even if you kill me, let my brother go.
When I think of our mother, she is like a mother in a dream.
If she were here now, how wonderful that would be.

She wept as she spoke, but the ministers did not listen and led them to the main gate of the Mandal Gang palace. There the people of the city had gathered and in union they wailed:

The royal children, like the sun and the moon,
are as beautiful as blossomed flowers,
but will never be taken as offerings for the temple
and will be carried away by the frost. So sad!

Although they grieved heavily, the demoness had such power that there was nothing they could do.
The children were brought before the demoness, who said to them:

Listen to me, you two orphans.
You are like the flags that do not touch the top
    of the pole,
and like the long yak hair that hangs below the yak.

You two orphans, devoid of mother and father,
tonight, rest easy from the pains of hell.
Tomorrow, as soon as the sun begins to rise,
you will be taken to two low-caste brothers, addicted
    to evil,
and they will cast you from a peak of the East Mountain
    in India.

She continued: "The peak of that mountain in its whiteness is as white as the snow-white color of Avalokiteśvara. In its redness it is as red as the face of Guru Drakmar. In its height it reaches to the blue skies. In its depth its base reaches the outer ocean. There, birds and wild animals utter their frightening cries. It is a place where criminals are thrown off cliffs. Therefore we will throw you into the darkness."

That night the demoness put the children in a dungeon. The guard was Durālabhā. They were not given food or clothing. Holding each other closely and being close to death, they rested for a short time under the gaze of their mother, Drowa Sangmo.

The next morning at daybreak the two outcaste brothers came to the demoness and asked for instructions, to which she responded: "You two outcaste brothers, take the two children and throw them off a cliff on the east Indian mountains. Whatever reward you desire you will have, and you can share it among the people. Go quickly!"

As the demoness instructed, the two brothers tied the children's hands behind their backs, took hold of both ends of the ropes, and, beating them with the handles of their knives, took them to the mountain. As they were being led up the mountain, the prince saw two deer on a mountain meadow with their offspring. He said to his sister:

Sister and princess Samantabhadrā,
Look over there at that high mountain meadow.
The male deer is the father and goes in front.
The female deer is the mother and is behind.
The herd of deer are between mother and father.
Though they are animals, there is recognition between
    mother and child.

Instead of being the children of a king as we are now,
how wonderful to be the children of those deer.
All this is the result of not having our mother.
We two children miss our mother.

And in floods of tears, they were taken to the top of the mountain. The younger outcaste brother picked up the dear prince and prepared to throw him into the sea. The prince addressed him:

Younger outcaste brother, hear these words.
I am about to be cast off this mountain.
On the point of death, allow me to make a small prayer.
If I can make a prayer, my wishes will be fulfilled.

The brother replied: "Then make your prayer." The prince sang the following request:

I make this request to the Embodiment of Qualities,
    Samantabhadra.
I make this request to the Embodiment of Enjoyments,
    Avalokiteśvara.
I make this request to the Incarnation Embodiment,
    Padmasambhava.
In particular, you five ḍākinī families, please hear
    these words.
Bless me to fulfill the wishes of this prayer.

Vajra ḍākinī of the east,
radiant with brilliant white body,
with silken crown, densely woven,
your right hand sounding a ḍāmaru drum,
your left hand sounding a bell,
your two feet sounding in dance,
stretch out your silken rope from the east,
make the path of this prince lead to the Dharma.
Look with compassion on princess Samantabhadrā.

All this is the result of not having our mother.
Supreme mother, Drowa Sangmo,
look upon your children with compassion.

And with these words he wept. The elder outcaste brother became
very sad and tears flowed from his eyes. He turned to his younger brother
and said:

Younger brother, listen to me.
Previously the younger and elder butcher brothers
spared the lives of these two children.
Similarly, the two fishermen let them go free.

When the mother and father of these children were present,
we would not even dare to step on their children's shadows.
Now, how can we possibly think of killing them?
It would be better to spare their lives.

The younger brother replied: "Brother, listen to me. What I value in this world is my life. If you cannot do this task, I will do it."

The elder brother replied: "Your share lies with the prince. As for me, even if it means my life, I will spare the life of the princess." With these words he released her.

The princess went to the younger brother. She prostrated to him and said:

> Listen to me, younger brother and outcaste,
> do not kill the prince. Let him go.
> For the rest of our lives, these two children
> will lavish many gifts upon you.

She wept as she spoke these words, but he would not relent. Then the prince spoke to his sister:

> Listen to me, sister and princess.
> This is our last meeting in this life.
> Sister, you are alive. Light is brought to this
>   dark world.
> I do not have the good fortune to be spared.
> This is the last meeting of brother and sister
>   in this life.
> I pray we shall meet again in the realm
>   of None Higher.

With tears in his eyes, he continued: "Now I am ready to die. I have no regrets. Cast me off the cliff."

The younger untouchable picked up the child and threw him off the cliff of an eastern mountain. He fell through the open skies like a bird. Just then, from the land of ḍākinīs, his mother Drowa Sangmo, shedding many tears, took on various manifestations. First, she transformed into a pair of vultures. The male vulture caught the prince on her wing just before he was about to crash into the rocks below. The female vulture said: "It seems as if the princess is not here," and vanished.

Just then, by the power of karma, the prince fell into the ocean. His mother transformed into two fish. The male fish took the prince on his back and carried him to the water's edge, so that no harm came to his life. The female fish said: "It seems that the princess is not here," and vanished.

THE PRINCE BECOMES KING OF PADMINĪ

On the side of the ocean the prince trembled and did not know where to go. Crying, and realizing he was lost, he sat down. From the land of Padminī his mother transformed herself into a talking parrot, and with one beat of her wings she was by his side. She said:

> Beautiful young boy sitting here,
> from where have you come?
> Where will you stay this night?
> What are the names of your parents?
> Who are your siblings and companions?

The prince replied:

> Parrot, I wonder if you can help me.
> For one thing, I have a human form of leisure
>   and opportunity.
> For another, I was born the son of a king.
> And third, I have been affected by the obstructions of Mara.

> My mother, Drowa Sangmo, disappeared into the skies.
> My father, Kālendra, was thrown into prison by a demoness.
> My sister's name is Princess Samantabhadrā.
> My name is Prince Samanta Sādhu.

> The demoness sent two butchers to kill us,
> but they did not carry it out and set us free.
> Because we are young we went out to play in the garden.
> The demoness saw us and handed us to two fishermen.

> They took us to the shore of the great ocean.
> I made a prayer, and the fishermen felt sorrow.
> They released me and my sister.

> We traveled to a thick forest in east India.
> There in its middle we were captured by the demoness's
>   ministers.
> We were taken to two evil outcastes.

The younger outcaste threw me off a cliff of the eastern
   mountains.

From the skies a male vulture put me on his wing.
Not being dashed against the rocks, I fell into the ocean.
There I was put on the back of a fish.
Taken to dry land, I was not harmed.

I came originally from Mandal Gang.
Tonight I will stay here by the ocean.
I have no food to eat or clothes to wear.
I have no one to show me the way.
Parrot, will you be my companion?

"Follow me," said the bird. And with one flap of its wings, it flew off. The
prince followed.

The parrot turned and said to the prince: "In my land of Padminī the
people have great faith in Avalokiteśvara. They recite the six-syllable heart
mantra. Because of this the royal lineage is finished. Would it not be won-
derful if you came and were the king of Padminī?"

"Will I become king?" asked the prince. The parrot nodded its head once
in the four directions as if to make prostrations. The prince did the same.
Suddenly from the sky fell a saffron robe, a red belt, white leather boots, and
a square head cloth. The parrot placed the cloth on the prince's head, pre-
sented the robe to him, tied the belt around his waist, and gave him the white
leather boots to wear. "Am I to be the king of Padminī?" asked the prince.

"You are," replied the parrot.

The parrot flew off, quickly flapping its wings, until it came to a place
where a great brahman meditator lived. It addressed the brahman: "The
royal lineage in Padminī is at an end. A three-year-old manifestation of
Avalokiteśvara now sits in the shade of a sandalwood tree."

The brahman meditator was overjoyed. He took his stick and left for
Padminī. Having made three circumambulations of the town he addressed
the people: "Because we people of Padminī are devoted to the deity
Avalokiteśvara, it has been reported that a three-year-old manifestation now
sits in the cooling shade of a sandalwood tree. This was told to me by a talking
parrot. If we welcome him as our new king, power and prosperity will grow."

The people of Padminī gathered and said: "Except for you, there was no one who welcomed the royal lineage coming to an end. We should kill you!" And they became agitated.

Others said: "Don't do this. Listen to what the elders say. Look to how birds flap their wings.[110] This is the prophecy of a talking parrot."

Everybody went to see for themselves. When they saw the prince sitting under the sandalwood tree, they were all overjoyed. A golden-colored horse from Padminī was ornately saddled and the prince seated on it. With the accompaniment of parasols, victory standards, banners, music, and incense, and an extraordinary welcoming procession, the prince was invited to Padminī and crowned king. The land prospered as never before.

BROTHER AND SISTER MEET AGAIN

The princess thought to herself: "My dear brother and prince has been cast off a mountain cliff and is no more. I too must end my life."

She prepared to jump, but the elder outcaste who had spared her life prevented her from doing so and, putting her on his back, carried Princess Samantabhadrā down the mountain. He thought to himself: "Because of the evil karma I collected in my previous life, I have been born with the body of a wicked outcaste. In this life too, I have done many evil acts and brought all this hardship on these two children. If I die, there is no place for me to go other than the Vajra Hell. Therefore it is better that I die."

He placed the princess on the ground. Taking his foot-long curved knife, he prepared to stab himself and die. The princess thought to herself: "It is not right that for a girl like me who is no better than a fly, a man should kill himself." With her hand, which was smoother than silk, she caught hold of the outcaste's hand, which was rougher than a claw. She said to him: "I was like an insect about to fly into the flame and you saved my life. Now I am saving yours. If you kill yourself, you will have to repeat that action for five hundred lifetimes. Give up the thought of killing yourself."

The outcaste stood up quickly and, with tears streaming down his face, said:

Hear me, princess Samantabhadrā.
Do not stay here. Go to the land of Padminī.
Cross over the pass from here, and on the other side
you will find a large Padminī nomad camp.
Seek food and drink from them.

With great sadness the outcaste set off for his own country. The princess continued down the mountain side. Previously the two fisherman brothers had led her over many passes and through many valleys. The ministers of the demoness and the two outcastes had done likewise. Now her legs were in great pain. She felt unable to continue and sat down on the mountainside. At that moment a young goddess descended and sucked on her knees. This cured her legs.

The princess thought to herself: "I wonder if I can see the body of my dear brother where he was thrown from the cliff of this eastern mountain. If not, maybe I can find some of his hair or pieces of his bones." She went to the side of the ocean. There she did not find the body of her brother. Furthermore, there were many white, black, and multicolored bones of criminals who had been thrown off the cliff. She did not think that those of the prince were among them. So she gathered the shorter hair and the smaller bones and took them to the brahman meditator, who made them into votive images, one for each year of the prince's life. These were placed into a shrine, and the princess made many prostrations to and circumambulations of them.

Nearby was the Padminī nomad camp, and the princess approached them to beg for food and drink. "Give this beggar of bad karma some sustenance," she begged. One nomad woman gave her some food and drink. As she was doing so, a dog bit the princess's leg from behind, forcing her to remain in the nomad camp for three months. When it had healed sufficiently, the nomads gave her a blanket made from black, white, and multicolored patches, a stick to protect herself from dogs, and a bowl. "Girl, over the next pass is the palace of the king of Padminī," they said. "The people of Padminī delight in virtue. Girl, go there and beg for food and drink." They pointed out the way.

With tears streaming down her face, the princess arrived at the gates of the palace. Facing the palace, she cried out in a long but thin voice: "Mighty king, hear what I have to say. Please give this beggar of unworthy karma food, possessions, clothes, ornaments, and the like."

The prince was on the roof of the palace, and his sister's voice struck his ears like an arrow fired by a great warrior. "This is like my sister's voice," he thought. He turned to his minister Sucandra and said: "Minister, go to the gate. Ask that beggar girl which country she comes from and who her parents and brothers and sisters are."

The minister went to the gate and said:

Beggar girl, from where have you come?
In the meantime, where have you been?
And finally, where do you plan to go?

Who are your parents, your brothers,
your sisters, and your relatives?
Tell me the truth. Do not hide.
I must report to the mighty king.

The princess replied:

Hear me, great minister.
My country is the land of Mandal Gang.
The name of my father is Kālendra.
He was put in prison by a demoness.

My mother's name is Drowa Sangmo.
She flew into the skies and disappeared.
My brother's name is Samanta Sādhu.
He was thrown off the eastern mountain and killed.

My name is Princess Samantabhadrā.
I have no food for my mouth or clothes for my body.
Please hear me, great minister.
Please ask the king for some gifts.

She made this plea with tears down her face and with many prostrations. The minister returned to the palace and told the king the princess's words. The prince began to cry, saying, "I too come from Mandal Gang. That is my sister." He ran down the long stairs and jumped down the short ones, until he came to the main gate. Seeing that it was indeed his sister, they hugged each other until they fainted. Ministers sprinkled them with sandalwood water and they regained consciousness.

Princess Samantabhadrā was bathed in the bathing pool, dressed in silk, adorned with precious jewelry, and led into the palace. There Prince

Samanta Sādhu was seated on a golden throne and Princess Samantabhadrā was placed on a turquoise throne. From these two thrones they ruled the kingdom of Padminī in accordance with the Dharma. The prosperity of the country increased as it had never done before.

THE DEFEAT OF THE DEMONESS

Sometime later in Mandal Gang, the demoness hoisted great flags from the top of the palace, sounded great conches, and beat the great drums. The ministers and people of the kingdom assembled. They addressed her:

> Hear us, supreme queen.
> You have hoisted flags where previously there were none,
> beat the great drums that previously remained unbeaten,
> and blown the great conches that had never been blown.
>
> What actions have threatened the laws of the kingdom?
> Where is the enemy army that invades our country?
> We ministers and people are wealthy and prosperous.
> What is the problem?

The demoness replied:

> Listen to me, assembled ministers.
> The two outcaste brothers, steeped in evil,
> did not throw the prince and princess
> from the peaks of the east Indian mountains.
> Now they have become the rulers of Padminī.
>
> Affairs cannot possibly remain like this.
> If a spark is not snuffed out when it is small,
> it can become a grass fire the size of Mount Meru.
> If water is not stopped when it is a mere trickle
> it can swell and flood the entire valley.
>
> Three days from now, when the sun rises,
> a great army from Mandal Gang will march to Padminī.
> The general of that army will be me, the demoness.
> Ministers and people, go and make preparations.

With these words she returned to her rooms.

On the morning of the third day the hundred-thousand-strong army of Mandal Gang assembled quickly in front of the main gate of the palace. The demoness Hachang saddled a black demonic horse, donned her armor, took her iron bow and iron arrows, and mounted her black horse. On the horse she bared her fangs three times. The evil ministers were happy. The Dharma ministers despaired, but there was nothing they could do against such a powerful demoness.

The demoness led the army forth until they came to the head of the Padminī Valley. The people of Padminī became aware of their arrival. The king, his ministers, and all the people were weighed down with sadness. Minister Sucandra said:

> Hear us, great king.
> Do not give way to this sadness.
> Great king, there is no need for despair.
> I will go to face this black demonic army,
> and be the general with an army of thirty thousand.

The prince replied:

> Great king and father, please hear me.
> Great mother, splendor of virtue, think of me.
> Whether I live, whether I die, I will go to fight.
>
> From the royal armory fetch me
> the golden armor studded with rubies,
> the golden arrows with the turquoise feathers,
> the iron arrows with owl feathers,
> all tipped with copper arrowheads.
> If the omens are bad, I will have to use them.
> Bring these all to me.
>
> Supreme goddesses from above,
> grant me today a celestial golden horse that can fly.
> I will be the general of the thirty thousand soldiers.
> Be the warrior helper of this prince today.

Minister, you have no method to defeat the demoness.
The time has come to finish the hordes of demons,
as exemplified by this demoness Hachang.
If today I do not conquer this demon,
the whole world will be in danger from her.

The father said with great delight: "At such a young age, my son is very brave."[111]

The prince put on his armor, took the iron bow and the iron arrows, mounted his celestial golden horse that could fly, and as general of his thirty-thousand-strong army, led his soldiers to the head of the Padminī Valley. Merely seeing the prince, the demoness Hachang flew into a temper. From her horse she notched an arrow and said:

Hear me, you wicked prince.
A man at the end of his life arrives at the door of the cannibal.
An insect at the end of its life arrives at the door of the ant.
By the middle of the day, if I am not able
to drink the warm blood of your heart,
then take me, protector spirits of this land.

With her upper fangs half-bared and her lower fangs upright, she suddenly attacked. The prince was a little afraid, and sang this prayer:

Buddhas and bodhisattvas dwelling in the ten directions,
and in particular the five classes of ḍākinī, please hear me.
Today be my protectors, come to my aid.
May I today conquer the demoness!

The upper part of this bow I entrust to the gods on high.
The lower part I entrust to the nāgas below.
The middle I entrust to the spirits on earth.
May the bowstring be pulled by the Three Jewels.

This arrow that I aim with my hand
will not hit the gods on high. Remain in your upper realms.
It will not hit the nāgas below. Remain in your waters.
It will not hit the spirits on land. Remain here on earth.

Celestial armies of the gods, come today to help.
Spirit armies, come here today to give help.
Nāga armies below, come here today to give help.
May this arrow be guided by the Three Jewels.

With these words the prince loosed an arrow. It hit the demoness in the
heart and she fell headfirst from her horse. The Mandal Gang army, realizing
that it was the prince, made many prostrations to him and offered him their
bows and arrows as symbolic gifts. The prince dismounted from his golden
horse, pointed his bow at the demoness, and said:

Listen to me, demoness Hachang.
Don't you recognize this youth before you?
If you do, you will know it is Prince Samanta Sādhu.
If you do not, know that it is the king of Padminī.

With sweet-sounding words on her lips, she replied:

Prince, hear these words I speak.
I did not know you were an enlightened being.
You are truly an enlightened being,
and so just this once, please spare my life.

I will be like a mother to you.
You will be like a son to me.
With you and I as mother and son
we can rule over the kingdom of Mandal Gang.

Your sister, Princess Samantabhadrā,
can reign over the kingdom of Padminī.
Together we can rule over these kingdoms as one.
Please, I beg that you spare my life today.

The prince replied:

Listen demoness Hachang.
My great mother, Dowa Sangmo,
took to the skies and disappeared.

Her two children who suckled on her milk were
 left behind.

To my great father, King Kālendra,
you gave madness water,
and though he was guilty of no crime,
you threw him in a dark dungeon.
When I think of this, how can I spare your life?

First, you put us two children in the hands of butchers.
Then you gave us to two fishermen brothers.
Third, you sent us to two outcastes.
The younger outcaste threw me off Eastern Mountain.

When I think of these three deeds,
how can I possibly spare your life?
Now that I have my enemy in my hands,
how can I spare her life?

Suddenly arrows, knives, and spears rained down on the dying demoness
from all directions, and she was dead. Her corpse was buried in a pit nine
levels deep, and a black reliquary was built on top. The prince declared:

As long as the Buddha's doctrine lasts,
the black doctrine of the demoness will not flourish.
All types of demonic influenced have here been
 suppressed,
and all sentient beings will live in happiness.

When in the snowy land of the north,
I am reborn as Gyalwai Jungné,[112]
may I spread the Buddha's teachings far and wide.

The prince laid on a lavish victory feast for the Mandal Gang soldiers.
When news of the demoness's death reached Padminī, the minister and peo-
ple were overjoyed and huge celebrations were held.

The King Is Released from Prison and Happiness Is Restored

The prince announced:

> I will not stay here but return to Mandal Gang.
> My father, the great king Kālendra,
> was cast into a dark dungeon by the demoness Hachang.
> Thinking on this, I will return to Mandal Gang.
> Minister Sucandra, saddle my celestial horse.

He continued: "Five hundred attendants headed by Minister Sucandra, prepare to leave for Mandal Gang."

Taking with him three pouches of restorative medicine for his father, the prince set off for Mandal Gang. When they arrived at the main gate of the palace, the servant Durālabhā was seized and dispatched to an uninhabited region of the country. They entered the palace and opened the door of the deep dungeon. The king lay there, emaciated and close to death. Seeing his father, the prince fell into a faint. When he had recovered, he held his father close and lamented:

> Great king and father, the hardships you have suffered
> have come about because of the wicked demoness Hachang.
> How could she have inflicted such punishment on you!
> Years have passed since I last saw your face.
> Father, I ask you. Please speak to me.

His father did not comprehend. His sunken eyes stared wildly and he was unable to speak. The prince went into the storeroom, fetched some milk of a white cow, and added to it a dose of the restorative medicine. He offered some of this mixture to his father to drink and rubbed some of into his body. Heat began to return to his father's body. The prince again offered some of the mixture to drink and rubbed the remainder on his father's body. The king was then able to speak a little:

> Is this young man who stands here today
> my dear son, Prince Samanta Sādhu?
> The hardships that father, son, and daughter have endured
> have been brought about by the wicked demoness.

A few days ago she and her ministers left for war.
Now the demoness must be about to return.
Do not stay here. Flee to Padminī.
Otherwise the demoness will eat you.

The prince replied:

Great father and king. Please hear me.
The demoness and her army came to Padminī.
The great army of the king of Padminī
put an end to this hated and deadly foe.
Therefore I have come here.

The prince asked his father to come to his own room. There the two were seated on golden thrones, and three months passed.

One day minister Trinadhara, minister Kāntimān, and the other ministers assembled. They prostrated to the prince and said:

Father and son, please give us your attention.
We ministers were caught under the sway of the demoness
and perpetrated these evils deeds against father and children.
Against our will we cast the great king into a dungeon
and initiated many methods to kill son and daughter.

But now you have been exonerated from all these.
When the brother and sister were in the forest,
we ministers deceived them and caught them.
Now we suffer such deep remorse.
Whatever wealth and jewels we have, we offer to you.

The ministers brought an inconceivable array of offerings, including gold coins, silver coins, elephants, horses, buffalos, and much more. The king said:

Ministers, listen to what I say.
Although you have committed such unimaginable deeds,
it was because you were under the power of the demoness's
    orders.
Hence do not let them trouble your minds.

From now on, do not commit any wicked deeds.
Give up the ten nonvirtuous acts.
Immerse yourselves in the ten virtues.
Meditate that the deity Avalokiteśvara is upon
    your head.
Recite the six-syllable mantra, the very essence
    of the Dharma.

Again the king spoke:

The older and younger butcher brothers,
the older and younger fishermen brothers,
they were very kind to me.
Bring them to me now.

A minister left and quickly fetched them. They were brought before the king. All the gold, silver, and offerings presented by the ministers, as well as an inconceivable amount of gold, silver, and jewels from the king's treasury and an equal amount of grain from the storehouse, were offered to the butchers and the fishermen. The king said:

Older and younger butcher brothers,
older and younger fishermen brothers,
you who have been very kind to me,
hear what I have to say.

Older and younger butcher brothers,
you will become inner ministers in Mandal Gang.
Older and younger fishermen brothers,
you will become inner ministers in Padminī.

The prince said that he would return to Padminī, and so father and son set out with five hundred attendants. They remained in Padminī for three months, holding great celebrations.

The king, ministers, and the all people lived in happiness and prosperity, enjoying everything that they desired.

Thus ends the story of Drowa Sangmo.

6. The Brothers Amogha and Siddhārtha (Dönyö and Döndrup)

Namo Guru Dharmāsūrya

> Amitābha, lord of the Realm of Bliss,
> noble Avalokiteśvara, chief of his disciples,
> arising as the form of the most kind guru,
> I prostrate to the supreme Buddha and his disciple.

THE BIRTH OF SIDDHĀRTHA

In the past, in the noble land of India, the great Dharma king Baladeva ruled over the great region of Tāmradvīpa. The kingdom was prosperous, his power was great and widespread, his law was obeyed, and his subjects were happy. He was a magnanimous king who loved the Dharma. His queen, Samantabhadrā, worshipped the Three Jewels and was endowed with great faith and devotion. She was honest and sincere and had affection for all. Her compassion was great and she strove in the practice of Dharma.

For many years the royal couple had been unable to produce a son. The king and queen, and the people, worried that the royal lineage would come to an end and the rule of law would degenerate. The lack of an heir caused everybody much consternation, and the Dharma ministers assembled to discuss it. Then unanimously they addressed the king:

> Lord of men, ruler of the land, and precious king,
> lend your ears to this assembly of ministers.
> If it is deemed necessary to perform extensive rituals,
> to make devotions to the deities, and to suppress demons
> in order to produce a son endowed with love and compassion

who will preserve the royal lineage of our king
and who will care for the people and ministers with joy,
we ask that we ministers be allowed to make efforts in these.

The king replied:

Welcome, assembly of wise Dharma ministers.
These words of yours spoken with one voice
are in accord with my thoughts and are agreeable.
Therefore if it is necessary to perform extensive rituals,
such as making devotions to the Three Jewels and
   so on,
bring here those soothsaying women who clearly know
the difference between right and wrong,
and ask them what methods and rituals we
   must follow.

Thus the king gave his consent to perform extensive rituals, such as the higher ritual of making offerings to the Three Jewels, the lower ritual of giving alms to the poor, and the intermediate ritual of making donations and providing service to the monastic community.

At that time in that land there was a soothsaying woman called Kaṇṭi, who was very learned in all forms of divination. She was called before the king, who said to her:

To the infallible objects of refuge, the Three Jewels,
I devotedly prostrate with body, speech, and mind.
Please bless us that the wishes of the king and ministers
here in Tāmradvīpa be fulfilled.

The essence of our request is that you endeavor
in divinations to search out a method to produce a son
who will continue the royal lineage, rule according to
   the Dharma,
bring under control all opposing forces,
and be endowed with compassion that shows impartiality
   to all.

The soothsaying woman replied:

> King and ruler of the land,
> those words are heavier than gold.
> Not to follow them and not to produce results
> would cause me great harm.
> Therefore I will conduct divination with all due care.
> Please care for me, lord of the land.

The soothsaying woman promised to do as the king asked and returned to her home. There she prepared extensive offerings for the deities and gurus and spoke these words of truth:

> By the truth of the meditation deities and the Three Jewels,
> and by the power of the assembly of oath-bound protectors,
> show to me the unmistaken, unconfused methods
> for bringing a son to the king of Tāmradvīpa.

With this prayer and by various divinations, she received only excellent omens. Delighted, she returned to the king:

> I bow with devotion to Mañjuśrī, primordial Buddha
>   and supreme deity.
> Please bestow upon me the light of wisdom.
> Lord of men, ruler of the land, and precious king,
> please hear me for a while.

> About one hundred leagues' journey from this place,
> across the ocean, is the deity island known as Kośa.
> If there you make offerings and prayers to the Three Jewels,
> and offerings to the deities and nāgas while urging them to act,
> you will without doubt be delivered of an incomparable son.

The king replied:

> Soothsaying woman, hearing your words,
> I am overjoyed and my body and mind are content.

I will do as you suggest. If a son is born to me,
I will give you gifts to your heart's desire.

The king addressed his ministers:

As the ministers suggested, the soothsaying women were called.
By their divinations and other calculations they have declared
that on the small island of Kośa, one hundred leagues from here,
making offerings to the Three Jewels
and requests to the nāgas and the deities
will fulfill our great desires.

Therefore three days hence at an auspicious time,
accompanied by one thousand ministers,
I will travel to Kośa to request deities and protectors.

Thus the king and queen, together with about a thousand ministers and
subjects, all suitably adorned and with ample provisions for the offerings
loaded on the backs of elephants, set out for the edge of the ocean. From
there they boarded ships and boats and sailed for five days until they arrived
at the pure land of Kośa, inhabited by deities and protectors. There for seven
days they made offerings to the Three Jewels, gave tormas to Dharma pro-
tectors such as Devī Camuṇḍī, and gave offerings and tormas to the eight
classes of spirits and deities. After this, the king said:

Gurus, deities, and the Three Jewels,
ḍākinīs and you hosts of Dharma protectors,
eight classes of deities, such as local spirits and earth lords,
accept these vast and pure offerings and tormas,
which are consecrated by the three syllables,
and offered within the state of inseparable bliss
    and emptiness,
and grant us the miracle of a son
to fulfill the wishes of the king and ministers of Tāmradvīpa
and, in particular, to preserve lineage of the king.

Seven days later in the same place, the king had a dream in which a white
spiritual master holding a crystal rosary appeared. He addressed the king:

Great king, you have come to this place,
made offerings, and given praise with faith
    and devotion.
To you will soon come two princes.
One will be my heart-son Lokeśvara,
and the other an emanation of Mañjuśrī.
Rejoice! Bathe, and make everything pure.

The king asked:

You, whose body is of a brilliant white color,
you have given us the joy of reassurance.
Who are you? From where do you come?
What is your name? Tell me truly.

The answer came:

I come from the western realm of Sukhāvatī.
My name is the protector Amitābha.
Devī Camuṇḍī, the lord of Kośa,
is the protector of you, your queen, and your
    children.
Make offerings and tormas for her,
and continually entreat her to act for you.
Practice love and compassion to the poor.

With the prophecy and all auspicious omens for the coming of a son in place, the king and ministers were overjoyed and set out for the palace.

A few months later, in the tiger year, Queen Samantabhadrā conceived a child in her womb. At that time flowers falling from the sky, rainbow canopies, and many other good omens were seen. In particular, on special days a goddess dressed in white would come and bathe the queen's body. This was witnessed by everyone.

At that time the queen went to the king and said:

Lord of men, ruler of the land, and precious king,
Put your mind at ease and consider these words.
Last night in my dreams I experienced extraordinary signs.

My body was a blissful mandala of the Buddha,
whose main deity was in the form of Avalokiteśvara,
surrounded by an entourage of a host of bodhisattvas.

I dreamt that the buddhas sang praises,
that pure-realm goddesses came and bathed me,
that gods and goddesses prostrated and made offerings.
From the deity's body came a limitless stream of light rays,
dispelling the heat and cold of the hell realms.

From his fingers came streams of pure milk,
relieving the thirst and hunger of the hungry ghosts.
I dreamt that the Dharma melody of the six-syllable mantra
put an end to the sufferings of gods and men.

The appearance of bliss and emptiness in my mind
relieved my body of even a trace of fatigue and pain.
I believe such extraordinary omens in a dream are good,
and my mind is full of joy.

The king replied:

I go for refuge! Protector Amitābha!
How wonderful! Great noble one, Avalokiteśvara!
Hearing this, my mind is full of joy.
In Kośa, Amitābha prophesized that two sons would appear
as emanations of Avalokiteśvara and venerable Mañjuśrī.
Therefore an incarnation of Lokeśvara is without doubt in
    your womb.
So be tranquil in all your activities.
Bathe and be sure to dwell in clean places.

After almost ten months had passed, a very special son was born, adorned
with auspicious marks and with a light-radiating syllable *hrīḥ* embossed at
his heart. As soon as he was born, the child spoke:

Oṃ maṇi padme hūṃ
Compassionate Avalokiteśvara,

look upon us wretched beings with love.
In this human life of leisure and opportunity
gained by millions of virtuous acts in previous lives,
we are thoroughly distracted by worldly activity
and waste this precious human life. How sad!

Although we wander constantly in the three lower realms,
here in this human life, which is like a resting place,
we accomplish the needs of this busy life
and plan to stay here forever.

The sufferings of the lower realms are unbearable.
Nevertheless, under the sway of our selfish desires
we accomplish the glorious heights of this life.
Later we fall like a stone into the lower realms,
where the name of happiness is never heard. How sad!

Great birth celebrations were held and offerings of gratitude were made
to the Three Jewels, local deities, and Dharma protectors. A brahman sign
reader called Bhadra arrived. As soon as he saw the young radiant prince
adorned with special marks and features, he was amazed and said:

Extraordinary prince, embodiment of the compassion
    of all the buddhas!
Aglow with special marks and features, an incarnation
    of Lokeśvara!
In your life, great king, he will take over the rule of a kingdom,
but for we of little merit, it will be difficult to follow him.

He will bring the world under his control
and look after his attendants and subjects with affection.
His name shall be He Who Accomplishes the Needs
    of All Beings.[113]

Upon hearing this, the king, ministers, and people were overjoyed. Flags
were hoisted, conches were blown, and great festivities were held. The sooth-
saying woman and the reader of the signs were rewarded handsomely. The
soothsaying woman was promoted to minister.

THE QUEEN DIES AND THE KING SEEKS A NEW WIFE

From then on, the king's rule flourished even more virtuously, and when Siddhārtha was five years old, everyone witnessed the astonishing occurrence of the sounds of the six-syllable mantra naturally coming from his mouth. At that time his mother Samantabhadrā became very ill, and not long after she died. The whole country was plunged into grief. "Now that this noble lady has passed away, the richness of the soil will deteriorate," they wailed, and they performed much purification practice.

After about a year had passed, the ministers and people talked among themselves and all agreed that even if the whole world were to be searched, a woman like the noble Samantabhadrā could not be found. However, as the king was still young, he should seek out another wife. For many months they searched for a wife, but none suitable was found.

In the meantime, a large offering festival was being held in the city and the king and his son were invited to it. All the women had gathered in the streets, and among them the king saw an ordinary young woman called Padminī. He was very attracted to her. He called his inner minister, Dhari, to him and secretly whispered:

> In the midst of these many women is the attractive Padminī.
> She is very beautiful and has all the charm of youth.
> To see if she is suitable to be the queen of a true king,
> secretly make enquiries to discover her race,
> where she lives, and who her family is.

The minister pleaded:

> She is beautiful, but if I were to give to the king
> a woman of low caste, an ordinary woman,
> the ministers and people would revile me.
> And would they not secretly criticize you?

The king replied:

> The most important caste is that of the father.
> How can the caste of an ordinary woman do damage?
> If a king takes a suitable woman as his bride,
> why would the ministers and people criticize that?

Minister Dhari went to see Padminī and said:

> Young and beautiful woman, Padminī, what is your caste?
> Who are your parents? What is your age?
> Tell me truthfully. I am a messenger of the king.
> I must report the facts back to him.

The girl addressed the minister:

> Listen to me, wise inner minister.
> This girl before you is an ordinary girl.
> My mother and father are ordinary people.
> How can one such as I be queen to the king?
>
> A stone can be dyed and will shine brightly,
> but it is not fit to adorn the neck of the king of the gods.
> Therefore, as we are but ordinary folk,
> please excuse me from being queen to the king.

The minister again spoke:

> It is difficult for race and family to come between
> a couple connected by the karma of previous lives.
> A lotus that grows from the dirty swamps is brought
> to the offering temple and becomes a celestial ornament.

The following day the king went to the side of the bathing pool in the royal park. There, minister Dhari brought the girl Padminī and offered her to the king. Without any marriage ceremony, the king took her as his bride. Therefore the people slandered the king, whispering that the girl was not fit to be a queen.

Sometime later Padminī had a dream in which someone who said he was the son of Protector Amitābha appeared wearing a yellow *atsara*[114] robe and holding a wheel, saying that he needed a place to stay. Then he dissolved into the crown of her head. The next day the queen went to the king and said:

> Last night I had a dream in which
> a prince who called himself the son of Amitābha,

and who was wearing a yellow robe, appeared
and said that he needed somewhere to stay.

He then dissolved into the crown of my head.
Immediately my body and mind were filled with delight.
This is an auspicious dream, I feel. Please interpret it.

The king replied:

The heart-son of Amitābha, and incarnation of Mañjuśrī,
in the form of a son will without doubt come to me.
Now he abides within your womb.
Bathe and follow only clean practices, Padminī.

The months and days passed and the unworthy queen gave birth to a
son who was at once radiant and who displayed extraordinary signs and fea-
tures. A great celebration was held in which offerings were made to the Three
Jewels and Dharma protectors. The child was shown to the sign reader brah-
man Bhadra, who remarked as soon as he saw the infant:

By your pure intent, by the compassion of the Three Jewels,
and by your righteous rule of the kingdom,
another son has been born to you.

Without doubt he is the incarnation of Mañjuśrī.
He comes as the granter of happiness to all us living beings.
His name: He who is effective in creating the path of freedom
for the five classes of living beings.[115]
It will be difficult for him to remain in Tāmradvīpa.

As soon as he had announced the child's name, a rain of flowers fell from
the skies, the earth shook, and many other auspicious omens were observed.
The radiant wheels on the palms and soles of his hands and feet were visible
to all.

After birth, apart from taking his mother's milk, he did not entrust him-
self to his parents but remained day and night in the company of his elder
brother Siddhārtha. Whenever he saw his brother he was very happy. They

ate together, and when sleeping shared the same pillow and the same blanket and mattress.

The two princes became youths, and one day they climbed to the top of the palace to look around. Prince Siddhārtha looked on all those persecuted by transience and suffering. Turning to his younger brother, who was standing in the midst of attendants, he said:

> This prime of youth that we now enjoy
> is touched by the passing of years, months, and days.
> Like a lamp run out of oil, it will disappear.
> This too is in the nature of transience!
> Think about the onset of death, my companions.
> Protect us from the suffering of impermanence, Avalokiteśvara.

> This contaminated body composed of the four elements
> is destroyed by the ailments of wind, bile, and phlegm.
> Like the flowers of autumn, it will fade and disappear.
> This too is in the nature of transience!
> Think about the onset of death, my companions.
> Protect us from the suffering of impermanence, Avalokiteśvara.

> Nowhere are found those who escape death.
> At the time of death, friends, relatives, and possessions,
> like the tools of a dead blacksmith, are left behind.
> This too is in the nature of transience!
> Think about the onset of death, my companions.
> Protect us from the suffering of impermanence, Avalokiteśvara.

> Therefore, without allowing your life to be carried away
>   by distraction,
> make efforts in the practice of the sacred Dharma.

The attendants turned their minds to the Dharma. They were unwavering in their recognition of Prince Siddhārtha as a guru.

Later Queen Padminī went to palace roof also. Between the balustrades, she looked around. In the south on the great plain men were amusing themselves shooting arrows, playing jumping games, lifting stones, and so on. In

the west the women were weaving and spinning wool. They spent the after-
noon in gossip. In particular, they sang about why Prince Siddhārtha was
worthy of the throne and why Prince Amogha was not:

> Prince Siddhārtha is the elder brother,
> his mother too was the daughter of a king,
> and so he is worthy to sit on the throne.
> As for Amogha, his mother is an ordinary woman,
> and he is the younger, and so not worthy of the throne.

Looking to the east and the north, Queen Padminī saw children play-
ing and chattering how Prince Siddhārtha was worthy to rule the kingdom.
Some children had built a throne of mud bricks. One child sat on it, saying
that he was Prince Siddhārtha being enthroned. Some children pretended to
be ministers and were giving him advice. Others played at being the subjects
and were respectfully giving the king coronation gifts. One child pretended
to be Prince Amogha and sat by the side of the throne. All of them sang
in unison:

> Prince Siddhārtha has become the king,
> and the sun of happiness rises over the land of Tāmradvīpa.
> Young men and women of intelligence,
> why would you not busy yourself with the practice of Dharma?

The Queen's Wicked Plan

At around the same time, the ministers were all in agreement and decided
that Prince Siddhārtha should be installed as king. The queen thought to
herself: "Whether I look at what the people are saying and doing or at what
the ministers are saying and doing, the elder brother will be the one who
takes the throne, and it seems that my son will not become king. If a son does
not ascend to the throne, his mother will gain no respect. Therefore I will
devise a way to get rid of Prince Siddhārtha." In this way wicked thoughts
began to form in her mind.

Sometime later the queen stuffed ochre in her right cheek and indigo in
her left cheek to produce quantities of reddish-blue saliva. She ate herbs and
elephant brains to bring on coughing and sneezing. Coming down the steps
onto the path where the king and his sons were circumambulating images of

the enlightened body, speech, and mind, she fell to the ground and lay there moaning and spitting out quantities of colored saliva.

"What ails you?" asked the king. Writhing in pain, she did not answer. Having lost his previous wife, the king was concerned. "What can be done?" he wondered anxiously. Many rituals were performed, but to no avail. The king called in a soothsaying woman possessed of clairvoyance:

> Listen to me, clairvoyant soothsayer.
> This illness that ails my supreme queen,
> is it caused by wind, bile, or phlegm?
> What remedial treatments and rituals are there?
> If a cure is not found soon, her future life cannot be far away.
> I am troubled and I do not know what to do.
> Tell me completely and honestly what is the cure.

The woman replied:

> The illness that ails our supreme queen
> is not caused by wind, bile, or phlegm,
> but is the fault of a disturbance in her mind.
> Better to ask the queen herself for a cure.

The king became worried. "What can it be?" he wondered. "I must go and ask her myself." He went to the sick queen and said:

> My beautiful Padminī, both upright and beguiling,
> if you know the remedy for your illness, tell me truthfully.
> I will go to the ends of the kingdom if need be.

The queen replied:

> Alas! There is a way to cure me of this illness,
> but how can I possibly ask you for it?
> This woman of evil karma, tormented by this fatal illness,
> will die, and so I ask that I be left in silence.
>
> If, however, you are considering helping me by any means,
> I ask that you take an oath in front of the shrine.

The king swore an oath that he would do whatever the queen asked. Then she said:

> Our so-called Prince Siddhārtha is a nonhuman demon,
> come to weaken your life and your power, and to endanger
>   my life.
> When he was born, even his peerless mother, Samantabhadrā,
>   died.
> If he is killed and his heart given to me, it will be of great
>   benefit.
>
> Such things I have clearly been told in dreams.
> If this is not the case, then it would be better to send me
> to Kośa, that land of gods, demons, and wild animals.

The king reflected: "In the past when my special queen was alive, we made requests to the Three Jewels, as well as presenting offerings and tormas to the Dharma protectors. As a result, a son was given to us. The brahman sign reader prophesized that he would rule a kingdom before I died. If he were not to rule our kingdom, it would make no sense that he would rule another. The prediction of the soothsaying woman did not seem to be the work of a demon. This problem that has come upon me. Is it a dream? Is it real? What shall I do? Still, this queen also has a son. I cannot go back on my oath." With these thoughts, he replied to the queen:

> Listen to me, my supreme queen.
> Listen with attention to the words of a king.
> We are of the lineage of Dharma kings.
> Generally, we have forsaken harm to all living beings.
>
> In particular, this Prince Siddhārtha is a son
> born by the compassion of the Three Jewels.
> To initiate his killing would be a heinous crime.
> Therefore, to help you, he will be expelled.

With this promise, the queen showed a little improvement in her illness. The king assembled the ministers and announced:

This Prince Siddhārtha of ours is an incarnation of a demon.
He poses a great threat to the kingdom and its people.
In particular, he is great danger to the life of the queen.

This son was first given to us by the gods of Kośa,
and now he will be sent back to the land of Kośa.
Make necessary provisions for the journey, ministers.

The ministers talked together and addressed the king:

This land of Kośa is a land of gods and demons,
uninhabited by humans, a far-off place of unhospitable
    terrain,
whose paths are subject to terrifying floods,
and where the fear of wild animals and snakes is unbearable.

Should the prince be sent to such a land,
there will be no outcome other than his death.
If you have affection and compassion,
we ask that you refrain from sending him there.

The king replied:

Not long after this son was born,
the peerless Samantabhadrā died.
Now if he is not killed or expelled,
Padminī will without doubt die.
However, if you can take responsibility for her life,
tell me and I will do as you say.

The ministers had no reply. The following day a few ministers addressed
the king:

He who was granted by the meditational deities,
how could he be an incarnation of a demon?
He who is wise and so compassionate,
how could he be a fool without discernment?

He who is adorned with special marks and worshipped by all,
how could he destroy the kingdom and its people?
He who is the very epitome of compassion and love for all,
how could he pose a threat to the life of the queen?

Therefore we ask the king not to send the prince
to this far-off hostile land of gods and demons.

The king replied:

When a house dog bites back at his master,
and a minister refuses to obey commands,
other than beating them with sticks and kicking
   them out,
why should we continue to rely upon them?

Thus the ministers were driven out with sticks. Once the king had spoken, the ministers could not say anything against it. However, secretly, they said that if their Prince Siddhārtha was expelled from the country, it would without doubt be bad for living beings in general and, specifically, would weaken the kingdom. Therefore the king must have fallen under the spell of the queen, or else he was confused. There was a general unhappiness and criticism of the king's decision. Some ministers approached Prince Siddhārtha:

Great protector and refuge for the people of Tāmradvīpa,
compassionate prince, hear our words.
The ordinary queen has taken a perverted mind toward you.
She has plotted to break the bond between father and son.

In particular, she has spoken wickedly of killing you,
saying that your severed heart would be of benefit to her,
or that if you were to be sent at once to a far-off hostile land,
it would without doubt be of benefit in curing her of her illness.
Otherwise, she says, this demon-incarnated prince
will destroy the kingdom and its people.

The poisoned water of this queen's jealousy
has turned the mind of this foolish king to evil.

We do not know what bad event will occur.
Be clever, be cautious, great prince.

The prince thought to himself: "Anything is better than being killed. It is best that I flee." He thought of how he had been nurtured by the kindness of his mother, Samantabhadrā, and spoke aloud:

Three Jewels, infallible refuge,
guard the life of this protectorless one.
Where are you now, most kind mother, who nurtured me
with your milk and the three white foods?

Though blameless, I am being persecuted by
    punishment of death.
Do you not see the karma of this callow youth?
These events cause me to lose trust in samsaric relatives.
Thinking on this, my mind becomes deeply confused.

For this prince who is venerated by the devotion
    of attendants,
his brocaded garments and his silken pillows
will be left behind as he travels alone to a far-off land,
with cold earth as his mattress and cold stones as his pillow.
These events cause me to lose trust in samsaric wealth.
Thinking on this, my mind becomes deeply sad.

This prince who enjoys all the food and drink he
    could desire,
while enjoying the delights of the flute and the vina,
must wander among wild and ferocious beasts,
undergoing hardships and subsisting on meager food
    and clothing.
These events cause me to lose trust in samsaric companions.
Thinking on this, my mind becomes deeply troubled.

This fate that has befallen me is a reminder
not to have trust in the phenomena of samsara,
and is an inducement planted in my heart.

By the power of these excellent teacher-like inducements,
may my mind travel along the path to enlightenment.

Mother, although I do not have the fortune to see you,
I hold you vividly in my heart, and it is unbearable.
Although you are just an appearance in a dream,
protect this wretched son, compassionate mother.

From that time onward, the two brothers slept in the same bed. They
kept whatever food was left over and accumulated it. One time their parents
asked Prince Amogha to come to them to see if new boots and new clothes
would fit. Although a messenger was sent, because of the strong affection
between the two brothers, the prince did not go. Prince Siddhārtha turned
to his younger brother and said:

In accord with the orders from my mother and father,
soon I must leave for a far-off uninhabited land of gods
    and demons.
As you will no longer be the companion to this brother,
devote yourself to mother and father and rule the kingdom.

Meditate always on the mind of enlightenment and the
    meditation deity.
Foster love and compassion toward all the subjects.
Strive in the profound Dharma, training the mind
and following the law of cause and effect.

If we two do not meet again in this life,
I pray that we will meet in a pure realm in the future.
This final testament on the parting of two brothers,
do not forget it, keep it in your mind and follow it.

Amogha replied:

Though you go to an uninhabited land of gods and demons,
brother, I ask that you take me with you.
How could I bear staying here without you?

He threw his arms around his brother's neck. Siddhārtha said:

> Wandering through this desolate country,
> there will be only fruit for food and water for drink.
> On the roads will be many terrifying wild animals.
> In the end we would be thrown into the great sea.
>
> Therefore remain here in the kingdom.
> Rule over the kingdom. Become the lord of wealth.
> Not to obey the instructions of our parents
> will bring heavy retribution and great danger
>   to your life.

In tears, the younger brother said:

> Brother, because this dreadful event has come about,
> the royal lineage is at an end and its rule is finished.
> Whether we two brothers live or die,
> Please, I ask that you take me with you.

With these words he refused to take a single step from his brother's side. Hearing this, their parents addressed the ministers:

> Hear us, ministers assembled here.
> Soon Prince Siddhārtha will be banished to Kośa.
> However, the two brothers are very close,
> and we cannot be sure that Amogha will not follow him.
> Therefore, ministers, prevent Amogha from doing so.

Prince Siddhārtha thought to himself: "There is no way I can be separated from my brother. If we both leave, Amogha will no longer be here and my mother and father will surely be upset. Moreover, the royal lineage will come to an end." Therefore in the middle of the night he suddenly got up and prepared to leave. His brother heard him and said:

> Brother, if you are leaving, take me with you.
> How can we brothers bear to be apart?

He put his arms around his brother's neck and lay there, thereby preventing the prince from leaving that night.

THE BROTHERS LEAVE THE PALACE

At that time the elder brother was thirteen and the younger brother was six. Prince Siddhārtha was still intent on leaving alone. He had packed some food in a bag and placed it by his pillow, and for several nights had tried to leave, but his brother heard him and so he was unable to go. "Whatever happens I can stay here no longer," he thought. Therefore, at a time when Jupiter and the constellation Puṣya were in conjunction, he put his bag on his shoulder and made to leave. His young brother, thinking that the prince would leave, had not taken his boots off and heard him. He got up suddenly and said:

> Brother, how could you leave me here?
> Is it not uncompassionate to abandon me?

Thus in tears he followed his brother. Siddhārtha said to him:

> We bring suffering upon ourselves.
> Is it now the same for you?
> I am suffering, you are suffering too.

> Though I thought to leave you, I cannot do it.
> If I am to take you, it will be frightening.
> Gurus, meditation deities, and the Three Jewels,
> look upon the dreadful things happening to us.

Thus he took his brother and they left. Two Dharma ministers, Sudṛḍha and Jayadhara, became aware of the brothers leaving. They took them inside, grieved over their leaving, and waited on them. Ensuring that the mother and father did not hear, they provided the brothers with horses and laden elephants. Then the ministers accompanied the brothers as escorts for half a month. As it was time to take their leave, the ministers prayed:

> Great sages who dwell on the paths of the three vehicles,
> you who perform feats through word of truth,
> as our good fortune, we the people of Tāmradvīpa have received

from the dance of the wisdom and compassion of countless
    buddhas
these two Dharma princes, who are as rare as the udumbara
    flower.

However, by the sudden obstructive actions of demons,
we now lack the opportunity to drink the nectar of their speech
and follow instructions at their lotus feet.
Thinking on this, we are plunged into sorrow.

Keep us in your mind. For these two young brothers
in the frightening and uninhabited land of Kośa,
where tigers, leopards, bears, poisonous snakes,
spirits, gods, demons, and yakṣa ghosts
are malicious to one another in thought and deed,
pacify these creatures and endow them
with thoughts of love toward one another.

For these two brothers to wander in a far-off land
is like the lord of the seven horses[116] almost shining,
and then setting, hidden behind the western mountain.
Thinking on this, we are plunged into sorrow.

From now on, in life after life, may we devote ourselves
at the lotus feet of these two brothers,
and by pleasing them with our accomplishments
of the paths of the three vehicles,
may we soon achieve the stage of the four embodiments.

The people who had accompanied the brothers were also overcome by the
grief of having to part and were in tears. Prince Siddhārtha spoke to them:

Living beings of the six realms experience their individual
    karma.
Companionship ending in parting is the way of things.
Coming together is as transient as the crowds in the market
    place.
This life is as transient as the bees in autumn.

Wealth is as transient as the wares of a trader.
Meditating upon transience is important.
Return home. I will pray that we all meet again.

They lamented:

Day and night, at all six periods, we will examine our minds.
Give us ministers and people profound instructions
on fusing the sacred Dharma with our minds.
We pray that in the succession of our lives,
we will meet and recognize you.

The prince replied:

Composite phenomena are not permanent, they will end.
Youth is transient, like a rainbow in the sky.
With the exhortation that is the remembrance of death,
and the whip of remembering the suffering of the lower realms,
meditate always on the great deity Avalokiteśvara.
Make prayers from your heart, with all sincerity.

With your mind moistened by love and compassion,
develop the mind of enlightenment, the supreme path
    of the buddhas.
Practice the six perfections and the four ways of gathering
    disciples,
which will ripen as benefit to yourselves and others.
Do this and you will gain the great fruit of permanent
    happiness.

In this or in all other lives,
I will recognize you and take care of you.
Now leave this place and return to your homes.
Make prayers that we will soon meet again.

For all mother sentient beings of the six types,
death at the end of birth is the way of things.

Good and bad deeds, by the law of karma, never just disappear.
Generate effort to remove the bad and cultivate the good.

Return to your home and tell these words to all.
I will pray that we meet again in a Buddha realm.

With this, they parted. They gradually sold the horses and elephants in towns they came across on their journey. After about fifty leagues there was no more habitation and they came to a large desert where no path was discernible. The younger brother was tired and weary, and so his elder brother took him by the hand. They ate the remainder of their food as they walked on.

Meanwhile, their parents had finished preparations for sending Siddhārtha into exile. The king called a minister:

Minister, do not tarry. Go now.
Bring Siddhārtha to his mother and father.

The minister returned and reported that the two princes were nowhere to be seen. The king replied:

Minister, how can your words be true?
Prince Amogha is but a young boy.
He could not go anywhere.
The people must be hiding him.
Go, search for him now!

The ministers went out and searched the homes of all the people, but the princes were not to be found. The king and queen became very upset. The queen, no longer faking illness, actually became ill. The people cried, saying that now the two young brothers were undergoing the ordeal of being in that uninhabited land of gods and demons. They slandered the queen, saying that this was what she deserved.

Meanwhile, the two brothers had left behind the desert and a few leagues later had arrived on a grassy plain where no sound of dogs or human was to be heard, and which was inhabited by many vicious ghosts, cannibals, and wild animals. Amogha said to Siddhārtha:

Brother, Prince Siddhārtha, hear me.
Listen to your younger brother, Amogha.
Here in this deserted land, this lonely plain,
where nothing is familiar except the land and sky,
vicious ghosts and cannibals cackle incessantly,
and wild animals let forth their frightening roars.

Hearing this, my heart is torn apart.
Alas! Alas! Such suffering as this.
May it never befall any living thing.
If we stay for long here, we will surely die.
Brother, show us the path.

Siddhārtha replied:

My dear brother, Prince Amogha,
listen carefully to your brother.
The suffering we two are experiencing has come about
because we have been parted from our loving mother.

Our affectionate father has banished us to an
    endless forest.
Even our friends and loved ones are far away.
Now we wander alone to the ends of the earth.
To think on this makes me very sad.
However, put your trust in the Three Jewels.
Be brave. Follow your brother.

By the kindness of this bodhisattva brother, the ghosts and cannibals, and the wild animals, befriended the brothers like companions and pet dogs, and no harm came to them.

For many months they wandered on this desolate plain. The elder brother had eaten about five balls of dough, and his brother had never received less than a handful. A few days later their provisions ran out and they wondered what they would do. They even cut up the leather food bag and ate that as they traveled on. Because of the salty taste of the bag they experienced a relentless and burning thirst. Amogha said to his brother:

I am so thirsty, I fear I may die.
Brother, please give me some water.

Siddhārtha searched everywhere for water but found none. So he took
saliva from his own mouth and gave it to his brother. As they had been trav-
eling a long time on this desolate plain, they had become very weak. Seeing
a tree, they rested in its cooling shade. Siddhārtha saw that there were many
delicious-looking mangos on the tree, and in great joy he picked them. The
two brothers feasted on the fruit and were transformed like gentle flowers
receiving the rain. Prince Siddhārtha took five mangos in his hand, offered
them to the Three Jewels, and made this prayer:

Gurus, meditation deities, Three Jewels,
ḍākinīs, Dharma protectors, local spirits, earth lords—
I offer this pure torma to you. Please accept it,
and by doing so, please be our refuge and guides.

Although we are tormented by this bodily hindrance,
by the bond of obeying the instructions of our parents,
may we become the guides and refuge to lead to freedom
the six classes of beings in these degenerate times.

Traveling on, they came to a land devoid of water. The younger brother
could not continue on and so Siddhārtha carried him on his back for about
eight furlongs. But still there was no water. Siddhārtha saw a hill shaped like
an elephant trunk. He said to his brother:

Stay here for a while, brother.
I am going off in search of water.
If we do not find water to relieve our thirst,
we will without doubt be facing our death.

He began to leave, but his brother started to cry and called out:

Last night as I lay asleep I had a dream
in which I experienced unbearable suffering.
This life of leisure and opportunity was brought to an end,
and I was left alone in a hostile land.

I dreamt that two sages came and helped us.
It appears that you are abandoning me, brother.
With your compassion, please take me with you.

Siddhārtha replied:

Young brother, how could I possibly leave you?
If there is no water, we will both die of thirst.
Therefore I must go in search of water.
I will quickly return.

He walked about a furlong but found no water. Still he continued on his journey. When he reached a mountain ridge, a voice called out, "Brother!" Looking back, he saw his brother face down on the ground. With great speed he urged himself down the mountain. He found his brother unable to speak, his eyes barely open, and his breath almost spent. Siddhārtha took him on his lap, loosened his belt, and pressed him close. Tears from his eyes fell onto his brother's face, and he revived somewhat. Amogha looked into his brother's eyes and said:

This suffering my brother and I are undergoing,
may it never fall on any living being.
The sufferings of thirst and hunger of all living beings,
may they all ripen on us and be experienced by us.

In the future, by drinking the sweet nectar of the Dharma,
may the tormenting suffering of living beings be dispelled.
Although we will never be apart in all our lives,
now my life here is spent.

Brother, do not grieve for me.
Make prayers that we will quickly meet again.

At that moment two kalaviṅga birds appeared and prayed:

In all our future lives, may we be reborn
in the presence of the two brothers,

and by becoming their devoted servants,
carrying out exactly their every instruction,
may we be nourished by the nectar of their words.

Then a kalandaka bird appeared and prayed:

In all my lives may I take with devotion
the lotus feet of the two brothers,
and by bringing to mind their past deeds,
may I become a wise composer of treatises.

A cuckoo appeared and prayed:

In all my lives may I be the wise one who
performs proper service to the two brothers,
and with clairvoyance, may I become a great translator
of the works of sutra and tantra.

Just then, the younger brother stopped breathing. Siddhārtha held the head of his brother and cried. "I have sent my brother away," he said. Placing his head against his brother's, he wept. Sitting by his brother's body, he mourned:

Three Jewels, infallible objects of refuge,
be the protector and support of this helpless one.
My mother and father from the land of Tāmradvīpa,
the kingdom, those companions who waited upon me,
my silk and brocade clothes, the three sweet foods, and more
have all been left behind, and I wander in this remote place
where nothing is familiar except the earth and sky.

Alas! Alas! What am I to do?
When we wandered on that desolate plain,
the suffering of heat and cold, hunger and thirst, was unbearable.
When we were on paths that were narrow and dangerous,
the suffering of the fear of ravines and robbers was unbearable.

When we came to the thick forests,
the fear of wild animals and snakes was unbearable.
When we walked through the steep gorges,
the fear of ghosts, gods, and demons was unbearable.

Here in this land, my younger brother Amogha
has left this life, and the suffering is unbearable.
Mother, mother, Samantabhadrā,
I think of you, and the suffering is unbearable.

My younger brother lies here. Who knows if I am to die?
Persecuted as I am by a hundred sufferings,
yet still I have not yet died.
Is this heart of mine made of iron?

Thus he called on his mother and sat there for a long time. After a while
he found his courage, lifted his spirits, and made this prayer:

Do not be sad, good Siddhārtha.
You already have the best of supports.
While you remain alone in this remote land,
you have as your best companion the self-arising wisdom.
For protection against sufferings of heat and cold, hunger
   and thirst,
you have contentment, able to put up with any suffering.

For protection against the fear of ghosts, gods, and demons,
you have the supreme refuge of love and giving.
For protection against the unbearable sufferings of the
   lower realms,
you have the supreme refuge of the ethics of the ten
   virtuous ways.

For protection against the sufferings of samsara,
you have the supreme refuge of wisdom and renunciation.
For protection against the fears of samsara and nirvana,
you have the supreme refuge of compassion and emptiness.

Here in the midst of this lonely forest, as praised by the buddhas,
transform your mind into the Dharma, Siddhārtha.
Keep transience and death at the center of your mind,
and may you find a safe and stable birth.

On the path of compassion with the teachings and practice
    of the Mahayana,
may you bring living beings to the path of the ten virtuous acts.
In the realm of the mind of enlightenment of benefitting others,
may you train in the practice the six perfections.

Having found conviction in the three baskets of scripture,
may you attain to the level of the regent of the Buddha.
In particular, may we two brothers in these very bodies
meet again and recognize each other.

In this way he made countless prayers, and for a while he entered into
meditation. At that time the birds and the wild animals circumambulated
him, the earth shook in six ways, flowers fell from the sky, and the gods
played celestial music. Apes and monkeys prostrated to him and circumam-
bulated him while saying this prayer:

Brave youth, with the selfless mind of enlightenment.
How wonderful! This celestial youth, this incarnation.
Here in this life, in the intermediate state, and in all future lives,
other than you there is no object of refuge in which we
    place our hopes.
By continually achieving the four great accumulations,[117]
may we always practice according to your words.

A tiger appeared. He had a perverse perception of the situation, thinking
to himself: "What is the point of making these prayers to some human!"
Nevertheless, just for the sake of mouthing flattery, he prayed:

May I too in all my lives from now on,
be before the lotus feet of the two brothers,
and by performing service and following their words,
may I become a wise and discerning scholar.

After a while Siddhārtha emerged from meditation, thinking that it had not been of any help. He put his brother's body on his back and walked over eight passes until he saw on the mountainside a forest of sandalwood, acacia, myrobalan, and other trees. It was a beautiful and pure place ornamented by rock clefts and milk streams flowing down its sides. There he spied a white sandalwood tree shaped like a canopy. Approaching, he saw the canopy like a rainbow canopy of five colors. There under the shade of the white sandalwood tree, he made a stone tomb. Making sure that it would not be harmed by animals, he placed his brother's body in it. The cooling shade of the tree produced sparkling dew drops.

Although he felt very attracted to the place, it was a haunt of wild animals and the heat was unendurable. He could not stay there, and so looking back for as long as he could see the tomb, and with tears of unbearable separation, he traveled on, crossing over thirteen mountain ridges.

Seven days later Śakra, the king of the gods, manifested as a sage carrying a small bag of medicine to revive the dead. Brahma manifested himself as a brahman carrying clothes made of Benares silk. They went to the body of Amogha. The sandalwood dew dropping into the tomb meant that the body had not decomposed or dried out and had a radiance as if it were alive. The sage added a little camphor to a cup of sandalwood water and said:

> This supreme potion, this life-restoring nectar stream,
> I offer to the lips of this young prince.
> Great guide, do not pass into nirvana,
> I ask that this body of yours is restored to its living state.

Two spoonfuls of the medicine were poured into the prince's mouth and warmth returned to the body. With a third dose his consciousness returned. After a further dose was fed to him and another dose rubbed into his body, he was able to stand. The brahman said to him:

> These soft, gentle, and light clothes of Benares silk,
> I happily offer to the body of the prince.

The prince replied:

> So kind, so kind! Miraculously appearing sages.
> Who are you? Where do you come from?

Have you seen my kind brother?
Where has he gone? Where is he? Please tell me.

The two sages replied:

Young and compassionate prince,
Brahma and Śakra could not bear you dying,
and we have been sent from the celestial realms
to offer you these clothes and this life-restoring
      medicine.

The prince said:

You have the power and ability to travel
from the celestial realms to the human realm.
Show me a way to quickly meet with my kind brother.

The two sages replied:

By now your brother Siddhārtha
has crossed thirteen passes and is gone.
However, we will accompany you in your search.
Keep this in your mind, celestial prince.

After about a furlong the two sages vanished like a rainbow. The young prince thought to himself: "There is nothing but wild animals and deer in this forest, but the brahman and the sage will protect me by being my celestial guardians. Now I must search for fruit." With this, a monkey miraculously appeared and offered the prince much fruit, then without a sound disappeared back into the forest.

For food he ate fruit, for drink he drank water, and for clothes he wore leaves. He piled up the first portions of the fruit he ate, and prayed:

These portions of fruit with their perfect flavor,
may they be the shares for my most kind brother.
If I and Siddhārtha, the jewel of my heart,
could meet in this place, how happy I would be.

With these words he wept, and in great grief called out for his brother. Day after day he wandered over mountains and through forests. Driven on by the pain of separation, he searched high and low for his brother.

SIDDHĀRTHA MEETS HIS GURU
Having crossed thirteen ridges, Prince Siddhārtha rested on a plain between mountains. The mountains to the west were high and large. Their upper regions were a mixture of slate and grassy slopes and the lower were covered with thick forests. In the southern part where the forest and the slate slopes met he saw a small flag waving. "There are no towns or nomad camps over there," he thought to himself. But looking at the flag, he was sure somebody was there and set off toward it. Arriving at the slopes of the mountain, he saw footprints in the dust. "There must be some kind of hermitage here," he thought. Continuing on, he saw under the flag a hollow in the mountains. From the hollow he heard the clear sound of cymbals. He was certain that there was a hermitage there and was overjoyed. Climbing up, he came to a spring at the head of the hollow where an elderly monk, wearing a hemp robe, was casting a torma at the spring. The prince prostrated and said:

> In this solitary place hidden by thick forest canopy,
> whose trees are verdant and lush with leaves,
> the sound of cymbals coming clearly to my ears
> and teaching the presence of the Mahayana
> has led me to this great being living here,
> who reveals the path of liberation,
> having shunned all attachment to samsara.

> With your love, compassion, and great wisdom
> give attention to this helpless youth,
> who wanders the land without protection.

The guru rose from his meditation and looked at the prince, who made many prostrations. The prince had been wandering on empty plains and over many mountains. He had been deprived of regular food, and in particular he was grieving for his dead brother. As a result, his hair was standing on end, he was emaciated, his clothes were in tatters, and even his private parts were exposed. The guru looked at this figure that resembled a ghost. With his clairvoyance he could see that this was a prince forced to wander abroad, but he pretended he did not know and said:

> Infallible refuge of the Three Jewels and the meditation
>   deities,
> I give to you my offering of practice.
> Please care for the six realms with your compassion.
>
> You with unkempt hair, rags for clothes,
> of poor complexion, and like a wretched urchin,
> are you human or a ghost? Tell me true.
>
> If human, what is your race? Who are your parents?
> Where are you going? Where do you stay?
> With a calm mind, tell me all in detail.

The prince prostrated and said:

> I take refuge in you, precious guru.
> I bow to you with respect.
> Hold me with the hook of your compassion.
>
> I am the son of the king of Tāmradvīpa.
> By the force of bad past-life karma I now wander abroad.
> Seeing from afar the guru's meditation place, I came here.
> As soon as I saw you, great faith made my hairs stand on end.
>
> If I am allowed to be an attendant for your practice,
> to serve you, and to follow your every word,
> please give me the nectar of the sacred Dharma.

Boundless compassion arose in the mind of the guru. "We should go to my hut," he said. To the east of the spring was a large rock about the size of a two-story house. On it were the self-emanated, embossed figures of Amitābha and the three protectors of the three families, each the size of an eight-year-old child. In front of the rock and built onto a cave was a pleasant grass hut. Inside the hut the guru asked the prince about his country, his story, and so on:

Prince Siddhārtha, you who have wandered far,
turn your ears without distraction to this guru.
What is the name of your father?
What circumstances led you to wander from your land?
Tell me of your lineage, tell me of your story.

The prince went down on one knee and said:

Hear me, precious teacher.
Listen well to this young prince.
The land I come from is called Tāmradvīpa.
My father is known as King Baladeva.
My most kind mother was called Samantabhadrā.
She passed away when I was very young.

Because of this an ordinary woman arrived
and became the powerful queen.
To her a son was born—my younger brother Amogha.

Under the sway of envy, the queen faked an illness,
whose cure, she said, was to have me banished.
My brother, Amogha, out of great love for me,
could not bear the thought of separation,
and so we wandered off into the forests together.

In the day we had no food, in the night no clothes.
Such endless suffering we had to endure.
My brother succumbed and his life came to an end.
I wandered off alone and have come to this place.

Now whatever befalls me, good or bad, I ask that you,
great guru, take care of me with your compassion.

The guru was delighted. "The meditation deities and the Dharma protectors have brought you here as if you were my son."

The prince set about collecting kuśa grass to repair the guru's mattress. He sprinkled water over the ground and made the place clean. Each day he gathered fruit and firewood as he settled in as the guru's attendant. At sunrise on the seventh day the prince's hair was shaved. He bathed and was given new clothes and food. He made offerings to the meditation deities, invocations of the protectors, and many other prayers. Then he entered meditation for a while. After he rose from meditation, the guru looked at the prince and with his clairvoyance made this prophecy:

> From the Potala mountain, greatest of pure realms,
> the mighty Avalokiteśvara came for the benefit of living beings.
> Amazing son, you are one of extraordinary courage.

> In the future, before you part from this body,
> you will meet your brother and together will become
> great protectors of the teaching and living beings.

> Until then, though we may be beset by the hindrances of Mara,
> by the compassion of the meditation deities and the Three
>   Jewels,
> our lives will not be put under threat.

> Extraordinary youth, of stainless royal lineage,
> Having been banished to wander in far-off lands
> by the force of the three poisons and envy,
> the king and queen will become weak
> and their minds will be tormented with worry.

The prince continued to serve the guru, and after a month guru said to the prince: "The grass of my mattress has never before become frayed and rotten. You are a manifestation of Avalokiteśvara. Is this fraying and rotting of my seat a sign that you have something on your mind? Tell me truthfully."

The prince replied: "If I cannot tell my guru, who can I tell? I miss my dear brother greatly. Though I lie down, I cannot sleep. Though I eat, it does not nourish me. I think to myself, if only I could gather some of my brother's bones."

His guru replied: "Then we, father and son, will go to where your brother's bones lie. You will be the guide."

The following day the guru and his disciple set out. After two days they rested at a spot abounding in fruit trees, between the plains and the mountains. Birds and deer circumambulated them. Apes and monkeys piled up wonderful fruits before them. With many prostrations and circumambulations, they addressed the guru and his disciple:

> Hear us, guru and your disciple.
> Pay heed to us apes and monkeys.
> These wondrous fruits, full of nourishment,
> supreme in flavor, gotten without dishonesty,
> we offer with minds of faith and ask that
> in all our lives you will care for us.

The prince said to his guru:

> Here in this delightful place, the birds and animals
> day and night prostrate and circumambulate us.
> Monkeys and apes, in particular, serve us with fruit.
> Please tell me, what is the cause of this?

The guru smiled and said:

> Listen well, my fortunate son.
> For the sake of living beings I have come here
> from the body of Amitābha in the pure realm
>   of Sukhāvatī.

> The animals know this and thus they circumambulate and
>   prostrate.
> In the future these birds and animals will become our disciples
> in the doctrine of the Buddha, in the northern land of snow.
> With the seven deities and doctrines of the Kadampa tradition
> they will raise the doctrine of the Buddha in a hundred
>   directions.

The guru gave this and many other prophecies, and the prince made many prostrations.

Eventually they arrived at the spot where the brother's body had been laid. The tomb remained intact and by its side were signs of human activity, such as the skins of fruit and the remains of a homemade straw mattress.

However, his brother's bones where nowhere to be found. Guru and disciple stayed there for seven days, and each day the guru made dedications, prayers, and tormas for the prince's younger brother.

Feeling sad, the prince set off in search of fruit, and in doing so, said:

> My dearest brother, Amogha, where are you?
> Please send me a message.

The guru said: "It is true that you have your brother heavily on your mind." He placed his robe in the sunlight and sat. The prince went off to pick fruit and in search of his brother.

At that time a yakṣa with three heads, six arms, and carrying a red spear appeared in front of the guru, saying that he was the lord of this locality. He spoke to the guru:

> Precious guru, you who have gone to the ends
> of all that is to be known and all that is to be abandoned,
> two sages, who were manifestations of Brahma and Indra,
> came before the stainless body of Amogha.
> They gave him life-restoring medicine and clothes of
>   Benares silk,
> bringing him back to life, and now he has left in search
>   of his brother.
> He travels over mountains and through valleys,
> all the time crying out for his brother.
> Until now they have not had the fortune to meet,
> but one day they will be reunited, compassionate one.

In reply the guru said:

> Yakṣa of vicious race, with three faces and six arms,
> tell me truthfully your name, race, and so on.

The demon replied:

> Mighty Vajradhara, lord of all ḍākinīs, I am the yakṣa Vekeca.
> With faith and admiration I have come to meet you.
> I have come for blessing and to establish a bond with you.

In the future, as the regent of the Buddha,
when you both perform great works for countless living beings,
I will act as the guardian of the doctrine of sutra and tantra.

"This is excellent," said the guru. He gave commands to the yakṣa and established a bond with him.

That evening as the sun was about to set, the prince returned. The guru said to him: "Today, a frightening demon with three heads and six arms, who is the lord of this area and whose name is Vekeca, came to me. He said that we two should not be sad about Prince Amogha, as a great sage had come to this place and had given Amogha life-restoring medicine. He revived and has wandered off over mountains and through valleys in search of his brother. Although you have not yet had the good fortune to meet him, you will be reunited. He promised, 'In the future when guru and disciple become masters of the teachings, and work for countless living beings, I will be your protector.' I gave him commands and established a bond with him. Therefore, our wishes will be fulfilled. No longer carry this burden in your mind."

The prince was delighted and expressed his gratitude for the guru taking this responsibility.

The guru and disciple set off for home. On the road they encountered nine poisonous snakes. Two were lying across the path. The guru, who was in front, stepped over the snakes, and in doing so slipped and fell on them. The prince was able to pull him up. The two snakes, suffering the pain of being squashed in this way, thought: "If it weren't for this young man pulling up the guru we would have definitely killed him." Therefore they developed a perverse view and made this evil prayer:

In the future, in all our lives,
may we serve respectfully at his lotus feet,
and may our divisive words have the power
to repeatedly sow discord and dissension.

Likewise, the other seven snakes make similar perverse prayers and scuttled off amid the rocks. The guru generated immense compassion for them and spoke these words of truth:

Over many lives these obstructive forces have hindered,
have held wrong views, and have made perverse prayers.
By the power of these brief spoken words of truth,
may their power never come to fruition.

May the knot of this vajra bond between guru and disciple
never loosen over many lives, and may we never separate.
By the power of the infallible refuge of the three precious jewels,
may this well-intentioned prayer be fulfilled.

Guru and disciple returned home. One day the guru said to his disciple:

Prince Siddhārtha, wise and of excellent lineage,
listen with attention to the word of this stainless teacher.
I have lived a long time in singular seclusion,
and through my concentrated meditation
I have no tension that tires my body and mind.

However, for you working as my attendant,
the suffering of being apart from your brother,
and of being alone with no one to talk to
causes you tension in body, speech, and mind.

Therefore, to ease that pain, a short distance from here
is a shady tree, delightfully green and lush.
We will go there to relax and take our pleasure.

They spent some time relaxing in the shade of a tree a short distance from the hut. There the guru spoke much on impermanence.

At one time, the prince asked: "On the side of the rock by our hut are various depictions of deities. How did these come about?"

The guru replied: "In the past when the Buddha Samantabhadra was in the world, this place was where he stayed. As his main disciples he had two young brahmans who were incarnations of Avalokiteśvara and Mañjuśrī. While they were making offerings to him, that Buddha prophesized that in the future the two disciples would meet again in this place and do great things for living beings. At that time these likenesses of the buddhas, together with the śrāvakas, miraculously appeared."

Again the guru spoke:

> Hear me this one time, brave young prince.
> Siddhārtha, pay attention, listen to me.
> That Buddha Samantabhadra, who came in the past,
> do not think him to be anyone other than me.

> You are Avalokiteśvara, the embodiment of compassion.
> Your brother Amogha is Mañjuśrī, the lord of wisdom.
> By the power of past prayers, we two meet here today.
> It will not be long before you meet Prince Amogha again.

The prince was overjoyed. He made prostrations and circumambulated the guru, saying:

> You who are the actuality of every buddha,
> possessed of the name of stainless guru,
> I ask that you turn your attention to me for a while.

> By the glorious perfection of your clairvoyance
> and your mastery of the ten great powers,
> you have spoken of these wonderful past and
>   future events.

> By the kindness of the guru I am blessed with a joyful body
>   and mind.
> Please continue to care for me with your great compassion.

The prince prostrated again and again like a falling wall.

Just then two cranes appeared. One offered a pair of cymbals, the other offered a jewel. Together they prayed:

> In the future, when guru and disciple
> become the leading lights of the teachings,
> may we be born as the first of your entourage,
> and may we become powerful patrons of giving,
> to please you with offerings of our wealth.

To this the guru replied:

> With harmonious minds you have made a wonderful prayer.
> By the power of words of truth, may it all be fulfilled.

Just then a partridge appeared, thinking: "What a pretentious liar this guru is." The guru responded:

> Partridge, do not have perverse thoughts.
> Rejoice with a harmonious mind.

The partridge bowed its head three times and said:

> May I too become your personal attendant
> and never be separated from you in all my lives.

The guru and disciple continued to perform funeral rituals for the younger brother, Amogha.

One day the prince went to look at a nearby town. On a plain he saw children playing and went to watch them. The children were struck by his extraordinary presence and said:

> Youth born of the gods, with your beautiful form
> and the glories of youth, where are you from?
> What is your purpose here? Where are you headed?
> Tell us truthfully of these matters.

The prince replied:

> I am the son of a beggar, bereft of food,
> who wanders the land aimlessly.
> I have not eaten today. My belly aches with hunger.
> Make me the gift of some food, children.

The children offered him copious quantities of rice and other foods. He returned to the hut and told his guru what had happened. The guru replied: "Son, it is good you were not truthful. If you had told them everything, there would have been danger of being seized by the king."

Then, from time to time, the prince would visit the plain where the children played. There he would act as the group leader. He would engage in tests of strength with those of his age and would always win, prompting him to proclaim:

> I was born in the year of the thunder dragon.
> My fame like thunder resounds in all directions.

The Prince Is Seized by the Minister

Around that time, about five leagues from the guru's hut was a large royal palace surrounded by a hundred thousand dwellings. Its beauty and glories were such that it was as if it had been transferred from the celestial realms of Indra, Śiva, and Viṣṇu. Inside lived a king called Pṛthivi Mahābrahma Varma, an incarnation of Vajrapāṇi who ruled his kingdom according to the ways of Dharma. He had a beautiful princess daughter but no sons. Two leagues from the palace was a large lake six leagues in circumference. There on the fifteenth day of the first of the three summer months, a turquoise dragon would descend from the sky into the lake and swim around with a great roar. The ministers and the people came and made vast offerings to it. As a result, the rains came on time, human illness vanished, disease in cattle disappeared, and many an auspicious occurrence was seen. However, in recent times, due to some obstruction in fortune, the dragon had not been coming to the lake. Consequently, the rains failed, cattle disease returned, illness among the people was on the rise, famines occurred, and so on. The king called in a soothsaying woman and said to her:

> Hear me, soothsaying woman.
> Listen attentively to the words of your king.
> Here in this great kingdom of ours,
> on the fifteenth day of the early summer month,
> a turquoise dragon would descend into the lake
> and our ministers and people would make offerings
> and place various offering substances in the lake.
>
> As a result, the rains come on time, harvests were
>   bountiful,
> and all manner of prosperity was seen.

But now the dragon does not come to the lake,
the rains no longer arrive on time,
and much misfortune occurs in the land.

What has brought this situation about?
Perform well your divinations, and so forth.

The soothsaying woman performed her divinations and said to the king:

Hear me, lord of men and great Dharma king.
Listen and consider these divinations and so forth.
As for the cause of the bad omens in our land,
I performed the three-hundred-and-sixty divination round.
In them I found the following.

This lake is the home of many nāga kings, such as Upananda.
Take a youth, eighteen years of age, born in the dragon year,
and load him with befitting incense and offering substances.
Tie nāga-summoning mantras and mystic-wheel diagrams
around his neck and cast him into the lake.

This will bring about the return of the good fortune,
the plentiful harvests, and all else.
Consider this well, great king and ministers.

The king and his ministers performed this ritual each year, and as a result, youths born in the dragon year fled as best they could. When the time came around again, the king addressed his ministers:

Listen to me, ministers assembled here.
It is time to cast the substances into the lake.
Make ready an eighteen-year-old born in the dragon year
and prepare the various substances.

The ministers searched high and low but could find no such youth. However, the talk of the children playing on the plain had spread, and an evil-minded minister called Triśu, through the power of a perverse prayer made in the past, had heard that such a youth born in the dragon year, eighteen years of age, was living as the student of guru Sādhumatī. He was delighted and approached the king:

> Hear me, precious king.
> Listen one time to minister Triśu.
> In accordance with the king's instructions,
> we have searched for a dragon-year youth.
> Others have searched everyone but not found one.

> Yet I have heard that in an upper valley in our land,
> in the residence of the monk called Sādhumatī,
> an eighteen-year-old dragon-year disciple has arrived.
> He is fit to carry the substances to the nāga kings.
> King and ministers, consider these words.

The king replied:

> If what the minister says is proven true,
> bring that youth to me now.

The minister said: "One step, two steps, three steps and I am there!" Thus he set off and quickly arrived at the guru's hut. Addressing him, the minister said:

> Listen to me, Sādhumatī.
> Listen carefully to this minister.
> Monk, you have a son here.
> Where is he? Take me to him.

The guru replied:

> Listen to me, minister of the king.
> I am a solitary monk meditating and practicing.
> For there to be a son here with no parents makes
>   no sense.
> Do not say these things, minister. Please leave it.

Triśu replied: "If you do not tell me, it will not be good for you." He raised his hand, his body quivered with aggression, he crooked his eyebrows, and he made various other wrathful expressions.

The guru replied: "I have nothing to tell. I am a solitary practitioner. I have no attachment to anything. If you want to kill me, then do it."

In desperation the minister searched outside and in but could not find anyone. He grabbed the guru by his chest, brandished his sword, and said:

> Listen to me, Sādhumatī.
> Listen carefully to the words of this minister.
> For an elephant who does not understand,
> a stick is more powerful than the words of a king.
> Likewise, if you do not tell me truthfully, monk,
> you will feel the sharp blade of this sword.

As he made to strike, the prince could bear it no longer. He appeared from nowhere and said to the minister:

> Great minister, do not do this.
> Please release my most kind guru.

The minister went to seize the youth by the arm. The guru pleaded with him, but to no avail. The minister developed a perverse view and said: "Is there a more deceptive, degenerate monk than this? If he has no wife, then is it possible in this world for there to be a son whose mother and father cannot be said to live anywhere?" With that he beat the guru a few times, who fell to the ground. The minister took the prince at once to the king.

The guru made prayers day and night, and spoke these words of truth to the Three Jewels:

> Infallible Three Jewels, who dwell in the unapparent realm,
> please hear me, and with your compassion, quickly grant
>   me refuge.
> By the great compassion of the Three Jewels,
> I have found this incarnated young prince,
> a precious wish-fulfilling jewel rare in the three worlds.

However, he has been snatched away by the force of perverse
    prayers.
May he not be harmed by the torments of body and mind.
May we be together in all lives as teacher and disciple,
and may father and son be quickly reunited.

The prince was brought before King Varma, who said:

Welcome! Extraordinary youth.
You have returned, minister Triśu.
Handsome youth, son of the gods,
it is good that Triśu found you and brought you here.
Therefore, young prince, stay and be happy in the palace.

The prince spent seven days in the palace. The princess daughter of the
king was called Bhāsvarā. She was radiant and beautiful, and one day she
came to the prince and said:

Deities, gurus, and the compassionate Three Jewels,
fulfill the wishes of this maiden according to the Dharma.
Listen to me, great incarnated prince.
Turn your attention to Princess Bhāsvarā.

Like the bright sun shining in the skies above,
opens and blooms the lotus here on earth.
Prince, the mere sight of your beautiful face
turns my mind and fills me with unbearable joy.

Therefore, with an oath of love and affection,
I will never give you up.
Look on me with your net of compassion.

The prince replied:

Beautiful, alluring maiden, with the glories of youth,
Princess Bhāsvarā, listen to me.
It is true that the mighty sun befriends the lotus,
but how can a tiny star do the same?

Similarly, how could a lowly beggar such as I
possibly be a loving companion to a princess such as you?
Beautiful maiden, do not say these things.
If the king should hear, we will both be punished.

The princess replied:

Just as the tides of crested waves of the mighty ocean
always arrive on time and never vary,
the power of karmic connections made in the past
can never be halted, even by the most powerful of men.
Therefore, handsome prince, grant this desirous maiden
the fruit of her hopes and longing.

The prince thought to himself: "The love that princess has for me is without doubt brought on by the ripening of a connection made by past karma." He said to her:

This love that you have for me is without doubt
the awakening of good karma of the past.
And so, I too rejoice and am overjoyed.
Be happy, my beautiful maiden.

From then on they could not be apart for even a minute. Therefore when the time came to cast him into the lake, the king thought to himself: "My maiden loves this youth. If he were cast into the lake, it could well be the end of her life." He addressed his ministers:

Listen to what I say, ministers assembled here.
Pay attention to these words of your king.
My daughter, Princess Bhāsvarā, and this young man
cannot be apart from each other for even a minute.

Therefore, ministers, quickly seek out another youth
of dragon-year birth to cast into the lake.

The other ministers could not say anything, but the evil minister Triśu addressed the king:

Great king, do not say this.
Usually a king says things just the once.
If he says too much, the rule of law is lost
and the minds of the people will turn bad.

Therefore, in keeping with your previous command,
it would be wise to cast this youth into the lake.
Besides, his guru is a shameless, deceiving monk.
If he was not wrongfully keeping a secret wife,
how could a child exist without mother and father?

The prince thought: "This maiden loves me, and I cannot do it, but if I don't go, then someone else would be sent in my place, and that would be so sad." With the attitude of cherishing others more than himself, he addressed the ministers:

Hear me, ministers assembled here.
Listen without distraction to Siddhārtha.
This daughter of the king, Princess Bhāsvarā,
    loves me.
She holds me and will not let me go.

Tomorrow when we set off in the boat,
the ministers and we two will be together.
When the princess has fallen asleep,
I will give you a signal, and you must hold her.
For the sake of the six realms of living beings,
without hesitation, I will enter the lake.

The ministers and the people were astonished. Two Dharma ministers, Somadatta and Kīrti, stood up, made prostrations, and with tears in their eyes, said:

Hear us, supreme incarnated prince.
Siddhārtha, listen to we two ministers.
You give up any thoughts for your self,
and for others you sacrifice your precious life.

When we think of this courageous act of yours,
the hairs of our bodies tingle with faith and stand on end.
Therefore may we never be apart in all our lives.
Hold us with your great compassion, celestial prince.

THE PRINCE ENTERS THE LAKE

The king, ministers, and people boarded the boat and set off on the lake.
Day and night the princess held on to the prince and would not let go. After
a while her hand loosened its grip. The prince gave a sign to the ministers.
They held the princess while the prince with a mind of compassion leapt
into the lake.

At that time a rainbow appeared in the sky, showers of flowers fell from
the sky, the earth shook in six ways, and many other miraculous signs were
seen. The princess, held by the ministers, returned to the palace and sang
this sad song:

Oh, woe is me! This mind of mine is weaker than others!
When I think of this all, it is wearier even than my body!
By the awakening of karma, I met an incarnated prince.
After we had met, I never thought that we would part.
My dearest prince has jumped into the depths of the lake,
and this maiden of little merit is left alone on this earth.
Prince, if you have magical powers, come here now.
See the torment of sadness in this young maiden's mind.

Around that time, all the nāgas living in the lake had assembled in Upa-
nanda's palace. To the astonishment of Upananda and the other nāgas, the
prince arrived. They addressed the prince:

Listen to us, incarnated prince.
Pay attention and turn your ears this way.
In the past humans were cast into this lake,
but the suffering of their minds parting from their bodies
was an impure obstruction bringing rains of hot sands
    to our land,
and all nāgas suffered countless pain and torment.

Now, Dharma king, by the power of love and compassion,
you have come here, and beautiful melodies ring out.
There have been rains of nutmeg, muskroot.
and many other excellent nāga medicines,
because of which we nāgas are covered with joy and happiness.
Even if we die here, we will be reborn in happy realms.
And so, most kind prince and savior of living beings,
we ask that you remain with us as our guide.

The prince replied:

Hear me, great lord of the nāgas.
Upananda and all others, listen to this prince.
In order to work for the benefit of living beings,
it matters not in which land I dwell.

However, my refuge and guide, Sādhumatī,
now dwells in a state of great concern,
and so I ask you not to be resentful or jealous
but to return me this one time to the human world.

The prince told the nāgas of all the events leading to the present situation.
The nāgas rejoiced in and were astonished at the prince's deeds. They prostrated and requested:

Siddhārtha, supreme incarnation,
extraordinary treasure of excellent qualities;
from the thick clouds of your love and compassion,
bring us the rains of the vast and profound Dharma.

For three months the prince gave countless teachings on the Dharma,
beginning with the law of cause and effect. Finally, he concluded by saying:

Listen carefully, you nāga lords.
Keep in mind the essence of what I have taught.
If you truly desire everlasting happiness,
With body, speech and mind, strive in the sacred Dharma.

With your lungs, heart, and chest,
entrust yourself to the Three Jewels.
Think again and again on the transient nature of things.
The pleasures of samsara are not to be relied upon.
Regard them as you would the fire within a pile of hay.

Think on the kindness of all living beings, and meditate
    constantly
on benefiting others with love and compassion.
Without grasping to samsara and nirvana as being true,
understand their natures as forever unestablished.

Constantly recite the six-syllable mantra and so forth.
and take again and again the eight precepts and so on.
Do this and you will fulfill your desires.
Do not forget them. Hold them at the center of your being.

The nāga kings were overjoyed. They held up in their hands countless
kinds of jewels, exemplified by a wish-granting jewel the size of an egg, and
together made this prayer:

The essence of the teachings you have given us,
we will follow and practice purely.
Through your kindness the land has prospered greatly.
To repay such kindness, we offer to you these jewels.

Henceforth, we will not require that a human be cast alive
    into the lake,
and we pray that in all our lives we are cared for
constantly by the guru and his disciple.

The prince accepted the gifts and said:

I have no need for jewels, but I accept them
in order to complete your accumulation of merit.
By the power of the deities, the guru, and the Three Jewels,
may the words of truth in this prayer be fulfilled.

SIDDHĀRTHA RETURNS TO HIS GURU

The prince thought that he would again be with his guru and offered these words of truth prayer:

> By the power of my pure intention of helping others,
> may I arrive now in the presence of my guru.

He sat and closed his eyes. Immediately he was at the door of his guru's solitary hut. He spoke to his guru:

> Most kind and precious guru,
> Siddhārtha has arrived from the depths of the lake.

The guru said: "My son, to be cast into that lake, to disappear, and then to return is unheard of. You have fulfilled my dreams. What has happened?" In a state of extreme anxiety, the guru fell unconscious. The prince sprinkled water from a pot over his face and revived him. Throwing his arms around his guru's neck, he said:

> I am your disciple, Siddhārtha.
> By your kindness, I survived the lake.
> I taught the nāgas and have come to this place.
> Do not be concerned. Please be at ease.

The guru was overjoyed and said:

> Incarnated prince, welcome! Welcome!
> You who work for all beings, welcome! Welcome!
> How wonderful that you have come from the depths of the lake!
> How wonderful that you care compassionately for the six classes
>   of living beings!
> An incarnated king such as yourself is so rare in the world!
> I take joy in the knowledge that we two will not be apart!

The prince offered the wish-granting jewel and the other gems to the guru, and told him in detail of the recent events. From then on, when they sat they sat on the same seat and when they ate they ate from the same bowl, so much was their desire not to be apart.

THE PRINCE BECOMES KING

King Varma thought to himself: "Since I cast the guru's disciple into the lake, the harvests have improved, wealth has increased, illness and disease have vanished, and prosperity and happiness are as good as it could be. In gratitude I must invite him here." He spoke to the ministers:

> Listen to me, assembled ministers.
> By casting Siddhārtha, disciple of the guru, into the lake,
> harvests have improved and all manner of prosperity
>   has arrived.
> To repay such kindness, is it not good to invite him here,
> to honor him with devotion and service?

All other ministers thought it was a suitable invitation and agreed with the king. However, Triśu said:

> How can nobility repay the kindness of the subjects?
> Great king, do not be so foolish. Best to abandon this idea.

He continued by telling the king how unfitting it would be to invite the guru. However, the other ministers had agreed with the king, who then said:

> Hear me, assembled ministers.
> Pay attention. Listen to your king.
> From among you, one with faith in the Dharma,
> one who is a man of courage, should go now
> and ask this kind and precious guru
> to come soon to this king's city.

The Dharma minister Śrījvalati stood up, went down on one knee, and said to the king:

> Lord of men, and precious king,
> listen to this Dharma minister, Śrījvalati.
> Hearing these words today of the king,
> we assembled here feel nourished with joy.
> To be the messenger sent to fetch Sādhumatī
> falls on me, and so I will quickly leave.

He took with him eleven attendants and set off. Arriving at the remote hut of the guru, he stood at the entrance and addressed the guru:

> Most kind and precious guru,
> listen a while to this Dharma minister.
> Your attendant, Prince Siddhārtha, we sent into the lake.
> And since then the land has been blessed with prosperity
> and all manner of happiness and fortune has ensued.
>
> Therefore the king, his ministers, and his people
> have spoken, and in order to repay your kindness,
> I as messenger have been sent here to invite the guru.
> Please summon up your compassion and fetch
>   your horse.

The guru replied:

> Welcome! Welcome Dharma minister Śrījvalati.
> Welcome here, you eleven attendants.
> For a long time in solitude I have meditated
>   single-pointedly
> and therefore I cannot wander among people.
> But in the face of a command from the king,
> as delivered by this minister,
> I will travel to the palace of the king.
>
> However, as is the way of a monk, I must fetch my robes
> and so forth, and then I will quickly come.
> Therefore minister take your attendants and wait
> at the crossroads by the foot of this mountain.

The minister left. The guru thought to himself: "I cannot leave the boy here. If I take him and the king sees him, there is the risk that he will be seized."

"I will disguise myself as a beggar," said the prince. "I will cover my face with a cloth and come as your attendant. If the cloth has a tear in it, I can travel."

The prince dressed as a beggar and covered his face with a cloth mask. He put the guru's robes, cloak, and ritual implements on his back and they set off.

The minister asked the guru to mount his horse, to which the guru replied: "I have given up four-legged mounts and have no horse." With this he set off on foot, with the prince holding his hand in support.

The minister asked:

> Sādhumatī, hear me.
> What is the country of your attendant?
> In particular, why does he not show his face?

The guru replied:

> This young disciple of mine
> was given to me by a destitute beggar.
> Out wandering on the desolate plains,
> his face was damaged by the poison of bees.
> It has swollen and, until the wound heals,
> he wears this cloth to protect it from the sun.

They arrived at the palace of King Varma. The guru was given a seat with three layers of cushions, while the prince sat on a lower seat. Each were presented with welcoming gifts of fruit. The king requested the guru to stay for seven days, which he accepted. The guru was lavished with service and devotion. The king then addressed the guru:

> Hear me, precious guru.
> Turn your ears to this king.
> Recently we had to send your chief disciple into the lake.
> For this I beg forgiveness for any upset we have caused you.
> Since this incarnated youth entered the lake,
> this land has seen a wonderful increase in its prosperity.
> This is all arisen from the kindness of the guru,
> and to repay such kindness I have invited you here.

The guru replied:

> Excellent! Great king, ministers, and people,
> how wonderful that you repay kindness!
> This son of mine, prince Siddhārtha, is not an ordinary child.

He was the son of the king of Tāmradvīpa.
The queen, out of jealousy, had him cast into exile.

Eventually he came to be my disciple.
His story is extraordinary beyond belief.
I will tell it in detail. King and ministers, pay heed.

The guru related the story of the prince. All were amazed, and they prostrated to the guru. After four days had passed, the prince remained unrecognized. On the fifth day the guru and the prince went to the top of the palace to walk around its perimeter. At the same time Princess Bhāsvarā took a rhinoceros horn, an elephant's tusk, and the skin of an antelope to the roof and offered them to the guru. She prostrated, asked for blessing, and said:

My refuge and incomparable Dharma king
Sādhumatī, please hear this princess.
Prince Siddhārtha, who was so close to my heart,
was sent into the lake by the king and his ministers.
Whatever wicked deeds of past lives brought this about
have now been purified. Please hold me with your
    compassion.

The guru replied:

Listen one time, princess, Tārā of the Dharma.
Turn your ears in the direction of Sādhumatī.
Princess, pay careful attention to these words.
By the compassion of the guru and deities,
the karma between you and the prince is unfinished.

Just then a strong gust of wind arose and blew off the guru's hat. The prince ran to fetch it, and in doing so he hit his head, breaking the string that held the mask, and his face was revealed. The ministers assembled there exclaimed:

Welcome! Incarnated prince, this is astonishing.
How wonderful that you are here!

They prostrated to him. The king and the princess recognized him. The princess ran to him and said:

> What a great kindness! Today I have met the prince.
> Is it possible that death can come together with life?
> Is this a dream or is it for real?
> If it were real, how happy I would be.

The prince said in return:

> By the compassion of the deities and the guru,
> I am freed from the fear of losing my life.
> I returned from the land of the nāgas
> and traveled here as the attendant of my guru.

> The remaining karma has awakened
> and death has come together with life.
> Be happy, my beautiful Bhāsvarā.

King Varma and the ministers marveled at this sight. Beginning with single jewels, they made countless offerings to the guru and prince. "How did all this come about?" they asked the guru. He told the assembled crowd the story of the prince. The king, his ministers, and the people all rejoiced at the wonderful life story of the great being. They were visibly moved by great faith and bowed their heads to his feet.

The guru took from his hut the jewels offered by the nāgas and gave as gratitude gifts the wish-granting jewel to the king and one jewel to each of the ministers. The king again addressed Prince Siddhārtha:

> Great incarnation, Prince Siddhārtha,
> under the sway of ignorance and misunderstanding,
> I have disturbed the mind of the guru and brought
>   you harm.
> All the wicked deeds of body, speech, and mind
> I confess them all and ask for your forgiveness.
> May I be cared for by you and never part from you
>   in all my lives.

The guru, the prince, and the princess were each invited to sit on jeweled thrones, where they were honored and waited upon in devotion.

Then the king said to the guru: "Prince Siddhārtha is of fine body and fine family. He is possessed of the glories of great merit and is a true treasure of love and compassion. Such a person is rare in the world. My daughter too has such a strong past-life connection with the prince that they cannot be apart for a moment. I too am oppressed by the fears of old age, a characteristic of samsara. My body is bent and my senses are weak. I can no longer bear the responsibilities of the kingdom. I ask that I install the prince as my regent."

The guru said: "Mighty king of great merit, for a long time you have enjoyed a connection made by the force of prayer with this guru and his disciple. My son is an incarnation of Avalokiteśvara, and so it is truly wonderful that these thoughts arise in your mind. In thirteen days from now, during the moon's waxing, when the constellations and planets are in a harmonious arrangement, you should hold the coronation. Therefore you must give the signal to the ministers and the people to begin the preparations."

The king made many prostrations to the guru and made the following request: "I too, in order to work for the attainment of permanent happiness, wish to become a monk, and ask that the guru and I build a monastery in a mountain retreat at the head of a valley, and there I will live, striving day and night in my practice of the three aspects of the path and the Mahāmudrā."

The guru accepted the request. The king was delighted. He addressed the ministers and the people:

> Listen to me, assembled ministers.
> Do not be distracted. Hear your king.
> Above, the sun and moon in the sky shine brilliantly,
> but through the wicked deeds of Rāhu, they are darkened.
> Below, the ocean is of a depth hard to fathom,
> but when the end of the eon comes, it will be emptied.
>
> Likewise, although a king possesses every power,
> the threat of the transience of death is always there.
> Therefore as my successor I will appoint Siddhārtha,
> who is from the noble lineage of kings.

Thirteen days from now, on a day of the waxing period,
when planet and constellation are harmoniously joined,
Prince Siddhārtha will be installed on the throne of King Varma.
People and ministers, dress in your best finery, make your
　devotions,
and immerse yourselves in happiness to your heart's content.

On the day of the auspicious planetary arrangement, the prince, the guru, and the princess were seated on thrones. The king made offerings of many wish-granting jewels of both superior and ordinary kinds, whole volumes of writings bound in gold and beryl bindings and headed by the most extraordinary scriptural representations of the Buddha's speech, copious quantities of silk, and large amounts of gold and silver coins, all of which were laden upon elephants, as well as gifts of horses, buffalos, and so on. He addressed the prince:

Son of the gods who fulfills the needs of living beings,[118]
you are now crowned as the supreme regent.
Nourish your subjects with the ten virtuous ways.
Spread Dharma traditions in all directions.

The guru too spoke these words of benediction:

Buddhas of the ten directions, and in particular, lord of
　immortality,
grant Prince Siddhārtha the glory of power over his life.
Buddhas of the five families from all directions,
anoint him on the crown of his head with the vase
containing the nectar of the mind of enlightenment.

Deities and gurus, with your excellent benediction,
anoint the king on the golden throne of fearlessness,
and from this day on, may the sun of happiness shine
　in every direction.

May his subjects too be free of fear,
and with the glory of happiness of Dharma
may their desires be fulfilled and there be joy everywhere.

Prince Siddhārtha and Princess Bhāsvarā became husband and wife and began their rule over the kingdom. For many days flags were flown, conch shells blown, musical instruments were played, songs were sung, dances were performed, and so on.

A hundred ministers served the king for a hundred days, each serving for a single day. The minister Triśu thought to himself: "It is not right that the king has enthroned this beggar boy as his regent. However, this shameless monk has deceived the king with his trickery." Although he had not developed even a single moment of faith, he pretended that he had and said to the prince:

> May I too, in my succession of lives, never be apart
>   from you,
> may I always be in your presence and have the glory
>   of serving you.

The prince accepted by saying:

> From now on, in the succession of your lives,
> you will, without doubt, be the main attendant of mine.

King Varma took novice monastic ordination from the guru. Three hundred subjects also became monks. A special monastery was founded at the head of a valley and the guru, when requested to name it, called it Sukara. The law of the Dharma was tied as tight as a silken knot. The guru gave full monastic ordination to the king and the three hundred subjects. The king's Dharma name was Bhadraśrī. Each of the three hundred also received new names. The king and the other monks stayed in the monastery. The new king and his queen ruled the kingdom, which in turn flourished and prospered.

After two years had passed, King Siddhārtha addressed the ministers and his people:

> Listen to me, ministers assembled here.
> Pay attention. Hear my words.
> At this time of happiness aplenty,
> We must go to a green and pleasant forest

to enjoy ourselves and do as we please.
Prepare provisions. Make ready the horses and elephants.

The ministers replied:

In accordance with your instructions,
mighty king, we will willingly do these things.

The ministers made the necessary preparations and gathered provisions.
The king said:

Now we should wait here no longer.
King and ministers will leave for a pleasant forest.

The king and queen were in a golden carriage pulled by the finest of
horses, followed by the ministers astride the finest horses, and together they
leisurely set off. After a few days the king and his entourage came to the place
where his young brother had died. The king made prayers for a while. While
they were there, the king heard something like a human voice coming from
far away. He turned to his ministers and said:

Stay here for a while. Do not leave.
Enjoy yourselves to your heart's content.
I want to engage in some solitary contemplation
and look at the extraordinary fruit and flowers.

With these words he crept quietly away. Suddenly a frightening-looking
creature with the body of human, but covered in hair, appeared. It was carry-
ing the flesh of a deer and some fruit. It kept saying:

My dear brother, Prince Siddhārtha,
where can he be? I have his share of food.

The prince became very upset. In tears, he said:

Sole eye of compassion, brother Amogha,
where are you?
Your brother Siddhārtha is here now.

Amogha pricked up his ears. The prince kept on saying, "Your brother is here," and he ran toward Amogha. The younger brother said to himself, "It is my brother," and ran to him. They met and hugged each other. The elder brother said:

> What a wretched state my brother is in.
> Though he has attained the state of leisure
> that is the body of a human, he looks like an animal.
> Though he is a prince, he wanders alone in the forest.
> May no one else experience these things.

Amogha replied:

> Today the sun of my happiness has risen.
> I have met my dear brother in this place.

They both cried tears of joy. They returned to the spot where the ministers were waiting. His head and body were shaved, he was bathed in pure, scented mountain water, and he was fed with the five kinds of nectar. At the same time, he uttered this prayer:

> By the power of this sharp blade cutting my hair,
> may I cut all mental afflictions with the sword of wisdom.
> By partaking of this nectar endowed with the eight great tastes,
> may I constantly partake of the nectar of the mind of
>   enlightenment.

After taking the nectar, Amogha's complexion was almost as radiant as his brother's. At the spot where the young brother died, the prince built a beautiful lotus pool filled with water possessing the eight excellent qualities. He founded a monastery there and completed many other virtuous works. On the way back he gave instructions for villages to be built and so on.

He sent a messenger ahead to the palace, who told everyone the younger brother's story. The ministers and people were amazed and they hurriedly set about making preparations for a celebration. As the two brothers approached the palace, many women headed by Princess Bhāsvarā, and many men headed by the Dharma ministers Jayadhara and Ānanda, came to welcome them.[119] Around the palace flags were flown, conch shells were blown, instruments played, drums beaten, and cymbals sounded. There was singing and dancing and a huge celebration was held.

At that time the prince said:

> Listen this way, ministers assembled here.
> Pay attention for a while. Listen to me.
> By the kindness of the deities and the guru,
> my dear young brother Amogha has been
>   restored to life.
>
> At this time of joy and happiness, it is only fitting
> that my sole refuge, the precious guru Sādhumatī,
> and the great lord Bhadraśrī are invited here,
> where they can be honored and served.
> Ministers, see that this happens.

Accordingly, the ministers invited the guru and the king Bhadraśrī. They in turn were astonished at the recent events.

At that time minister Triśu thought to himself: "This deceiving monk by his trickery has installed his son as king. Not only that, he has brought his younger brother in from his wanderings, and now both of them are together. I am supreme among the ministers, but these two do not like me, and that bodes ill for me."

The former king and the two brothers were sat on high golden thrones. The guru intoned these words of benediction:

> The power of the compassion of the precious
> and infallible Three Jewels gathered as one,
> and hosts of truth-speaking sages—
> by the glorious blessing of your ability
> to nourish all that is good and virtuous,
> may these brothers enjoy all happiness here and now.
>
> Life-granting goddess Cintācakra White Tārā,
> lord of limitless life and limitless light of wisdom,[120]
> and supreme goddess of longevity Vijayā,
> grant the power of long life to these brothers.

In this land may the king and his ministers be in harmony.
May the citizens be sated with the joy and happiness
that comes from being possessed of the wealth of Dharma.
May there be an end to all strife and disharmony,
and may all places be suffused with happiness and prosperity.

With these words of benediction, great festivities followed.

The Final Battle

Minister Triśu developed perverse thoughts and joined forces with a bandit leader who had captured the region of Ganga Paṭa. When war was approaching, Prince Amogha became general and made a prayer to the god of war before setting out:

Ki ki so so! Victory to the gods!
Fierce god of war, mighty and powerful!
Crush the enemy on his neck!
Destroy the demonic hordes!

During the battle, from the enemy side minister Triśu mounted his horse and sang this song:

Offerings to you, rakṣa lord of the demons.
May the doctrine of the black demons flourish!
Listen to me, Prince Amogha.
Turn your ears to minister Triśu.

In the past I was supreme among the ministers of King Varma.
But these days he is swayed by the deception
of this monk Sādhumatī, and has crowned his beggar son,
who goes by the name of prince, king.

I, with a minister's legacy, have been humiliated.
Despair has been visited upon this minister.
An old dog shut out behind the door
has no choice but to show its teeth.
Before this day is out, a black dog will meet you.
That has been written on your skull.[121]

From my tiger-skin quiver I take one arrow.
As quick as lightning I take one arrow.
From my leopard-skin holder I take my bow,
a bow bound in wild goat skin.
I do not let loose an arrow, but a thunderbolt
straight to your heart, beggar boy! Homaya!

He pulled back an arrow. The prince turned in his saddle and avoided the
shot. He turned back to face the minister and sang this song:

Hear me, deities! I offer to the Three Jewels.
Let this angry enemy be crushed upon his neck!
Listen to me, minister Triśu.
Turn your ears to Amogha.

Your words are boastful like thunder,
and your arrows are powerless
against this dragon-like opponent.
These countless bows and arrows all around me,
today I will not use. Put them aside!

This white lasso that I hold in my hand
was miraculously created from renunciation and compassion,
and its workings are the iron ring of the mind of enlightenment
and the hook of the understanding of the no-self of phenomena.

Though the enemy of mental affliction is great,
I have no fear, and today I have no choice but to use it.
Deities and Three Jewels, by your great compassion,
today bring this enemy to defeat.
May I bring under my control this minister.

With these words he cast the white lasso. Immediately it latched itself
around the neck of the minister, and with no possibility of breaking free he
was led away. The opposing army was terrified and surrendered. The men
offered up their weapons and armor and sought refuge in the prince, who
gave them assurances they would not be harmed.

Triśu was brought before King Siddhārtha, who possessed the mind of enlightenment that repaid harm with kindness. With such an attitude he increased threefold the size of the minister's estate.

THE BROTHERS RETURN HOME

At that time Siddhārtha thought to himself: "For we two brothers death has become life. At this happy and prosperous time in this land, we should go to our parents to relieve their troubled minds." He related this to Amogha:

> Listen to me, younger brother.
> Princess Bhāsvarā, hear the words of this king.
> These days we enjoy happiness and prosperity.
> My dear young brother has returned from death.
>
> Our prayers have been answered and we live in peace.
> The people are rich with the wealth of Dharma.
> At such a time is it not right to meet and serve our kind parents?

In unison, they replied:

> Greatest of men, who nourishes his people in keeping with
>   Dharma,
> Listen a while to Amogha and Bhāsvarā.
> As the lord of the land has said, it would be excellent
> to meet with mother and father. Please do this.

The Dharma minister Śrījvalati and Triśu were installed in the palace. Gifts that included the seven types of precious gems headed by wish-granting jewels, as well as gold, silver, provisions, and so on, were gathered in copious quantities to form many elephant loads. Accompanied by thousands of ministers, and led by the Dharma ministers Jayadhara and Ānanda, they left in golden chariots.

After awhile they were seen by laborers rebuilding King Baladeva's castle. His minister went to the king:

> Hear us, precious and mighty king.
> Give your attention to these ministers.
> The renowned King Varma from a far-off land

has built many new villages close to our kingdom
and is busy making many provisions for living.
Therefore maybe he is preparing to seize our kingdom.
What do you think, mighty king?

King Baladeva replied:

Hear me, my ministers.
In the past we had great power,
but my two dear sons wandered off afar,
and now my royal lineage is close to an end.
Therefore, we are beset with suffering.
Ministers, see what is best to do.

Mother and father had not gotten over the loss of their sons and were still in despair.

The two princes quickly sent one hundred messengers to the palace of their parents. The people said that war had arrived and made other wild, exaggerated claims. Then the Dharma minister Jayadhara and four attendants went to palace and addressed the king:

Emaho! Greetings and prosperity to you!
Maharaja, listen to us ministers.
Your son and prince, Siddhārtha, with his queen
as well as his younger brother, Prince Amogha,
have come to meet again with their mother and father.
We have come in advance to give you this news.

The king thought: "How is this possible? I think Varma plans to seize my kingdom by way of this deception." He addressed the minister:

Listen to me, great minister.
Pay attention. Listen to this king.
A good few years have passed since
my young son, Siddhārtha, wandered far away.
How is it possible that he could return?

Do not take pleasure in my suffering.
The renowned King Varma from a far-off land
has desires to seize my kingdom.

The minister replied:

Great king, please pay attention.
Lend your ears to this minister.
My name is Jayadhara, and since the time
  of my father
I have been a Dharma minister.

I have long given up divisiveness, lies,
deception, and other nonvirtuous ways.
So generally how could I bring harm to other beings?
Specifically, how could I cause dissension between
  kingdoms?

Doing so would be to amass evil deeds,
and then what would it mean to be a Dharma minister?
Therefore, great king, have no fear.
Make preparations to meet your two sons.

The king was overjoyed and said:

Excellent news, Dharma minister!
What great kindness, Jayadhara!
My two dear sons, through the power of divisive calumny,
were cast out to wander in the dark forests.
With all hope of meeting gone, they were like a dream.

But now by the power of the kindness of the Three Jewels,
today father and sons will meet again!
I am so happy and my mind is full of joy.
Dharma minister, stay awhile in the palace
and enjoy yourself to your heart's content.

Listen to me, ministers assembled here.
Pay attention. Listen to King Baladeva.
I will without doubt meet my sons today.
Go and prepare the celebrations in the palace.

The ministers replied:

Lord of men, ruler of the land, your instructions are like gold.
We will carry them out to the best of our ability.

All the roads were swept. The palace was decorated with beautiful adornments. Flags were flown, conches were blown, and all manner of preparation was made.

The king and queen set up camp on a plain near the palace and spent a day there. A succession of three messengers arrived at the camp to deliver scrolls to the king. The first was delivered by the minister, his four attendants, and the messengers who had been originally sent to the palace. It contained the details of the sons going into exile and their subsequent trials and hardships. The second scroll delivered by a nobleman and his four attendants told of how Amogha died and of the guru's kindness. The third scroll delivered by a messenger described how the younger son was brought back to life, the journey to the nāga realm, ascending to the throne of King Varma, and so on.

The king and queen, and their ministers and people, were astonished at these accounts and were full of joy. Immediately the skies were filled with flags. The earth rang with the sounds of song and dance, of music, and of general enjoyment.

Although King Baladeva had not previously walked over the palace threshold, with a turquoise walking stick in his hand he announced that he was going to meet his sons and queen. Accordingly, with many ministers, he set off to welcome the princes.

At the tent of the two princes gifts were exchanged, and as soon as they had met, the king said:

Welcome! Welcome! My young son, Siddhārtha.
Welcome! Welcome! Young Amogha.
For your aged father, today the sun of happiness has arisen.
How wonderful that today I have met with my two dear sons.

Were you not weary and beset by hardship
in your far-off wanderings, my two young princes?
Alone without companions in the faraway forests,
were you not tormented by hunger and thirst?

Nevertheless, without hindrance to your life,
we meet again and your father's wishes are fulfilled.
What great kindness, lord of men, ruler of the land.

With great joy they hugged each other and vowed not to be apart again.
The elder son addressed his father:

Most kind and gracious father,
turn your attention to these princes.
Today under the joyous sun of perfect auspiciousness
father and sons have met again.

When we were wandering through far-off lands,
were you, great father, healthy in body?
Was the palace and the kingdom happy and prosperous?
Were the people nourished with happiness in keeping
    with Dharma?

That we did not succumb to obstacles to our lives
was because of the kindness of that great being Sādhumatī,
whose supreme compassion cared for us,
and I was installed upon the throne of King Varma.

I fulfilled the wishes of that Dharma king Bhadraśrī,
and cared for the people through the ways of Dharma.
Then I quickly left to meet again with my kind parents.
Now we have met, my mind is very content.

The family stayed in the encampment for three days, and the whole area
took on the form of the eight auspicious signs.

Queen Padminī came and made huge offerings of special jewels, quartz,
aquamarine, emeralds, sapphires, the seven types of gems, horses, elephants,
silks, and so on. She prostrated and said:

Great Dharma king, entity of every buddha.
You work for the welfare of others, please hear me.
I was lost in the darkness of unknowing ignorance,
and therefore I did not see your excellent qualities.

Under the power of pride, perverse in thought and deed,
I carried out wicked deeds, such as casting you out of the
     kingdom.
From my heart I am full of remorse, and by confessing
     to you,
I ask that you, great treasure of compassion, forgive me.
Look upon the wretched situation of this aged mother
     and father.

In tears, she took the feet of the prince to her head in reverence.
Siddhārtha addressed her:

Listen to me, my great queen, Padminī.
Hear what Siddhārtha has to say.
In the recognition of all beings as one's parents,
what room is there for grudges and revenge?

Being free from concepts of attachment and anger,
How can there be closeness and distance?
You of great kindness, whatever you have done,
has become an aid to the practice of Dharma.

Do not despair, my great mother, Padminī.
Rest your mind and be at peace.

With these words the king, queen, ministers, and people were filled with
faith. The ministers and people were welcomed into Mangalkūṭa Palace.
There the king, who was of an advanced age and longed to enter the practice
of Dharma, decided to install the younger brother as king. Calling the min-
isters and people together, he announced:

Listen here, my assembled ministers.
Pay attention to the words of your king.

Though we may be endowed with youth and good family,
the Buddha has said that once born, death will surely come.

Accordingly, the vigor of youth of this king has gone,
and he is now oppressed with the fears of old age.
The color in his face has faded, his hair and whiskers are white.
Wrinkles cover his face and his eyes are sunken.

Now the fears of death are approaching.
For the sake of my future life I wish to pursue
    Dharma practice.
My younger son, the precious Amogha,
I will install as king. Ministers, make preparations.

In keeping with the instructions of the king, everything was organized
well and on an auspicious day the younger brother, Prince Amogha, was
installed on the throne. His father said:

Prince Amogha, of my royal lineage,
I enthrone you as the Dharma king,
lord of the land, to nourish the two traditions
here in this country of Tāmradvīpa.

Always rule by the law of the ten virtuous ways.
Honor those of noble and decent behavior.
Punish those who live in ignoble and wicked ways.
Constantly take the Three Jewels to the crown of your head.
Bring the people to happiness through the path of Dharma.

Amogha in reply proclaimed:

Although in my heart I long to pursue the Dharma,
I cannot go against the words of my father,
and therefore will become the king and ruler of Tāmradvīpa.

Ministers and people, follow these practices.
Constantly, with firm faith and devotion,
venerate and make offerings to the Three Jewels.

With the six-syllable mantra, and so forth,
make efforts in the practice of the sacred Dharma.

In brief, follow even the smallest of virtuous ways.
Do not pursue evil acts. Guard your minds well from these.
If you should do the opposite and devote yourself
to thievery, cheating and harmful ways in thought and deed,
the force of the law of the realm will fall upon you.
Do not deviate from these practices.
Follow them, all of you.

With this proclamation he was enthroned as king.

The two brothers made both kingdoms as one and ruled with one queen between them. The number of subjects increased and they ruled over two-thirds of the world. Minister Triśu was made commander of the army, and all the minor kingdoms of the four directions naturally fell under their auspices.

One time Prince Siddhārtha thought to himself: "I must invite my kind guru and King Bhadraśrī to the palace." He called the Dharma ministers Śrījvalati and Somadatta and said:

Listen to me, Dharma minister Śrījvalati.
Pay attention to the king, Somadatta.
Now that mother, father, and sons have been reunited,
and the whole land is nourished with goodness and happiness,
I will invite my most kind guru Sādhumatī,
and former king Bhadraśrī, to honor and serve them.
You two, go quickly and invite them.

The two ministers accordingly traveled to the monastery where the guru lived, and said to the king and the guru:

Hear us, give us your attention, noble lord.
Sādhumatī, listen to us two for awhile.
The Dharma king Siddhārtha and younger brother Amogha
set out for Tāmradvīpa to meet again with their parents.
Once reunited, King Baladeva offered his throne to the
    younger brother,
whereby Amogha brought the citizens to happiness.

King Siddhārtha has sent us as messengers to invite
our supreme guru, the great father Bhadraśrī, and all the monks.
Please do all you can to come to the palace.

The guru replied:

Welcome! Welcome! Dharma minister Śrījvalati.
Welcome! Welcome! Minister Somadatta.
Are you not weary after your journey here?
Are the two princes in the best of health?

Having brought the land of Tāmradvīpa to joy,
how excellent that you come here to invite us.
In your company we will proceed to the palace.

Prince Siddhārtha waited at the palace gate to greet them. As soon as the
guru dismounted, the prince prostrated to him said:

Welcome! Welcome! Precious guru.
Welcome! Welcome! King Bhadraśrī.
Has your meditative concentration increased in your
    solitary retreat?
Are all the conducive conditions for your Dharma
    practice in place?
Look upon us with your great love.
What kindness that you grace the palace today.

The guru replied:

Hear me this one time, Prince Siddhārtha.
Have you reunited with your father and is all well?
As is the king's wish, I have come to Tāmradvīpa.
We will strive to speak of the Dharma in this Dharma land.

The precious guru with King Bhadraśrī and thousands of monks; the
soothsaying woman Kanti; the reader of signs Bhadra with many brahmans;

the Dharma ministers Jayadhara, Ānanda, Somadatta, Kīrti; and many thousands of other ministers were treated to a sumptuous celebration.

The minister Triśu still harbored bad views and thought to himself: "This deceiving guru has used his power to take over two kingdoms for his two sons. Now there is no way I can overcome the guru and the princes. Therefore it would be best if I fled to another land." Taking a hundred bandits with him, he left the kingdom. But on a narrow mountain path, part of the mountain collapsed and they were all killed.

For three months and twenty days the guru gave teachings, primarily on cause and effect. He related the astonishing story of Prince Siddhārtha, and at the end gave the following prophecies:

Hear me this one time, ministers assembled here.
Pay careful attention, turn your ears this way.
At this time, in this virtuous land of Tāmradvīpa,
we have come together and made many pure prayers.
By the power of these prayers, at a time in the future,
the following events will occur.

In the era of troubles when the lifespan will be one hundred
    years,
the great guide of gods and men, the teacher Gautama,
    will appear.
At that time, north of here there will be a far-off snowy land,
populated by many wild animals, ghosts, and cannibals.

In that land, gradually the number of humans will increase,
and the teachings and doctrine of the Buddha will flourish
    and prosper.
This sacred place will be the supreme realm for you to tame
your disciples in harmony with their dispositions.

In the beginning, you will take three or seven births,
in all of which you will hold the title of emperor,
and you will establish the tradition of the sacred Dharma.
At that time, Amogha will be reborn as my son.

Sometimes I will be your father, but mostly in the form
    of a guru.

You will spread the teachings of the Buddha in a hundred
    directions
and accomplish the needs and wishes of many beings.
The demons and cannibals will be tamed and the land blessed.
A hundred doors will be opened for the Buddha's teachings
    in general,
and specifically for the ultimate excellent path, the great
    secret path
for attaining the state of enlightenment in a single life.

Then, a few human years later,
a demonic incarnation, the result of evil prayers,
possessing the name of Lang, will appear.
The Buddha's teachings, like blood mixed with milk,
will fade until only the name remains.

At that time, in the noble land of India,
I will be the fully ordained vajra-holding monk.
Prince Siddhārtha, in that northern land of snow,
you will be a celibate layman known as Jaya.

Again you will invite me from Central India to Tibet.
The victory standards of the teachings of the Buddha in general,
and those of the Kadampa tradition with its seven deities and
    doctrines,
will be raised and flown in a hundred directions.

Amogha, at that time you will be known as Prajñā.[122]
You will devote yourself to me and assist greatly
in the propagation of the sacred Dharma.
We three will cleanse the teachings of the Buddha.

Therefore, at the end of the degenerate era of troubles,
Siddhārtha and I will be inseparably guru and disciple.
Young Amogha, you will take the form of a patron king,

and with faith and devotion toward the teachings,
you will serve and venerate us.

For you fortunate ones gathered here,
some will be mothers and fathers, others will be disciples,
others patrons or monks who follow the three trainings.

All of you, on seeing or hearing this guru and his disciple,
will shut the door to the lower realms of suffering,
and having cast far away the seeds of evil deeds,
will reach the firm shore of the path that leads to
the states of enlightenment of the three vehicles.
Rejoice, you ministers and people gathered here!

Having given these reassuring prophecies, Sādhumatī, Bhadraśrī, and the many thousands of monks returned to their solitary hermitage.

The two brothers continued to nurture their respective kingdoms with the principles of Dharma. Countless minor kingdoms from the four directions were gathered into their fold by influence of their power and glory. All their subjects held to their heads in reverence the good law of the ten virtues. As a result, there was not even a trace of the hardship that comes from causing harm to one another. Everyone enjoyed the prosperity and happiness of being endowed with the wealth of Dharma. The happiness was such that the pride of the gods who lived in the Realm of Thirty-Three would have been helplessly swept away.

* * *

This has been *The Sun That Brings on the Smile of the Lotus of Faith*, the secret biography of the two young brothers Amogha and Siddhārtha.

7. The Story of Rūpasūrya (Sukyi Nyima)

Namo Ārya Lokeśvaraya.

THIS STORY OF RŪPASŪRYA, the daughter of a sage, follows those stories of the oral tradition. In this tradition are found the *Parable of the Birds*, *Vetala Stories*, *The Story of Monkey God Hanuman*, *The Story of King Pañcamātā*, *The Story of Manoharā*, *Treatise of the Old Fish*, and *Treatise of Bearded Sugrīva*. Also, many such stories are found in the Vinaya and Sutra teachings.

The story of the brahman girl Rūpasūrya, whose message is to urge those of great desire to renounce samsara, was translated into Tibetan long ago by Lotsāwa Vairocana and She'u Lotsāwa. This version follows the translation of She'u Lotsāwa.

Those who listen to stories from the oral tradition should first make three pledges: not to knowingly follow improper behavior, to listen with full attention, and not to distort what you have heard.

RŪPASŪRYA IS BROUGHT TO THE PALACE TO BECOME QUEEN

In India, in the city of Cittamaṭi, there lived a king called Candrasena, or Dawa Depön in Tibetan. His queen was Devaśrī, or Lhai Palmo in Tibetan. Their elder son was Candrasiṃha, or Dawa Sengé in Tibetan. The younger son was Candrakumāra, or Dawa Shönu in Tibetan.

As for his power and wealth: he ruled over 3,600,000 towns and cities; possessed inconceivable wealth, including three hundred and sixty treasuries full of jewels; owned a white parasol with a golden handle; a meditative-concentration begging bowl that produced whatever he wished for; a golden-colored horse that could fly; the powerful *airāvata*[123] elephant whose trunk was as red as vermillion; a wish-fulfilling cow; a buffalo that produced much milk; a speaking parrot; a *phalka* pig;[124] a dog that would bite and

A large crowd of spectators watches *Rūpasūrya* in the round, Tibet, 1940s.

not let go; a magic lasso; a garden that was always in bloom; a wise minister called Negi; the son of a low-caste hunter; and much more.

One day King Candrasena said to his elder son, Candrasiṃha: "Alas! A bird with broken wings, a tiger without stripes, a snow lion without snow, a fish thrown out of the lake, and a king without a royal dynasty—I am like these examples. Therefore it is time to hand over the subjects of Cittamaṭi to you. I am old and you are young. Rule over the kingdom!"

The son replied:

At first, the kingdom was ruled by grandfather and uncle,
then it was reigned over by father and brother.
Now the kingdom has been entrusted to me.

Father and mother, of the two ways of ruling a kingdom,
Buddhist and non-Buddhist, please give me advice
on which is the best.

His father replied: "As you have said, there are two ways to rule a king-dom—the Buddhist and the non-Buddhist. If you rule according to the Buddhist way, you will gain peace and happiness now and reap a fruitful result in future lives. If you follow the non-Buddhist way, you will quickly gain pow-ers and be able to perform magical feats. You will have might, a great army,

A TIPA production of *Rūpasūrya* in Dharamsala, 1977.

and all necessary conditions will be met. We are in the age of degeneration and it is difficult to tame living beings by peaceful methods. Therefore you should rely on wrathful means, practice the deity Maheśvara,[125] and so for a while follow the non-Buddhist path. In the end, however, you should make prayers and arrangements to rule by the Buddhist way." With these words he handed over power to his son Candrasiṃha.

One day King Candrasiṃha loaded many provisions, including jewels, on elephants headed by the powerful *airāvata* elephant whose trunk was as red as vermillion, horses, buffaloes, and various kinds of chariots. He also gathered fresh meat, warm blood, moist hides, and many thousands of animals to be offered in a flesh-and-blood sacrifice. The king himself was seated on a black *meghavegin*[126] horse with a retinue of thousands, including the minister Negi leading the horsemen and the son of a low-caste hunter.

To the east of the city was a terrifying place called the Forest of Poisonous Snakes. In that forest was a self-emanated stone statue of the non-Buddhist god Maheśvara, which did not touch the ground but hovered in space. It was to this place the king was traveling in order to make offerings and seek blessings. On the road they came across a low-caste beautiful girl washing her hair. While doing this, adorned with ornaments, she performed a joyful dance, made beautiful movements, and sang sweet songs. She was intoxicating to look at. With the arrow of the sideways glance loaded on the bow of a sweet smile, the king's mind went in search of this deer-like girl. He said to minister Negi:

Negi, what is the name of this girl's father?
What is the name of her mother?
What is her own name?
What is her brahman family?
What is her wealth and her retinue?

The minister realized that the king had become infatuated with this low-class girl, and replied:

Of this beguiling and beautiful girl,
her father's name I do not know,
her mother's name I do not know.
Her caste and family are that of commoners.
Her wealth and retinue can be understood likewise.

He took hold of the king's reins and led him to the statue of Maheśvara. There the king and his entourage set up vast offerings to the god. The warm blood of various animals was used for a bathing ritual. Fresh meat was added to the offerings. There were human skins complete with arms and legs, canopies with intestines for guttering, and so on. Countless offering rituals were performed in order to please Maheśvara, and much effort was put into bathing and cleansing. After they had received initiation, blessings, and siddhis, they returned home.

Once more they came across the beautiful girl on the road. She had washed herself clean. A beautiful smile played on her face as she danced as an offering to the king. This girl who had smitten the king had anointed her body with sandalwood powder, her cheeks were rouged, and the mandala of her face was blessed with a welcoming white-toothed smile. She was adorned with ornaments that far outstripped those of the gods, and she stood there a hundred times more beautiful than before. She came before the king, who took her by his right hand and said:

A face possessed of the splendor of a full moon,
holding the rabbit of a brilliant white-tooth smile;[127]
girl who radiates a thousand cooling moonbeams,
will you not shine to open up the nighttime flowers
in my white lotus pleasure grove?

Minister Negi immediately intervened:

> Great king, please listen to me!
> Yellow brass may be of a color beautiful,
> but it is no match for the yellow of gold.
> False blue turquoise is of a color beautiful,
> but it is no match for the blue of turquoise.
> A low-caste maiden may be very beautiful,
> but she is not fit to be queen for a king.

The king replied to his minister:

> Without climbing the high snowy mountain,
> how will you ever see the white snow lioness?
> Without venturing into the thick forest,
> how will you ever see the striped tiger?

> Without plunging to the depths of the ocean,
> how will you ever find the wish-fulfilling jewel?
> Without mixing with the talk of common people,
> how will you ever find your beloved companion?

Before the minister had time to plead with him again, the king pulled the maiden onto his horse and they rode off to Cittamaṭi. Two days' journey from the palace, the hunter's son was sent ahead to deliver a message to the father and mother telling them to prepare a celebration. The hunter's son delivered the message accordingly. Mother and father and subjects were delighted. Everybody washed their hair and dressed in the best clothes and finest ornaments. All the junctions and crossroads of the city were filled with dancers and singers as they waited in welcome. Finally, the king and his bride reached the palace. There the talking parrot perched itself on the back of the king's golden throne, and in an exaggerated manner said:

> Great king, hear what I say!
> This beautiful queen of yours,
> she is the daughter of which king?

What is the name of her mother and father?
Of what family and caste is she?
What dowry and gifts did she bring?
What share of her inheritance does she have?

Of the qualities possessed by a noble and wise woman,
such as serving her lord above, caring for her subjects below,
increasing wealth and progeny on her own level,
how many of these qualities does she have?

Of the skills possessed by a noble and wise woman,
such as the preparation of food, and so on,
how many does she know?

The king looked ashamed and said: "I do not know these things. But she is good-looking, beautiful, astonishing, and very attractive. These qualities she has. In particular, it was because I was smitten by her that I have enthroned her as my queen."

The parrot was a little unhappy at this reply. Bobbing his head three times, he said to the king:

Ha, ha! Precious king!
This astonishing, astonishing maiden of astonishing appearance,
a ruinous, ruinous woman who will bring you to ruin.
The beautiful appearance of this beautiful maiden!
Is the king deluded or is this parrot babbling?

The king looked angrily at the parrot and said:

Parrot, do not speak so much.
Though clever in speaking, you talk nonsense.
Though you know a lot, you are of the race of ignorance.
Though intelligent, you belong to the animal realm.

I have pursued beauty.
As for caste, family, and lineage,
entourage, retinue, and wealth,
I have five hundred queens with all of these,

but they are no match for this maiden.
Therefore, parrot, go to your place.

The parrot looked out of the corner of his eyes, and in a lowered voice
said humbly:

Ah! Precious king!
An axe with a poor handle may be sharp, but will be
    uncomfortable.
A bow poorly made may be hard, but it will break.
A low-caste maiden may be beautiful, but she will
    deceive.

I too was only jesting.
This year I make clairvoyant predictions.
Next year I will suffer regret.
If I am fault, would be better that I leave.

The parrot flew off to its home under the eaves by the golden victory stan-
dard on the roof of the temple.

Along with five-hundred maidens from outlying kingdoms, the low-caste
maiden was crowned queen. The king was seated on a golden throne, the
low-caste maiden on a turquoise throne, and the other queens were seated
on thrones of silver, copper, iron, bronze, and so on. There they unabashedly
indulged themselves in the five pleasures of the senses. In particular, the low-
caste maiden enjoyed herself without restraint.

During the celebrations, around midnight, a wild pig came into the king's
garden. It ate all the old flowers, ruined the new ones, dug up the earth, and
covered the whole area in pig dung. The person in charge of the garden was
the hunter's son. He thought to himself: "In the past, no deer or wild animal
would dare damage the garden, and now a wild pig has done this."

Taking his bow and arrow he went in search of the pig. As dawn
approached, he was closing in on the pig when suddenly a musk deer leapt
out of nearby bushes. The hunter thought to himself: "Killing the pig would
only yield its meat. But to kill this deer would yield meat and hide." There-
fore he left the exhausted pig and pursued the fresh-legged deer. The say-
ing "Increased anger becomes avarice, like the hunter chasing the wild pig"
comes from this story.

He pursued the deer for half a day. Suddenly a stag leapt out of nearby woods. The hunter reflected: "If I kill the deer, its meat is not much, and apart from flesh and hide, I will get nothing else. If I kill this stag, I get meat, hide, and its antlers." Therefore he abandoned the tired deer and set off in pursuit of the fresh-legged stag. The saying "With the body of a beggar of great desire, like the hunter in pursuit of the stag" comes from this story.

He chased the stag until the sun went down. As nightfall descended, the stag disappeared into a thick and seemingly endless forest. As the saying goes:

> The first task not completed,
> the second cannot be accomplished.
> The first lies unattained,
> the second is given up.

Think about this advice and its examples. Householders who continually take up with masters and then abandon them, and those who enter the Dharma and continually take up with gurus and deities and then abandon them, are just like the hunter who pursued the wild pig.

The hunter became lost in the thick forest and could not find his way. He did not know the direction to Cittamaṭi, and he had strayed from the path. Now he could not find it. He was hungry and thirsty, and all alone. That night he made a bed from leaves and ate some fruit. In fear of robbers and wild animals, he put his bow and arrows by his head and laid down under a pine tree.

The next morning he awoke, and when the sun rose he was still unsure of which way to go. Feeling hungry, he went off to pick some fruit. He came across a four-sided spring of pure water endowed with the eight excellent qualities of water, on which were the recent impressions of a pot and a ladle. The hunter thought to himself: "By the appearance of this spring there is certainly someone living around here." Therefore he sat and waited.

Before long a beautiful maiden appeared. She was astonishing to look at. On her right cheek was the design of a golden vajra, on her left the design of a silver lotus. On her forehead was the form of a precious jewel, at the tip of her nose was the design of a vermillion sun, and on her chin the design of a crystal moon. Her teeth were as white and perfect as a conch, and from her mouth came the sweet aroma of sandalwood. Her body was white with a reddish hue. She was unlike the daughter of any human and resembled the daughter of a god. In her right hand she carried a ladle and in her left a pot, and she had come to fetch water.

The hunter thought to himself: "If I offer this maiden as a bride to the king, he will be delighted and I too will be rewarded with many gifts." He approached the maiden:

> Maiden, what is your father's name?
> What is your mother called?
> What is your own name?
> What is your family and your lineage?
> What servants and wealth do you possess?

> I am from the city of Cittamaṭi.
> In that city lives the king father Candrasena.
> His elder son is Candrasiṃha.
> Would it not be desirable to be his bride?

The maiden did not answer and did not look his way. Instead she quickly filled her pot and, like a deer that had seen a hunter, hurried away. The hunter thought to himself: "She will definitely return tomorrow to collect water. Today I did not mention the king's wealth and power." That evening he ate more fruit and stayed in the same place. The next day the maiden came again. The hunter's son again asked her: "Maiden, do you have a master or not? If not, wouldn't it make sense to become the queen of King Candrasiṃha? He rules over 3,600,000 towns and cities, headed by the city of Cittamaṭi, and possesses inconceivable wealth. He has a white parasol with a golden handle, a golden-colored horse that can fly, the powerful *airāvata* elephant whose trunk is as red as vermillion, a wish-fulfilling cow, a buffalo that produces much milk, a meditative-concentration begging bowl, a magic lasso, a *phalka* pig, a dog that bites and will not let go, a garden that is always in bloom, and much more. Will you not become his queen?"

The maiden filled up the pot even quicker than she did before and, without looking at the hunter or speaking, ran off like a deer that had seen a hunter. He thought to himself: "I do not even know the way home. There is nothing I can do except to ask this maiden which road to take. She may be human, she may be nonhuman. Whatever she is, she will surely know the area." Again he ate fruit and stayed in the same place.

The next day, the maiden again came to fetch water. The hunter said to her: "Maiden, for a few days now I have been asking you questions, but you have chosen not to give a single word in reply. Are you human or not? Are you a yakṣa? Are you the mistress of this area? Are you a Dharma practitioner? Whatever you are, I am lost in the midst of this thick forest and I cannot find my way. Help me find the way home and show the path. Also, do you have effective protection against robbers, wild animals, and so on?"

The maiden showed him the direction and the path. She also consecrated and empowered with mantras a handful of kuśa grass and gave it to him. She told the hunter not to tell anyone there was such a maiden living in the forest. The hunter thought to himself: "With my ugly face and dark skin, she probably has no liking for me in these ragged clothes. I will bring the king here. If he comes he might take her as queen. At that time he will need protection against robbers and animals."

Again he asked the maiden: "Maiden, you give me only this much protection. If I lose it on the path, my life will be in great danger. Please give me a little more protection." Again the maiden gathered a handful of kuśa grass, consecrated and empowered it, and gave it to the hunter. With this protection, he covered the day-and-a-half journey very quickly.

As he approached the city of Cittamaṭi, his sons had called out to their neighbors and relatives, saying: "Our father has been away hunting deer for five days. He must have gathered much meat and hide. He will definitely give you some. Help us bring in the meat." They filled a large copper vessel in the kitchen and fanned the flames with bellows.

Seeing the smoke, the hunter thought: "I have not eaten human food for five days. They will have cooked food when I arrive." And he ran hungrily toward his home. Seeing him his family thought: "Our father must have killed many deer, and not being able to carry them all he has come to call us." They went out to greet him and accompany him back to the house. "Shall we help you bring back the meat?" they asked. "Or do we need help from friends and relatives? If that is not enough, we will have to request the king for labor."

The hunter replied: "Where is the meat? I see no sign of it. You have no heart. I have been five days without proper food. Did you not think to send me a single provision?"

The sons became annoyed and agitated. "How useless it is to be born to someone like you! It would be easier to be a servant. It is not only you who went without food. What about us?" In great anger some of them threw dust at him, while others beat him with tree branches and chased him. As the saying goes, "An old man hopes for hot food. An old woman hopes for the leftovers."

The hunter thought to himself: "If I go to the king and tell him all that happened in the forest, he will reward me with gifts and, more important, he will give me something to eat." The king was protected by seven guard posts arranged from outer to inner. The hunter went to the outmost guard post and said to the sentry: "Take me to the king. I have the gift of good news to offer him."

The sentry replied: "It is not possible for someone like you to bear good news. Besides, you are of a low caste and contaminated. We would be punished if we let you through." The second sentry heard this and passed it on to the third. Soon all seven had heard it. In turn it was heard by the king, who said to the seventh sentry: "What did the hunter say?"

"He has some good news to offer to the king," replied the sentry. "He is hungry and has probably come to beg food. I don't think he has any good news."

The king replied: "If someone who runs over mountains and through the valleys has no good news, then what good news do you have, who spend all your time at the gate? Bring the hunter in."

The sentries washed the dirt and grime off the hunter's body, rubbed sandalwood paste into his body, and dressed him in clean clothes. He was then taken to the king. "What good news do you have?" asked the king.

"For good news to be expressed, the mouth must be empowered with the auspicious substances of food and drink," replied the hunter. In response he was given molasses, rice beer, the three white foods, the three sweet foods, and so on. Then the king was seated on a gold throne, the hunter on a turquoise throne, and the five hundred queens each on their own thrones.

"Now," said the king, "if you have some good news to tell me, say it."

The hunter thought to himself: "I if tell everything honestly, it will upset the five hundred queens, especially the low-caste queen, and I will be in danger of severe punishment. Therefore I must communicate what I have to say in a hidden way." He said to the king:

> Great king, hear what I say!
> I ventured into the deep forest,
> and there I heard this wonderful news.

Within the great king's mighty palace,
there are a thousand astonishing springs,
in which are seen to swim golden fish.
To the side of each of these springs
is a cavity with a copper opening.

If you place a metal rivet in each cavity,
the jewel that fulfills every wish
will come into the king's hands.
The mighty king's life will be long,
the kingdom will spread and flourish,
and the people will be happy and content.

Do you understand, you of great mind?
Do you hear this news, son of the gods?

The five hundred queens were delighted at this news. Some gave the hunter their uneaten food. Some gave him their drink. Others removed some of their garments and ornaments and presented them to him. They said of all the good news they had heard, the news of the hunter was the best. And so without understanding its meaning they talked happily among themselves. The king, however, sat there in reflection without saying anything. He thought to himself: "When he spoke about a thousand springs in my palace, he was probably talking about the left and right eyes of the five hundred queens. The golden fish in these springs is probably their yellow-eyed avarice. The copper cavities are their slender, silk-like ears. Putting a rivet in these cavities means ensuring they do not hear. The wish-fulfilling jewel coming into my hand means that a supreme queen will be mine."

He knew he had to question the hunter closely without the queens hearing. He gathered the queens together and in their midst said to them: "If this precious jewel is coming to our palace, it is very important that we all are washed and clean. Therefore, you five hundred queens take your water pots and bathing stands to your bathing places. I too will go and bathe. Hunter, prepare my towel, water pots, bathing stand, and other requirements." The queens at once collected their items and went to the bathing pools.

The king gave his bathing items to the hunter and they went off to the king's bathing pool. The king said to the hunter: "If you have something to say, say it." The hunter told the king everything, from the wild pig coming into the king's garden and eating the flowers up to the account of his own family refusing to give him any food.

In particular, he told the king of the beautiful maiden he had come across in the forest: "She was extraordinary to look at. On her right cheek was the design of a golden vajra, on her left the design of a silver lotus. On her forehead was the form of a precious jewel, at the tip of her nose was the design of a vermillion sun, and on her chin the design of a crystal moon. Her teeth were as white as a conch. Her white body had a reddish hue. From her mouth came the sweet aroma of the finest sandalwood. Her conduct was peaceful and disciplined. She was unlike the daughter of any human and resembled the daughter of a god. All the excellent qualities of the present queens as one could not match a fraction of the physical qualities of this maiden, not to mention her qualities as a perfectly beautiful woman. If the king were to take her as his queen, all his people would rejoice."

At this news the king reacted with a myriad of expressions and his face broke out in a radiant smile. He said to the hunter: "Clever hunter, if such a woman exists, we must go right now. If we don't, she might move elsewhere, or another king might take her for his own, and that would not be good. We will go now!"

The hunter said: "Great king, how can it be right for master and servant to just get up and go like this? You should adorn yourself with ornaments. I too will dress appropriately. To guard you from bandits, thieves, and wild animals, tie this protection around your neck. I will prepare provisions. Isn't this best?"

"One's appearance is changed by clothes. Women are seduced by adornments, people are nourished by food," said the king. "So let it be done." The king dressed in clothes made of the finest Benares cotton. On the front at the heart was embossed the auspicious endless knot. The upper garments were ablaze with precious jewels and adorned with the eight auspicious symbols. The garments were smooth to the touch and light to wear. In the winter they withstood the cold. In the summer months they protected the wearer from the heat. In the world they were priceless.

Countless gorgeous ornaments adorned the king. Around his neck he wore a necklace beautifully constructed of different varieties of celestial sapphire. On his arms and hands he wore jeweled bracelets and rings of gold, silver, pearls, lapis, and coral. He gave all these ornaments to the hunter and they set off on their journey.

That evening master and servant slept by the spring in the forest. In the morning at sunrise the hunter said to the king: "I will go in search of fruit.

Great king, please stay here. The maiden will come to fetch water, and you must speak to her."

The hunter left and soon after, from the southwestern part of the woods, the maiden appeared as the hunter predicted. Their desire to look at her was insatiable. On her right cheek was the design of a golden vajra, on her left the design of a silver lotus. On her forehead was the form of a precious jewel, at the tip of her nose was the design of a vermillion sun, and on her chin the design of a crystal moon. Her teeth were as white as a conch. Her white body had a reddish hue. From her mouth came the sweet aroma of the finest sandalwood.

These were the innate ornaments of the maiden. She wore no outer ornaments, such as bracelets or ankle bracelets, but was still astonishing to gaze upon. She walked gracefully, her manner was peaceful and disciplined. When you looked at her, your eyes were transfixed. When you smelled her, you were held by her aroma. When you listened to her, your ears were captivated. When you touched her, your body was captivated. In her right hand she carried a ladle, in her left a pot. Such a one had come to fetch water. The king spoke to her:

> Beautiful young woman, listen to me.
> Fetching wood and water is the work of servants.
> Giving counsel, eating, and drinking is the work of masters.
> I am a king who reigns over a kingdom.
> Like iron filings to a magnet,
> will you not follow me?

He continued: "I am Candrasiṃha, the elder son of King Candrasena of the city of Cittamaṭi. Will you not be my queen? I rule over 3,600,000 towns and cities and have a white parasol with a golden handle, a golden-colored horse that can fly, the powerful *airāvata* elephant whose trunk is as red as vermillion, a buffalo that produces a lot of milk, a wish-fulfilling cow, a meditative-concentration begging bowl that produces whatever is wished for, a magic lasso, a *phalka* pig, a dog that bites and does not let go, a garden that is always in bloom, and much more."

The maiden did not look in the king's direction and said not a single word. She quickly filled her water pot and, like a deer who had spotted a hunter, ran off. Then the hunter returned. "What did the maiden say?" he asked.

"Whatever I said, she said nothing in reply," said the king. "Moreover, she did not even look at me."

The hunter thought to himself: "I am the one who brought the king to this deserted place. If we are not able to bring this maiden back, then all my efforts will have been in vain." He said to the king:

> Precious king, if you travel without haste, you will arrive.
> If you eat appropriately, your body will be healthy.
> If you speak gently, everyone will understand.
> After a long time, even iron will break naturally.[128]
> With the tiny steps of a bird you will reach the
>   mountain pass.

"That is true," said the king. "Tomorrow we will see if we get an answer. If not, we will have to return home." That night they stayed in the same place.

The next morning the maiden arrived as before. The king saw her qualities as being a hundred times more than the day before. He came to a firm decision that if he did not gain this maiden, even if he died, he would not return home. He thought to himself: "Yesterday she was not happy that I spoke about my power, subjects, and so on. Now if I praise her qualities instead, she might answer me." He addressed the maiden:

> Indra, the asura gods, the kiṃnara spirits,
> Brahma, Viṣṇu, and Maheśvara,
> none of them can match your excellent form.

> Īśvara, Lakṣmī, Vedī, and the goddess Uma,
> you are all their beauty as one.
> Daughter of a god, a nāga, or a gandharva,
> in this human world you have no equal.

> I have fallen under your spell.
> Could you possibly abandon me now?

The maiden showed a little dislike for the king's flattering words. She filled her water pot quicker than before and disappeared like a deer who had seen a hunter.

The hunter arrived and asked the king what the maiden had said today. "She ran away, as she did yesterday," he replied. The hunter said:

> Best is not to begin.
> But once begun, to give up is not right.
> Like a drawing carved in stone,
> not to give up, even at the cost of life,
> is the best course of action.

The king said nothing. The next morning the maiden arrived as usual. The king thought to himself: "Probably this type of maiden likes to hear amorous talk. If I speak to her amorously, maybe I will get an answer." He addressed her:

> When I see the sun-disc of your face,
> the lotus grove of my body starts to shake.
> The blue lotus of my channel knot is opened,
> and the stamens of desire bloom.
> If you enjoy it, will you not take it in your hand?

As she did on previous days, the maiden did not look at the king or give him a reply but rushed off like a deer that had seen a hunter approaching. When the hunter arrived and asked the king what the maiden had said, the king replied: "Today also she said nothing."

The hunter thought to himself: "This maiden is hard to win over. Even if the king does win her over, she will be his queen, but if he has no power over her, all this hardship will be of little consequence." He said to the king:

> Great king, please hear me.
> A mountain without snow may be high,
> but it is no place for the snow lion.
> A clump of thorny trees may be dense,
> but it is no place for the tiger to crouch.
>
> An ocean devoid of jewels may be deep,
> but it is no place for the nāga kings.
> The solitude of the forest may be pleasant,

but it no place for a king to stay.
Lord of men, are you not discouraged?

But the king was attracted only to the maiden and gave no answer to the hunter.

The next day the maiden came to the spring again. The king thought to himself: "Yesterday I spoke gently to the maiden, and still she saw it fit not to reply. Women are timid, and so if I speak wrathfully to her, maybe she will give me an answer." He addressed the maiden:

Young woman, posing with your seductive charms,
proud of your fulsome youth and beauty,
if you have no desire for peaceful ways,
if you have no liking for sweet words,
I am of great power, a storm at the end of time.

You are a weak and helpless child of a honey bee.
I can blow you away in an instant.
Are you frightened, young maiden?

The maiden only half-filled the pot and ran off like an animal who had seen a butcher. The hunter arrived. "What did she say today?" he asked. "She again said nothing," replied the king. The hunter addressed the king:

Kyai! Great king, please hear me.
The best tastes are known by the tongue.
The depth of the ocean is known by the fish.
The inner thinking of this maiden is known by traveling.
Let us follow her to where she has gone.

"That is right," said the king, and master and servant set off in pursuit of the maiden. They arrived at a place about five hundred bow spans away. The land was as flat as the palm of a hand and stretched out for a league in all directions. It was surrounded on all sides by a bounded perimeter of fruit trees, including walnut, pear, pomegranate, mango, grape, and *visti* fruit, and by medicinal plants and trees, such as myrobalan, figwort, and so on. Inside this area there were no malicious sounds of jackals and fierce animals.

Instead, musk deer, red deer, saiga deer, spotted deer, wild goats, gazelles, and other types of peaceful horned animals played gently and happily among themselves. Birds such as peacocks, cuckoos, cranes, ducks, and kalaviṅgas sang their sweet songs. The ground was covered with flowers that came up to the ankle. Their colors were white, red, blue, yellow, and violet, and included blue poppies, lotuses, and more. Incense trees such as eaglewood, acacia, white and red sandalwood, and so on adorned the four directions.

In the middle of this area the ground rose up to about a bow span in height. On it was a flat moon-like stone two bow spans in length. Upon this stone were two grass huts erected like two tents, side by side. In one was a brahman meditator engaged in practice. In the other was the maiden, also engaged in practice. When the king and the hunter reached the door of the huts, the meditator and the maiden had washed the five parts of the body and were now sitting on kuśa grass seats in the eightfold posture of Vairocana, engaged in deep meditation. The hunter said to the king:

> Hear me, great king.
> If she is not won by sweet talk,
> I will show a wrathful side,
> and like a hawk snatches a bird,
> we will take her away in an instant.
> Is that not right to do, lord of men?

The king replied: "How can such a thought be right? First of all, they are engaged in religious practice and the karmic ripening would be heavy. Second, they are religious and monastics, and such a deed would harm the kingdom. Third, as the saying goes, 'If you want something important, you have to be patient.' Also it is said, 'Even if you are hungry, you do not eat the food of an oath-breaker. Even though you are cold, you do not wear clothes made from a black yak's hair.'"

The hunter replied:

> Great king, hear my words.
> I do not understand the nature of a river.
> When an ox crosses it, its back is not visible.
> When a duck crosses it, its feet are submerged.

I do not understand the nature of a king.
When he lives in the palace, he finds fault with the soft seats
and does not partake of the sweet foods.
When he stays in this solitary forest,
sitting on a seat of leaves from the pomegranate tree,
he is attracted to the taste of fruit.
Why is this, son of the gods?

The king said nothing. That night they stayed in that place. The next morning the maiden left to fetch water. The king took hold of her and said:

Beautiful and seductive maiden,
no matter how many questions I ask of you,
you give no answer at all.
Not even a single glance do you give me.
Now I have thrown my life away.
Is this the way of a Dharma practitioner?

The maiden trembled and in great fear said: "Great king do not lose your life for my sake. I will not come to be your queen. To know the reason why, ask my father, the great meditator. Now I am going to bring fruit for him. When I return, great king, come to the meditator." With these words she left.

After a short while she returned with a bowl of fruit and took it to the meditator. The king made three prostrations to the meditator, offered him a gold coin, and sat crouched before him. The meditator took the fruit from the bowl and divided it into four. One portion he offered to the guru and the Three Jewels with the words "*Vajra pūja megha.*" The second share he offered to himself with the words "*A la la hoḥ.*" The third portion he consecrated with the words "*Oṃ āh hūṃ,*" and placed it on a stone mound outside for the birds and deer. He consecrated the fourth portion with the words "*Tha ra thi,*" and offered it to the king.

The king addressed the meditator: "I have something to ask of you. If you grant it, I will eat this fruit. If not, I will not eat it."

The meditator replied: "If it does not pose any danger to my life, then ask."

The king continued: "I am Candrasiṃha, the elder son of Candrasena, king of the city of Cittamaṭi. You must give me your daughter."

The meditator replied:

> Great king, what are you saying?
> You may well be of a high caste,
> but you are making the mistake of a youth.
>
> She is not suitable to become a queen.
> She is not of royal descent, but of poor beginnings.
> Living here in this isolated forest,
> she knows no work apart from picking fruit.
>
> She is the child of that slothful animal, the deer.
> How could such a low-caste maiden
> maintain and preserve your royal domain?
> Best you return home, great king.

The king replied:

> Great meditator, do not say this. Listen to me.
> I am looking at the beautiful form of this maiden.
> As for queens of noble lineage, family, and name,
> I have five hundred, but they bring me no joy.
>
> I have come here to ask for your daughter.
> If you will not give her, I will kill myself.
> If I die, my mother and father will grieve and die,
> as will my younger brother, Candrakumāra.
>
> All the people and cattle of the 3,600,000 towns,
> headed by the city of Cittamaṭi, will have to be gathered
> in order to perform the ritual of dedicating the merits.
> In particular, minister Negi, this hunter's son,
> and many more will be overcome with suffering.
>
> The suffering will be beyond imagination,
> and does not the root cause of all this grief
> lie with your daughter?
> Think whether this contradicts your Dharma vows or not.

The meditator replied: "If it is come to that, it will be difficult not to give her to you. My daughter has taken refuge in the Three Jewels and therefore follows the Buddhist path. You have taken refuge in Īśvara and therefore follow the non-Buddhist path. As you both have separate objects of refuge, it will be difficult for your power to increase and for your subjects to be happy. Great king, can you also go for refuge to the Three Jewels and maintain the ten virtues? If you promise to do so, I will give you my daughter."

The king promised to do this. In the presence of the meditator, he committed to the precepts of refuge and bodhicitta and took the vows of a chaste layman. From then on the king pledged to abandon the non-Buddhist path and rule according to Buddhist principles.

The meditator called the maiden to him. "Maiden, you are an indispensable crutch for this frail body, but there is no choice but for you to become the queen of this king. If you do not, he has decided to kill himself. If this king were to die, the grief would kill his mother and father and all those close to him. In order to perform their dedication of merit ceremonies, everybody from the 3,600,000 towns, headed by the city of Cittamaṭi, would have to be gathered together. In particular, the minister Negi and the hunter's son would be tormented by grief, and the root of all these bad deeds is found in you. I am a Dharma practitioner who must avoid bad deeds, and therefore, by all means you must go.

"The purpose of practicing the Dharma is to benefit others. Therefore, as queen to this king, treat the people and those around you as your own children. I have dedicated the life and body of this old man for the benefit of sentient beings. Now you must go and do the same."

At these words the maiden fell unconscious. Her father sprinkled sandalwood water on her heart and she recovered consciousness. She stood up and performed the prostrations from the seven-limb ritual. Going down on both knees, she placed her hands together and addressed the meditator:

> What is this? What are you saying, precious guru?
> "Practice giving without avarice," you teach.
> But with a king's wealth, aren't you bringing me to avarice?
>
> "Make your morality firm and without pretense," you teach.
> But aren't you giving me away to be the wife of a lustful king?

"Meditate on patience as the response to harm," you teach.
But won't anger increase in the pit of desire and resentment?

"Develop enthusiasm for the ways of virtue," you teach.
But aren't you casting me into the swamp of idleness?

"Develop a meditative concentration without distraction,"
    you teach.
But won't distraction increase in the midst of the busy life?

"Rely on the lamp that dispels the darkness of ignorance,"
    you teach.
But aren't you placing me in the hole of darkest confusion?

"If you are attached to home life, there can be no Dharma,"
    you teach.
But by putting me in the palace, are you not casting me
    in prison?

"There is so much suffering in the lower realms," you teach.
But aren't you throwing me onto the millstone of hell?

Her father, the meditator, replied:

Clever maiden of humble mind, listen to me.
Intelligent maiden of innocent thought, listen to me.
Experienced maiden of little learning, listen to me.
In all these matters I am knowledgeable.

Using the coffers of a wealthy king,
you can engage in the practice of giving.
In a body that has abandoned morality,
you can guard morality with your mind.

Even though you indulge in idle behavior,
you can take joy in the ways of virtue.
Though there may be no affection from those close,
you can still meditate on patience for your enemies.

Though you have no place for meditative concentration,
the mind can always watch itself.
If by looking you do not see,
you can always look until you see.

Freed from object to look at and from the act of looking,
this is the thinking of this meditator.

From such desires are born the lotus stalks of the buddhas.
In the palace look after the six types of beings like your
    children.
When various suffering beset you,
take on the sufferings of others as your burden.
Do not complain about the responsibilities you have.
Dedicate all good you do for the sake of others.

The maiden said: "It would not be right for me to go against the word of my father. If by all means I have to go, then, great king, allow me first to serve my father for three years."

The king replied: "I cannot even leave it for a single day."

"Then put it off for three months," she pleaded.

But the king refused even that. The meditator addressed the king: "In order to fulfill the wishes of my daughter, let her stay with me for three days, and then she will leave."

The king agreed to this. The three days that the maiden spent with the meditator felt like three years to the king. At night his heart felt as dry as parched grain.

In those three days the meditator gave the maiden profound Dharma instructions by way of the ten virtuous and ten nonvirtuous ways, and advice that brings benefit to worldly beings. In particular, he gave her a pearl rosary of a hundred and one beads that had been a special object in his meditation, saying: "Maiden, in this time of degeneration, living beings love slander and divisiveness. The powers of the black forces, the spirit Pehar, and others, are strong. In particular, the female kind are prone to much talking and are not of powerful minds, and so are in great danger of hindrance and obstruction. Never be apart from this protection. If you are with this rosary at all time, no spirit of any kind will find any opportunity to attack you. Do not show it to anyone. Do not show it to your beloved king, or even to your own sons and daughters." He performed the initiation and blessing and gave her the rosary.

After the three days had passed, the king, his queen, and their entourage set off for the city of Cittamaṭi. Her father and meditator accompanied the party for a distance of five hundred bow spans. The maiden made farewell prostrations every seven steps, and finally said to him:

> Three Jewels, guides of the three worlds,
> Avalokiteśvara, protector of the three realms,
> my guru, master of the three bodies,
> I bow to you with body, speech, and mind.

> When the six classes of beings from the three worlds
> are tormented with the sicknesses of the three poisons,
> be the doctor who cures them with the three trainings.
> For this maiden at all moments of all three times,
> grant me the blessings of the Three Jewels.

The guru pledged to do this. Taking a handful of powdered incense flowers, he scattered them over the departing party and uttered these words:

> By the truth of the precious Three Jewels,
> by the truth of the two accumulations perfected
>   by the buddhas,
> by the truth of the infallible law of cause and effect,
> by the truth of the unchanging reality of suchness,
> by the truth of the sages who speak words of truth,
> and by the power of my pure intentions,
> may the king rule righteously over his kingdom,
> may his people be blessed with prosperity and happiness,
> and may this maiden's wishes and thoughts come
>   to fulfillment.

> May she accomplish completely every virtuous act.
> May she be blessed with the fortune of walking the path
>   to freedom.
> May she be granted the fortune of fortunes.

May she be granted in all ways the fortune of the
    unchanging Dharma.
May she have the fortune of her wishes being realized
    in the Dharma.

The party made prostrations to the meditator and touched his feet with
their heads. They carried his advice in their minds as they set out for the city
of Cittamaṭi. The maiden had left her heart behind in the forest, and with
her mind longing for her father, she made prostrations every seven steps and
uttered a verse of praise at each.

The meditator too was sad to see her go. He climbed to the top of a dry
tree to watch them as they left. His sadness caused him to shed many tears.
As he was so old, his vital winds and his mind were both weak, and these two
weaknesses combined to cause him to fall from the tree and die.

At that moment the skies in all directions became filled with rainbows
and light. Rains of flowers fell, the sounds of music were heard, and the earth
shook. Moreover, his remains produced countless relics and images. Among
them was a thumb-sized image of Avalokiteśvara and a container full of
musk that was probably taken to the god realms.

Meanwhile, in the city of Cittamaṭi, King Candrasena and his people
were grieving the loss of the elder son, Candrasiṃha. Bird's nests formed on
top of the palace, mouse nests were found below the palace, and all the door-
ways were infested with lice.[129] The king and his people had no wish to live
and were close to death.

Headed by the minister Negi, a party of a hundred wise ministers accom-
panied by thousands of soldiers scoured the countryside in all directions
searching for master and servant, but found nothing. Not a trace of them
was seen and no report of their whereabouts was heard. The ministers were
all plunged into grief. Minister Negi in particular had great affection for
the king, and the king held the minister close to his heart. With his strong
yearning for the king, he addressed the other ministers:

Three Jewels, who are our place of refuge!
Son of the gods and incomparable refuge,
sole refuge for us and for all your people,
moon that dispels the darkness of the four continents,
you are not to be found in the blue skies of existence.

Have you been taken by impermanence, the demon
   of death?

Snow lion, king of the beasts of prey in the snowy heights,
you are not to be seen in the cool, snowy mountains.
Have you been struck by the rock of the deceiving rabbit?

I think of you again and again, great king.
Like a bird for its eggs, I yearn for you.
Like a fish without water, I yearn for you.
Like a camel who has lost its calf, I yearn for you.

This longing is unbearable, my heart aches.
In such sadness, I have no wish to return.
All of you return to your homes.
Serve your master. See to the welfare of the people.

The ministers and the soldiers returned home. Negi stood alone in the
forest uttering long, grief-stricken cries of, "My king, my king!" His strength
was sapped, his mouth and nose became dry, and his sight grew weak. In so
much pain, he thought to himself: "Rather than suffer so much, it would
better that I end my life." He climbed to the top of a dry tree, placed a rope
around his neck, and prepared to jump. Suddenly he heard the murmur of
voices in the uninhabited woods. He cried out three times. Immediately, the
hunter arrived. The minister cried out:

Whether you are a god, a nāga, a yakṣa, or a kiṃnara—
Have you seen my beloved king?
If you have not seen my dear king,
do not stay here while I end my life.

The hunter seized the minister by the hand, saying: "Negi, do not do this.
The king with his queen is coming."

Negi said: "I am so happy, I could cry." Climbing down from the tree, he
began to cry and his eyes glistened with tears. After a while he regained his
composure. The hunter said to him: "Now go to the city of Cittamaṭi and
tell them the news. Dispel the grief of the mother and father, and ask them

to prepare a great festival and celebration. I will go and attend the king and his queen."

Minister Negi did what the hunter requested. The crossroads and junctions of the city were beautifully festooned with parasols, victory standards, banners, fluttering silk ribbons, tassels, flags, bags of incense powder, and so on. The ground was sprinkled with aloe, incense, Singhalese sandalwood, and so on. Handsome young men and beautiful young women moved playfully through the crowds singing, dancing, and making music.

With this welcome, the brahman maiden Rūpasūrya was enthroned as queen to King Candrasimha. Immediately birds such as the kalaviṅga broke into beautiful song. Fruit trees suddenly bore perfect fruit. Newly sprouting flowers all bloomed at once. Grain grew where no seeds had been planted. Many such extraordinary signs were witnessed all over the land. The people all experienced a truly wonderful happiness.

* * *

This has been the chapter on Rūpasūrya being brought to the palace to become queen.

Separation Brought on by Slander

King Candrasimha set out a code of ethics based on the ten virtues. He sent out messengers to the vassal kingdoms to explain this code. He beat the great drum of ethics on the ground. He flew the flags of ethics in the skies above and blew the conch shell of ethics in the spaces between the earth and the skies. The ministers and the people gathered and were treated to a festival of food and drink and gifts of clothes and jewelry.

The king announced that from this time onward the royal code of ethics for those living under the king's rule was that the physical acts of killing, taking what was not given, and improper sexual conduct were to be abandoned. The Three Jewels were to be worshipped and circumambulated. Effort was to be put into constructing images of the body, speech, and mind of buddhas. Contravention of these laws would result in severe punishments—eyes would be plucked out and knee joints severed. Therefore the laws should be followed carefully.

The verbal acts of lying, slander, harsh words, and idle gossip were to be abandoned. The scriptures were to be read, effort would go into recitation, and, in particular, it was important that the six-syllable mantra was repeated. Failure to comply with this law would result in harsh punishments—the face would be cut, the tongue cut out, the eyes removed, and so on. Therefore the law should be observed carefully.

The mental acts of avarice, hostility, and wrong views were to be abandoned. The mind of enlightenment was to be cultivated at all times by way of the four immeasurable states of mind. Those who broke these laws would be punished with death or with exile in remote lands. Adultery would be punished by cutting off the perpetrator's nose. Robbery was to be punished with fines two or eight times the amount stolen. Causing division between friends would result in amputation of the limbs.

In all, the king devised a hundred and one punishments, by which all fighting and trouble ceased among the people and peace and prosperity reigned.

Through great deeds, such as constructing temples and images of the body, speech, and mind of the buddhas, serving the monastics, giving to the poor, and so on, the king served the doctrine of the Buddha well. However, he had not conquered the demon of mental afflictions. In particular, in the early part of his life he had worshipped Īśvara, the non-Buddhist god, and had offered him by way of sacrifice the flesh and blood of many thousands of animals. As a result, the ripening effects of those deeds would occur in this very life. This chapter tells of how that came about.

The Dharma protector, King Candrasiṃha, and brahman Rūpasūrya sat on a golden throne and turquoise throne, respectively, exchanging words of the Dharma and enjoying drinks that produced an untainted bliss. As they did so, light passed between them. The radiance of the king fell upon the queen, and the radiance of the queen fell upon the king. The palace became transparent, like a building made of crystal. Looking from the outside, the inside was visible. Looking from the inside, the outside was visible.

The king was so attached to Rūpasūrya that he did not even glance at the five hundred queens headed by the low-caste queen. This made them very unhappy. The low-caste queen in particular had become someone whose heart had been snatched away by a hawk. In her retinue there was woman called Gandhabhadrā who had the power to eat the raw flesh of Rūpasūrya. She knew how to create illusions and to play tricks before the eyes. She had great supernatural powers and was learned in the use of mantra and magic substances. She acted only on evil thoughts. She came to the low-caste queen and said: "Great queen, you sit alone without your retinue. Are you unhappy? I will take on your immediate and other tasks."

The low-caste queen replied:

> In the midst of our firmament of stars,
> sits the moon, full in all its glory.
> For three times five days it increased.
> At dawn after fourteen whole days,
> the moon was eclipsed by the sun.

> Therefore would it not be right to
> entrust oneself to Maharishi Vishnu for guidance?
> The sage would then receive offerings.

Gandhabhadrā thought to herself: "I understand what she is saying. The firmament of stars refers to her and the queens. The full moon is the King Candrasiṃha. 'For three times five days it increased' refers to the fifteen waxing days of the moon. In talking of how the moon was eclipsed by the sun after fourteen whole days, the 'sun' is Rūpasūrya.[130] 'Entrusting oneself to Maharishi Vishnu for guidance' refers to me. 'Receiving offerings' means that if I could get rid of Rūpasūrya, I would be well rewarded."

Gandhabhadrā said to the queen: "Great queen, what you say is true. In the past the king had great affection for you and the five hundred queens. On top of that, he had special affection for you. Even if you pierced his eye, he would feel no pain. Now, since Rūpasūrya has arrived, none of you even catch his eye. He does not even see the palace he lives in. What you all say is true. But it will not be difficult for me to destroy her. You and the queens should not worry."

Gandhabhadrā was skilled in music and dance. She brought lutes, flutes, clay drums, and many other musical instruments to the entrance of the king's palace. There she played sweet music, acted out delightful scenes, and performed joyful dances. The king's perception was hindered by his ripened karma, and his head was turned somewhat by this show. "Ah! Gandhabhadrā is skilled in music and dance," he said. He called her inside and asked her to lift the spirits of Rūpasūrya.

Gandhabhadrā offered songs and dances to the king and queen, bringing much comfort to Rūpasūrya. In the evening when the sun went down, Gandhabhadrā managed to feed thirty-two intoxicating and stupefying substances to the king and his retinue. After this, she went to the home of the low-caste queen and said: "In the middle of the night I will get rid of Rūpasūrya. As gratitude you must grant me whatever I ask." And the two women continued in gleeful conversation.

As the middle of the night approached, Gandhabhadrā took a rope three bow spans in length and a gold knife and went to the palace. There she found the king and his retinue happily spending the night engaged in Dharma conversations and being entertained with song and dance. She thought to herself: "In the past just the smell and luster of these black substances would be enough to put people to sleep for three days and nights. Now that I have administered them, not only are they not in a state of stupefaction but they have not even taken a wink of sleep. Is this the blessing of Rūpasūrya? She has power, it seems. Is she a siddha? Maybe she is a yakṣa? Or a daughter of Brahma or Īśvara? Does she have some powerful protection? Whatever the answer, I must think about this." She returned to the home of the low-caste queen and explained what had happened the previous night.

The low-caste queen said: "Now, using divination, a prognostic mirror, and prophetic calculations, I must see what kind of woman this Rūpasūrya is." She laid out a mirror that revealed hidden calculations and spread out divining pebbles. In her hand she took a top-knot arrow tied with ribbons that liberates upon seeing. Using divination techniques from China and India, such as those of the sixty yearly houses, she made her calculations. She also used cord divination, mirror divination, and many more. All divinations were in agreement that Rūpasūrya was in possession of a powerful protection far superior than any invisibility stick, and that as long as she was not parted from it, all the armies from the four directions and the demons and their kind could not harm her.

The next day the low-caste queen spoke with Gandhabhadrā. She again went to the palace with her musical instruments. "Gandhabhadrā is skilled in music and dance. Come in and entertain Rūpasūrya," said the king.

Gandhabhadrā sang and danced for the couple. When she had finished she sat by Rūpasūrya and talked with her in a very friendly and affectionate manner. In particular, she gave Rūpasūrya much seemingly heartfelt advice about caring for her subjects, serving the king, and giving orders to the outer and inner ministers. Rūpasūrya, being young and, in particular, being a woman, thought: "Her words are so true." In return, she happily engaged in relaxed conversation with Gandhabhadrā and served her drinks of sweet ale and other sweet drinks.

The next day Gandhabhadrā went to the palace as before. The king called her in and asked her to sing and dance to lift the spirits of Rūpasūrya. After the performance, Gandhabhadrā said to the queen: "Ruling a kingdom in this degenerate age is difficult. You cannot speak from the heart to your children. You should not speak harshly to your enemies. Don't praise those close to you. Don't sell your complaints to your subjects. In particular, here you have the attention of the king and are surrounded constantly by an entourage, and there is a danger that others will come to the king and attempt to break this apart with slander. Therefore you must take care, as your body is very important. Moreover, since you arrived here, the five hundred queens, headed by the low-caste queen, have had no opportunity to be with the king. They do not even cross the palace threshold. In the past, even if they pierced the king's eye, he would not feel it. So now they find this situation unbearable. There is a danger that they will poison your food or bribe some official to secretly kill you. You must examine your food well. Most important, do not remain alone without a companion. This I tell to you. Please do not repeat it to the king, ministers, or anyone else."

Rūpasūrya replied: "Ah, Gandhabhadrā, I have no truer friend than you. Not even my parents who gave birth to me could give me such loving advice. Such kindness is greater than that of my mother and father who bore me."

Gandhabhadrā thought to herself: "In a short time it seems that I will have her." She said to the queen:

> Listen to me, my queen.
> For the five hundred queens,
> headed by the low-caste queen,
> you are like dust in their eyes,
> and they suffer as if fire were in their hearts,
> or that their very hearts had been torn out.
>
> There is a danger that they will summon a tantrika
> to perform rituals of suppression, curses,
> casting of tormas, and so forth. You must be careful.
> We of the female race are of poor and simple minds.
> Take this to mind and think about it deeply.

To avert these dangers, make offerings to the Three Jewels.
Request a good guru for initiation and transmissions,
and it is very important to wear upon your body
implements of protection such as the protection that
    guards merit,
the protection of invisibility, and so on.

Rūpasūrya replied: "Others, as you say, are like that. For protection against evil acts my father, the great meditator, has given me a powerful protection, which cannot be overcome by any human or nonhuman. Will that suffice?"

Gandhabhadrā thought to herself: "Now I have cast her under my power." And she rejoiced at such a thought. Outwardly, she showed complete respect for the queen, and said: "Last night I had auspicious dreams. They pertain to hearing these words today. Please grant me the blessing of this protection."

Rūpasūrya replied: "In other circumstances I would show it to you. My father, the meditator, told me not to show this special protection to anyone—not to the king who is so close to me, not even to my flesh and blood children, and I have promised to do this. Do not be upset."

Gandhabhadrā said: "I prostrate to the great meditator. Your father is a great source of blessing and of advanced insight. It is said that if you understand celestial Dharma you understand worldly Dharma as an aside. Therefore what the great meditator said was true. If you show it to the king, not only will he have power over all the ministers and all the people, but he will have power over you. Therefore there is the possibility that he may seize it from you. If you show it to your sons and daughters, they will gain their parents' wealth, and so there is the possibility that they will take it from you. I will not seize it from you. I will not gain it by theft. I will not take it and give it away. I would not dare tell anyone the properties of this protection. Please show it to me. Give me its blessing. It is my heart's desire."

Rūpasūrya thought that this was all very true. "It is very important not to tell anyone about it," she said. Gandhabhadrā vowed she would not, and with this Rūpasūrya showed her the protection. Gandhabhadrā took the pearl rosary in her hand. Tapping it three times on her head she said: "May I receive blessing by way of the enlightened body." Placing it three times at her throat, she said: "May I receive blessing by way of the enlightened speech." Pressing it three times at her heart, she said: "May I receive blessing by way of the enlightened mind." Tapping it three times under her arm, she uttered:

"May I receive blessing by way of the enlightened body, speech mind, qualities, and activities." In her mind she cursed: "In particular, may I receive blessings to fulfill all my wishes." She ran the rosary through her fingers, looked intensely at the color, shape, and size of the beads, and so on, and handed it back to Rūpasūrya, thanking her profusely.

She returned to the home of the low-caste queen. As it is said:

> A murderer disguised as a child
> will destroy a brave warrior.
> A deceiver who speaks sincerely
> will bring the wise to a vulgar level.

Gandhabhadrā said to the low-caste queen: "You are in charge of the king's treasury. Go there and bring me the types of pearl you find. Rūpasūrya has an extraordinary consecrated pearl rosary. First we must fool her."

The low-caste queen ran off as if her head were on fire, striding over the longer steps and jumping down the shorter. Coming to the king's treasury, she gathered seven bowls of pearls and returned. Gandhabhadrā took pearls from the bowls and made a rosary exactly like that of Rūpasūrya. Placing it under her arm, she engaged in wicked conversations with the low-caste queen.

Once more Gandhabhadrā brought musical instruments to the palace and performed. "You are skilled in music and dance," said the king. "Come inside and lift the spirits of Rūpasūrya." Again she entertained the king and queen, and once again she sat down by Rūpasūrya, where she engaged in beguiling talk that brought pleasure to the queen. In particular, she said: "Your guru is indeed one of great blessing. Last night I had a very auspicious dream:

> I dreamt that the sun and moon arose within me.
> I dreamt that I drank the ocean in a gulp.
> I dreamt that I ate the mountains as food.
> I dreamt that I threaded the stars as a rosary.

Rūpasūrya was hindered by obstruction and made no attempt to analyze the dream. She considered Gandhabhadrā's dream to be honest and not a lie. She said: "Your dream is very auspicious. My father, the meditator, is a yogi with great powers, a veritable Avalokiteśvara, it is said." She talked a lot about his excellent qualities.

Gandhabhadrā said: "Yes, yes! To him I go for refuge. Please give me the blessing again today. I too have boundless reverence for your father, the great meditator. I have made a prayer to be able to meet him."

Rūpasūrya thought to herself: "It has been said that Gandhabhadrā was hostile to the Dharma. Now this devotion she has developed must be a sign that the blessings of the Three Jewels have entered her. Why shouldn't she have faith in the Dharma?" She again gave the pearl rosary to Gandhabhadrā.

Gandhabhadrā was very pleased and, like before, made a show of blessing her head, throat, heart, and under her arm. As she did the last of these, she exchanged it for the rosary she and the low-caste queen had made after their wicked conversations the night before. This she handed back to Rūpasūrya, and said: "Oh queen, I hand you back your rosary undamaged and unchanged. You are of the ruling class and your words carry great authority. Do not say later that yesterday when you gave me the rosary I handed it back to you incomplete in some way." With this she left and bounded joyfully over the steps, hurrying back to the low-caste queen.

Through the celestial realms it reverberated:

> Such an intelligent one as this
> has not remained within her guru's command.
> Giving her heart and mind to this enemy
> is the result of being born a woman.

If the dream of Gandhabhadrā is examined, it can be seen that "the sun and moon arose within me" is a sign that the she has taken over the king and queen. "I drank the ocean in a gulp" portends that the happiness and prosperity of the people will be on the wane. "I ate the mountains as food" refers to the destruction of the king's treasury. "I threaded the stars as a rosary" indicates that she will inflict misery on the ministers. This the brahman soothsayers had understood and discussed in other lands.

Gandhabhadrā told the low-caste queen: "Now we have in our hands her powerful protection. Soon all your desires will be fulfilled." This made the queen very happy.

Once more Gandhabhadrā went and performed at the palace. "Gandhabhadrā, come and lift Rūpasūrya's spirits." Again she performed songs and dances for the couple. Afterward she sat with Rūpasūrya and spoke of things that gladdened the queen's heart. When the sun had set, she plied the king and queen, and their retinue, with thirty-two intoxicating and stupefying black substances, and then returned to the home of the low-caste queen.

She took a rope and a knife and returned to the palace in the middle of the night. The king and his retinue were like lifeless corpses, completely unconscious in sleep. She went to the powerful *airāvata* elephant whose trunk was as red as vermillion, and which was draped in golden lacework, and killed it. She took the body inside the palace. There she placed its upper torso on the right side of the sleeping queen, its lower abdomen on her left side, and its innards by her head. She made it so that blood was dripping from the queen's mouth and then returned to the low-caste queen's home.

The next morning at dawn the king awoke. The queen had not awoken, and so the king went to her. There he saw his beloved elephant in a scene that resembled a cannibal's palace. He was frightened and alarmed. He thought to himself: "The great meditator himself said she was not the daughter of a human. Is she a yakṣa demon? A cannibal? Maybe she is a flesh-eating piśāca. Having her as a companion will harm my royal lineage and the people will be brought to ruin." He took his sword from its sheath and went to cut her throat, when suddenly the speaking parrot appeared before the king:

> Great king, please hear me.
> Every act should be considered before it is done.
> It is not right to perform deeds without consideration,
> as taught by the story of the ox keeper and the crow.

"So, tell the story of the ox keeper and the crow," said the king. The parrot replied: "Great king, do not stand. Please sit. Put your sword back in its sheath, and I will explain."

The king agreed and sat down. The parrot continued:

> There once was an ox keeper
> who looked after many oxen,
> and one day an ox was missing
> and he set off in search of it.

> He did not find it but instead
> became hungry, thirsty, and exhausted.
> Nearby, water was dripping down a crevice.
> "I must gather this in a palm leaf and drink it," he thought.

When the leaf was filled, a crow suddenly appeared
and with the beating of its wings scattered the water.

Again he gathered the water, and again the same event occurred.
He became angry and struck out with a stick.
It hit the crow on the head and the bird died.

"What is happening here?" wondered the keeper.
He looked at the spilled water and saw
that all the creatures around it had died.
"What is this? I do not know," he said.

Searching for the source of the water,
he saw a sandalwood tree further up the valley,
around which was coiled a sleeping poisonous snake,
from whose mouth was dripping the water.

Though full of regret, there was nothing he could do.
A good deed had been repaid with bad.
What is this? I do not know.

The king said: "This is true." He went to the bedside of Rūpasūrya and
said: "Rūpasūrya, you are in a deep sleep. You are probably dreaming. Wake
up." He pulled her up by her right hand. She awoke and said: "Great king, I
was in a deep sleep. I was unconscious and had no dreams."

In the middle of the next day Gandhabhadrā again performed songs and
dances. "Gandhabhadrā is skilled in music and dance. Come inside and lift
the spirits of Rūpasūrya," said the king.

Once more Gandhabhadrā performed, and that evening she plied the
king and his retinue with forty-two intoxicating and stupefying black sub-
stances before returning to the home of the low-caste queen. Toward the
middle of the night she took a rope and a knife and went to the cemetery.
There she took a corpse and carried it to the palace. The king and his entire
retinue were sleeping like wild boar drunk on honey beer. From their throats
came the sound of snoring and from their mouths came heavy breathing.
She carried the corpse to the bedside of Rūpasūrya and cut it up. She placed
the upper part on the right side of the sleeping Rūpasūrya, the lower part

on her left side, and the innards piled up by her head. She made it so blood was coming from Rūpasūrya's mouth. Then she returned to the home of the low-caste queen.

The next day at sunrise, the king awoke before his retinue. He went to the bedside of Rūpasūrya, where he saw the butchered body. The torso was on her right side, the lower part on her left, and the innards were piled up by her head. Blood was coming from her mouth. The king was angry. He took his sword from its sheath and prepared to strike her. The talking parrot suddenly appeared by his side:

> Great king, please hear me.
> Every act should be considered before it is done.
> It is not right to perform deeds without consideration,
> as taught by the story of the brahman and the mongoose.

"So, tell the story of the brahman and the mongoose," said the king.
The parrot replied: "Great king, please sit down. Put your sword back in its sheath." The king agreed and sat down. The parrot continued:

> In the great city of Kapilavastu,
> there lived a brahman weaver woman.
> One day she thought, "I must fetch some water."
> She had a child but no one to watch over it.
> Up to then she would entrust the child to another,
> but at that time there was no one to be seen.
>
> Running here and there, she found no one
> except a mongoose, known in Sanskrit as *nakula,*
> and in Tibetan as *semo takchung*.[131]
>
> Turning to this creature, she said:
> "Until I return from fetching water, watch over
>   this child
> and I will give you a reward."
> Taking her pot, she went to fetch water.
> The mongoose placed the child at the foot of a tree
> and climbed to its top, where he kept his watch.

After a while two fire-breathing snakes appeared.
The mongoose thought to himself:
"This young human child is a piece of flesh cut
    from another.
To entrust it to an animal such as me,
is not to entrust a child, but to entrust a life.
I must honor this entrustment."
He jumped down upon the snakes,
bit their throats, and killed them.

He then went off and met the brahman mother.
She thought to herself: "This mongoose has blood
    on its mouth.
These creatures like to kill. It has killed my son."
She hit the mongoose with an iron ladle,
and the animal died there and then.

Returning home she saw her son
sleeping safely under the tree.
She was full of regret, but what could she do?
A good deed had been repaid with bad.

"This is true," said the king. He cleaned up the mess in the room and
went to Rūpasūrya: "Rūpasūrya, today you slept deeply. Did you have any
dreams? Get up. Let us have pleasant talk and delicious food."

Rūpasūrya replied: "Great king. Last night I slept so heavily that I had
various confusing dreams. Also, my mind is not clear, and because of that
I have nothing to say. Also, right now I am not feeling well, and so have no
desire for food. Some obstruction or contamination weighs upon me, I feel."

The king wondered what had brought this on, and together they talked
about the possible reasons.

Meanwhile, Gandhabhadrā and the low-caste queen discussed how pre-
viously they had killed the elephant and taken it to Rūpasūrya's room, and
how they had recently done the same with a corpse, and yet the king had
done nothing to Rūpasūrya. Then Gandhabhadrā said: "Today I will per-
form even greater magic than before." In the morning she took her musical
instruments and set off for the palace.

"Gandhabhadrā, you are skilled in song and dance," said the king. "Come and gladden the heart of Rūpasūrya." Gandhabhadrā performed for the couple, and as she did so, the speaking parrot hopped in front of the king and his entourage and said:

> Great king, hear these words.
> At the painted red door, the color of precious copper,
> with its white conch-shell threshold
> is the little unseen dog in a display of silken clothes.

> To it the queen has turned her head,
> and now the sun and moon falls to earth,
> the great nāgas of the oceans are disturbed,
> and Mount Meru is spinning round.

Gandhabhadrā thought to herself: "This parrot might tell of my plot." Immediately she took a twelve-stringed lute that could transform the listener's experience and placed it against her right thigh, supported it with her left leg and her chest, and plucked it gently with her fingers. Striking a seductive pose, she sang a beautiful song. Then she stood up and danced while playing the lute at the same time. The king and his entourage were entranced. The king turned to the parrot and said: "Have you ever seen such a performance?"

The parrot replied:

> Great king, hear these words.
> Greater performances than this I have seen.
> I have seen fangs in one with no teeth.
> I have seen an old woman of five years of age.
> I have seen the spinning of a thread of water
> from the plucking of hot tongues of fire.
> If this is a great show, then so are these.

Everyone became angry at the parrot: "These are lies. They make no sense. How can one with no teeth have fangs? How can a five-year-old girl be an old woman? Who can pluck hot tongues of fire? Who has seen the spinning of threads of water? Gandhabhadrā, your show is far greater than these lies. Be the mistress of dance!"

The parrot said:

Listen to me, everybody.
Last year's clairvoyant predictions
this year will come to pass.
The show will become greater by the day.
You who enjoy the show, have no regrets.

The parrot returned to his place. After sunset when the performance finished, Gandhabhadrā plied the king and his retinue with sixty-two intoxicating and stupefying black substances. In particular, she made sure that Rūpasūrya ingested the substances. Then she returned to the home of the low-caste queen.

Gandhabhadrā said to the low-caste queen: "At the palace a speaking parrot almost told the king of our plot. This evening I must take decisive action."

They discussed what to do in great detail. Finally they decided that they would steal the younger son, Candrakumāra, from his father's arms that night and take him to Rūpasūrya's bedside. There they would cut his body in two, take out the innards, and place them by her bed. They would make it seem as if Rūpasūrya had done the killing. The king and his entourage would then kill her. "Would you have any regrets about killing the younger son, Candrakumāra?" asked Gandhabhadrā.

The low-caste queen replied: "If it gets rid of Rūpasūrya, then apart from myself, you, and the king, there is no one else I care about. Do it. If it results in the destruction of Rūpasūrya, you will have such wealth that you will never know poverty."

When about a third of the night had passed, Gandhabhadrā went to the palace. There the king and his retinue were asleep. Through the power of the substances, they had taken off their clothes and lay there naked. Some were lying the wrong way around on their beds. Some were lying face down, others were grinding their teeth while mucus dripped from their mouth and noses.

Without a second thought, Gandhabhadrā went to King Candrasena's chambers. There his son Candrakumāra, only six years old, beautiful and fresh-faced like the son of a god, was lying in his arms, his little body half out of the bedclothes. She snatched him away and took him to Rūpasūrya's room. There she cut his body in half, and as before placed the top half on

Rūpasūrya's right and the bottom half on her left. She placed the innards of the child by her head and made it so that blood was dripping from Rūpasūrya's mouth. "Now Gandhabhadrā's work is done," she said to herself, and with great glee she went to the low-caste queen's home.

It is said that when the child is gone, the heart knows it. As dawn approached, King Candrasena felt in his mind that his son was gone. He woke up and looked. His son was nowhere to be seen. He searched in the room and everywhere in the palace. Finally he called his elder son, Candra-siṃha, and together they went to Rūpasūrya's room. There they saw the top half of the child's body on the right of Rūpasūrya, the bottom half on her left, his innards by her head, and his blood coming from her mouth. Father and son flew into a rage and Candrasiṃha went to cut her throat. Suddenly the parrot appeared before the king and said:

> Great king, please hear me.
> Every act should be considered before it is done.
> It is not right to perform deeds without consideration,
> as taught by the story of the king and the parrot.

The king replied:

> The hunter has deceived me.
> This flesh-eating ḍākinī
> killed my precious elephant here.
> As I was about to kill her,
>
> I made the mistake of listening to this parrot.
> Because of this dishonest, beguiling parrot,
> the palace has become filled with corpses.
> This parrot's words are baseless.

"I will send this parrot to the abode of the Lord of Death." With his sword he struck at the parrot and killed it. He then went to cut the throat of Rūpasūrya. When he saw her face, it was so beautiful the king was over-come with compassion and could not kill her. He handed the sword to his father and said: "I have been with her a long time, and went through much hardship to bring her here from a place far away. I cannot kill her. You do it."

Immediately his father took the sword and went to cut her throat. But when he beheld her face, it was so extraordinarily beautiful that he could not do it and returned to his son.

The king, his father, and the ministers discussed what was to be done. There was much disagreement. Some said she should be exiled. Others said that it would be hard to find another queen like her, and that she should be punished appropriately and allowed to stay. There was one evil minister called Viṣajatila. He was angry and fierce, and enjoyed the act of killing. Headed by this minister, a few bad ministers stood up and said: "If this is to be decided by what she deserves, then is right that her flesh be cut into pieces and fed to dogs and animals at junctions on the city roads. The king and his son cannot do this, and so she should be given to three butchers and taken to a cemetery called Boiling Ocean of Blood, three days from here in the southwest. It is a frightful place, where malicious spirits roam. In particular, it abounds with flesh-eating piśācas and cannibal demons with terrifying forms. In the daytime it is a swirling ocean of blood and fat. At night everywhere is ablaze with deadly tongues of fire. Foxes, jackals, bears, wild apes, and other fierce animals howl out their fearsome cries. The air is thick with the vapor of many poisonous snakes. Foul demons constantly wander there to snatch the life-breath of living beings. Skeletons, corpses, and parts of corpses naturally dance and cackle. Send her there and tell the three butchers to scatter her flesh and blood. As reward, give them a third of your lands. If you fail to do this, father and son will lose their lives and the kingdom will be ruined."

Everyone obeyed the wicked ministers, and Rūpasūrya was handed to the three butchers with these instructions: "Take her to the Boiling Ocean of Blood cemetery and kill her. Do this and as a reward the king will grant you a third of his lands." The butchers immediately bound her limbs with iron chains. They tore off her clothes, took away her jewelry, and whipped her with twigs of thorns. They wrapped black cloth around the lower part of her body, and a black noose around her neck. Her hands were tied and, with the butchers holding both ends of the rope, she was led out of the palace.

All at once the earth shook from its depths and the sun and moon refused to shine. The pleasure grove known as Without Sorrow was plunged into sorrow. Lotuses, utpala, and other flowers died and were taken by the frost, never to bloom again. Leaves, blossoms, and fruits withered on the trees. Pleasant meadows blessed by eight qualities became parched deserts and beautiful pools dried up. Sweet-sounding birds such as the kalaviṅga beat their breasts on the ground and let out cries of anguish. Jackals, wolves, and wild dogs howled blood-curdling cries and were seen attacking at the junctions and crossroads in the city. The whole land was filled with these and other bad omens.

"What are these bad omens?" cried the people of the city. "Is there a threat to the lives of the king and queen? What do these events portend? Let us go to the palace to see," they said. There they saw their extraordinary and beautiful queen, Rūpasūrya, tied up and being dragged along and beaten by three butchers. Greeted by such a sight, they beat their breasts and clenched their fists. Some threw themselves on the ground. Some fainted, while others were in shock and stared with open mouths. The whole city was plunged into the black hole of grief.

Rūpasūrya too was suffering immense pain as she was dragged and beaten by the three butchers. She cried out to the people:

> Listen to me, all people gathered here!
> Alas! Alas! Such pain as this!
> What has this girl done wrong!
> Alas! What is the king thinking!
>
> I cannot bear this!
> No one can help me!
> This must be the ripening of some bad karma.
> Think on this and avoid the ten nonvirtuous acts.

The wise and intelligent among the crowd called out to Queen Rūpasūrya:

> Beautiful and alluring princess and queen,
> you are being taken from your people alone and friendless.
> You have been stripped of your jewels, shorn of your clothes,
> taken from your beloved companions and those dear to you,
> to be thrown into the clutches of these terrifying servants
>   of the Lord of Death.
>
> Your throat, from which comes your Brahma-like melodious
>   voice,
> is clasped tightly by an evil black noose.
> Your soft and gentle limbs are bound by iron chains.
> What fault could possibly bring this upon you?

Has the great Dharma king been possessed by demons?
Do not cry. Though tears fall from your eyes, wipe them away.
If you cry, a rain of blood will fall from your eyes.
Though your mindfulness is firm, your consciousness runs wild.
Though your body is straight, your feet stagger.

For such a hardship as this, what wrong did you do?
Having offered you our wealth and jewelry,
if you are at fault, please tell us truly.

Rūpasūrya replied:

Listen to me, all people gathered here!
This maiden has done no wrong.
If I have, then say what it is.

When I look at suffering such as this,
I think that without practicing the worthy Dharma,
what is the essence of a worldly existence?
Where is the control over this transient life?

What is the point in being conscientious
toward those who take on many new friends?
What is the point in entrusting yourself
to those who flatter you?

Whether going or staying, it is like this.
Give up all worldly existence.
Immerse yourself in virtue.

The king in his palace heard the wailing and lamenting of his people.
Not able to bear it, he went outside to see. The people addressed him in
one voice:

Our great Dharma king, please hear these words!
In samsara, where our own suffering is experienced
    by ourselves,
where hungry ghosts eat their own flesh,

where moths take their own lives,
where someone tears out his own heart
and gives his own warm flesh to murderous butchers,
do not bring such disgrace upon your own head,
son of the gods!

The wicked ministers were furious and came to the king: "Great king, it is said that the actions of a king and a maiden are done one time only. The decree of your former words has been superseded by later words. The saying goes, 'Officials do not protect the wicked. Gurus do not save evildoers.' The word of a king is spoken only once. Great king, if you stay here at this place where the fate of criminals is decided, you run the risk of suffering contamination to your body. Go inside the palace." With that, they led him away.

Rūpasūrya thought to herself: "I am not escaping from this terrible crime, and now the people are slandering the king with words of abuse." She said to the crowd:

In the past this place was populated by non-Buddhist
    barbarians.
And then it became like a delightful Dharma garden,
where the bees of great scholars drank the honey
    of wonderful teachings,
giving out the sweet melodic sounds of Dharma.
And then the hail and storms of demonic forces
destroyed the lotus groves and scattered the bees.

The moon of king Candrasiṃha is obscured by the clouds
    of evil ministers.
The sun of Rūpasūrya has been eclipsed by murderous
    butchers.[132]
And now I must lose my life in some far-off place.
This is not the doing of the king. This maiden is not
    at fault.
Do not cast your flowers of abuse at the king.

The people were overwhelmed with emotion, and tears flowed from their eyes like blood. They addressed the queen:

Refuge for us who have no guide or shelter,
mother of us motherless orphans,
giver of food and wealth for us penniless beggars,
wish-fulfilling jewel granting us every happiness.

Leaving us behind, where are you going?
Lamp that dispels the darkness of ignorance, where are
        you going?
If you, who free us from all misery, do not stay here,
then like orphans abandoned by mother and father,
who can we turn to?

They began to cry. Rūpasūrya too, looking at their faces, shed many tears.
Great love and compassion was born inside her and she said to them:

Three Jewels, our only hope!
Three Jewels, our only refuge!
Precious Three Jewels, please hear me!
Unfailing Three Jewels, supreme refuge for living beings!

These people who have such intense longing for me,
the pots of tears that fall from their eyes
bathe their faces like a celestial bathing ritual.
The mandalas of their faces are summoned to the essential drops
        of their fingers.
The flowers of their own hair they scatter with their hands.
The drums of their breasts they beat with the sticks
        of their hands.
On the stage of their own throats they sing their songs
        of lamentation.
Their bodies are in the pose of being unable to stand by
        themselves.
On the plains of sorrow they perform their dances of suffering.

These beings, devoid of refuge, devoid of protection,
hear them and look upon them with compassion!

They have no one else to turn to.
Shelter these leaderless beings with your undivided
     compassion.

As soon as she had finished speaking, the three butchers led Rūpasūrya off to the Boiling Ocean of Blood cemetery, as if they were driving forward an ox cart. The people decided to accompany her, saying it would better to die with her. However, some were too attached to their wealth and soon dropped off. Other became exhausted and turned back. Some became hungry and thirsty and returned home. However, most traveled for two days with the queen. Then the butchers too became tired and that evening they stopped. The people gathered around Rūpasūrya and said:

Your body, a snow mountain encircled by the light of the sun,
your melodious voice, the unchanging and unending drum,
your mind is the sun, friend to the lotus, illuminating all.
You are the earth, the oceans' garment, producing the harvest
     of joy.
You are the wish-granting jewel fulfilling all hopes.
Supreme queen, please hear us.

They continued: "You are one whose body is extraordinary and attractive. Beautiful to look upon, gentle to touch, irresistible to gaze upon. Such a body these butchers will cut up and feed to the hordes of flesh-eating demons. If they can do that, then why can they not do the same to our bodies, which are ugly to look at, of poor complexion, and the lowest of human bodies? Therefore we are going to give our lives too. Or why don't we offer our clothes, jewelry, and food to the butchers, and together we could all flee to another kingdom?"

Rūpasūrya said: "Do not say these things. I must give up my life without choice. You have gained this rare human form of leisure and opportunity. To give up your life needlessly would mean that for five hundred lifetimes you would have to bear the pain of giving up your life again and again. Do not think like this. Moreover, it is not right to bribe the butchers with gifts and flee to another country. For one thing, the butchers will not listen to you. They favor one-third of the king's lands over your jewelry and clothes. Second, it would go against king's word. The lands would be lost and the butchers would be punished. There is little point in amassing such wrong deeds. Therefore return to your homes. Serve the king, follow the customs of your kin, look after your children, and so on. Do these things well and abandon the ten nonvirtuous acts and follow the king's law.

"Only I will die. What suffering is that for you? If you cannot bear my death, then for my sake, make the higher offerings to the Three Jewels, the intermediate offering of performing service to the monastic community, and the lower offerings of alms to the poor. In this way amass a great store of virtuous deeds. In the presence of a good guru take vows as best you can and guard them preciously. With this my wishes will be fulfilled."

In their suffering the people wailed and lamented, as blood fell from their mouths. Some fainted, some beat their chests. After a while they said to her: "Precious queen, if you have decided not to take us with you and wish that we return home, please give us some advice to help our minds and teachings to turn our minds from samsara. Whatever you say, we will without question willingly follow.

Rūpasūrya responded with the following:

> Is there any need to seek advice elsewhere?
> Just look at the situation that I am in.
> Do the things of this world have any essence?
>
> At this time of being cast into the jaws of the Lord of Death,
> are friends and relatives of any help?
> Do our bodies and wealth offer any help?
> Do our citizens and kingdoms provide any help?
> Are our masters and children of any help?
> Are our houses and land of any help?
> Are the men who are our companions of any help?
>
> There is no need of these fleeting bubbles.
> There is no need of friends and relatives.
> There is no need of our bodies and wealth.
> There is no need of our servants and people.
> There is no need of our masters and children.
> There is no need of our houses and lands.
> Nothing do we need. This short life is just a dream.

Do those who do not think about the sacred Dharma
have time to amass their wicked deeds?

Listen to me, people gathered here.
All you brazen, reed-like maidens,
in the midst of women, you open your upper mouth.
In the midst of men, you open your lower mouth.
Like a dog wandering throughout the town,
you carry the discarded food of deception and slander.

Seeing wealth, you wish it was your adornment.
Seeing other women, you befriend them.
Seeing men, you wish them to be your husbands.
Look at this woman on whom the status
of becoming a mistress has fallen!

Listen to me, all you men.
If I were to explain to you your qualities,
it would expose your faults.
Look at the king, Candrasiṃha.
Not satisfied with one queen, he kept five hundred,
and in the end caused pain to everyone. Think about this!

Would it not be better from a young age
to become ordained and practice the Dharma?
Listen, all you people gathered here.
There is no time. Look now to death!

She continued: "Even the Buddha, who had attained the vajra body,
passed into nirvana. Even those great male and female yogis who have con-
trol over their own minds pass away. Therefore we people of this country—
neighbors, young and old, friend and enemy—will go before the Lord of
Death. Think about this. In particular, this maiden Rūpasūrya is now before
you, but tomorrow she will be taken to a cemetery by three heartless butch-
ers. There her limbs will be torn off and her flesh and blood will be por-
tioned out and given to birds and animals. Nothing will be left of her except
for a few scattered bones and some strands of hair. At that time Rūpasūrya,

queen to the king, will be dead, and only her empty name will remain. All of this, put it in your minds. Apart from the Dharma, what can help? If you think about this and do what you can, it would be good.

"None of you know when your death is coming. Who can say with certainty they will be here next year? You too will lie for the last time on your bed, eat your last meal, speak your last words, drink your last drink. Your succession of breaths will continue to a point from which they can no longer be extended. You will gaze at the faces of your relatives and friends. The light fades, your consciousness wavers, and the darkness begins. The things of this life subside, those of the next life begin to appear. As the Lord of Death leads you along the precipitous path of the intermediate state, it is you alone separated from all those friends and relatives who must wander along this path. At that time the suffering of fear is unbearable. Ask yourselves if you will be able to bear it. At that time this body that you hold as your own will be left behind. The consciousness led by karma and ripening, who knows where it will go.

"Alas! This empty name does not carry on alone. Imprints that are the power of karma will lead you to one of the six realms. There are three lower realms. If you are to be born in the realm of hell, you will suffer the excruciating agonies of being burned alive, boiled alive, butchered, skinned, and so on. Could you bear this? Could you stand this? Could you tolerate this?

"If born as a hungry ghost, you will suffer greatly from hunger, thirst, and poverty. Could you bear this? Could you stand this? Could you tolerate this? Born as an animal, you will be dumb and stupid, used by humans, and killed for your skin and flesh. Could you bear this? Could you stand this? Could you tolerate this? Wherever you are born in samsara, there is no happiness but only pain and suffering. Wouldn't it be wonderful to be free from this samsara?

"Listen to me! Since entering the doorway of Dharma, how much Dharma have you practiced? How much of your conduct is in accord with the Dharma you speak? The bad deeds and thoughts, not in accord with the Dharma, how much of it was necessary? Think well.

"Now your minds mock such conviction. I have spoken in detail about life in the hell, ghost, and animal realms, but you do not think they are true. You doubt that your life will be taken by demons, Pehar, flesh-eating demons, and so on, and that all this is of little consequence. I have explained in detail how all phenomena are transient, but this ever-increasing grip on your body as your own means that you doubt that you will be taken away suddenly by some unforeseen circumstance and that this is all of little consequence. I have talked much about the certainty of death and the uncertainty of its arrival, but you do not think that death will come. You doubt that you will fall prey to the Beggar of Death, and that this is of little consequence.

"Listen again! Hoping to be happy without doing good, hoping to become enlightened without amassing merit, are useless thoughts that only serve to lie and deceive yourselves. Do not involve yourselves in actions that lead only to misery.

"Day and night without stopping, our lives run toward death. At that time best is to have joy. Will you have that? Second best is not to be afraid. Will you have that? At least, you should have no regrets. Will you have that? Having joy at the time of death is to have recognized your mind as a buddha. Not to be afraid at the time of death is to have applied yourself to virtuous ways from your heart. Not to have regrets at the time of death is not to have tainted the vows and pledges you have taken with the bad smell of degeneration. I ask that you please practice these, whatever is suitable, as much as you can.

"At that time meditate strongly on love and compassion by thinking that all living beings are your kind mother and father. Generate your mind toward the supreme and highest enlightenment for the sake of living beings and protect it with the three trainings. Develop the six perfections, which ripen your own mind-stream, and the four ways of gathering disciples, which ripen the mind-stream of others. Practice by way of reading, study, and contemplation. Whether I live or die, I have no last testament other than this."

A profound understanding of the Dharma was born in the minds of the people there. With great emotion and reverence, they said to the queen:

> We have understood. What great kindness!
> We have received the blessing. Treasure of venerable wisdom!
> We will do as you ask. Sole refuge of living beings!
> Wherever you go, look on us with compassion.

All the people gathered there, young or old, man or woman, began to cry, and said: "You know such profound teachings, and yet without having the time to practice them, you will suffer the hardship of being killed by these three terrifying butchers who will cut up your body, which is as extraordinary and beautiful as that of a goddess."

Rūpasūrya replied: "Do not call it a hardship. If I die now, I have no regrets." And she sang this song of confidence and no regrets:

> I bow down to the infallible Three Jewels.
> This brahman maiden, confident and free of regret,
> studied, contemplated, and meditated at the feet
>   of the guru.
> I even placed the king's rule within the Dharma.
> I cared for the people with love and compassion.
> Now if I die, I have no regrets.
> You too should perform deeds that bring no regret.

> When I was beset with great suffering,
> I meditated on the joy of perfecting the contemplation
> of taking the suffering of others onto myself.
> Now if I die, I have no regrets.
> You too should perform deeds that bring no regret.

> Without thinking of my own welfare for even a moment,
> I meditated from my heart solely on the welfare of others.
> This is the main practice that will bring enlightenment.
> Now if I die, I have no regrets.
> You too should perform deeds that bring no regret.

> Even though everyone rises up as a pernicious enemy
>   to me,
> I greet them all with the smile of a loving mind,
> and have never discarded the garments of patience.
> Now if I die, I have no regrets.
> You too should perform deeds that bring no regret.

> Even though living beings that I have cared for with kindness,
> harshly malign me with words of hate and anger,
> I greet them with a joyful smile free of anger.
> Now if I die, I have no regrets.
> You too should perform deeds that bring no regret.

Confusion holding to reality obscures seeing the truth.
Truth is not to be sought from the midst of confusion,
but in the midst of that confusion I have found the truth.
Now if I die, I have no regrets.
You too should perform deeds that bring no regret.

Why do I say these things?
All phenomena are imputed by thought.
If they are held to exist, banish such holding.
Leave them as just names, as they are known when unexamined.
Cut the life-blood of holding to nonexistence,
for if even the ultimate dharmakāya cannot stand on its own,
you should have no concern about the destruction
of this conventional illusory body.
Now if I die, I have no regrets.
You too should perform deeds that bring no regret.

Great reverence for the queen was born in everyone there. They turned
their backs on samsara and developed the mind of supreme enlightenment.
Because she had given them many teachings even more vast and profound
than before, they thought to themselves: "These teachings have helped our
minds. She must be a Buddha." They requested of her: "Please make a prayer
that in all lives we will be cared for by you. We too will pray that in all our
lives we be born in your presence."

Rūpasūrya replied: "As all that is good and happy depends on aspiration
and prayer, I will do that." She continued:

Buddhas, bodhisattvas, śrāvakas, and solitary realizers
who abide in the myriad realms of the ten directions,
gurus, meditation deities, ḍākinīs, Dharma protectors,
male and female spiritual warriors, sages who fulfill prayers—
come and be witnesses for the fulfillment of my prayer.

At the lotus feet of the Three Jewels,
I prostrate with body, speech, and mind.
I make offerings and confess all wrong deeds.
I rejoice in the amassing of a store of virtue

and plead that you turn the great wheel of Dharma,
and that the gurus remain without passing into nirvana.

She continued: "These three murdering butchers with their terrifying
forms, their black complexions, and ugly scowling faces have bound me
body and limb with iron chains and an evil noose. Just as they will cut up
my body with knives and swords, may I, in some future time, through the
power of the roots of virtue that I have planted with body, speech, and mind
in past, present, and future, slay the evil mind of holding to a self that is
within these three butchers with the sharp knives of study, contemplation,
and meditation, and with the open mouth of the two truths and the snarling
fangs of method and wisdom.

"Just as these three butchers have bound me body and limb with iron
chains, may I, in some future time, bind the gateways of their senses and their
mental consciousnesses with the iron chains of mindfulness and awareness.

"Just as they have covered my body with a cloth, placed an evil noose
around my neck, and will lead me down a path unbounded on either side,
may I, in some future time, cover them with the cloth of conscientiousness
and awareness and lead them with the noose of love and compassion down a
path unbounded on either side.

"Just as these butchers will take me to a cemetery, where they will separate
body and limb and cut them into pieces of flesh, may I, in some future time,
separate out the three poisons of their minds and cut into pieces the evil
obscurations of their erroneous and degenerate ways.

"Furthermore, for all those men and women, headed by the wicked min-
isters, who practiced deception by way of slander to separate King Candra-
siṃha and me, may I at some future time separate them from samsara and
the three lower realms with the act of renunciation. May I constantly be able
to empty samsara and the three realms.

"Furthermore, just as I was driven from the palace and placed into the
hands of these murdering butchers to be led away to a cemetery, may I drive
the king and his entourage from the palace into the hands of a qualified spir-
itual teacher and friend, where they will be led to the plains of method and
wisdom, and may I be able to send them to the plains of nirvana.

"In short, those beings who on my account have committed evil deeds
by way of envy, resentment, anger, and pride will suffer the suffering conse-
quences of the evil karma they have amassed. Therefore, having developed
the mind of enlightenment and vowed that whatever physical, verbal, or

mental action I undertake will bring help and happiness to all, may that vow be perfected, and may I lure all living beings. In that way may I be lured by the Three Jewels.

"By the blessings of the Three Jewels and the power of my pure intent, may these beings who have amassed a store of bad karma through acts of body, speech, and mind be freed from the results of such acts, which are the sufferings of the lower realms.

"Also, these men and women who have followed me here and who cry and grieve unbearably for my sake, may I in some future time bring them to the Dharma, and on the plain of great happiness may I sing and perform the songs of bliss and emptiness, and may I dance with the joy of experience and insight.

"May I gather a circle of disciples about me by the practice of giving Dharma and material things, speaking kindly, encouraging others to act according to the teachings, and being an example myself, which are the four ways of gathering disciples. May I instill them with pure ethics and bring them to the three trainings, which comprise the entire path.

> By the truth of the precious Three Jewels,
> and the power of my pure intent,
> may this pure prayer be realized."

She said to the people: "Now it is time for me to go. Do not try to stop me but return to your homes. In body, speech, and mind, do what accords with the Dharma. If you insist on following me, you should know that one furlong from here is a place where tigers, leopards, bears, jackals, and other wild animals will feed on warm flesh. One furlong further on is a place where crows, owls, black vultures, and other birds will pluck out your eyes and carry off your brains. About one furlong from there is a place where the breath of poisonous snake is as thick as fog and your bodies will crack open. About one furlong from there is a place where terrifying cannibal demons will carry your entire bodies into the sky. About one furlong from there is the great Ocean of Boiling Blood cemetery, a place where all kinds of beings gather. There are found the great residences of devils, cannibals, malicious spirits, female demons, and so on. It is a sacred place for spiritual warriors, ḍākinīs, and others to perform their tantric feasts. It is a place where birds, wild animals, deer, and humans all lose their lives. Therefore you should return home. These three butchers are bringers of food to the cemetery denizens, and so they are not harmed."

At that moment the three butchers led Rūpasūrya away to the Ocean of Boiling Blood cemetery like a little bird being carried away by a hawk.

At the cemetery the two younger butchers talked to each other, and they agreed: "Such a beautiful woman as this we two cannot possibly kill. Let us give the reward to the older butcher. As for the killing, it would be better if we urged him to do it."

They went to the older butcher and said: "If this queen is to be killed, you do it. We will give our reward to you."

"I will do it. Bring your reward to me." With that, he took out his knife and went to cut the throat and limbs of Rūpasūrya. But when he gazed on her extraordinary and beautiful face, he too was unable to kill her and returned to the other butchers, saying: "You can have my reward. You two kill her. I cannot do it."

They replied: "We weren't able to do it either, but now we must." They went to the queen in order to kill her. But on seeing her extraordinary beauty, again they were unable to carry it out and returned to the elder butcher.

They talked about what they should do. The elder butcher said: "None of us is able to kill her. If we return home without killing her, there will no possibility of a reward, and the king will punish us by wiping out our entire families. Therefore it is best that we leave her here in the middle of the cemetery. The wild animals and the flesh-eating piśāca demons will probably devour her raw flesh and blood."

As the sun set, they carried Rūpasūrya to the middle of the cemetery. There they took off her chains and removed the cloth covering her. In the cemetery was a large stone slab called Swirl of Blood and Fat, where the flesh of all the corpses was laid. Rūpasūrya was placed naked and face down on this slab, her hands and feet outstretched and tied to four bamboo stakes. The butchers left and journeyed to a place two furlongs away called Grove of Overhanging Cliff.

Meanwhile Rūpasūrya, in a state of firm equilibrium, uttered this prayer for the practice of severing:[133]

So kind, you three precious jewels!
My wishes today have been fulfilled.
Gurus, meditation deities, ḍākinīs,

spiritual warriors, Dharma protectors, and guardians,
tonight I have this special request
concerning my life and this illusory body of four elements.

Tonight I will not call for help.
Tonight I will repay my karmic debt with a great feast.
Tonight I separate the flesh and bones of samsara and nirvana.
Tonight I offer a great feast of flesh and blood.

From the very peak of samsara
down to the eighteen realms of hell,
come all, without exception, to this place.

The eighty thousand hindering devils,
the three hundred and sixty classes of demons,
divinities, nāgas, harm bringers, elemental spirits,
flesh eaters, animal-headed ghouls, cannibals,
serpents, Īśvara, and hungry ghosts,
come here and share this flesh.

Feast greedily on this mountain of flesh.
Come here and stir the blood.
Gulp down this ocean of blood.
Come here and peel off this skin.
Wear this human skin for your clothing.

Māraya to this self-cherishing!
Jvala raṃ on this demon of selfish desire!
Hūṃ hūṃ on this holding of self!
Phaṭ phaṭ on this pride of self!
Svahā on nonattachment, on no clinging!

May this great offering of flesh and blood
please the Sugata Buddhas and their sons,
and dispel the hunger, thirst, and poverty of the six classes
    of beings.
Let it be taken as flesh payment of my karmic debt,

and may the six classes of living beings be satisfied
with uncontaminated bliss!

As soon as she had uttered these words, all the wild animals and flesh-eat-
ing demons in the cemetery came with great reverence to Rūpasūrya. Like
faith-filled disciples that had found a spiritual teacher, some prostrated,
some circumambulated, some made offerings, some confessed their evil
deeds, some praised her and made heartfelt requests.

At dawn the three butchers returned to the cemetery to see what had hap-
pened to Rūpasūrya. Not only had the flesh-eating demons, tigers, leopards,
bears, and jackals not harmed her, but they were all prostrate at her feet in
varying forms of veneration. When the demons and wild animals saw the
butchers, whereas previously they had shown them expressions of happiness,
now they emitted terrifying roars and snarled with frightening expressions
on their faces, if they had just seen an enemy. They bared their fangs, wagged
their tails, and beat the ground.

The butchers said to themselves: "We could not kill her, and now the ani-
mals and the demons, not only are they not eating her, but they are vener-
ating her with faith and devotion. If she is not killed, and we return home,
not only will we get no reward, but the king will punish us with our lives.
Therefore we should flee to another country and send Rūpasūrya back to
where she first came from."

They released her from the four bamboo stakes and said to her: "Return
to where you came from. We cannot kill you. We are fleeing to another
country. Please pray that we will always be cared for by you."

The queen replied:

By the virtuous deeds I amass in the three times,
may these three butchers in all their future lives,
shed the very root of the three poisonous afflictions,
and apply themselves through the three gateways to the
     ways of virtue.

By my virtuous deeds may we four beings become wise
in the four truths and practices of abandoning and cultivation,
and may we attain the four enlightened forms of a buddha
and enhance living beings with the four ways of gathering
     disciples.

Having taught the Dharma that destroys the five afflictions
for the sake of the five classes of mother living beings,
may I place them on the five Mahayana paths,
and may they gain the five forms of the Buddha.

From now on, in all my lives may I never be apart from you,
and having left behind anger and all malicious intent,
may we always be in harmony and mutual joy.

Although the six classes of living beings
wander by the force of karma in the city of existence,
driven on by the power of mental affliction,
may they never hear words of hate and anger
and, like mother and child, may they dwell in harmony.

By the power of being cared for by Avalokiteśvara,
may we enjoy forever the glory that is the Dharma,
and be maintained by minds in harmony with each other.

She continued: "You released me from this cemetery and saved my life.
Likewise, I will release you from the prison of samsara, place you on the road
to freedom, and deliver you unto the bliss of nirvana."

The three butchers offered their ornaments, clothes and weapons to
Rūpasūrya. They vowed to give up the ten nonvirtuous acts and said that
from now on they would not commit such wicked deeds and pursue only
virtuous ways. They left for another country. Rūpasūrya too set out joyfully
for the place where she was born, hoping to meet again the great meditator,
her father.

This has been the chapter on separation brought on by slander.

ABSOLVED FROM ALL WRONGDOING

As Rūpasūrya approached the place where she had lived with her father, the
great meditator, she saw that the leaves and fruit on the trees had withered.
They had become as stiff as a corpse, and birds such as the kalaviṅga no longer
sat there but had flown off elsewhere. The pools and bathing ponds, whose
water possessed the eight excellent qualities, had dried up and become holes
in the ground. Flowers, such as the utpala and lotus, no longer bloomed, but
had withered and died. Winds had spread red, gray, and black dust over the

land, so that it was almost obscured. The two grass huts lay scattered and in ruins like birds' nests beaten by sticks. Apart from one deer, there were no other animals to be seen. This deer showed no interest in eating and drinking but laid its head down by the ruined huts.

Rūpasūrya thought to herself: "My father, the great meditator, must have gone to the land of another king or governor. Or maybe he has gone to meditate in a quieter hermitage up in the hills or snow mountains."

She went to where the huts once stood and looked inside the ruins. There she saw her guru's bell and drum lying undamaged. Half hidden under the earth were his monk's robes, rotting and covered with green growth. The scriptures lay there tangled like grass. She realized: "With his possessions in such a state, my guru has not been invited by another king or governor, and neither has he gone to meditate in a quieter hermitage up in the hills or snow mountains. He must have passed away. There must be some remains of his body somewhere." She searched but found nothing.

Returning to the ruined huts, she cried with great sadness, her tears falling like rain. She made this prayer:

> Master and precious guru, composite of the Three Jewels,
> unparalleled father and dharmakāya;
> though you have attained the unchanging vajra form,
> you are no longer here in front of me.
>
> Whether you be in a ḍākinī pure realm
> or in the highest realm of Akaniṣṭa,
> please care for me with your great compassion.
> Bless the speech of this maiden
> and grant me an appearance of your emanated form.

By the power of such a heartfelt plea, something like a rainbow or light emerged from the hut in a ball of red light and dissolved into the head of the deer outside. The deer stood up, snorted three times, shook the dew off his back, circumambulated the hut three times, and set off in an easterly direction. Rūpasūrya followed its hoof prints. After a distance of about five hundred bow spans, she came to a place graced by a canopy of light. Nonhumans were circumambulating and making offerings. At once Rūpasūrya performed the seven-limbed practice of prostration and offering. When she entered the canopy of light she saw a thumb-sized statue of Avalokiteśvara, transparent and flawless, that had emerged from the precious master's body, as well as a Magadha[134] measure of relics.

The light again absorbed into the deer. It immediately stood up, circumambulated Rūpasūrya three times, and returned to the grass hut. Rūpasūrya also entered the hut, where she collected the ragged remains of the guru's robes and made them into a garment for herself. She looked at the scriptures and was able to understand about half of them. The guru's meditation rosaries, made from beads of wood, crystal, and skull, were broken and scattered around the hut. She collected the beads and made a rosary containing a hundred various beads, which she used for her practice.

She thought to herself: "Now if I leave for another place, I could search for an excellent guru, but it will be difficult to find one. Moreover, I have the body of a woman and, like an enemy, it can cause great hindrances to my practice of Dharma. Therefore wouldn't it be better to stay here, make prayers to my guru, and when I attain the Mahāmudrā supreme siddhi, I will work for sentient beings."

She remained in single-pointed endeavor in order to achieve this accomplishment. By the power of her excellent qualities, the trees and flowers were restored to their former state and the kalaviṅgas and other sweet-sounding birds returned.

For twelve years she prayed to the guru and engaged in a meditation on the Mahāmudrā. Yet no matter how hard she tried, because of the karma and ripening of going against her guru's words and not following his advice, she gained no results from her meditation and had no significant dreams or signs of progress. One evening she dreamt of a young boy holding a crystal rosary. In her mind she was sure this was a manifestation of her deity. Without waking, and in her dream voice, she poured out this lamentation to Avalokiteśvara:

Conquering Amitābha, leader without equal,
compassionate Maitreya, appointed by the Buddha,
noble Avalokiteśvara, supremely compassionate,
noble beings, renowned for your great love,
please hear this wretched lamentation.

In the infinite past I have been beset by much suffering.
Tied by the ropes of tightly binding samsara,

.   I am cast helplessly in the dark pit of ignorance.
Great compassion, lift me up with your hook of love.

Since the beginning of time up to now,
I have wandered endlessly in samsara.
As I have wandered, the river of my mental afflictions
    has swelled.
As it swells, so am I tormented by much suffering.
With such fierce suffering, I have gained no happiness,
but with my strong attachment, I continue to wander
    in samsara.

As much as I try, I can find no opportunity for liberation.
This body of leisure and opportunity has been wasted,
and now that the troubles of illness, old age, and death fall
    upon me,
supreme refuge, won't you be my protector and guide?

Having taken on the pledge of great and powerful practice,
I have thought since the beginning of time to liberate
    living beings.
Yet, deprived of merit, I still wander in samsara.
Great guide, Maitreya, are you leaving me in indifference?
Great compassion, with your hook of your love,
lift up those disciples blessed with the karma and good fortune.

Fallen into the great ravine of wrong views,
I am left alone with no guide, no refuge.
Great compassionate one, are you not showing partiality?

If you perceive without obstruction all existing phenomena,
but you don't see me wandering lost and alone
in this prison of mistaken conception of subject and object,
then your excellent wisdom is simply one-sided.

If I have not fallen under the sway of bad karma,
and except for you I have forsaken all other refuges,
then are you not the refuge for all those who seek refuge?

In my distraction and laziness, instantly I think of you and pray.
But if soon I am not delivered from the great ocean of samsara,
then, great compassionate one, what does your name mean?

Alas! Please hear me, compassionate Maitreya!
Great compassionate one, noble Avalokiteśvara!
If this unfortunate maiden is in such a state,
what is the point of your great compassion?

By the force of great familiarity with it in the past,
I am sunk in this ocean of samsara, source of all faults,
crushed by the huge mountain of dark ignorance,
and thrown into the mouth of the monsters of the three
    poisons.

All these faults I alone am responsible for,
and yet if by thinking of you in this way,
your blessings, great guide Maitreya, do not enter me,
what is the point of making these efforts?

From now until I attain enlightenment,
being cared for by you, protector Maitreya,
for the sake of all sentient beings equal to the reaches
    of space,
may I train in the supreme mind of enlightenment.

May I become like the brave bodhisattvas
in spreading throughout the ten directions
the Buddha's teachings, foundation of the happiness
of all my mother sentient beings.

So that I might understand correctly,
as the buddhas and bodhisattvas have done,
the word and meanings of the sutras and commentaries,
and be able to teach them to others,
grant me your blessings, mighty guide.

For as long as this great ocean of samsara and suffering
has not dried up, for so long may I, as you have done,
take on the great pledges and become a guide for all beings.

After this lamentation, the white boy in the dream dissolved into a
mass of light, and from a state of shimmering light he spoke to Rūpasūrya:
"Maiden, you did not guard the pledges made to your guru's words. As a
result of going against the instructions of your guru, you do not possess
the merit to attain the mahāmudrā power in this life. Therefore go about
the towns and cities. Teach the vast Dharma of the six-syllable mantra and
bring living beings to happiness. Repair the transgressions of the pledges
you have made with the body, speech, and mind of your guru. In particu-
lar, dispel the suffering of those beset with grief and sorrow. Do this and,
in the intermediate state between death and a new life, you will attain the
mahāmudrā power."

As soon as she heard these words, she dreamt that the mass of light cir-
cumambulated her three times and dissolved into the crown of her head. She
awoke and thought to herself: "I have not broken any pledges made with
my guru except when he told me not to show the pearl meditation rosary
to anyone. I showed it to Gandhabhadrā, and this is the result of that act."

In order to purify herself of the obscurations brought on by transgressions
to the body, speech, and mind of her guru, she built one hundred shrines.
For the consecrating material to be placed inside each one, she used the rel-
ics formed from her guru's body, robes, and scriptures. She performed the
consecration ceremony herself. After that she thought: "In order to purify
myself, I will recite the six-syllable mantra as instructed and bring living
beings to happiness."

She wrapped a coarse blanket around her body, covered her upper body
with the guru's ragged robes, and picked up a begging bowl and a stick. "If I
go like this," she thought, "this beautiful face has got me into trouble before
and it could do so again." She smeared her cheeks with honey and black dust
and rubbed it in. She traveled from town to town bringing everyone into
contact with the enlightened activity of Avalokiteśvara. She became known
as Yogini Mahāmuni.

Meanwhile, in the city of Cittamaṭi, the people and King Candrasiṃha
were tormented by the grief of being without Queen Rūpasūrya. The king
in particular was suffering greatly the loss of his queen, who was far more
perfect than any other queen. Not only did he not enjoy the company of his

five hundred queens, headed by the low-caste queen, he did not even look at them. He forgot to eat and drink, and under the weight of his anguish he became weak and thin and was little more than a skeleton.

Seeing this, his father wondered why his son was in such a pathetic state:

> Listen to me, son of royal breeding and in the prime of youth.
> Without being struck by any illness arising from
> any imbalance in the four elements of the body,
> your full and youthful body has become emaciated.
> Untroubled by illness, what ails your mind?
> When your power, wealth, and kingdom are undiminished,
> you have no need to be unhappy about anything.

King Candrasiṃha made this plea to his father:

> Lords of the gods, my sole father, hear me.
> The friend that I searched long and hard for,
> the beautiful sun whose form[135] tortured me,
> has been eclipsed at noon by the Rāhu butchers,
> and my mind is plunged into a dark hole of grief.
> There is no light to illuminate what is right or wrong,
> and so my mind knows no joy, and my body too is ailing.
> Great father, look on me with your compassion.

His father replied:

> My young and intelligent son, listen to me.
> That sun performs in two distinct ways.
> It brings the joy of a good harvest,
> and it can dry up the huge and bountiful ocean.
> Which this is I do not know. Let it be.

> This sun has two distinct capabilities.
> From afar its light relieves the suffering of cold.
> Close to, it can blind and turn a body to ashes.
> Which this is I do not know. Let it be.

This sun has two distinct powers.
It can dispel the greatest of darkness,
and burn the world and its inhabitants.
Which this is I do not know. Let it be.

Here in the palace you have five hundred queens,
all alluring and adorned with every mark of beauty.
Immerse yourself in the pleasures of the five senses.
Lift this despairing mind. Let it be free and at ease.

His son again replied:

A king, in the great open skies of his kingdom,
may have queens about him like hosts of stars.
But if the lord of those stars, the sun of seven horses,
is not there, those stars alone cannot dispel the darkness.

Alas! Father and king. Please hear me.
I cherish my sun with her beautiful form
like a mother bird cherishes the egg in her nest.

Those heartless butchers took her to a cemetery,
and now she is probably dead.
Demons such as the lion-headed yama demon,
the powerful jackal-faced yama demon,
and the red-mouthed demon of cannibal form
have probably torn her apart by now.
All my efforts have been in vain.

Again his father spoke:

Prince Candrasiṃha, listen to me, my son.
Do not hold as a goddess the butcher
who slew your younger brother, Candrakumāra,
as well as your powerful airāvata elephant.

King Candrasiṃha replied:

The daughter of Indra, lord of the gods,
from the high celestial realm of Tuṣita,
the daughter of Takṣaka, lord of the nāgas,
from the pure realm of the underworld,
were they to hold a competition of beauty,
they could not possibly compete with her.

My mind has been plunged into the depths of sorrow by this.
Heal me soon of this despair, great brahman.

Feeling the desperate sorrow of yearning for the queen, the king and the people dedicated two-thirds of their possessions to the merit of Rūpasūrya. The father, with Rūpasūrya in mind, made fervent pleas day and night to the great sages. As a result of this and by the power of former prayers, he received a prediction from his meditation deity.

Yogini Mahāmuni, after wandering throughout the land, finally arrived in the city of Cittamaṭi. "Alas! I am in in this city again," she thought. "If I stay here, some hindrance will surely arise." She prepared to leave for another town. Meanwhile the townsfolk had invited her to a Dharma celebration. There many people asked her for Dharma teachings and for the transmission and initiation of the six-syllable mantra. Therefore she stayed in the city for a few days.

At that time Gandhabhadrā was in the crowd. She thought to herself: "I have committed much wrong. This is a special yogini. I will ask her for Dharma. Also, the root of the evil that has plunged the king and his people into so much sorrow lies with me. I will also offer my confession to her."

On the evening of the fifteenth of the month Gandhabhadrā erected a high throne adorned with jewels and set amid a vast array of offerings, and invited Rūpasūrya to take her place upon it. She told her family and entourage: "Return home. I am receiving a very profound teaching from this yogini."

They returned home. Gandhabhadrā went down on her knees in front of the yogini. Placing her hands together, she uttered these words of confession: "I am one of great evil. Yogini, please hear me. Please care for me."

She then offered her confession by way of the four powers: "Buddhas and bodhisattvas dwelling in the ten directions, great spiritual masters, please hear me. I, Gandhabhadrā, from time without beginning in samsara until now, motivated by the three poisons, I have performed wicked deeds and rejoiced in wicked deeds done by others. In particular, I listened to the words of a low-caste queen. She told me of the brahman queen called Rūpasūrya. She possessed as her protection a pearl rosary of a hundred and one beads. I tricked her with various methods and eventually plied her and the king with intoxicating substances to drug and stupefy them. Then I killed the king's beloved *airāvata* elephant. I placed its flesh and blood by Rūpasūrya's head, and wickedly made it appear as if she had killed it. Then I procured a corpse from the cemetery and placed it at her bedside. After that, I killed the elder king's younger son, Candrakumāra, and placed his flesh and blood by Rūpasūrya's head as she slept. Because of this, the king killed his talking parrot and Rūpasūrya was taken by three butchers to a cemetery to be killed. The root culprit of all these evil acts is me. Moreover, the grief of King Candrasiṃha in losing his queen, Rūpasūrya, has brought him close to death. If he were to die, all the people and cattle of the 3,600,000 towns, headed by the city of Cittamaṭi, would have to be dedicated for the merit of the king. The root of all this evil is me. I confess before you, yogini, all this evil. I do not conceal any. I do not deny any. From this day on I will cease from this evil and vow to restrain myself from evil."

Three times she repeated this confession. After this she made extraordinary offerings of precious jewels, headed by the pearl rosary she had gained by deceit.

Rūpasūrya thought to herself: "This is the person that sent me to the cemetery. I should grab her by the hair and bite her." But then she thought: "Sentient beings are capable of any kind of action," and instead practiced patience and accepted her confession.

Then Gandhabhadrā petitioned the yogini: "I plan to offer this confession on the last day of the waning period of the month. Please, yogini, care for this wicked one with your compassion."

The yogini promised that she would.

The intelligent minister Negi thought to himself: "A very special yogini is in the city. I should invite her to the palace and she could offer teachings in order to cure the father and his son of their sorrow."

He went to invite the yogini and met her on a lonely road where three roads crossed. He prostrated to her and sought her blessing. He presented her with his upper garment as a meeting gift, and said: "Will you come to the palace and give teachings to relieve the king and his son of their sorrow? In the past the king had a queen called Rūpasūrya. She was taken by three butchers to a cemetery. No trace of her body was ever found and the three butchers did not return home. I do not why this is. In the places you have been, have you heard rumors of where they are? Have you seen them?"

The yogini replied: "I have heard of their whereabouts, but I have not seen them." She smiled. As soon as he saw her full white set of teeth, the discerning minister knew it was her.

"Yogini, I think it is you?" he asked.

As she had taken the vow not to lie, she replied: "It could be."

"Ah! You are a special yogini," he exclaimed. He took her by the hand and told her how the king was oppressed by sorrow.

"What you say is true. Those responsible for these deeds are Gandhabhadrā and the low-caste queen. On the last day of the month Gandhabhadrā is offering me confession. Come and listen, and you will know the reasons why I say this."

Minister Negi replied:

> My beautiful sun-like form, when I first met you,
> I thought you were a goddess from the celestial world.
> Then when you were taken away by the three butchers,
> it was if I had been born in hell.

> Those times have remained with me,
> but now I have found you,
> and I am full of joy, most kind queen!
> I will happily do whatever you say.
> Stay in this place. Go nowhere.

He left at once for the palace. Addressing the king, he said: "Hear me, great king. The three butchers and Queen Rūpasūrya are in the kingdom. Cease your sorrows. Go and bathe."

The king replied: "Have you heard that she has risen from the dead? Do not tell lies, Negi."

"It is no lie. Without a doubt, it is true," replied the minister. "If you ask why, a yogini who has abandoned the telling of lies has said so."

The king was heartened by this news. "Maybe it is true," he thought, and went to bathe in order to wash away his sorrows.

Negi strapped his sword to his side and invited the king and his son to the house below that of Gandhabhadrā. There they hid. On the last day of the month Gandhabhadrā invited the yogini to her house. There she waited on her with great hospitality. As night approached, Gandhabhadrā sent her servants away and seated the yogini on a jeweled throne in the midst of an array of offerings. As she recounted all the evil deeds she had done, the king and his son could barely control themselves and had to be restrained by the minister. When she had repeated her confession three times, all three leapt out with raised swords and crowded over Gandhabhadrā. The yogini sheltered her and said to the king, his son, and the minister:

> Precious king and son,
> a kingdom is to be fostered in peace.
> The people are to be treated with love.
> Wrongdoers are to be treated with compassion.
> One's learning is to be examined with one's mind.
> Wealth is to be used wisely at the right time.
> The heart of this one is with mine.
> The retribution for killing an evil one
> will fall on me.

The king replied:

> Women are in the nature of ignorance.
> Rūpasūrya is like an illuminating beacon.
> We will do as you ask.
> Women are in the nature of anger.
> Rūpasūrya is as gentle as silk.
> Women are in the nature of desire.
> Rūpasūrya is like the wish-granting cow.
> We will do as you ask.

The yogini was a little annoyed with the king's flattery. She said to him:

> I, Rūpasūrya, was living with my old father,
> and then, unable to counter the demands of the king,
> I was brought to the palace, where I was placed into the hands
> of three wicked butchers and taken to a cemetery.

> While there, nine times I lost consciousness.
> Three times the flow of my breath ceased.

Five times I came close to death.
I suffered unimaginably from heat and cold.
I almost lost this precious life.
I only just survived.

The king replied:

The moon, so bright and clear,
can be obscured and hard to see.
The lotus, so gentle and smooth,
can have stamens as sharp as thorns.
A crystal shrine, so pure and translucent,
can become tainted by dust and dirt.
Scholars, so wise and learned,
can sometimes be mistaken.
Through the force of ignorance, I have erred.
Please forgive my wrongdoing.

Minister Negi said:

In the great sea of ignorance and samsara
was formed the great mountain of the king's pride,
surrounded by the peopled continents of desire.
The advice of the virtuous was cast downward,
the heels of the decadent were placed on their heads.
The root of all this wrongdoing is right here.

At once the ministers were called, and they fell into discussion. For her yellow-eyed resentment, it was decided that the low-caste queen would have her eyes plucked out. As for Gandhabhadrā, for her deceptive singing and dancing, and for her trickery and drugging of the king in order to falsely apportion blame to Rūpasūrya, her mouth was disfigured, her eyes torn out, her nose and ears were cut off, her knee tendons were severed, and she was cast out onto the market road.

Rūpasūrya thought to herself: "As the deity instructed, now I should go and wander throughout the land as propagator of the six syllables." She made preparations to leave.

Seeing this, the people told her of the immeasurable pain and suffering the king, ministers, and people had experienced since she had left the kingdom. They continued: "If you do not remain as queen, the suffering of King Candrasiṃha will never end. Please care for us. If you seek only your own peace and happiness and abandon us here, then what does your vow to develop the mind of supreme enlightenment mean?"

Queen Rūpasūrya thought to herself: "The words of the people have real substance. The instructions of the deity also said to dispel the suffering of those beset with grief and sorrow." Therefore she accepted the people's request.

Immediately, the ministers headed by Negi and the people of the city put up ceremonial parasols, victory standards, banners and flags, decorative tassels, drapes, and so on. Music was played and the seven royal emblems and the eight auspicious signs were displayed. The yogini Mahāmuni was led into the palace and again installed as queen.

This has been the chapter on how Rūpasūrya was absolved from all wrongdoing.

Enjoying Happiness and Entering the Path to Liberation

Namo Lokeśvaraya! Again the brahman Rūpasūrya was enthroned as queen. As a result, many auspicious omens were observed. The earth shook in six ways. Birds such as the kalaviṅga sang sweet songs. Fruit trees bore exceptional fruits. Omens a hundred times greater than her previous enthronement were seen. In the king's garden called Always in Bloom there was a lotus surrounded by other flowers. For years the lotus had not bloomed. Nobody knew why. On one auspicious day a light of five different colors radiated from the lotus and permeated the garden. Everybody witnessed this. From that day on, the king and his entourage came to the garden every day and made immeasurable offerings. Rūpasūrya alone realized that a special being would emerge from that lotus. With the vast number of offerings presented to the king, offering substances unowned by anyone, and the peerless offering of practice, she made offerings and chanted with innumerable melodies of praise:

Guide of living beings, possessed of the forms of the buddhas,
taming living beings in accord with their disposition,
child endowed with the thousand petals of enlightened activity,
within this lotus born from mud but untainted by mud,

crack open the egg of ignorance that is my mind[136]
and become the eye ambrosia for all living beings.

By the light of my sun-like form,
may this lotus grove of excellent teaching blossom,
and with the honey whose taste gives untainted bliss,
satisfy the hungry bees that are the people of this kingdom.

After Rūpasūrya made this prayer, all the flowers and trees except the central lotus bloomed at once. The flowers, petals, and fruits were exceptional, and their beautiful aroma spread over a hundred leagues. Each petal was one league in length. No one petal interfered with another and each was transparent.

Soon a red light shot from the west and struck the petals of the central lotus like a comet. Immediately the earth shook in six ways and all musical instruments played themselves. In the center of the lotus sat a small white child, his hair in five knots, the hide of an antelope covering his left breast, adorned in celestial clothes. His right hand held a hundred-bead rosary, his left a white blooming lotus that nestled by his ear. With a radiant smile, he spoke: "Great king, in the earlier part of your life you held wrong views and went for refuge to the non-Buddhist god Īśvara. You deprived countless animals of their lives and caused them much suffering. As a ripening result, you will have to experience much suffering in this life. In your future life too, you are destined to spend many tens of thousands of eons in the deepest Hell Without Respite, experiencing unbearable suffering for each animal you have killed. However, by becoming attracted to this brahman woman, who is cared for by me, you have developed faith and devotion. Moreover, you went for refuge to the great meditator and took vows from him. Since then you have ruled your kingdom in accordance with the Dharma. This has reversed any immediate bad fortune. Finally, you have the auspicious omen of meeting me.

"Now, in order to purify yourself of all obscuration, you should create ten thousand images of each of the representations of the enlightened body, speech, and mind. You should build one hundred and eight monasteries and establish ten thousand monks in each, serving and honoring them as best you can. Treat your people with love and compassion and bring them to the path of enlightenment. Finally, you should give up the kingdom and all possessions and go and live in solitude, there to tame your mind and eventually practice the two stages of yoga. If you do this, in the intermediate state you will gain the supreme siddhi. If you do not follow what I have said, after this life you will be reborn in the Hell Without Respite for ten million eons, after which you will wander in the realms of ghosts and animals."

The king replied:

You in whom there are no faults,
in whom every excellent quality is complete,
child who holds a white lotus and crystal rosary,
care for me with your compassion.

My mind since time without beginning
has not understood the ways of karma.
Therefore, protector, that you with your compassion
care for me is truly a wonder.

This fortunate being has seen your face!
And met with this brahman maiden.
I will practice in keeping with the words of you both.
Wherever you are from, wherever you stay,
look after me with your compassion.

The child replied:

I have no coming, going, or staying.
Unborn, I come from the unborn dharma realm.
Unceasing, I am liberated in the unceasing realm
of nonproliferation.
Not abiding, I disappear into the nonabiding bliss
and emptiness.

With this, the child transformed into rainbow light and vanished into space.

The king and queen, in keeping with the deity's instructions, spent seven years constructing ten thousand images of each of the representations of the enlightened body, speech, and mind, together with accessories, as well as one hundred and eight monasteries, which on the outside resembled large shrines and inside were in the form of temples. In the center of these monastic complexes was a temple constructed from the five precious gems, one league long and half a league wide, on top of which was a white parasol with a golden handle. On the roof and in the four directions and four intermediate directions were hoisted golden victory standards topped with aquamarine. In between were rows of bells and bangles that gave out sweet sounds. The parapets were strung with lattice work adorned with jewels, while the whole was beautifully adorned with flags, silk tassels, and so on.

Inside, upon a throne supported by figures of strong men, elephants, horses, peacocks, cranes, and lions, was a statue of Avalokiteśvara made of refined crystal and adorned with jewels. In front of the statue were unimaginable offerings that exceeded the possessions of the gods and that were headed by a meditative-concentration begging bowl that produced whatever was wished for.

Ten thousand monks were invited to reside in each of the monasteries, where they were served and venerated with the best offerings. These monks spent their time in practice before the Three Jewels. Some prostrated, some made offerings, some performed confession rituals, some rejoiced in the virtues of others, some prayed for the wheel of Dharma to be forever turning, some prayed that the gurus would never pass into nirvana.

Two thirds of the king's dominion was given over in service to the Three Jewels and the monastic community. The people too spent their time immersed in the ten virtues and left behind all wrongdoing.

An exceptional child was born to Queen Rūpasūrya, beautiful to look at and with a radiant smile. Everyone who saw him was captivated. He was the ambrosia of the eyes of all men and gods. Taking parts of the names of his mother and father, he was called Sūryasiṃha. The brahman seers who were summoned to examine him said in unison:

> Dispeller of the darkness of living beings,
> bringer of the harvest of happiness and prosperity,
> this prince is the flawless sun.
> Terrifying opponents, the lord of all beasts,
> this prince is the lion, king of the animals.
> The three realms he will bring under his control.

When Prince Sūryasiṃha reached the age of eight, Queen Rūpasūrya said to King Candrasiṃha:

There is no knowing when death will come.
We are powerless to have control over our lives.
Even though it may appear otherwise,
the happiness of samsara is without any essence.
Therefore, as the deity instructed,
it is time to dwell in solitude without any attachment,
and seek the great freedom of enlightenment.

The king could not go against the words of Rūpasūrya. However, his mind was still a little attached to his kingdom and its pleasures. As these doubts plagued his mind, one day he saw behind the palace a monk wearing the orange robe and carrying a begging bowl, a staff, and a pot. He was calm and serene, and was walking slowly with his eyes focused on the ground just a yoke's length away. The king said to him: "Noble arhat,[137] where are you from? Where are you going?"

The monk replied: "I am not an arhat. I am a king from another world who ruled over its four continents, but understanding that my kingdom had no essence, I became ordained into the doctrine of the Buddha, and I have come here to see the disciples of Śākyamuni Buddha.[138] The amount of happiness found in this city-of-ghosts kingdom is the size of a needle point. If you are attached to that, then why would you not become a monk?"

These words struck the heart of the king like an arrow. He went straight to his son and said:

Intelligent and all-powerful son, listen to me.
The Lord of Death is not idle, for he will come,
and there is no way to flee from him.
It is time to seek the great goal of freedom.
Look after the kingdom, my son.
Your mother and father are going to the Dharma.

His son replied:

To lie unclothed in the high snowy ranges
in the first of the three periods of winter,
except for the turquoise-maned snow lion,
is not within the capabilities of animals.

To swim and dart beneath the thick ice
in the last of the three periods of spring,
except for the little golden-eye fish,
is not within the capabilities of creatures.

To harness the power of a great king
in the period of the five degenerations,
except for the great lord, Candrasiṃha,
is not within the capabilities of lesser kings,
and especially not in one so young as me.

His father replied:

When the dangers of the snow mountain mist approach,
who better than the son whose father is the lord of beasts?
When the dangers of the thick ice forming arrive,
who better than the son whose mother is the golden-eye fish?
If it is not known how to foster a kingdom,
who better than the son of me, Candrasiṃha?
Keep this in your mind. Look after the kingdom.
Your mother and father will now immerse themselves
    in Dharma.

His son, Sūryasiṃha, replied:

In that case, noble father, please listen.
After the father, the son rules the kingdom.
For that, who should be my objects of offering?
Who are the wise that I can ask questions of?
What kind of queen is best for nurturing a family?

His father, King Candrasiṃha, replied with the following advice:

Those who guard their morality as they would their eyes,
with great knowledge of the practices of the four truths,
compassionate to others, trained in the mind of
    enlightenment—

for your objects of offering, devote yourself to such a
    monastic community.

Those who are intelligent and possessed of noble birth,
with great liking for virtue and of a resolute mind,
showing affection to the people and respecting their master—
rely constantly on such ministers.

One who is of a good family and of noble ways,
who is kind to the people, who respects her companions,
who has a wide knowledge of food and drink,
and who will increase your wealth of sons—
seek out such a queen.

In all matters outer and inner, consult and come to
    a decision.
Never be stubborn, but be in harmony with all.
If you are wise in maintaining harmony,
you will be revered by all.
From a father to a son, keep this in your mind!

Then Prince Sūryasimha went to his mother and said:

I cannot go against the words of my father, the king,
but the load of an ox has been placed on a calf.
With regard to all affairs, both outer and inner,
how am I to carry them out?

His mother gave this advice:

Tread carefully with enemies and you will have long-term
    friends.
Have little desire for wealth and finally you will become rich.
Always follow virtue and finally you will become a Buddha.

Listen to me this one time, my son.
Whenever you see wicked deeds done by those close to you,
be brave, but inwardly hold them to be false.

Whenever you think on what is good and bad,
what is and what is not, do not talk of it much,
but consult your own mind.

Always put your trust in the Three Jewels.
From a mother to her son, keep this in your mind!
Do not forget this heartfelt talk.
Your mother and father now go to the sacred Dharma.

Then the hunter spoke to the child:

Stones in clods of earth are the curse of the castle.
Spoiled servants are the curse of tsampa.
Losing yourself to women and society is the curse
    of ambition.
The ill-intended moving to the head of the row
    is the master's curse.
Dispel these four curses and rule the kingdom in
    accord with Dharma.
I too am minded to the Dharma and will follow
    the king and queen.

Minister Negi thought to himself: "What the hunter said is correct. I too will speak to the prince and then follow the Dharma." He went before the prince and said:

Fill your mouth with noble words and you will
    become noble.
Speak sincerely to your children and they will
    become sound.
Outwardly be content with food and drink and
    you will be a great adornment.
Keep your wealth hidden and you will become rich.

Keep no favorites among your circle and you will
    be respected.
Always follow the ways of virtue and you will reap
    a great reward.

These are sincere words, and so hold them in your mind.
I too am minded toward the Dharma
and will request to be allowed to follow the Dharma.

Headed by his mother and father, the prince addressed the minor rulers, the ministers, and the people:

Mother, father, ministers, people, and all attended here,
listen to what I have to say.
Under your reign the kingdom is as vast as space.
Under my reign it will not diminish.
I will do all you say and not go against the words of my parents.

If you will not be persuaded to stay, but will follow the Dharma,
then I request that I be allowed to take care of you.
I will arrange all necessary provisions and offer them to you.
I ask that in the future you lead me to higher realms of birth.

The 3,600,000 towns and cities, headed by the city of Cittamaṭi, and every piece of the land, far and near, without exception, was offered to Prince Sūryasiṃha.

Then the king and his queen, together with their ministers and entourage, went to the remote monastic community in the forest of Bodhividhi. There they attained the great liberation of the precious state of a buddha.

King Sūryasiṃha ruled his kingdom in keeping with Dharma, and his minister and people enjoyed unprecedented prosperity and happiness.

Thus ends the story of Rūpasūrya.

8. The Story of Padma Prabhājvālya (Pema Öbar): Incarnation of Great Siddha Padmasambhava

Ripening within the womb of a lotus flower,
in the Sindhu ocean that possessed the hue
of the five wisdoms of the self-arising conqueror,
taking the form of the lotus-born vajra body,
outshining all appearance and existence—
the dust from your feet I take to my head.

Your abode of the Glorious Copper Mountain,
in the shape of a wish-fulfilling jewel,
its base descending into the realm of the Naga king,
its magnificent middle accommodating the Dharma of the
    ḍākinīs,
its peak reaching the realms of Brahma.
On the right, the male skeletons in line.
On the left, the female skeletons in line.
Extraordinary king of the mountain, I prostrate to you.

NOW I WILL RELATE a chapter from his life story. Long ago in the country of India there was a destitute non-Buddhist kingdom, whose palace was called Nakhamuṇi, and whose king was called Mithyāyajña. This king was an incarnation of the demon Maṭmaṭa. His minister was called Janghākarika, who was an incarnation of the demon Kṛṣṇa Devadatta.

Not far from the palace was a beautiful little house called Temple of Tārā. There an incarnation of Avalokiteśvara was to be born, whose father was a merchant called Sudhana and whose mother was called Devaputra brahman. This merchant traded goods from upper parts of the country to the lower, from the lower parts to the upper, from south to the north, and from the

A performance of *Padma Prabhājvālya,*
at the Norling Shotön Festival in Lhasa, 1937.

north to the south. In this way he filled the king's coffers with valuables and
made a destitute king wealthy.

SUDHANA IS SENT TO SIṄGALA

One day the non-Buddhist king fell into a perverse state of mind and
thought to himself: "If I do not find a way to get rid of this merchant, there
is a danger that he will become greater than me." He turned to his minister,
Janghākarika, and said:

> My supreme minister, so dear to my heart,
> Janghākarika, hear what I have to say.
> Near here in a house called the Temple of Tārā,

there lives a merchant by the name of Sudhana.
Bring him to me.

Minister Janghākarika changed over the left and right black flaps of his
coat, strapped one knife on his right side and one on his left, and set off for
the Temple of Tārā in an even gait. On arriving, he knocked on the door and
shouted out: "Devaputra brahman!"

From inside the house Devaputra brahman wondered who was calling
and looked outside. Seeing that the demon minister Janghākarika was at the
doorway, she went to the door and said:

> Welcome, minister to the king.
> Welcome here, minister Janghākarika.
> Minister, please relate to me
> the reason for coming to this place.

The minister replied:

> Listen to me, Devaputra brahman.
> Listen to what Janghākarika has to say.
> Your husband, the merchant Sudhana,
> has been told to come before the king.

Devaputra brahman returned inside and went to her husband, saying:

> Alas! Hear me, merchant Sudhana.
> Listen to this wife, Devaputra brahman.
> The demon minister Janghākarika has come to our door,
> saying that the non-Buddhist king, Mithyāyajña,
> has commanded that you are to go before him.
> What should we do? What is best to do?

The merchant replied:

> My wife, Tārā of the mind of enlightenment,
> my lady, Devaputra brahman, listen to me.
> Whatever punishment the king might have for me,
> I will go to him.

Do not worry, my lady. Be at ease.
Have you heard me, Devaputra brahman?

The minister and the merchant went before the king. The king addressed
Sudhana:

Welcome, merchant Sudhana.
I trust the journey here was not tiresome?
The purpose of our talk today concerns the fact
that as king and official, our positions are reversed.

I hold the position of being a king of a country,
and yet my wealth consists of a few silk cloths.
You are an official in a kingdom,
and yet you have all the wealth you want.
As a result, I have very little wealth.

Therefore, in the nāga realm known as Padminī,
the king Śaṅkhapāla Śuklā holds in his hand
a great treasure of a jewel, one known as
Fulfilling All Needs, Destroying All Armies.

This jewel would fulfill all needs within Nakhamuṇi
    Palace,
as well as accomplishing the defeat of all enemies
    outside.
Therefore you are to obtain this jewel.
If you do, your reward will be extraordinary.
If you do not, you will be punished.

The merchant replied:

Great king, please hear what I say.
I ask that you do not give me such a heavy task.
When I was young and my teeth were white,
I alleviated your poverty with riches.

A staging of the *Padma Prabhājvālya* opera in India.

Now that I am old and my hair is white,
how could I possibly find jewels from within
    the great ocean?
I cannot go. Please excuse me from this task.
Have you heard me, my precious king?

The king replied:

Merchant, if you do not obey the words of a king,
then I will deliver this punishment on you.
Janghākarika, go and bring Devaputra brahman here now.
Both husband and wife will receive the punishment.

As the minister was making ready to leave for the Temple of Tārā, the merchant thought to himself: "My wife is going to be punished for something I have done. It would be better that I went to the great ocean." He again addressed the king:

Hear me, great king, Mithyāyajña.
Listen to this traveler, Sudhana.
Please, I beg of you, do not visit punishment
on the old mother, Devaputra brahman.

I can travel to the realm of the great ocean.
For traveling to such a fearsome place,
I ask that the king provide all I need.

I will need a boat that is both speedy and sturdy.
Upon that boat I will need a cabin of the finest wood.
Atop that cabin should be a roof of gold,
crowned with the horsehead wish-granting jewel.

I will need five hundred helpers, all loyal.
I will need four large sails to gather the large winds.
I will need four lesser sails to set against the lesser winds.
I will need a lead anchor that will resist the pull of the four
    directions.

I will need a live pigeon to look out for sea monsters.
I will need a variety of grains to feed the pigeon.
I will need a white conch shell to tame the sea monsters.
I will need the curd of a cow to maintain the conch shell.
I will need good grass to feed the cow.

I will need a talking parrot who can tell the future.
I will need much sesame grain to feed the parrot.
I will need a red rooster to signal daybreak.
If you can grant these provisions, great king,
I will set off for the great ocean.

The king promised to provide whatever the merchant needed. Again the merchant addressed the king:

Great king, please hear these words.
Before setting out to the great ocean,
please grant me a stay of three years,
or, at the very least, of three months.

The king replied:

Before the merchant sets out for the ocean,
how can I grant him a stay of three years?
How can I grant him three months?
I will grant you seven days, starting from now.
During that time you may do as you please.

At this, the merchant set out for the Temple of Tārā with a heavy heart.
Meanwhile his wife, Devaputra brahman, was wondering if the king had punished her husband and had climbed to the top of the house to look out for him. Seeing him approaching, she came down to him and said:

Listen to me, merchant Sudhana.
Listen to this mother, Devaputra brahman.
What punishment did the king inflict on you?
Tell me truthfully and fully.

The merchant replied:

My wife, Tārā of the mind of enlightenment,
my lady, Devaputra brahman, listen to me.
The words of the non-Buddhist king were as follows,
and were a punishment like no other.

In the nāga realm known as Padminī,
the nāga king Śaṇkhapāla Śuklā holds in his hand
a great treasure of a jewel, one which is known as
Fulfilling All Needs, Destroying All Armies.

This I must obtain as a support for the palace, he has said.
Should I obtain it, I will receive extraordinary rewards.
If I do not, both of us will be subject to the law.

Therefore I will leave for the great ocean.
I have been granted seven days before I leave.
During this time I may do as I please.
Have you understood this, Devaputra brahman?

Devaputra brahman was overcome with grief and said:

Alas! Such suffering upon us!
Alas! What is to be done!
If it is true that the merchant must go to sea,
who can this mother turn to?
The waters have dried up on the land.
The risen sun has set and grown old.

Thus she cried out aloud in her grief and fell unconscious to the floor. The merchant sprinkled sandalwood water on her face, and she recovered. He spoke to her:

My wife, Tārā of the mind of enlightenment,
Do not be upset. Be at ease.
If I do not return within three years,
then I will have died and faced my death.

After me, continue in the ways of virtue.
Make offerings to the Three Jewels,
give alms to the poor and the beggars.
Cherish the child you carry in your body,
make sure that you bring him up well.[139]

If after today we do not meet again in this life,
I pray that we meet on the road to the land of the ḍākinīs.

He took her by the hand and made this prayer.

Seven days later, in the morning, the merchant left for the palace of the king. His beautiful wife, Devaputra brahman, realizing that she would be without him, was overcome with grief.

At the palace the king addressed Sudhana:

Listen to me, traveler Sudhana.
Listen to the song of me, the king.
All the provisions for your journey to the ocean,
without error I have arranged for you.

You will have your five hundred helpers,
all of whom are loyal and led by Subhavya.

The merchant with his helpers and provisions, which included excellent horses, oxen, and buffalos, set out for the ocean. They traveled over the grass plains of India, where the horses, oxen, and buffalos were employed. Finally, the helpers set about building a boat. Some were employed in woodwork, some in metalwork, and some worked with gold. In three months they built the boat. All climbed into the boat and set out for sea.

When rowing the boat, the ropes were slack.
When sailing the boat, the ropes were tight.
After some leagues they came to a part of the ocean,
under which lived fearsome nāgas.

The ocean tossed and threw up great waves. The speaking parrot, with tears in his eyes, said to the merchant:

> Listen to me, merchant Sudhana.
> Listen to this speaking parrot.
> Under our boat are two nāgas,
> one black and one white, and very fierce.
> They manifest as scorpions, the size of yaks.
> Our boat is about to be destroyed.
> If you have any methods or prayers to prevent this,
> make them now. Otherwise, help me return home.

With these words, the parrot flapped his wings three times, and flew out of the boat. Then the black and white nāgas manifested as scorpions the size of yaks, seized the boat at either end, and tore it apart. With great effort the merchants were able to cling to the timbers of the broken boat and were carried off into the ocean. Instead of being taken to their desired destination of the nāga land of Padminī, they were carried to the undesired female cannibal land of Siṅgala. The cannibals there put their hands to their foreheads and looked out to sea. Seeing many merchants clinging to the ship's timbers, they talked among themselves:

> Listen here, we race of female cannibals.
> Today a group of merchants from eastern India
> have lost their boat and have been carried by the sea.
> This is food for our families. We should see to it.

They went down to the shore and addressed the merchants:

> Hear us, you merchants! Listen to us women!
> We will rescue you from this endless ocean.
> Welcome to this happy land of Siṅgala.

Each cannibal rescued a merchant and took him as her companion.

One day the merchant Sudhana thought to himself: "These companions of ours regularly walk up the valley to where the land is flat. What are they doing there?" One day he went up the valley to see. At the head of the valley was a fortress. "Where is the way in?" he wondered. Walking around on all four sides, he could see no way in. By the fortress was a dead tree. He climbed it and looked into the fortress. Inside he saw many people. Some

had a torso but no bottom half. Some were without eyes, ears, and so on.
Many were crying out. The merchant called out to them:

> You men, who have collected no bad karma,
> what are you doing in this fortress?
> Imprisoned inside this hell-like place,
> what have you done to deserve such suffering?

The men inside the fortress replied:

> Listen to us, man on top of a tree.
> Listen to us without distraction.
> Where have you come from?
> Why have you come here?

Merchant Sudhana replied:

> Listen to me, men inside the fortress.
> Listen to me without distraction.
> I have come from eastern India.
> I am a merchant in the service of King Mithyāyajña.

> In keeping with his instructions, I set out on the ocean
> to fetch the jewel called Fulfilling All Needs, Destroying All Armies.
> Because of a disturbance caused by fearsome nāgas,
> the sea became turbulent and the boat was destroyed.
> Clinging on to timbers from the broken boat,
> we came to this land of ḍākinīs.

> I am known as Sudhana the merchant.
> My five hundred helpers are in the homes of the ḍākinīs.
> We have become companions of the ḍākinīs.
> This is the tale of how I came here.

The men inside the fortress replied:

> Listen to us, merchant Sudhana.
> Listen to us without distraction.

This is not a land of ḍākinīs.
It is a land of flesh-eating cannibals.

We too are merchants, in the service of King Candra.
We came to the ocean in search of jewels.
Because of a disturbance caused by fearsome nāgas,
the sea became turbulent and the boat was destroyed.
Like you, we were rescued from the sea by the cannibals.

When we were young, we were kept as their companions.
When we became old we were cast into this fortress.
The reason why some here have no bottom halves to
    their bodies
is that when full human flesh is unavailable
they eat away at these parts.
The same fate will fall upon you.

If we have not accumulated bad karma, then our karma
    is the same.
Have you understood all this, merchant Sudhana?

In response, merchant Sudhana said:

Listen to me, merchants of King Candra.
Listen to me without distraction.
If it is true that this is not a ḍākinī land,
then tell me a way to escape from it.

The men in the fortress replied:

Listen to us, merchant Sudhana.
We will tell you of a way of escape.
Further on up the valley of this land
is a place called the Great Golden Desert,
where is found a turquoise spring and turquoise grass.

On the full moon of the first summer month,
the king of horses comes to that place.

He takes three mouthfuls of the turquoise grass,
three mouthfuls from the turquoise spring,
and three times he rolls on the desert ground.

If you make a single-pointed prayer to him,
the king of horses will lead you from this place.

That evening Sudhana went to the homes of the cannibals and spoke to his five hundred companions:

Listen to me, my five hundred companions.
Listen to me without distraction.
This land is not a land of ḍākinīs.
It seems that it is a land of cannibals.
We must find a way to escape from here.
Have you understood this, my five hundred companions?

The five hundred merchants became afraid. That evening the cannibals returned from the flatlands. Sudhana addressed them:

Listen to me, my ḍākinī companions.
Listen to Sudhana without distraction.
This land looks like a ḍākinī land.
If it really is a land of ḍākinīs,
day and night you should be holding festivities.

The place should be filled with dancing and singing,
and with the sounds of secret mantra and melody.
But every day you wander off to the flatlands.
Is this the activity of a ḍākinī land?

Sudhana and the merchants discussed a way to escape. They prepared much beer and spirits. Sudhana said: "Only pretend to drink. Give as much as you can to the cannibals."

The cannibal women brought beer and spirits to the merchants. The merchants pretended to be drunk and plied as much drink as they could on the cannibals. Gradually the cannibals became completely intoxicated and fell asleep. Sudhana said: "Now, all of you, follow me." As instructed by the men in the fortress, they fled up the valley to the Golden Desert, where they waited.

After some time, out of the clouds, Baladeva, the king of horses, appeared, and with a whooshing sound landed on the desert. From the turquoise spring he took three mouthfuls of water. He took three mouthfuls of turquoise grass and rolled three times on the ground. Sudhana and his five hundred helpers went down on one knee, place their hands together, and made this prayer:

Mighty king of horses, guide of living beings,
please hear the words of these merchants.
Our land is that of Nakhamuṇi,
and we are merchants of King Mithyāyajña.

We were sent to fetch a jewel from the ocean,
but because of hindrance from a black nāga,
the ocean churned and our boat was destroyed.

We were saved by clinging on to the timbers of the boat,
but instead of landing at our desired destination of Padminī,
we came instead to this dreaded place of Siṅgala.
Show us a way to escape from here.

The king of horses neighed three times and said:

Listen to me, merchant and helpers.
Listen to what Baladeva has to say.
If you have a metal ring to hook on to, say so.

For I have a hook to lift you up.
Those who can fit, sit upon me.
Those who cannot, take hold of my mane and tail.

Do not look back into the cannibal's mouth.
You have made a single-pointed prayer, now jump!
Let us flee! If others come to know, it will be a bad omen.
Baladeva knows this. You are indeed fortunate.

Sudhana and the merchants climbed onto the horse. Those who could not fit held on to his mane and tail, and with a whoosh they flew into the skies.

Gradually the cannibals awoke one another from their sleep. "Our companions are not here," they said. "We must go and look for them." They roused themselves quickly from their sleep and went in search, but could not find them. Looking up, they saw the merchants on Baladeva flying through the sky. They ran to their houses and brought out their children. Holding them aloft, they cried out:

Shameless Sudhana and his merchant helpers!
Listen to your wives down here.
Even if you do not think of your wives,
think of your children and come back.
If you are determined not to return,
then at least look back one last time.

Their cries rang out through the skies for a long time. Sudhana's merchant helpers thought to themselves: "They are cannibals, but they do have our children." With this thought they all looked back, and like grains falling into the threshing machine, they fell into the cannibals' mouths. The cannibals said:

You shameless five hundred merchant helpers,
the great horse has miraculous powers of flying,
but nothing can help you now.

With this, they ate the helpers.

Because he had made a single-pointed prayer, the king of horses took Sudhana to the celestial realm of Tuṣita.

THE BIRTH OF PRABHĀJVĀLYA
From his abode on Glorious Copper Mountain, the Orgyen Guru, Padmasambhava, was gazing at the world. He thought to himself: "There is no one sadder than Devaputra brahman in her Tārā Temple. To relieve her sadness I must borrow a place to live for almost ten months."

From Glorious Copper Mountain he sent out a ray of light into Devaputra brahman. From that day on, she found joy in all she did. At night she slept peacefully. In the daytime she enjoyed her food. Finally, after almost ten months, a son was born to her. As soon as the child was born, he spoke to his mother:

> Mother, Devaputra brahman, listen to me.
> I will be the protector for those without friends.
> I will be the refuge for those without shelter.
> The doctrine of the Buddha I will establish.
> The profound tantric path I will establish.
> I will crush the doctrine of the demon Maṭmaṭa.

His mother thought to herself: "A child speaking as soon as he is born? Either he is an incarnation of Buddha or a manifestation of a demon."

How an ordinary child would develop in a month, he developed in a day. How an ordinary child would develop in a year, he developed in a month. Therefore he was given the name Padma Prabhājvālya (Radiant Lotus).

One day the children from the neighboring houses went out to collect wood. Padma Prabhājvālya thought that he too would like to go gather wood. He went to his mother and said:

> Listen, mother, Devaputra brahman.
> Hear what Padma Prabhājvālya has to say.
> The children of the neighboring houses
> have gone outside to collect wood.
> Mother, give me a sack and a rope.
> I too will go to gather wood.

His mother replied:

> Little child, so dear to my heart,
> Padma Prabhājvālya, listen to your mother.
> These children from the neighboring houses
> are doing worked suited to their ability.
>
> You are a child of only three.
> How can you possibly gather wood?
> Stay here in the Temple of Tārā, child.
> I will provide you all you need for living.

However, he did not listen to his mother. Secretly he took a sack and a rope and went up the valley to collect wood with the other children. There on the upper fields he played games with the children. In the morning the other children won all the games, but in the afternoon Prabhājvālya won them all. The children remarked:

Listen, children gathered here.
His confidence is high, but he has no father.
Ours is lower, but we have a mother and father.
Let us return to our mother and father.

With these words they put their sacks on their backs and returned home. Prabhājvālya gathered wood from the high fields. As he did so, he saw a mother and father deer together. He thought to himself: "Even grass-eating animals have a mother and father, and so I must have a father. I will ask my mother about my father." He put his sack on his back and returned to the Temple of Tārā. He put the wood by the kitchen door and went to his mother, saying:

Listen, mother, Devaputra brahman.
Hear what Padma Prabhājvālya has to say.
Today I went to where you said I should not go,
up to the high Indian plains where I collected
aloe, mulberry, and other wood.

There on the plains I saw a mother and father deer.
The father walked in front, the mother behind.
Their children walked in between the two.
Grass-eating animals have mothers and fathers,
and surely I must have a father.
Mother, tell me about my father.

His mother replied:

My dear son, Padma Prabhājvālya,
listen to your mother, Padma.
Why ask about your father?
Be quiet. Do not say such childish things.

The next day Padma went to gather wood at the foot of the valley. There he saw a lake and noticed a mother and father duck swimming with their brood. He thought to himself: "Those with the bodies of birds have mothers and fathers, and so surely I must have a father. I will ask my mother about him." He picked up the wood and returned to the Temple of Tārā. Going to his mother, he said:

> Listen, mother, Devaputra brahman.
> Hear what Padma Prabhājvālya has to say.
> Today I went to a lake on the high Indian plains.
> On the lake were a mother and father duck.
> The father was in front, the mother was behind,
> and their children swam in between the two.
> Those with the bodies of birds have mothers and fathers.
> And so for sure I have a father.
> Tell me about him, Mother.

His mother replied:

> My dear son, Padma Prabhājvālya,
> listen to your mother, Padma.
> I will tell you of your father.

> One time our king, Mithyāyajña,
> organized a great feast for the beggars.
> At that time I picked a beggar child as my foster son.
> That is the story of your mother and father.
> Do you understand, Padma Prabhājvālya?

His mother took a sandalwood stick and beat him severely. Padma became very upset and pleaded with his mother:

> Listen, mother, Devaputra brahman!
> Hear what Padma Prabhājvālya has to say!
> Woe is me! I am so sad. I have no parents.
> Of such little merit am I!
> I will not stay here but go in search of my parents.
> If I find my father, I can repay his kindness.

In tears he ran down the stairs of the house. His mother came after him and said:

> My dear son, Padma Prabhājvālya,
> listen to your mother, Padma.
> Do not be upset, my son. Be at peace.
> Come inside the Temple of Tārā.
> I will provide everything you need.
>
> Do not go wandering throughout the country.
> Enter a retreat here in the Temple of Tārā.
> Otherwise the non-Buddhist king might hear
>   of you.
> If that should happen, he will show no mercy.

Padma entered a retreat in the scripture room of the Temple of Tārā. One day he looked out on a market that had suddenly sprung up. The bigger traders were dealing in elephants and horses, while the smaller merchants were selling needles and thread. He thought to himself: "I want to sell some thread." He took a sheaf of wool from his mother's wool cupboard and, without her knowing, spun eighteen large balls and nineteen small balls of yarn that radiated light. Leaving the temple by the back door, he went to the market.

At a junction of three roads he met an old woman whose hair was whiter than a conch and who was carrying a bag of coins on her back. Padma said to her:

> Old woman, shall we two do business?
> Old woman, we could be buyer and seller.
> Old woman, what do you have to sell?
> I have quality wool to sell.

The old woman replied:

> Ah! What a clever little boy.
> This child speaks so well.
> If we are to discuss business where three roads meet,
> some will say the price is high, others that it is low.

This will cause the winds in my blood to rise.
Let us go among those palm trees over there.
We can conduct our business there.

The old woman had thought to cheat Padma Prabhājvālya, and led him to the palm trees. They agreed on an exchange of one coin for one ball of yarn. As they were about to trade, the boy said:

Old woman, tell me of the qualities of your coins.
I will tell you of the qualities of my yarn.

The old woman replied:

As you ask me about my coins,
in India they are known as *kārṣāpaṇa*.
In Tibetan they are called *drönbu*.
The larger ones are called in Chinese *drönbu*.

"Now tell me about your woolen yarn," she said. Padma replied:

As you ask me about my woolen yarn,
first, it comes from the body of a fine female sheep.
Second, it was sheared with the knife of a young man.
Third, it was packed in the wool closet of my mother.
Fourth, it came into the hands of this young child,
where it was wound, stretched, and dipped.
These are the qualities of this woolen yarn.

The yarn can be long as a road,
and as short as is necessary.
The lowest quality is like casting off a friend.
The best is like a whistled song.

They began trading. When only half of the yarn was sold, the old woman ran out of coins. At this, she became tormented by a rise of the winds in her blood:

Woe, woe is me! What pain is this!
Alas, alas! What can I do!
All the wealth I have amassed in my life
has been taken away in one morning by him.

To a father who was like a sandalwood tree,
comes a son, who is like a red willow tree.
A good father who dealt in jewels,
has a bad son who deals in yarn.

With this, the old woman fell into a faint. Padma thought to himself: "This old woman has something to say about a father who was like a sandalwood tree." He took her by the hand and said:

Old woman, do not complain so much. Get up.
Tell me about this sandalwood-tree father.
If it is a story about my own father,
I will give you back all your coins
and the other half of the yarn as a present.
Do you understand, old woman with your sweet words?

The old woman was delighted. She got up, put her hands together, and said:

Listen to me, Padma Prabhājvālya.
I will tell the story of the sandalwood-tree father.
Your father is the merchant Sudhana.
Your mother's name is Devaputra brahman.

Your father, the merchant Sudhana,
was sent to the ocean by the king.
Because of hindrance from fearsome nāgas,
they did not return from the ocean.
This is the story of your parents.
Have you understood, Padma Prabhājvālya?

He gave the radiant yarn to the old woman. Like a hawk hearing the sound of thunder, he was overjoyed on hearing her story. He returned home

from the market on the main road, whistling as he went. He went to his
mother and said:

> Listen, mother, Devaputra brahman.
> Hear what Padma Prabhājvālya has to say.
> Today I sing a song for the good of all,
> for today I have a mother and a father.
>
> The merchant Sudhana is my father.
> My father, the merchant Sudhana,
> was a very successful man.
> I will do the work that he has done.
> I will carry on his legacy and serve you, mother.

Mother and son were very happy at this turn of events.

One day the non-Buddhist king and his officials were taking a walk on
the roof of the palace. He looked toward the market that had sprung up.
There he saw the bigger traders dealing in elephants, horses, and all kinds of
precious jewels. He saw the old woman selling her coins, and in front of her
he saw the yarn. Its radiant light was so bright he almost fell off the roof. He
ran down to the palace and said to a minister:

> Janghākarika, my minister, listen to me.
> Hear what I say, Janghākarika.
> In a market that has just sprung up,
> in front of an old woman selling her coins,
> is a treasure unlike no other that radiates with light.
>
> The greater light is like that of the sun and moon,
> the lesser light is as bright as the stars themselves.
> It is yarn that has been spun by the old woman herself,
> or it is yarn that has come from another kingdom.
>
> Minister, go and discover the story of this yarn.
> Go this minute, Janghākarika.
> Have you understood, Janghākarika?

Minister Janghākarika changed over the left and right black flaps of his coat, strapped one knife on his right side and one on his left, and set off for the market. He went to the old woman selling her coins and said:

Old woman with your sweet talk, listen to me.
Listen to this minister Janghākarika.
This yarn that sits in front of you,
does it come from another kingdom,
or is it yarn you have spun yourself?
Do not hide anything from me. Tell me honestly.

The old woman rose unsteadily to her feet, and said to the minister:

Minister of the king, Janghākarika,
listen to this old woman.
This yarn that sits in front of me
does not come from another kingdom.
This old woman spun it in her leisure time.
Have you understood, Janghākarika?

The minister became angry and said:

If you do not tell me the truth,
I will kill you. You will face death.

Three times he slapped the old woman so that she almost blacked out. He took out his black knife and went to stab the old woman in the heart. She put her hands together and pleaded with the minister:

Janghākarika, minister to the king,
do not kill this old woman. Spare her life.
I will tell you truthfully of where the yarn came from.

There was a father, known as the merchant Sudhana.
He had a son called Padma Prabhājvālya.
The child and I were talking business.
I told him of his father, who was like the sandalwood tree.
As a reward, he gave me the yarn.

I offer this yarn to the king.
Do not beat me or kill me, I beg of you.
Do not, I beg, send me into forced labor
or impose a heavy tax on me.

The minister took the yarn to the king and said:

Hear these words, precious king.
If I am to tell the story of where the yarn came from,
there was a father known as merchant Sudhana.
He had a son who was called Padma Prabhājvālya.
It was by this son that the yarn was made.
Have you understood, great king?

The king was disturbed to hear this. He replied:

This is very strange indeed,
that a child should come without a father.
This merchant's son is very intelligent.
At such a young age, he showed much skill
in the business of selling yarn and gaining those coins.
Seems as if he is cleverer than his own father.

If I do not get rid of this young child,
he could well prove a danger to my rule.
Janghākarika, go at once and bring the boy to me.

PRABHĀJVĀLYA IS SENT TO THE OCEAN
The minister set out at a steady pace until he arrived at the Temple of Tārā.
There he knocked on the doors and called out long and loud: "Elegant lady,
Devaputra brahman!"
From behind the many doors of the temple, Devaputra brahman looked
out to see Janghākarika at her door. She went upstairs to her son and said:

My dear son, Padma Prabhājvālya.
Padma Prabhājvālya, listen to your mother.
Previously I said to you, my little son,
not to go wandering throughout the country.

Now the demon minister, Janghākarika, is at our door.
Son, hide among the stacked scriptures in your room.
I will go down to see the demonic minister
and see what commands the king has issued.

The child hid among the scriptures while his mother went to the door.
There she addressed the minister:

Minister, pray tell the reason you have come here.
Please, speak honestly and truthfully to me.

Janghākarika replied:

Hear me, Devaputra brahman.
Listen to this minister Janghākarika.
The command of our king, Mithyāyajña,
is of great significance and unlike others.

Your young son, Padma Prabhājvālya,
is to be brought into the presence of the king.
Now bring the child to me.
Have you understood, Devaputra brahman?

His mother, Devaputra brahman, could not possibly show her son to the
minister, and so she replied in a roundabout way:

Janghākarika, minister and messenger for the king,
please hear these words, Janghākarika.
My companion and husband, the merchant Sudhana,
was long ago sent to the ocean and has not returned.
How can a son be born without a father?
Have you understood, minister Janghākarika?

Janghākarika became very angry and replied:

Listen to me, woman! You conch-like beautiful woman,
listen to the words of this minister Janghākarika!
The whole of India is talking about your son.

If you do not speak truthfully to me,
I will kill you and you will face death.

Three times he threw her face down on the ground and drew out his knife
to stab her in the heart. Padma Prabhājvālya had heard his mother's words
and thought to himself: "My old mother is being punished on my behalf."
He ran down the long steps and jumped over the short ones. Taking the
minister by the hand, he said:

Janghākarika, minister and messenger to the king,
do not kill my mother. Spare her life.
Regardless of what he has determined for me,
I will go before the king.

The minister stopped short of killing Devaputra brahman and went to
the king accompanied by Padma. The child prostrated three times to the
king, causing him to almost fall off his throne. The king said:

Welcome, Padma Prabhājvālya.
I trust you experienced no hardship on the way here.
You, a son, do not have a father.
I, a king, do not have the fortune to have a son.

The son does the work of his father,
the minister does the work of the king.
The feather does the work of the arrow,
the gums do the work of the teeth.

If the son were to venture out, it would be worthwhile.
If this father stays at home, it would be worthwhile.
It is a wonderful practice in the nāga realm of Padminī,
to reward with gifts those who fulfill the wishes of the fish.

Go and bring for me the great treasure of a jewel,
known as Fulfilling All Needs, Destroying All Armies,
which the nāga king Śaṅkhapāla Śuklā holds in his hand.
Do that and you will receive a great reward.
Fail, and you will be subject to the law.

Padma got up, prostrated to the king, and said:

Great king, please pay attention to me.
Do not turn your ears to another.
My father, Sudhana, was successful in his work,
and yet he did not bring this jewel from the ocean.

I am just a three-year-old child.
How can I possibly bring back this jewel?
Please, do not give this command to me.

The king replied:

If you are not to heed the command of a king,
there is no option other than punishment.
Minister Janghākarika, go quickly now.
Bring the boy's mother to me.
Mother and son will both be punished.
Have you understood, Janghākarika?

The minister got ready to leave for the Temple of Tārā. Padma Prabhā-jvālya thought to himself: "For my sake my own mother will be punished. Even if it costs me my life, I must go to the ocean." He said to the king:

Please hear these words, precious king.
Listen to this child, Padma Prabhājvālya.
If I have to journey to the great ocean,
please grant me at best a time of my own choosing
or a period of three years before I leave.
Or at least please grant me three months.

The king replied:

Listen to me, Padma Prabhājvālya.
Listen to the melody of a king.
For preparing to journey to the ocean,
how I can I grant you a time of your choosing?

How can I grant you up to three years?
How can I grant you even three months?
I will grant you only seven days from now.
During that time you may do as you please.

He added: "Whatever you need for your journey, speak of it now." Padma Prabhājvālya replied:

Concerning what I will need for the journey,
please provide for me what you provided for my father.

And with a heavy heart and in tears, he returned to his mother. She said to him:

My dear son, Padma Prabhājvālya.
Hear me, my Padma Prabhājvālya.
What was the command of the non-Buddhist king?
Tell me truthfully. Hold nothing back.

Her son replied:

Hear me, mother, Devaputra brahman.
Listen to these words of Padma Prabhājvālya.
The words of the non-Buddhist king are as follows.

The son does the work of his father,
the minister does the work of the king.
The feather does the work of the arrow,
the gums do the work of the teeth.

I am to bring from the nāga realm known as Padminī
a great treasure of a jewel, one which is known as
Fulfilling All Needs, Destroying All Armies,
which the nāga king Śaṅkhapāla Śuklā holds in his hand.

Should I succeed, I will be rewarded greatly.
If I fail, we will both be punished.

His mother replied:

> Woe! Alas! Such suffering is this!
> Woe! Woe! What is to be done?
> In Nakhamuṇi, there is no one so sad as we two!

> Previously your father, the merchant Sudhana,
> was sent out to journey over the great ocean.
> But by the hindrance of ferocious nāgas,
> he lost his life and did not return.

> Now, my son, even more precious than his father,
> is to be sent out to the ocean. How is this possible!
> Rather than you, my son, be sent to the ocean,
> it would be better that I go before the king and die.

With cries of grief and lamentation, she made to go before the king. Padma took her by the hand, and said:

> Do not go before the king, mother.
> This non-Buddhist king has no mercy.
> This is the result of past karma and of circumstance.
> If it is past karma, I will purify the karmic obstruction.
> If it is circumstance, I will fulfill your aspirations.

> If I do not set out on the great ocean,
> we both will suffer the king's punishment.
> Seven days has he granted me leave.
> For that time mother and son may do as they please.
> Do you hear and understand, my great mother?

Devaputra brahman remained in a state of distress. That night a ḍākinī dressed in silk came to her in a dream and said:

> Old mother, Devaputra brahman.
> Devaputra brahman, hear what I say.
> If your little child, Padma Prabhājvālya,
> is to travel far to the great ocean,

come tomorrow to the shrine of the descending deity
and a ḍākinī will give to you a profound mantra,
one that cannot be undone by fire or by water.
Have you understood, Devaputra brahman?

The next day, as soon as she awoke, Devaputra brahman went to her son
and said:

My dear son, Padma Prabhājvālya.
Listen to your mother, Devaputra brahman.
Stay here in the Temple of Tārā.
I must go to the shrine of the descending deity.

Devaputra brahman went to the shrine. There she prepared offerings,
the tallest being the height of an arrow, the shortest, the length of spindle.
As she made inconceivable offerings, she prayed: "May the smoke clouds of
these offerings block out the sky." Putting her hands together, she looked to
the sky and chanted:

I prostrate to you, ḍākinī in the east, of the vajra family,
white in color, as white as the white conch,
with your entourage of a hundred thousand white ḍākinīs.

Rat-a-tat-tat! In your right hand a sandalwood drum.
Ting-a-ling-ling! In your left hand a white silver bell.
Upright as upright, on your crown the buddhas of the
    five families.
Flat as flat, your eastern crown upon your head.

Tap-tap-tap! Your feet perform a dance.
Rattle, rattle! Your bone ornaments from the graveyard.

Come today to the shrine of the descending deity.
My little son, the child Padma Prabhājvālya,
is being punished by the non-Buddhist king.
He must travel out to the great ocean.
Mantra ḍākinīs of the five classes, give me a prophecy.

From the skies came the drawn-out melodic sound of the ḍākinīs. From the east came white ribbons. From the south yellow ribbons, from the west red ribbons, from the north green ribbons, and from the center came dark-blue ribbons. From high above in the skies the ḍākinīs of the five classes spoke to Devaputra brahman:

> Old mother, Devaputra brahman,
> listen to us, the ḍākinīs of the five classes.
> For your little son, Padma Prabhājvālya,
> his life there will be of three periods.
>
> In the first, he will travel out to the great ocean.
> In the second, he will go to the land of the cannibals.
> In the third, on the peak of the high eastern
>   mountain,
> the butchers will perform a fire sacrifice.
>
> We ḍākinīs will grant you a profound mantra,
> one that cannot be overcome by fire or by water:
> *Namo buddhāya, namo dharmāya, namo sangha
>   guru ḍākiya.*

Three times they gave her the verbal refuge mantra. Devaputra brahman was overjoyed. The ribbons disappeared into space like a rainbow. She made her way back to the Temple of Tārā, and went to her son:

> My dear little son, Padma Prabhājvālya,
> Padma Prabhājvālya, listen to your mother.
> I have been to the shrine of the descending deity.
> There the ḍākinīs of the five classes gave me a prophecy.
>
> They bestowed on me a profound mantra,
> one that cannot be overcome by fire or by water.
> Keep it in your mind, my son.
> I will give it to you fully and clearly:
> *Namo buddhāya, namo dharmāya, namo sangha
>   guru ḍākiya.*

Three times she repeated the verbal refuge mantra, and Padma kept it in his mind.

When the seven days were over, Padma went before the king, who said to the boy:

Listen to me, Padma Prabhājvālya.
The provisions you need for your journey
are as was given to your father in the past.
Padma Prabhājvālya, prepare to travel to the ocean.

Padma said to the king:

Great king, please hear this request.
While I am gone to the great ocean,
please impose no heavy tax on my mother
or send her into bonded labor.

With five hundred companions, headed by Subhavya,[140] the provisions were loaded upon excellent horses, oxen, and buffalos, and together they set out for the ocean. They traveled to the Golden Desert. There the companions set about building a boat. Some worked with gold, some with copper, some with metal, and others were employed in woodwork. In three months they built the boat. On the fifteenth day of the first summer month they launched the boat, climbed in, and set sail. When rowing the boat the ropes were slack, and when sailing the boat the ropes were tight.

About one league out to sea, the speaking parrot began to shed tears. Padma Prabhājvālya said to him:

Listen to me, you speaking parrot.
Turn your attention to Padma Prabhājvālya.
When the parrot is hungry, there are sesame seeds to eat.
When thirsty, there is the nourishment of milk.

Considering this, why is it that you are not happy,
and instead shed these tears of sadness and grief?
Do you miss the happy place that is the thick clusters of trees?
Do you miss your mother and father from your realm of birds?

The parrot replied to Padma Prabhājvālya:

Listen to me, enlightened one, Padma Prabhājvālya.
Turn your attention to this parrot, Padma Prabhājvālya.
The reason that this parrot is shedding tears
is not because he misses his thick clusters of trees
or that he misses his parents from the bird realm.

Under our boat there are two nāgas,
one black and one white, and very fierce.
They manifest as scorpions, the size of yaks.
Our boat is about to be destroyed.
If you have any methods or prayers that will prevent this,
I plead that you do them now.

After some leagues the boat arrived at the part of the sea directly above the abode of the nāgas. The seas became turbulent, the sails were stretched. The waves were as tall as Mount Meru. Some thought that the boat would be tossed into the air. Others thought it would be thrown to the bottom of the sea. Some of the five hundred called out to their fathers, some to their mothers, some to their wives and children. Padma Prabhājvālya addressed them:

Do not be afraid, have no fear, my five hundred companions.
From this great ocean of samsara, I have the power to save you.
My mother, my mother, three times she uttered it.
Devaputra brahman, three times she called it out.

I have instructions given to me by my mother.
There was a teaching given to her by a ḍākinī.
It has power. It has ability.

This ocean, turbulent like boiling milk,
will become like poured cold water.
Namo buddhāya, namo dharmāya, namo sangha guru ḍākiya.

Three times he repeated the refuge mantra. The ocean, once as turbulent as boiling milk, became as calm as poured cold water. The pride and hostility of the nāgas were pacified. They revealed their forms and brought to Padma Prabhājvālya a wish-granting jewel and an indranīla sapphire. Bowing before him, they said:

> Little enlightened one, you are a wonder,
> a little child with such great power.
> You possess a verbal mantra that no eye can see,
> a profound mantra that no hand can hold.
> We ask that you grant us nāgas this profound mantra.
> We nāgas are a malicious and hostile race.
> It was we two who interrupted your father.
> Therefore we give you this promise, that from now on
> we will not harm the life of another living being.

With this vow, they offered the wish-granting jewel to Padma Prabhājvālya. Three times he repeated the refuge mantra that had conquered the pride and hostility of the nāgas, and he accepted their vow never to harm the life of another living being.

Witnessing this, the five hundred companions addressed Padma Prabhājvālya:

> Hear us, enlightened one, Padma Prabhājvālya.
> Listen to these five hundred merchant companions.
> From this ocean of samsara, navigator and child emanation,
> you have rescued us, and for doing so,
> we will repay your kindness upon returning to our homes.

After a while they saw the golden spires of the nāga land of Padminī. Padma Prabhājvālya thought to himself: "If I take my five hundred companions down to the nāga land, it will lessen my chances of gaining the jewel. It would be better if they remained on this plain." He spoke to his companions:

> Listen to me, my five hundred companions.
> Pay attention to Padma Prabhājvālya.
> Our boat has arrived at dry land.
> I will make a coracle big enough to hold me alone,
> and by myself I will travel out on the ocean.

The companions were unhappy about this and said:

Hear us, enlightened one, Padma Prabhājvālya.
Listen to these five hundred merchant companions.

When we left Nakhamuṇi to travel with you,
we did not think of our mothers, fathers, and relatives,
but only of you, enlightened one.
We did not think of our homes or our children,
but only of you, enlightened one.

Wherever the enlightened one goes, take us with you.
If you do not take us with you,
we five hundred companions will kill ourselves.

Again, Padma Prabhājvālya addressed his companions:

Alas, listen to me, my five hundred companions.
You could indeed come with me,
but we would not escape from Padminī.
Therefore stay here on this sandy beach.
Once I have got the jewel, I will quickly return.
Do you understand, my five hundred companions?

Leaving his companions, Padma Prabhājvālya built a small black coracle, big enough to hold him alone, and set off to the nāga land of Padminī.

Reaching land after a few leagues, he weighed down the little black coracle with a stone, thinking that it might carried away by the wind, and left it on the ocean. Arriving at the second enclosure surrounding Padminī, he was met by many tigers, leopards, and poisonous snakes. He became afraid and spoke aloud:

My mother, three times she uttered it.
Devaputra brahman, three times she called it out.
I have instructions given to me by my mother.
I have a teaching given to her by a ḍākinī.
If it is blessed with power and ability,

then may these snakes, tigers, and leopards, with their
    fangs bared,
become as tame as our house dogs.

Three times he uttered the mantra as before. All the animals became as
friendly as his pet dogs. Wagging their tails, they showed him the way.

At the third enclosure he was met by two young nāga maidens who held
in their hands two lassos formed from live snakes, eighteen male arm spans
and nineteen female arm spans in length. They spoke to Padma Prabhājvālya:

My! My! This looks like a human.
A person has arrived we think,
arrived at the door of the nāgas.

The approach to the nāga land of Padminī
is guarded by three levels of protection.
This human has escaped from the first,
which was the mouth of the fierce nāgas.

He has also escaped from the second,
which was the mouths of the wild animals.
Look and see if he will escape from third,
which is the hands of we two nāgas.
Will he escape or won't he? Watch the show!

They threw the black snake lasso around Padma. He thought his skin
would crack and his bones would break. He spoke out loud:

My mother, my mother, three times she uttered it.
Devaputra brahman, three times she called it out.
I have instructions given to me by my mother.
I have a teaching given to her by a ḍākinī.
If it is blessed with power and ability,
may this black snake lasso in the hands
    of the nāgas
be broken into one hundred and eight pieces.

He uttered the mantra as before. The lasso broke into a hundred and eight pieces, and Padma Prabhājvālya stood up unharmed. The two nāga sentries were astonished. They bowed low and said:

> Little enlightened one, you are a wonder.
> A young child with such powers!
> From where have you come?
> What business do you seek in this nāga land?

Padma Prabhājvālya addressed the two nāgas:

> Sentry nāgas, hear what I say.
> I have come from the eastern part of India.
> I am following the command of a non-Buddhist king.
> I have come to the nāga land of Padminī
> to seek the great treasure of a jewel,
> one which is known as Fulfilling All Needs, Destroying All Armies.
> Nāga sentries, please heed this petition.

The two sentries went to the palace and addressed the nāga queen:

> Hear us, great nāga queen.
> Give your attention to these two sentries.
> At the gate of our nāga palace,
> an extraordinary enlightened one has arrived.

The nāga queen was astonished. She addressed the two sentries:

> Listen to me, you two sentry maidens.
> If an extraordinary enlightened one has arrived
> at the gate of our nāga palace, invite him inside.

At the queen's command, the two sentries brought Padma Prabhājvālya into the palace. When he came face to face with the queen she was sitting on a jeweled throne. She addressed him:

> Hear me, child incarnation.
> Pay attention to this nāga.

From where have you come?
What business do you seek in this nāga land?

Padma Prabhājvālya replied:

Hear me, great nāga queen.
Please turn your attention this way.
I have come from the eastern part of India.
I am following the command of a non-Buddhist king.
I ask that you consider with great compassion
granting me the great treasure of jewel known as
Fulfilling All Needs, Destroying All Armies.

The nāga queen replied:

Listen to me, enlightened one, Padma Prabhājvālya.
Listen to this queen of the nāgas.
How can I possibly give to you the jewel,
Fulfilling All Needs, Destroying All Armies?
It is the life source of the nāga king Śaṇkhapāla,
and of many lesser nāga kings besides.

Padma Prabhājvālya replied:

Alas! Hear me, great nāga queen.
Turn your attention to Padma Prabhājvālya.
In the east of India I have a mother.
If you do not give me this jewel,
she will suffer the punishment of the non-Buddhist king.
Consider this request with your compassion.
Please grant me the jewel.

The nāga replied:

Listen to me, enlightened one, Padma Prabhājvālya.
Listen to this queen of the nāgas.
If I am to give you the jewel that fulfills all needs,
then you must identify the key to its whereabouts.

Padma Prabhājvālya replied:

> The jewel is not in the treasure house.
> It lies beneath the tongue of the nāga queen.

The queen replied:

> If I am to give you the jewel Fulfilling All Needs, Destroying
>   All Armies,
> then you should know that in this nāga palace
> there are many of our kind who are blind and deaf.
> Grant us the profound mantra to cure them.

Padma spoke these words about the mantra:

> I have instructions given to me by my mother.
> I have a mantra given to her by a ḍākinī.
> If it is blessed with power and ability,
> may the blind and deaf nāgas be cured
> and, in particular, may you, great nāga queen,
> become as a youth of fifteen.

Three times he uttered the mantra. The blind and deaf nāgas were freed from their disabilities and shone with a new radiance. The queen took on the appearance of a young maiden of fifteen. From beneath her tongue she took the jewel wrapped in silks of five colors. Holding it in her hand, she prayed:

> Working for the welfare of living beings,
> first it goes to the east of India.
> May the reign of the kings of India be long!

> Working for the welfare of living beings,
> second it goes to the land of China.
> May the reign of the kings of China be long!

> Working for the welfare of living beings,
> third it goes to the land of snows.

May the reign of the kings of Tibet be long!

May the people and ministers be prosperous and happy!
It dwells within the form of the Jowo wish-fulfilling jewel.
On the plain of the celestial Lubuk Leu
is the place called Luguk, not Lubuk.
There lies a palace of a hundred thousand nāgas.
May it finally return to this land of the nāgas.[141]

The nāga queen presented the jewel to Padma Prabhājvālya. The two sentries escorted him back to the gate. With the jewel in his hand he made his way back to the spot where he left his little black coracle. However, it had been carried away by the wind. Padma said:

My mother, my mother, three times she uttered it.
Devaputra brahman, three times she called it out.
I have instructions given to me by my mother.
I have a mantra given to her by a ḍākinī.
If it is blessed with power and ability,
may I be transported on a road made of five colors.

He uttered the refuge mantra three times and was transported on a road made of the five rainbow colors. Soon he arrived at the place where his five hundred companions were waiting. They were overjoyed to see him. They said: "Our guru has returned! Our guide has returned!" They were blessed with the jewel.

Padma Prabhājvālya addressed his companions:

Listen to me, my five hundred companions.
Pay attention to Padma Prabhājvālya.
Remain here on this plain for one month.
I miss my mother, and it is unbearable.
I miss my mother, and so I will go ahead.

PRABHĀJVĀLYA RETURNS HOME
With the jewel in his hand Padma Prabhājvālya left his companions and traveled home. When he arrived at the Temple of Tārā, he found the doors had been gnawed away by dogs. In great sadness, he went inside. The scriptures

of the Buddha and the commentaries had all disappeared. In the kitchen he found his mother lying down. She was disheveled. Birds had nested in her hair and she had become blind. In tears, Padma Prabhājvālya said:

> Mother, Devaputra brahman, hear me.
> Listen to Padma Prabhājvālya.
> You little son has returned from the ocean.
> Mother, do not lie there. Get up.
> Do you hear me, my precious mother?

His mother replied:

> Demonic minister, Janghākarika.
> Messenger Janghākarika, listen to me.
> My son, Padma Prabhājvālya, went to the ocean.
> How could he have returned?
>
> Demonic minister, do not upset me like this.
> This old woman is sick. Let her be sick.
> If you cannot bring this old woman back from the dead,
> then plunge your evil knife in her.

Padma said to his mother:

> Mother, Devaputra brahman, hear me.
> I am not the demonic minister.
> I am your little son, Padma Prabhājvālya,
> who has returned from the reaches of the ocean.
> I did not die. I am alive.
> Do you hear me, Devaputra brahman?

His mother replied:

> My little son, Padma Prabhājvālya.
> Padma Prabhājvālya, listen to me.
> If you are my Padma Prabhājvālya,
> before you set out to travel the ocean,

I recited for you three times a profound mantra,
which could not be undone by fire or by water.
Recite that mantra now three times before your mother.
Do you hear me, Padma Prabhājvālya?

Padma Prabhājvālya said to his mother:

I have instructions given to me by my mother.
I have a mantra given to her by a ḍākinī.
If it is blessed with power and ability,
may her eyes be restored to a sight clearer than before.

Three times he repeated the refuge mantra, *Namo buddhāya, namo dharmāya, namo sangha guru ḍākiya.* Immediately his mother's eyes were restored to a sight clearer than before.

In the happy home of the Temple of Tārā, without anyone else knowing, mother and son celebrated with a joyous feast and enjoyed themselves to their heart's content.

While they were doing so, the people of Nakhamuṇi had heard that Padma Prabhājvālya had arrived back from the ocean, and eventually the gossip reached the ears of the non-Buddhist king Mithyāyajña. He was displeased and sent the minister Janghākarika to the Temple of Tārā.

Arriving at the house, he knocked on the door and called out in long, drawn-out voice:

Lady, hear me. Devaputra brahman,
listen to the minister Janghākarika.
It is said that your little son, Prabhājvālya,
has returned from his journey over the ocean.
You must now send him to the king.
Have you understood, Devaputra brahman?

His mother said to Padma:

My little son, Padma Prabhājvālya,
listen to your mother, Devaputra brahman.
Janghākarika, the minister to the king,
has arrived at the door of the Temple of Tārā,

saying you must now go with him.
Do you hear me, Padma Prabhājvālya?

Padma, with the jewel, set out with the minister to go before the king. In the palace the king said to the boy:

Listen to me, Padma Prabhājvālya.
Pay attention to this king.
Before you set out on your journey,
I provided as necessities for attaining the jewel
a hundred loads of cut male tree birch wood,
a hundred loads of female tree willow wood,
and all provisions for your boat.

You were given five hundred companions,
all loyal and headed by the companion Subhavya.
Where are these companions? Bring them here now.

Moreover, the jewel Fulfilling All Needs, Destroying
   All Armies
you fetched but did not deliver into my hands,
taking it instead to the Temple of Tārā.
Why did you take it there?

Padma replied to the king:

Hear me, king Mithyāyajña.
Give your attention to Padma Prabhājvālya.
At the time that I set out for the ocean,
there was only an agreement to fetch the jewel,
not one to deliver it into your hands.

The five hundred companions await on the golden plains.
I will offer all the boat's provisions back to you.
I missed my mother and so went ahead alone.
However, I present this jewel to you.
I beg, do not punish mother and son.

The king was not happy to hear this. He addressed his ministers:

> Council of ministers, headed by Janghākarika,
> listen with attention to this king.
> This child, Padma Prabhājvālya,
> though he was sent far away over the ocean,
> escaped from the jaws of the fierce nāgas
> and has returned unharmed with the jewel.
>
> In this he has exceeded his father.
> If I do not find a way of getting rid of him,
> there is a danger he will take over my kingdom,
> and an ordinary person will become greater than a king.
>
> Council of ministers, discuss this matter.
> Do you understand, ministers?

The ministers addressed the king:

> Great king, please hear us.
> Listen attentively to us ministers.
> To subject this child to the law and punishment,
> would it not be right to drain his blood?
> Or to pierce him with arrows and spears?

From their midst a Dharma minister called Mitrakīrti stood up and said:

> Hear me, great king.
> Hear me one time, council of ministers.
> How can you overcome this child, Prabhājvālya,
> by subjecting him to arrows, knives, and spears?
> Even by subjecting him to the three elements,
> how could you possibly overcome him?
>
> Instead, in land of the cannibals, in the southwest,
> is the cannibal palace called Garuḍa Dharma.
> There the twelve thousand cannibals possess

a golden pan with agate handle and horse-tail tassel.
Send Padma Prabhājvālya to get it.
How will be possibly escape the jaws of the cannibals?
Do you hear, great king and ministers?

Everyone agreed with the minister's suggestion.

PADMA PRABHĀJVĀLYA IS SENT TO THE LAND OF THE CANNIBALS
About one month later, the five hundred companions, along with horses,
elephants, buffalos, and so on, returned from the ocean and presented them-
selves to the king. Later Padma was called to the king, who said:

Listen to me, Padma Prabhājvālya.
Pay attention to this king.
You traveling to the nāga land of Padminī,
and fetching the jewel, is nothing special.

Now you and I have something to discuss.
In land of the cannibals, in the southwest,
is the cannibal palace known as Garuḍa Dharma.
There the twelve thousand cannibals possess
a golden pan with agate handle and horse-tail tassel.

You are to go there and bring it back.
Do this and you will be well rewarded.
Fail, and you shall suffer punishment under the law.
Have you understood, Padma Prabhājvālya?

Padma addressed the king:

Great king, please hear me.
Do not give your attention elsewhere.
My father, Sudhana, was successful in his work,
and yet he did not bring this jewel from the ocean.
I am just a three-year-old child,
but I was able to bring the jewel from the ocean.

Now if I must take a golden pan with tassel
from the land of cannibals in the southwest,
how will I escape from the jaws of the cannibals?

I ask that you do not impose a heavy tax or forced labor
on my dear mother, Devaputra brahman.
If she is sick, please provide her with help, great king.

If she dies, please provide someone to help with
    the funeral.
Place her corpse on the top of the mountain.
Give her flesh, bones, and blood to the vultures.

In response, the king said:

Listen to me, Padma Prabhājvālya.
While you are away in land of the cannibals,
I will provide a helper for your mother.
If she dies, I will provide a funeral helper.

What provisions do you need to get the golden pan?
Tell me honestly, now.

Padma Prabhājvālya replied:

For traveling to the land of the cannibals,
please give me the five hundred companions I had before
and provisions enough for five hundred.

With enough provisions for the five hundred companions, headed by
Subhavya, they set out for land of the cannibals. In the Temple of Tārā, his
mother, Devaputra brahman, thought to herself: "My son, who exceeds even
his father, will not return from the mouths of the cannibals," and was over-
come with grief.

After journeying for many leagues, the travelers came to a land. Padma
thought: "Taking the five hundred companions to the land of the cannibals
will make it more difficult to escape from the cannibals. They should return
home." He addressed his companions:

Subhavya and my five hundred companions,
if you travel on to the land of the cannibals,
we will not escape from the cannibals' mouths.
You should all now return to your homes,
and there live a life in keeping with Dharma.

To my mother, Devaputra brahman,
be a nurse and a helper in death.
Have you understood, my five hundred companions?

The companions replied:

Hear us, enlightened one, Padma Prabhājvālya.
Listen to these five hundred merchant companions.
Before when we traveled out to the ocean,
our navigator was you, the child incarnation.

Now even if he falls into the mouths of the cannibals
in land of the cannibals in the southwest,
there is nothing we can do.

Wherever you go, take us with you.
If the enlightened one does not take us with him,
we, your five hundred companions, will kill ourselves.
Have you understood, child incarnation?

Padma uttered the refuge mantra three times for the companions to
return home and, having acquiesced, they turned back.

Padma Prabhājvālya, taking a share of the provisions, set off for the land
of the cannibals. After about a league he came across a tall rock, standing like
a pillar to the sky. He climbed to the top and thought to himself: "If I return
to my country, there will be no escape from the eye of the non Buddhist
king. If I travel on to the land of the cannibals, there will definitely be no
escape from the mouths of the cannibals. Therefore I should jump from this
peak and kill myself." He put his hands together and prayed:

Ḍākinī in the east, of the vajra family,
accept this offering of the flesh and blood of Prabhājvālya.

Ḍākinī in the south, of the jewel family,
accept today this offering of this child's flesh and blood.

He made similar prayers to the ḍākinīs of the west, north, and center. He closed his eyes and, as he was about to jump, suddenly his mother appeared clearly to him. Then a little lark, who said he was from the Temple of Tārā, perched on the rock and said to Padma:

Hear me, enlightened one, Padma Prabhājvālya.
Listen to the words of this little lark.
Do not jump from this rock and kill yourself.
Please continue your journey to the land of the cannibals.
The time has come for you to take the golden pan and tassel.
Mother and son will be together again.

Padma spoke to the bird:

Listen to me, little lark.
Listen to these words of Padma Prabhājvālya.
The realm of birds is wise in clairvoyance.
I will go to the land of the cannibals.
Little bird, what land are you from?
Tell me clearly and honestly.

The little bird replied:

Hear me, enlightened one, Padma Prabhājvālya.
Listen to the words of this little lark.
The land of my birth is the east of India.

In the day I search for food.
At night I sleep in the same place,
in the gaps of the tamarisk eaves
of the Temple of Tārā.

The little bird flew off in the direction of the Temple of Tārā. Padma Prabhājvālya climbed down the tall rock and continued on to the land of the cannibals.

After some leagues he came to a small pass the width of a jute rope. Beyond that was a great plain, from which came the terrifying howls of jackals, and on which was a black hide tent. The valleys were the color of iron, the rivers were like molten coal. Into this place Padma journeyed.

In the black valley a cannibal weaver had set the upper part of her loom in the higher reaches of the valley and the lower part in the mouth of the valley. Padma ventured into the weaving area and said:

> Old weaver woman, listen to Padma Prabhājvālya.
> Please give me a place to sleep this night.
> And tomorrow please show me the way I must go.

The cannibal stopped her work and stood up quickly. She looked at Padma Prabhājvālya:

> My! My! This looks like a human.
> A person has arrived I think,
> arrived at the door of the cannibals.
> A human's life is over when it arrives at the cannibal's door.
> An insect's life is over when it arrives at the ant's door.

Tossing her hair behind her, she seized Padma Prabhājvālya and then stroked him and swallowed him. Padma was terrified and felt that outside his skin had split and inside his bones had broken:

> My mother, my mother, three times she uttered it.
> Devaputra brahman, three times she called it out.
> I have instructions given to me by my mother.
> I have a mantra given to her by a ḍākinī.
> If it is blessed with power and ability,
> may I be vomited out, like foul-tasting saliva,
> from the mouth of this cannibal from these black
>   iron valleys.
> *Namo buddhāya, namo dharmāya, namo sangha guru ḍākiya.*

Uttering the refuge mantra three times, he was vomited out unharmed from the cannibal's mouth. She ran off several steps away. Turning around, she prostrated and said:

Little enlightened one, you are a wonder;
a little child with such great power.
You possess a verbal mantra that no eye can see,
a profound mantra that no hand can hold.

I ask that you grant me this profound mantra.
This night you will stay in my home.
Tomorrow I will show you your way.
Have you understood, child incarnation?

That night Padma stayed in the home of the black valley cannibal. She said to him:

I who eat the human flesh of others
have nothing else to offer you.
If you want horse or human flesh,
I can offer these to you.

Padma Prabhājvālya ate some flesh from the corpse of a horse and a human. He performed a dedication ritual and offered a small portion. The black-valley cannibal asked Padma Prabhājvālya:

Listen to me enlightened one and child incarnation.
Listen to this wicked cannibal.
Where have you come from?
Where will you go from here?

Padma Prabhājvālya replied:

Hear me, old lady of the black valley.
Listen to Padma Prabhājvālya.
I have come from east India.
I am following the command of the non-Buddhist
    king.
From here I travel to the land of the cannibals,
to fetch a golden pan with horse-tail tassel.

The cannibal spoke:

> If you want refined iron, take as you want.
> If you want the best blue silk, take as you want.
> Best would be to stay with me as my step-child.
> If not, then better you return to your home.
>
> I am the first sentry of land of the cannibals.
> You will face different levels of sentry posts.
> How will you possibly escape from their clutches?
> Even if I was your parent, I would have no better advice
>   than this.

Padma replied to the cannibal:

> When I came from the east of India,
> I did not come because I wanted refined iron.
> I did not come because I desired the best blue silk.
> I came because I seek the golden pan with horse-tail tassel.
> Old woman, please show me the path.
> I will not stay here but go to the land of the cannibals.

The black-valley cannibal escorted him for a long way. Padma crossed over a small pass and went on his way. After a while he came to a large plain that was terrifying to look at. The valleys were the color of copper, the streams and rivers the color of blood. The cannibal of the copper valley was weaving like the previous cannibal. He ventured into the weaving area and asked the same question as before:

> Old weaver woman, listen to Padma Prabhājvālya.
> Please give me a place to sleep this night.
> And tomorrow please show me the way I must go.

The cannibal stopped her work and stood up quickly. She looked at Padma Prabhājvālya:

> In a place where there are no humans,
> I hear a human voice.

It is probably a young Tibetan,
whose life is about to end.

She tossed her hair behind her. As a sentry, she put her hand to her brow
and looked. Seeing Padma, she said:

One long year has gone by
since human flesh has come this way.
One long year has gone by
since human blood has come this way.
Ha la la! Something to eat!
Ha lu lu! Something to drink!

She grabbed hold of him, stroked him three times, and swallowed him.
Padma recited the refuge mantra as before, and the same events occurred as
told above.

At the third sentry post in the conch valley, the same thing happened.
Finally Padma came to the cannibal of the yellow golden valley. He entered
the weaving area and spoke as before. The cannibal jumped up:

My! My! This looks like a human.
A person has arrived, I think,
arrived at the door of the cannibals.
Today my friend-pulse[142] is telling me
the flesh of a Tibetan to cook has arrived.

This cannibal had taken a vow in the presence of the cannibal queen Pretā
Sukhanāth not to eat raw meat. Therefore she seized Padma, put him in a
large golden pot on top of a golden gate, and placed it on top of a blazing
fire. Padma recited the refuge mantra three times. He escaped from the pot
unhurt, and the pot, grate, and fire were thrown a league away. The cannibal
was filled with faith:

Little enlightened one, you are a wonder;
a little child with such great power.
You possess a verbal mantra that no eye can see.
I ask that you grant me this profound mantra.

I am the fourth cannibal sentry.
Some leagues from here is the Garuḍa Dharma Palace,
home to Pretā Sukhanāth, queen of the cannibals.
She is the mother of sixty children.
How will you escape from her mouth?

If you want refined gold, take as you want.
If you want the best yellow silk, take as you want.

Padma did not listen to her and continued his journey to the southwest.
The Garuḍa Dharma Palace was surrounded by three iron hills. Passing over these, he came to the outer door of the palace itself. On the right of the door was chained a white lion, and on the left a tiger. There was no way to get between these two animals, and so he uttered the refuge mantra three times. At once the lion and the tiger became as friendly as pet dogs. Passing through the gate he saw the Garuḍa Dharma Palace, a vast building ninety-eight stories high. Inside was the cannibal queen Pretā Sukhanāth. Her hair was reddish brown and shot upward. She had fangs like snow-mountain peaks. The folds of skin on her chest reached her knees. The folds of skin on her knees reached the ground. She wore clothes of human skin and a necklace of fresh and dried human heads. She sat there sucking on a dry human head. She was a terrifying sight.
Padma came into her presence and said:

Hear me, cannibal queen.
Listen to Padma Prabhājvālya.
I have come from the east of India.
I ask for a place to stay for the night.

The cannibal jumped up:

My! My! What delight is this!
Today I have been sent ḍākinī food.
Many years since I tasted hot human flesh.
Many years since I drank warm human blood.
Today is my lucky day.
Ha la la! Something to eat!
Ha lu lu! Something to drink!

She seized Padma, stroked him, and swallowed him. Padma was terrified. Taking hold of her two fangs he kicked at her uvula and recited the refuge mantra three times. She spat him out of her mouth unharmed like bad-tasting saliva. The cannibal was astonished and developed great faith. She prostrated to him and said:

> Little enlightened one, you are a wonder.
> A young child with such powers!
> From where have you come?
> What business do you seek here?

Padma replied:

> Pretā Sukhanāth, queen of the cannibals,
> listen to Padma Prabhājvālya.
> I have come from east India,
> following the command of the non-Buddhist king.
>
> I have come to ask for the golden pan with horse-tail tassel,
> from the cannibal palace of Garuḍa Dharma.
> Please give me the golden pan with horse-tail tassel.
> Have you heard me, cannibal queen?

The cannibal queen said to Padma:

> How will you ever gain the golden pan?
> Give you the golden pan, you say?
> In general, it is the life-force source of the cannibals,
> and specifically, the life-force source of my sixty sons.
>
> How can I give such a golden pan to you?
> Tonight sleep inside my fingernails.
> My sixty sons are coming here from the valleys.
> How will you escape from their mouths?

That evening the cannibal placed Padma in her fingernails. Then the sixty sons, from different fathers, arrived. Thirty came from the upper valley, thirty from the lower valley. They came to their mother and said:

Mother, Pretā Sukhanāth, hear us.
Listen to your sixty sons.
Here in the Garuḍa Dharma Palace
is the hot smell of a Tibetan human.
Give us some hot human flesh, mother.
If you have warm human blood, give us some.

Their mother replied:

Sixty sons of this mother,
since you went wandering through the valleys,
no warm flesh of a Tibetan has come this way.

For a mother who stays always in an empty house,
how could there be the warm flesh of a Tibetan?
If you want the flesh from a horse or human corpse,
take as much as you can eat.

The sixty sons replied:

Mother, Pretā Sukhanāth, hear us.
Listen to your sixty sons.
If you have no warm flesh of a human,
show us your fingernails and toenails.

The sons started to search her fingernails. She said: "Children, don't talk so much. It makes my head itch." She pretended to scratch her head, and as she did so, Padma Prabhājvālya hid in her hair. The children searched as much as they wanted in her fingernails and toenails, but they found nothing. The oldest son said:

If mother will not give us warm human flesh,
bring us the divination text and the divination vessel.
Do not move them from your right hand to your left.
Do not pass them under the hindquarters of a red bitch.
Do not pass them inside the bolt of the door.
Clean them as much as you can and lend them to us.

The mother brought the divination text and vessel. She passed them from her right hand to her left and passed them under the behind of a red female dog. She passed them inside the door bolt and gave it to her sixty sons. The divination was performed, and it clearly stated: "It is now the time for Padma Prabhājvālya, an incarnation of Guru Padmasambhava who will suppress us cannibals at the end of a future eon, to arrive here in this land of cannibals."

When asked where he was now, the divination was not that clear and said only: "He is hiding in a thick forest."

The next day the sons returned to the valleys. Padma emerged from the hair of the cannibal. She said to him:

> Listen to me, enlightened one, Padma Prabhājvālya.
> Listen to this wicked cannibal.
> If I am to give you the golden pan with horse-tail tassel,
> give me the mantra so that I might enter the Dharma.
> Don't leave me here. Take me to east India.

Padma recited:

> I have instructions given to me by my mother.
> I have a mantra given to her by a ḍākinī.
> If it is blessed with power and ability,
> then may this cannibal queen, Pretā Sukhanāth,
> turn into a meat-eating ḍākinī.
> *Namo buddhāya, namo dharmāya, namo sangha guru ḍākiya.*

Three times he uttered the refuge mantra. The cannibal became endowed with a loving mind and transformed into a buddha family ḍākinī of central direction. The Garuḍa Dharma Palace of that ḍākinī was:

> Just one cubit short of touching the sky,
> which is the pathway of the sun and the moon.
> Just one cubit short of touching the earth,
> which is the pathway of the fish and the otter.

She took the golden pan from the top of the ninety-eighth story. "What other wealth do you need?" she asked.

"No need to bring any more wealth, but bring that washing pot," he replied.

They climbed to the top of the palace and, banging the golden pan, flew off. As they did so, they passed over the cannibal of the golden valley, who looked up to the skies and said:

> This flash of light in the wide skies above
> is probably my mistress, Pretā Sukhanāth.
> Mistress, if you are leaving and going to Tibet,
> don't leave me here. Take me with you.
> Take me, so that I can be of service to you.
> Take me, so that I can receive initiation from the child.

Mistress Pretā Sukhanāth said:

> Listen to me, enlightened one, Padma Prabhājvālya.
> The golden-valley woman asks to be taken to Tibet.
> If we take her, what other wealth do you need?
> Will you take her or not, Padma Prabhājvālya?

He agreed to take her. "I need no other wealth, but bring that hook and rope," he said. He recited the mantra three times and the cannibal transformed into a jewel-family ḍākinī of the southern direction. She climbed into the golden pan and they flew off.

They passed over the conch-valley cannibal, who looked up to the skies and said:

> This flash of light in the wide skies above
> is probably my mistress, Pretā Sukhanāth.
> Mistress, if you are going to the land of snows,
> don't leave me here. Take me with you.
> Take me, so that I can receive initiation from the child.
> Take me, so that I can be of service to you.

The queen asked if he would take her. "Bring her," he said. He recited the mantra three times and the cannibal transformed into a vajra-family ḍākinī of the eastern direction.

"What other wealth do you need?" she asked.

"I need no other wealth, but bring that dose of medicine," he said. With the golden pan as their vehicle, they flew off.

They passed over the copper-valley ḍākinī. She too looked up into the skies and petitioned as the others had done. Padma agreed to take her. He recited the mantra three times and she transformed into a lotus-family ḍākinī of the western direction. "What other wealth do you need?" she asked.

"I need no other wealth, but bring that leather bag," he said. With the golden pan as their vehicle, they flew off.

They passed over the iron-valley ḍākinī. She too looked up into the skies and petitioned as the others had done. Padma agreed to take her. He recited the mantra three times and she transformed into an action-family ḍākinī of the northern direction. "What other wealth do you need?" she asked.

"I need no other wealth, but bring that tail fan," he said. With the golden pan as their vehicle, they flew off.

The ḍākinīs of the five families and child tapped the golden pan and the earth shook. They struck it forcefully and it resounded as the sound of emptiness, the sound of the Dharma, and the whole sky lit up. They struck it forcefully again and they landed on the roof of the Temple of Tārā. His mother, Devaputra brahman, was overjoyed to see her son again, and they spent day and night in joyous festivities and celebration.

The people of the country heard that Padma Prabhājvālya had not only escaped from the cannibals but had returned with the golden pan and five companions. When this news reached the king, he called for his minister Janghākarika:

> Listen to me, Janghākarika.
> Pay attention to your king.
> It is said that the child Padma Prabhājvālya
> has returned from the land of the cannibals.
>
> He has brought with him the golden pan,
> and is accompanied by five maidens.
> Summon Padma Prabhājvālya here.
> Bring the pan and the five maidens.

Minister Janghākarika changed over the left and right black flaps of his coat, strapped one black knife on his right side and one on his left, and set off

for the Temple of Tārā at an even gait. On arriving, he heard, as the people
had reported, sounds of the singing and dancing of a returning-home festiv-
ity. "Lady Devaputra brahman!" he shouted out in a long, drawn-out voice.
Devaputra brahman went to the minister, who said:

> Listen to me, Devaputra brahman.
> Listen to these words of Janghākarika.
> It is said that your son, Padma Prabhājvālya,
> has returned from the land of the cannibals
> and has brought with him five maidens.
> Now you must all come before the king.

The child and the five ḍākinīs, taking the golden pan, went before the
king. He addressed them:

> Welcome, you companion maidens.
> Welcome, you group of ḍākinīs.
> Padma Prabhājvālya, when you first set out for the ocean
> you obtained the jewel, but instead of giving it to me,
> you took it back to the Temple of Tārā.
>
> Now you have returned from the land of the cannibals
> and have brought the golden pan, but rather than give
>   it to me,
> you take it to the house of your old mother.
>
> I am the king of a kingdom,
> and I have only one wife.
> You are a subject of me, the king,
> and not only do you have a wife,
> but you have brought five of them.
> Now you will face punishment.

The king discussed with his ministers: "We sent him to the ocean but he
did not die. Even when placed in the mouths of cannibals, he does not die.
He is either a manifestation of a devil or an incarnation of a buddha. If I do
not get rid of him, he will become king of Nakhamuṇi and rule the entire
kingdom."

One demonic minister stepped forward:

> Deliver this child, Padma Prabhājvālya,
> into the hands of our butchers,
> and on the top of the high eastern mountain,
> offer his body as a fire sacrifice.

All agreed. Three butchers, who were ignorant of good and bad deeds and the law of karma, were summoned. The king said to them:

> Listen to me, you three butcher brothers.
> Take this child, Padma Prabhājvālya,
> to the peak of the high eastern mountain,
> and perform a fire sacrifice on his body.

> All the ash from his burnt body,
> scatter into the winds of the four directions.
> I will reward you well.
> Have you heard me, you three butcher brothers?

The three butchers stripped Padma of his soft clothes and his beautiful ornaments, bound his hands, and took him to the top of the mountain. There they made a pyre of juniper, offered his body as a fire sacrifice, and scattered his ashes to the winds of the four directions and so on.

* * *

This ends the story of the first, second, and third periods of the heart disciple Padma Prabhājvālya.

PADMA PRABHĀJVĀLYA IS REBORN

When the Nakhamuṇi king, Mithyāyajña, had sent Padma Prabhājvālya to the peak of the eastern mountain as a fire sacrifice, it was as if a piece of grit had been removed from his eye, and he celebrated with great festivities. The ḍākinīs stayed with him as his wives.

One day the ḍākinīs had a change of mind and said to the king:

> Hear us, Mithyāyajña.
> Listen to your companion maidens.

Grant us seven days to spend on the mountain peak
where Padma Prabhājvālya was burnt in sacrifice.
We are not cleansed of the grief for this child.
Send us this one time to the eastern mountain peak.

The king replied:

Listen to me, my companion maidens.
Hear these words, you group of ḍākinīs.
There is no need to carry this grief for Prabhājvālya.
I will give you your seven days' leave.
Today you should do as you please.
Do you understand, you ḍākinīs?

They replied:

Please send one of the butchers
to show us the site of the fire sacrifice.

The youngest of the three butchers was sent along with the ḍākinīs. Without uttering a word he pointed out the spot and returned home.

The ḍākinīs spent the night on the mountain. The next day at dawn the iron-valley maiden said:

I have a mantra given to me by the child.
If it is blessed with power and ability,
may all the ashes of his burnt body
be called here now in this very place.
Namo buddhāya, namo dharmāya, namo sangha guru ḍākiya.

Three times she recited the refuge mantra and waved the tail-fan in the four directions. A whirlwind sprung up and gathered the ash into one spot. Then the copper-valley maiden stood up:

I have a mantra given to me by the child.
If it is blessed with power and ability,
may his consciousness be carried like a feather on the wind
and be gathered here in this leather bag.

She recited the refuge mantra three times and waved the bag in the four directions. The ash that had been amassed by the wind entered the bag, causing it to bulge.

Then the golden-valley maiden stood up:

> I have a mantra given to me by the child.
> If it is blessed with power and ability,
> may the mind if this child, wherever it may be,
> be summoned to this place now.

Three times she uttered the refuge mantra and waved the rope and hook in the four directions. From the bag two eyes stared out.

Then the conch-valley maiden stood up:

> I have a mantra given to me by the child.
> If it is blessed with power and ability,
> may the child be even more radiant than before.

She uttered the refuge mantra three times and placed the dose of medicine in the leather bag. The child was born not from a womb but miraculously from within the petals of a lotus flower, emerging with a complexion more radiant than ever.

Then the queen of the cannibals stood up:

> I have a mantra given to me by the child.
> If it is blessed with power and ability,
> may the karmic obstructions created by the butchers
> and by the blacksmith all be purified.

Three times she uttered the refuge mantra and washed the child with the water from the washing pot.

The beauty of the iron-valley maiden was greater than that of the other ḍākinīs, and so the child was happier in her company. Consequently, she stayed a further seven days to look after the child while the four other ḍākinīs returned to Nakhamuṇi. There they addressed the king:

> Hear us, King Mithyāyajña.
> Pay attention to us maidens.

The iron-valley maiden has not overcome her grief.
She asks for another seven days' leave.

We four maidens are freed from our grief.
Please lend us the golden pan with horse-tail tassel.
We will not stay but will go out to play.
Great king, come and look from the palace roof.

The king took the golden pan from the treasury and gave it to the maidens. They climbed inside, flew up into the air, and circled the Nakhamuni place three times on the outside and three times on the inside before landing again. They placed all the Dharma ministers inside the pan and again lifted up into the sky, flying back and forth over Nakhamuni. The king, watching this great spectacle, said:

Hear me, you ḍākinīs.
This spectacle in the golden pan is astonishing.
I too will see the sights from the golden pan.
Bring the golden pan to land, ḍākinīs.

The ḍākinīs brought the golden pan to ground. The Dharma ministers climbed out, and the ḍākinīs said:

Listen to us, ministers gathered here.
Pay attention to us ḍākinīs.
Dharma ministers and demon ministers
should not be together inside the golden pan.
Else we will be punished by the non-Buddhist king.
All demon ministers, headed by the *kārṣāpaṇa* seller,
now climb in this golden pan.

The king and the demon ministers were placed inside the golden pan, and they flew up in the sky. The ḍākinīs tapped the golden pan and the earth shook. They struck it forcefully and it resounded as emptiness, the sound of the Dharma, and the whole sky lit up. They struck it forcefully again and headed off to the land of the cannibals. When they flew over the iron valley the king became very afraid:

Hear me, my companion ḍākinīs.
Please steer the golden pan away from here.
I have enough of this show. I am afraid.
The whole land looks like cannibal land.

The ḍākinīs replied:

Come further. There is a greater show ahead.
This is the first path taken by the child.
There is yet a greater show than this.
The shows get greater day by day.

They beat the golden pan forcefully and came to rest over the Garuḍa
Dharma Palace. The king again pleaded:

Listen to me, ḍākinīs.
Listen again, my companion ḍākinīs.
Turn this golden pan to east India.
I will give you the Nakhamuṇi kingdom.

The ḍākinīs replied:

Listen to us, King Mithyāyajña.
Listen again, council of demon ministers.
A slingshot made of goat hide hits the goat.
Bad actions in the end fall back on you. What a shame!

Sixty sons, your mother has a gift,
brought for you from east India.
Warm human flesh we have brought for you.
Sons do not sleep. Get up!

With these words they tipped over the golden pan.

The sixty sons had been overcome by the grief of not having their mother
day after day, and by the forced sleep of not having their life-force golden
pan. Hearing their mother's voice that day, they awoke suddenly and looked
up at the sky. They saw the king and his ministers falling out of the black-
ness and onto the ground. They caught them and ate them. The fleet-footed

Janghākarika managed to flee eighty steps before he was caught. The youngest of the sons said: "If you have the legs to flee, then I have the mouth to eat," and so stroking him, he ate him.

Their mother said:

> From this day on, my brood of sixty sons,
> refrain from eating human flesh.
> Place your minds and desires into the Dharma.
> Your mother will not stay but goes to Tibet.

From that day on the sons gave up eating human flesh. The ḍākinīs returned to Nakhamuṇi and went to the peak of the eastern mountain to where the child and the iron-valley ḍākinī were. They addressed the child:

> Hear us, enlightened one, Padma Prabhājvālya.
> Listen to this assembly of ḍākinīs.
> The doctrine of the Maṭmaṭa has gone.
> Please establish the excellent doctrine of Secret Mantra.

The child said: "Alas. That is something I am yet to do." He remained on the mountain engaged in working for the benefit of living beings.

The land of Nakhamuṇi was without a king and the ministers held discussions. Some suggested inviting an Indian king. Some suggested a Chinese king, others suggested a Tasik king. There was no agreement. One Dharma minister, Mitrakīrti, stood up and said: "There is no need to invite an Indian king or a Chinese king. Here in our own land, on the peak of the eastern mountain, the heart-son Padma Prabhājvālya has been born with a radiance greater than before. We should entrust our kingdom to him."

The ministers gathered a vast array of offerings and went before the child, saying:

> Guide of living beings, child incarnation,
> please listen to the people of this land.
> The black demonic doctrine has vanished.
> Please establish the white doctrine of virtuous deeds.
> Rule the kingdom of the Nakhamuṇi Palace
> in accordance with the teachings of the Dharma.

The child replied:

> Listen to me, assembled ministers.
> Pay attention to what I say.
> If you want me to rule the kingdom of the Nakhamuṇi Palace,
> Erase the black paint of the palace and replace it with white.
> Pull down the black flags and replace them with white.

This was done as requested.

Finally, to the sounds of tambura, cymbals, bells, flutes, and lyres; amid the decorations of banners, parasols, victory standards, and waving fans of silk and horse hair; and to the celebration of song and dance, he was enthroned upon the golden throne of Nakhamuṇi.

Thus ends the story of Padma Prabhājvālya.

Table of Tibetan Transliteration

Buchung Lhau Darpo	Bu chung Lhau Darpo
Chaktra	Lcags phra
Chaktsampa	Lcag zam pa
Chokrong	Cog rong
Chongyé	'Phyong rgyas
Chung	Gcung
Chung Riwoché	Gcung ri bo che
Chusur	Chu tshur
Dampa Sangyé	Dam pa sangs rgyas
Dampa Sönam Gyaltsen	Dam pa bsod nams rgyal mtshan
Dangsang Lhamo	Dwang bzang Lha mo
Dawa Depön	Zla ba ded dpon
Dawa Sengé	Zla ba sen ge
Dawa Shönu	Zla ba gzhon nu
Dedruk	Sde drug
Desi Sangyé Gyatso	De srid sangs rgyas rgya mtsho
Deyang Shar	Bde yangs shar
Dingchen Tsering Wangdü	Sdings chen tshe ring dbang 'dus
Dokham	Mdo kham
Dorjé Lekpa	Rdo rje legs pa
Drachen	Sgra chen
Draklha	Brag lha
Drakmar	Brag dmar
Drakpa Samdrup	Grags pa bsam grub
Driseru Gongtön	'Bri se ru gong ston
Driza Tökar	'Bri bza' thod dkar
Drowa Sangmo	'Gro ba bzang mo
Dzomkyi	'Dzoms skyid

Gyal Khar	Rgyal mkhar
Gyalu	Rgya lu
Gyalwa Jungné Dromtönpa	Rgyal ba 'byung gnas 'brom ston pa
Gyangtsé	Rgyal brtse
Gyatak Ramoché	Rgya stag ra mo che
Gyekhuk	Gyes khug
Jang Phekhu Nangpa	Jang phad khud nang pa
Jangding	Byang ldings
Jema Shingdrung	Bye ma shing drung
Jikmé Wangyal	'Jigs med dbang rgyal
Kagyü	Bka' rgyud
Khedrup Gyatso	Mkhas grub rgya mtsho
Kongjo	Kong jo
Kongyul	Kong yul
Kundeling	Kun bde gling
Kunsang Dechen	Kun bzang bde chen
Kyirong	Skyid grong
Kyipo Yalung	Skyid po gya' lung
Kyormo Lung	Skyor mo lung
Labrang Rapsal	Bla brang rab gsal
Lachi	La phyi
Lang	Glang
Langkhor	Glang 'khor
Latö Dingri	La stod ding ri
Lha Yulma	Lha yul ma
Lhaga	Lha dga'
Lhai Palmo	Lha'i dpal mo
Lhokha	Lho kha
Lhorong	Lhorong
Lön	Rlon
Luding	Klu sdings
Luga	Klu dga'
Maldro Gyama	Mal gro rgya ma
Meru Gönsar	Rme ru dgon gsar

Migyur Ling	Mi 'gyur gling
Mila Shepai Dorjé	Mi la bzhad pa'i rdo rje
Namlingv	Rnam gling
Namri Songtsen	Gnam ri srong btsan
Namthar	Rnam thar
Nangsa Öbum	Snang sa 'od 'bum
Nangsa Shalü	Snang sa sha lus
Nangsa Yulma	Snang sa yul ma
Nangtsé	Snang rtse
Nenying	Gnas snyin
Ngamring	Ngam ring
Ngari	Mnga' ri
Ngok Lekpai Sherap	Rngog legs pa'i shes rab
Norsang	Nor bzang
Nyangtö Gyangtsé	Myang stod rgyal rtse
Nyangtsa Saldrön	Myang tsha gsal sgron
Nyimo Netso Lek	Snyi mo ne tso legs
Otang	'O thang
Pehar	Pe har
Pema Öbar	Padma 'od 'bar
Phalha	Phal ha
Phungpo	Phung po
Pundun Drok Kharpa	Spun bdun grog mkhar pa
Rapsal	Rab gsal
Rechungpa	Ras chung pa
Rinang Tsochen	Ri nang mtsho chen
Rinpung	Rin spung
Rongtön Lhaga	Rong ston lha dga'
Śākya Gyaltsen	Shākya rgyal mtshan
Sershung Ringmo	Gser gzhung ring mo
Shalü	Sha lus
Shang	Shangs
Shedra	Bshad sgra

Shotön	Zho ston
Sönam Gyalmo	Bsod nams rgyal mo
Sönam Palkyé	Bsod nams dpal bskyed
Songtsen Gampo	Srong btsan sgam po
Sukyi Nyima	Gzugs kyi nyi ma
Taradzé	Ta ra mdzes
Tashi Chödé	Bkra shis chos sde
Tashi Trigo	Bkra shis khri sgo
Tasik	Stag gzigs
Thanglha	Thang lha
Thangtong Gyalpo	Thang stong rgyal po
Thönpa Nyemo	Thon pa snye mo
Tö	Stod
Tö Yeru	Stod gyas ru
Tönmi Kuntu Sangpo	Thon mi kun tu bzang po
Trisong Tsen	Khri srong brtsan
Tsang	Gtsang
Tsari	Tsa ri
Tsechen Gashi	Rtse chen dga' bzhi
Tshomé	Mtsho smad
Tsöndrü Sangpo	Brtson 'grus bzang po
Ütsang	Dbus gtsang
Yarlung	Yar lung
Yarlung Kyorpo	Yar klung skyor po
Yeru	Gyas ru

Notes

1. *Garland of Past Lives, Jātakamālā, Skyes pa'i rabs kyi rgyud,* Toh 4150, *hu.*
2. Kṣemendra, *Wish-Fulfilling Tree of the Bodhisattva's Lives, Bodhisattvāvadā-na-kalpalatā, Byang chub sems dpa'i rtogs pa brjod rin po che dpag bsam gyi 'khri shing,* Toh 4155, skyes rab *khe.* The Kangyur is a collection of the Buddha's teachings in their Tibetan translation, and the parent collection of the Kangyur is the Tengyur, which gathers the Indic treatises and commentaries on the Buddha's teachings in Tibetan translation.
3. *Ma ṇi bka' 'bum* (Delhi: Trayang and Jamyang Samten, 1975).
4. *Rgyal rabs bsal ba'i me long,* trans. Per K. Sørensen (Wiesbaden: Harrassowitz Verlag, 1994).
5. A collection of stories centering on a "risen corpse" (*ro langs, vetala*), which was activated by the great Indian master Nāgārjuna and then turned into gold. Carried on the back of his disciple, the corpse told stories as its bearer traveled through India.
6. A description of Gesar's birth, early years, and coronation can be found in *The Epic of Gesar of Ling,* trans. Robin Kornman, Sangye Khandro, and Lama Chönam (Boston: Shambhala Publications, 2012).
7. Daṇḍin, *Mirror of Poetics* (*Kāvyādarśa*), Toh 4301, sgra mdo *se,* 322a1. The term "ornament of poetics" refers to a variety of literary devices and effects that make up a poem, the analysis of which gained importance and evolved into the discipline of Alamkarasastra, the science of ornaments.
8. *Rol mo'i bstan bcos.*
9. Tashi Tsering's paper is on this point and he says that like many before him, he has not been able "to find any written evidence of Thangtong Gyalpo being the founder of Aché Lhamo" (2001, 43).
10. Being "secular" did not mean the performance was inappropriate for monastic audiences. The monks enjoyed the dancing as part of their culture [GK].
11. The following descriptions of the ten groups are taken primarily from Snyder 2001, and partly from Schuh 2001.
12. Tashi Tsering mentions a written record of a Shotön Festival in 1635 (2001, 57).
13. The famous mantra of the deity of compassion.
14. *Dri med kun ldan.* "Viśvantara" is not a translation of the Tibetan name, but as this story is clearly based on the Viśvantara parable found in the Jataka literature, as mentioned in the introduction, it was felt that some literary license could be taken here.
15. Deity of compassion.

16. Here and elsewhere, the term *pañcāli* refers to a kind of plant, possibly a form of silk or cotton, from which clothes and cushions are made, but I am unable to identify it.

17. The flower from a udumbara tree blossoms only very rarely.

18. A yoke presses down equally on the shoulders of all.

19. *Gyen la 'dren pa'i 'gyogs su gyur.* Such a refusal would cause great difficulty.

20. *Skye rgu 'dzin pa'i bdag mo.* Description that back-translates into Sanskrit as Prajā-pati, who was the Buddha's aunt or foster mother, and became the first nun. Indra later prophesizes that the prince's mother will incarnate in the future as Prajāpati.

21. Taken literally in accordance with the early part of the story, the prince was already married and had three children by this time.

22. *Gnan ne.* Tibetan term for which I cannot find any Sanskrit equivalent.

23. *Bu ram, ikṣvāku,* one belonging to the sugarcane lineage—the ancestral race of the Buddha—referred to as the Śākya king in the last line of this verse.

24. Dingchen Tsering Wangdü was an eighteenth-century official at Shelkar Dzong Monastery in southern Tibet. According to Gene Smith in his *Among Tibetan Texts—History and Literature of the Tibetan Plateau,* ed. Kurtis R. Schaeffer (Somerville, MA: Wisdom Publications, 2001), 176, this work was written between 1770 and 1780.

25. *Padma bla mtsho.* Although the story is set in India, many place names are repli-cated in Tibet. In Bön mythology a lake by this name would reveal signs indicating the imminent condition of the life force of the king. It is also the lake south of Lhasa where Yeshé Tsogyal, consort of Padmasambhava, was born.

26. *Skam thun.* These are grains and seeds that are ritually transformed and then thrown at an opponent. Liquid ritual substances (*rlon thun*) are such things as blood, mentioned in the previous sentence.

27. This vernacular form of the famous mantra is repeated throughout the text. Some-times it reads *Oṃ mo oṃ mo maṇi padme hūṃ,* as Dingchen has in this instance. The Mimang edition has *Oṃ maṇi padme hūṃ.*

28. *Mkha' lding.* The garuḍa is a mythical hawk known for its ability to kill snakes. The deity with this form, therefore, is especially suited to killing nāgas, who often take the appearance of snakes.

29. In Tibet and India tea is boiled, not brewed!

30. In other words, "You will die!"

31. *Don yod zhags pa,* "effective noose." Here it is a jewel with the power to bind oth-ers. It is also an implement in the form of a rope or chain, held by various deities such as Śiva, whose purpose is to bind others effectively. It is also an epithet of Avalokiteśvara, the Buddhist deity of compassion.

32. *Tshangs pa 'du ba, brahmasabhā,* the hall or court of Brahma, a term applied to bathing pools. Cleanliness is often associated with the god Brahma.

33. Puṣya (*rgyal*) is the eighth of the twenty-eight lunar mansions, and is found in the astrological sign of Cancer.

34. *Tshe thar.* The practice of saving the lives of animals about to be slaughtered as a way to extend one's own life.

35. *(D)ger mtsho gnyan po.* The personal protector of the northern land.

36. The thirteenth letter of the Tibetan alphabet.

37. The first four letters of the Tibetan alphabet: *ka, kha, ga, nga.*

38. *'Jol mo.* Described as "a bird with a sweet voice." Some have suggested nightingale, but it could be another species of bird.
39. *Ki ki bsvo bsvo.* Described as pre-Buddhist Bön praise and invocation of the local gods.
40. There seems to be a line missing, as only seven types of fat are listed.
41. *'Jam dar yug cig.* Expression meaning that the entire country can be governed by compassionate rule.
42. *Ka bshad.* Here the acrostic is alphabetic, in which each line begins with succeeding letters of the Tibetan alphabet. It is impossible to reproduce these lines using the same poetic device in English, but I have included the letters of the Tibetan alphabet at the beginning of each line.
43. According to tradition, the sun is pulled on its orbit by seven horses. According to ancient Indian cosmology, Jambudvipa, or the southern continent on which we live, is named after the river Jambu, which in turn is named after the Jambu tree whose fruits fall into the river. Some of these fruits remain in the river and gradually turn into gold.
44. "Turaṃvadana," the name of the gandharva king, means "with horse's head."
45. A famous discourse of the Buddha (*Ratnākarasūtra*, vol. 7, Toh 124, mdo sde, *tha*).
46. The phrase "knowledge illuminates" is a play on the name of the sage Prakāśa (illuminate) and *mati* (knowledge).
47. *Bkra shis dbang po.* This is clearly an indigenous Tibetan name, and back-translation into Sanskrit serves no purpose here.
48. *Yid 'phrog, manoharā.* Lit. "capture the mind." A play on the name of the goddess.
49. Cavalry, chariots, elephants, and infantry.
50. Estimated by many Tibetan scholars to coincide with 617 CE.
51. Gar Tongtsen and Tönmi Kuntu Sangpo were later to become renowned ministers to the king.
52. The three sacred mountains around Lhasa are described in terms of their resemblance to various animals. In some descriptions the analogy above is ascribed to another of the three mountains.
53. *Tsan dan sbrul gyi snying po, Uragasāracandana.* A rare and precious species of sandalwood tree.
54. *Tsan dan go shir sha, gośrīṣacandana.* Another rare species of sandalwood tree.
55. River near Bodhgaya, India, where the Buddha sat in ascetic meditation for six years.
56. A wrathful form of the goddess Tārā.
57. Milk Plain Lake, the site on which Lhasa was built.
58. This statue is known as Akṣobhyavajra and until recently resided in the Lhasa Ramoché Temple.
59. A revered ancient wooden statue of Avalokiteśvara that for a long time resided in the region of Mangyul Kyirong in western Tibet.
60. A bronze statue of the future Buddha, Maitreya, showing the Turning of the Wheel of Dharma mudra, and which resides in the main temple of Lhasa.
61. A white sandalwood statue of Tārā that resides in the main temple of Lhasa.
62. No mention is made of how the other statues were transported. This is in keeping with *Maṇikabüm. Mirror Illuminating the Royal Genealogies* states that the Śākyamuni statue and the Maitreya statue were placed on manifested yaks.

63. These three perceptions are described in Maṇikabüm (116b–17a) and in Gyal (220).
64. A *yojana* is usually described as a distance of about four miles. Considering the length of each of the four sides as one *krośa*, as given below, it may be that the area mentioned here refers to the circumference. A *krośa* is usually one eighth of a *yojana*, but in some systems it is described as a quarter of a *yojana*. Four of these would then make up the circumference of the walls. However, this would make the length of each wall a mile! From here and other *yojana* measurements in texts elsewhere, I feel it would make more sense if a *yojana* was estimated to be about a mile.
65. This was the residence of the Nepalese princess. Here a stone statue of the Buddha was carved out of the surrounding rock, giving it its name Draklha (Rock Deity).
66. The palace of Indra, king of the gods.
67. Island-fortress capital of the legendary King Ravana in the great Hindu epics, the *Ramayana* and the *Mahabharata*.
68. 636 CE, according to this reckoning.
69. *Zin zhing*. Written in *Mirror Illuminating the Royal Genealogies* as Zimshing, from which this part of the text is taken almost verbatim.
70. Although this translates as "Gate to the Throne of Auspiciousness" (*bkra shis khri sgo*), it seems to refer to the city rather than the gates to the palace. See *Mirror*, note 613.
71. The princess is also called Wencheng. According to some sources, Kongjo means "lotus in the lake."
72. *Stag gzigs*. A Tibetan corruption of "Tajikistan," used to refer generally to the Persian countries west of Tibet.
73. The text previously stated that the minister was given a hundred gold coins to give to the emperor. However, this part of the text is taken almost verbatim from *Mirror Illuminating the Royal Genealogies*, which states that seven coins were intended for the emperor.
74. The text here is a little corrupt and I have relied on *Mirror Illuminating the Royal Genealogies,* which also states that the foals were given grass but denied water.
75. *Rgya nag rtsis*. Sometimes this term is translated as "astrology," but it has more to do with the reading of the earthly elements than the planets and stars.
76. The red spot daubed by Indian women on their foreheads.
77. Previously the hostess told Gar that the princess would be "after the sixth maiden." But here there are seven previous maidens.
78. An expression meaning there is nothing more you can do.
79. In the more elaborate versions of this story the "beggar" plays an important part in Gar's escape, but here no further mention is made of him.
80. It was possible for doctors to examine a patient "remotely," if the patient was holding the other end of a piece of rope, for instance. The pulse travels along the rope like an electric current.
81. This and the preceding passage have been taken verbatim from *Maṇikabüm*. However, in *Mirror* there are other intervening events that make this jump in the narrative more plausible.
82. Food left behind at funerals for spirits.
83. This verse refers back to the way Gar disguised the Chinese hostess's description of the princess.

84. *Spor thang.* A system of divination originating in China based on applying six elements to the sixty-year cycle to give 360 possibilities.
85. *Rgyal mo tsha ba rong.* Often abbreviated to Gyalrong; a place in Kham, in eastern Tibet.
86. *Srid pa chags pa'i lha dgu.* These are local protector deities of Tibet. According to Bon teachings, these nine came into existence at the same time the land of Tibet was created.
87. *Rgya chu.* Chi. Minjiang.
88. *Ldan ma brag.* In Khams. See note 696 in *Mirror Illuminating the Royal Genealogies* for a short discussion on this rock.
89. *Sgo gdong sgo mo.* A place on the Minyak to Lhasa Road. It is also known as Garthar, because this was the place from which Gar was finally freed (*thar*) from Chinese captivity.
90. Caused by Gar tricking the emperor into burning the forests, slaughtering the sheep, destroying the crops, and losing all divination works.
91. The city hosting the palace of the emperor.
92. This refers to the text of both *Maṇikabüm* and *Gyal,* which say that people from each part of the town each welcomed an emanation of the princess, and gives reasons for these assertions.
93. *Mirror* elaborates on this, identifying two forests by the type of tree, and saying that the trees of one forest fell to the left and the other to the right.
94. A fabulous mountain, home to Avalokiteśvara, said to be in India or in southeast Sri Lanka.
95. Nang (snang) = "appear," Sa (sa) = "earth," Ö ('od) = "light," and Büm ('bum) = "hundred thousand."
96. *Gzungs sgrub.* Rituals in which mantra scrolls and other objects are consecrated before being enclosed into sacred objects.
97. A blue stone resembling a turquoise.
98. *Nu rin.* Money given to the bride's mother.
99. Symbolic accumulation of good deeds and bad deeds done throughout life.
100. In tantra practice there are ten harmful conditions, such as various types of contempt, wrong views, a total lack of compassion, and so on, which when present in someone makes them suitable to be destroyed.
101. Fabulous park of the nāgas.
102. There is a saying here in the Tibetan text, *mgyogs pa'i sngon la slebs chen,* which translates literally as "To arrive before the speedy one brings great profit." However, I am unable to provide any reference for it, and scholars I have asked cannot do so either. Nevertheless, it clearly refers to the fact that sending Nangsa home will also be of great value to the husband and father.
103. I am indebted to Nyima Tso, production manager at Norbulingka Institute, Sidhpur, Dharamsala, for help in identifying parts of this now-defunct type of loom.
104. "Great compassion" is *brtse chen* (*tsechen*), which phonetically is also the name of the bridge.
105. The following exchange of songs between Nangsa and the Lama is in acrostic verse, in which each line begins with succeeding single consonants of the Tibetan alphabet. There are thirty-two lines here because the last two letters of the thirty-letter

alphabet are repeated. It is impossible to reproduce these lines using the same poetic device in English, because in English the letters of the alphabet rarely form words. However, that is not the case in the Tibetan alphabet, and it is possible to see from some of the unusual analogies and sayings used how the author has forced each line to begin with a single consonant.

106. Proverb illustrating getting one's responsibilities wrong.

107. "Forgetting the bridge over the river" is a proverb meaning forgetting to repay the kindnesses of others.

108. The gandharvas are celestial beings skilled in music. They have the ability to magically create cities wherever they are. Hence "city of the gandharvas" is a metaphor for something that is illusory even though it appears real.

109. Each line begins with a successive letter of the Tibetan alphabet. Drowa Sangmo continues the alphabet in her reply.

110. A saying meaning "You can know something by examining it well."

111. At this time, his father still languishes in prison far away, and such a conversation must have been made by mystical means.

112. More popularly known as Dromtönpa (1004–64), the chief disciple of Atiśa.

113. Siddhārtha means "accomplishing the needs" and is thus the shortened form of this name.

114. Corruption of the Sanskrit "Ācārya" (*slob dpon*), which is a title given to a recognized scholar-practitioner.

115. Amogha (*don yod*) means "effective" and is thus the shortened form of this name.

116. The sun.

117. Being reborn in a land conducive to the practice of virtuous ways, devoting oneself to the great beings, taking joy in being virtuous as a result of karma and prayers of past lives, having a store of virtuous merit.

118. Siddhārtha means "fulfilling the needs," and often in these addresses the prince's name is interwoven with its meaning.

119. The princess had originally set out to the forest with the prince.

120. This line treats Amitābha and the long-life deity Amitāyus as a single deity.

121. It has been ordained or destined.

122. The vajra-holding monk is the Indian master Atiśa. Jaya and Prajñā are the Sanskrit names of his two Tibetan disciples, Dromtön Gyalwa Jungné and Ngok Lekpai Sherap.

123. *Rab brtan*. Strong and dependable.

124. *Phal ka*. Unable to identify.

125. *Dbang phyug chen po*. Epithet of Śiva.

126. *Sprin gyi shugs can*, "with the power of clouds."

127. According to Tibetan folklore, the visible structures on the full moon form the picture of a rabbit.

128. There are three variations of this line in three editions. This translation follows the meaning most likely intended.

129. *Shig tshang*. Other versions have *shing sna skyes* (trees grew).

130. "Sun" in Sanskrit is *sūrya*.

131. I have been a bit creative here in inserting the English term "mongoose." Otherwise only the Sanskrit or Tibetan would appear. The word used here and elsewhere for mongoose is *ne'u le*, which must be a corruption of *nakula*, and here I have used

the extant Sanskrit. As for the Tibetan, the critical edition has *dred mong*, which is a kind of bear. Other editions have *sre mo*, or *sred mong*, which is either a weasel or mongoose. *Takchung (stag chung)* means "little tiger."

132. A play on their names: *candra* means moon, and *sūrya* means sun.

133. *Gcod.* The advanced practice of dwelling in charnel grounds and offering one's body to the demons that live there, as a way of lessening the clinging to oneself.

134. Magadha was an ancient Indian kingdom frequented by the Buddha. Presumably this measure was a standard measure of that kingdom.

135. In the name Rūpasūrya, *rūpa* means "form" and *sūrya* means "sun."

136. For this line, I have followed another edition that makes more sense.

137. Practitioner on the Buddhist path who has reached the state of being permanently liberated from all suffering and its causes.

138. The Buddha of this world who was born into the royal Śākya clan in northern India.

139. This is a reference to his wife being pregnant, or rather a foretelling of her pregnancy, because later in the text it is clear that she became impregnated by Padmasambhava's miraculous intervention while Sudhana was away.

140. Previously, Subhavya was one of his father's five hundred helpers, and it was related that he along with the others was eaten by the cannibals.

141. This verse has resonance with the story of the famous Jowo statue of Buddha housed in the Jokhang, or central temple, of Lhasa. It is said that after the statue had been in the human realm it went to the nāga realms. It then returned to India, after which it went to China, and was finally brought to Lhasa by the bride of the Tibetan king Songtsen Gyalpo. When it first left the nāga realm, the nāga king asked that it eventually be returned. When the statue arrived in Tibet, an embossed statue of a nāga miraculously appeared on the wall of a rock near Lhasa. The nāga was posed with his hand on his brow, and was said to be waiting for the statue. The place was named Luguk (*klu sgug,* the waiting nāga). Later the name became corrupted to Lubuk, hence the correction in the verse above.

142. In Tibetan medicine a type of pulse reading performed to divine the future.

Glossary

Amoghapāśa (*don yod zhags pa*). A fabulous jewel resembling a noose or lasso (*don yod*), it nevertheless is used for good intention and therefore is "meaningful" (*don yod*). Elsewhere it is a form of the deity Avalokiteśvara.

arhat (*sgra bcom pa*). A Buddhist practitioner who has permanently eradicated all mental afflictions, which are the inner causes for the accumulation of karma and suffering.

ārya (*'phags pa*). A noble being who has attained the advanced spiritual level of having a direct and nonconceptual perception of the ultimate truth of phenomena.

asura (*lha ma yin*). A class of celestial but worldly beings, often characterized as being envious of and in conflict with the higher class of gods (deva).

Avalokiteśvara (*spyan ras gzigs*). A Buddhist deity, often characterized as the personification of the Buddha's compassion.

bodhisattva (*byang chub sems pa*). A Buddhist practitioner of the Great Vehicle who, motivated by great compassion, is striving to become an enlightened being.

cakras (*rtsa 'khor / khor lo*). Psychic channels in the body grouped together at certain vital points, such as the heart, navel, and throat, often in a form resembling the spokes of a wheel or petals of a lotus.

Cakrasaṃvara (*'khor lo bde mchog*). Tantric meditation deity.

ḍāka (*dpa' bo*). Spiritual warrior and male counterpart to ḍākinī.

ḍākinī (*mkha' 'gro*). A female practitioner or yogini who has gained high spiritual realizations or is able to perform supernatural feats. She may be human, in human form, or from a celestial realm. The name means "sky-goer," thereby indicating her supernatural powers.

ḍāmaru (*ḍā ma ru*). A small ritual drum.

Dzokchen (*rdzogs chen*). The Great Completion. Simply put, it refers to the practice of recognizing the naked and clear entity of primordial awareness in its present state free of all mental contamination.

gandharva (*dri za*). A class of celestial musicians who feed off aromas.

Great Vehicle (*theg pa chen po, mahāyāna*). The Buddhist path followed by practitioners who wish to attain enlightenment for the sake of all beings.

Indra (*dbang po*). The "mighty" (*dbang po*) ruler of the celestial realms.

indranīla (*indra ni la*). Sapphire.

Kadampa (*bka' gdams pa*). The Tibetan Buddhist tradition founded by the Indian master Atiśa in the early eleventh century.

kalandaka (*ka lan ta ka / ka lan da ka*). Species of sweet-sounding bird.

kalaviṅga (*ka la ping ga / ka la bing ga*). Indian cuckoo.

kiṃnara (*mi'am ci*). An animal spirit with the body of a human and the head of a horse or another animal. The Tibetan term means "A human or what?"

kumbhāṇḍa (*grul bum*). Ocean-dwelling spirit.

kuśa (*ku sha / rtswa mchog, dharba*). A species of tussock grass long regarded as sacred and used to form a ritual meditation seat. Its pairs of leaves are so sharp that it symbolizes discriminating wisdom.

Mahāmudrā (*phyag rgya chen po*). A multivalent term referring to a body of teachings followed primarily by the Kagyü tradition of Tibetan Buddhism.

Maitreya (*byams pa*). The future Buddha.

Mañjuśrī (*'jam dpal dbyangs*). Buddhist deity, often characterized as the personification of the Buddha's wisdom.

Meru (*ri rab*). Mythical mountain forming the central structure of ancient Indian cosmology.

nāgas (*klu*). Semicelestial beings dwelling between the animal and the spirit realm, sometimes taking on the form of snakes, and with a fondness for water.

Pehar (*pe har*). Originally a mischievous spirit that caused harm to people.

phurpa (*phur pa*). A ritual dagger.

piśācas (*sha za*). Flesh-eating demons.

pratyeka (*rang rgyal / rang sangs rgyas*). Buddhist practitioner who prefers to practice without reliance on a teacher, especially in his or her last life before attaining the goal of nirvana.

Rāhu (*sgra gcan*). The "shadow" planet to which solar and lunar eclipses are attributed.

rākṣas (*srin mo*). Demonic cannibals.

Realm of Thirty-Three (*sum cu rtsa gsum*). Celestial abode in the realm of desire, primarily consisting of Indra, the king of gods, in its center, and eight gods as his entourage in each of the four directions.

samsara (*'khor ba*). Our existence in which we circle or wander from life to life through the force of our mental afflictions and karma.

seven jewels of the ārya (*'phags pa'i nor bu dun*). Seven qualities found in ārya beings: faith, ethics, learning, wisdom, giving, modesty, conscientiousness. They are jewels because just as ordinary jewels bring worldly happiness, these spiritual jewels bring limitless joy to self and others.

siddhis (*dngos grub*). Supernatural powers gained by tantric practice.

śrāvaka (*nyan thos*). A "hearer" or "listener." Buddhist disciple who hears the Buddha's teachings and passes them on to others. The goal of the śrāvaka path, like that of the pratyeka, is to reach the stage of an arhat, where all personal suffering is at an end.

tathāgata (*de bzhin gshegs pa*). Epithet of a buddha.

Three Jewels (*dkon mchog gsum*). The Buddha, the Dharma, as represented by his teachings, and the monastic community, or Sangha, who are living examples of his teachings. These three are Buddhist objects of refuge.

torma (*gtor ma*). "That which is thrown." An edible-substance offering for deities, protectors, nāgas, spirits, and so forth. It is cast away at the end of the ritual in order to reduce attachment.

tsampa (*tsam pa*). Roasted barley flour; a staple of the Tibetan diet.

udumbara (*u dum war a*). A type of fig tree, or a fabulous lotus, whose flower blossoms rarely; according to some sources, only when a buddha is in the world.

utpala (*utpal*). A species of blue lotus or a type of blue poppy.

vajra (*rdo rje*). Ritual implement symbolizing indestructability.

Vajradhara (*rdo rje 'chang*). The Buddha in his form of the teacher of the tantras.

vetāla (*ro langs*). Zombie or risen corpse, in which a dead body is inhabited by a spirit.

yakṣa (*gnod sbyin*). Type of spirit, but also a class of gods. Consequently, they may help or hinder.

Bibliography

PRIMARY

The Epic of Gesar of Ling. Translated by Robin Kornman, Sangye Khandro, and Lama Chönam. Boston: Shambhala Publications, 2012.

Garland of Past Lives. Jātakamālā, Skyes pa'i rabs kyi rgyud, Toh 4150, *hu.*

Maṇikabüm. Ma ṇi bka' 'bum. Delhi: Trayang and Jamyang Samten, 1975.

Mirror Illuminating the Royal Genealogies. Rgyal rabs bsal ba'i me long. Translated by Per K. Sørensen. Wiesbaden: Harrassowitz Verlag, 1994.

Mirror of Poetics. Kāvyādarśa, Toh 4301, sgra mdo *se.*

Wish-Fulfilling Tree of the Bodhisattva's Lives. Bodhisattvāvadāna-kalpalātā, Byang chub sems dpa'i rtogs pa brjod rin po che dpag bsam gyi 'khri shing, Toh 4155, skyes rab *khe.*

SECONDARY

Henrion-Dourcy, Isabelle. "Explorations in the Vocal Art of the Lhamo Performer: Commenting a Demonstration by Tenzin Gonpo." In Tsering, *Lungta 15, The Singing Mask,* 119–41.

Jamyang Norbu. 1986. "The Role of the Performing Arts in Old Tibetan Society." In Norbu, *Zlos-Gar,* 1–6.

———, ed. 1986. *Zlos-Gar: Performing Traditions of Tibet. Commemorative Issue on the Occasion of the 25th Anniversay of the Founding of Tibetan Institute of Performing Arts (1959–84).* Dharamsala, India: Library of Tibetan Works and Archives.

———, 2001. "The Wandering Goddess: Sustaining the Spirit of the Aché Lhamo in the Exile Tibetan Capital." In Tsering, *Lungta 15, The Singing Mask,* 142–58.

Jamyang Norbu and Tashi Tsering. 1986. "A Preliminary Study of Gar, the Court Dance and Music of Tibet." In Norbu, *Zlos-Gar,* 132–43.

Jikmé Wangyal, and Beri Geshé. 2009. *Bod gzhung zlos gar tshogs pa'i lo rgyus kun bzang zhing gi mchod sprin mig yid rna ba'i dga' ston* (The History of TIPA). Delhi: Tibetan Institute of Performing Arts.

Lǐ Liánróng (李連榮). 2001. "History and the Tibetan Epic Gesar." http://journal.oraltradition.org/files/articles/16ii/li_lianrong.pdf.

Lobsang Samten. 2001. "Script of the Exordium of the Hunters, the Bringing Down of Blessings of the Princes, the Songs and Dances of the Goddesses, and the Auspicious Conclusion." In Tsering, *Lungta 15, The Singing Mask*, 61–96.

Richardson, Hugh E. 1986. "Memories of Shoton." In Norbu, *Zlos-Gar*, 7–12.

Samuel, Geoffrey. 1986. "Music of the Lhasa Minstrels." In Norbu, *Zlos-Gar*, 13–19.

———. 2005. *Tantric Revisionings: New Understandings of Tibetan Buddhism and Indian Religion*. Delhi: Motilal Banarsidass.

Schuh, Dieter. 2001. "The Actor in the Lhamo Theatre." In Tsering, *Lungta 15, The Singing Mask*, 97–118.

Snyder, Jeanette. 2001. "Preliminary Study of the Lhamo." In Tsering, *Lungta 15, The Singing Mask*, 8–35.

Tashi Tsering, ed. 2001. *Lungta 15, The Singing Mask*. McLeod Ganj, India: Amnye Machen Institute.

———. 2001. "Reflections on Thangtong Gyalpo as the Founder of the Aché Lhamo Tradition of Performing Arts." In *Lungta 15, The Singing Mask*, 35–60.

Thupten Jinpa Langri, Geshé. 2012. *Bod kyi lha mo'i 'khrab gzhung che khag gces btus la sngon gleng ngo sprod.* (Introduction to the Tibetan Critical Edition of *Selected Great Folk Operas of Tibet*.) Delhi: Institute of Tibetan Classics.

Credits

page 31 © Patrick Willoughby Rosemeyer 1998_286_144_1
page 33 © Harry Staunton 1999_23_2_32
page 570 © Hugh Richardson 2001_59_12_76_1

The Newark Museum
page 47 (top) © The Reverend Roderick A. Macleod

Gabinetto Vieusseux Collection, Fratelli Alinari
page 47 (bottom) © Fosco Maraini

© Patrick Sutherland
page 107 (bottom) Photo taken for the Austrian Science Fund research project Society, Power and Religion in Pre-Modern Western Tibet, directed by Dr. Christian Jahoda, Institute for Social Anthropology, Austrian Academy of Sciences, Vienna.
page 321 (bottom)
page 439 (bottom)

James A. Cannavino Library, Special Collections, Marist College, USA
page 650 © Lowell Thomas

Color Plates

Gabinetto Vieusseux Collection, Fratelli Alinari
insert page 1 (top left & top right) © Fosco Maraini

Pitt Rivers Museum, University of Oxford
insert page 1 (bottom) © Rabden Lepcha 1998_285_159_1

Royal Geographical Society
insert page 2 (top) © Ato Photographic Association

James A. Cannavino Library, Special Collections, Marist College, USA
insert page 2 (bottom) © Lowell Thomas

Tibet Images Collection
insert page 3 (top) © Jirina Simajchlova
insert page 7 (top) © John Miles

© Christiane Kalantari
insert page 3 (bottom) Photo taken for the Austrian Science Fund research project Society, Power, and Religion in Pre-Modern Western Tibet, directed by Dr. Christian Jahoda, Institute for Social Anthropology, Austrian Academy of Sciences, Vienna.

Getty Images
insert page 4 (top) © Ernst Haas

© Pascale Dollfus
insert page 4 (bottom)

Courtesy Tibet Museum, Dharamsala
insert page 5 (top)

Courtesy Tibet Foundation London
insert page 5 (middle & bottom) © Ralph Hodgson

© Shyam Sharma
insert page 6 (top & bottom)

Creative Commons
insert page 7 (middle) © John Hill

exploretibet.com
insert page 7 (bottom)

© Matthieu Ricard
insert page 8 (top and bottom)

Index

on marriage to Kālendra, 447
meets Kālendra, 445
pregnancy of, 437–39, 440
receives teachings from daughter,
440–41
Sūryasiṃha, 643, 644–48
Sutra Vehicle, 432, 433, 569
Svara, 58
Swirl of Blood and Fat, 624
Swirling Turquoise Lake, 228
Switzerland, 39
syllables, 494, 587

Takṣaka (nāga lord), 635
Tāmradvīpa, 491, 498, 510–11, 512, 562
Tang Taizong, Emperor, 320, 328–30,
338–40, 343, 344
tantra, 116, 138, 423, 433
tantric activities, four types, 122
Tantric dances, 25
Tārā, 157, 352, 449, 546, 553
bardo prayer to, 383–84
emanations of, 320, 322, 721n56
homage to, 351, 354, 355, 357, 435
incarnations of, 422
as inner mother, 355
prayers to, 327
Princess Kongjo and, 334, 336, 347,
349, 722n76
sign of blessings of, 353
speaking turquoise statue, 285–86, 287,
363
white sandalwood statue of, 325, 326,
721n61
Tārā Temple (in *Drowa Sangmo*), 449,
451, 452, 453, 454
Taradzé, 50, 56–57
Tashi Chödé Monastery, 317
Tashi Palsang encampment, 297
Tashi Shöl troupes, 27, 28
Tashi Trigo, 328, 347, 723n91
Tashi Wangpo, 293, 295
Tasik (Tajikistan), 328, 330, 335, 722n72
tastes, eight great, 552
tathāgatas. *See* buddhas
Temple of Tārā (in *Pema Öbar*), 649,

650, 655, 665, 666, 667, 672–74,
679, 688–90, 694, 696, 706–7
ten great powers, 530
ten harmful conditions, 386, 723n100
ten nonvirtuous deeds, 339, 431, 448,
489, 627
ten perfections, 67
ten virtues, laws of, 323, 329, 339, 562,
567, 595–96
ten virtuous deeds, 409, 434, 448, 449,
489, 518, 519, 549, 589
Tengyur, 13, 719n2
Thanglha, 227
Thangtong Gyalpo, 3, 6, 24–25, 27, 28
thigh-bone horn, 83
thigh-bone trumpet, 119, 134
Thönmi Saṃbhota, 2
Thönpa Nyemo troupe, 28
three families, 523
Three Jewels, 167, 282, 403
blessings of, 623
compassion of, 187, 243, 255, 293, 301
devotion to, 355
faith in, 148, 185
grace of, 205
homage to, 149, 289, 592, 620
inspiration of, 220
invoking, 218
kindness of, 398
never-ending companionship of, 362
offerings to, 200, 214, 235, 291, 372,
492, 587
prayers to, 77, 83, 128, 216, 242, 252–53,
484, 485, 535, 614–15
requests to, 454–55
stopping offerings to, 112
trusting in, 70, 284, 514, 541, 647
visualization of, 472
as witnesses, 279, 280
worship of, 491, 562, 595
See also refuge: in Three Jewels
three kāyas. *See* buddhas: three bodies of
three poisons, 187, 284, 307, 525, 592,
622, 626, 635–36, 638
three trainings, 432, 567, 592, 619, 623
three vehicles, 567

About the Contributors

GAVIN KILTY has been a full-time translator for the Institute of Tibetan Classics since 2001. Before that he lived in Dharamsala, India, for fourteen years, where he spent eight years training in the traditional Geluk monastic curriculum through the medium of class and debate at the Institute of Buddhist Dialectics. He also teaches Tibetan language courses in India, Nepal, and elsewhere, and is a translation reviewer for the organization 84000: Translating the Words of the Buddha.

THUPTEN JINPA LANGRI was educated in the classical Tibetan monastic academia and received the highest degree of *geshé lharam* from Ganden Shartse Monastery. Jinpa also holds a PhD in religious studies from the University of Cambridge, England. Since 1985, he has been the principal English translator for the Dalai Lama, accompanying His Holiness on tours to the West and translating and editing many of his books. In addition to publishing his own books and scholarly articles, Jinpa serves on the advisory board of numerous educational and cultural organizations, and he currently chairs the Mind and Life Institute and the Compassion Institute. He is the president and the editor in chief of the Institute of Tibetan Classics, based in Montreal.

The Institute of Tibetan Classics

THE INSTITUTE OF TIBETAN CLASSICS is a nonprofit, charitable educational organization based in Montreal, Canada. It is dedicated to two primary objectives: (1) to preserve and promote the study and deep appreciation of Tibet's rich intellectual, spiritual, and artistic heritage, especially among the Tibetan-speaking communities worldwide; and (2) to make the classical Tibetan knowledge and literature a truly global heritage, its spiritual and intellectual resources open to all.

To learn more about the Institute of Tibetan Classics and its various projects, please visit www.tibetanclassics.org or write to this address:

Institute of Tibetan Classics
304 Aberdare Road
Montreal (Quebec) H3P 3K3
Canada

The Library of Tibetan Classics

"This new series edited by Thupten Jinpa and published by Wisdom Publications is a landmark in the study of Tibetan culture in general and Tibetan Buddhism in particular. Each volume contains a lucid introduction and outstanding translations that, while aimed at the general public, will benefit those in the field of Tibetan Studies immensely as well."

—Leonard van der Kuijp, Harvard University

"This is an invaluable set of translations by highly competent scholar-practitioners. The series spans the breadth of the history of Tibetan religion, providing entry to a vast culture of spiritual cultivation."

—Jeffrey Hopkins, University of Virginia

"Erudite in all respects, this series is at the same time accessible and engagingly translated. As such, it belongs in all college and university libraries as well as in good public libraries. *The Library of Tibetan Classics* is on its way to becoming a truly extraordinary spiritual and literary accomplishment."

—Janice D. Willis, Wesleyan University

Following is a list of the thirty-two proposed volumes in *The Library of Tibetan Classics*. Some volumes are translations of single texts, while others are compilations of multiple texts, and each volume will be roughly the same length. Except for those volumes already published, the renderings of titles below are tentative and liable to change. The Institute of Tibetan Classics has contracted numerous established translators in its efforts, and work is progressing on all the volumes concurrently.

1. *Mind Training: The Great Collection*, compiled by Shönu Gyalchok and Könchok Gyaltsen (fifteenth century). NOW AVAILABLE

2. *The Book of Kadam: The Core Texts*, attributed to Atiśa and Dromtönpa (eleventh century). NOW AVAILABLE

3. *The Great Chariot: A Treatise on the Great Perfection*, Longchen Rapjampa (1308–63)

4. *Taking the Result As the Path: Core Teachings of the Sakya Lamdré Tradition*, Jamyang Khyentsé Wangchuk (1524–68) et al. NOW AVAILABLE

5. *Mahāmudrā and Related Instructions: Core Teachings of the Kagyü Schools.* NOW AVAILABLE

6. *Stages of the Path and the Ear-Whispered Instructions: Core Teachings of the Geluk School*

7. *Ocean of Definitive Meaning: A Teaching for the Mountain Hermit*, Dölpopa Sherap Gyaltsen (1292–1361)

8. *Miscellaneous Tibetan Buddhist Lineages: The Core Teachings*, Jamgön Kongtrül (1813–90)

9. *Sutra, Tantra, and the Mind Cycle: Core Teachings of the Bön School*

10. *Stages of the Buddha's Teachings: Three Key Texts.* NOW AVAILABLE

11. *The Bodhisattva's Altruistic Ideal: Selected Key Texts*

12. *The Ethics of the Three Codes*

13. *Sādhanas: Vajrayana Buddhist Meditation Manuals*

14. *Ornament of Stainless Light: An Exposition of the Kālacakra Tantra*, Khedrup Norsang Gyatso (1423–1513). NOW AVAILABLE

15. *A Lamp to Illuminate the Five Stages: Teachings on the Guhyasamāja Tantra*, Tsongkhapa (1357–1419). NOW AVAILABLE

16. *Studies in the Perfection of Wisdom*

17. *Treatises on Buddha Nature*

18. *Differentiations of the Profound View: Interpretations of Emptiness in Tibet*

19. *Elucidation of the Intent: A Thorough Exposition of "Entering the Middle Way,"* Tsongkhapa (1357–1419)

20. *Tibetan Buddhist Epistemology I: The Sakya School*

21. *Tibetan Buddhist Epistemology II: The Geluk School*

22. *Tibetan Buddhist Psychology and Phenomenology: Selected Texts*

23. *Ornament of Abhidharma: A Commentary on the "Abhidharmakośa,"* Chim Jampaiyang (thirteenth century). NOW AVAILABLE

24. *Beautiful Adornment of Mount Meru: A Presentation of Classical Indian Philosophies*, Changkya Rölpai Dorjé (1717–86)

25. *The Crystal Mirror of Philosophical Systems: A Tibetan Study of Asian Religious Thought*, Thuken Losang Chökyi Nyima (1737–1802). NOW AVAILABLE

26. *Gateway for Being Learned and Realized: Selected Texts*

27. *The Tibetan Book of Everyday Wisdom: A Thousand Years of Sage Advice.* NOW AVAILABLE

28. *Mirror of Beryl: A Historical Introduction to Tibetan Medicine*, Desi Sangyé Gyatso (1653–1705). NOW AVAILABLE

29. *Selected Texts on Tibetan Astronomy and Astrology*

30. *Art and Literature: An Anthology*

31. *Tales from the Tibetan Operas.* NOW AVAILABLE

32. *A History of Buddhism in India and Tibet*, Khepa Deu (thirteenth century)

To receive a brochure describing all the volumes or to stay informed about *The Library of Tibetan Classics*, please write to:

info@wisdompubs.org

or send a request by post to:

Wisdom Publications
Attn: Library of Tibetan Classics
199 Elm Street
Somerville, MA 02144 USA

The complete catalog containing descriptions of each volume can also be found online at wisdompubs.org.

Become a Benefactor
of the Library of Tibetan Classics

THE LIBRARY OF TIBETAN CLASSICS' scope, importance, and commitment to the finest quality make it a tremendous financial undertaking. We invite you to become a benefactor, joining us in creating this profoundly important human resource. Contributors of two thousand dollars or more will receive a copy of each future volume as it becomes available, and will have their names listed in all subsequent volumes. Larger donations will go even further in supporting *The Library of Tibetan Classics*, preserving the creativity, wisdom, and scholarship of centuries past, so that it may help illuminate the world for future generations.

To contribute, please either visit our website at www.wisdompubs.org, call us at (617) 776-7416, or send a check made out to Wisdom Publications or credit card information to the address below.

Library of Tibetan Classics Fund
Wisdom Publications
199 Elm Street
Somerville, MA 02144
USA

Please note that contributions of lesser amounts are also welcome and are invaluable to the development of the series. Wisdom is a 501(c)3 nonprofit corporation, and all contributions are tax-deductible to the extent allowed by law.

If you have any questions, please do not hesitate to call us or email us at advancement@wisdompubs.org.

To keep up to date on the status of *The Library of Tibetan Classics*, visit the series page on our website, and subscribe to our newsletter while you are there.